OFFICIAL
RULES OF

INCLUDING
Instructions
& Strategies

Published by
Redwood Editions
an imprint of
Hinkler Book Distributors Pty Ltd
17–23 Redwood Drive
Dingley, Victoria, Australia

© Copyright for design, editing and typesetting:
Hinkler Book Distributors Pty Ltd, 2000

Reprinted in 2000 (twice), 2001

ISBN 186515 153 X

Edited by Deborah Doyle (Living Proof – Book Editing)
Typeset by Midland Typesetters, Maryborough, Victoria
Printed and bound in Australia

Editor's note:
*Throughout this book, for the purposes of readability and the book's cost
effectiveness, I have retained the masculine gender for nouns such as 'men'
and pronouns such as 'his'. However, because of the dated nature of the
text and the glaringly sexist overtones, I have deleted all references to
women's inferiority and the more outmoded cultural details.*

CONTENTS

iv Contents

vi Contents

PAGE

viii Contents

THE BRIDGE FAMILY

— · —

The parent of this popular family of games is 'straight' bridge, in which the dealer or his partner must make the trump, whereby their opponents have nothing to say about this except to double the value of the tricks. The dealer's partner is always the dummy, and either side may score toward game by making the odd trick or more. Auction bridge is a development, in which the privilege of making the trump is bid for, whereby the highest bidder plays the hand and his partner is dummy, regardless of the position of the deal, and his side is the only one that can score toward game, whereby the adversaries score nothing but penalties in the honour column if they defeat the contract.

Straight Bridge is practically no longer played, having been completely superseded by Auction Bridge, or simply Auction. For this game, in 1917 the revisers of the final official laws settled on what is called 'the new count,' for the values of the tricks, whereby each player at the table is given the privilege of bidding for the right to name the declaration on which the hand should be played. This is the game about to be described.

— · —

AUCTION BRIDGE
OR AUCTION

CARDS Auction is played with a full pack of fifty-two cards, ranking A K Q J 10 9 8 7 6 5 4 3 2, the Ace being the highest in play, but ranking below the deuce in cutting. Two packs should be used, whereby one pack is shuffled while the other is dealt. The still pack marks the position of the next dealer.

MARKERS   Suitable markers for scoring the various points made at Bridge have not yet been invented. Some people use the bezique marker, but it is not a success. The score is usually kept on a sheet of paper, and it should be put down by each side, for purposes of verification.

PLAYERS   Auction is played by four people, and the table is complete with six people. When there are more than four candidates for play, the selection of the four is made by cutting. These people cut again for partners, and for the choice of seats and cards.

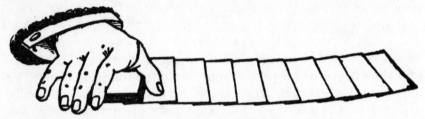

SPREADING THE PACK

CUTTING   At auction, the usual method of cutting for partners and so on is to shuffle the cards thoroughly and 'spread' them face downwards on the table; each candidate draws a card and turns it face upwards in front of him. The four who cut the lowest cards play the first game, or rubber.

   The four having been selected, the cards are again shuffled and spread, and partners are cut for; the two lowest pair against the two highest. The lowest of the four is the dealer, and has the choice of cards and seats. His partner sits opposite him, and the next-lowest cut has the choice of the remaining seats.

TIES   As between cards of equal value in cutting, the spade is the lowest, then hearts, then diamonds next, and then clubs.

POSITION OF THE PLAYERS   The four players at the bridge table are indicated by letters. A and B are partners against Y and Z. Z always represents the dealer, who always makes the first bid; A is the second bidder, Y the third, and B the fourth.

```
        Y
  A          B
        Z
```

DEALING The cards having been properly shuffled, the dealer, Z, presents them to the pone, B, to be cut. At least four cards must be left in each packet. Beginning at his left, the dealer distributes the cards one at a time in rotation until the pack is exhausted. When two packs are used, the dealer's partner shuffles one while the other is dealt, and the deal passes in regular rotation to the left until the rubber is finished. If no one makes a bid, the deal passes to the next player.

IRREGULARITIES IN THE DEAL If any card is found faced in the pack, or if the pack is incorrect or imperfect, the dealer must deal again. If any card is found faced in the pack, or is exposed in any way; or if more than thirteen cards are dealt to any player; or if the last card does not come in its regular order to the dealer; or if the pack has not been cut, there must be a new deal. Attention must be called to a deal out of turn, or with the wrong cards, before the last card is dealt, or the deal stands.

There are no misdeals in auction; that is, whatever happens, the same dealer deals again. Minor irregularities are provided for in the laws.

The cards having been dealt, each player sorts his hand to see that he has the correct number: thirteen; the player or players keeping the score should announce it at the beginning of each hand.

There is a penalty of 25 points in honours for every card lifted and looked at before the deal is complete.

STAKES In auction, the stake is a unit, so much a point. The number of points won or lost on the rubber may be only two or three or may run into the hundreds. The average value of a rubber at auction is about 400 points. Any much larger figure shows bad bidding. In straight bridge the average is about 180. In settling at the end of the rubber, it is usual for each losing player to pay his right-hand adversary.

MAKING THE TRUMP The dealer begins by passing or naming any one of the four suits, or no trumps, for any number of tricks he pleases up to 7. Each player in turn to the left then has the privilege of passing, bidding higher, or doubling. When three players pass a bid or a double, it is known as the Winning Declaration or Contract.

In order to understand the principles that govern the players in their declarations, you should be thoroughly familiar with the values attached to the tricks when specific suits are trumps. The first six tricks taken by the side that has made the winning declaration do not count. This is the 'book,' but all over the book count towards making good on the contract, according to the following table:

When	Clubs		are	trumps,	each	trick	counts	6	points
"	Diamonds	"	"	"	"	"	"	7	"
"	Hearts	"	"	"	"	"	"	8	"
"	Spades	"	"	"	"	"	"	9	"
"	there are no trumps,				"	"	"	10	"

These values are used only in the bidding and in scoring successful play. If the contract fails, every trick by which it fails is worth 50 in honours to the adversaries.

The game is 30 points, which must be made by tricks alone, so that three over the book, called three 'by cards,' will go game from love at no trump, or four by cards at hearts or spades. These are called the Major or Winning Suits. Because it takes five by cards to go game in clubs or diamonds, and on account of the difficulty of this undertaking, these are called the Minor or Losing Suits.

RANK OF THE BIDS   In order to overcall a previous bid, whether of the partner or of the opponent, the bidder must undertake to win the same number of tricks in a suit of higher value, or a greater number of tricks in a suit of lower rank, such as 4 clubs over 3 spades. Players should restrict themselves to the same form of expression throughout, and all bids, even passing, must be made orally and not by gesture.

Let's suppose this to be the bidding: The dealer, Z, begins with 'No bid,' and the second player, A, says, 'I pass,' or simply 'No.' The third bidder, Y, says, 'One club,' the fourth player, B, 'One spade.' The dealer, starting on the second round, says, 'Two clubs,' supporting his partner's declaration. The next player, A, who passed the first time, says, 'Two spades.' Both Y and B pass, but the dealer, Z, says, 'Three clubs.'

Suppose A doubles three clubs. Y passes, and B says, 'Three no trumps.' As will be explained presently, doubling does not affect the value of the declaration in bidding, so three no trumps overcalls three clubs doubled. Z, A and Y all pass, so three no trumps becomes the winning declaration and B is the declarer, A being the dummy, and Z to lead for the first trick.

In this example, had the bid been left at three clubs, doubled or not, that would have been the winning declaration, and the partner who first named that suit, Y, would be the declarer, Z being the dummy, although Z actually made the highest bid. It is only when the two players who have both named the winning suit are not partners that the higher bidder becomes the declarer.

DOUBLING No player may double his partner, but he may re-double an opponent who has doubled. All doubling must be strictly in turn, as for any other bid. Doubling does not affect the value of the bids, but simply doubles the value of the tricks or penalties when they are scored at the end of the hand. Suppose A bids two spades and Y doubles. B can take A out with three clubs, because, so far as the bidding goes, two spades, if doubled, are worth no more than two spades undoubled.

Any overcall annuls the double, or redouble. Suppose A says two hearts, Y doubles, B redoubles, and Z says two spades. The doubling is all knocked out, and were A to go three hearts and get the contract, hearts would be worth only 8 a trick in the scoring unless Y doubled all over again. A double reopens the bidding, just the same as any other declaration, allowing the player's partner, or the player himself in his turn, to take himself out of the double by bidding something else.

IRREGULARITIES IN DECLARING If any player declares out of turn, either opponent may allow the declaration so made to stand, in which case the next player to the left must bid, or he may ignore the bid and declare it void. If a player passes out of turn there is no penalty, and the player whose turn it was must declare himself. The player who has passed out of his proper turn may re-enter the bidding if the declaration he passed has been overcalled and doubled. A double out of turn gives the opponents the option of a new deal.

If a player makes a declaration that is not enough to overcall the last bid, either adversary may call attention to it. Suppose the last bid is three hearts, and the next player says three clubs. This is not enough. Unless the player in error corrects himself at once, and makes it four clubs, either adversary may demand it be four clubs, and the partner of the corrected player cannot bid unless this four-club bid is overcalled or doubled. A player correcting himself must stick to the suit named; he is not allowed to say three spades when he sees that having three clubs is not enough.

If an insufficient declaration is passed or overcalled by the player on the left, it is too late to demand any penalty, and the insufficient bid stands as regular. Suppose A bids four hearts, Y says four clubs, and B and Z pass. A can repeat his bid of four hearts if he likes, because that is enough to overcall four clubs.

A player is always allowed to correct an erroneous bid without penalty, provided he does so before the next player acts, and he may correct it in either of two ways. If he made a slip of the tongue and named the wrong suit, he may change it. If he has named the right suit, but not enough tricks, he may bid more tricks, but he cannot reduce the number of tricks if he has inadvertently bid too many.

METHOD OF PLAYING The winning declaration settled, whether doubled or not, the player on the left of the declarer leads for the first trick, and dummy's cards go down, whereby the declarer plays the combined hands. The declarer gathers the tricks for his side, but either adversary may gather for the other. The first six tricks taken by the declarer make a book, and all over the book count towards his contract. The adversaries have a book when the number of tricks they have taken in is the difference between the number of tricks bid and seven. If the contract is 4, their book is 3, and all over that book are worth 50 apiece in honours. All tricks should be laid so that they may be readily counted by any player at the table.

There is a penalty of 25 points in honours for looking at a trick once turned down.

DUMMY Until a card is led by the proper player, the declarer's partner has all the rights of any other player, but as soon as the player to the left of the declarer leads and dummy's cards are laid on the table, dummy's duties and rights are restricted to the following:

He may call attention to too few cards played to a trick; correct an improper claim of either adversary; call attention to a trick taken by the wrong side; ask his partner whether he has none of a suit to which he renounces; correct an erroneous score; consult with the declarer as to which penalty to exact for a revoke; and, if he has not intentionally overlooked the hand of another player, he may call his partner's attention to an established revoke made by the adversaries, or to a card exposed by them or a lead out of turn. He may also ask a hand to be played out.

THE REVOKE Should a player fail to follow suit when able to do so, it is a revoke, and the revoke is established when the trick in which it occurs is turned down and quitted by the side that won it, or when the revoking player, or his partner, in his right turn or otherwise, has led or played to the following trick. If a player asks his partner whether he has none of the suit led, before the trick is turned down, the revoke may be corrected, unless the player in error replies in the negative, or has led or played to the next trick.

Dummy cannot revoke under any circumstances.

The penalty for the revoke depends on the side in error. If the declarer revokes, he cannot score anything but honours as actually held, and the adversaries take 50 points' penalty in the honour column, in addition to any points they may be entitled to for defeat-ing the declaration. If an adversary revokes, they score honours only, and the declarer may either take the 50 points or take two actual tricks and add them to his own. If he takes the tricks, they may aid him in fulfilling his contract, because the score is then made up as the tricks lie, but the declarer will not be entitled to any bonus in case he was doubled.

Suppose Z is the declarer, and is playing three hearts doubled. He wins two odd tricks only, but detects a revoke, for which he takes two tricks. This gives him four by cards, doubled, worth 64 points towards game, but he does not get any bonus for making his contract after being doubled, or for the extra tricks, because they were taken in penalty and not in play.

EXPOSED CARDS   After the deal but before the winning declara-tion is settled, if any player exposes a card, his partner is barred from bidding or doubling, and the card is subject to call. If the partner of the offending player proves to be the leader to the first trick, the declarer may prohibit the initial lead of the exposed suit. If the player is the declarer, the card is not exposed, because the declarer may expose cards without penalty.

All cards exposed by the declarer's adversaries after the original lead are liable to be called and must be left on the table, face upward. Exposed cards are cards played two at a time, dropped on the table face up, or so held that the partner might see them, or cards mentioned as being in the hand of the player or his partner.

LEADING OUT OF TURN   If either adversary leads out of turn, the declarer may call the card exposed, or call a suit when it is the turn of either adversary to lead. If the declarer leads out of turn, from his own hand or dummy's, there is no penalty, but he may not correct the error unless directed to do so by an adversary. If the second hand plays to the false lead, it must stand. If the declarer plays from his own hand or from dummy to a false lead, the trick stands. In case the dealer calls a suit and the player has none, the penalty is paid.

CARDS PLAYED IN ERROR   If any player but dummy omits to play to a trick, and does not correct the error until he has played to the next trick, the other side may claim a new deal. If the deal stands, the surplus card at the end is supposed to belong to the short trick, but is not a revoke.

OBJECT OF THE GAME   The object in auction is for the declarer to fulfil his contract, and for the adversaries to defeat it.

The highest card played to the trick, if of the suit led, wins the trick, and trumps win all other suits. At the end of the hand, the declarer counts up the tricks he has won over the book, and if he has made good on his contract, he scores the value of those tricks towards game. As soon as either side reaches 30, it is a game, but the hands are played out and all the tricks are counted.

RUBBERS   Three games, 30 points or more each, make a rubber, but if the first two are won by the same partners, the third game is not played. The side that first wins two games adds 250 rubber points to its score.

SCORING   Apart from the game score, which is made entirely by tricks won on successful declarations, there are several additional scores that have no influence in winning or losing the game, although they may materially affect the ultimate value of the rubber. These are all entered under the heading 'Honour scores,' or 'Above the line.'

HONOURS   Honours are the five highest cards in the trump suit: A K Q J 10; when there is no trump, they are the four Aces. The partners holding three, four or five honours between them, or four honours in one hand, or four in one hand and the fifth in the partner's, or all five in one hand, are entitled to claim and score them, according to the following table. It will be seen that their value varies according to the trump suit, and it must be remembered that this value cannot be increased by doubling.

TABLE OF HONOUR VALUES

Declaration	♣	◇	♡	♠	No trump
Each Trick above 6	6	7	8	9	10
3 Honours...........................	12	14	16	18	30
4 Honours...........................	24	28	32	36	40
4 Honours (All in 1 hand)	48	56	64	72	100
5 Honours...........................	30	35	40	45	
5 Honours (4 in 1 hand)........................	54	63	72	81	
5 Honours (All in 1 hand)	60	70	80	90	

The leftmost label **HONOURS** runs vertically alongside the honours rows.

Rubber 250, Grand Slam 100, Little Slam 50.

When one side has nothing but the odd honour, three out of the five, it is called *simple honours.* The value of simple honours is always the same as two tricks.

SLAMS Little Slam is made by taking twelve of the thirteen tricks; it counts 50 points. Grand Slam is made by taking the thirteen tricks, and it counts 100. Either score must be exclusive of revoke penalties. Either side can score slams.

PENALTIES If the declarer succeeds in making his contract, he scores below the line for tricks and above the line for honours according to the table of values already given, and he scores for as many tricks as he wins, regardless of the smaller number he may have bid.

However, if the declarer fails to make good on his contract, he scores nothing but honours as actually held, and his adversaries score 50 points' penalty in the honour column for every trick by which the declaration falls short, no matter what the declaration was, but they never score anything towards game, no matter how many tricks they win, because they are not the declarers. They may, however, score slams.

If we suppose the winning declaration to be three hearts, and the declarer makes the odd trick only, holding simple honours, he scores 16 above the line, and the other side scores 100 points above the line for defeating the contract by two tricks, worth 50 each.

If a winning declaration is doubled and fails, the adversaries score 100 points, instead of 50, for every trick by which they defeat the contract. If it is redoubled, they score 200. However, if the declarer succeeds after being doubled, he not only scores double value for the tricks toward game; he gets 50 points for fulfilling a doubled contract and 50 more for any tricks over his contract if he makes them. These figures are 100 in each case if he redoubles.

Suppose the declaration is three no trumps, doubled, and the declarer makes five by cards. He scores 5 times 20 towards game, aces as held, and then 150 in penalties, 50 of which are for fulfilling his contract and twice 50 for the two tricks over his contract.

The adversaries cannot score any penalties for the declarer's failure to fulfil his contract if they have revoked, even if the two tricks he may take as revoke penalty are not enough to make good his bid. In this case, the declarer would take 50 points, and each side would score honours as actually held.

KEEPING SCORE Two styles of score-pad are now in general use. In one, the tricks and honours are entered in the same vertical column, one above the other, and are all added in one sum at the end. In the other style of pad, the tricks are in one column and the honours and penalties in another, so that four additions are required in order to find the value of the rubber, which is always the difference between the total scores after giving the winners of two games 250 points. The following table shows both styles of pad.

WE	THEY
	36
	30
18	100
16	
8	
	40
	36
	250
42	492
	42
	450

WE		THEY	
8	16		
	18		100
		40	30
		36	36
8	34	76	166
	8		76
	42		250
			492
			42
			450

The scoring on which this rubber is won and lost was as follows: WE started with a contract to win one heart, and made it, with simple honours, whereby THEY scored 8 towards game and 16 above for honours. Then THEY set a contract for two tricks, whereby THEY got 100 in penalties, against simple honours in spades, scored as 18 above for WE and 100 for THEY. Then THEY made four odd at no trump and 30 aces, whereby THEY won the first game, under which a line is drawn.

On the next deal, THEY made four odd in spades, with four honours, 36 each way, whereby THEY won the second game and also the rubber, for which they add 250 points. Both scores are now added up and the lower deducted from the higher, whereby it is shown that THEY win 450 points on the balance.

CUTTING OUT At the conclusion of the rubber, if there are more than four candidates for play, the selection of the new table is made by cutting; the people who have just played cut the cards to decide the outgoers. The players who cut the highest cards sit out for one rubber, after which they re-enter without cutting in. A player leaving a table must declare a return if he wishes to continue, and must be in the room when his turn comes. If he leaves to make up another table, he must declare to return or not. For other deals, see the Laws.

CHEATING Most of the cheating done at the bridge table is of a character whereby that it cannot be challenged without difficulty, although there is enough of it to be most annoying.

Some players will place a high and low card when they shuffle and spread the pack, and because they are the last to draw, can get the partner they want. Second dealing is a common trick, whereby the aces are slipped back if they would fall to an adversary dealing them to the partner instead, who can go no trumps and score a hundred aces several times in an evening. Some players are great offenders in trifling matters, such as asking the dealer whether he passed it, when nothing has been said; looking over the adversaries' hands as dummy, and then pushing dummy's cards forward, as if arranging them, but in reality indicating which one to play. A lot of petty cheating is done in putting down the score, and also in balancing it by cancellation. Some players are so eager to win a prize that they will stoop to all kinds of private signal, and some go so far as to make up a table and agree to double everything, so that some one of the four will have a big score. Another common trick is to have a stool pigeon overlook another player's hand and signal it up to the cheating player.

There might be some remedy for cheating, but so far no one has found it; or at least he lacks the courage to put it in practice and expose the offenders.

SUGGESTIONS FOR GOOD PLAY The great secret of success playing in auction lies in bidding soundly, so that no bid will have a double meaning and the partner will be able to completely rely on the information that the bid should convey. The complications of the situation are so numerous, because of the variations introduced by each succeeding bid as the players overcall each other, that it would be impossible to cover them in a work of this kind, and you would do well to consult a work such as *Foster on Auction* or Whitehead's *Auction Bridge Standards*. The first named gives the play, as well as the bidding.

A few general hints might be of assistance in showing the principles that govern the more common situations.

THE DEALER'S BIDS These can be divided into three classes: minor suits, major suits, and no-trumpers. Passing without a bid on the first round does not necessarily imply that you will have nothing to say on the second round, because bids on the second round show length, without the sure tricks required for original bids.

The dealer should never call any suit on the first round of bids unless he has two sure tricks in it, such as A K, or K Q J, or A Q J. If he has only one trick in the suit itself, he should have at least one sure and one probable in some other suit to fill up the holes. The A J 10 of clubs is not a club bid, but the ace and queen of any other suit would justify it. The bidder should have at least five cards in a major suit, or four with the three top honours, to justify him in declaring it, because his partner is likely to leave him to play it.

It is not once in a year that you will be left to play a one-club or one-diamond bid, and these suits are never bid originally with any idea of having them for the trump unless the bid is two or three instead of one. The shorter these suits the better, because they are less likely to be trumped. Minor-suit bids offer assistance to the partner; major suit bids ask the partner to assist them.

THE SECOND HAND   He should declare just as if he were the dealer when the dealer refuses to make a bid. He may even go no trump on a lighter hand. When the dealer bids a suit, second hand should overcall only when he can make his contract or wishes to indicate a lead in case third hand should go to no trumps. If the dealer bids no trump, second hand should pass, unless he is prepared to overcall any ensuing bid for three tricks.

THE THIRD HAND   He should be a trick or two stronger than he would have to be to declare as dealer on the first round. When the dealer bids no trump, third hand should take him out with any weak five-card suit and nothing else, simply to warn him that there are no winning cards in the hand. Always take him out with five cards in a winning suit, no matter how strong the rest of the hand. Experts may depart from this rule, but beginners should not.

HIS SUIT   Take him out of a winning suit with no trump, only to deny his suit and show strength in each of the three other suits. If the dealer bids no trump and second hand calls a suit, double if you can stop the suit twice; otherwise, show any good suit of your own, but do not go two no-trumps unless you can do it all yourself. Leave that to your partner. Do not assist your partner's suit bids with less than three tricks if second hand overcalls.

If third hand has a suit that is much stronger than any average declaration the dealer is likely to have made a bid on, such as six spades to four honours, he should overcall his partner's bid.

THE FOURTH HAND   He bids on the bidding much more than on his cards. He must be cautious when 'no-bid' is passed up to him. If the dealer bids a losing suit, and second and third hands pass, leave him in unless you can go game and are not afraid of a shift. If the dealer bids a winning suit, and second and third hands pass, make any sound declaration. If the dealer starts with no trumps, show any suit that might save the game if led at once by your partner, such as five to A Q 10 and another ace for re-entry.

SUBSEQUENT BIDS   Any suit bid on the second round but not on the first shows length without the tops. When a winning suit is taken out by the partner, a losing-suit bid on the second round shows tops in it. Any suit re-bid on the second round, without waiting for the partner's assistance, shows six or seven probable tricks in hand.

Never bid a hand twice, unless its strength is greater than indicated by the first bid. Having bid a club on ace king small, that is the end of it. If you have an outside ace, which the club bid did not show, you can assist your partner once on that trick, but no more. Having assisted your partner's suit bid with three tricks, do not bid again unless you have a fourth trick in hand, but if he re-bids his suit without waiting for you, you may assist on one trick, especially a high honour in trumps.

Do not double simply to get penalties, unless you are not afraid of a shift. Do not give up a fair chance for going game yourself simply to double an adversary, unless you are sure of 200 in penalties at least, and do not give up the rubber game for less than 300. Always remember that a double may enable an adversary to go game, and will often show the declarer which hand to finesse against.

FREE DOUBLES These are opportunities to double when the declarer will go game anyway if he makes his contract, but they should never be made if there is any chance he will shift.

CONVENTIONAL DOUBLES These are doubles that are intended not to penalise the contract but to get the partner to show what he has. There are three rules governing them: The double must be made at the first opportunity. It must be a double of not more than one no-trump, or three is suit. It must be made before the partner of the doubler has made any declaration other than passing. If a no-trumper is doubled, the partner must call any four hearts or spades, otherwise his longest suit, unless he is sure of defeating the no-trumper for at least 300. If a major suit is doubled, the partner must call the other major suit if he has four of it; otherwise his longest suit; or no-trump if he can stop the doubled suit twice. If third hand intervenes with a bid, taking out the double, the doubler's partner need not make a bid unless he has a suit of five cards, or is very strong in a major suit.

OPENING LEADS The position we have to consider first is that of the eldest hand, usually designated by the letter 'A,' who sits on the declarer's left.

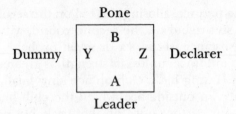

Pone

Dummy   Y   Z   Declarer

Leader

SELECTING THE SUIT TO LEAD   If your partner has declared a
suit, lead the best card you hold of it, regardless of number, unless
you have an ace–king suit of your own, in which case lead the king
first and have a look at dummy. If your partner has not declared
anything, lead your own suit. With high cards not in sequence, such
as ace–queen, king–jack, or even queen–ten, in every suit but
trumps, lead the trump.

There is a great difference between playing against a trump declaration and against no-trumpers. In the first case, the leader is
opposed to unusual trump strength, and his object must be to make
what he can of his winning cards, before the declarer gets into the
lead and discards his weak suits, so as to be ready to trump them.
However, in the second case, there being no trumps, the leader's
object should be to get a suit established against the dealer, if he
can, and the longer the suit is, the better. The dealer's strength in
a no-trumper is usually scattered, and he can often be found with a
weak or missing suit, which is usually the suit in which the eldest
hand or his partner is long.

We will first consider the leads against trump declarations, because
they are more common and are also the more useful. If a player
makes a trump-hand lead against a no-trump declaration, he will not
do nearly so much harm as if he were to make a no-trump-hand lead
against a trump declaration. For that reason, if a player cannot
master both systems of leading, it is better for him to learn the leads
against trumps than those against no-trumps.

RULES FOR LEADING HIGH CARDS   With a suit such as A K Q
2, no one need be told not to begin with the deuce. Whenever a
player holds two or more of the best cards of a suit, he should play
one of them. If he holds both second and third best, playing one of
them will force the best out of his way, leaving him with the commanding card.

The cards that are recognised by bridge players as being high are
the A K Q J 10, and if we separate the various combinations from
which a player should lead each of these cards, a study of the groups
so formed will greatly facilitate our recollection of them.

In the first group are the hands that contain two or more of the best cards. In this and all following notation, the exact size of any card below a Ten is immaterial.

So far as trick-taking is concerned, it is of no importance which of the winning cards is first led; however, good players lead the King from all these combinations in order that the partner may be informed, by its winning, that the leader holds the Ace also.

In the second group are the hands that contain both the second and third best, but not the best.

The *King* is the proper lead from these combinations. If it wins, the partner should have the Ace; if it loses, the partner should know that the leader holds at least the Queen.

Both these groups, which contain all the King leads, can be easily remembered by observing that the King is always led if accompanied by the Ace or Queen, or both. Beginners should follow this rule for leading the King, regardless of the number of small cards in the suit.

There is only one combination from which the *Queen* is led: when it is accompanied by the Jack, and there is no higher card of the suit in the hand. Whether or not the Ten follows the Jack does not matter. With any two high cards in sequence, the lead is a high card when you are playing against a declared trump.

The *Jack* is never led except as a supporting card. It is always the top of the suit, and the suit is usually short. The object of making this opening is to avoid leading suits headed by two honours that are not in sequence. These are good Jack leads:

The *Ten* is led from one combination only:

The *Ace* should not be led if it can be avoided; however, it is better to lead it from suits of more than four cards, so as to make it at once. If the Ace is accompanied by the King, the King is the card to lead, not the Ace. If the Ace is accompanied by other honours, such as the Queen or Jack, it is better to avoid opening the suit, unless you have five or more cards of it. But if you do lead a suit headed by the Ace, *without the King*, be sure that you lead the Ace, when you are playing against a trump declaration, or you may never make it.

All combinations such as the following should be avoided, if possible, because more can be made out of them by letting them alone.

However, with three honours: A Q J, the Ace should be led.

RULES FOR LEADING SHORT SUITS It will sometimes happen that the only four-card suit in the leader's hand is trumps or a suit headed by honours not in sequence, which it is not desirable to lead. In these cases, if there is no high-card combination in any of the short suits, it is usual to lead the highest card, unless it is an Ace or a King. Many good players will not lead the Queen from a three-card suit, unless it is accompanied by the Jack. All these leads are called *forced*, and are intended to assist the partner, by playing cards that can strengthen him, although they are of no use to the leader. The best card should be led from any combinations such as the following:

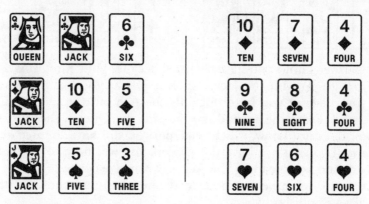

SMALL-CARD LEADS If the suit selected for the lead does not contain any combination of high cards from which it would be right to lead a high card, good players make it a rule to begin with the fourth-best, counting from the top of the suit. This is called the 'card of uniformity,' because it indicates to the partner that there are remaining in the leader's hand exactly three cards higher than the one led.

Should the player be forced to lead any of the undesirable combinations shown on the previous page, he would begin with the Ace if he held it; otherwise, he would lead the fourth-best. In each of the hands shown, this would be the four, and this card would be led, even if there were five or six cards in the suit. From the following hand, for example, the five is the proper lead.

RULES FOR LEADING SECOND ROUND   If the leader wins the first trick, having the best of the suit in his hand, he should follow with the winning card, but if he has several cards that are equally winning cards, he should lead the lowest of them. This is an indication to the partner that the card led is as good as the best; therefore, the leader must hold the intermediate cards. When a King wins, your partner knows you have the Ace, if he does not hold it. Then tell him what he does not know: that you have the Queen also.

Suppose you have led the King from these combinations:

    |

Your partner knows you have the Ace, because your King wins. From the first, go on with the Jack, which is just as good as the Ace but tells your partner you have not only the Ace but the Queen still in your hand. From the second, go on with the Queen, the card your partner does not know, which tells him you still have the Ace *but not the Jack*. If you do not have the Queen, you will have to go on with the Ace, and your leading the Ace *will deny the Queen*.

If you do not have the best, lead one of the second- and third-best, if you hold both:

    |

From the first of these, having led the King, if it wins, go on with the Ten, whether or not you have any smaller cards. From the second, if the King wins, go on with the Jack, which denies the Ten but tells your partner you still have the Queen. No mistake is more common among beginners than leading a low card on the second round, on the assumption that the partner must have the Ace. If you have led from King and Queen only, you must go on with the fourth-best, because you do not have both the second- and the third-best. This fourth-best is the card that was the fourth-best originally. Having led the King from this:

the card to follow the King is the Six, if the King wins the first trick.

THE FOURTH-BEST From any combination of cards, if you do not have the best, or both the second- and the third-best, in your hand for the second round, lead your original fourth-best. From all the following, the proper lead on the second round would be the fourth-best, in each case the four of the suit:

LEADING TRUMPS A trump lead is sometimes adopted when all the plain suits are bad ones to lead away from, such as A Q, or A J, or K J in each and no length. If a player holds high cards that are not in sequence, such as the major tenace, Ace and queen, it is very probable that the declarer holds the King. By refusing to lead these suits, and waiting for them to come up to the tenace, the declarer's high card may be caught and a valuable trick saved. When a good player opens his hand with a trump, right up to the declaration, his partner should lead his best supporting cards boldly up to Dummy's weak suits.

THE PONE'S LEADS When the pone gets into the lead, if he does not return his partner's suit, he should open his own suits according to the rules already given for all the high-card combinations. If he has no high-card combination, it is usually better for him to lead some card that will beat Dummy than to lead his fourth-best. Suppose he wishes to lead a diamond, in which he holds Q 10 8 4 3, and Dummy has only the 9 and 6. It is better to lead the ten of diamonds than the fourth-best, because if the declarer does not follow with an honour, your partner will not have to sacrifice an honour to keep Dummy from winning the trick with the 9.

After the opening lead, when Dummy's cards are exposed, the knowledge of his cards may change the aspect of the game greatly; however, the proper cards to lead to and through Dummy will be better understood in connection with the play against no-trumpers.

NO-TRUMP LEADS The main difference in the leads against no-trumpers is that there is no hurry to make your aces and kings: the main thing is to make some of the smaller cards good for tricks. When you are long in a suit, if you lead out the winning cards first, your partner might have none to lead you later on, and if you cannot make every trick in the suit before you lose the lead, you might never make anything but your one or two high cards.

The difference in the leads at no-trump is covered by a very simple rule: if you have only two honours in sequence, do not lead either of them, but begin with the fourth-best, even if your honours are the Ace and King. However, if you have three honours in the suit, and two of them are in sequence, always lead an honour against a no-trumper.

The exception to this rule is that when you are so long in the suit that you might catch some high cards with your high cards, you lead them first. With six or seven in suit to the A K, for example, lead the King, on the chance of dropping the Queen. With seven in suit headed by the Ace, lead the Ace, but never with less than seven without the King. With six in suit, you may lead the King from K Q, without either Jack or 10; but with less than six in suit, never lead the King from K Q unless you have the 10 or the J also.

THIRD-HAND PLAY The leader's partner must do his best to inform his partner as to the distribution of his suit. The method of doing this is entirely different when there is a trump from that which is adopted when there is no trump. In the first case, all your partner wants to know is who is going to trump his suit if he goes on with it. In the second case, what he wants to know is his chance for getting his suit cleared or established.

WITH A TRUMP When third hand makes no attempt to win the trick, either because his partner's or Dummy's card is better than any he need play, he plays the higher of two cards only, the lowest of three or more. This is called playing *down and out*. Suppose third hand holds 7 and 2 only, and the lead is a King. The 7 is played. The leader goes on with the Ace, denying the Queen, and third hand plays the deuce. If the Queen is not in the Dummy, the declarer must have it. In any case, the leader knows that if he goes on, his partner, third hand, can trump that suit. With three cards, the lowest falling to the first round, followed by a higher card, will show the leader that third hand still has another of that suit. Many players use this echo to show the Queen, when the King is led.

It is not necessary to play down and out with an honour, because the leader can read the situation without it. Suppose third hand holds the J 5. He plays the 5 to the first round, because one of his two cards is an honour. The leader goes on with the Ace, and the Jack falls. Now third hand must have the Queen or no more, and no matter which it is, he can win the third round, with either the Queen or a trump.

AGAINST NO-TRUMPERS   When there is no trump, third hand uses what is called the *Foster echo*. This consists of playing always the second-best of the suit, when no attempt is made to win the trick. Suppose the leader begins with the King. Third hand holds 10 8 7 4, and plays the 8. This marks him with only one card higher than the 8, and is a great exposer of false cards played by the declarer.

On the second round, the rule is to always to keep the lowest card of the suit until the last. If third hand held four originally: 10 8 7 4, his play to the second round would be the 7, and he would keep the 4. If he held 10 8 7 only, his play to the second round would be the 10, and he would keep the 7. This makes it clear to the leader how many and what he holds.

HIGH CARDS THIRD HAND   When third hand tries to win his partner's lead, he does so as cheaply as possible; that is, holding both King and Queen, he plays the Queen, not the King. If his cards are not in sequence, he should always play the best he has. With Ace and Queen, for example, he must play the Ace if the King is not in the Dummy. To play the Queen would be to throw it away if the declarer has the King. If the leader has the King, third hand gets out of his way by giving up the Ace.

FOSTER'S ELEVEN RULE   In trying to win tricks as cheaply as possible, third hand can often be guided by the Eleven Rule, which can be applied to any lead of a small card.

By deducting from eleven the number of pips on any low card led by his partner, the pone may ascertain definitely how many cards there are *higher than the one led* that are not in the leader's hand. This rule, which was invented by R. F. Foster in 1881, in connection with the game of whist, is used by anyone who wants to be a good bridge player. The rule itself is this:

When the eldest hand leads any card that is not an honour, deduct the spots on it from eleven. From the remainder thereby found, deduct the number of cards *higher than the one led* that are in neither your own hand nor Dummy's in that suit. This final remainder is the number of cards that are in the declarer's hand that are higher than the card led. The main thing to remember is that it is only the cards higher than the one led that you need worry about. By way of example:

Suppose you are third hand, and your partner leads the seven of clubs, Dummy lays down the Q 9 2, and you hold A J 3, therefore:

Leader

Dummy

Third hand

Deducting seven from eleven, you find it leaves four. These four cards, higher than the one led, are all in sight: Q 9 in Dummy, and A J in your own hand; therefore, the declarer cannot have any card higher than the seven. If he has, your partner's lead is not his fourth-best, as you will see if you lay out the cards.

RETURNING SUITS   When third hand returns his partner's suit, he should lead the higher of two cards, and the lowest of three, unless he has a card that will beat anything Dummy might hold in the suit, in which case he should *always beat Dummy*.

PLAYING AGAINST DUMMY   Some of the fine points in bridge arise in situations in which careful consideration of the Dummy's cards is required.

There are three great principles in playing against Dummy:
● First, lead through the strong suits, and up to the weak.
● Second, do not lead through a fourchette.
● Third, do not lead up to a tenace.
These rules must not be blindly followed in every instance. They are simply general principles, and some of the prettiest *coups* arise from the exceptional cases.

LEADING THROUGH DUMMY   The eldest hand, when he does not deem it advisable to go on with his own suit, can be guided in his choice by the strength or weakness of specific suits in Dummy's hand. The play against Dummy is especially important at no trumps.

Suits that it is good policy to lead through are A x x x, K x x x or any broken sequences of high cards.

Suits in which Dummy either is long or holds any of the regular high-card combinations should be avoided; winning or high sequences are especially dangerous. To lead these suits through Dummy's strength is an invitation to your partner to force you in the suit led.

It is not necessary for you to be strong in a suit that you lead through Dummy, and if both of you are weak, it is often advantageous, especially if it avoids leading one of his strong suits.

With A Q 10 x, Dummy having J x x x, play the 10. If your partner has the King, you make every trick in the suit.

With A Q 10 x, Dummy having K x x, play the Q. If Dummy passes, you make two tricks; if he covers, you have tenace over the Jack.

With A 10 9 x, Dummy having J x x x, play the 10. If your partner has the K, your A 9 is tenace over the Q.

With A J 10 x, Dummy having Q x x x, if the suit must be led, play the Jack; however, these positions should be avoided, except in the end game, or when you play for every trick.

With A J 10 x, Dummy having no honour in the suit, if you must lead the suit, play the 10.

In trumps, with K Q x x, Dummy having A J x x, play the Queen. If Dummy wins with A, play a small card for the second round, and he might refuse to put on the J. The declarer who does not have the 10 would make Dummy cover, but nothing is lost if he does, and it marks the 10 with your partner.

With King and others of a suit in which Dummy does not have the Ace, avoid leading the suit until the Ace has fallen.

With King alone, play it if Dummy has the Ace; keep it if he has not.

TRUMPS   If a player in this position is strong in trumps, he should keep quiet about it and let the maker of the trumps develop the suit. False-carding is perfectly legitimate in trumps, and will deceive the declarer more than your partner.

END GAMES   There are cases in which it is necessary to play as if your partner was known to have a specific card, because unless he has it, the game is lost. For example, you want one trick and have Q 10 x x, and Dummy has K x x, of an unplayed suit. The Queen is the best play, because if your partner has any honour, you must get a trick; otherwise, it is impossible.

You have K x in one suit, a losing card in another, and a winning card. You want all four tricks to save the game. Play the King, and then the small card; because if your partner does not have the Ace and another winning card, you must lose the game.

You have a losing trump, and Q x x of a suit in which Dummy has K 10 x. If you want one trick, play the losing trump, and count on your partner for an honour in the plain suit. If you must have two tricks, lead the Queen, and trust your partner to hold Ace.

LEADING UP TO DUMMY The best thing for the third hand, or pone, to do, when he does not return his partner's suit, and has no very strong suit of his own, is to lead up to Dummy's weak suits, and to lead a card that Dummy cannot beat, if possible.

The general principle of leading up to weakness suggests that we should know what weakness is. Dummy can be considered weak in suits of which he holds three or four small cards, none higher than an 8; Ace and one or two small cards; or King and one or two small cards. In leading up to these suits, your object should be to give your partner a finesse, if possible, and in calculating the probabilities of success, it must be remembered that there are only two unknown hands, so that it is an equal chance that he holds either of two unknown cards. It is 3 to 1 against his holding both, or against his holding neither. Of three unknown cards, it is 7 to 1 against his holding all three; or none of them; or about an equal chance that he holds two of the three; or one only.

If Dummy holds any of the weak suits just given, and you hold nothing higher than the Ten, you should lead it. Suppose you have 10 9 6, and Dummy has A 3 2. The K Q J can be distributed in eight ways, in any of which your partner will pass your Ten if second hand does not cover. In four cases, second hand would cover with the King, and in one with the Queen and Jack. In the remaining three, your partner's hand would be benefited.

If Dummy has King and one or two small cards, it is not as disadvantageous to lead up to the King as it would at first seem, because it is forced out of his hand on the first round, unless declarer plays Ace, and it is usually good policy to force out Dummy's cards of re-entry early in the hand.

In leading from high-card combinations, the usual bridge leads should be followed, but exceptions must be made on the second round when specific cards are in Dummy's hand; For example, with A K J and other cards, it is usual to stop after the first round and wait for the finesse of the Jack. This is obviously useless if the Queen is not in Dummy's hand; therefore, with K Q 10, unless Dummy has the Jack; or K Q 9, unless Dummy has the 10. The lead from A Q J should be avoided if Dummy has the King.

With A Q 10 and other cards, and J in Dummy's hand, begin with the Queen.

With A J 9 and other cards, and 10 in Dummy's hand, lead the Jack.

With A J 10, and if Dummy has K Q x, play the Jack, and do not lead the suit again.

In trumps, with K Q and other cards, if Dummy has the J singly guarded, begin with the King as usual, but follow it with the Queen instead of the smallest, because declarer might have passed in the hope of making a Bath coup with both Ace and Jack. In plain suits this is a dangerous lead: because declarer has Ace and wishes to force Dummy, he would hold his Ace as a matter of course.

With short suits, such as K x, Q x; or even with King or Queen alone, the honour is a good lead if Dummy has no court cards in the suit. The Queen is rather a better lead than the King, the only danger being that second hand holds fourchette.

With Q J x, or J 10 x, one of the high cards should be played. With Q 10 x, and if Dummy has Ace or King, the Queen should be led.

With K 10 x, and if Dummy has Jack, the suit should not be led.

With combinations such as K x x x, and if Dummy has Q x, the suit should not be led.

When you have a suit that is both long and strong, such as A K x x x, and Dummy has no honour in the suit, it is a common artifice to underplay, by beginning with the smallest, if you are playing against no-trumps and you have a card of re-entry. This should not be done unless you have the general strength to justify this finesse.

If you open a long suit, Dummy has only small cards, and your partner wins with Q, J, or 10, and does not return it, he has evidently a finesse in the suit and wants it led again.

END GAMES   In the end game, there are several variations that are made possible by the fact that the cards on your right are exposed.

With A J x, and if Dummy has Q x x, the small card should be led.

With Q x, and an odd card, and if Dummy has K x x of the first suit, it is better to play the odd card; however, if for any reason this should not be done, lead the Q, and hope to find A 10 with your partner.

The state of the score must be a constant guide in all end games; for example, you hold Q 10 x, and Dummy has J 9 x. If you want only one trick, play the Queen, but if you want two, play the small card.

SECOND-HAND PLAY The easiest position to play as second hand is, of course, with Dummy on your left, because Dummy's cards will show what is best to be done. If a small card is led, and you have King, put it on if Dummy does not have the Ace, unless you want your partner to get the lead. If Dummy has only two cards of the suit, and neither of them is the Ace, always play your King.

When the declarer leads a suit, it is often important to count how many he and your partner can possibly hold; for example, you have four: K x x x, Dummy has four: A J 10 x, and declarer leads the Queen. It is useless to play your King, because either the Queen is a singleton, and the declarer cannot continue the suit, which will compel Dummy to lead it to you eventually, or the third round will be trumped, perhaps by your partner. If you have only two small cards with the King, put it on the Queen. You cannot save it, but you might establish your partner's 9.

In the last three tricks, if you find yourself with a doubtful card, and the best and a small card of a suit that the declarer leads through you, win the trick and lead the doubtful card, because if the declarer held the best of that suit, he would have led it first, to be sure of a trick.

DUMMY ON THE RIGHT When Dummy leads through you, your skill in avoiding any traps the declarer might be setting for you will depend on your knowledge of how he manages his hand, and your ability to infer what he holds.

As a general principle, it can be assumed that any high card led by Dummy forms part of a combination, the unseen part of which is in the declarer's hand. If Dummy leads a Queen from Q x x, and you hold A J x, it is almost a certainty that the declarer holds the King. If you have A K x, the dealer must have J 10 and several other cards. If you have K x x, the declarer probably holds Ace, or a long suit headed by J 10.

When Dummy leads strengthening cards, they must be to give the declarer a finesse. If he leads a small card from small cards, some high-card combination must be in the declarer's hand. In these cases it is useless for you to finesse. If you have any sequence superior to the card led, cover with the lowest. There should be no false-carding in this, because your partner is the only player who can be deceived.

With A K and other cards, play the King, whatever Dummy leads.

With A Q and other cards, and if Dummy has nothing higher than the 9, play the Ace.

With K Q 10, play the Queen on a small card led, unless Dummy has the Jack.

With A J 10 x, play Ace if Dummy has no honour in the suit. However, if Dummy leads the 9, cover with the 10; if it loses, you lie tenace over the declarer.

With A J x, play the Jack on a 9 led. This prevents the finesse of the 9, and retains command of the suit. If Dummy has both K and Q, play your Ace. It is useless to play the Bath coup, because the declarer knows your cards, and your partner is only deceived.

With K x x, if Dummy does not have the Ace, do not play the King, no matter what is led.

With Q x x, unless Dummy has both A and K, do not play the Queen. If your partner has the Jack guarded, one of you must make a trick. If Dummy has A J, and leads J, put on the Queen; it might make the 9 or 10 good in your partner's hand.

With A x x, and if Dummy leads Jack, play the Ace.

With any fourchette, cover the card led.

If Dummy remains with one or two small cards of a suit that has been led, and you have the best, play it on the second round. Dummy's play is evidently for the ruff, and if the declarer does not have the second best, your partner has.

If you have King and only one or two small cards, and Dummy leads Queen from Q 10 x x, play your King. You cannot save yourself, but you may make the 9 good in your partner's hand. If you have three or more small cards, do not play the King, because either your partner or the declarer must be short in the suit. Therefore, if Dummy leads Jack from J 10 and other cards, play the King with a short suit. If your partner has Queen, you establish it; if not, you cannot make a trick in the suit.

With short suits it is usually best to cover an honour with an honour; however, with several small cards, such as K x x x, and if Dummy leads a singleton Queen, you should pass.

With K 10 x, and if Dummy has J and other cards, play honour on honour, and small card on small card, whichever Dummy leads.

It is often important for second hand to cover with what is called an *imperfect fourchette*. A true fourchette is the card immediately above and below the one led, such as K J over the Q, or Q 10 over the J. An imperfect fourchette is the card above the one led, and another next but one below it, such as K 10 over a Q led, or Q 9 over a J led. Covering forces the opponents to play two honours to win one trick, and will often make an intermediate card good in your partner's hand.

THIRD-HAND PLAY In addition to the methods of echoing on the partner's leads of high cards in the suit first opened, third hand must be ready to adapt himself and his play to any change of suit, and will require constant practice in putting himself in his partner's place, asking himself what the object is in leading specific cards through Dummy's hand. The inferences from the conventional leads should be sufficiently familiar to require no further explanation, but even good players occasionally overlook indications that the partner holds specific cards. For example, A leads a small card, and Y, Dummy, holds Q x x, and plays Q. You play the King and win the trick. This marks not only the Ace, but the *Jack* in your partner's hand, because the declarer would not play a twice guarded Queen from Dummy's hand if he had the Jack guarded himself.

False cards should be avoided by third hand as much as possible. The declarer will give your partner enough to puzzle over without your adding to the confusion. There are some exceptions in trumps, for example you have K Q x; Dummy has A J x x, and your partner leads. Unless Dummy plays Ace, you should put on the King, and change the suit.

If you hold Ace and other cards in a plain suit, and your partner leads Jack, pass it if Dummy has no honour. Perhaps by winning the second round you can give the invited force. With any honours other than the Ace, pass a partner's Jack led.

If your partner leads you a suit of which he knows, or should know, you do not have the best, he must have a good finesse in the suit that he does not lead, and you should take the first opportunity to lead that suit to him.

In returning your partner's suits, some modification can be suggested by way of the condition of Dummy's hand. For example, with K x x, and if Dummy has A Q J x, if you win, third hand, on Dummy's finesse, you can be sure your partner's lead was a weak suit. If Dummy is weak in the other two plain suits, your partner might have a good finesse in one or both of them.

When your partner wins the first round of an adverse suit, and immediately returns it, he is inviting a force.

DUMMY ON THE LEFT   When the player is third hand with Dummy on his left, his main concern will be to divine his partner's object in leading specific cards up to Dummy.

The general principles of inference are the same as in the preceding case, and cards can often be inferred in the same way from the evident intention of your partner. For example, you hold K x x, your partner leads J, and declarer covers with Queen. A glance at Dummy's cards shows him to have 10 x x, so your partner can be credited with A 9. You have x x; your partner leads Q, covered by declarer with K; and Dummy has J x x. You can credit your partner with A 10. You have x x, your partner leads Q, and declarer wins with Ace; Dummy holds 10 x x. Your partner must have J 9 and other cards, and the declarer has the King.

There are several cases in which you should not allow Dummy to win the trick. If you have only one card of a suit in which your partner leads Ace then Queen, and Dummy has the King twice guarded, trump at once, if you can, to prevent Dummy from getting into the lead. Your partner leads Queen, you hold A 10 x, and Dummy has K x x. Let the King make on the first round.

If your partner leads a small card up to strength in Dummy's hand, he is either inviting a force or trying to establish a long suit. Under these circumstances, if you have the Ace, play it, and lead a second round of the suit immediately, whereby the question will be settled.

If you have Q J 10 of a suit in which your partner leads King, play the Jack, so that he will count you for Q or no more, and will not go on with the Ace.

IN GENERAL Both the adversaries of Dummy should adopt the usual tactics for unblocking, and so on, especially in no-trumpers, and in some cases Dummy's exposed cards will make the matter more simple. For example, you hold A Q alone, of a suit that partner leads. If you are the pone, and Dummy does not have the King, play Ace and return the Queen.

FOURTH HAND There is only one difference from the usual methods in playing fourth hand, and that is in indicating sequences by winning with the best and returning the lowest to show the intermediate cards. For example, fourth player, who holds K Q J x, wins with King and returns the Jack, or with A K Q, wins with Ace and returns the Queen. The reason for this is that the declarer gains nothing by the information, because he knows from the first what cards are out against him; however, the information might be valuable to your partner, the second hand. If it is not the intention to return the suit at once, the lowest of the sequence should be played.

PLAYING TO THE SCORE This is a most important element, and there is no surer indication of a careless or weak player than his inattention to the score.

You cannot be too early impressed with the importance of saving the game before trying to win it, although great risks can be taken to win a game that cannot be lost that hand.

Never risk a sure contract in the hope of making more, unless the two will win the game, and the odd trick will not win it. Never risk a trick that will save the game in the hope of winning more, and always set a contract while you can.

DISCARDING This is one of the still unsettled questions of bridge tactics: some people believe in discarding the weak suit always, others the strong suit always, and others one or the other according to the declaration. Against a trump declaration, almost everyone agrees that it is best to discard the best suit, so that if your partner gets in before you do, he can have something to guide him as to what your best chance is for any more tricks.

Against no-trumpers, most players hug even possible tricks in their long suit and discard their weak suits, on the ground that it is foolish to throw away cards that might win tricks. Although this is true, it is also true that in discarding their weak suit they too often enable the declarer to win tricks that they might have stopped. For this reason, many players *discard the suit they are not afraid of,* that is, their best protected suit, and keep what protection they have in the weak suits, even if it is nothing but three to a Jack or ten. Unfortunately, no one has yet been able to advance any argument sufficiently convincing for either system to demonstrate that it is better than the other. Some of the best teachers of the game advocate the discard from strength against no-trumps; others teach the weak discard.

ENCOURAGING DISCARDS In order to distinguish between discards from weakness and those from strength, many players use what is called an encouraging card. This is anything higher than a six, if they have protection in the suit, or want it led. A player with an established suit, and A 8 2 of another suit, for example, would discard the 8, to encourage his partner to lead that suit and put him in. In case there is no card higher than the six, the reverse discard is used. With A 4 2, the play would be the 4 and then the 2. Some players use this reverse, or encouraging, card to induce the partner to continue the suit he is leading.

THE DECLARER'S PLAY The main difference between the play of the Dummy and partner and that of their adversaries is that there is no occasion for the former to play on the probability of his partner's holding certain cards, because a glance will show whether or not he holds them. There is no hoping that he might have specific cards of re-entry, or strength in trumps, or that he will be able to stop an adverse suit, or anything of that sort, because the facts are exposed from the first. Instead of adapting his play to the slowly ascertained conditions of his partner's hand, the declarer should have it mapped out and determined before he plays a card. He might see two courses open to him: to draw the trumps and make a long suit, or to secure the discards that will give him a good cross-ruff. A rapid estimate of the probable results of each line of play, a glance at the score, and his mind should be made up. Several examples of this foresight will be found in the example hands.

Another point of difference is that the declarer should play false cards whenever possible. He does not have a partner who, if he plays the King, might jump to the conclusion that he can trump a suit, or does not have the Queen. The more thoroughly the adversaries are confused, the greater the advantage to the declarer, especially in the end game.

WITH A TRUMP When the winning declaration is a suit for trumps, the declarer's first consideration on getting into the lead must be whether or not to lead trumps. As a rule, the trumps should be led at once, so as to exhaust the adversaries; however, there are exceptional cases, the main ones being:

Do not lead trumps from the strong trump hand if it would be to your advantage to put the other hand in the lead with a plain suit, so as to let the trump lead come from the weaker hand to the stronger, as when a finesse in trumps is desirable.

Do not lead trumps if you have no good plain suit, and can make more tricks by playing for a cross-ruff.

Do not lead trumps if the weaker hand can trump some of your losing cards first. It often happens that a *losing trump* can be used to win a trick before trumps are led.

AT NO-TRUMP The declarer's first concern in a no-trumper must be to select the suit that he will play for. Four simple rules cover this choice:

1. Always lead from the weak hand to the strong if the suit is not already established.

2. Play for the suit in which you have the greatest number of cards between the two hands, because it will probably yield the greatest number of tricks.

3. If two suits are equal in number, play for the one in which you have the greatest number of cards massed in one hand; that is, if you have two suits of eight cards each, select the one that has six of those cards in one hand, in preference to the suit that has four in each hand.

4. Everything else being equal, play for the suit that is shown in the Dummy, so as to conceal from the adversaries as long as possible the strength in your own hand.

A suit is said to be *established* when you can win every remaining trick in it, no matter who leads it. Because it is very important that the hand that is longer in the suit should be able to lead it without interruption when it is established, good players make it a rule to always *play the high cards from the shorter hand* first, so as to get out of the way. With Q 10 and three other cards in one hand, and K J and one other in the other hand, the play is the K and J from the short hand, keeping the Q 10 in the long hand.

If there is any choice, the suit should be selected that contains the longest sequence, or the sequence that has the fewest breaks. It should be noticed that the sequence need not be in one hand, because it is almost as valuable if divided, and it is especially advantageous to have the higher cards concealed in the declarer's hand. Its continuity is the main point. For example, declarer and Dummy hold between them one suit of K J 9 7 5 4 3, and another of Q J 10 9 8 7 5. The latter should be selected, because two leads must establish it.

In establishing a long suit it is very important to note the fall of the missing cards in the sequences. In the first of the two combinations just given, the declarer should be as careful to watch for the fall of the 8 and 6 as for the A Q and 10.

LEADING It is quite unnecessary to follow any system of leads, other than to distinguish between the combinations from which high or low cards are led. However, it is important to remember that although a high-card combination can be divided, it should be played as if in one hand. For example, the declarer holds Q J x x x of a suit, and Dummy has A x x. By leading Q or J, Dummy is enabled to finesse, as if he held A Q J. The declarer holds K J x x x, and Dummy has Q x x. The play is to force the Ace, as if the combination of K Q J x x were in one hand.

Many opportunities arise for leading the Ace first from a short suit, in order to secure a ruff on the second or third round.

SECOND-HAND PLAY If any card is led by the adversaries that the fourth hand cannot win, the second hand should cover it if possible, because unless he does so, his weakness will be exposed, and the suit will be continued. This is especially true of cases in which the second hand holds single honours, such as Jack and other cards, or Queen and other cards. Even the King should be played second hand in these cases, unless it is so well guarded that the Ace must fall before the King can be forced out.

If the fourth hand can win the card led, it is seldom necessary to cover the second hand. For example, if the Jack of trumps is led, the dealer holds Q 9 7 4, and Dummy has A 6 3 2, there is no need to play the Queen. If the King is with the third hand, this play would establish the Ten. If the King is with the leader, it or the Ten must make. If Dummy were second hand with the same cards, and Jack was led, he should not play the Ace, because third hand must play the King to shut out the Queen.

With A Q 9, and if your partner has K and other cards, it is best to play A on J led.

If the dealer has Ace and several other cards of a suit led, and Dummy has only two small cards, a force can definitely be secured by passing the first round. If Dummy has the Ace and passes second hand, and the dealer fails to win the trick, the adversaries will of course see that the play is made in order to force the dealer on the third round.

If Dummy is weak in trumps, and has only one card of a suit in which the dealer has Ace and others, the Ace should be played, and Dummy forced, unless there is a better game.

It is a disadvantage to play in second hand from suits in which each has a guarded honour. If the dealer has Q x x, and Dummy has J x, they must make a trick in that suit if they play a small card second hand, and avoid leading the suit. The same is true of the adversaries, but they must play on the chance that the partner has the honour, whereas the dealer knows it.

FINESSING   This is a very important part of the strategy of the game for the dealer. The adversaries of the dealer never finesse in bridge, but the dealer himself relies on finessing for any extra tricks he might want.

A finesse is any attempt to win a trick with a card that is not the best you hold, nor in sequence with it. Suppose you have Ace and Queen in the hand that is longer in the suit, and lead from the shorter hand a small card. If you play the Queen, that is a finesse, because you hope to take a trick with it, although the King is against you.

It is usually bad play to finesse when there are nine cards of the suit between the two hands, dealer's and Dummy's, because there is a good chance that the card you wish to finesse against will fall.

When it will be necessary to take two finesses in the same suit, the lead must come twice from the weaker hand. Suppose the dealer holds A Q J and other cards. If the first finesse of the Jack wins, he should put Dummy in again, so as to take a second finesse of the Queen. Suppose the dealer holds A J 10, and finesses the ten the first time. If it falls to the Queen, he should get Dummy in again, so as to take the second finesse with the Jack. The idea is to take advantage of the fact that the odds are against both King and Queen being in one hand. If they are both on the right, one of them will be played on the small card led from Dummy, and then the dealer can win it with the Ace and force out the other high card with his Jack, which will have become one of the second- and third-best of the suit.

RE-ENTRY CARDS   After a suit has been *cleared*, or established, it will be necessary to get into the lead with it. For this purpose the dealer must be careful to preserve a re-entry card in the hand that is longer in the suit. Suppose that Dummy's long suit is clubs, but that the Ace is against him, and that his only winning card outside is the Ace of diamonds. If diamonds are led, and the dealer has the Queen, he must let the lead come up to his hand so as to keep Dummy's Ace of diamonds for a re-entry to bring the clubs into play after the Ace has been forced out and the suit established. Many of the prettiest plays in bridge are in the management of re-entry cards.

UNDERPLAY   When the dealer is afraid of a suit that is opened against him, and has only one winning card in it, such as the Ace, he should hold up that card until the third hand has no more of the suit to lead to his partner. The original leader will then have to get in himself, because his partner cannot help him; however, if the dealer gave up the Ace on the first trick, it would not matter which partner got into the lead: they would return to the suit first opened.

DUCKING   This is a method of play by which the dealer hopes to make his own suit even when the hand that is longer in it has no re-entry card. Suppose Dummy holds six clubs to the Ace King, and not another trick in his hand. The dealer has only two small clubs to lead. If the two winning clubs are led right out, it is impossible to catch the Q J 10, no matter how those cards lie; therefore, the dealer leads a club, but makes no attempt to win the first round. No matter what is played by the adversaries, he *ducks* the first round, and keeps his Ace and King. Next time the dealer gets in, he leads another club, is now able to win the second and third rounds of the suit, and will probably catch all the adverse cards and establish it.

The dealer's play always requires careful planning of the whole hand in advance.

THE NULLO   Although not yet in the official laws of the game, this bid seems to be a popular one with many players. It is a contract to lose tricks instead of win them, and is mainly a defence against overwhelmingly strong no-trumpers. A bid of three nullos means that the declarer will force his opponents to win nine tricks, and he wins four only, so that each trick under seven counts for the nullo player on his side.

SCORING There is some difference of opinion as to the proper value for the nullo, but the general verdict seems to be to put it just below the no-trumper at 10 a trick, no honours. Two no-trumps will outbid two nullos. If the adversaries of a nullo revoke, the declarer can give them two of his tricks, or take 50 in honours as penalty. If he revokes, they take 50 penalty as usual.

SUGGESTIONS FOR BIDDING The dealer should never bid a nullo originally, because it gives his partner no information as to the distribution of the suits. When any player has one long suit good for either no-trumps or nullos, such as A K Q 6 4 2, he should 'shout,' bidding a trick more than necessary. Singletons and missing suits are valuable parts of a nullo hand, because they afford opportunities for discards. It is always dangerous to bid a nullo without the deuce of the longest suit. If the dealer bids a spade, his partner can safely bid one nullo, because the contract is seldom or never obtained for less than two or three, but he should not persist in the nullo if his partner does not assist it. The greater the opposition from a no-trumper, the more probable that the nullo will succeed, but it is a dangerous declaration in any case. The player with aces and kings is sure to win tricks, regardless of his partner's hand, but deuces and treys are not sure to lose, because the partner might have all high cards, although not the tops.

SUGGESTIONS FOR THE PLAY The declarer should count up the tricks he must win, and as a rule win them early, bunching his high cards as much as possible. Suits with two small cards and two high ones must win one trick, but should escape with that. The great point is to lead losing cards from one hand and discard dangerous cards in other suits from the other hand whenever possible.

The opponents of a nullo should lead their shortest suits, so as to get discards later, keeping their eyes on the dummy and forcing it to win tricks whenever possible, but never allowing it to get a discard. The partner's leads should be returned unless a singleton can be led at once. It is usual to lead the top of two cards, the intermediate of three or more, and to avoid leading suits that are safe, with small cards at the bottom.

ILLUSTRATIVE AUCTION HANDS

Z is the dealer in both cases, but Y makes the winning declaration, so that B leads for the first trick. The first illustration is straight auction; the second is a nullo. The underlined card wins the trick, and the card under it is the next one led.

A	Y	B	Z		A	Y	B	Z
Q ♠	2 ♠	9 ♠	♣ 2	1	**A ♢**	Q ♢	J ♢	9 ♢
A ♠	6 ♠	8 ♠	♡ 3	2	**K ♢**	6 ♢	8 ♢	5 ♢
K ♠	10 ♠	4 ♠	♡ 7	3	**10 ♢**	4 ♢	♡ A	3 ♢
5 ♠	**J ♠**	3 ♠	♡ J	4	J ♠	3 ♠	9 ♠	**A ♠**
2 ♢	**Q ♢**	4 ♢	5 ♢	5	5 ♠	Q ♠	**K ♠**	6 ♠
10 ♢	9 ♢	7 ♢	**J ♢**	6	♣ Q	♣ 6	♣ J	**♣ K**
♡ 4	3 ♢	8 ♢	**A ♢**	7	7 ♢	♡ 7	♡ 5	**♡ 10**
7 ♠	♡ 5	♡ 9	**K ♢**	8	**10 ♠**	♡ 7	♡ Q	♡ 9
♡ 8	♣ 3	♡ 2	**6 ♢**	9	**♣ 5**	♣ 4	♣ 2	♣ 3
♣ 4	**♣ Q**	♣ 10	♣ 9	10	**7 ♠**	2 ♠	4 ♠	♡ K
♣ 5	**♣ A**	♡ 6	♣ 7	11	♣ 10	♡ 4	**♣ A**	♡ 8
♣ 8	**♣ K**	♡ 10	♡ Q	12	♣ 8	♡ 3	**♣ 9**	♡ 6
♣ J	♣ 6	♡ A	♡ K	13	♣ 7	2 ♢	**8 ♠**	♡ 2

In the first example, the dealer, Z, bids a heart. A says one spade and Y two clubs. This bid of Y denies any support for his partner's hearts, but shows a supporting minor suit, in case Z is strong enough to go on with the hearts. B bids two spades because he can stop the hearts twice and ruff the clubs. Z cannot pursue the hearts, but shows his supporting minor suit, bidding three diamonds. This says to Y, 'Go no trumps if you can stop the spades.' When A passes, having bid his hand on the first round, Y goes two no-trumps and makes game. B leads the top of his partner's declared suit, and A leads a fourth round, hoping to get in with the club jack. At tricks 8 and 9, B signals control in hearts. A keeps the protection in clubs to the end and saves a trick by it. Y keeps two clubs in dummy, so that if club is led, he will have one to return after he has made his diamonds.

In the second example, they are playing nullos, and Y is declaring. The points in the play are holding the spade queen, so as to lead a diamond or a spade at trick 6. This B prevents, hoping to force two clubs on Y and Z and set the contract. At trick 7, if the hearts are split, the queen must win the ten. If not, Z must win one heart trick. Y makes his contract, losing four odd.

ILLUSTRATIVE AUCTION HANDS

Following are two illustrations of use of the conventional double. Z is the dealer in both hands, but B is the final declarer, so that Z leads. The underlined card wins the trick, and the card under it is the next one led.

A	B	Y	Z	#	A	Y	B	Z
♡ 3	♡ 2	♡ 4	♡ K	1	♣ Q	♣ 2	♣ 6	♣ 10
5 ♢	♡ 9	♡ 6	♡ Q	2	♡ 10	♡ 2	♡ 3	♡ A
3 ♠	5 ♠	Q ♠	2 ♠	3	♣ A	♣ 3	♣ 7	♣ J
Q ♢	6 ♢	2 ♢	3 ♢	4	♡ Q	♡ 4	♡ 7	♡ 5
6 ♠	7 ♠	A ♠	4 ♠	5	♡ 6	2 ♠	♡ J	♡ 9
A ♢	9 ♢	4 ♢	K ♢	6	2 ♢	3 ♢	A ♢	6 ♢
K ♠	8 ♠	♡ 7	10 ♠	7	K ♢	9 ♢	5 ♢	J ♢
J ♠	9 ♠	♡ 8	♡ 5	8	7 ♢	3 ♠	4 ♢	Q ♢
8 ♢	10 ♢	J ♢	♣ 5	9	♣ 5	♣ 9	♡ 8	♣ K
♣ 4	♣ 3	♣ J	♣ A	10	4 ♠	6 ♠	A ♠	5 ♠
♣ 8	♡ J	7 ♢	♡ A	11	♡ K	7 ♠	8 ♠	K ♠
♣ Q	♣ 6	♣ 10	♣ 9	12	10 ♢	10 ♠	9 ♠	♣ 4
♣ K	♣ 7	♣ 2	♡ 10	13	8 ♢	Q ♠	J ♠	♣ 8

In the first illustration, Z deals and bids a heart, which A doubles, showing that he has a no-trumper, but is weak in hearts. Y passes and B bids two diamonds, because he is not long enough to call the spades. Z goes to two hearts, A to three diamonds, all of which pass.

Z might as well lead another heart, because the declarer can ruff dummy if he does not. A leads a small spade, so as to get the finesse in trumps, and then leads another spade to get out of dummy's way. After the king of trumps is caught, there is no hurry about catching the ten: it is more important to discard the losing hearts on the spades. If Y trumps the spades, B can over-trump. After the hearts are discarded and Y's trump is picked up, the ace of clubs is the only trick lost. Five odd. Game.

In the second illustration, Z deals and bids no-trump. Instead of bidding two no-trumps, A doubles to get a suit bid from B. Y bids two spades, which he would have done whether or not A had doubled. B passes, because the take-out relieves him from bidding on four small hearts. He could double, to show two stoppers; or he could have gone two no-trumps; or he could have bid the hearts. When he passes, A doubles two spades, to insist on a bid from B, who says three hearts.

Having so many re-entries, Z leads his own suit: clubs. The finesse holds. In leading trumps, B keeps high ones in each hand. After picking up the trumps, B clears the diamonds; he trumps the clubs himself, and lets dummy trump the spade and make the diamonds; five odd and game.

– –

VARIETIES OF AUCTION

THREE-HAND AUCTION   This is a game for three active players only, but four may form a table. Each player is for himself, there being no partnerships except the temporary combination against the declarer for each deal. The player who cuts the lowest card chooses his seat and cards, and the player with the next-lower cut sits on his left, the other on his right.

The cards are dealt one at a time into four packets, of thirteen each, just as in the ordinary game of auction, and the odd hand remains untouched until the winning declaration is decided. The dealer makes the first bid, and then each bids in turn until two pass. The penalty for bidding out of turn is 50 points added to the score of each opponent; for doubling out of turn it is 100. If both pass the irregularity, there is no penalty, but if only one passes, the third can call attention to it.

The highest bidder takes up the dummy hand, sorts it and lays it on the table opposite him, face up, as soon as the eldest hand leads a card. If there is a player sitting opposite the highest bidder, he moves to the vacant seat.

The game is 30 points, and the winner of a game adds 125 points to his score at once. The first player to win two games not only adds the 125 for the second game; he adds 250 more for winning the rubber. Honours are scored by each player separately, and every honour is worth as much as a trick in that suit. Four or five in one hand count double. At no trump, the aces count for 10 each to the holders, four in one hand 100. The declarer scores his dummy's honours.

At the end of the rubber, each wins from or loses to each of the others. The score is usually made up in the following way, whereby the final amounts to the credit of each are shown in the top line:

A, 240	B, 980	C, 456
− 740	+ 740	+ 215
− 215	+ 524	− 524
− 955	+1264	− 309

DUPLICATE AUCTION   This game can be played in any of the ways described for the movement of trays and players under the head of duplicate whist. Tricks and honours are scored as usual, but there are no games or rubbers. Should the declarer make 30 or more points on a single hand, he gets 125 points' bonus in the honour column.

AUCTION FOR THREE   There are two ways of arranging matters for three players, one of which is a development of the other.

STOP GAP   The idea of this game is to allow three people to play while waiting for a fourth to make up a rubber. Seats, cards and deal are cut for as usual, and dummy's cards are to the left of the dealer, who has the first bid. If he passes, the bidding goes round as usual, but the first bid made must be in suit, never in no-trumps, and for one trick only. This is to prevent the old way of making shut-out bids as a gamble on dummy. After the first bid, there are no restrictions on bids or doubling. The highest bidder sorts dummy's cards and places them between his adversaries, as soon as the first card is led.

Every deal is a game in itself, and tricks, honours and penalties are entered in a lump. If 30 or more is made by tricks, 100 bonus is added for a game won. Suppose the bid is four spades, doubled and set for one trick, less four honours. Each of the adversaries takes 64 points, the declarer nothing. The moment a fourth candidate for play appears, the game can be abandoned, and the scores balanced, as on the preceding page.

DUMMY UP   This is an improvement on stop gap, whereby the limitations on the first bid are removed, as well as the gamble on the dummy, by turning dummy's cards face up before a bid is made. Each player then proceeds to bid, dealer first, on his cards in combination with what he sees will be his dummy, when placed between his two adversaries.

Dummy-up can also be played by four people, whereby the dealer's cards are the dummy, and the actual dealer takes no part in the bidding or play, but shares in the fortunes of the winning declaration. This requires four separate scores to be kept.

AUCTION FOR TWO   There are three ways of playing, and each is suitable to the varying abilities of the people engaged.

CHINESE AUCTION   The lower cut deals, whereby he gives twenty cards to his adversary and twenty to himself, one at a time, face down. Separately from these he then deals six more to each, one at a time. These six are the 'playing hand'. Each player then takes up the twenty and lays out any ten of them face down, in two rows of five each. On these he places the remaining ten, face up.

The playing hands are then taken up and sorted, so that each sees twenty-six cards on which to bid or double.

The winning declaration, doubled or undoubled, settled, the non-declarer leads a card, from either his hand or the table, and the declarer plays to it, from hand or table. The non-dealer then plays again, and the declarer again, whereby the four cards form a trick, and the winner leads for the next trick. The moment a card is played from the table, the card under it must be turned face up. Every deal is a game, and 100 is added for reaching 30 in tricks.

No card that covers another card can be shifted, but the moment a card that was turned face down is turned up, it becomes playable, on either that trick or the next.

BLIND AUCTION   This is another form of the game for two players. Thirteen cards are dealt to each player, one at a time, and the remainder of the pack is laid aside, face down. The dealer examines his hand and makes the first bid, which his opponent can over-call or double. The bidding finished, the hand is played, but there are only two cards to a trick. The result is scored, and 100 is added if game, 30 points in tricks, is reached. The remaining twenty-six cards are now taken up, bid, played and scored. The secret of success in this game is a good memory for what cards fell in the first twenty-six.

DRAW AUCTION   The deal being cut for, thirteen cards are dealt to each player, one at a time, and the twenty-seventh is turned up, being left on the top of the remaining twenty-five, all of which are face down. There is no bidding, the hand is played at no-trumps, and the non-dealer leads for the first trick. The winner of this trick takes into his hand the turned card; the loser of the trick takes the next card, which he puts into his hand without showing it, but turns up the next card, to be played for as before, whereby the winner of the trick takes it.

When the stock is exhausted, there will be twenty-six cards played away, and thirteen in each hand still to play. Now the dealer can make a bid, and his opponent can overcall or double or pass, just as in auction. The result of the play on these last thirteen tricks is scored as at auction, and 100 is added for going game on the deal. The skill in this game is in drawing and holding cards that will be valuable for the final bidding, and in weakening the opponent by forcing him to give up valuable cards in following suit during the first thirteen tricks of the no-trumper. A strong point is in avoiding the necessity of taking in the worthless exposed cards, by letting your opponent win the tricks.

PIVOT BRIDGE   This is simply a movement of the players, and is very popular in social games. It requires that the four originally seated at a table remain at that table until the game is ended and do not cut for partners after the first rubber, but change in regular order. The usual way is for the first dealer to sit still all the time, and for the three other players to move round him in a circle at the end of each rubber. This will compel the player on his left to pass behind him and take the seat on his right. At the end of three rubbers, each will have had each of the others for a partner. When there are a number of tables in play, it will be necessary to have a prize for each, whereby the first choice is given to the player who has the highest score in the room.

When this method is adopted, it is not necessary to deduct the lower score from the higher at the end of each rubber, so that each player can keep what he gets: the comparative result is the same if the players remain at the same table. This method is open to the objection that if two strong players are opposed to weak ones all the time, it is a great advantage. It is also liable to abuse, if four players agree to double everything, so that someone at the table will score highly.

A method for obviating any possibility of collusion to win a large or special prize was tried out on 28 March 1916 at the Ritz-Carlton, New York, in a charity bridge for the Women's League for Animals, when the prizes were cars, chow dogs, boxes at the opera and so on. It was based on the following idea:

The average score for three rubbers, when the lower score is not deducted, will range between 1400 and 2100 points. From these you select 100 numbers, according to the following schedule, which represents the proportionate probability of the various scores:

Every 4th number between 1400 and 1500 =	25
Every 4th number between 1500 and 1600 =	25
Every 5th number between 1600 and 1700 =	20
Every 10th number between 1700 and 1800 =	10
Every 10th number between 1800 and 1900 =	10
Every 20th number between 1900 and 2000 =	5
Every 20th number between 2000 and 2100 =	5
Total selected numbers:	100

The manager can start the numbers at any point. If he begins with 1404, and goes to 1408, 1412, and so on, he will end that series of 25 at 1498 and start the next with 1502, ending at 1596. It is advisable to have them at regular intervals after the starting point has been fixed on.

These 100 numbers are placed in a sealed envelope, each on a slip of paper or a small card. After all the players' scores have been turned in to the committee at the end of the game and sorted out into numerical order, each group in a specific 100 by itself, all the 1500s in one pile, for example, one number is publicly drawn from the envelope containing the 100 selected scores, and the player whose score most closely approaches that number wins the first prize; the next-nearest number, above or below, second prize, and so on.

In the game referred to at the Ritz-Carlton, the number drawn was 1442, and the winning scores in their order were 1443, 1438, 1447, 1448, 1435 and 1434. In case of ties, the equal scores made by the players are turned face down and shuffled, and one is drawn by the committee; the player to whom it belongs is the winner of the tie.

Because no one can have the faintest idea what number will be drawn, except that the chances are in favour of the average scores, and that no one can expect to win a prize who cannot get at least 1400 points on three rubbers, this scheme is as fair for one person as for another, and its use has practically eliminated the undesirable element in any large semi-public games at which a few valuable prizes might be offered.

PROGRESSIVE AUCTION   This is simply a movement of the players from table to table, much as described under the heading of *Compass whist*. The players can either agree that all the north and south pairs will sit still and all the east and west pairs will move one table or they can arrange for the winners to move in a specific direction. In all progressive games, sometimes called *Drive Auction*, there are no rubbers or games, because one table would keep all the others waiting. An even number of deals, usually four, is the rule for each round before moving.

DUPLICATE AUCTION   This is auction with the hands kept separate and put into trays to be carried from table to table. The methods will be found fully described under the titles for duplicate whist.

CONTRACT BRIDGE   This is a variation of the regular game of Auction Bridge, in which the only difference is in the scoring. The amount that can be scored below the line, towards game, is the number of tricks bid, so that if the bid is three spades, and the dealer makes five odd, all he scores towards game is 27. For each trick he wins over his bid, he scores 10 points in honours, no matter what the final declaration might be.

In order to prevent reckless bidding, the penalty for the first trick by which a contract fails is the usual 50 points; however, for the second trick it is 100, and for the third and any further it is 150. These amounts arc doubled if the losing contract is doubled. There is the usual 50 points for fulfilling a doubled contract, 50 for each trick over, and 100 if redoubled.

There is no score for honours less than four in one hand; however, there is a bonus of 50 for little slam, and 100 for grand slam. If a little slam is both bid and made, it is worth 250, and if a grand slam is bid and made, it is worth 500. The partners who win the first or second game add 100 points in honours immediately. For winning the rubber game, they add 300, so that two games running are worth 400; two out of three are worth 300 only.

The revoke penalty is always two actual tricks, taken from the side in error. These might help to fulfil a contract, but carry no bonus if the contract was doubled. Tricks taken previous to the revoke cannot be taken, because they are obviously not affected by the error. Rubbers run about twice as large as at regular auction, so due allowance must be made for this in arranging the amount of the stakes.

PIRATE BRIDGE   In this form of the game of Auction Bridge, not only the final declaration but the partner is bid for. When a bid is made, it must be 'accepted' by some other player, or it is void. The player accepting becomes the partner without changing his seat. Any other player may overcall, in the same declaration if he likes, even after it has been accepted. If a bid of two hearts is accepted, a bid of three hearts is a try to get the original heart bidder to accept. No higher bid can be made until the preceding one is accepted, whereby a partnership is established. When a bid is not accepted, the player to the left of the unaccepted bidder has a chance to declare. Any bid not accepted goes back to the last acceptance. Four individual scores must be kept. The bidder is the declarer; the accepter is the dummy.

PAR AUCTION   This is simply a method of marking the backs of an ordinary pack of playing cards so that they can be dealt again and again in order to bring about the same distribution, instead of having to place them in trays, as in duplicate. There is supposed to be a definite score possible on each deal, if the bidding and play is perfect, and this score is called 'par'. The players who make this score exactly are winners. The cards are practically a set of twelve puzzles, because there are twelve deals in each pack. In order to learn how the hands were supposed to be bid and played, you have to purchase a book.

––

THE AMERICAN LAWS
OF AUCTION BRIDGE

HOW PLAYED

1. The game of Auction is played by four players, two against two playing as partners. Two partners constitute a side.

CARDS

2. Two packs[1] of cards that have different backs are used. A correct pack contains four suits of thirteen cards each: one card of each denomination to a suit. A pack becomes imperfect when one or more cards are torn, soiled or otherwise marked whereby they can be identified from their backs.

RANK OF CARDS

3. In the play, Ace is high, then King, Queen, Jack, Ten and so on; Deuce is the lowest. In drawing cards, Ace is low, then Deuce, Trey and so on; King is the highest.

RANK OF SUITS

4. In the declaration,[2] Spades are high, Hearts next, Diamonds next and Clubs lowest. In drawing cards, as between cards of equal denomination, Spades are low, Hearts next, Diamonds next, and Clubs highest.

LEAD

5. The player at the left of Declarer leads[3] to the first trick, and thereafter the winner of each trick leads to the next.

TRICK

6. After the lead, each player in his turn to the left plays[4] a card. A trick consists of four cards thereby played.

---

[1] The game can be played with one pack; legal provisions require that two packs be suspended by consent.

[2] In the declaration, No Trump ranks above any suit.

[3] A player leads or plays by placing one of his cards face upwards near the centre of the table.

[4] The first lead of a hand, when legally made, is called the initial lead.

FOLLOWING SUIT

7. A player must follow suit, that is must play a card of the suit led if he has one. When leading, or when void of the suit led, he may play any card he holds.[5]

WINNING THE TRICK

8. A trick is won for his side by the player who, (*a*) if the trick does not contain a trump,[6] plays the highest card of the suit led, or who (*b*) plays the highest trump, if the trick contains one or more trumps. A trick once turned and quitted[7] may not be looked at[8] until the end of the hand.

ODD TRICKS

9. Odd tricks are tricks won by Declarer in excess of six tricks. If Declarer fulfils his contract, his side counts the value of all odd tricks; otherwise, nothing is counted in the trick score.

TRICK VALUES

10. Odd tricks count in the trick score as follows:

With	Clubs	trumps,	each	trick	counts	6	points
"	Diamonds	"	"	"	"	7	"
"	Hearts	"	"	"	"	8	"
"	Spades	"	"	"	"	9	"
"	no trumps,		"	"	"	10	"

Doubling doubles the above values; redoubling multiplies them by four.

HAND

11. A hand[9] begins with the cut[10] and ends when the last card is played to the thirteenth trick.

GAME

12. A game is won when one side has a trick score of thirty (30) or more points. A game may be completed in one hand or more; each hand is played out[11] whether or not the game is won during it.

---

[5] To 'refuse' is to fail to follow suit. To 'renounce' (Law 55) is to refuse when able to follow suit. See Law 56 for 'revoked'.

[6] As a result of the bidding (Law 30), the hand may be played without a trump (that is, 'No Trump') or with one of the four suits as the trump. Any trump is a winner as against any card of a plain (non-trump) suit.

[7] Footnote to Law 56 (*a*) defines 'quitted'.

[8] Law 61 (*e*) prescribes penalty.

[9] 'Hand' is also used to mean the cards held by a player. When the word is used in this way, the sense is obvious. Also used to designate players, as in 'second hand', 'third hand' and so on.

[10] See Law 25.

[11] All points won are counted whether or not they are needed to make game.

RUBBER

13. (*a*) A rubber begins with drawing for partners (Law 22) or cutting out (Law 23) and is completed when one side has won two games. The side that has won two games adds a bonus of 250 points to its honour-score. The side that has the greater number of total points[12] wins the rubber.[13]

(*b*) When a rubber is started with the agreement that the play will terminate (that is, no new hand will commence) after a specified time, and the rubber is unfinished at that hour, the score is made up as it stands, and 125 is added to the honour-score of the winners of a game. A hand if started must be played out.

(*c*) If a rubber is started without any agreement as to its termination, and before its conclusion one player leaves, or if, after this agreement, a player leaves before the appointed hour without appointing an acceptable substitute (Law 21-a), the opponents have the right to consult and decide whether the score is to be cancelled or counted as in (*b*).

HONOURS

14. The Ace, King, Queen, Jack and Ten of the trump suit are the honours unless the declaration is No Trump, in which case the four Aces are the honours. Honours count in the honour-score of the side that received them in the deal.

HONOUR VALUES

15. Honour values are based on trick values (Law 10). They are not increased by doubling (Law 35) or redoubling (Law 36).

WHEN THERE IS A TRUMP

3 honours[14] between partners have the value of 2 tricks.

4 honours between partners have the value of 4 tricks.

4 honours held by one partner have the value of 8 tricks.

5 honours, held 3 by one and 2 by the other partner, have the value of 5 tricks.

5 honours, held 4 by one and 1 by the other partner, have the value of 9 tricks.

5 honours held by one partner have the value of 10 tricks.

WHEN THERE IS NO TRUMP

3 aces held between partners count 30 points.

4 aces held between partners count 40 points.

4 aces held by one partner count 100 points.

---

[12] See Law 17.

[13] Therefore, a side may win two games and still lose the rubber.

[14] 'Simple honours' means 3 honours.

SLAMS

16. A side that wins all thirteen tricks[15] scores 100 points for Slam.[16] A side that wins twelve tricks scores 50 points for Little Slam.[17] Slam points are added to the honour-score.[18]

SCORING

17. Each side has a trick-score, which includes only points won by odd tricks, and an honour-score for all other points, including bonuses for honours, penalties, slams and undertricks.

At the end of the rubber, the total points of a side are obtained by adding together its trick-score and honour-score.[19] Subtracting the smaller total from the greater gives the net points by which the rubber is won and lost.[20]

A proved error in the honour-score may be corrected at any time before the score of the rubber has been made up and agreed on.

A proved error in the trick-score may be corrected at any time before the next declaration begins (Law 29) or, if the error occurs in the final hand of the rubber, before the score has been made up and agreed on.

FORMING TABLES

18. A table consists of four, five or six members, four of whom are players. A complete table consists of six members. In forming a table, candidates who have not played rank first and in the order in which they entered the room. Candidates who have played but are not members of an existing table rank next. Candidates of equal standing decide priority by drawing[21] cards. Low wins.

ENTRY

19. Before the beginning of a rubber[22] a candidate may enter any incomplete table by announcing his desire to do so, and these announcements in the order made entitle candidates to places as vacancies occur. In case there are more candidates than there are vacancies, the provisions of Law 18 apply.

---

[15] Without counting tricks received as penalty for a revoke.

[16] Also called Grand Slam.

[17] When Declarer's contract is seven and he wins six odd, he counts 50 for Little Slam although his contract fails.

[18] Slam or Little Slam may be scored by either side.

[19] The 250-point bonus for winning two games (Law 13-*a*) is included.

[20] Law 13 (*a*) explains who wins a rubber.

[21] Method of drawing is described in Law 22.

[22] Law 13 (*a*) stipulates that the rubber begins when any player draws for either partners or cutting out.

MEMBERS LEAVING TABLE

20. If a member leaves a table, he forfeits all his right at that table unless he leaves to make up a table that cannot be formed without him and, when leaving, he announces his intention of returning when his place at the new table can be filled. In this case, if he returns, he has prior rights over any players who have joined the table in his absence, and he may displace one of them. When a member[23] leaves a table to make up a new table that cannot be formed without him, and does not claim the right to retain his membership in the old table, he will be the last to draw out of the new table.

PLAYERS LEAVING TABLES

21. (*a*) A player who leaves a table may, with the consent of the other three players, appoint a substitute to play in his absence; this appointment becomes void on return of that player or on conclusion of the rubber. In any case, the substitute when released regains all his previous rights.

(*b*) A player who withdraws from a table of four at the end of a rubber, or who, after availing himself of the privileges of paragraph (*a*) fails to return before the end of the rubber, thereby breaking up the table, cannot claim entry elsewhere as against the other three players from that table.

DRAWING FOR PARTNERS AND DEAL

22. A table having been formed, the members draw[24] cards. He who draws lowest becomes the dealer of the first deal and has the choice of packs and seats.[25] He who draws second lowest is Dealer's partner and sits opposite him. The third lowest has the choice of the two remaining seats; the fourth lowest takes the remaining seat. The members, if any, who draw higher than fourth lowest remain members of the table but do not play in the current rubber.

In all cases when drawing cards, should anyone show two or more cards, he must draw again.

A player having made a choice of packs or seats must abide by his decision.

CUTTING OUT

23. If at the end of a rubber a table consists of five or six members, the players who have played the greatest number of consecutive

---

[23] Should two members make up a new table, both rank ahead of the other members.

[24] One pack is spread face downwards on the table and each member draws one card. All draw from the same pack.

[25] A player may consult his partner before choosing.

rubbers are the first to lose their places as players (but do not lose their standing as members). The draw (Law 22) decides between claimants of equal standing; low wins.

THE SHUFFLE

24. After drawing for partners, second hand[26] shuffles the pack that Dealer has chosen (Law 22), and third hand[27] shuffles the still pack.[28] Thereafter, at the beginning of each deal, third hand shuffles the still pack.[29] After being shuffled, the still pack is placed between second and third hands, where it remains until the next deal.

During the shuffle, the pack must not be held below the table nor so that the face of any card can be seen.

Dealer has the right to shuffle last, but must not shuffle after the cut except as in 25 (*b*).

The deal must not proceed until the pack has been shuffled as herein provided.

THE CUT

25. (*a*) Dealer, immediately before the deal, places the pack before his right-hand opponent, who lifts off the top portion and places it beside the bottom portion, preferably towards Dealer, who then places the bottom portion on top. This constitutes the cut.

(*b*) If the cut leaves fewer than four cards in the top or bottom portion, or if during it any card is faced or displaced, or if there is any doubt as to where the pack was divided, or if any player shuffles after the cut, there must be a new shuffle and a new cut.[30]

THE DEAL

26. (*a*) The deal begins after the cut and ends when the last card has been placed in proper order in front of Dealer.

(*b*) After the first deal, players deal in turn to the left. A player may not deal for his partner if either opponent objects.

(*c*) Dealer gives the first card to the player on his left, and so on, until all fifty-two cards are dealt, the last one to Dealer.

(*d*) A player may not look at any of his cards during the deal. Penalty: 25 points in the adverse honour-score.

[26] The player on Dealer's left.
[27] Third hand is Dealer's partner.
[28] The 'still pack' is the pack not being dealt or used in the play of the hand.
[29] A player may not cut or shuffle for his partner if either opponent objects.
[30] A player may not cut or shuffle for his partner if either opponent objects.

NEW DEAL (Compulsory)

27. There must be a new deal:[31]

(*a*) If the cards are not dealt into four distinct packets in accordance with Law 26 (c).

(*b*) If, during the deal, any card is found faced in the pack or is exposed on, above or below the table.

(*c*) If it is discovered during the hand that more than thirteen cards were dealt to any player.

(*d*) If, during the hand, one player holds more than the proper number of cards and another player holds fewer.

(*e*) If during the hand the pack is proved incorrect (Law 2). The pack is not incorrect on account of a missing card or cards if it is or they are found in the still pack, among the quitted tricks, below the table, or in any other place whereby it is made possible that this card or these cards were part of the pack during the deal. Any player may search anywhere for missing cards, including the still pack and the quitted tricks (face downwards). See also Law 56 (*e*).

NEW DEAL (Optional)[32]

28. During the deal, any player who has not looked at any of his cards may demand a new deal:[33]

(*f*) If the deal is out of turn.

(*g*) If the pack is imperfect (Law 2).

A new deal may be demanded by either of Dealer's opponents[34] who has not looked at any of his cards:

(*h*) If Dealer omits the cut.

(*i*) If Dealer deals with the wrong pack.

If any player, after looking at a card, makes a claim under this law, or, if no claim is made, the deal stands as regular, and the player to the left deals next. In case of a deal with the wrong pack (*i*), the next dealer may choose either pack for the remainder of the rubber.

THE DECLARATION

29. The declaration[35] begins when the deal ends, and ends when all four players pass[36] (Law 38) their first opportunity to declare[37] or,

---

[31] Always by the same dealer, and with the same pack except (*e*) when a missing card is not found. See Law 62 about new cards.

[32] A new deal may also be demanded under Laws 37 (*d*), 37 (*e*) and 54 (*i*).

[33] By the same dealer except as in (*f*), and with the same pack except as in (*g*) and (*i*).

[34] 'Opponent' is always used in the general sense; 'adversary' is always an opponent of Declarer.

[35] Declaration also means bid, double, pass or redouble.

[36] The player next in turn then deals with his own pack.

[37] To declare means to bid, double, pass or redouble.

after a bid (Law 30), when three players in succession have legally passed. The first legal act of the declaration is a bid or pass by the Dealer. Thereafter each player in his turn to the left must pass, bid if no bid has been made previously, make a higher bid[38] if a bid has been made previously, double the last bid made by an opponent, or redouble an opponent's double provided no bid has intervened.

BID DEFINED

30. A bid is made by specifying any number from one (1) to seven (7) inclusive, together with the name of a suit or No Trump, thereby offering to contract that with suit such as trump or with No Trump; the bidder will win at least the specified number of odd tricks.

HIGHER BID DEFINED

31. To make a 'higher bid', a player must (*a*) name a greater number[39] of odd tricks in a suit or No Trump than the number named in the last previous bid, or (*b*) name at least an equal number of odd tricks in a suit of higher rank (Law 4) than the suit named in the previous bid.

INSUFFICIENT BID

32. A bid following any previous bid is 'insufficient' if it is not 'higher' according to Law 31.

When an insufficient bid is made:

(*a*) The insufficient bidder, if he does so before an opponent has declared or called attention to the insufficiency, may make the bid sufficient by changing the number of odd tricks named, in which case the declaration proceeds as if the bid had been sufficient.

(*b*) When either opponent calls attention to an insufficient bid before it is changed, the insufficient bidder must make his bid sufficient by increasing the number[40] of odd tricks named, and if the player on the left of the insufficient bidder then passes, the partner of the insufficient bidder must pass and may not re-enter the declaration unless an opponent subsequently bids or doubles.

(*c*) If neither opponent calls attention to the insufficiency and the player on the left of the insufficient bidder bids, doubles or passes, the previous insufficiency is waived.

(*d*) Either opponent, after the bid has been made sufficient as provided in (*b*), may in turn made a higher[41] bid, in which case the declaration proceeds as if no bid had been insufficient.

[38] Law 31 defines 'higher bid'.
[39] Seven is the greatest number that may be named.
[40] Not exceeding seven.
[41] That is, higher than the bid after it has been made sufficient.

BID OUT OF TURN DEFINED

33. A bid is out of turn[42] (not an illegitimate bid, Law 41):

(*a*) If, before Dealer declares, a bid is made by any other player.

(*b*) If, after Dealer declares, any player bids otherwise than in his turn.

BID OUT OF TURN PENALISED

34. After a bid out of turn:

(*a*) Either opponent of the offender may cancel it. The proper player then proceeds with the declaration,[43] and the out-of-turn bid is ignored, but the partner of the out-of-turn bidder must thereafter pass whenever his turn comes.[44]

(*b*) When the player on the left of the out-of-turn bidder declares before the improper bid is cancelled, the out-of-turn bid is thereby accepted as if made in turn and there is no penalty.

(*c*) When the player on the right of the out-of-turn bidder is the proper declarer and declares[45] without otherwise cancelling the improper bid, this act cancels the out-of-turn bid, and (*a*) applies.

DOUBLE DEFINED

35. When, during the declaration and in proper turn, a player doubles, it doubles the trick value (Law 10) of the last previous bid. Doubling changes neither bidding values (Laws 4 and 31) nor the values of honours (Law 15), Slam or Little Slam (Law 16).

REDOUBLE DEFINED

36. When, during the declaration, and in proper turn, a player redoubles, it doubles the double (Law 35); that is, it multiplies the original trick value (Law 10) by four. A redouble, as for a double, affects only trick values (Law 35).

IMPROPER DOUBLES AND REDOUBLES

37. The penalties for improper doubles or redoubles follow:

(*a*) A double or redouble before a bid has been made is void.

(*b*) For a double or redouble after the declaration ends, Law 41(g) prescribes the penalty.

(*c*) A double or redouble made when it is the turn of the right-hand opponent to declare is subject to the same penalty as a bid out of turn (Law 34-a) unless the partner of the offender has passed the

---

[42] When a bid is out of turn and also insufficient (Law 32), either opponent may elect to apply either Law 32 (*b*) or Law 34 (*a*).

[43] The 'proper player' must pass if he is the partner of the player in error.

[44] The offending player, because he has not received improper information, may subsequently declare in turn.

[45] When he doubles, it is a double of the last legal bid.

bid involved, in which case the double or redouble is void and there is no penalty.

(*d*) A double or redouble when it is the partner's turn to declare can be accepted by the opponents, after consultation, as if it had been in turn; or the opponents can demand a new deal; or they can call the bid that was doubled final and elect whether the double or redouble should stand. Any of these penalties may be exacted even though the partner of the offender calls attention to the error; however, if the player to the left of the offender declares, he thereby accepts the out-of-turn double or redouble.

(*e*) A double of a double is a redouble; a redouble when there has been no double is a double. a redouble of a redouble is void and is penalized by a new deal or 100 points in the adverse honor-score. Doubling a partner's bid or, redoubling a partner's double is penalized by 50 points in the adverse honor-score. Either opponent may exact any of these penalties.

PASS DEFINED

38. When, during the declaration and in proper turn, a player passes, the turn to declare is thereby passed to the next player to the left.

PASS OUT OF TURN DEFINED

39. A pass is out of turn:

(*a*) If made before Dealer declares.

(*b*) If made (after Dealer declares) by any player except in turn.

PASS OUT OF TURN PENALISED

40. After a pass out of turn:

(*a*) If the opponent at the left of the offending player declares[46] before attention is called to the error, the pass is accepted as regular.

(*b*) If an opponent calls attention to the error, the pass is void and the player whose turn it was when the error was made resumes the declaration, but the offending player may not thereafter bid, double or redouble unless the declaration he passed is over-bid, doubled or redoubled.

ILLEGITIMATE DECLARATIONS

41. (*a*) A bid, double or redouble made after the declaration is ended is not penalised if made by Declarer or his partner. But should the error be committed by an adversary, Declarer may call a lead from the partner of the offending player the first time it is that partner's turn to lead.

[46] See footnote to Law 29, which provides that a pass is a declaration.

(*b*) When a player who has been debarred from bidding or doubling bids, doubles or redoubles, either opponent may decide whether or not this bid, double or redouble should stand and in either case both the offending player and his partner must thereafter pass.

(*c*) A pass after the declaration is ended is void.

DECLARING AND CHANGING

42. If a player passes, bids, doubles or redoubles, and then attempts to change[47] to some other form of declaration or attempts to change the size of a sufficient bid, this attempted change may be penalised as a bid out of turn.[48]

REPEATED ERRORS

43. When any player commits an error for which a penalty is provided in Laws 32, 34, 37, 40, 41 or 42 at a time when an error has previously been committed under those laws, for which the penalty has not already been fully paid:

(*a*) If the previous error was committed by the other side, the penalty for it (or as much as remains unpaid) is cancelled and the side newly in error is liable for the penalty provided for the new offence;

(*b*) If the previous error was committed by the same side, the opponents, after consultation, may elect which error to penalise.

CARDS EXPOSED DURING DECLARATION

44. If, during the declaration,[49] any player leads or exposes[50] a card, this card must be left face upwards on the table, and the partner of the player in error must thereafter pass whenever it is his turn to declare.

If the player in error later becomes Declarer or Dummy, the card in question is no longer exposed; otherwise, it remains an exposed card until played.

If the player on the left of the player in error later becomes Declarer, he may, on the first trick, forbid a lead of the suit of the exposed card.[51]

---

[47] A player who inadvertently says, 'No Bid,' and who means to say, 'No Trump' or vice versa, or who inadvertently says, 'Spade,' 'Heart,' 'Diamond,' or 'Club,' and who means to name another of these cards may correct his mistake, provided the next player has not declared. 'Inadvertently' refers to a slip of the tongue, not a change of mind.

[48] Unless it is an attempt to change the third or fourth consecutive pass that closes the declaration (Law 29).

[49] Law 29 specifies when the declaration begins and ends.

[50] Law 51 defines exposed cards.

[51] When two or more cards are exposed, all are subject to the provisions of Law 44, but the Declarer may not forbid the lead of more than three suits.

CONTRACT AND DECLARER

45. With the completion of the declaration, the side that has made the highest bid assumes a contract to win at least the number of odd tricks[52] named in the bid: the partner of that side who first named the suit or No Trump specified in this bid is Declarer.

For every trick Declarer falls short of his contract, the adversaries score 50 points in their honour-score for under-tricks. All tricks won by adversaries beyond their 'book' are under-tricks. The adversaries' book is the number of the bid subtracted from seven. Declarer's book is his first six tricks. In the case of a double, the under-tricks count 100 each; in the case of a redouble, they count 200 each.

When there is a double and Declarer fulfills his contract, he counts in his honour-score a bonus of 50 points, and another bonus of 50 points for each trick, if any, that he wins beyond the number called for by the contract. When there is a redouble, these bonuses are 100 points each instead of 50.[53]

THE PLAY

46. After the declaration, the play proceeds according to Law 5. Until the initial lead has been legally made, Declarer's partner is not subject to any of the limitations[54] imposed on Dummy.

DUMMY

47. As soon as the initial lead is legally made, Declarer's partner places his cards face upwards on the table and becomes Dummy.[55] Declarer plays Dummy's cards as well as his own. Dummy takes no part in the play and has no rights except as provided in Laws 48 and 49.

DUMMY'S RIGHTS (Unconditional)

48. Dummy always has the right:

(a) To call attention to the fact that too many or too few cards have been played to a trick,

(b) To call attention to the fact that the wrong side has gathered in a trick,

(c) To ask Declarer whether he has any of a suit he has refused,[56]

(d) To correct an error in the score,

(e) To participate in the discussion of any disputed question of fact after it has arisen between Declarer and an adversary,

[52] Law 9 provides that a Declarer whose contract fails scores nothing for tricks.
[53] These bonuses are in addition to the increased trick score; see Law 10.
[54] Except consultation as to the penalty provided in Law 54 (a).
[55] 'Dummy' is sometimes used in the obvious sense of dummy's cards.
[56] 'Refuse' is defined in the footnote to Law 7.

(*f*) To correct an improper claim of either adversary, and

(*g*) To assist Declarer as allowed by Law 54(*j*).

DUMMY'S RIGHTS (Conditional)

49. If Dummy has not intentionally looked at a card held by any player, he has the following additional rights:

(*h*) To claim an adverse revoke,

(*i*) To call attention to an adverse lead out of turn,

(*j*) To call attention to a card exposed by an adversary,

(*k*) To call Declarer's attention to any right he might have under the laws, and

(*l*) To suggest playing out the hand when Declarer would concede any of the remaining tricks (Law 59-*b*).

DUMMY PENALISED

50. (*m*) Should Dummy call attention to any matter that volves a right of Declarer or a penalty incurred by the adversaries, and this matter is not covered by Law 48, paragraphs (*a*) to (*g*); or should he, after having intentionally looked at a card held by any player, seek to exercise any of the rights mentioned in Law 49, paragraphs (*h*) to (*l*); this right or penalty is cancelled and may not be exercised or exacted.

(*n*) Should Dummy, by touching a card or otherwise, suggest a play by Declarer, either adversary may require Declarer to make this play (if legal) or to refrain from making it.

(*o*) Should Dummy warn Declarer that he is about to lead from the wrong hand, either adversary may designate the hand from which Declarer will lead.

EXPOSED CARDS

51. The following are 'exposed' cards:

(*a*) Two or more cards led or played simultaneously (all are exposed).

(*b*) A card dropped face upwards on the table, even if snatched up so quickly that it cannot be named.[57]

(*c*) A card dropped other than on the table if the partner sees the card's face.[58]

(*d*) A card held in such a way by a player that the player's partner sees any portion of the card's face.

---

[57] If an adversary throws his cards face upwards on the table, they are exposed (except as in 59*a*) and liable to be called, but if the other adversary retains his hand, he cannot be forced to expose it.

[58] The fact that an opponent sees it does not make it an exposed card.

(*e*) A card mentioned by either adversary as being in his own or his partner's hand.

(*f*) If an adversary who has legally played to the twelfth trick shows his thirteenth card before his partner plays his twelfth, the partner's two cards are exposed.

(*g*) A card designated by any law as 'exposed'.

CALLING EXPOSED CARDS

52. After a card has been 'exposed' as defined in Law 51, it must be left face upwards on the table, and Declarer may 'call' it (that is, require its owner to lead or play it)[59] at any time when it is the owner's turn to lead or play, except when the playing of the 'called' card would cause the holder to renounce.

Declarer may call an exposed card any number of times until it can be legally played, but the owner may play it even if it is not called.

PLAY OF DECLARER AND DUMMY

53. A card from Declarer's hand is not played or led until quitted.[60] If Declarer names or touches a card in Dummy's hand, he must play it.[61] If he touches two or more cards simultaneously, he may play either.

Declarer and Dummy are not liable to the call of exposed cards.[62]

LEADS OUT OF TURN AND CARDS PLAYED IN ERROR

54. (*a*) After the declaration and before a legal initial lead, should the partner of the proper leader lead or expose a card, Declarer may either call a lead[63] from the proper leader or treat the card[64] as exposed. Declarer's partner may call Declarer's attention to the offence, but should they consult about the penalty, it will be cancelled. Should Declarer's partner spread any part of his hand before Declarer selects the penalty, Declarer may not call a lead.

(*b*) Should an adversary who has played a card that, as against Declarer and Dummy, is a winner lead, another or several of these winning cards without waiting for his partner to play, Declarer may require said adversary's partner to win, if he can, the first or any of these tricks, after which the remaining card or cards thereby led are exposed.

---

[59] Declarer and Dummy are not liable (Law 53).

[60] A card is 'quitted' when the player no longer touches it.

[61] Unless Declarer says, 'I arrange,' or words to that effect, or unless his touching the card is obviously for the purpose of uncovering a partly hidden card or to enable him to get at the card he wishes to play.

[62] However, see Law 54(*a*).

[63] If the player called on to lead a suit has none of it, the penalty is paid.

[64] Or cards.

(*c*) Should the adversaries lead simultaneously, the correct lead will stand, and the other card is an exposed card.

(*d*) Should Declarer lead out of turn from either his own hand or Dummy's, either adversary may direct that the error be rectified, but Declarer may not rectify it unless so directed.

(*e*) After a lead by Declarer or Dummy, should Fourth Hand play before Second Hand, Declarer may require Second Hand to play his highest or lowest card of the suit led, or to win or lose the trick.[65] If Second Hand has none of the suit led, Declarer may call his highest of any designated suit. If Second Hand holds none of the suit called, the penalty is paid.

(*f*) Should Declarer lead from his own or Dummy's hand and then play from the other hand before Second Hand plays, Fourth Hand may play before Second Hand without penalty.

(*g*) Should any player (including Dummy) lead out of turn and next hand[66] play without claiming the penalty, the lead stands as regular.

(*h*) If an adversary leads out of turn, Declarer may call a lead as soon as it is the turn of either adversary to lead, or may treat the card so led as exposed.

(*i*) If a player (not Dummy) omits playing to a trick and then plays to a subsequent trick, Declarer or either adversary (as the case may be) can demand a new deal whenever the error is discovered. If no new deal is demanded, the surplus card at the end of the hand is considered played to the imperfect trick, but does not constitute a revoke therein.

(*j*) Whenever it is suspected that any of the quitted tricks contains more than four cards, any player (including Dummy) may count them face downwards. If any are found to contain a surplus card and any player is short, either opponent may face the trick, select the surplus card and restore it to the player who is short, but this does not change the ownership of the trick. The player who was short is answerable for revoke as provided in Law 56 (*e*).

RENOUNCE

55. When a player who has one or more cards of the suit led plays a card of a different suit, his act constitutes a renounce.[67]

---

[65] Except as provided in (*f*).

[66] Declarer accepts a wrong lead if he plays next from either his own or Dummy's hand.

[67] See also 'Refuse,' Law 7, footnote.

REVOKE DEFINITIONS

56. A renounce (Law 55) becomes a revoke and subject to penalty (Law 57):

(*a*) When the trick in which it occurs is turned and quitted[68] by the rightful winners, except as provided in Law 58 (*c*).

(*b*) When the renouncing player or his partner, whether in turn or otherwise, leads or plays to the following trick.

(*c*) When one side has claimed a revoke, and either opponent mixes the cards before the claimant has had reasonable opportunity to examine them.

(*d*) When a player has incurred a penalty whereby he is required to play the highest or lowest of a suit, or to win or lose a trick, or to lead a specific suit, or to refrain from playing a specific suit, and fails to act as directed when able to do so.

(*e*) If at any time a player is found to have fewer than his correct number of cards, and the other three players have their correct number, the missing card or cards, if found (see also Laws 27-*e* and 54-*j*), belong to the player[69] who is short, and, unless the player is Dummy, he is answerable for any revoke or revokes as if the missing card or cards had been in his hand continuously.

REVOKE PENALTY

57. The penalty for each revoke is:

(*a*) When Declarer revokes, he cannot score for tricks, and his adversaries, in addition to any bonus for under-tricks,[70] add 50 points to their honour-score for each revoke.

(*b*) When either adversary revokes, Declarer for the first revoke may either score 50 points in his honour-score or take two tricks[71] from his adversaries and add them to his own.[72] These tricks may assist Declarer to make good his contract, but will entitle him to neither any other bonus[73] in the honour-score by reason of the bid having been doubled or redoubled nor a Slam or Little Slam not otherwise obtained. For each revoke after the first, Declarer adds 50 points to his honour-score.

---

[68] A trick is 'quitted' when it is turned and the player no longer touches it.

[69] The fact that this player made no claim of irregularity at the time of the deal is conclusive, in the absence of evidence to the contrary, that the missing cards were dealt to him.

[70] The fact that Declarer revokes does not permit adversaries to score for under-tricks, provided Declarer has won (even with the help of the revoke).

[71] The value of the two tricks—undoubled, doubled or redoubled as the case may be—is counted in the trick score.

[72] Dummy may advise Declarer which penalty to exact.

[73] They may enable him to win a game, and if that game ends the rubber, give him the 250-point bonus.

(*c*) The value of honours as held is the only score that can be made by a revoking side unless both sides revoke; if one side revokes more than once, the other side scores 50 points for each extra revoke.

REVOKE AVOIDED

58. A renounce (Law 55) may be corrected, and the revoke (Law 57) avoided, under the following circumstances:

(*a*) If made by Dummy, the renounce may be corrected before the trick is turned and quitted. After the trick has been turned and quitted, whether by the rightful winners or otherwise, the renounce may not be corrected. In both cases there is no penalty.

(*b*) A renouncing player, other than Dummy, may not correct his error (except as in *c*) after the trick is turned and quitted, nor after he or his partner has led or played to the following trick. If the correction is made in time, there is no revoke penalty, but the player in error (except as in *e*) may be required to play his highest or lowest card of the suit led. Any player who played after the renounce may withdraw his card and substitute another.

(*c*) If, before the trick is turned and quitted, the partner of the renouncing player asks him whether he has any[74] of the suit refused, subsequent turning and quitting does not establish a revoke until the renouncing player has answered in the negative, or until he or his partner has led or played to the following trick.

(*d*) If the renouncing player is an adversary and the renounce is corrected in time, declarer, instead of calling the highest or lowest, may treat the card played in error as exposed.

(*e*) The highest or lowest may not be called from Declarer unless the adversary to his left has played to the trick after the renounce.

(*f*) Should Dummy leave the table after requesting protection from revokes,[75] Declarer would not be able to be penalised, following a renounce, unless an adversary in due time should call the renounce to his attention.

(*g*) The revoke penalty cannot be claimed after the next ensuing cut (Law 25), nor, if the revoke occurs during the last hand of a rubber, after the score has been agreed on, nor if there has been a draw for any purpose in connection with the next rubber (for example as in Law 23).

[74] Or none.
[75] Sometimes called 'courtesies of the table'.

CLAIMING AND CONCEDING TRICKS

59. (*a*) If Declarer says, 'I have the rest,' or any words that indicate the remaining tricks or any number thereof are his, either adversary may require him to place his cards face upwards on the table and play out the hand. Declarer cannot then take any finesse not previously proven a winner[76] unless he announced it when making his claim; he also cannot call any cards either adversary has exposed.

(*b*) If Declarer concedes one or more tricks, and either adversary accepts the concession before Dummy lawfully demands that the hand be played out (Law 49-*l*), this trick or these tricks belong to adversaries, even though, had the hand been played out, Declarer could not have lost them.

(*c*) If an adversary concedes a trick or tricks to Declarer, and this concession is accepted before the other adversary objects, it is binding on both adversaries.

PENALTIES AND CONSULTATION

60. Laws that give 'either partner', 'either opponent' and so on the right to exact a penalty do not permit consultation.

(*a*) If either partner suggests or names a penalty, he is deemed to have selected it.

(*b*) If either partner directs the other to select a penalty, the latter must do so, and if an attempt is made to refer the privilege back, the penalty is cancelled.

(*c*) If either partner asks (in effect), 'Which of us is to select the penalty?' the penalty is cancelled.

(*d*) A proper penalty once selected may not be changed.

(*e*) If a wrong penalty is selected,[77] the selection must be corrected on request of either opponent.

(*f*) If a wrong penalty is selected and paid without challenge, the selection may not be changed.

(*g*) A reasonable time must be allowed for selection of a penalty, and the selection must be made within a reasonable time.

(*h*) If, instead of exacting a penalty at the proper time, either opponent of the side in error plays or declares, no penalty may be exacted.

---

[76] 'Proven a winner' means that the adversary who plays last to the trick in which the finesse is to be taken has previously refused that suit; the fact that a finesse in the same suit has previously won is not enough.

[77] If the 'penalty' selected is something not described in the Laws, no penalty may be exacted.

INFORMATION

61. (*a*) During the declaration, information must be given about its details up to that time, but after it is ended, should either adversary or Dummy inform his partner about any detail of the declaration except the contract, Declarer or either adversary (as the case may be) would be able to call a lead the next time it is the turn of the offending side to lead. At any time during the play, any player who inquires must be informed what the contract is.

(*b*) Any player except Dummy may, before a trick is turned and quitted, demand that the cards so far played be placed before their respective players; however, should either adversary, in the absence of this demand, in any way call attention to his own card or to the trick, Declarer would be able to require the partner of the offender to play his highest or lowest card of the suit led, or to win or lose the trick.

(*c*) Either adversary, but not Dummy (Law 50-*o*), may call his partner's attention to the fact that he is about to play or lead out of turn; however, if, during the play, an adversary makes any unauthorised reference to any incident thereof, or to the location of any card, Declarer may call the next lead when it becomes an adversary's turn.[78]

(*d*) If, before or during the declaration, a player gives any unauthorised information about his hand, his partner may be barred from subsequent participation in the declaration.

(*e*) The penalty for looking at quitted tricks (except when the Laws permit examination) is 25 points in the adverse honour-score for each offence.

NEW CARDS

62. One new pack must be produced to replace an incorrect one (Law 27-*e*) or an imperfect one (Law 28-*g*); otherwise, when new cards are demanded, two packs must be furnished, and the opponents of the player demanding them must have the choice, unless the demand is made at the beginning of a rubber, in which case Dealer has the choice.

THE ETIQUETTE OF AUCTION

In the game of Auction, slight intimations can convey improper information. To offend against etiquette is more serious than to offend against a law, because in the latter case the offender is subject to prescribed penalties, and in the former his opponents are without redress.

---

[78] Any reference of this type by Dummy can be similarly penalised by either adversary.

1. Declarations should be made in a simple way: 'One Heart', 'One No Trump', 'Pass', 'Double'; they should be made without emphasis.

2. Except by his legitimate declaration, the player should not indicate by word, manner or gesture the nature of his hand, nor his approval or disapproval of a play, bid or double.

3. If a player demands that the cards be placed, he should do so for his own information, not to call his partner's attention to any card or play.

4. An adversary should not lead until the preceding trick has been turned and quitted; nor, after having led a winning card, should he draw another card from his hand before his partner has played to the current trick.

5. A card should not be played in a way so as to draw attention to it; nor should a player detach one card from his hand and subsequently play another.

6. A player should not purposely incur a penalty; nor should he make a second revoke to conceal a first.

7. Conversation that might annoy players at the table or at other tables in the room should be avoided.

8. Dummy should not leave his seat in order to watch his partner play; nor should he call attention to the score.

9. If Declarer says, 'I have the rest,' or any words that indicate that the remaining tricks, or any number thereof, are his, and an adversary exposes his cards, Declarer should not allow any information so obtained to influence his play.

10. A player who has been cut out of one table should not seek admission to another unless he is willing to cut for the privilege of being admitted to it.

THE WHIST FAMILY

— · —

CARDS   Whist is played with a full pack of fifty-two cards, ranking A K Q J 10 9 8 7 6 5 4 3 2; the Ace is the highest in play, but ranks below the deuce in cutting. Two packs are usually used, whereby one is shuffled while the other is dealt.

MARKERS   These are necessary for keeping the score. The most common markers are red and white circular counters, whereby the white is used for the points in each game, and the red for the games themselves, or for rubber points. It is better to have two sets, of different colours, whereby each set consists of four circular and three oblong counters, and the latter are used for the rubber points, or for games.

PLAYERS   Whist is played by four people. When there are more than four candidates for play, five or six may form a 'table'. If more than six offer for play, selection of the table is made by cutting.

When the table is formed, the four people who will play the first rubber are determined by cutting, and they again cut for partners and the choice of seats and cards.

CUTTING   The methods of cutting are the same as the ones described in connection with Bridge, and ties are decided in the same way.

PLAYERS' POSITIONS   The four players at a whist table are usually distinguished by the letters A, B, Y and Z; the first two letters of the alphabet are partners against the last two, and their positions at the table are indicated as follows.

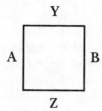

Z is always the dealer; A is the original leader, or first hand; Y is the second hand; B is the third hand; and Z is the fourth hand. After the first trick, some other player may become the leader, whereby the one on his left is the second hand, his partner is the third hand, and the player on his right is the fourth hand. B is the pone.

DEALING   When the cards have been properly shuffled, the dealer presents them to the *pone* to be cut. The American laws require that after separating the pack, the pone will place the cut part, which he lifts off, nearer the dealer. Beginning at his left, the dealer distributes the cards one at a time in rotation, until the pack is exhausted. The last card is turned face upwards on the table, and the suit to which it belongs is the trump for that hand.

When two packs are used, one pack is shuffled by the dealer's partner while the other is being dealt, and the shuffled pack is placed on the left of the player whose turn it will be to deal next. Each player deals in turn until the conclusion of the game or rubber.

IRREGULARITIES IN THE DEAL   The following rules for the deal should be strictly observed.

If any card is found faced in the pack, the dealer must deal again. If the dealer turns over any card but the trump while dealing, the adversaries may, if they please, demand a new deal. A player who deals out of turn may be stopped before the trump card is turned, but after that, the deal must stand, whereby afterwards it is passed to the left in regular order. On completion of the deal, each player should take up and count his cards to see that he has thirteen; if he does not have thirteen, it is a misdeal, and unless the pack is found to be imperfect, the deal passes to the player on the misdealer's left. The dealer loses the deal if he neglects to have the pack cut, if he deals a card incorrectly and fails to remedy the error before dealing another card, if he counts the cards on the table or the ones remaining in the pack, if he looks at the trump card before the deal is complete, or if he places the trump card face downwards on either his own cards or any other player's cards.

STAKES   When stakes are played for, it should be distinctly understood at the beginning whether the unit is for a game, for a rubber, for rubber points or for tricks. Traditionally, in England the game was invariably played for so much a rubber point, sometimes with an extra stake on the rubber itself. In America, it was usual to play for so much a game; however, in some cases the tricks were the unit, whereby the loser's score was deducted from seven, or was the last hand played out and then the loser's score deducted. A very popular method was to play for a triple stake: so much a trick, whereby each hand was played out; so much a game; and so much a rubber. These three stakes were usually in the proportion of 10, 25 and 50. In clubs, it was customary to have a uniform stake for whist, and to fix a limit for all betting on the game beyond the 'club stake'. It was good practice for the people at the table to be able to refuse any bet made by a player before it was offered to an outsider.

METHOD OF PLAYING   The player on the dealer's left begins by leading any card he chooses, and all the other players must follow suit if they can. Failure to follow suit when able to is called *revoking*, the penalty for which, under the American laws, is loss of two tricks; under the English laws, it is three tricks or points. Any player who has none of the suit led may either trump it or throw away a card of another suit, which is called *discarding*. When it is the dealer's turn to play to the first trick, he should take the trump card into his hand. After it has been taken up it must not be named, and any player who names it is subject to a penalty (see Laws); however, a player may ask what the trump *suit* is. If all the players follow suit, the highest card played wins the trick; trumps win against all other suits, and a higher trump wins a lower. The winner of the trick may lead any card he pleases for the next trick, and so on until all thirteen tricks have been played.

CARDS PLAYED IN ERROR   Cards either played in error or dropped face upwards on the table, or two or more cards played at once, are called *exposed cards* and must be left on the table. They can be *called* by the adversaries but the fact of their being exposed does not prevent their being played when the opportunity offers. Some people imagine that the adversaries can prevent an exposed card from being played, but this is not the case.

LEADING OUT OF TURN   If a player leads out of turn, the adversaries may call a suit from the player in error, or from his partner, when it is next the turn of either of them to lead. The American laws require the call to be made by the player on the right of the one from whom the suit is called. The English laws give the adversaries the option of calling the card played in error an exposed card. If all the players have played to the trick before discovering the error, it cannot be rectified, but if all have not played, the ones who have followed the false lead must take back their cards, which are not, however, liable to be called.

REVOKING PLAYERS Revoking players cannot win the game that hand, no matter what they score, but they may play the hand out, and score all points they make to within one point of game.

Any player may ask the other players to **draw cards** in any trick, provided he does so before the cards are touched for the purpose of gathering them. In answer to this demand, each player should indicate which of the cards on the table he played.

In the English game, any player may look at the last trick turned and quitted; in the American game, he may not.

TAKING TRICKS As the tricks are taken, they should be neatly laid one on the other in a way so that any player at the table can count them at a glance. There are several methods of stacking tricks; the first shown below is probably the best.

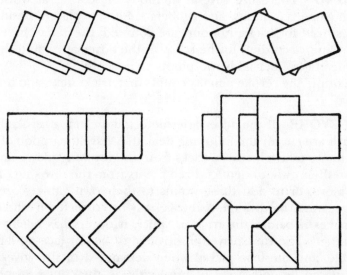

When six cards have been taken by one side, they are usually gathered together to form a **book**; any subsequently taken are laid apart, because they are the only cards that count. It is customary for the partner of the player who wins the first trick on each side to gather the tricks for that deal. In some places it is the custom for the partner of the winner of each trick to gather it, so that at the end of the hand each player has tricks in front of him. Although this method saves time, the practice is not recommended, because it hinders the players in counting the tricks already gained by each side.

Immediately on completion of the play of a hand, the score should be claimed and marked. Any discussion of the play should be postponed until this has been attended to. The adversaries must detect and claim revokes before the cards are cut for the following deal.

The laws of whist should be carefully studied.

OBJECT OF THE GAME   The object of all whist play is to take tricks, of which there are thirteen in each hand or deal. The first six tricks taken by one side are called a *book*, and do not count, but each trick above that number counts one point towards game. The seventh trick is called the *odd*, and two or more over the book are called *two, three*, and so on, *by cards*. At the conclusion of each hand, the side that has won any tricks in excess of the book scores those tricks; the opponents count nothing. As soon as either side has scored the number of points previously agreed on as a game, which must be 5, 7 or 10, the cards are again shuffled and spread for the choice of partners, and so on, unless it has been agreed to play a rubber.

SCORING   There are several methods of scoring at whist. The English game is 5 points, and rubbers are always played. Besides the points scored for tricks, honours are counted; the games have a different value, according to the score of the adversaries, and the side that wins the rubber adds two points to its score.

In scoring, the revoke penalty counts first, tricks next, and honours last.

THE REVOKE   If the adversaries detect and claim a revoke before the cards are cut for the following deal, they have the option of three penalties: to take take three tricks from the revoking player and add them to their own, to deduct three points from the revoking player's game score, or to add three points to their own game score. The penalty cannot be divided. A revoke may be corrected by the player who makes it before the trick in which it occurs has been turned and quitted. The card played in error must be left face upwards on the table, and must be played when demanded by the adversaries, unless it can be gotten rid of previously, in the course of play. In America, the revoke penalty is two tricks.

THE HONOURS   The honours are the four highest trumps: A, K, Q and J. *After tricks have been scored*, partners who held three honours between them are entitled to count two points towards game; four honours count four points. If each side has two honours, neither can count them. It is not enough to score them; after the last card has been played, they must be claimed by word of mouth. If they are not claimed before the trump is turned for the following deal, they cannot be scored. Partners who at the beginning of a deal are at the score of four cannot count honours; they must get the odd trick to win the game. If one side is out by tricks, and the other side by honours, the tricks win the game, and the honours count nothing.

RUBBER POINTS At the conclusion of each game, the rubber points are scored, either with the oblong counters or on the small keys of the whist-marker. If the winners of a game are five points to their adversaries' nothing, they win a *treble*, and count three rubber points. If the adversaries have scored, but have one or two points only, the winners mark two points, for a *double*. If the adversaries have reached three or four, the winners mark one, for a *single*. When the rubber points have been marked, all other scores are turned down. The side that wins the rubber adds two points to its score for doing so. The value of the rubber is determined by deducting from the score of the winners any rubber points that might have been made by their adversaries. The smallest rubber possible to win is one point, the winners having scored two singles and the rubber, equal to four, from which they have to deduct a triple made by their adversaries. The largest rubber possible is eight points, called a *bumper*, the winners having scored two triples and the rubber, to their adversaries' nothing.

It is sometimes important to observe the order of precedence in scoring. For example, if, at the beginning of a hand, A–B have three points to Y–Z's nothing, A–B make two by honours and Y–Z win three by cards, Y–Z mark first, so that A–B win only a *single*, instead of a *treble*. On the contrary, if A–B make two by cards, and Y–Z claim four by honours, A–B win a treble, because their tricks put them out before it is Y–Z's turn to count.

In America, where rubbers are played without counting honours, it is not usual to reckon rubber points; some agreed value is simply added to the score of the players who win the odd game.

Where single games are played, whether for 5, 7 or 10 points, some people consider the game is finished when the agreed number of points is reached. Other people play the last hand out, and count all the tricks made, so that if two partners are at the score of 6 in a 7-point game, and make five by cards, they win a game of 11 points. When this is done, it is usual to deduct the score of the losers from the total, and to call the remainder the value of the game. In the American Whist League, the rule was to stop at seven points, and to determine the value of the game by deducting the loser's score from seven.

When long sittings occur without changing of partners or adversaries, it is common practice to count the tricks continuously, and when the play is concluded, to deduct the lower score from the higher, whereby the winners are credited with the difference.

CUTTING OUT   If rubbers are played, there is no changing of partners, or of rotation in the deal, until one side has won two games, whereby the rubber is ended. If the first two games are won by the same partners, the third game is not played. If more than four players belong to the table, the ones who have just played cut to decide which players will give place to the ones waiting; the ones who cut the highest cards go out. If six players belong to the table, there will be no more cutting out, because the players who are out for one rubber re-enter for the next, and take the places of the ones who have played two consecutive rubbers. If five players belong to the table, the three who remained in for the second rubber must cut to allow the fifth to re-enter. At the end of the third rubber, the two players cut who have not yet been out, and at the end of the fourth rubber, the player who has played every rubber goes out without cutting. After this, it is usual to spread the cards, and to form the table anew. In all the foregoing instances, the partners and the deal must be cut for, after the cut has determined which people are to play.

MARKING   There are various methods of using the counters. At the beginning of the game, they may be placed at the left hand, and transferred to the right as the points accrue. Another method is to stack the four circular counters one on the other at the beginning of the game, to count a point by placing one of them beside the others, to count two points by placing another on the first, to count three points by placing a third beyond these two, and to count four points by placing them all in line.

Nothing   One   Two   Three   Four

In the seven-point game, the score is continued by placing one counter above and to the right or left of the other three counters, to indicate five points, and above and between the other three counters to indicate six points.

Five   Or this   Six

When counters are not used, one of the standard forms of whist-marker is used, the most legible and convenient of which is the 'Foster Whist Marker', in which the counting keys are always level with the surface and can be seen equally well from any position at the table.

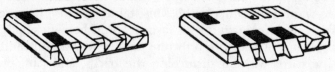

THE FOSTER WHIST MARKER

The four large keys on one side are used to count single points, and the single large key on the opposite side is reckoned as five. The three small keys are used for counting rubber points, or games.

In ten-point games, the scoring to four points is the same, but beyond four, a single counter placed *below* two or more other counters, is reckoned as three; *above* two or more others, is reckoned as five.

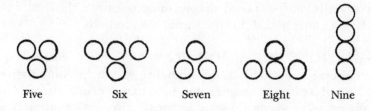

Five   Six   Seven   Eight   Nine

When proper markers are not obtainable, many people cut eight slits in a visiting card, and turn up the points.

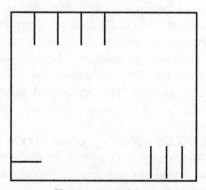

VISITING-CARD MARKER

Whatever the apparatus used, it should be such that every player at the table can distinctly see the state of the score without drawing attention to it.

METHODS OF CHEATING Whist offers very few opportunities to the card-sharper. When honours are counted, the cheat might be able to keep one on the bottom of the pack until the completion of the deal by *making the pass* after the cards have been cut. A *cheat* who had sufficient skill to do this without detection would be very foolish to waste his talents at the whist table, because however large the stakes, the percentage in his favour would be very small.

When whist is played with only one pack, a very skilful shuffler can gather the cards without disturbing the tricks, and can, by giving them a single *intricate* shuffle, then drawing the middle of the pack from between the ends and giving another single intricate shuffle, occasionally succeed in dealing himself and his partner a very strong hand in trumps, no matter how the cards are cut, so that they are not shuffled again. A hand dealt in this way was framed on the walls of the Whist club in Columbus, Ohio, in the United States, whereby eleven trumps had been dealt to the partner, and the twelfth trump turned up. In this case the shuffling dexterity was the result of fifteen years' practice, and was used simply for amusement: the dealer never bet on any game and did not conceal his methods.

SUGGESTIONS FOR GOOD PLAY Although whist is a game of very simple construction, the immense variety of combinations it affords renders it very complicated in actual practice; there is probably no game in which there is so much diversity of opinion as to the best play, even with the same cards, and under similar conditions. It has been repeatedly remarked that in all the published hands at whist that have been played in duplicate, or even four times over, with the same cards, no two hands have been alike.

It would be useless to formulate rules intended to cover every case that might arise, because the conditions are frequently too complicated to allow the average person to select the exact rule that would apply. All that can be done to assist the beginner is to state some general principles that are well recognised as being fundamental, and to leave everything else to experience and practice at the whist table.

GENERAL PRINCIPLES Nothing obstructs the progress of the beginner so much as his attempts to cover all the ground at once. The more ambitious he is, the greater his necessity for keeping in view the maxim 'One thing at a time; all things in succession.' You must master the scales before you can produce the perfect melody!

The novice should first thoroughly understand the object, and the fundamental principle of the game.

THE OBJECT   The object is to win tricks, not to give information, or to count the hands, or to remember every card played, but simply and only to win tricks.

THE PRINCIPLE   The principal is to secure for specific cards a trick-taking value that does not naturally belong to them, by either getting higher cards out of the way of lower or placing the holder of intermediate cards at a disadvantage with reference to the lead.

If any person takes the trouble to deal out four hands, and after turning them face upwards on the table counts how many tricks each side will probably take with its high cards and trumps, he finds that the total is hardly ever exactly thirteen tricks. Let's suppose the following to be one of the hands so dealt, whereby Z turns up the ♡ 6 for trumps:

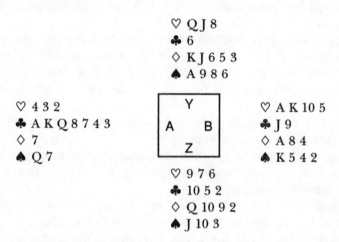

When we look over this hand, it seems that A could make only one trick in Clubs, of which the second round would be trumped. His partner can count on five tricks: the two best would and the fourth trumps; the ♢ A, and the ♠ K: a total of six tricks. On counting the adversaries' probable tricks, Y should make one of his three trumps, and the ♠ A. Diamonds will not go around twice without being trumped, so we cannot count on Y's ♢ K. We cannot see any sure tricks for Z. Where are the five other tricks necessary to bring our total up to thirteen? They must be there, because there are thirteen tricks taken in every hand played.

If we play over the hand, we find that A–B can make six, seven, nine or ten tricks, according to their good management and the good or bad play of their adversaries. In *Foster's Whist Tactics*, Illustrative Hand No. 13 contains the various ideas of sixteen of the best players in the American Whist League with reference to the proper management of this hand. The players played it in four ways, and the score had very different results.

This must show that the accidental distribution of the Aces, Kings and trumps is not everything in whist, and that there must be ways and means of securing tricks that do not appear on the surface.

There are four ways of taking tricks at whist:

1. By playing high cards, the suit of which the other cards must follow. This A does, in the example, on the first round of the Club suit.

2. By playing low cards, after the higher cards have been exhausted, and the adverse trumps are out of the way. This Y will do with his Diamonds, or A with his Clubs, according to circumstances.

3. By trumping winning cards played by the adversaries. This Y will do if Clubs are led a second time, or A will do if Diamonds are led twice.

4. By being able to take tricks with cards that are not the best of the suit, whereby the player who holds better cards has already played smaller. This B will do with the ♡ 10 if A leads trumps, and Y does not play either Q or J. If B leads trumps, he will lose this advantage.

These four methods of winning tricks suggest four systems of play, which are commonly used by experts:

1. Playing high cards to the best advantage, so as to secure the best results from the combinations that might be held. This is the basis of all *systems of leading*.

2. Leading from the longest suit, so that higher cards can be forced out of the way of smaller ones, whereby the smaller ones are left 'established', or good for tricks after the adverse trumps are exhausted. This is called the *long-suit game*.

3. Trumping good cards played by the adversaries. This is called *ruffing*. When two partners each trump a different suit, it is called a *cross-ruff*, or *saw*.

4. Taking advantage of the *tenace* possibilities of the hand by placing the lead with a specific player, or by avoiding the necessity of leading away from tenace suits. For example, a player holds A Q 10 of a suit, and his right-hand adversary holds K J 9. These are known as the *major* and *minor* tenaces. Whichever leads makes only one trick, but if the holder of the major tenace can get the suit led twice, he makes all. This is called the *short-suit game*, or *finesse and tenace*. Its resources can be added to by finessing against specific cards. For example, if A Q 3 of a suit led by the partner are held, to play Q is a finesse against fourth hand having the King.

Each of these systems has its advantages, and almost every hand will offer opportunities for practice in all of the systems.

The most important thing to impress on the beginner is that whist cannot be played by machinery. Some authorities would have us believe that specific theories alone are sound, that specific systems of play alone are good, and that if you persevere in following specific precepts, in matters such as leading, management of trumps and so on, the result has to be more than average success at the whist table.

Nothing can be further from the truth. As in all other matters largely controlled by chance, there is no system, as a system, whereby you win at whist. You cannot succeed by slavishly adhering to either the long or the short-suit game, by invariably giving information, or by continually playing false cards. The true elements of success in whist lie in the happy combination of all the resources of long and short suits, of finesse and tenace, of candour and deception, continually adjusted to varying circumstances, so as to result in the adversaries' losing tricks.

HOW TO STUDY WHIST   Any person who is anxious to become an expert whist player can attain considerable proficiency in a short time if he contents himself with mastering the following general principles, one at a time, and puts each into practice at the whist table before proceeding to the next.

The science of modern whist can be divided into two parts: 1. *Tactics*, or the purely conventional rules for leading, second- and third-hand play, returning partner's suits and so on, all of which can be learnt from books or gathered from more experienced players. 2. *Strategy*, or the advantageous use of the information given by the conventional plays. This is largely dependent on personal ability to judge the situation correctly, and to select the methods of play best adapted to it.

CONVENTIONAL PLAYS   These can be divided into two parts: plays used by the partners who attack, either with their strong suits or by leading out trumps, and plays used by the partners' adversaries, who are defending themselves against these suits or wishing to prevent their trumps from being drawn. We will first consider the conventionalities used in attack.

LEADING   The player who has the original lead should have a double object in view: to secure the best results for his own hand and to indicate to his partner when he is in need of assistance.

The first matter for his consideration will be whether to begin with a trump or with a plain suit. There are two main uses for trumps. The most attractive to the beginner is ruffing the adversaries' winning cards, and the most important to the expert is leading trumps to prevent this. No matter how strong or well established a plain suit is, it is of uncertain value as long as the adversaries have any trumps with which to stop it. A suit is established when you can probably take every trick in it. If a player who has a good established suit is sufficiently strong to make it probable that he can, with his partner's assistance, exhaust the adverse trumps, he should do so by leading trumps. If his adversaries are probably stronger than he is, he must *force* them, by leading the established suit that they will be compelled to trump, thereby weakening their hands and gradually reducing their trump strength until it is possible to exhaust what remains by leading. Because it is to the advantage of the player who has a good suit to exhaust the trumps, it must be desirable to his adversaries to keep theirs, if possible, for the purpose of ruffing this good suit.

Trumps are also useful as cards of re-entry, when a player has an established suit, but has not the lead; however, their most important use is in defending or stopping established suits.

RULES FOR LEADING TRUMPS With five or more trumps, the beginner should always begin by leading them, regardless of the rest of his hand. With three or less, he should never lead them, unless he has very strong cards in **all** the plain suits. With four trumps exactly, he should lead them if he has an established suit and a card of re-entry in another suit. A card of re-entry in plain suits is one that is pretty sure to win a trick, such as an Ace or a guarded King. The following are examples of hands from which trumps should be led originally by a beginner; Hearts are trumps in every case:

     ♡ J 8 6 4 2; ♣ K 3 2; ◇ 10 9 2; ♠ 7 5.
     ♡ Q 10 2; ♣ A K 5; ◇ K Q 10 9 ; ♠ A Q 3.
     ♡ K J 8 3; ♣ A K Q 10 7 3; ◇ 3; ♠ A 7.

The following are examples of hands from which trumps should not be led:

     ♡ A K Q; ♣ J 8 7 5 3; ◇ Q 4; ♠ K 4 2.
     ♡ Q J 10 2; ♣ 5 2; ◇ A K Q 2; ♠ 6 4 3.
     ♡ A Q 5 4; ♣ K Q J 6 3; ◇ A 9 2; ♠ K.

If at any later stage of the hand a player finds himself with an established suit and a card of re-entry, he should lead trumps if he has four. For example, the player who has the last example should lead trumps if the first round of Clubs either forced the Ace out of his way or found it with his partner.

RULES FOR LEADING PLAIN SUITS   It is safest for the beginner to select his longest suit for the original lead, unless he has a four-card suit that is much stronger. Length and high cards, the two elements of strength, are often very nearly balanced. In the following examples, the player should begin with the longest suit:

      ♡ A 4 3; ♣ J 10 9 8 3; ◇ A K Q; ♠ K 2.
      ♡ K 10 8 3; ♣ 4 2; ◇ K Q 10 8 2; ♠ A Q.

In the following examples, the four-card suit should be selected:

      ♡ J 3; ♣ 6 5 4 3 2; ◇ J 10 5 3; ♠ Q 8.
      ♡ Q 4 2; ♣ 7; ◇ 10 6 4 3 2; ♠ A K Q 10.

The principle by which you should be guided in selecting a plain suit for the original lead is that if there are a number of small cards in one suit, and a few high cards in another, by leading the long suit first, the higher cards in it are forced out of the way, and the high cards in the shorter suit will then bring the holder of the established small cards into the lead again. However, if the high cards of the short suit are first led, the long suit of small cards is dead.

Having determined whether to lead the trump or the plain suit, the next point is to select the proper card of the suit to lead. At first, the beginner need not trouble himself about making any distinction between trumps and plain suits; that will come later.

RULES FOR LEADING HIGH CARDS   If you have a strong suit, but without cards of re-entry or trump strength to support it, the best policy is to make tricks while you can. With a suit such as A K Q 2, no one need be told not to begin with the deuce. The various combinations from which high cards should be led, and the card to lead, have been given in detail in connection with Auction Bridge, to which you are referred.

AVOID CHANGING SUITS   When a player has begun with a suit, for the purpose of either establishing it or taking tricks in it, he should not change it until he is forced to do so. Running off to untried suits is one of the beginner's worst faults. There are five good reasons for changing suits, and unless one of them can be applied, the suit should be continued:

   1. In order to lead trumps to defend it.
   2. In order to avoid forcing the partner.
   3. In order to avoid forcing both the adversaries.
   4. Because it is hopeless, and there is some chance in another.
   5. To prevent a cross-ruff, by leading trumps.

SIMPLE INFERENCES Simple inferences from the fall of the cards are usually the best guide in the matter of changing suits.

If the Jack is led from K Q J x x, and wins the trick, the partner may be credited with the Ace, and if the original leader has four trumps, and a card of re-entry, he should quit his established suit, and lead trumps to defend it.

If the King and Ace have been led from A K x x, and the partner has dropped the Queen on the second round, the suit should be changed, unless the original leader is strong enough to risk weakening his partner by forcing him to trump the third round. Four trumps are usually considered to be sufficiently strong to justify a force in this position. Some players will force, even with a weak hand, if the two cards played by the partner are small, and the partner has not availed himself of an artifice known as *calling for trumps*, which we will consider.

If the King and Ten have been led from K Q J 10, and on the second round one adversary has dropped the Eight and the other the Nine, the suit should be changed, because the partner must have the Ace, and neither of the adversaries have any more. To lead this suit again is called *forcing both adversaries*, because it enables one adversary to make a small trump and the other to get rid of a losing card.

If the Four has been led from J 8 6 4, and the adversaries have won the first trick with the Nine or Ten, A K Q must be against the leader and his partner, and the suit should be abandoned as hopeless, unless it is feasible to force the partner.

If at any time there is a strong indication that the adversaries will have a cross-ruff, it is usually best to stop leading plain suits, and to attempt to get out the trumps.

THE LEADER'S PARTNER The leader's partner, or the Third Hand, has several conventional plays to remember, the most important of which are the following:

WHEN PARTNER LEADS HIGH CARDS In this case, the Third Hand usually has little to do but play his lowest of the suit. The exceptions are:

If he holds A J alone, on a King led, the Ace should be played.

If he holds A Q alone on a Ten led, the Ace should be played. With A Q x, the Ten should be passed. With Ace and small cards, the Ace should be played on the Ten. With Queen and small cards, the Ten should be passed. When Third Hand plays Queen on a Ten led, it should be a certainty that he has no more of the suit.

If Third Hand holds A K and only one small card, the King should be played on a Queen led.

If Third Hand holds Ace and only one small card, the Ace should be played on the Jack led. If Third Hand has four trumps and a card of re-entry, the Ace should be played on the Jack led, regardless of number, in order to lead trumps at once, to defend the suit.

WHEN PARTNER LEADS LOW CARDS   In this case, the Third Hand should do his best to secure the trick. If he has several cards of equal trick-taking value, such as A K Q, or K Q J, he should win the trick as cheaply as possible. The only *finesse* permitted to the Third Hand in his partner's suit is the play of the Queen, when he holds A Q and other cards; the odds are against Fourth Hand's having the King.

FOSTER'S ELEVEN RULE   By deducting from eleven the number of pips on any low card led, the Third Hand may ascertain how far his partner's suit is from being established. For example, if the card led is the Seven, Second Hand is playing the Eight, and Third Hand is holding A J 6 3, from which he plays Ace, and Fourth Hand is playing the Five, the only card against the leader must be the King or Queen; the leader cannot have both, otherwise he would have led one. If the Second Hand does not have the missing card, he has no more of the suit. The number of inferences that can be made in this way by observant players is astonishing. A great many examples and exercises in them are given in *Foster's Whist Manual.*

IF THIRD HAND HAS NONE OF THE SUIT   This should trump anything but an Ace or a King on the first round. On the second round, if there is only one card against the leader, his partner should pass with four trumps, and allow the suit to be established. For example, if the leads have been Ace, then Jack and Third Hand holds only one of the suit, he should pass if the Second Hand does not play King.

THIRD HAND ON STRENGTHENING CARDS   Unless Third Hand has both Ace and King of the suit, he should pass any forced or strengthening lead that is not covered by the Second Hand. The Fourth Hand is thereby obliged to open another suit, or to continue at a disadvantage.

Third Hand who wins the first round has the choice of four lines of play:

1. To lead trumps, if he is strong enough.
2. To return the best card of his partner's suit, if he has it. This is imperative before opening any suit other than trumps.

3. To lead his own suit, if he can do anything with it. It is considered better play for the Third Hand to return the original leader's suit than to open a long weak suit of his own, such as one headed by a single honour.

4. To return his partner's suit, even with a losing card, in preference to changing.

When the original lead is a trump, it should be returned in every case, either immediately or as soon as the player can obtain the lead.

The same reasons for changing suits as those given for the original leader will apply to the Third Hand.

RULES FOR RETURNING THE PARTNER'S SUITS   When the original leader's suit is returned by his partner, either immediately or when the leader has regained the lead, it is usual to show, if possible, how many cards remain in the Third Hand, so that by adding them to his own, the leader can estimate the number held by his adversaries. This consideration is secondary to the return of the best, or one of the second and third best; however, in the absence of these cards, the Third Hand should always return the higher of only two remaining cards, and the lowest of three or more, regardless of their value.

In addition to the foregoing conventionalities, which are proper to the leader of a suit and his partner, there are two usages that apply equally to any player at the table. These are discarding and forcing.

DISCARDING   When a player cannot follow suit, and does not wish to trump, his safest play is to discard whatever seems of least use to him. It is not considered good play to unguard a King or to leave an Ace alone; however, this can be done if the partner is leading trumps, and there is a good established suit to keep. Beginners should be careful to preserve cards of re-entry, even if the beginners have to discard from their good suit in order to do so.

When the adversaries have shown strength in trumps, or are leading them, there is little use in keeping a long suit together. It is much better to keep guard on the suits in which your adversaries are probably strong, and to let your own and your partner's suits go.

A player who has full command of a suit can show it to his partner by discarding the best card of it. Discarding the second-best card is an indication that the player does not have the best one, and in general, the discard of any small card shows weakness in that suit.

FORCING   We have already observed that a player who is weak himself should not force his partner. An exception can be made in cases in which he has shown weakness, or has had a chance to lead trumps and has not done so. On the contrary, an adversary should not be forced unless he has shown strength, or the player forcing him is weak. The hope of a player who has a good suit is to defend it by leading and exhausting the trumps. His adversary tries to keep his trumps in order to stop that suit, and at the same time forces the strong hand, by leading cards that he must trump, hoping that this force will weaken his adversary so much that he will be unable to continue the trump lead.

It is usually very difficult to convince the beginner that the weaker he is himself, the more reason he has for forcing the adversaries to trump his good cards. He is constantly falling into the error of changing from a good suit, which the adversaries cannot stop without trumping, to a weak suit, which enables them to get into the lead without any waste of trump strength. If an adversary refuses to trump a suit, it is imperative to keep on with it until he does, because it is always good play to force an adversary to do what he does not wish to do.

Any player can convince himself of the soundness of this theory of forcing by giving himself the six highest cards in any suit, three small cards in the others, and four trumps, thereby giving another player the four best trumps, and nine of the highest cards in two suits. If the first player forces the second with his good suit, and continues every time he gets the lead, he must win six tricks; if he does not, the second player makes a slam.

A deliberate force from a partner should always be accepted, if he is a good player.

We can now turn our attention to the conventionalities used by players who are opposed to the establishment of suits in the hands of the leader and his partner. These are divided between the Second and the Fourth Hand, the former being the more important. Generally speaking, they are the tactics of defence.

SECOND-HAND PLAY   The player who is second to play on any trick is called the Second Hand. It is his duty to protect himself and his partner, as much as possible, in the adversaries' strong suits. The main point for the beginner to observe in Second Hand play is the difference between the circumstances in which he is required to play high cards and those in which he should play low ones.

HIGH CARDS LED   When a card higher than a Ten is led on the first round of a suit, the Second Hand usually has nothing to do but play his lowest card, and make what inference he can as to the probable distribution of the suit. However, if he holds the Ace, or cards in sequence with it, such as A K, he should cover any card higher than a Ten. If he holds K Q he should cover a J, 10 or 9 led, but it is useless for him to cover an honour with a single honour, unless it is the Ace.

LOW CARDS LED High cards are played by the Second Hand when he has any combination from which he would have led a high card if he had opened the suit. The fact that a player on his right has already laid a small card of the suit on the table should not prevent the Second Hand from making the best use of any combinations he might hold. The only difference between leading from these combinations and playing them Second Hand is that in the latter case, no attempt is made to indicate to the partner the exact nature of the combination held. The general rule is to win the trick as cheaply as possible, by playing the lowest of the high cards that form the combination from which a high card would be led. These are as follows:

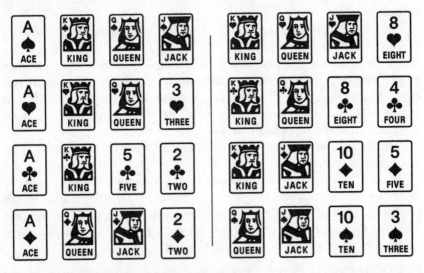

The beginner must be careful with these:

The combination that makes the first of these a high-card lead is the A K, and the King must be played Second Hand. The Jack has nothing to do with it. In the second, the Ten does not form any part of the combination, and the Queen is the card to play Second Hand.

Some players will not play a high card second hand with K Q x x unless they are weak in trumps.

An exception is usually made with these combinations, from which the proper lead is the Ace:

     |

Many players will not play Ace Second Hand in any case, and will play the Queen with the first combination only when they are weak in trumps. The reason for this exception is the importance of retaining command of the adverse suit for as long as possible.

ON THE SECOND ROUND The Second Hand should follow the usual rule for playing the best of the suit if he holds it, or one of the second and third best, if he holds them. He should also be careful to estimate, by the eleven rule, how many cards are out against the leader, which will sometimes guide him to a good finesse. For example, the first player leads Ace, then Eight. If the Second Hand holds K J 9 2, instead of playing the best card to the second round, which would be King, he should finesse the Nine.

WITH SHORT SUITS When Second Hand holds short-suit combinations such as:

   |

and a small card is led, his proper play is one of the high cards, because he cannot save both of them.

ON STRENGTHENING CARDS LED This is a difficult point for the beginner, and his best plan is to follow the rules already given for covering cards higher than the Ten. One of the most common errors is to cover a Jack led with a Queen, when holding A Q and other cards. The Ace should be put on invariably. To play the Queen in this position is called *finessing against yourself*.

SINGLY GUARDED HONOURS Many players put on the King Second Hand, if they hold only one small card with it, and a small card is led. This will win the trick as often as it will lose it, but it betrays the hand to the adversary, and enables him to finesse deeply if the suit is returned. It can be done in order to get the lead, and in trumps the practice is very common, and is usually right. With

Queen and only one small card, it can be demonstrated that it is useless to play the Queen Second Hand, except as an experiment, or to get the lead in desperate cases.

With any combination weaker than J 10 x, it is useless to attempt to win the trick Second Hand, and it only makes it difficult for the partner to place the cards correctly.

THE FOURCHETTE When the Second Hand has cards immediately above and below the one led, he should cover. The beginner might have some difficulty in recognising the fact that he holds fourchette if the suit has been round once or twice, and the intermediate cards have been played. Cards such as a Queen and a Seven may be fourchette over a Nine, if Jack, Ten and Eight have been played.

WHEN SECOND HAND HAS NONE OF THE SUIT LED When this is the case on either the first or second round, Second Hand must decide whether or not to trump it. If the card led is the best of the suit, he should certainly do so, but if it is not, and there is any uncertainty as to who will win the trick, it is usual for the Second Hand to pass when he has four trumps. With five trumps, there should be some good reason for keeping the trumps together, because a player who has so many trumps can usually afford to trump. If he does not trump, his play comes under the rules for discarding.

FOURTH-HAND PLAY The Fourth Hand is the last player in any trick. He is the partner of the Second Hand, but he does not have as many opportunities for the exercise of judgement; his duties are simply to win tricks if he can, and as cheaply as possible. If he cannot win the trick, he should play his lowest card.

A bad habit of Fourth Hand players is holding up the tenace A J when a King or Queen is led originally. This is called the *Bath Coup*, and the suit must go around three times for it to succeed in making two tricks. The holder of the tenace should equally make two tricks by playing the Ace at once, provided he does not lead the suit back.

THE TURN-UP TRUMP When trumps are led by the adversaries, it is a common practice to play the turn-up as soon as possible, unless it is a valuable card. On the contrary, it is usual to keep it for as long as possible when the partner leads trumps.

CHANGING SUITS If the Second or Fourth Hand wins the first or second round of the adversaries' suit, it is seldom right to return it, because that would probably be playing their game. The player should open his own suit, as if he were the original leader. If he is strong enough to lead trumps under ordinary circumstances, he might be deterred from so doing if the adversaries have declared a strong suit against him. The same consideration can prevent his leading trumps in the hope of making a suit of his own, because the adversaries might reap the benefit by bringing in their suit instead. On the contrary, when the Second or Fourth Hand holds command of the adverse suit, they may often risk a trump lead that would otherwise be injudicious. Once a suit is started, it should not be changed, except for one of the reasons already given for the guidance of the First Hand.

WHEN THE ADVERSARIES LEAD TRUMPS When this is the case, and the Second Hand has a chance to either establish a suit against them or force his partner, he should stop the trump lead if he can. If his partner has led trumps, the Second Hand should usually play his winning cards on his right-hand opponent's plain-suit leads, to stop them, and continue the trumps.

These are about all the conventionalities necessary for the beginner. After at least a year's practice with them, he will either discover that he has no aptitude for the game or be ready to go into more detail. A beginner who attempts to handle the weapons of the expert simply plays with edged tools that will probably cut no one but himself and his partner.

———

THE SIGNAL GAME Having become thoroughly familiar with the elementary conventionalities of the game, so that they can be used without the slightest hesitation at the whist table, the player can proceed to acquaint himself with the details of what is commonly known as the Signal Game, which comprises all the methods of signalling up hands between partners, according to specific arbitrary and pre-arranged systems of play. Many players object to these methods as being unfair, but the methods are now too deeply rooted to yield to protest, and the best thing for a player to do is familiarise himself with his adversaries' weapons.

THE TRUMP SIGNAL A player who is anxious to have trumps led but who has no immediate prospect of the lead can call on his partner to lead trumps at the first opportunity, by playing any two cards of a suit led, the higher before the lower. Let's suppose he holds five good trumps, with the Six and Two of a suit of which his partner leads King, then Jack. By playing first the Six, and then the

Two, he calls on his partner to quit the suit and lead a trump.

Among some players, the lead of a strengthening card when an honour is turned is a call for trumps to be led through that honour at the first opportunity, but it is not good play.

Passing a certain winning card is considered by most players to be an imperative call for trumps.

The discard of any card higher than a Seven is known as a single-card-call. Even if it were not so intended, it is assumed that a trump lead cannot injure a player who has nothing smaller than a Nine in his hand.

ANSWERING TRUMP SIGNALS   In response to his partner's call, a player should lead the best trump if he holds it, one of the second and third best if he holds them, the highest of three or less, the lowest of four, and the fourth best of more than four. If he holds any of the regular high-card combinations in trumps, he should lead them in the regular way in answer to a call.

AFTER A FORCE   If the player is forced before he can answer the call, he may indicate the number of trumps originally held by playing them in this way:

With 3 or less, trumping with the lowest and leading the highest.

With 4 exactly, trumping with the third best and leading the highest.

With 5 or more, trumping with the third best and leading the fourth best.

These methods of taking the force must not be carried to extremes. For example, a player who holds K J 10 2 would hardly be justified in trumping with the 10 to show number. Some experts who hold the best trump with at least four others will not lead it; they prefer to show number first, by leading the fourth best. Other players who hold four lead the lowest after trumping with the third best.

THE ECHO IN TRUMPS   When the partner leads high trumps, the Third Hand should echo with four or more, by signalling in the trump suit. The universal form of the echo is to play first the third best, then the fourth best. When a player has called, and his partner leads, it is unnecessary for the caller to echo. Players seldom echo on adverse trump leads, even with five trumps.

THE FOUR-SIGNAL   There are several ways of showing four or more trumps without asking your partner to lead them. Among some players, the original lead of a strengthening card is evidence of four trumps, and is called an *Albany Lead*. A player who holds three cards of any plain suit, such as the 3, 4, 5, may show the number of his trumps by playing these small cards as follows:

Number of trumps	1st trick	2nd trick	3rd trick
3 or less	3	4	5
4 exactly	4	5	3
5 "	4	3	5
6 "	5	3	4
7 or more	5	4	3

The second of these is the four-signal; the last three are trump signals. They are used only in following suit.

The four-signal is sometimes used in the trump suit as a *sub-echo*, to show three trumps exactly.

Apart from being signalled, trump strength can often be inferred, especially from players passing doubtful tricks, forcing their partners, and so on.

TRUMP SUIT LEADS   When trumps are not led for the purpose of exhausting them immediately, but simply as the longest suit, the fourth best may be led from the following:

If the Ten accompanies the King and Queen, in the third combination, it is best to adhere to the usual lead of the King.

In leading trumps from combinations that contain a winning sequence, such as the following:

many players begin with the lowest of the winning cards and continue with the next above it.

SPECULATIVE TRUMP LEADS   The whist player will often find himself with a single good suit, a card of re-entry, and few trumps. Some conditions of the score can prompt him to make a speculative trump lead from this hand. If his trumps are high, such as A K x, he can safely begin by leading them, but if they are weak, and he is depending largely on his partner's possible strength, he should show his suit first by leading it once.

OVER-TRUMPING This is usually considered to be bad policy when a player has a good suit and sufficient trump strength to justify him in hoping to do something with it. The refusal to overtrump unless the trump played is a high one should be considered by the partner to be a call.

It is sometimes necessary to overtrump the partner in order to get the lead. For example, a player holds the two best trumps, and all winning cards of a plain suit, whereas the player on his right has a losing trump. In this position, the player who has the two best trumps should trump any winning card his partner leads, or over-trump him if he trumps, so as to prevent the adversary from making that losing trump.

UNDERTRUMPING, OR THE GRAND COUP This is playing a low trump on a trick that the partner has already trumped with a higher, in order to avoid the lead. For example, a player holds major tenace in trumps with a small one, and knows that the minor tenace is on his right. Four cards remain in each hand. The player on the left leads, Second Hand trumps, and Third Hand follows suit. If the Fourth Hand keeps his three trumps, he must win the next trick, and lose the advantage of his tenace.

A player will sometimes have the best card in two suits, and a small trump, and will know that the two best trumps and an unknown card are on his right. If the missing suit is led, and the player on the right trumps, his unknown card must be one of the other two suits, and the player who has command of them should keep both and throw away his small trump. The discards on the next trick can enable him to determine the suit of the losing card on his right.

THE LAST TRUMP If two players have an equal number of trumps, and each of them has an established suit, it will be the object of both to remain with the last trump, which must bring in the suit. The tactics of each will be to win the third round of trumps, and then, if the best trump is against him, to force it out with the established suit, thereby coming into the lead again with the last trump. So often is it important to win the third round of trumps that few good players will win the second round, unless they can win the third also. With an established suit, a card of re-entry, and four trumps King high, a player should lead trumps, but if his partner wins the first round and returns a small trump, the King should not be put on, no matter what Second Hand plays, unless the card next below the King is fourchette. Some of the most brilliant endings in whist are skirmishes for possession of the last trump; the player who is at a disadvantage often persistently refuses the fatal force: he hopes the leader will either be compelled to change his suit or lose the lead.

DRAWING THE LOSING TRUMP It is usually best to draw losing trumps from the adversaries, unless a player can foresee that he might want the best in order to stop a strong adverse suit.

A THIRTEENTH CARD A thirteenth card played by the partner is usually considered to be an invitation to put on the best trump. The Second Hand should not trump a thirteenth card unless he is weak in trumps.

AMERICAN LEADS Advanced players, who have had so much practice that they can infer the probable position of the cards without devoting their entire attention to it, have adopted a system of leading from the four following combinations, in order to show the number of small cards in the suit:

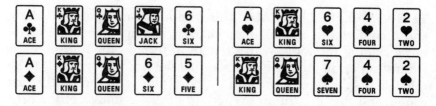

From these the King is never led if there are more than four cards in the suit. If there are more than four, the lowest of the sequence of high cards is led. From the first this would be the Jack, from the second the Queen, from the third the Ace (because the King is barred), and from the fourth the Queen. The Ten is not ranked among the high cards in American Leads.

On the second round, with the first two combinations, the difference between a suit of five and one of six cards can be indicated by following with the Ace if five were held originally, the King if more than five. Seven cards can be shown with the first combination, by leading the Queen on the second round.

The main difference these leads make in the play of the Third Hand is that he should not trump any court card led, even if he is weak in trumps. Misunderstanding as to the meaning of the first lead, especially if it is a Queen, often causes confusion and loss, but this is claimed to be offset by the value of the information given. Some lead 10 from Q J 10, fourth best from K J 10.

To the adversaries these leads are often of value, because the adversaries are frequently enabled to place the cards very accurately from the information given by the lead itself, regardless of the fall of the cards from the other hands. For example, Second Hand holds A J of a suit in which King is led, Third Hand plays the Four, Fourth Hand plays the Nine. The leader remains with Q 3 2, Third Hand still has 8 7 6 5, and if he also has the 10, Fourth Hand has no more. Again: The leader shows a suit of six; Second Hand holds two only. If the suit is led a third time it is a doubtful trick, and with four trumps the Second Hand should pass. If the leader shows the exact number of the suit originally led, and then changes to a four-card suit, the adversaries know at least nine of his cards.

This is so obvious it is an almost invariable rule for a player, on quitting his suit, to conceal the length of the second suit led by leading the highest card of a short suit.

If it were allowable to exercise some judgement in using these leads, the leads might not be open to so many objections; however, they are worse than useless unless the partner can depend on their being uniformly adopted.

THE MINNEAPOLIS LEAD   This is another variation in the leads, and is confined to one combination: Ace and any four other cards, not including the King. With strength in trumps, the fourth best is led instead of the Ace; the theory is that the Ace is more likely to be valuable on the second or third round of this suit than on the first round, and that the trump strength justifies the finesse of the original lead. With weak trumps, the Ace is led. Some players extend this principle to the Second Hand, and play Ace on a small card led, when they are holding A x x x x with weak trumps. This is open to the objection that it gives up command of the adverse suit too early in the hand; however, it saves many a trick.

THE PLAIN-SUIT ECHO   This is another device for giving information about number. When the original leader begins with a high card, the Third Hand should play his third best if he holds four or more cards, and on the second round his second best, always retaining his fourth best and any cards below it. The value of this echo is much disputed, and the adversaries can usually render it ineffective by holding up small cards; this practice is very much in vogue with advanced players.

LOW'S SIGNAL   This is the most recent system of indicating to the leader the number of cards in his suit held by the Third Hand. With four or more of the suit, the third best is played to the lead of a high card, or when no attempt is made to win the trick. In returning the suit, the second best is led if three or more cards remain, and on the third round, or in a discard, the highest card is played, whereby the fourth-best card and the cards below it are always retained. For instance: With the 8 7 5 2 of a suit that the partner leads, the 5 is played to the first round. If the suit is returned, the 7 is played, and next time the 8. If only three cards are held originally, the lowest is played to the first round, and the higher of two returned, in the usual way. The main value of this signal is that the return of the lowest card of a suit shows absolutely no more, instead of leaving the original leader in doubt as to whether it is the only card, or the lowest of three remaining cards. It is also a great exposer of false cards.

DISCARD SIGNALLING This is another method of indicating plain suits. When a player is known to have no trumps, and therefore cannot be calling for them, he can use the trump signal in any plain suit that he wishes led to him. As a general rule, a player should not use this signal unless he has a specific trick in the suit in which he signals. Some players use what is called the reverse discard: when a signal in one suit means weakness in it, and there is an invitation to lead another. This avoids the necessity of using the good suit for signalling purposes.

UNBLOCKING When the original leader shows a suit of five cards, and the Third Hand has four exactly, the latter should keep his lowest card, not for the purpose of echoing, but in order to retain a small card that will not block the holder of the longer suit. If the Third Hand has three cards of the suit led, and among them a card that might block his partner, he should give it up on the second round. For example, when K 4 3 are held and partner shows a five-card suit by leading Ace then Jack, Third Hand should give up the King on the second round. Again, when Q 9 3 are held, partner leads Ace then Eight and Second Hand plays King second round, Third Hand should give up the Queen. Again, when K Q are held, and the partner leads the 8 originally, won by Fourth Hand with Ace, the King should be discarded or otherwise gotten rid of at the first opportunity.

SHORT-SUIT LEADS Many players will not lead a long weak suit unless they have sufficient strength to justify them in hoping to establish, defend and bring it in, with *reasonable* support from the partner. With a long suit, headed by a single honour, weak trumps and no cards of re-entry, these players prefer to select a strengthening card for the original lead, hoping it will be of some assistance to the partner by affording a successful finesse. It is claimed that it is better for a person, especially one who has a strong hand, to play with the knowledge that his partner is weak than for him to be under the impression that he might be strong. This opening lead should warn the Third Hand to finesse deeply, to hold any tenaces he might have, and to let nothing pass him that might be too much for his weak partner to attend to. This is a very difficult game to play well, and is seldom resorted to except by the most expert players.

DESCHAPELLES COUPS It often happens that after the adverse trumps are exhausted, a player finds himself with the lead, but unable to give his partner a card of his established suit. In these cases, the best course is to sacrifice the King or Queen of any suit of which he does not have the Ace, in the hope that it will force the best of the suit and leave the partner with a card of re-entry. For example, the leader has established the Club suit; his partner has exhausted the trumps, Hearts; and because he has no Clubs, he leads the King of Spades from K x x x. If the holder of the Club suit has Spade Queen, and the King forces the Ace, the Club suit will be brought in. If he does not have the Queen, the Clubs are probably hopeless. The *coup* risks a trick to gain several tricks.

Players should be careful not to fall into this trap in the end game, and it is usually right to hold up the Ace if the circumstances are at all suspicious.

TENACE POSITIONS Many expert players will not lead away from a suit in which they hold tenace. If they have two suits, and one contains a tenace and the other does not, they will select the latter, although it might be much weaker. It is noteworthy that players who disregard the value of holding a tenace in the opening lead are well aware of its importance towards the end of the hand. When one player holds tenace over another, the end game often becomes a struggle to place the lead, and players frequently refuse to win tricks in order to avoid leading away from tenaces, or to compel another player to lead up to them.

UNDERPLAY This is often resorted to by the Fourth Hand in suits in which the Third Hand has shown weakness. For example, a small card is led, Third Hand plays the Ten, and Fourth Hand holds A Q J x. It is a common artifice to win with the Queen, and to return the small card. When the original leader is underplayed in his own suit, he should invariably put up his best card.

FINESSING The expert can finesse much more freely than the beginner. When a player has led from a suit such as K J x x and his partner has won with Acc and returned a small card, the Jack can be finessed with strong trumps. If the adversaries lead trumps, and the Ace wins the first round, a player who holds the King second hand on the return can finesse by holding it up and trusting his partner for the trick.

In all cases that mark the best of the suit against a player, and on his left, he may finesse against the third best's being there also. For example, a player leads from K 10 x x x. Third Hand plays Queen and returns a small card. The Ten should be finessed, regardless of trump strength, because the Ace must be on the left, and the finesse is against the Jack's being there also. Many varieties of this finesse occur.

PLACING THE LEAD This is usually a feature of the end game. A player might have an established suit, and his adversary might be the only person who has any small cards of it. If the lead can be placed in the hand of this adversary, he must eventually lead the losing cards.

A player begins with a weak suit of four cards, on the first round of which it is evident that his partner has no more and the adversaries have all the high cards. The suit is not played again, and for the last six tricks, the original leader finds himself with three cards of it and the Q x x of another suit. If the adversaries play King and Ace of the latter suit, the Queen should be given up, whereby the partner is trusted for the Jack, because the Queen will force the holder of the three losing cards into the lead. It is sometimes necessary to throw away an Ace in order to avoid the lead at critical stages of the end game.

FALSE CARDS It requires more than ordinary skill to judge when a false card will do less harm to the partner than to the adversaries. There are some occasions for false-card play about which there is little question. Having a sequence in the adverse suit, the Second or Fourth Hand can win with the highest card, especially if the intention is to lead trumps. If only K Q are held, Second Hand can play the King, especially in trumps. If A K x are held, the Fourth Hand should play Ace on a Queen led by an American leader. With a suit such as K J 10 x, after trumps have been exhausted, the Ten is not a safe lead; Jack or fourth best is better. Holding up the small cards of adverse suits is a common stratagem, and it is legitimate to use any system of false-carding in trumps if it will prevent the adversaries who have led them from counting them accurately.

PLAYING TO THE SCORE The play must often be varied on account of the state of the score, to either save or win the game in the hand. If the adversaries seem to be very strong, and likely to go out on the deal, all conventionalities should be disregarded until the game is saved; finesses should be refused, and winning cards should be played Second Hand on the first round. If the adversaries are exhausting the trumps, it will often be judicious for a player to make what winning cards he has, regardless of all rules for leading, especially if the cards are sufficient to save the game.

It often happens that the same cards must be played in different ways according to the state of the score and the number of tricks in front of the player. A simple example will best explain this. Hearts are trumps; you hold two small ones, and two better are out against you, but you cannot tell whether they are in one hand or not. You also have two winning Spades, and one smaller is still out. The game is seven-point whist. The importance of playing to the score will be evident if you consider your play in each of the following instances, whereby your score is given first:

Score 6 to 6: you have 5 tricks in front of you.
Score 6 to 6: you have 4 tricks in front of you.
Score 6 to 5: you have 4 tricks in front of you.
Score 5 to 4: you have 5 tricks in front of you.

INFERENCES   The great strength of the expert lies in his ability to draw correct inferences from the fall of the cards, and to adapt his play to the circumstances.

Inferences from the various systems of leads and returns are too obvious to require more attention, but attention can be called to some inferences that are often overlooked, even by advanced players:

If a suit led is won by Third Hand with King or Ace, and the original leader wins the second round with King or Ace, the adversaries must have the Queen.

If the Third Hand plays Ace first round, he has neither King nor Queen. If he plays Queen on a Ten led, he has no more. If he plays Ace on a King led, he has the Jack alone, or no more.

If the Second Hand plays King first round on a small card led, he has Ace also, or no more. If he plays Ace under the same conditions, he has no more. [See Minneapolis Lead.]

If a suit is led, and neither Third nor Fourth Hand has a card in it above a Nine, the original leader must have A Q 10, and the second player K J. When neither Third nor Fourth Hand holds a card above the Ten, the major and minor tenaces are divided between the leader and the Second Hand. If it can be inferred that the leader held five cards in the suit originally, he holds the minor tenace.

When a player, not an American leader, begins with a Jack and wins the trick, the adversaries can conclude that his partner had two small cards with the Ace and did not have four trumps and another winning card.

When a good player changes his suit, he knows that it will not go around again, or that the command is against him. This is often a valuable hint to the adversaries. When the player quits his original suit and leads trumps, without his partner having called, the adversaries can conclude that the suit has been established.

When a player puts Ace on his partner's Jack led, and does not lead trumps, the adversaries can count on him for only one small card of the suit led.

When an adversary finesses freely, he can be credited with having some strength in trumps.

When a player changes his suit, the adversaries should note carefully the fall of the cards in the new suit. As already observed, the leader almost invariably opens the new suit with the best he has. Suppose a player leads two winning cards in one suit, and then the Eight of another, which the Second Hand wins with the Ten; the four honours in the second suit must be between the Second and Fourth Hands.

Having won the first or second round of the adverse suit, and having no good suit of his own, the Second or Fourth Hand might be able to infer a good suit with his partner, by the play. For example, a player opens Clubs, and shows five; his partner wins the second round, and opens the Diamond suit with the Jack, on which Second Hand plays Ace, and his partner drops the 9. Having the lead now, and no good suit, it is evident for the player that the play should be continued on the assumption that the partner is all Spades and trumps.

———

THE AMERICAN GAME Since the revolt against the invariable opening from the longest suit, which was the style of game advocated by the old school of Pole and 'Cavendish,' many systems have been tried out by the various clubs that meet at American national tournaments. E. C. Howell was the first player to attempt to set the short-suit game in order, but his methods have long since been superseded by more elastic tactics.

The fundamental principle of the short-suit game, as first explained to world players in the *New York Sun*, is to use the original or opening lead to indicate the general character of the hand rather than any details of the individual suit. In the long-suit game, the original leader is always assuming that his partner might have something or other, and plays on that supposition. The short-suit player indicates the system of play best adapted to his own hand, without having the slightest regard as to the possibilities of his partner. It is the duty of the partner to indicate his hand in turn, and to shape the policy of the play on the combined indications of the two partners.

This does not mean that the player will always lead a short suit; it means that he should combine the best features of both systems without slavishly adhering to either system. This idea was brought to perfection in practice by the famous American Whist Club of Boston, under the able leadership of club captain, Harry H. Ward. It was demonstrated that Ward could take any kind of team and beat any of the old-style long-suit players, no matter how skilful they were.

FIVE-TRUMP HANDS With five trumps, and the suits split, 3, 3, 2, players always open a trump, unless they have a tenace over the turn-up card. From five trumps and a five-card plain suit, players open the suit if it is one that will require some help to establish; otherwise, the trump is used. From five trumps with a four-card plain suit, players open the trump with hands of moderate strength; otherwise, the plain suit is used.

FOUR-TRUMP HANDS From four-trump hands, players invariably open a suit of five cards or more, but prefer to avoid a four-card suit headed by a single honour. These are the suits in which the best chance for a single trick usually occurs when the suit is led by someone else. For example, Hearts trumps:

$$\heartsuit\ 8\ 7\ 6\ 3 \qquad \clubsuit\ 9\ 8 \qquad \diamondsuit\ K\ 8\ 3\ 2 \qquad \spadesuit\ K\ 4\ 2$$

The best opening from this hand is the club nine.

When players are forced to open single-honour suits, the lead of the lowest card shows an honour as good as the Queen, whereas the lead of an intermediate card denies this honour, as in the following examples. Hearts trumps:

$$\heartsuit\ 10\ 8\ 3\ 2 \qquad \clubsuit\ K\ 6 \qquad \diamondsuit\ Q\ 7\ 6\ 4 \qquad \spadesuit\ Q\ 5\ 4$$

From this, players should lead the four of diamonds, but if they hold

$$\heartsuit\ 10\ 8\ 3\ 2 \qquad \clubsuit\ K\ 6 \qquad \diamondsuit\ J\ 8\ 7\ 4 \qquad \spadesuit\ Q\ 5\ 4$$

they should lead the seven of diamonds.

From hands that contain four trumps and three three-card suits, players use their own judgement: sometimes they lead the trump, sometimes a plain suit. They prefer the plain suit if it is a desirable one to open, such as hearts trumps:

♡ K 8 3 2   ♣ J 10 4   ◇ A 10 3   ♠ 8 4 3

From this, players would open the Jack of clubs, but from

♡ K 8 3 2   ♣ J 3 2   ◇ A 10 3   ♠ Q 6 3

they should lead the deuce of trumps. If in this hand the club suit were Q J 3, the Queen of clubs would be the best opening.

It might seem paradoxical that a weaker hand should call for a trump lead; however, the opening is not an attack; it is a move to await developments.

THREE-TRUMP HANDS From hands that contain three trumps or fewer, players' opening leads vary from the ordinary player's game more than in any other detail. Players always open a long suit from three-trump hands if the suit is a good one, such as A K and other cards, K Q and other cards, or even Q J and other cards. However, without this strength in the long suit, they let it alone completely, and develop the hand with a short-suit or 'gambit' opening.

With three trumps and a five-card suit that contains two honours that are not in sequence, players still open the long suit if they have a sure re-entry in another suit. For example, hearts trumps:

♡ K 6 2   ♣ 8 6 2   ◇ A Q 6 4 3   ♠ A 10

The trey of diamonds is the best opening. If there were no re-entry, such as only 10 2 of spades instead of A 10, players should open the 10 of spades.

Although players open a great many short suits, they avoid weak three-card suits except in rare instances.

Although the American system, like all other systems, entails losses at times, it seems to avoid many of the pitfalls that confront the player who always opens his long suit, regardless of the possibilities of ever bringing it in. In many instances, players find this player places himself in the worst possible position for any chance to make even one trick in the suit he opens.

We admit that if a team adopts straight American leads, it is much easier for them to count the partner's hand accurately; however, it seems that this advantage is more than overcome by the fact that in American openings, we have a clear idea about the general character of the partner's hand while there is still time to take advantage of the knowledge. In the long-suit game, this element is entirely wanting.

IN CONCLUSION The first-class whist player is usually developed gradually. If he possess the faculty of paying close attention to the game while he is playing, nothing should prevent him from rapidly progressing. At first, he might care little or nothing for 'book' whist, but after some experience with book players, he is rather in danger of running to the other extreme, and putting more book into his game than it will carry. Having passed that stage, his next step is usually to invent some system of his own, and to experiment with every hand he plays. By degrees, he finds that all special systems of play have some serious defects that overbalance their advantages, and this discovery gradually brings him back to first principles. If he gets so far safely, his game for all future time will probably be sound, commonsense whist, without any American leads, plain-suit echoes, or four-signals, and free from any attempts to take fourteen tricks with thirteen cards.

When a whist player reaches that point, he is probably as near the first class as the natural limitations of his mental abilities will ever permit him to go.

THE LAWS These are found at the end of the Whist Family of Games.

ILLUSTRATIVE WHIST HANDS

A and B are partners against Y and Z. A is always the original leader, and Z is the dealer. The underlined card wins the trick, and the card under it is the next one led.

Number 1: Long Suits; ♡ 5 turned.

A	Y	B	Z	TRICK
♣ K	♣ 5	♣ 7	♣ 3	1
♡ 10	♡ J	♡ Q	♡ 5	2
♣ Q	♣ J	♣ 2	♣ 10	3
♡ 7	♡ 3	♡ 9	♡ 8	4
J ♠	9 ♠	2 ♠	5 ♠	5
♣ A	♡ 4	♡ 6	5 ♢	6
4 ♠	♡ K	A ♠	6 ♠	7
J ♢	7 ♢	2 ♢	K ♢	8
♡ 2	3 ♢	4 ♢	A ♢	9
♣ 9	6 ♢	3 ♠	8 ♢	10
♣ 8	9 ♢	7 ♠	8 ♠	11
♣ 6	10 ♢	K ♠	10 ♠	12
♣ 4	Q ♢	♡ A	Q ♠	13

Number 3: Short Suits; ♡ Q turned.

A	Y	B	Z	TRICK
Q ♢	K ♢	A ♢	2 ♢	1
2 ♠	A ♠	J ♠	5 ♠	2
4 ♢	10 ♢	3 ♢	J ♢	3
♡ 2	♡ 5	♡ 3	♡ Q	4
♡ 6	♡ A	♡ 4	♡ J	5
♣ 8	♣ 2	♣ 3	♣ K	6
♡ 7	8 ♢	5 ♢	7 ♢	7
♡ K	4 ♠	6 ♢	♡ 9	8
K ♠	7 ♠	6 ♠	8 ♠	9
Q ♠	♣ 4	♣ 5	10 ♠	10
9 ♠	♣ Q	♣ 6	♡ 10	11
♡ 8	9 ♢	♣ 7	♣ J	12
3 ♠	♣ A	♣ 10	♣ 9	13

Number 2: American Game; ♡ 8 turned.

A	Y	B	Z	TRICK
6 ♢	J ♢	A ♢	9 ♢	1
♡ 3	3 ♢	2 ♢	10 ♢	2
♣ 9	♣ K	♣ A	♣ 3	3
♡ 6	4 ♢	5 ♢	♣ 4	4
♣ Q	♣ 8	♣ 2	♣ 7	5
♣ 6	♡ 4	♡ 9	♣ 10	6
♡ 10	7 ♢	8 ♢	♣ J	7
♣ 5	♡ K	♡ A	7 ♠	8
4 ♠	Q ♢	♡ Q	♡ 5	9
2 ♠	5 ♠	♡ J	♡ 7	10
A ♠	6 ♠	Q ♠	K ♠	11
J ♠	9 ♠	3 ♠	10 ♠	12
8 ♠	K ♢	♡ 2	♡ 8	13

Number 4: Play to Score; ♡ J turned.

A	Y	B	Z	TRICK
K ♠	4 ♠	3 ♠	A ♠	1
♡ 3	♡ 9	♡ Q	♡ 2	2
2 ♠	7 ♠	5 ♠	♡ 4	3
♣ 2	♣ K	♣ 6	♣ 3	4
♡ 5	♡ 7	♡ 8	♡ J	5
♡ 10	♣ 5	♡ K	♡ A	6
♣ 8	♣ J	3 ♢	♣ 4	7
5 ♢	J ♢	A ♢	2 ♢	8
10 ♠	9 ♠	8 ♠	♡ 6	9
♣ Q	♣ 7	4 ♢	♣ A	10
Q ♠	J ♠	6 ♠	♣ 10	11
10 ♢	7 ♢	6 ♢	♣ 9	12
Q ♢	8 ♢	9 ♢	K ♢	13

Number 1: This is a fine example of the *Long-suit Game.* The leader begins with one of the high cards of his long suit. Missing the 2, he knows someone is signalling for trumps, and because it is very unlikely that the adversaries would signal while he was in the lead, he assumes it is his partner, and leads his best trump. His partner

does not return the trump, because he holds major tenace over the king, which must be in Y's hand. At trick 5, B still holds major tenace in trumps, and leads a small card of his long suit to try to get A into the lead again. If A leads trumps again, his only possible card of re-entry for his club suit is gone. At trick 7, if B draws Y's king, he kills A's card of re-entry at the same time.

Number 2: This is an excellent example of the **American Game**. A has a three-trump hand, but his long suit is not headed by two honours in sequence, and the Queen of clubs cannot be considered as a re-entry, so A makes the gambit opening of the singleton diamond. His partner, having nothing in plain suits, immediately returns the diamond. A now leads an intermediate club, and B forces him again. At trick 6, A avoids changing suits. If the long spade suit is opened, and Z returns the diamond 10, A–B will make four tricks fewer on this hand.

Number 3: This example of the **Short-suit Game** is from Val Starnes' *Short-Suit Whist*. This is sometimes called the Gambit opening. The leader, having no reason to lead trumps, even with five, and not having three honours in his long suit, prefers the gambit opening of the singly guarded queen. Y holds what is called a potential or imperfect fourchette, and covers, in order to make A–B play two honours to get one trick. B also makes a gambit opening by returning a supporting spade. Three tricks are gained by the two leads of the supporting cards, and five would have been made but for Y's covering on the first trick.

Number 4: This is an example of **Playing to the Score**. The game is *English Whist*, 5 points, counting honours. The first lead of trumps shows Z that honours are divided, and that he must make 11 tricks to win the game. At trick 3, he must trump; to discard clubs would be inconsistent with refusing to trump in order to bring them in. At trick 4, if Y cannot win a trick in clubs and give Z a finesse in trumps, Z cannot win the game. At trick 7, both black queens are against Z, and he must take the best chance to win if the diamond ace is also against him. The adversaries cannot place the club ace, so Z underplays in clubs as his only chance for the game.

PRUSSIAN WHIST This is the ordinary 5-, 7- or 10-point whist, with or without honours, except that instead of turning up the last card for trump, the player to the left of the dealer cuts a trump from the still pack, which is shuffled and presented to him by the dealer's partner.

FAVOURITE WHIST This is the regular 5-, 7- or 10-point whist, with or without honours, except that whichever suit is cut for, the trump on the first deal of the rubber is called the favourite. Whenever the suit turns up for trump, after the first deal, tricks and honours count double towards game. There must be a new favourite at the beginning of each rubber, unless the same suit happens to be cut again.

A variation is to attach a progressive value to the four suits, whereby tricks are worth 1 point when Spades are trumps, when Clubs 2, when Diamonds 3, and when Hearts 4. Honours do not count, and the game is 10 points, made by tricks alone. The hands are played out; the winners score all tricks taken, and the winners of the rubber add 10 points for bonus. The value of the rubber is the difference between the score of the winners and that of the losers. For example, if the rubber is in A–B's favour with the score shown in the margin, A–B win a rubber of 8 points.

1st game:	10 to 6
2nd game:	4 to 16
3rd game:	14 to 8
Rubber:	10
Totals	38 to 30

This is a good game for superstitious people who believe that specific trump suits are favourable to them.

— —

DUPLICATE WHIST

Duplicate whist is not a distinct game; it is simply the name given to that way of playing whist whereby a number of hands are played over again with the same cards but by different people.

CARDS The cards have the same rank as at whist; they are dealt in the same way, and the same rules apply to all irregularities in the deal, except that a misdealer must deal again. The objects of the game are the same, and so are all the suggestions for good play. The only differences that require attention are the positions of the players, the way of counting the tricks, and the methods of keeping and comparing the scores.

THEORY It can briefly be stated that duplicate proceeds on the principle that if two partners have made a specific number of tricks with specific cards, under specific conditions with reference to the lead, distribution of the other cards in the adversaries' hands, and so on, the only way to decide whether or not two other players could have done better, or annot do so well is to let them try it, by giving them the same cards under exactly the same conditions.

This comparison can be carried out in various ways; however, in every instance it depends entirely on the number and arrangement of the players engaged. The most common forms are club against club, team against team, pair against pair and player against player. The reason for the arrangement of the players will be better understood if the method is first described.

METHOD OF PLAYING   There is no cutting for partners, and no choice of seats and cards as at whist, because the players take their places and deal according to a prearranged schedule.

The player to the left of the dealer begins by placing the card he leads face upwards on the table and in front of him. The second player follows by placing his card in front of him in the same, as does the third, and as does the fourth. The four cards are then turned face downwards, and the dealer takes up the trump. The partners who win the trick place their cards lengthwise, pointing towards each other; the adversaries place theirs across. At the end of the hand, the number of tricks taken by each side can be seen by glancing at any player's cards. If there is any discrepancy, a comparison of the turned cards will show which trick it occurs in, and the cards can be readily faced and examined.

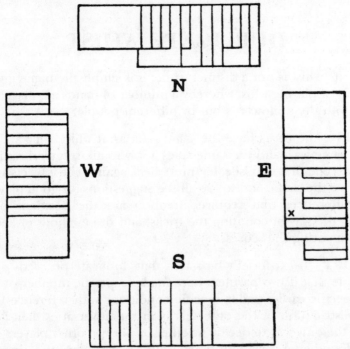

N and S: 6; E and W. 7. East has made a mistake in turning the fifth trick.

COUNTERS In some places,13 counters are placed on the table, and the winner of each trick takes down one counter. This system often leads to disputes, because there can be no check on it, and there is nothing to show which trick the error occurred in.

COUNTING TRICKS At the end of each hand, the players sitting North and South score the *total* number of tricks they have taken, instead of the number in excess of a book. Their adversaries, sitting East and West, do the same. Each player then slightly shuffles his 13 cards, so as to conceal the order in which they were played, and the four separate hands of 13 cards each are then left on the table, face downwards; the trump is turned at the dealer's place.

TRAYS When any apparatus is used for holding the cards, such as trays, boxes or envelopes, each player puts his 13 cards in the compartment provided for them. Each tray has a mark on it, usually an arrow, showing which end of the tray should point towards a given direction, usually the north. The pocket into which the dealer's cards go is marked 'dealer', and it is usual to provide a trump slip for each tray. When the hand is first dealt, the trump is recorded on this slip, which travels around the room with the tray. After the dealer has turned up the designated trump, he places the trump slip in the tray, face downwards. When the play of the hand is finished and the cards are replaced in the tray, the dealer puts his trump slip on the top of his cards. The four hands can then be conveniently carried or handed to any other table to be overplayed.

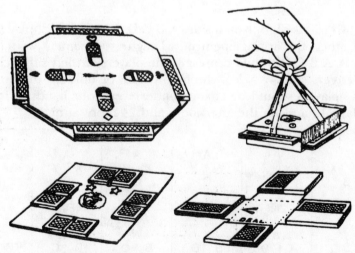

VARIOUS TYPES OF APPARTATUS FOR DUPLICATE WHIST

SCORING   There should be two score-cards at each table. The various methods of putting down and comparing the scores can best be described in connection with the variety of competition to which they belong. It is a common practice to note the trump card on the score sheets.

POSITION OF THE PLAYERS   The four players at each table are distinguished by the letters N, S, E and W; North and South are partners against East and West. West should always be the dealer in the first hand, and North have the original lead. In all published illustrative hands, North is the leader, unless otherwise specified.

The deal passes in rotation to the left, and the number of hands played should always be some multiple of four, so that each player can have the original lead an equal number of times. Twenty-four hands at each table is the usual number, and is the rule at all League tournaments. The partners and adversaries should be changed after each eight hands. Three changes in 24 hands will bring each member of a set of four into partnership with every other member for an equal number of hands.

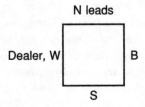

If two teams of four on a side, A B C D, and W X Y Z, play against each other, the arrangement in a League tournament would be as follows: A B C D should represent the players of the visiting club, or challengers, and W X Y Z the home club, or holders; the positions of the players should be changed after every four hands. It is usual to play 24 hands in the afternoon, and 24 more at night.

A W X B	A Y Z B	A W Y C	A X Z C	A X Y D	A W Z D
1st	2nd	3rd	4th	5th	6th
Y C D Z	W C D X	X B D Z	W B D Y	W B C Z	X B C Y

If more than four players are engaged on each side, this arrangement must be repeated with every additional four; the tables are
always in sets of two each, but in these cases, and in fact in anything
but League matches, it is usual to play only the 1st, 3rd and 5th sets.

CLUB AGAINST CLUB   The smaller club should put into the
field as many multiples of four as it can; the larger club presents an
equal number to play against them. The opposing sides are then so
arranged that half the members of each club sit North and South,
the other half East and West. If we distinguish the clubs by the marks
O and X, and suppose 16 to be engaged on each side, they would
be arranged at 8 tables, as follows.

X	X	X	X
O 1 O	O 3 O	O 5 O	O 7 O
X	X	X	X
1st set	2nd set	3rd set	4th set
O	O	O	O
X 2 X	X 4 X	X 6 X	X 8 X
O	O	O	O

If an apparatus is used, the players can sit still for four hands,
whereby they put the trays aside and then exchange them for the
four trays played at the other table in the set. If not, the cards are
left on the table, as already described, and the fours change places;
the players at table 1 go to table 2, and the ones at table 2 go to
table 1; the other sets change in the same way. This brings them into
this posi- tion:

X	X	X	X
O 1 O	O 3 O	O 5 O	O 7 O
X	X	X	X
O	O	O	O
X 2 X	X 4 X	X 6 X	X 8 X
O	O	O	O

The two O's who have just played the N and S hands at table 1
proceed to play at table 2: the N and S hands that have just been
played by two X's, whereas the two O's who played the E and W
hands at table 2 overplay at table 1: the E and W hands just held by
the two X's.

It is now evident that the four O's have held between them all the 52 cards dealt at each table, because the first pair have held all the N and S hands dealt at both tables, and the second pair have held all the E and W hands. The same is true of the four X players, and if there is any difference in the number of tricks taken by the opposing fours, it is supposed to be due to a difference in skill: other matters have been equalised as much as the limitations of the game will permit.

When the overplay is finished, the cards are gathered, shuffled, cut and dealt afresh, and East now has the original lead. It must be remembered that the deal can never be lost, and that no matter what happens, the player whose proper turn it is to deal must do so.

NUMBERING HANDS   The hands simultaneously played are scored under the same number but distinguished by the number of the table at which they are first dealt. Each pair of partners in a team plays two table 1 hands, in one of which they are N and S, in the other E and W.

SCORING   The result of the hand is entered on the score sheets, which the opposing players at each table should then compare, and turn face downwards, leaving them on the table when they change places.

Let's suppose the N and S partners of the O team make 7 tricks at table 1, and that the E and W partners of the X team make 6. Each pair enters on its own score-card the number it makes. The E and W partners of the O team now come to table 1, and play the 26 cards that the other members of their team did not hold. They are not permitted to look at the score-card until the hand has been overplayed. They then enter the result, which should be 6 tricks. If the total of the tricks taken by the same team on the N and S and E and W hands is not 13, it must be a loss or a gain. At the end of the 24 hands, the result of the match can be immediately ascertained by laying side by side the score cards of the East and West hands played at the same table. The North and South scores are not compared, because the laws state they might be incorrect, but the East and West must be officially right.

On pages 108 and 109, we give an illustration of the full score of a match. The check marks in the 6th column show that the N and S players compared the score with the E and W before turning down their cards. The figures in the 2nd column are the gains on the various hands. The figures in the 7th column show which of the four players whose names are written at the top of the score-card were partners for that series of hands. The result shows that the O team had a majority of one trick at table 1, whereas the X team had a majority of three tricks at table 2, whereby they were the winners of the match by two tricks.

If sixteen players were engaged, it would be necessary to institute a similar comparison between each set of tables, and there would be sixteen score-cards to compare, two at a time, instead of four.

TEAM AGAINST TEAM   The methods just described for a match of club against club are identical to the ones used in a contest between two teams of four; the only difference is proportion. In the latter case, there will be only one set, of two tables, and only four score-cards to compare.

The change of partners should be exhaustive in team matches, which will require six sets.

TEAMS AGAINST TEAMS   When several quartette teams compete with each other, Howell's system of arrangement will be found to be the best. There are two methods: for odd and for even numbers of teams.

ODD NUMBERS OF TEAMS   This is the simplest form of contest. Let's suppose five teams offer for play. We will distinguish them by the letters *a, b, c, d* and *e,* and arrange each team at its own table:

N	a	b	c	d	e
W + E	a 1 a	b 2 b	c 3 c	d 4 d	e 5 e
S	a	b	c	d	e

The names of the N and S and of the E and W members of each team should first be entered on the score-cards; all the N and S players then move to the next table east. The players at table 5 go to table 1, and each table deals and plays four hands, after which they put the hands away in trays.

	e	a	b	c	d
	a 1 a	b 2 b	c 3 c	d 4 d	e 5 e
	e	a	b	c	d
Hands:	1 to 4	5 to 8	9 to 12	13 to 16	17 to 20

The peculiarity of this system is in the movement of the trays: the ones at the middle table always go to the extreme West of the line, and the others move up as many tables at a time as might be necessary to follow them. In this instance, the trays at table 3 go to table 1, and all others move up two tables. At the same time, the N and S players all move one table further east, whereby the position shown on the top of page 110 is brought about.

MANHATTAN WHIST CLUB

Table No. 7....... X Team

1. D. Jones   3. M. Boyce
2. E. Wilson   4. H. Jones

B-W	Gain	Trump	HAND	N-S	Check	
6		DK	1	7	✓	3+4
9	1	H7	2	5	✓	
4	2	HJ	3	11	✓	
5		S4	4	7	✓	2+4
3		S9	5	10	✓	
7		D3	6	5	✓	
9	1	C5	7	3	✓	1+4
9		HQ	8	5	✓	
4	1	DK	9	8	✓	
3		SA	10	9	✓	
8		S3	11	6	✓	
10	+5	C2	12	2	✓	
			13			
			14			
			&c			

MANHATTAN WHIST CLUB

Table No. 7....... O Team

1. Finery   3. Bullock
2. Lewis   4. Izard

B-W	Gain	Trump	HAND	N-S	Check	
6		DK	1	7	✓	1+2
8		H7	2	4	✓	
2	1	HJ	3	8	✓	
6		S4	4	10	✓	1+3
3	11	S9	5	6	✓	
8		D3	6	4	✓	
10	11	C5	7	4	✓	1+4
8		HQ	8	9	✓	
6	1	DK	9	10	✓	
4		SA	10	5	✓	
7		S3	11	3	✓	
11	+6	C2	12		✓	
			13			
			14			
			&c			

MANHATTAN WHIST CLUB

Table No. 7......

X Team

1 D. Jones   3 M. Boyce
2 E. Wilson   4 H. Jones.

B-W	Gain	Trump	HAND	N-S	Check	
4		CJ	1	8	✓	3+4
8	1	S3	2	5	✓	
3		CA	3	8	✓	2+4
7	2	HQ	4	6	✓	
7	1	D4	5	3	✓	1+4
11	1	D7	6	3	✓	
6		C6	7	9	✓	
6	3	S4	8	8	✓	
2		C7	9	12	✓	
11	1	S4	10	5	✓	
9		D3	11	7	✓	
5		DQ	12	9	✓	
			13			
	+9		14 &c			

MANHATTAN WHIST CLUB

Table No. 2......

O Team

1 Chinery   3 Bullock
2 Lewis   4 Izard

B-W	Gain	Trump	HAND	N-S	Check	
5	1	CJ	1	9	✓	1+2
8		S3	2	5	✓	
5	2	CA	3	10	✓	1+3
10		HQ	4	6	✓	
10	3	D4	5	6	✓	1+4
4		D7	6	2	✓	
5		C6	7	7	✓	
1		S4	8	7	✓	
8		C7	9	11	✓	
9		S4	10	2	✓	
4		D3	11	7	✓	
		DQ	12	8	✓	
			13			
	+6		14 &c			

2nd set d	e	a	b	c
a 1 a	b 2 b	c 3 c	d 4 d	e 5 e
d	e	a	b	c
Hands: 9 to 12	13 to 16	17 to 20	1 to 4	5 to 8

This movement of the trays and players is continued for two more sets, which completes the round:

3rd set c	d	e	a	b
a 1 a	b 2 b	c 3 c	d 4 d	e 5 e
c	d	e	a	b
Hands: 17 to 20	1 to 4	5 to 8	9 to 12	13 to 16

4th set b	c	d	e	a
a 1 a	b 2 b	c 3 c	d 4 d	e 5 e
b	c	d	e	a
Hands: 5 to 8	9 to 12	13 to 16	17 to 20	1 to 4

If we now take any two of the teams engaged, *a* and *d* for example, we will find that the E and W *a* and the N and S *d* pairs of those teams have played hands 9 to 12 at table 1, in the 2nd set, and that N and S *a* and E and W *d* pairs have overplayed the same hands at table 4, in the 3rd set, so that we have really been carrying out a number of matches simultaneously, between five teams of four players each.

If there are 5, 7, 9 or 11 tables in play, the movement of the trays must be 2, 3, 4 or 5 tables at a time; however, the movement of the players remains the same: one table at a time, in the direction opposite to that of the trays.

GILMAN'S SYSTEM Another method, recommended by Charles F. Gilman, of Boston, which prevents any possibility of players' giving hints to their friends as they pass the trays, is to have each team play at its own table first, so as to get an individual score. The E and W players then move to the next table but one, in either direction: they go from 11 to 9, from 9 to 7, and so on, and the N and S players sit still. This movement is continued until the E and W players have gone twice around. The trays move in the same direction as the players do, but only one table at a time: they go from 11 to 10, from 9 to 8, and so on. This brings about the same result as that of the Howell's system.

EVEN NUMBERS OF TEAMS This method of arranging even numbers of teams is also Gilman's; however, it requires considerable care in the movement of the trays, because half of them lie idle during each round, which is the same as skipping a table in other methods.

Suppose we have ten tables, arranged in two rows as follows, with a team of four players at each.

1	2	3	4	5
6	7	8	9	10

Taking 30 deals as the number to be played, we place trays 1, 2 and 3 to be played and overplayed by tables 1 and 6, which are opposite each other in the rows. Trays 4, 5 and 6 we lay aside. Trays 7, 8 and 9 are to be played and overplayed by tables 2 and 7. Tables 10, 11 and 12 are laid aside, and so on, until we get to tables 5 and 10, which play and overplay trays 25, 26 and 27. The easiest way to manage this is to give tray 2 to table 6, while tray 1 is at table 1, and then to let table 1 take tray 2, while table 6 plays tray 3. Then table 1 will get tray 3, while table 6 overplays tray 1. This will make all the trays come in numerical order to table 1, and will act as a check.

When the play of the first round, three deals, is finished, the E and W players all move one table: 2 goes to 1, 3 to 2, and so on. The umpire now brings into play the trays that were idle, giving trays 4, 5 and 6 to tables 1 and 6; trays 10, 11 and 12 to tables 2 and 7; and so on down the line, for all the trays that were used in the first round lying idle.

Again the players move, and now table 1 gets the 7, 8, 9 set of trays to overplay with table 6, and so on, so that all the sets move up a table after each intervening round, and table 1 will get all the trays from 1 to 30 in order.

SCORING In both the foregoing systems, each pair should have its own score-card, and should mark the name of the team it plays against for each series of four hands. These score-cards are more for private reference than anything else in tournaments, because there is always a professional scorer, for whose use small slips are filled out and collected from the tables at the end of each round. The winner is the team that wins the most matches, not the one that gains the most tricks. In the case of ties, the number of tricks won must be the deciding factor. If the number of tricks taken by each side is a tie in any match, the score is marked zero, and each team counts half a match won. At the top of page 112 an illustration of the final score in a match between five teams. The *c* and *d* teams are tied for second place in the number of matches, but the *c* team takes third place, because it has lost one more trick than the *d* team lost. The *b* and *c* teams score a half match; so do the *c* and *e* teams.

Teams	a	b	c	d	e	Matches	Tricks
a	╲	+5	−1	+1	+4	3	+9
b	−5	╲	0	−1	+2	1½	−4
c	+1	0	╲	−2	0	2	−1
d	−1	+1	+2	╲	−2	2	0
e	−4	−2	0	+2	╲	1½	−4

PAIR AGAINST PAIR This is the most interesting form of competition, especially for domestic parties, because the arrangement of the players permits great latitude in the number engaged: table after table are added as long as players offer to fill them.

TWO PAIRS When only four players are engaged at a single table, the game is called Memory Duplicate, which is forbidden in all first-class clubs. The players retain their seats until they have played an agreed number of hands, which are laid aside, one by one, in trays. No trump is turned in Memory Duplicate: one suit is declared trumps for the entire sitting.

Instead of the players' changing positions for the overplay, the trays are reversed. If the indicators pointed N and S on the original deals, they must lie E and W for the overplay.

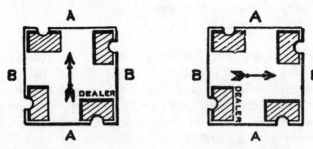

ORIGINAL POSITION OF TRAYS   POSITION FOR OVERLAY

SCORING The E and W hands only are scored; the card is laid aside after the original play is completed, and a new card is used for the overplay. The difference in the totals of these two sets of score-cards will show which pair gained the most tricks.

FOUR PAIRS These should be arranged at two tables, and adversaries should be changed after every 8 hands. The third set will exhaust the combinations, and it will then be found that each pair has played and overplayed an equal number of hands against every other pair.

1st set	2nd set	3rd set
b	c	d
a a	a a	a a
b	c	d
Hands: 1 to 8	9 to 16	17 to 24
d	b	c
C c	d d	b b
d	b	c

Four hands are dealt at each table in each set, and then exchanged. The trump card is turned for every original deal.

SCORING Each pair carries its own score-card with it from table to table, until the 24 hands have been played. The 7th column is used to designate the pair played against. The pairs at the second table should begin scoring with hands numbers 5, 13 and 21, respectively, because they will presently receive from the first table the series beginning 1, 9 and 17, respectively. Eight hands complete a match, and the result must be tabulated in the same way as for teams of four; ties are decided by the majority of tricks won. Following is an example.

Pairs	a	b	c	d	Matches	Tricks
a	\	+3	-2	+5	2	+6
b	-3	\	+4	-1	1	0
c	+2	-4	\	-2	1	-4
d	-5	+1	+2	\	2	-2

The *a* pair wins the tie with *d* 6 tricks plus.

SIX PAIRS This is a very awkward number to handle, and should be avoided if possible. The whole game could be played at three tables simultaneously, but this course would necessitate the players' changing places ten times and following a very complicated schedule in doing so. The simplest way to handle six pairs is to arrange them at three tables, two of which are constantly in play, and the third only half the time. This is the first position:

```
        b                        d                        f
      a 1 a                    c 2 c                    e 3 e
        b                        d                        f
```

Tables 1 and 2 deal and play two hands each, and then exchange trays with each other. At table 3, two hands are dealt and played, and both are left in the trays.

The players at tables 1 and 2 then change adversaries: they deal, play and exchange two fresh hands. The players at the third table remain idle, or look on.

```
        c                        d                    |        f
      a 1 a                    b 2 b                   |      e 3 e
        c                        d                    |        f
Hands 5 and 6 played and exchanged                    |     None.
```

The *b* and *c* pairs now give way to *e* and *f*:

```
        e                        d                    |        b
      a 1 a                    f 2 f                   |      c 3 c
        e                        d                    |        b
Hands 7 and 8 played and exchanged                    |    3 and 4.
```

While tables 1 and 2 are playing two fresh hands, the trays that contain hands 3 and 4 that were left at table 3 are overplayed by the *b* and *c* pairs, which makes a match between them and the *e* and *f* pairs.

Again the pairs at the first two tables change adversaries: they deal, play and exchange two more hands, and the third table remains idle.

```
        f                        d                    |        b
      a 1 a                    e 2 e                   |      c 3 c
        f                        d                    |        b
Hands 9 and 10 played and exchanged                   |     None.
```

The pairs *a* and *d* now give way to *b* and *c*, and the *b c e f* pairs play two hands and exchange them, then change adversaries for two more hands; *a* and *d* remain idle all the time. All the pairs have now been matched but *a* and *d*, and they take seats E and W at two tables; the N and S positions are filled up by any of the other players in the match.

```
      any              any
   a  1  a          d  2  d
      any              any
```

No notice is taken of the scores made by the N and S hands in the last set, because it is simply a match between the *a* and *d* pairs.

SCORING Each pair against each is considered a match, and the winner of the most matches wins; tricks decide ties.

COMPASS WHIST When we come to handle large numbers, the changes of position become too complicated, and the simplest plan is to arrange them at as many tables as they will fill, and to place on each table an equal number of trays. At the Knickerbocker Whist Club, New York, which was famous for its compass games, they played a minimum of 24 trays, or got as near that number as possible. If there were 14 tables, they played two deals at each. If there were only 10 tables, they played 30 trays.

All the N adn S players sit still, and at the end of each round, two or three deals as the case may be, all the E and W players move up one table, whereby 2 go to 1, 3 to 2, and so on. Each pair keeps its own score card, on which the number of the tray is written; andthe number of the pair played against, which is always the number of the table at which the pair started. One of the pairs that remains there is number 3 N and S, and the other, which is number 3 E and W, moves away.

Each pair adds up its score card at the end, and writes the total number of tricks it has won. The names of the players have previously been written on the blackboard, and their scores are written opposite their names. Each side—N and S and E and W—is then added up in order to find the average, and all scores above average are plus, whereas all below average are minus.

The following is an example of the averaging of a game in which five tables took part and 30 deals were played:

	N and S			E and W	
a	201	−6	f	189	+6
b	204	−3	g	186	+3
c	211	+4	h	179	−4
d	207	=	j	183	=
e	212	+5	k	178	−5
5	1035		5	915	
Aver 208, N and S			Aver 183, E and W		

The *e* and *f* pairs make the best scores N and S and E and W respectively; the *f* pair, having won the greatest number of tricks above the average of the hands, would be the winners.

HOWELL PAIR SYSTEM   A very popular system of managing pairs in club games, and also in the national tournaments for the Minneapolis trophy, was called the Howell Pairs. In this system, indicator cards are placed on the tables. These cards show each player the number of the table and the position at that table to which he should move next. Sometimes he will sit N, sometimes S, and sometimes E or W, but he always finds his partner opposite him, and at the end of the game will have had every other pair in the game for an adversary once, and will have played all the hands dealt.

A different set of indicator cards is required for every different number of tables in the game. They were invented by E. C. Howell of Washington, D. C., and are arranged for any number of pairs from four to thirty-four.

INDIVIDUALS   When four people play memory duplicate, one of the four, usually S, retains his seat and keeps the score; the other people change places right and left alternately, whereby each person plays with S as a partner for 8 hands. These changes successively bring about the three following positions:

```
          c          |          b          |          a
       a     b        |       a     c        |       c     b
          S          |          S          |          S
Hands: 1 to 4        |       5 to 8         |       9 to 12
```

For the overplay, the trays are reversed, whereby the hands originally dealt N and S are placed E and W, but the players continue to change right and left alternately. This brings the same partners together, but on different sides of the table:

```
          c          |          b          |          a
       b     a        |       c     a        |       c     b
          S          |          S          |          S
Hands: 1 to 4        |       5 to 8         |       9 to 12
```

SCORING   The names of the four players should be written at the head of each score-card, and because there is no trump turned in memory duplicate, the third and seventh columns can both be used for the numbers of the players who are partners; the sixth column can be used for the N and S gains.

When the match is finished, a tabulation of the tricks lost or won by each player will readily show who is the winner. In the following illustration, number 3 finishes plus 6, number 4 plus 2, number 1 minus 4, and number 2 minus 4.

MANHATTAN WHIST CLUB

Table No.........
1 _Chimery_   3 _Bullock_
2 _Lewis_   4 _Izard_

E-W	Gain	Part's	HAND	N-S	Gain	Part's
8			1	10	2	
4		1&2	2	5	1	3&4
6	1	−4	3	5		+4
3			4	5	2	
7			5	8	1	
6	2	1&3	6	4		2&4
3		+1	7	4	1	−1
10	1		8	9		
5			9	6	1	
9		1&4	10	10	1	2&3
10	2	−1	11	8		+1
2			12	3	1	

Summary	1 to 4	5 to 8	9 to 12	Total
No 1	−4	+1	−1	−4
2	−4	−1	+1	−4
3	+4	+1	+1	+6
4	+4	−1	−1	+2

It must be remembered that the hands that are here scored N and S, in the 5th column, were E and W when originally dealt, so that the 1st and 5th columns are really the same hands. The score-card should be folded down the middle during the overplay, so that the original scores cannot be seen. It is even better to use a new card.

FOSTER'S SYSTEM This system of playing two pairs at one table was used at all the matches for the Utica Trophy, in which one pair from a club challenged the pair that held the trophy for another club. It consisted of having an umpire to transpose the suits between the original and the overplay of the deals. The trays that contained the hands were sent into the umpire's room, and the umpire had an extra pack of cards, from which he duplicated each hand of thirteen cards as he took it out of the pocket to which it belonged; however he changed the suits, whereby he made clubs trumps instead of hearts, and so on. This system was found to do away with the memory part of the game, because ot was very difficult to recognise a hand unless it had some startling feature.

Coupled with the current practice of throwing out all hands in which there is found to be a suit of more than six cards, and dealing it over again, Foster's system for two pairs is the best so far suggested.

EIGHT INDIVIDUALS This form of contest is seldom used, because players dislike the continual changing of position and the delay in arriving at the results of the score. It would require seven sets to exhaust the combinations, and at each table, two hands would have to be dealt, played and exchanged with the other table in the set before the players could change positions. This would require 28 hands to complete the match.

SAFFORD'S SYSTEM This system for arranging the players is to have indicator cards on the tables:

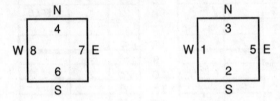

The players take their seats in any order for the first set, after which they go to the next higher number: 8 keeps his seat, and 7 goes to 1.

SCORING Each individual must keep his own score, whereby he adds up the total tricks taken in each set of four hands. These totals must then be compared with those of the player occupying the same position: N, S, E or W, at the other table in the set, and it will save time in the end if these totals are tabulated at once, on a sheet prepared for the purpose. For example, let this be the arrangement of eight players in the first set:

```
    b                              f
  a 1 c        Hands 1 to 4      e 2 g
    d                              h
```

If *a* and *c* take 34 tricks E and W, *e* and *g* take only 30 with the same cards, either *a* and *c* must have gained them or *e* and *g* must have lost them. It is a waste of time to write both losses and gains, and all that is necessary is to call the top score zero and charge all players with the loss of as many tricks as their total is short of the top score. In this case, we charge *e* and *g* with a loss of 4 each. It must be obvious that *f* and *h* have also made 4 more tricks than have *b* and *d*, and that the latter must be charged with a loss of 4 on the same hands that *e* and *g* lose on.

Following is an illustration of a sheet balanced in this way, showing the losses of the various players. The totals at the end of the match show that *c* is the winner, because he has lost fewer tricks than has any other player.

Players	a	b	c	d	e	f	g	h
Set 1	–	4	–	4	4	–	4	–
2	–	2	–	2	–	2	–	2
3	5	5	–	–	–	–	5	5
4	1	–	–	1	1	–	–	1
5	–	–	3	3	–	–	3	3
6	–	–	–	–	3	3	3	3
7	4	–	–	4	–	4	4	–
Totals	10	11	3	14	8	9	19	14

LARGE NUMBERS OF INDIVIDUALS   Several ingenious methods have been devised for handling large numbers of players, especially in domestic parties; both Safford and Mitchell distinguished themselves in this line. The simplest form has been suggested by Mitchell, and is especially adapted for social gatherings both sexes.

As many tables as possible are filled, whereby all the ladies sit N and E and the gentlemen S and W.

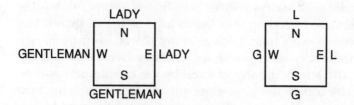

The number of hands dealt at each table must be adjusted to the number of tables filled and the time to be devoted to play. The trays that contain the hands are passed to the West; all the gentlemen move one table to the East, and the ladies sit still. In all the changes, each gentleman keeps to his original point of the compass: South or West. When he arrives at the table he started from, the round is finished. If an odd number of tables are engaged in play, the' changes can take place in regular order to the end. If the number is even, a dummy must be put in; however, because this is objectionable in a social gathering, it is better to adopt one of the two following systems, unless half the number of tables is an odd number, whereby the method already described can be used.

1ST METHOD　Some table in the series, which must not be either the first or the last series, deals no original hand, but overplays all the hands that come from the other tables to the East of it. The four players sit still and take no part in the progression, thereby obliging the people whose turn it would be to play at their table to pass on to the next.

2ND METHOD　Each gentleman should carefully note the number of the hand originally dealt at the table from which he starts. He progresses until he meets this hand again. The first to observe this should give notice to the company by way of a bell tap, because all the gentlemen must meet their original hands at the same time. Instead of stopping at the table at which this tray is encountered, all the gentlemen move on to the next, leaving the trays as they are. This skip enables each person to finish the round without playing any of the hands twice.

SCORING　There must be four winners: the ladies who have the best scores for the N and E hands, respectively, and the gentlemen who have the best S and W scores. If a choice is necessary, the lady and the gentleman who take the greatest number of tricks above the average should be selected as the winners.

MARRIED COUPLES　Safford had an ingenious schedule for eight married couples, arranged in two sets so that no husband and wife are ever in the same set at the same time. When seven sets have been played, every lady will have overplayed four hands against every other lady and gentleman, including four hands held by her husband. The same will be true of every man. Indicators are placed on the tables to show players their successive positions. The numbers represent the husbands and the letters the wives, whereby the couples are a–1, b–2, and so on. The couple a–1 always sits still; the ladies go to the next higher letter of the alphabet, and the men go to the next higher number: *h* goes to *b* as *a* sits still, and 8 goes to 2.

	N				N				N				N	
	6				3				f				c	
W a	1　2	E	W d	2　8	E	W 1	3　b	E	W 4	4　h	E
	g				e				6				5	
	S				S				S				S	

One hand is dealt at each table, and is overplayed at each of the other tables. A different point of the compass should deal at each table, in order to equalise the lead.

SCORING　The score of each four hands should be added up by each player, and the results should be tabulated at the end of every four hands, in the way described for eight people. The winner is the player who loses the fewest tricks. This is the only known system for deciding whether or not a man can play whist better than can his wife.

PROGRESSIVE DUPLICATE WHIST   This is the generic name by which the systems of duplicate are known whereby the purpose is to have as many as possible of the players meet each other during the progress of the match. Most of the systems we have been describing belong to this class.

— -—

THE LAWS OF DUPLICATE WHIST
DEFINITIONS

The words and phrases used in these laws are construed in accordance with the following definitions unless the construction is inconsistent with the context:

(a) The thirteen cards received by any one player are termed a 'hand'.

(b) The four hands into which a pack is distributed for play are termed a 'deal'; the same term is used to designate the act of distributing the cards to the players.

(c) A 'tray' is a device for retaining the hands of a deal and indicating the order of playing them.

(d) The player who is entitled to the trump card is termed the 'dealer', whether the cards have or have not been dealt by him.

(e) The first play of a deal is termed 'the original play'; the second or any subsequent play of this deal is termed the 'overplay'.

(f) 'Duplicate Whist' is the form of the game of whist in which each deal is played only once by each player, and in which each deal is overplayed so as to bring the play of teams, pairs or individuals into comparison.

(g) A player 'renounces' when he does not follow suit to the card led. He 'renounces in error' when, although he holds one or more cards of the suit led, he plays a card of a different suit; if this renounce in error is not lawfully corrected, it constitutes a 'revoke'.

(h) A card is 'played' whenever, in the course of play, it is placed or dropped face upwards on the table.

(i) A trick is 'turned and quitted' when all four players have turned and quitted their respective cards.

LAW I—Shuffling

SEC. 1. Before the cards are dealt, they must be shuffled in the presence of an adversary or the umpire.

SEC. 2. The pack must not be shuffled so as to expose the face of any card; if a card is exposed in this way, the pack must be reshuffled.

LAW II—Cutting for the Trump

SEC. 1. The dealer must present the cards to his right-hand adversary to be cut. The adversary must take from the top of the pack at least four cards and place them towards the dealer, leaving at least four cards in the remaining packet. The dealer must reunite the packets by placing the packet not removed in cutting on the other packet. If, in cutting or in reuniting the separate packets, a card is exposed, the pack must be reshuffled and cut again; if there is any confusion of the cards or doubt as to the place where the pack was separated, there must be a new cut.

LAW III—Dealing

SEC. 1. When the pack has been properly cut and reunited, the cards must be dealt, one at a time, face downwards, from the top of the pack, the first to the player at the left of the dealer, and each successive card to the player at the left of the player to whom the last preceding card has been dealt. The last, which is the trump card, must be turned and placed face upwards on the tray, if a tray is used; otherwise, it must be placed at the right of the dealer.

SEC. 2. There must be a new deal—

(a) If any card except the last is faced or exposed in any way in dealing.

(b) If the pack is proved to be incorrect or imperfect.

(c) If either more or less than thirteen cards are dealt to any player.

(d) If, after the first trick has been turned and quitted on the original play of a deal, one or more cards are found to have been left in the tray.

LAW IV—The Trump Card

SEC. 1. The trump card and the number of the deal must be recorded, before the play begins, on a slip provided for that purpose, and must not be elsewhere recorded. This slip must be shown to an adversary, then turned face downwards and placed in the tray, if a tray is used.

SEC. 2. The dealer must leave the trump card face upwards until it is his turn to play to the first trick; he must take the trump card into his hand and turn down the trump slip before the second trick is turned and quitted.

SEC. 3. When a deal is taken up for overplay, the dealer must show the trump slip to an adversary, and thereafter the trump slip and trump card will be treated as in the case of an original deal.

SEC. 4. After the trump card has been lawfully taken into the hand and the trump slip turned face downwards, the trump card must not be named nor the trump slip examined during the play of the deal; a player may, however, ask what the trump suit is.

SEC. 5. If a player unlawfully looks at the trump slip, his highest or lowest trump can be called; if a player unlawfully names the trump card, or unlawfully shows the trump slip to his partner, his partner's highest or lowest trump can be called.

SEC. 6. These penalties can be inflicted by either adversary at any time during the play of the deal in which they are incurred before the player from whom the call can be made has played to the current trick; the call can be repeated at each or any trick until the card is played, but cannot be changed.

SEC. 7. When a deal has been played, the cards of the respective players, including the trump card, must be placed in the tray face downwards and the trump slip placed face upwards on top of the dealer's cards.

SEC. 8. If, on the overplay of a deal, the dealer turns a trump card other than the one recorded on the trump slip, and this error is discovered and corrected before the play of the deal is commenced, the card turned in error is liable to be called.

SEC. 9. If this error is not corrected until after the overplay has begun, and more than two tables are engaged in play, the players at that table will take the average score for the deal; if fewer than three tables are in play, there must be a new deal.

SEC. 10. If a player records on the trump slip a different trump from one turned in dealing, and the error is discovered at the next table, there must be a new deal. If the deal has been played at one or more tables that have the wrong trump, the recorded trump must be taken as correct, and the players at the original table take the average score for the deal; if fewer than three tables are in play, there must be a new deal.

SEC. 11. By the unanimous consent of the players in any match, a trump suit can be declared and no trump turned.

LAW V—IRREGULARITIES IN THE HAND

SEC. 1. If, on the overplay, a player is found to have more than his correct number of cards, or the trump card is not in the dealer's hand, or any card except the trump card is faced so as to expose any of the printing on its face, and fewer than three tables are engaged, there must be a new deal. If more than two tables are in play, the hands must be rectified and then passed to the next table; the table at which the error was discovered must not overplay the deal, but will take the average score.

SEC. 2. If after the first trick has been turned and quitted on the overplay of a deal, a player is found to have fewer than his correct number of cards, and the other players have their correct number, this player will be answerable for the missing card or cards and for any revoke or revokes he has made by reason of its or their absence.

LAW VI—PLAYING, TURNING AND QUITTING THE CARDS

SEC. 1. Each player, when it is his turn to play, must place his card face upwards before him and towards the centre of the table, and let it remain in this position until all have played to the trick, whereby he must turn it over and place its face downwards and nearer to himself, placing each successive card as he turns it, so that it overlaps the last card played by him, and with the ends towards the winners of the trick. After he has played his card and also after he has turned it, he must quit it by removing his hand.

SEC. 2. The cards must be left in the order in which they were played and quitted until the scores for the deal are recorded.

SEC. 3. During the play of a deal, a player must not pick up or turn another player's card.

SEC. 4. Before a trick is turned and quitted, any player can require any of the other players to show the face of the card played to that trick.

SEC. 5. If a player names a card of a trick that has been turned and quitted, or turns or raises any card of this type so that any portion of its face can be seen by himself or his partner, he incurs the same penalty he would incur had he led out of turn.

LAW VII—CARDS LIABLE TO BE CALLED

SEC. 1. The following cards are liable to be called:

(a) Every card placed on the table so as to expose any of the printing on its face, except the cards that these laws specifically provide, will not be liable in this way.

(b) Every card held by a player so as to expose any of the printing on its face to his partner or to both of his adversaries at the same time.

(c) Every card, except the trump card, named by the player who holds it.

SEC. 2. If a player says, 'I can win the rest,' 'The rest are ours,' 'It makes no difference how you play,' or words to that effect, or if he plays or exposes his remaining cards before his partner has played to the current trick, his partner's cards must be laid face upwards on the table and are liable to be called.

SEC. 3. All cards liable to be called must be placed face up on the table and left that way until played. A player must lead or play them when lawfully called, provided he can do so without revoking; the call can be repeated at each or any trick until the card is played. A player cannot, however, be prevented from leading or playing a card liable to be called; if he can get rid of it in the course of a play, no penalty remains.

SEC. 4. The holder of a card liable to be called can be required to play it by only the adversary on his right. If this adversary plays without calling it, the holder can play to that trick as he pleases. If it is the holder's turn to lead, the card must be called before the preceding trick has been turned and quitted, or before the holder has led a different card; otherwise, he may lead as he pleases.

LAW VIII—LEADING OUT OF TURN

SEC. 1. If a player leads when it is the turn of an adversary to lead, and the error is discovered before all the players have played to this lead, a suit can be called from him or from his partner, as the case may be; the first time thereafter, it is the right of either of them to lead. The penalty can be enforced by only the adversary on the right of the one from whom a lead can lawfully be called. The right thereto is lost unless this adversary calls the suit he desires led, before the first trick won by the offender or his partner subsequent to the offence, is turned and quitted.

SEC. 2. If a player leads when it is his partner's turn and the error is discovered before all the players have played to this lead, a suit can at once be called from the proper leader by his right-hand adversary. Until the penalty has been exacted, waived or forfeited, the proper leader must not lead; should he so lead, the card led by him is liable to be called.

SEC. 3. If a player when called on to lead a suit has none of it, he can lead as he pleases.

SEC. 4. If all the players have not played to a lead out of turn when the error is discovered, the card erroneously led and all cards played to this lead are not liable to be called, and must be taken into the hand.

LAW IX—PLAYING OUT OF TURN

SEC. 1. If the third hand plays before the second, the fourth hand can also play before the second.

SEC. 2. If the third hand has not played and the fourth hand plays before the second, the latter may be called on by the third hand to play his highest or lowest card of the suit led, and, if he has none of that suit, to trump or not trump the trick; the penalty cannot be inflicted after the third hand has played to the trick. If the player liable to this penalty plays before it has been inflicted, waived or lost, the card so played is liable to be called.

LAW X—THE REVOKE

SEC. 1. A renounce in error can be corrected by the player who makes it, except in the following cases, whereby a revoke is established and the penalty therefore incurred:

(a) When the trick in which it occurs has been turned and quitted.

(b) When the renouncing player or his partner, whether in his right turn or otherwise, has led or played to the following trick.

SEC. 2. At any time before the trick is turned and quitted, a player can ask an adversary whether he has any of a suit, to which this adversary has renounced in that trick, and can require the error to be corrected in case this adversary is found to have any of the suit.

SEC. 3. If a player, who has renounced in error, lawfully corrects his mistake, the card improperly played by him is liable to be called, and, if he is the second or third hand player and his left-hand adversary has played to the trick before attention has been called to the renounce, he can be required by this adversary to play his highest or his lowest card to the trick in which he has renounced, and will not play to that trick until this adversary has inflicted or waived the penalty. Any player who has played to the trick after the renouncing player can withdraw his card and substitute another; a card so withdrawn is not liable to be called.

SEC. 4. The penalty for a revoke is the transfer of two tricks from the revoking side to adversaries. If more than one revoke during the play of a deal is made by one side, the penalty for each revoke, after the first, is the transfer of one trick only. The revoking players cannot score more, nor their adversaries less than the average on the deal in which the revoke occurs, except that in no case will the infliction of the revoke penalty deprive the revoking players of any tricks won by them before their first revoke occurs.

In Pair Matches, the score will be recorded as made, independently of the revoke penalty, which will be separately indicated as plus or minus revoke ('−R' for the revoking side, and '+R' for its adversaries). In these matches, the penalty for a revoke will not increase the score of the opponents of the revoking players above the maximum, as made at the other tables, on the deal in which the revoke occurs, provided, however, that if the opponents win more tricks than this maximum, independently of the revoke penalty, their score will stand as made. Nor shall the score of the revoking players be reduced, by the infliction of the revoke penalty, below the minimum so made. Nor will the score of the revoking players be thereby reduced below the minimum score made at the other tables unless the injured side can establish to the satisfaction of the committee in charge that the full penalty should be enforced.

SEC. 5. A revoke cannot be claimed if the claimant or his partner has played to the following deal, or if both have left the table at which the revoke occurred. If the revoke is discovered in season, the penalty must be enforced and cannot be waived.

SEC. 6. At the end of the play of a deal, the claimants of a revoke can examine all the cards; if any hand has been shuffled, the claim can be urged and proved if possible; however, no proof is necessary, and the revoke is established if, after it has been claimed, the accused player or his partner disturbs the order of the cards before they have been examined to the satisfaction of the adversaries.

LAW XI—MISCELLANEOUS

SEC. 1. If anyone calls attention in any way to the trick before his partner has played thereto, the adversary last to play to the trick can require the offender's partner to play his highest or lowest of the suit led, and, if he has none of that suit, to trump or not to trump the trick.

SEC. 2. A player has the right to remind his partner that it is his privilege to enforce a penalty, and also to inform him of the penalty he can enforce.

SEC. 3. A player has the right to prevent his partner from committing any irregularity, and for that purpose can ask his partner whether or not he has a card of a suit to which he has renounced on a trick that has not been turned and quitted.

SEC. 4. If either of the adversaries, whether with or without his partner's consent, demands a penalty to which the advertsaries are entitled, this decision is final; if the wrong adversary demands a penalty or a wrong penalty is demanded, or either adversary waives a penalty, none can be enforced except in the case of a revoke.

SEC. 5. If a player is lawfully called on to play the highest or lowest of a suit, to trump or not to trump a trick, to lead a suit or to win a trick, and unnecessarily fails to comply, he is liable to the same penalty as if he had revoked.

SEC. 6. If anyone leads or plays a card, and then, before his partner has played to the trick, leads one or more other cards, or plays two or more cards together, all of which are better than the cards that any of his adversaries hold of the suit, his partner may be called on by either adversary to win the first or any subsequent trick to which any of these cards are played, and the remaining cards so played are liable to be called.

For the Rules of Etiquette of Duplicate Whist, see page 85.

SINGLE TABLE, OR MNEMONIC DUPLICATE

The laws of Duplicate Whist govern when applicable, except as follows:

Each player plays each deal twice, and the second time plays a hand previously played by an adversary. Instead of turning the trump, a player can declare a single suit trumps for the game. On the overplay, the cards can be gathered into tricks instead of being played as required by law (Law VIII, Sec. 1). In the case of discovery of an irregularity in the hands, there must always be a new deal.

MNEMONIC DUPLICATE FOR MORE THAN ONE TABLE

Except a contest played in comparison with a progressive match, the replaying of the cards by the same players—'up and back,' as it is sometimes called—is the only possible method of approximating to Duplicate Whist for one table; however, when eight or more players participate, this form of the game is extremely undesirable, because the element of memory enters into the replay and destroys the integrity of the game and its value as a test of Whist skill. It has been well described as 'a mongrel game—partly Whist and partly Dummy, but lacking in the best features of each'.

In the early days of Duplicate Whist, Mnemonic Duplicate was, to some extent, played even when several tables of players were participating. It survives in a few circles, mainly ones in which Duplicate Whist has never been tried. It can be played under any of the Duplicate Whist schedules by playing the schedules through twice—the second time whereby the North and South hands are given to the East and West players, and vice versa. Because each deal is played twice by each pair, double the time is required to play the same number of deals, as at Duplicate Whist. Allowance must be made for this in fixing the number of deals to be played.

The Snow System of movement, when practicable, is preferable. When the Howell pair system of movement is used, the scores do not require 'equating', because they are equalised on the replay. Under other systems, only the North and South scores have to be kept, because the comparison can be made quite as readily as by direct comparison of these scores.

—-—

DUMMY

There are three forms of Dummy: the English game, for three players; the French game, for three or four; and the game now generally known as Bridge, or Bridge Whist. Dummy is not recognised in any form by the American Whist League, and there are no American Laws that govern it. We will describe each variety of the game in its turn, beginning with the English.

CARDS *English Dummy* is played with a full pack of fifty-two cards, ranking as at whist both for cutting and playing. Two packs are usually used.

MARKERS These are necessary, and are of the same patterns as those used in whist.

PLAYERS According to the English usage, Dummy is played by three people, and the table is complete with that number.

The players cut for partners and for the deal. The player who cuts the lowest card takes dummy for the first rubber, the one who cuts the next lowest takes dummy for the second rubber, and the one who cuts the highest takes it for the last rubber. It is considered obligatory to play three rubbers, in order that each can have whatever advantage or disadvantage might be supposed to attach to the dummy. The three rubbers so played are called a Tournée. It is sometimes agreed that one player will take dummy continuously, on condition that he concedes to his adversaries one point in each rubber. When this is done, the largest rubber that the dummy's partner can win is one of seven, and he can win nothing, whereas his adversaries can win a rubber of nine, and must win at least two. This concession of a point is not made, as many people imagine, because it is an advantage to have the (dummy) partner's hand exposed, but because it is an advantage to have the player's hand concealed. He knows the collective contents of the adversaries' hands; each of them knows only the contents of dummy's hand and his own.

CUTTING The player who cuts the lowest card has the choice of seats and cards, but he must deal the first hand for his dummy, not for himself. The methods of spreading, cutting, deciding ties and so on described in connection with whist are those used in dummy.

POSITION OF THE PLAYERS The players are distinguished, as at whist, by the two first and last letters of the alphabet, and their positions at the table are indicated in the same way. There is no mark to distinguish the dummy hand, a defect that is remedied in the French system.

DEALING At the beginning of a rubber, dummy's partner presents the pack to his *left-hand* adversary to be cut, and deals from right to left, beginning with the player on his right, and turning up the last card for dummy's trump. When two packs are used, there is no rule as to which player will collect and shuffle the still pack. On this point the French rules are very explicit.

The general rules with reference to irregularities in the deal are the same as the ones for whist.

When the cards have been dealt, it is usual for dummy's partner to take up and sort the dummy first. There are several ways of laying out dummy's hand, the most common of which is to run the suits down in rows, with the turn-up across and to the right of the other trumps, if any.

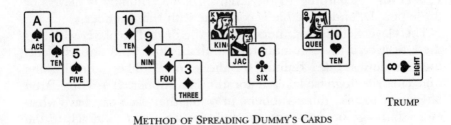

METHOD OF SPREADING DUMMY'S CARDS

STAKES The remarks made on this subject in connection with whist apply equally to dummy. Dummy's partner must pay to or receive from each adversary the amount agreed.

METHOD OF PLAYING The general method of playing is identical with that for whist, with the following exceptions:

When it is dummy's turn to play, his partner selects the card.

THE REVOKE For this, dummy is not liable to any penalty, because his adversaries can see his cards. Even if the revoke is occasioned by dummy's cards being disarranged, or one of them covered up, the adversaries should be as able to detect the error as the partner. If dummy's hand revokes, it cannot be remedied after the trick in which it occurs has been turned and quitted, and the game must proceed as if no revoke had occurred. All the penalties for a revoke can be enforced against dummy's partner, should he renounce in error and not correct it in time. Because there are no American laws for dummy, the English penalty of three tricks or three points can be enforced, and the revoking player cannot win the game that hand.

CARDS PLAYED IN ERROR   Dummy's partner is not liable to any penalty for cards dropped face upwards on the table, or for two or more cards played at once, because it is obvious that Dummy cannot gain any advantage from these exposed cards.

LEADING OUT OF TURN   If either dummy or his partner leads out of turn, the adversaries can call a suit from the one who should have led. It should be noticed that if it was not the turn of either player to lead, there is no penalty, because neither player can have gained any advantage from knowing what suit the other wished to lead, or from the exposed card. If all the players have played to the erroneous lead, the error cannot be corrected, and no penalty remains.

The methods of *Taking Tricks, Scoring, Claiming and Counting Honours, Marking Rubber Points* and so on are the same as in whist, and the counters are used in the same way.

CUTTING OUT   As already observed, there is no changing of partners, or of the rotation of the deal, until the completion of a rubber, but at the beginning of each rubber, dummy must deal the first hand. If one side wins the first two games in any rubber, the third game is not played. At the end of the tournée, if any player wishes to retire, and another offers to take his place, the cards must be shuffled and cut as at the beginning; a player's position in one tournée gives him no rights in the next. There is nothing in the English game to recognise that there can be more than three candidates for dummy, because it is supposed that if four were present, they would prefer playing whist.

SUGGESTIONS FOR GOOD PLAY   Because these are equally appropriate to any form of dummy, we will postpone considering them until we have described the other varieties of the game French dummy, and—Bridge—and give them all at the end of the chapter Bridge.

DOUBLE DUMMY

CARDS Double Dummy is played with a full pack of fifty-two cards, and rank as at whist for both cutting and playing. Two packs are usually used.

MARKERS These are necessary, and are of the same description as those used in whist.

PLAYERS According to the English usage, double dummy is played by two people, and the table is complete with that number.

CUTTING The players cut for the deal. The player who cuts the lowest card deals for his dummy first, and has the choice of sitting to the right or left of his opponent. It is usual to select the seat on the right of the living player, because it is possible that you will forget whether or not specific cards have been played, and under these circumstances it is better to lead up to an exposed hand than to a hand the contents of which you are not sure of.

The methods of spreading, cutting, deciding ties, etc., are the same as those employed at whist.

POSITION OF THE PLAYERS It is not usually considered necessary to distinguish the players more than to indicate which hand had the original lead. For this purpose the whist notation is used, whereby A is the leader and Z the dealer.

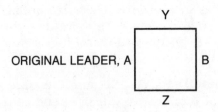

DEALING When two packs are used, the still pack should be shuffled by the non-dealer, and placed on the left of the player or dummy whose turn it will be to deal next.

The general rules with reference to irregularities in the deal are the same as in whist.

When the cards are dealt, it is usual to sort the dummy hands first, running the suits down in rows, with the turn-up trump across, and to the right of the others.

STAKES   The remarks already made on this subject in connection with whist and dummy apply equally to double dummy, except that there is no double payment, but each player wins from or loses to his living adversary the unit agreed on.

METHOD OF PLAYING   This so closely resembles dummy as to require no description. Neither dummy can revoke, and there are no such things as exposed cards, or cards played in error. It is very common for one player to claim that he will win a specific number of tricks, and for his adversary to admit it and allow him to score them, without playing the hand out.

LEADING OUT OF TURN   If either of the dummies or the players leads out of turn, the adversary can call a suit from the one that ought to have led, but if it was the turn of neither, there is no penalty. If all four have played to the trick, the error cannot be corrected, and no penalty remains.

The methods of *Taking Tricks*, *Scoring*, *Claiming and Counting Honours*, *Marking Rubber Points* and so on are the same as in whist, and the counters are used in the same way.

RUBBERS   If the first two games are won by the same player and his dummy, the third game is not played. Tournées are not played, and the completion of the rubber breaks up the table.

CUTTING IN   When the table is complete with two, at the end of a rubber a new table must be formed.

SUGGESTIONS FOR GOOD PLAY   The player should first carefully examine the exposed hands, and by comparing them with his own, suit by suit, should fix in his mind the cards held by his living adversary. This takes time, and in many places it is the custom to expose the four hands on the table. Players whose memory is better than that of their opponents object to this, for the same reason that they prefer to sit on the right of the living player. It is not at all uncommon for a player to forget that specific cards have been played, to his very serious loss.

Once the hands are fixed in the mind, some time should be given to carefully considering the best course to pursue, after which the play should proceed pretty rapidly until the last few tricks, when another problem might present itself.

There is nothing in the game beyond skilful use of the tenace position, discarding and establishing cross-ruffs. Analysis is the mental power mainly used. There are no such things as inferences, false cards, finesse, underplay, speculative trump leads or judgement of human nature. The practice of the game is totally different from any other form of whist, and much more closely resembles chess.

The laws of Dummy are set out at the end of the English Whist Laws.

— ▪ —

HUMBUG WHIST

This is a variation of double dummy, whereby two players sit opposite each other. The deal and seats are cut for in the usual way; four hands of thirteen cards each are dealt, and the last card is turned for trump.

Each player examines the hand dealt to him, without touching the hands to his right or left. If he is content with his hand, he announces it; if not, he can exchange it for the one on his right. In the case of exchange, the discarded hand is placed on the table face downwards, and the other is taken up and played. If a player retains the hand originally dealt him, he must not look at the other hands. If the dealer exchanges, he loses the turn-up card, but the trump suit remains the same. Each player deals for himself in turn, and there is no deal for the dead hands. Whist laws govern the deal and its errors.

METHOD OF PLAYING   The dealer's adversary has the first lead; the other adversary must follow suit if he can, and the highest card of the suit led wins the trick. Trumps win all other suits.

SCORING   Each trick above six counts one point towards game. Of the four honours: A K Q J of trumps, if each player holds two, neither can count. However, if one player has only one honour, or none, the other counts 2 points for two honours, if he holds them; 3 points for three; and 4 points for four. The honours count towards games as in whist. The penalty for a revoke is three tricks, and it takes precedence over other scores; tricks count next, and honours last. Five points is game.

SUGGESTIONS FOR GOOD PLAY   It is considered best for a player who does not find four reasonably sure tricks in his hand to exchange, because there is an certain advantage to be gained by knowing thirteen cards that cannot be in the adversary's hand. Before changing, the player should fix in his memory the exact cards of each suit in the hand he is about to discard. By combining his knowledge of these cards with that of his own cards, he is often able to direct his play to advantage. Beyond this there is little skill in the game.

A variation is sometimes made whereby the dealer announces a trump suit after he has examined his hand, raher than turn up the last card. His adversary then has the right to either play his hand or exchange it for the one on his right; however, the dealer must play the hand dealt to him.

— —

THIRTEEN AND THE ODD

This is Humbug Whist without the discard. The dealer gives thirteen cards to his adversary and to himself, one at a time, and turns up the next for the trump. The trump card belongs to neither player. The winner of the odd trick scores a point. Five points is game.

— —

MORT
WHIST À TROIS, OR FRENCH DUMMY

'MORT' simply means 'the dead hand', and is the equivalent of the English word Dummy; the partner is known as *Vivant*, or 'the living hand'. In these words the English usually sound the *t*, as they do in words such as *piquet* and *valet*.

CARDS Mort is played with a full pack of fifty-two cards, and ranking is as at whist for cutting and playing. Two packs are usually used.

MARKERS These are necessary for counting the game points only. Four circular counters for each side, preferably of different colours, are used, or the ordinary whist markers can be used. At the end of each game, the score of the points won or lost by each player must be transferred to a score-sheet, which is kept for that purpose.

PLAYERS Mort is played by three people, but the table is usually composed of four. If there are more than four candidates, the methods described in connection with whist are adopted for deciding which four people will play the first tournée.

When the table is formed, the cards are again shuffled and spread in order to cut for partners and deal.

TIES These are decided in the same way as for whist.

CUTTING If there are three players, the one who cuts the lowest card takes dummy for the first game; he also has the choice of seats and cards, and can deal the first hand for himself or for Mort, as he pleases; however, once he had made his choice, he must abide by it. The player who cuts the intermediate card takes dummy for the second game, and the player who cuts the highest card takes it for the third game; each player in turn has the choice of seats and cards. These three games finish the rubber or tournée, because each has once had the advantage or disadvantage of playing with Mort. It is obligatory to finish the tournée: no player is allowed to withdraw and substitute another player without the consent of the other players. In Mort it is very unusual for one person to take dummy continuously.

If there are four players, the one who cuts the highest card of the four sits out, and takes no part in the first game. It is customary for him to take Mort's seat, and to make himself useful in sorting dummy's cards for him. He plays in the three following games, and takes Mort in the fourth, or last. Four games complete the tournée for four players.

POSITION OF THE PLAYERS The players or hands are distinguished by the letters M, V, L and R, which stand, respectively, for Mort, Vivant, Left and Right. The Mort is the dead hand, which is turned face upwards on the table. The Vivant is his partner, who sits opposite him and plays his cards for him. The Left and Right are the adversaries who sit on the left and right of *Mort*.

Special attention must be called to use of the term *adversaries* in any description of Mort. It is used exclusively to designate the two partners opposed to the Mort and Vivant. In all other cases in which opposition is implied, the term *opponents* must be used.

When it is necessary to distinguish the dealer from the first, second or third hand, it is usual to add the letters used for that purpose in whist, whereby the letters are placed inside the diagram of the table, as follows:

```
              V
          ┌───────┐
          │   z   │
       L  │b     a│  R
          │   y   │
          └───────┘
              M
```

This diagram shows that Vivant dealt, and that the adversary on the Right of Mort had the original lead.

WITH THREE PLAYERS When Vivant has selected his seat and cards, the adversaries can select their seats. It is usual for the strongest adversary to sit Right.

WITH FOUR PLAYERS In this case, we can best describe the arrangement by numbering them 1, 2, 3 and 4, respectively, whereby the lowest number, 1, has cut the lowest card, and the other numbers have the right to play Vivant in their numerical order. The first arrangement would be as follows:

For the three succeeding games the arrangement would be:

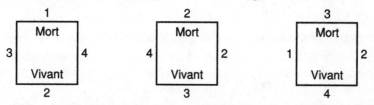

It will be seen that each player, immediately after being Vivant, sits out, or takes Mort's place, for the next game.

DEALING It is usual for Vivant to deal the first hand for himself, because the disadvantage of exposing fourteen cards is more than compensated for by the fact that the adversary is compelled to open the game by leading up to an unknown hand. If Vivant deals the first hand for Mort, he must present the pack to the player on dummy's right for cutting, and deal the cards from right to left, turning up the trump at Mort's place. If he deals for himself, he presents the pack to the pone for cutting, and proceeds as in whist.

When two packs are used, the French laws require that if the deal is for Mort, the Right will gather and shuffle the still pack, and that if Vivant deals for himself, the pone will gather and shuffle. We have found this to be awkward, because the player who is gathering and shuffling the cards of one pack is called on to cut the other. For this reason, we recommend that whichever adversary is the pone for the deal in hands should allow his partner to gather and shuffle the still pack. When either adversary deals, his partner will, of course, gather and shuffle the still pack.

The general rules with reference to irregularities in the deal are the same as those for whist, with the following exceptions:

A misdeal does not lose the deal unless the opponents so elect; they may prefer to have a new deal by the same dealer. The reason for this is that the deal is a disadvantage, especially for Mort.

If Vivant or Mort offers the pack to one adversary to cut, and then deals as if the other had cut, it is a misdeal, and it is not admissible to shift the packets in order to remedy matters.

It might be imagined that a card exposed in dealing, if dealt to Mort, would make no difference, because all his cards will presently be exposed. However, the laws give the opponents of the dealer the option of allowing the deal to stand, having a new deal or calling it a misdeal.

According to the French laws, if there is any discussion in progress with reference to the previous hand or play, the dealer may lay aside the trump card, face downwards, until the discussion is finished. If this law prevailed in America, I think the trump would very seldom be turned immediately.

STAKES In Mort, the stake is a unit, so much a point. It can help players, in regulating the value of the stake, to remember that six is the smallest number of points that can be won or lost on a single game, and that thirty-seven is probably the highest, although fifty, or even a hundred, is not impossible. The average is about twelve. The same customs as for whist prevail with reference to outside betting.

The Vivant must pay or receive double, because he has to settle with each adversary. If four people play, the one who sits out has nothing to do with the stakes, but can make outside wagers on the result of the game.

THE METHOD OF PLAYING This is practically the same as for whist, with the following exceptions:

When it is the turn of Mort to play, Vivant selects the card for him.

THE REVOKE The rules governing this are the same as those already given for English Dummy. Mort is not liable to penalty under any circumstances. If any other player revokes, his opponents may take three points from the score of his side, or add three points to their score, or take three of his tricks. The penalty cannot be divided; however, if two or more revokes are made by the same side, the penalty for each can be enforced in a different way. For example, if the score is 3 to 2 in favour of the adversaries, Vivant may take three points from their score for one revoke, and add three to his own score for the other. It is not permissible to reduce the revoking player's *tricks* to nothing. At least one trick must be left in order to prevent slams being made through revoke penalties.

CARDS PLAYED IN ERROR   Vivant is not liable to any penalty for dropping his cards face upwards on the table, but if he or Mort plays two cards at once to a trick, the adversaries may select which cards they will allow to be played. The adversaries are subject to the same penalties as in whist for all cards played in error.

LEADING OUT OF TURN   If Vivant or Mort lead out of turn, the adversaries may let the lead stand, or demand it be taken back. If it was the turn of neither Vivant nor Mort, no penalty can be enforced, and if all the players have played to the trick, the error cannot be corrected.

TAKING TRICKS   The methods of taking tricks, and placing them so that they can be easily counted, have been fully described in connection with whist.

OBJECT OF THE GAME   As in whist, the object is to take tricks; the highest card played of the suit led wins, and trumps win against all other suits. The first six tricks taken by one side, and that form a *book*, do not count, but all above that number count towards game. At the end of each hand, the side that has taken any tricks in excess of the book scores them, and their opponents count nothing. As soon as either side reaches five points, they win the game, but the concluding hand must be played out, and the winners are entitled to score all the points over five that they can make on that hand. For example, the score is 4 to 3 in favour of Vivant and Mort. They win the first seven tricks, which makes them game, but they do not cease playing. If they succeed in gaining eleven tricks out of the thirteen, they win a game of 9 points, instead of 5.

As already observed, Vivant loses or gains double the value of the points in each hand. In the three-handed game, this must be so, but in our opinion it would be a great improvement in the four-handed game to allow the player sitting out to share the fortunes of the Vivant, as in Bridge, and in many German games of cards, notably Skat.

SLAMS   The two great differences between French and English Dummy are that honours are not counted in Mort and that a special value is attached to slams. A slam is made when one side takes the thirteen tricks. These must be actually won, and cannot be partly made up of tricks taken in penalty for revokes. Players cannot score a slam in a hand in which they have revoked.

A slam counts 20 points to the side that makes it, but these 20 points have nothing to do with the game score. For example, the score is 4 all. Vivant and Mort make a slam. This does not win the game, but the 20 points are debited and credited on the score-sheet. The deal passes to the left, and the game proceeds with the score still 4 all, as if nothing had happened.

SCORING The number of points won on each game are written on the score-sheet, and each side is credited with the number of points that appears on their markers when the game is finished. To the winners' score is added 3 points, for a triple game, if their opponents have not scored; 2 points, for a double game, if their opponents are not halfway; or 1 point, for a simple game, if their opponents are 3 or 4. In addition to this, the winners add 4 points, for bonus or consolation, in every instance. From the total thereby found must be deducted whatever points have been scored by the losers, whether game points, slams or both. For example, Vivant and Mort win a game with the score 8 to 2 in their favour, which is a double. This is written on the score sheets as follows:

8 + 2 for the double, + 4 consolation = 14, minus 2 scored by the opponents; making 12 the net value of the game. Vivant therefore wins 24 points, and each of the adversaries, R and L, lose 12. Again:

R and L win a simple with a score of 5 to 4 and V and M have made a slam. 5 + 1 for the simple, + 4 for consolation = 10, minus 4 points scored, and 20 for the slam = 24 whereby it is shown that R and L lose 14 points each, although they won the game. Again:

V and M win a triple, with a score of 8 to 0; R and L have revoked. 8, + 3, + 4, + 3 for the revoke = 18, from which there is nothing to deduct.

The greatest number of points that can be made on a game, exclusive of slams and revokes, is 17, and the least number is 6.

MARKING The methods of using the counters in scoring the game points have already been described in connection with whist.

CUTTING OUT If there are more than four candidates for play at the conclusion of a tournée, the selection of the new table must be made as if no tournée had been played, and all players having equal rights to cut in.

CHEATING Mort offers even less opportunity to the cheat than does whist, because the deal is a disadvantage, and nothing is gained by turning up an honour, beyond possessing it.

——

CAYENNE
OR CAYENNE WHIST

CARDS   Cayenne is played with two full packs of fifty-two cards, which rank as at Whist for both cutting and playing.

MARKERS   These are necessary, and must be suitable for counting to ten points. A sheet of paper is used for scoring the results of the games.

PLAYERS   Cayenne is played by four people. When there are more than four candidates for play, the selection of the table must be made as for whist. Partners and deal are then cut for.

CUTTING   When one of the packs has been spread on the table, face downwards, each of the four players draws a card, and the two lowest pair against the two highest. The lowest of the four is the dealer, and has the choice of seats and cards. Ties are decided in the same way as for whist.

POSITION OF THE PLAYERS   The partners sit opposite each other, and are distinguished, as in whist, by the letters A–B and Y–Z. Z is the dealer, and A has the original lead.

DEALING   One pack of cards is shuffled and cut as in whist. The dealer then gives four cards to each player, beginning on his left, then four more, and finally five; no trump is turned. In many places, six cards are first dealt to each player, and then seven; however, the 4–4–5 system is better, and is the rule in the very similar game of Boston.

   The general rules with reference to irregularities in the deal are the same as for whist, except that a misdeal does not lose the deal. The misdealer must deal again, and with the same pack.

CAYENNE   After all the cards are dealt, the player to the left of the dealer cuts the still pack, which is shuffled and presented to him by the dealer's partner, and the top card of the portion left on the table is turned up for Cayenne. This card is not a trump, but is simply to determine the rank of the suits.

STAKES In Cayenne, the stake is a unit, so much a point. The largest number of points possible to win on a rubber is 24, and the smallest is 1. The result of the rubber can be a tie, which we consider to be a defect in any game. In settling at the end of the rubber, it is usual for the losers to pay their right-hand adversaries.

MAKING THE TRUMP The trump suit must be named by the dealer or his partner, after they have examined their cards. The dealer has the first say, and may select cayenne or any of the other suits; announce *grand*, playing for the tricks without any trump suit; or call *nullo*, playing to take as few tricks as possible, without a trump suit. If the dealer makes the choice, his partner must abide by it, but if he does not have a hand to justify him in deciding, he should leave the selection to his partner, who must decide one way or the other.

The considerations that should guide players in their choice are the scoring possibilities of their hands, in tricks and in honours. As in whist, the first six tricks taken by one side do not count, but each trick above that number counts one, two and so on, *by cards*. There are five honours in the trump suit in Cayenne: A K Q J 10, and the partners who hold most of them count 1 for each honour they hold in excess of their opponents' honours, and 1 in addition, for *honours*. For example, if A–B have three honours dealt them, they must have one more than their adversaries, and 1 for honours, whereby they are entitled to score 2. If they have four honours, they have 3 in excess, and 1 for honours: a total of 4. If they have five honours, they count 6 by honours.

At the end of the hand, the points made by cards and by honours are multiplied by the value of the trump suit. This value varies according to the suit that is cayenne, which is always first preference. If cayenne is also the trump suit, the points made by cards and honours are multiplied by 4. If the trump suit is the same colour as that of cayenne, the multiplier is 3. If it is a different colour, the multiplier is 2 or 1, according to the suit. The rank of the suits as multipliers will be readily understood from the following table:

If Cayenne is	♡	◇	♣	♠	If trumps, multiply by 4.
Second colour is	◇	♡	♠	♣	If trumps, multiply by 3.
Third colour is	♣	♣	♡	♡	If trumps, multiply by 2.
Fourth colour is	♠	♠	◇	◇	If trumps, multiply by 1.

In order to better understand the importance of considering this variation in value when making the trump, it should be noticed that although the game is 10 points, several games can be won in a single hand, because everything made is counted, and any points over 10 go to the credit of the second game. If more than 20 points are made, the excess goes on the third game, and so on. Another important point is the great value attached to honours, and the maker of the trump should never forget that he can better afford to risk his adversaries' winning 2 by cards with a trump in which he has three honours than he can to risk a trump in which they might have three honours, and he can probably win only the odd trick.

Another element might enter into his calculations: the state of the score. Tricks count before honours, and if he feels certain of making, by cards, the few points necessary to win the rubber, he may entirely disregard the honours.

With this hand, it would be better to play without a trump, and to announce a *grand*, in which there are neither trumps nor honours, and every trick over the book is multiplied by 8. Two by cards at grand is worth more than two by cards and two by honours with any trump but cayenne.

There is still another resource: to announce *nullo*, whereby there is no trump, and the object of the players is to take as few tricks as possible. In nullo, every trick over the book counts for the adversaries, and is multiplied by 8. A peculiarity of nullo is that the Ace of each suit ranks below the deuce, unless the player who holds the Ace wishes to declare it higher than the King. In the latter case, he must announce it when he plays it, and before his left-hand adversary plays to the trick.

If the dealer transfers the right of making the trump to his partner, he must use the phrase 'You make it, partner.' If a player makes the trump out of turn, his adversaries may consult as to the propriety of demanding a new deal.

METHOD OF PLAYING When the trump suit, grand or nullo is announced, the player on the dealer's left begins by leading any card he pleases, and all the other players must follow suit if they can. The penalty for a revoke is loss of three tricks or the value of three tricks in points, or addition of a like amount to the adversaries' score. The side that makes a revoke cannot win the game that hand, no matter what it scores; however, it may play the hand out, and count all it make to within one point of game, or 9. Revoking players cannot count points for slams.

The rules for cards played in error, leading out of turn and all irregularities of this type, are the same as in Whist. The last trick turned and quitted can be seen.

The methods of gathering and stacking the tricks is the same as for Whist.

OBJECTS OF THE GAME   The main object in Cayenne, either with a trump or in a grand, is to take tricks; in a nullo it is not to take them. In any case the highest card played of the suit led wins the trick, and trumps, if any, win against all other suits. At the end of each hand, the side that wins any tricks in excess of the book scores them, after multiplying their number by the unit of value settled on by the announcement. If a nullo is played, the adversaries score them. Honours are then claimed; however, the game cannot be won by honours alone, as in Whist; the players who hold honours must stop at the score of 9, unless they also win the odd trick. As soon as either side reaches or passes 10 points, it wins a game; however, the hand must be played out, and all tricks taken must be counted. If one side goes out by cards, the other cannot score honours. Thirteen tricks taken by one side is called a *slam*, and counts 6 points. Twelve tricks is a *little slam*, and counts 4. Either slam must be made exclusive of revoke penalties.

RUBBERS   The rubber is won by the side that first wins four games of ten points each, and the winning side adds 8 points to its score.

SCORING   The game score should be kept on a whist marker, whereby the four large keys on one side are used for single points, and the single large key on the opposite side is used for five points. The three small keys are used to show how many games of the rubber have been won by that side.

Two Games Won, and 2 Points Scored on the Third

The method of using counters for scoring 10-point games has already been described in connection with whist.

In addition to either markers or counters, there must be a sheet of paper for keeping the final results of the games.

In scoring, the revoke penalty counts first, tricks next, and honours last.

The first side that reaches 10 points wins a *quadruple*, or game of

4, if its adversaries have not scored; a *triple*, or game of 3, if their adversaries have not reached 4; a *double*, or game of 2, if its adversaries have not reached 7; and a *single*, or game of 1, if its adversaries are 8 or 9 up. These game points are written on the score-sheet, and all the points on the *adversaries'* marker are then turned down. If the winners make any points in excess of 10, these points are left to their credit on the marker, and count towards the next game. For example, the score is A–B, 6 and Y–Z, 8, shown on the markers as follows:

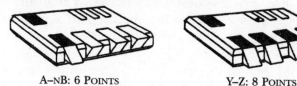

A–NB: 6 POINTS   Y–Z: 8 POINTS

Let's suppose that Z announces cayenne, and makes 2 by cards; A–B claim two by honours. Y–Z multiply by 4, making them 8, and bringing their total score on the marker to 16, that is, a game, and 6 points to their credit on the second game. This must now be written on the score-sheet. A–B's honours do not count, because Y–Z went out by cards, so the game is a double: A–B did not reach 7 points. The score and markers now stand:

	A–B	0						
Score:	Y–Z	2						

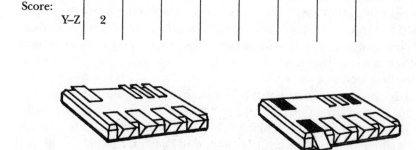

A–B's: NOTHING   Y–Z's: 1 GAME, 6 POINTS

Let's suppose A–B announce grand on their deal, and make four by cards, which, multiplied by 8, gives them 32 points, that is, three games, and 2 points to their credit on the marker. The first of these games is a double, Y–Z have 6 points up. The two other games are quadruples, written on the score-sheet as follows:

	A–B	0	2	4	4			
Score:	Y–Z	2	0	0	0			

A–B's: 3 Games, 2 Points   Y–Z's: 1 Game, 0 Points

In the next hand, let's suppose clubs are cayenne. Y deals, and plays in colour, spades. Y–Z win 6 by cards, and 4 by honours; 10 points multiplied by 3 = 30. For this they score three games, the first being a triple, and the others quadruples. These three games win the rubber, for which they add 8 points, and 4 points for the little slam. All this is written on the score-sheet:

	A–B	0	2	4	4	0	0	0	= 10
Score:									
	Y–Z	2	0	0	0	3	4	4	8 4 = 25

When both scores are added up, the value of the rubber won by Y–Z is found to be 15, after deducting the 10 points made by A–B.

CUTTING IN If there are more than four people belonging to the table, the ones waiting cut in, as for Whist.

METHODS OF CHEATING In all games in which the cards are dealt in bulk, four or six at a time, there is more or less temptation for the cheat to gather desirable cards in the pack, leaving them undisturbed in the shuffle. If he can pick up two tricks of the previous deal with eight good cards of the same suit in them, by placing any two tricks of other cards between them, and dealing six at a time, he can tell exactly how many of the eight located cards are in his partner's hand. For this reason, a player who does not thoroughly shuffle the cards should be carefully watched, and a protest should immediately be made against any disarrangement of the tricks as they are taken in during the play, such as placing the last trick taken under the first. If the player who does this is to be the next dealer, anyone who observes the movement should insist on the dealer's right to shuffle the cards thoroughly; if the dealer does not do this, he should leave the game.

We are strongly opposed to dealing the cards in bulk at Cayenne, and see no reason why the methods that prevail in the very similar game of Bridge should not be adopted.

SUGGESTIONS FOR GOOD PLAY There is little to add to the rules already given for Whist. The principles that should guide players in making the trump have been given in connection with the more important game of Bridge, and the suggestions for playing nullo are fully discussed in the games in which it is a prominent characteristic: Solo Whist, and Boston. Grand is practically Whist after the trumps are exhausted.

For the Laws of Cayenne, see the Whist Family Laws.

— —

SOLO WHIST

OR WHIST DE GRAND

CARDS Solo Whist is played with a full pack of fifty-two cards, which rank as for Whist for both cutting and playing. Two packs are usually used, whereby one is shuffled while the other is dealt.

MARKERS These are not used in Solo Whist: every hand is a complete game in itself, which is immediately settled for in counters representing money. At the beginning of the game, each player should be provided with an equal number of these counters. They are usually white and red, and the red is worth five times as much as the white. Twenty white and sixteen red is the usual allotment to each player when the game begins. One of the players should be the banker, to sell and redeem all counters.

PLAYERS Solo Whist is played by four people. If there are five candidates for play, they all sit at the same table, and each takes his turn to sit out for one hand while the four other people play. The dealer is usually selected to sit out. It there are only three players, one suit must be deleted from the pack, or the 2, 3 and 4 of each suit must be thrown out.

CUTTING When the table is formed, the players draw from an outspread for the deal, and for choice of seats and cards. The player who draws the lowest card deals the first hand, and it is usual for him to dictate to the other players what seats they will occupy in relation to him. Ties are decided in the same as at Whist.

POSITION OF THE PLAYERS The four players at Solo Whist are usually distinguished by the letters A, B, Y and Z.

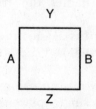

Z is the dealer, and A is known as the **eldest hand**. The position of the players does not imply any partnership, because as we see presently, any player may have any one of the other players for a partner, without any changing of their positions at the table.

When the players have taken their seats, they are not allowed to change them without the consent of all the other players at the table.

DEALING   When the cards have been properly shuffled, they are presented to the pone for cutting. Beginning on his left, the dealer distributes the cards three at a time, until only four remain. These he deals one at a time, and he turns up the last for the trump. When two packs are used, the player sitting opposite the dealer shuffles the still pack while the other pack is dealt. The deal passes in regular rotation to the left.

When three play with a pack of forty cards, the last card is turned up for trumps, but it does not belong to the dealer, and is not used in play.

The general rules with reference to irregularities in the deal are the same as for Whist, except that a misdeal does not pass the deal. The misdealer must deal again, and with the same pack.

When the cards are dealt, each player sorts and counts his hand to see that he has the correct number of cards: thirteen. If he does not have thirteen, he should immediately claim a misdeal, because a player who has more or fewer than his right proportion of cards cannot win anything on that hand, but will have to stand his proportion of all losses incurred by him or his side.

OBJECTS OF THE GAME   There are seven distinct objects in Solo Whist, and before play begins, each player has the opportunity to declare which of these objects he proposes to attain to. They are:

1. To win 8 of the 13 tricks, with the assistance of a partner. This is called a **Proposal**; the partner's share is an **Acceptance**.

2. To win 5 of the 13 tricks, against the three other players combined. This is called a **Solo**.

3. To take no tricks: there is no trump suit, and the three other players are opposed. This is called **Misère**, or **Nullo**.

4. To win 9 of the 13 tricks against the three other players combined; the single player names the trump suit. This is called **Abundance**.

5. To win 9 of the 13 tricks against the three other players combined, with the trump suit that is turned up. This is called **Abundance in Trumps**.

6. To take no tricks: there is no trump suit, and the three other players are opposed; the single player's cards are exposed face

upwards on the table after the first trick is complete. This is called
Misère sur table, or *A Spread*.

7. To win all 13 tricks against the three other players combined;
the single player names the trump suit, and has the original lead
whether eldest hand or not. This is called *Abundance Déclarée*, or *A
Slam*.

Whereas the object of the proposing player is to win or lose the
declared number of tricks, that of his adversaries is to prevent him
from doing so, if possible. There are no honours, and the only factor
in the count is the number of tricks actually taken. The highest card
played of the suit led wins the trick, and trumps, if any, win against
all other suits.

METHOD OF DECLARING The eldest hand has the first say,
and after examining his cards, he may make any of the several propositions just enumerated. The smallest proposal he can make is to
take 8 tricks with the assistance of a partner. To do this, he should
have four reasonably sure tricks in his own hand. Some players say
he should be strong in trumps, whereas others claim that the eldest
hand should propose only on general strength. The former is the
better plan. No other player should propose on trumps alone. This
announcement is made by saying, *'I propose.'* If a player thinks he
can take five tricks against the combined efforts of the three other
players, he announces, *'Solo.'* If he feels equal to a misère, he calls:
'Misère,' and so on, according to the strength of his hand. If he does
not feel justified in making a call, he says, *'I pass,'* and the next player
on his left has the opportunity, and so on, until some player has
proposed to do something, or all players have passed.

If any player has proposed for a partner, any of the other players,
in their proper turn, may accept him by simply saying, *'I accept.'* By
doing so, a player intimates that he has four probable tricks also, but
in the plain suits, and that he is willing to try for eight tricks with
the proposer for a partner. All the other calls are made by a single
player with the intention of playing against the three other players.
When any player except the eldest hand has once said, 'I pass,' he
cannot afterwards make or accept any proposal. The eldest hand,
after passing once, can accept a proposal, but cannot make one.

It is the custom in some places, when no one will make a proposal
of any sort, to turn down the trump, and play the hands without any
trump suit, each player for himself; the winner of the last trick loses
to each of the other players the value of a solo. This is called a *Grand*.

RANK OF THE PROPOSALS The various calls outrank each
other in the order in which we have given them. If one player says,

'I propose,' and another calls, 'Solo,' the solo call shuts out the proposal, even though it has been accepted by a second player. The call of a misère would in turn shut out a solo, abundance would take precedence of misère, and abundance in trumps would be a better call than simple abundance. The slam, of course, outranks all other bids. This making of a better proposition than one already made is known as 'Overcalling'.

A player who has made a call of any kind, or has accepted a proposal, may amend his proposition to a better one, only in case he is overcalled, or a player who cannot get a partner to accept him may amend his call to solo. For example, a player might have a hand that he feels sure is good for 8 tricks, perhaps 9. To be safe, he calls solo, and hopes to make three or four over-tricks. If he is outbid by some player who overcalls him with a misère, he might be tempted to amend his call to abundance.

No call is good until every player who has not already passed does so, by saying, distinctly, 'I pass.'

STAKES The losses and gains of the players are in proportion to the difficulties of the tasks they set themselves.

The most popular method of settling is to pay or take red counters for the various calls, and white counters for the tricks under or over the exact number proposed. If the callers succeed in their undertakings, their adversaries pay them; if they fail, they pay their adversaries. A red counter is worth five white ones.

Proposal and Acceptance wins or loses .... 1 red counter.
Solo wins or loses .... 2 red counters.
Misère, or Nullo, wins or loses .... 3 red counters.
Abundance, of any kind, wins or loses .... 4 red counters.
Open Misère, or Spread, wins or loses .... 6 red counters.
Declared Abundance, or Slam, wins or loses .... 8 red counters.
Each Over-trick or Under-trick wins or loses .... 1 white counter.

In Proposal and Acceptance, each of the partners pays one of his adversaries. In all cases in which a single player is opposed to the three other players, he wins or loses the amount shown in the foregoing table with each of them individually, so that a single player who calls a solo would win or lose 6 red counters. If he lost it, making only four tricks, he would also have to pay to each of his three adversaries a white counter. If he won it, making seven tricks, each adversary would have to pay him two red and two white counters.

Misères, Spreads and Slams pay no odd tricks. The moment a

Misère player takes a trick, or a Slam player loses one, the hands are abandoned, and the stakes paid.

The the early days, the value attached to the counters in America was usually 25 cents for the red, and 5 cents for the white; in England, the proportion was sixpence and a penny.

POOL SOLO   When players wish to enhance the gambling attractions of the game, a pool is introduced. For this purpose a receptacle is placed on the table, in which each player puts a red counter at the beginning of the game. Any person playing alone against the three other people, wins this pool if he is successful; if he fails, he must double the amount it contains, besides paying each of his adversaries in the regular way. In some places, it is the custom for each player to contribute a red counter when he deals. The proposals and acceptances do not touch the pool.

METHOD OF PLAYING   If a proposal is accepted, and no one overcalls it, the proposer and acceptor are partners, but make no change in their positions at the table. The eldest hand, sitting to the left of the dealer, begins by leading any card he pleases, and the play proceeds exactly as for Whist, whereby the tricks are stacked so that they can be readily counted at any time.

If a single player has called solo, misère or abundance, the eldest hand still has the original lead, and there is no change in the positions of the players. The position of the lead is often a serious consideration when a player calls a solo or misère.

In all calls except misères and slams, the hands must be played out, in order to give each side an opportunity to make all the overtricks it can. The moment a Misère player takes a trick, or a slam player loses one, the hands are thrown up, and the stakes paid.

When a spread is called, the trump is taken up, and the eldest hand leads. As soon as all players have played to the first trick, the caller spreads his remaining twelve cards face upwards on the table, so that each of his adversaries can see them; however, they have no control over the order in which the cards will be played. The adversaries play their hands in the usual way, and have no guidance other than that possible by inference from the play and the exposed hand. The caller plays according to his best judgement.

When a slam is called, the player proposing it has the original lead, but that does not alter the position of the deal for the next hand.

REVOKES   A revoke is a serious matter in Solo Whist. The penalty for it is loss of three tricks, and the revoking players must pay the *red* counters involved in the call whether they win or lose; however, they may play the hand out in order to save over-tricks. For example, a proposer and acceptor make 11 tricks, and their adversaries have claimed a revoke. After deducting the revoke penalty, 3 tricks, the callers still have 8 tricks left, enough to make good the call. They each lose a red counter, but no white counters, having saved their over-tricks. Had they taken only 8 tricks altogether, the penalty for the revoke would have left them only 5, and they would each have had to pay one red and three whites. If either adversary of the callers revokes, the individual player in fault must pay for all the consequences of the error. If the player in fault can show that the callers would have won in spite of the revoke, his partners must pay their share, but the revoking player must settle for the three tricks lost by the revoke. For example, Z calls solo; A revokes; and Z makes 6 tricks, which it can be shown he must have done in spite of the revoke. A, Y and B each pay Z 1 red and 1 white counter, and then A pays Z 9 white counters in addition, for the tricks taken as a revoke penalty.

If the single player revokes, on either solo or abundance, he loses the red counters involved, and must pay whatever white counters are due after three of his tricks have been added to the tricks of the adversaries as a penalty for the revoke. For example, A calls solo, and revokes, but wins 6 tricks in all. He pays two red counters to each adversary. They then take three of his tricks, leaving him three only, and demand two white counters each, for the two under-tricks. If a player who has called a misère or a slam revokes, he immediately loses the stakes. If a revoke is made by any adversary of a player who has called misère or slam, the player in fault must individually pay all the stakes.

CARDS PLAYED IN ERROR   In the simple proposal and acceptance, the rules with reference to cards played in error, or led out of turn, are the same as for Whist. In the case of a single player against three adversaries, the caller is not liable to any penalty for cards played in error, or led out of turn; however, his adversaries are subject to the usual whist penalties for all these irregularities, such as having the cards laid on the table as exposed, or a suit called, or the highest or lowest of a suit led demanded from an adversary who has followed suit out of turn.

For the better protection of the single player, who is much more liable to be injured by irregularities than are partners, he is allowed to prevent use of an exposed trump for ruffing, and to demand or *to prevent* the play of any exposed card in plain suits. If a suit is led of which an adversary has an exposed card on the table, the single player may call on him to play his highest or lowest of that suit.

If any adversary of a misère player leads out of turn, or exposes a card, or plays before his proper turn in any trick, the caller may immediately claim the stakes, and the individual player in fault must pay for himself, and for his partners.

METHODS OF CHEATING   Although the practice of dealing three cards at a time gives a little more opportunity to the cheat than would occur if they were dealt as in Whist, there is little to be feared if two packs are used, unless two cheats are in partnership. When these partners sit next to each other, there is more or less danger, if only one pack is used, that one will shuffle so that the other will cut understandingly, or that a good shuffler will run up six cards for a dealer who is not embarrassed by the cards' being cut. A shrewd cheat can often help a silent partner who is playing under the disguise of a single caller, especially in misère. People who played in the many public cafés of Europe had to be especially careful to avoid this style of partnership, because it was very common there.

SUGGESTIONS FOR GOOD PLAY   Apart from the general principles common to all forms of Whist, such as play of high or low cards, trumps or plain suits, and so on, there are several points peculiar to Solo Whist that require attention.

PROPOSING   It is better to propose on two or three sure tricks, with strong probabilities of several more, than on a certainty of four only. For example, the two highest trumps, and two suits that contain Aces, with no other trick probable, is not as good a hand for a proposal as one that contains four average trumps, with one plain suit of K Q J x x, and another of K Q x x. It is not improbable that the latter will be good for seven or eight tricks. Nothing but experience will teach a player what combinations of cards are 'probably' good for tricks; however, K x x, or Q J IO x, or K Q, can be counted on.

There should be some intelligible system of proposing, so that the players can understand each other. The eldest hand should not propose except on strong trumps, and this should be a warning to other players not to accept him on trump strength alone.

Four trumps with two or three honours can be called strong; or five trumps, even without an honour. Five trumps with two or more honours is great strength.

Any player other than the eldest hand should propose on general strength, and the player who accepts him should do so on trump strength. Some such distinction should be clearly understood, in

order that there can be no contretemps such as two players' proposing and accepting on trumps alone, and finding themselves
without a trick in the plain suits after the trumps are drawn.

If the eldest hand is strong in trumps, but does not have four sure
tricks, he should pass, whereby he will be given an excellent opportunity to accept a player who proposes on general strength in the
plain suits. If the proposal is accepted before it comes to his turn,
the eldest hand should be in a good position to defeat it.

If any player, other than the eldest hand, has sufficient trump
strength to justify a proposal, he will usually find that he can risk a
solo, or that by passing, he can defeat any proposal and acceptance
that might be made.

ACCEPTING A proposal by the eldest hand should not be
accepted by a player who has only one strong suit. The probability
of tricks in several suits is better than a certainty in one suit; however,
if one strong suit is accompanied by a card of re-entry, or by four
trumps, it should prove very strong, particularly in partnership with
the eldest hand.

When the partners sit next to each other, proposals can be
accepted on slightly weaker hands than would be considered safe
otherwise.

PLAYING PROPOSALS AND ACCEPTANCES If the eldest hand
has proposed, and his partner sits next to him on the left, the commanding trumps should be first led, in order to secure as many
rounds as possible. If the eldest hand has no high-card combination
in trumps, it is sometimes better to lead a small card from a weak
suit, hoping to put the partner in. If successful, the partner will first
show his suit, and then lead trumps through the adversaries. If the
acceptor sits on the right of the proposing eldest hand, trumps
should be led immediately, and the highest of them first, no matter
what they are. The Q or J at the head of five trumps can be of great
use to a partner who has an honour. When the eldest hand has
proposed, and his partner sits opposite him, trumps should be led
at once, and all combinations played as in Whist.

The foregoing principles equally apply when the eldest hand has
accepted a proposal, if the player can be depended on to have proposed on general strength.

When partners sit opposite each other, the general principles of
leading, establishing, defending and bringing in suits are the same
as for Whist, and the usual trump signals and echoes are made use
of. The game is practically Whist, and there is the additional knowledge that both proposer and acceptor have strong hands.

When partners sit next to each other, there are many opportunities for leading strengthening cards through the adversaries, especially in the partner's known or inferred strong suit.

FINESSE If neither proposer nor acceptor is the eldest hand, he should make no finesses; he should get into the lead as soon as possible, and exhaust the trumps. The greatest danger of defeat for a proposal and acceptance is that the adversaries, who have the original lead, can establish a cross-ruff, or get six tricks with their winning cards before the calling players get a lead.

It is a common artifice for the proposer and acceptor, after they have exhausted the adversaries' trumps, to each show a strong suit by leading it once, and then to lead the highest card of a weaker suit, thereby offering each other chances for successful finesse.

If a partner sitting on the right leads a suit, there should be no finesse, and, in general, finessing should be avoided until the declaration is assured. It can then be used to secure probable over-tricks.

ADVERSARIES' PLAY The players opposed to the call are always designated the adversaries.

Players opposed to a proposer and acceptor should make no finesses that they are not certain will win more tricks if successful than they will lose if they fail. If the adversaries sit together, and are the last to play on any trick, the third hand should not trust anything to his partner that he can attend to himself, unless he is very anxious to be the last player on the next trick.

When the adversaries sit opposite each other, their play will differ very little from that in Whist, except that they will make no efforts to establish long suits, and will not lead small cards from combinations that contain an Ace. Every trick possible should be made sure of at once, before the calling players get any chance to discard. Weak suits should be protected, as they are in Whist when they are opposed to strong hands.

If an adversary has the first lead, it is usually best for him to make what winning cards he has at once, unless he is pretty sure that the proposal will be defeated.

It is very seldom right for the adversaries to lead trumps. Some exceptions will naturally present themselves, such as when an eldest hand lead to his partner's turned-up King. In the middle or end game, it can be advantageous to bring down the caller's trumps together, or to draw two for one.

If an adversary finds himself with a pretty strong hand, he should utterly disregard his partner, and play as false as he can, because if the callers have eight probable tricks between them, it is impossible for the fourth player to have anything, unless there has been some mistake in the call.

IN GENERAL There are one or two exceptions to the methods of playing sequences in Whist, which depend on the position of the players who hold them. For example, if first or second hand holds any sequence of high cards, he should play the highest if his partner sits next to him on the left, and the adversaries are to play after him; otherwise, the partner might think the higher cards of the sequence were against the leader. If a caller holds K Q x second hand and plays the Q as in Whist, and his partner follows him and holds Ace, he would have to play it, thinking the King might be beyond.

SOLO When the players in a solo, misère or abundance are being spoken about, it is usual to distinguish the ones opposed to the single player by calling them, respectively, Left, Right and Opposite.

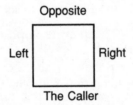

Opposite

Left   Right

The Caller

This arrangement does not affect use of the letters A Y B Z, and the terms first, second, third and fourth hand, for indicating the position of the deal and the lead.

CALLING Solos are easiest that are declared by the eldest hand, or by the dealer and the hardest are the ones called by second hand. The safest solos are the ones called on trump strength, but average trumps and winning cards in the plain suits are more advantageous if the caller is not eldest hand. To call a solo on plain suits alone, with only one or two trumps, is extremely dangerous, and a solo called on a single suit must have at least five or six good trumps in order to succeed.

PLAYING When a call has been made entirely on trump strength, it is much better to make tricks by ruffing, than by leading trumps. There is little use for a solo player to hold a tenace in trumps, hoping it will be led to him. If he has good suits, he should make sure of two rounds of trumps by leading the Ace.

When the solo player is depending on the plain suits for tricks, and has one long suit, he should make what winning cards he has in the other plain suits in preference to leading trumps, because his only danger is that his long suit will be led often enough to give his adversaries discards in the other suits.

If a proposal was made before the solo was called, it is better for the solo player to sit on the left of the player who proposed.

The caller should never play single honours second hand, unless he has only one small card of the suit, or unless the honour is the Ace.

With A Q x, second or third hand, the Q must be finessed if the caller has counted on both A and Q for tricks. If he can probably win without the finesse, he should play Ace. If he has tricks enough to win without either A or Q, he should play neither of them.

A solo player should be very sure of his call before finessing for over-tricks.

ADVERSARIES' PLAY The player to the left of the caller should not lead trumps; however, if the solo player has had a lead, and has not led trumps himself, the player on his right should take the first opportunity to lead them through him.

The player to the left of the caller should not lead from suits headed only by the King, nor from suits that contain major or minor tenaces. The best leads are from suits headed by Q J or 10, even if they are short.

With high-card combinations such as can be used to force the command in one round, such as K Q, or K Q J, the regular whist leads should be used. With suits headed by winning sequences, held by the player on the left, it is often right to lead them once, in order to show them, and then to lead a weaker suit to get rid of the lead. It is sometimes better to play winning sequences as long as it seems probable that the caller can follow suit.

Many persons use the Albany lead to indicate a wish for trumps to be led through the caller. In response to this signal, the best trump should be led, whatever it is.

When the adversary who leads in any trick is not on the left of the solo player, the caller will, of course, not be the last player, because at least one adversary must play after him. In these cases, it is best to lead the longest suits.

MISÈRE The great difficulty in misère is not in playing it but in judging what hands justify this undertaking.

CALLING As a general proposition, it can be stated that misère should not be called with a long suit that does not contain the deuce. However, the longer the suit, the less the danger there is for a player who is determined to risk it, because the deuce is more likely to be found alone in some adversary's hand. Short suits can be risked, even with no card smaller than a 5 or 6, and it is of course a great advantage to have a suit altogether missing.

LEADING The lead is a disadvantage to the caller, because he must begin with a small card, and the adversaries can play their highest. The only satisfaction to the caller is that he can usually locate the high cards of the suit under these circumstances. For example, suppose he originally leads a 4, second hand plays the 9, third hand plays the Ace, and fourth hand plays the 10. The third hand is marked with whatever cards of the sequence K Q J are not in the caller's hand.

Many players fall into the error of leading the highest card of a losing sequence, such as a 6 from 6 5 4 3. This accomplishes nothing, and only discloses to the adversaries the fact that the caller is safe in that suit. The three is the better lead.

FOLLOWING SUIT The caller should usually play a card as minimally inferior as he can to the highest already on the trick. When he has cards of equal value, such as the 5 and 2, the 3 and 4 being already on the table, he should play the lowest card of the fourchette, because although it can be said that the fourth player must take the trick, there is no certainty he will follow suit.

When second hand is playing, if there is a choice between two cards, such as the 6 and 2, an intermediate card having been led, it is often a nice point to decide whether or not to risk covering, and keeping the deuce. If the deuce is played. it must be remembered that the adversaries will follow with their highest cards, leaving two cards out against the caller, both of which are smaller than the 6.

DISCARDING The misère player should never discard from his long suits. The high cards of short suits, and single intermediate cards, such as 5's and 6's, should be gotten rid of at every opportunity.

ADVERSARIES OF THE MIS`ERE In playing against a misère, the main difficulty is to prevent the caller from discarding, and to place the lead with the player who can probably do him the most harm.

It is an axiom with solo-whist players that every misère can be defeated, if the weak spot in it can be found, because if the misère were absolutely safe, it would be played as a spread, which would pay the caller twice as much. This is not true, however, because it often happens that the cards are so distributed in the other hands that the call cannot be defeated, however risky it might have been.

The weak point in a misère is usually a short suit that has one high card, or a suit of intermediate length, without the deuce.

Because it is probable that the caller is short in suits in which the adversaries are long, and long in those in which they are short, he is less likely to get a discard if they lead their shortest suits first. If the misère player has overcalled a proposal or a solo, he is likely to be short in the trump suit, or at least safe in it. It is not good play to lead a single Ace; however, a King can be very effective, because for if no one plays the Ace on it, that card can be absolutely marked in the caller's hand. In this case, the adversary who has the greatest number of that suit should keep it for the attack. If this player can get into the lead, he is sure not only of preventing the caller from discarding but of allowing the other adversaries to discard to advantage.

With an honour and one small card, a player on the left should lead the small card first; if the player is on the right, the honour should be led first. A long suit that contains the deuce should be avoided as long as possible.

The caller's cards can sometimes be inferred if there has been a previous call on the hand. For example, a misère can be a forced call; that is, the player first called a proposal, and not having been accepted, was forced to amend his call, whereby he chose misère in preference to solo. This would indicate a long weak suit of trumps. If the dealer calls Misère, the turn-up trump should be carefully noted.

It is useless to persevere in suits in which the caller is evidently safe. If he plays a very low card to a trick in which there is already a high card, that suit should be stopped.

DISCARDING An adversary should get rid of some one suit, if possible, because when that suit is afterwards led, he will have free choice of his discards in the other suits. Short suits should be discarded in preference to high cards in long suits, unless the cards in the short suit are very low. Discards give great information to the adversaries if the rule is followed to discard the highest of a suit, because all cards higher than the ones discarded must be between the two other adversaries and the caller, and each adversary is thereby furnished with a guide. It is useless to discard a suit of which the caller is void, and it is best to keep discarding from one suit until it is exhausted, or until only the deuce remains. The trump signal is frequently used in discarding to indicate that the signaller wishes to get into the lead.

RETURNING SUITS Whether or not to return a partner's lead can often be decided by inferences from the fall of the cards. It is frequently an easy matter to locate the cards in the various suits, if it is borne in mind that adversaries who play after the caller get rid of their highest cards. For example, right leads the 9, caller plays the 5, left plays the 10, and the last player finds he holds K Q J 6 of the suit. He should know that the caller has nothing between the 5 and the 9 and must have the Ace, so his cards were probably A 5 4 3 2. Although it is manifestly impossible to catch him on that suit, it can still be led three times, in order to give the partners discards, because both of them must be short. If this estimate of the caller's cards is wrong in anything, it is not with reference to the Ace, so there is not the slightest danger in continuing the suit.

As a general rule, the suit first led by an adversary should be returned, unless the player who wins the trick has a singleton in another suit, whereby he should lead that.

The suit led by the caller, if he was eldest hand, should not be returned.

Some judgement of character must be used in playing on a caller's own lead. An adventurous player will sometimes call a misère on a hand that contains a singleton 5 or 6, and will lead it at once, trusting that second hand will imagine it to be safe, and cover it. Players should be aware of this trap, and never cover a misère player's own lead if they can help it, unless the card led is below a 4.

ABUNDANCE   Very few people will risk calling an abundance they are not pretty certain of; however, a player might be forced to the call on a doubtful hand, especially if he is overcalled on his original proposal to play a solo. The lead is a great advantage, because trumps can be exhausted immediately, and the suits protected. If the caller does not have the lead, he must calculate in advance for trumping in, and if his plain suits are not quite established, he will require more trumps than would otherwise be necessary. The greatest danger to an abundance player who does not have the original lead is that his best suit will be led through him, and trumped, on either the first or the second round. The caller is often trapped into unnecessarily high trumping when suits are led through him a second or third time.

THE ADVERSARIES   The adversaries have little chance to defeat an abundance unless they can over-trump the caller, or ruff his good cards before he can exhaust the trumps. It is best for the Right to lead his longest suit, and for the Left to lead his shortest. A guarded King suit should not be led under any circumstances, nor should a short suit Ace high. If an adversary has a single trump of medium size, such as a J or 10, it is often good play to trump a partner's winning cards, so as to be sure of preventing the caller from making a small trump. If an adversary has trumped or over-trumped, it is very important to lead that suit to him again as soon as possible.

The rules for discarding that are given in connection with Whist should he carefully observed, especially in the matter of showing command of suits.

SPREADS   These should not be called except with hands in which every suit contains the deuce, and all the cards are low enough to guarantee to the player that nothing short of extraordinary circumstances will defeat him. Open sequences, or Dutch straights, as they are sometimes called, in which the cards are all odd or all even, such as 2 4 6 8 10, are quite as safe as ordinary sequences, provided the deuce is among the cards.

The player who calls a spread must remember that it will be impossible for him to get any discards after the first trick without consent of the adversaries, because they will not lead a suit of which they see he is void. In order to reduce the caller's chances of a discard on the opening lead, before his cards are exposed, the adversaries should select their shortest suits, unless they have a bottom sequence to the deuce.

THE SLAM   This feature of Solo Whist is even rarer than the grand coup at Whist. It is not very marvellous for an abundance player to make twelve or thirteen tricks; however, to announce thirteen tricks before a card is played is something phenomenal. All the adversaries can do against this call is to show each other, by their discards, in which of the suits they have a possible trick. It is very annoying to have a player succeed in making a slam just because two of his adversaries keep the same suit.

SOLO WHIST FOR THREE PLAYERS

The best arrangement is to play with a pack of forty cards, and delete the 2, 3 and 4 of each suit. The last card is turned up to determine the trump, but is not used in play.

There is no proposal and acceptance, and solo is the lowest call. If all three players pass, the trump card is turned down, and each player in turn has the option of calling a six-trick abundance, naming his own trump suit. In some places, it is the custom to allow the players to overcall each other, after the trump is turned down, whereby each increase the number of tricks he proposes to take.

A misère overcalls eight tricks.

Kimberly Solo   This game is for four players. There is no proposal and acceptance, and solo is the lowest call. If all players pass, a six-trick solo with a different trump is allowed.

ILLUSTRATIVE SOLO-WHIST HANDS

The dealer, Z, turns up the heart 3 in both hands, and A leads. The underlined card wins the trick, and the card under it is the next one led.

A Solo				TRICK	*A Misère*			
A	**Y**	**B**	**Z**		**A**	**Y**	**B**	**Z**
10 ◇	8 ◇	Q ◇	K ◇	1	K ♠	7 ♠	J ♠	10 ♠
3 ◇	9 ◇	A ◇	2 ◇	2	Q ♡	5 ♠	9 ♠	8 ♠
♡ 6	♡ 2	♡ A	♡ 3	3	Q ◇	5 ◇	A ◇	J ◇
♣ 8	♡ 4	♡ Q	♡ K	4	9 ◇	4 ◇	K ◇	10 ◇
♣ 9	♣ A	♣ 4	♣ 7	5	♡ 6	3 ♠	6 ♡	8 ◇
A ♣	9 ♠	K ♠	4 ♠	6	♡ 7	2 ♠	4 ♠	♣ A
♣ K	♣ 2	♣ 6	♣ 5	7	♣ 10	♣ 8	♣ 7	♣ K
7 ♡	2 ♡	Q ♠	6 ♠	8	♣ 9	♣ 6	7 ◇	♣ Q
5 ◇	♣ 3	♣ Q	♡ 8	9	♣ 5	♣ 4	6 ◇	♣ J
6 ◇	3 ♠	♡ 5	J ◇	10	♡ 8	♣ 2	♡ K	♣ 3
7 ◇	♡ 10	♡ 9	♡ J	11	♡ A	♡ 2	♡ Q	♡ 3
8 ♠	5 ♠	♡ 7	4 ◇	12	2 ◇	3 ◇	♡ 9	♡ 4
J ♠	♣ J	♣ 10	10 ♠	13	♡ J	A ♠	♡ 10	♡ 5

Solo player wins.	*Misère player loses.*

In the first example, A and Y pass, and B calls Solo. A follows the modern practice of leading the top of his long weak suit, as a card of warning and support for his partners. Z knows Y must have 9 or Ace of diamonds, or no more, and he avoids the error of opening another suit, especially a weak one. B continues with the trump Queen, hoping to drop King and Jack together. At trick 5, Z cannot give up the command of trumps, and because A's lead and discard indicate he wants spades led up to him, Z's best chance is that Y has some clubs. Y leads to A. At trick 9, Z knows that B cannot have 10 and 9 of trumps, or he would have led one of them to prevent the J and 8 both making, so Y must have one of those trumps. At trick 11, if B leads the club, he loses his call. He must again take the chance of bringing the trumps down together.

In the second example, A proposes, or calls Solo, and Y overcalls him with Misère. The great point in playing against Misère is to continue leading suits in which he is known to be long, so as to give your partners discards. This B does with the two long spades; the caller is marked with the ace and others on the second trick. Z then allows B to discard his high diamonds on the clubs.

SCOTCH WHIST
OR CATCH THE TEN

CARDS   Scotch Whist is played with a pack of 36 cards, which rank in plain suits, A K Q J 10 9 8 7 6, and the Ace is highest in both play and cutting. In the trump suit, the Jack is the best card, and the order is J A K Q 10 9 8 7 6.

MARKERS   There are no suitable counters for Scotch Whist, and the score is usually kept on a sheet of paper.

PLAYERS   Any number of people from two to eight can play. When there are five or seven players, the spade 6 must be removed from the pack. In some places, this is not done: the thirty-fifth card is turned up for the trump, and the thirty-sixth is shown to the table and then laid aside.

CUTTING   Whatever the number of people who offer for play, the table is formed by cutting from the outspread pack for partners, seats and deal.

When two people play, the one who cuts the lowest card has the choice of seats and cards (if there are two packs).

When three play, the lowest deals, and chooses his seat and cards. The next lowest has the next choice of seats.

When four play, partners are cut for; the two lowest pair against the two highest, and the lowest of the four is the dealer, and has the choice of seats and cards.

When five play, each for himself, the lowest cut deals, and has the first choice of seats and cards. The next lowest has the next choice of seats, and so on.

When six play, they cut for partners; the two lowest pair together, the two highest together, and the two intermediates together. The player who cuts the lowest card of the six has the choice of seats and cards, and deals the first hand. If the six play, three on a side, the three lowest play against the three highest; the lowest cut of the six takes the deal, and the choice of seats and cards.

When seven play, each for himself, the lowest deals, and has the choice of seats and cards; the others choose their seats in the order of their cuts.

When eight play, they may form two sets of four each, or four sets of two each. In either case, the partnerships are decided by cutting, and the lowest cut of the eight has the deal, and the choice of seats and cards.

TIES   These are decided in the way already described in connection with Whist.

POSITION OF THE PLAYERS   Two players sit opposite each other. Three, five or seven sit according to their choice; four sit as in Whist, and the partners face each other. Six, playing in two partnerships, sit alternately, so that no two partners will be next to each other. Six, playing in three partnerships of two each, sit so that two adversaries will be between each pair of partners. Eight, playing in two sets of four each, or as four pairs of partners, arrange themselves alternately. If we distinguish the partners by the letters A, B, C and D, the following diagram will show us the arrangement of the tables.

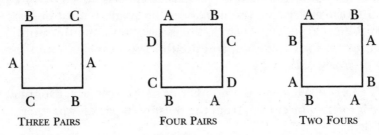

THREE PAIRS   FOUR PAIRS   TWO FOURS

The player to the left of the dealer is the original leader.

DEALING   The method of dealing varies with the number of players engaged. When only one pack is used, any player may shuffle, and the dealer shuffles last. The pack must be presented to the pone for cutting, and the entire pack is then dealt out, one card at a time.

When two play, the dealer gives each six cards, one at a time. These two hands are kept separate, and two more are dealt in the same way, and then a third two, whereby the last card is turned up for the trump. When the deal is complete, there will be six hands on the table: three hands belonging to each player.

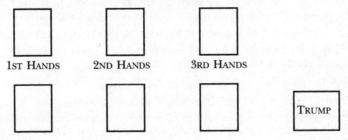

1st Hands   2nd Hands   3rd Hands

When three play, the cards are dealt in much the same way: two separate hands of six cards are given to each player.

When four, five, six, seven or eight play, the cards are dealt in rotation from left to right until the pack is exhausted, whereby the last card is turned up for the trump. When five or seven play, either the spade 6 must be thrown out of the pack or the thirty-sixth card must be shown, after the dealer has turned the thirty-fifth for the trump. When eight play, all four sixes are deleted.

The deal passes to the left, whereby each player deals in turn until the game is finished.

The general rules with reference to irregularities in the deal are the same as for Whist.

STAKES When stakes are played for, they are for so much a game. Rubbers are not played. It is usual to form a pool, whereby each player deposits the stake agreed on, and the winner takes all. In partnership games, each losing player pays the successful adversary who sits to his right. If three pairs were engaged, and A–A won, C and B would each pay the A who sits next to him. Before play begins, it should be understood who pays for revokes: the side or the player.

METHOD OF PLAYING The player on the dealer's left begins by leading any card he chooses, and all the other players must follow suit if they can. Failure to follow suit when able to is a revoke, the penalty for which, if detected and claimed by the adversaries, is immediate loss of the game. When there are more than two players or two sets of partners, the revoking player or side must pay the two or more adversaries as if each had won the game. In some places, the individual is made to pay, not the side. This should be understood before play begins. If seven are playing, and one is detected in a revoke, his loss is equal to six games. Any player who has none of the suit led may either trump or discard. The dealer should take up the trump card when it is his turn to play to his first trick, after which it must not be named, although a player may be informed of what the trump suit is. If all follow suit, the highest card played of the suit led wins the trick, and trumps win all other suits. The winner of the trick may lead any card he chooses for the next, and so on, until all the cards have been played.

It is not necessary to keep the tricks separate, as in Whist, but one player should gather for his side.

When two or three play, the hands must be played in the order in which they were dealt. For example, if these are the hands:

Adversary's:	1	3	5
	1ST SET	2ND SET	3RD SET

Dealer's:	2	4	6	TRUMP

The players first take up hands numbers 1 and 2; a card is led from number 1; the dealer follows suit from number 2, or trumps, or discards; and the play continues until these two hands are exhausted. The second set is then taken up and played in the same way, and the player who won the last trick in one set has the first lead in the next. Finally, the third set is played in the same way, and all the cards taken by each side are gathered into one pile by the player who has won them. The trump card must remain on the table until the dealer takes up the last hand. When three people play, the set of hands first dealt must be first played, and then the second set taken up.

The rules for cards played in error, leading out of turn and so on are the same as for Whist.

OBJECTS OF THE GAME The side first that scores 41 points wins the game, and the main object is to secure tricks that contain cards to which a specific value is attached. All these cards belong to the trump suit, and are as follows:

The Jack of trumps counts 11
The Ace of trumps counts 4
The King of trumps counts 3
The Queen of trumps counts 2
The Ten of trumps counts 10

The other trumps, and the plain-suit cards, have no counting value.

The Jack of trumps, being the best, must be taken in by the player to whom it is dealt; however, any court card in trumps will win the Ten, so that one of the main objects in Scotch Whist is to *catch the ten*.

At the end of each hand, the players count the number of cards they have taken in tricks, and are entitled to score one point for each above the number originally dealt to them. For example, if four people play, nine cards were originally dealt to each person, so each pair of partners held eighteen. If, at the end of the hand, the players have taken in eight tricks, or thirty-two cards, they score 14 points towards game, in addition to any score they might have made by winning honours in trumps, or catching the Ten. If five people play, beginning with seven cards each, and at the end of the hand one player has taken in fifteen, and another player ten, they score 8 and 3, respectively, for cards.

SCORING   At the end of each hand, each player or side should claim all honours won, and cards taken in. One player should keep the score, and announce it distinctly, so it can be known how many points each player or side requires to win the game.

In the case of ties, the Ten counts out first; then cards; then A K Q of trumps in their order; and the Jack last. A revoke, if detected and claimed before the cards are cut for the next deal, immediately ends the game.

METHODS OF CHEATING   When only one pack is used, the cheat can often succeed in dealing himself the Jack of trumps, and usually loses no time in marking the Ten, so that he can at least distinguish the player to whom it is dealt. A player should be carefully watched who keeps his eyes on the pack while he is shuffling, or who rivets his attention on the backs of the cards while he is dealing. Two packs should be used in all round games of cards.

SUGGESTIONS FOR GOOD PLAY   Because the main counting elements that are affected by the play are the trump Ten and the cards, it is usual to especially devote attention to winning them. With J A of trumps, or A K, it is best to lead two rounds immediately, but with a tenace, such as J K, or A Q, it is better to place the lead on your left if possible. The high cards in the plain suits are capable of being very skilfully managed in this matter of placing the lead. It sometimes happens that a player who has the Ten is fourth hand on a suit of which he has none, or that he catches the Ten with a small honour if it is used in trumping in. The partnership games offer many fine opportunities for playing the Ten into the partner's hand, especially when it is probable that this partner has the best trump, or a better trump than the player on the left.

In calculating the probabilities of saving the Ten by trumping in, it must be remembered that the greater the number of players, the less chance there is that a suit will go around more than once, because there are only nine cards of each suit in play.

Many players, in their anxiety to catch the Ten, overlook the possibilities of their hands in making cards, the count for which often runs into high figures.

Close attention should be paid to the score. For example, A wants 4 points to win, B wants 10, and C wants 16. If A can see his way to win the game by cards or small honours, he should take the first opportunity of giving C the Ten, or of allowing him to make it in preference to B. Because the Ten counts first, and cards and honours next, B might be shut out, even if he has the Jack.

LAWS There are no special laws for Scotch Whist. The whist laws are usually enforced for all irregularities such as exposed cards and leading out of turn. The most important matter is the revoke, and it should be clearly understood before play begins whether the revoke penalty is to be paid by the individual in fault or by the side to which he belongs. Some players think there should be some regulation for penalties in cases such as that of a player who takes up the wrong hand, when two or more are dealt to each player; however, because no advantage can be gained by the exchange, it is difficult to see what right the adversary would have to impose a penalty.

ILLUSTRATIVE SCOTCH-WHIST HAND

Following is a simple example hand, as an illustration of the way of playing with four people, two of whom are partners against the other two.

Z deals and turns heart 8.

	A	Y	B	Z
1	Q ◊	K ◊	8 ◊	9 ◊
2	♣ A	♣ K	♣ J	♣ 8
3	♣ 7	♣ 9	♣ 6	6 ♠
4	8 ♠	J ♠	K ♠	A ♠
5	J ◊	9 ♠	A ◊	Q ♠
6	7 ◊	10 ♠	♣ Q	7 ♠
7	♡ A	10 ◊	6 ◊	♡ Q
8	♡ 9	♡ 6	♡ K	♡ 7
9	♣ 10	♡ 10	♡ J	♡ 8

A–B win 30 by honours.

Y–Z win 2 by cards.

Trick 1. *Y* plays King second hand, hoping it will be taken by the Ace, so that he can become third or fourth player, and perhaps save his Ten. *B*, with the minor tenace in trumps, plays to avoid the lead as long as possible.

Trick 2. *Y* gets rid of another winning card, and *B* keeps a small card in order to avoid the lead.

Trick 3. *A* returns the Club, and reads *B* for the Q or no more. *B* still avoids the lead, and *Z* is marked as not having the trump Ten, or he would have saved it.

Trick 4. *Z* plays to win what cards he can.

Trick 5. *B* throws ◊ A in order to avoid the lead, knowing *Y* has the trump Ten, because *A* would have made it on the second round of Spades. *A* also marks it with *Y*, because *B* does not save it.

Trick 6. B is not sure whether *Y* has a Diamond or a Club left, and discards the winning card.

Trick 7. Z plays Queen in order to shut out the Ten, if it is with *A*. *A* knows each player has two trumps left, and that because the turn-up is still with *Z*, *B* must have J or K, because if he held only 7 and 6, he would have trumped in to make cards.

Trick 8. A leads trumps. If *Y* does not play the Ten, and *B* does not have the Jack, *B* must make four cards and the King by passing. If *B* has the Jack, he must catch the Ten, no matter how *Y* and *Z* play.

FRENCH WHIST   This is the name given to a variety of Scotch Whist in which the Ten of Diamonds counts ten to the players who win it, whether or not it is a trump.

— —

BOSTON

CARDS   Boston is played with two packs of fifty-two cards each, which rank as for Whist, for both cutting and playing.

MARKERS   These are not used in Boston: every hand is immediately settled for in counters. These are usually of three colours: white, red and blue, which represent cents, dimes and dollars, respectively. At the beginning of the game, each player should be provided with an equal number, the general proportion of which is 20 white, 18 red and 8 blue for each. A player should be selected to act as the banker, who sells and redeems all counters.

STAKES   The stakes in Boston depend on the value of the counters. One cent for a white counter is considered a pretty stiff game; because it is quite possible for a single player to win or lose a thousand white counters on one hand, and the payments very seldom fall short of fifty.

THE POOL   In addition to the counters won and lost on each hand, it is usual for the players to make up a pool at the beginning of the game by each depositing one red counter in a small tray provided for the purpose. This pool can be increased from time to time by penalties, such as one red counter for a misdeal or four for a revoke, or for not having the proper number of cards. The whole amount in the pool can be won or lost by the players, according to their success or failure in specific undertakings, which will presently be described. When the pool is empty, it is replenished by contributions from each player, as at first.

The pool proper is usually limited to 25 red counters. When it exceeds that amount, the 25 are set aside and the surplus is used to start a fresh pool. Any player who wins a pool is entitled to 25 red counters at the most. It will often happen that several of these pools accumulate, and each must be played for in its turn. At the end of the game, any counters that remain in the pool or pools must be divided among the players.

PLAYERS Boston is played by four people. If more than four candidates offer for play, five or six may form a table; if there are more than six, the selection of the table must be made by cutting, as in Whist.

CUTTING The four people who will play the first game are determined by cutting, and they again cut for the deal, with the choice of seats and cards. The player who draws the lowest card deals, and chooses his seat; the next lower card sits on his left, and so on, until all players are seated. Twelve deals is a game, at the end of which the players cut to decide which player will go out, as in Whist.

It is usual to count the deals by opening the blade of a pocketknife, which is placed on the table by the player on the dealer's right. When it comes to this player's turn to deal, he partly opens one blade. When he deals again, he opens it entirely, and the third time he closes it; that is the third round, and the last deal of the game.

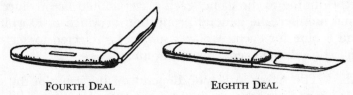

FOURTH DEAL   EIGHTH DEAL

POSITION OF THE PLAYERS The four players at Boston are distinguished by the letters A Y B Z.

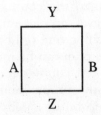

Z is the dealer, and A is known as the *eldest hand*. There are no partnerships in Boston, except that of three players combined against the fourth player, who is always spoken of as *the caller*. When the players have taken their seats, they are not allowed to change them without the consent of all the other players at the table.

DEALING At the beginning of the game, the two packs are thoroughly shuffled, after which they must not be shuffled again during the progress of the game. If a hand is dealt and not played, each player must sort his cards into suits and sequences before they are gathered and dealt again.

At the beginning of each deal, one pack is presented to the players for cutting; each player has the privilege of cutting once, and the dealer goes last. Beginning on his left, the dealer gives four cards to each player, then four more, and finally five; no trump is turned.

The general rules with reference to irregularities in the deal are the same as for Whist, except that a misdeal does not lose the deal. The misdealer must deal again with the same pack, after the players have sorted their cards into suits. It is a misdeal if the dealer fails to present the pack to the other players to cut, or neglects to cut it himself. If the dealer exposes any of his own cards in dealing, that does not invalidate the deal. The deal passes in regular rotation to the left, and each pack is used alternately.

MAKING THE TRUMP When the deal is complete, the player opposite the dealer cuts the still pack, and the player on his right turns up the top card for the trump. The suit to which this card belongs is called *First Preference*, and the suit of the same colour is called *Second Preference*, or *Colour*. The two remaining suits are known as *Plain Suits* for that deal.

When the cards have been dealt, and the trump turned, each player carefully sorts and counts his cards, to see that he has the correct number: thirteen. A player who has more or fewer cards than his right proportion should at once claim a misdeal, because if he plays with a defective hand, he cannot win anything that deal but must stand his proportion of all losses incurred, and pay a forfeit of four red counters to the pool.

OBJECTS OF THE GAME In Boston, each player has an opportunity to announce that he is willing to undertake to win a specific number of tricks, if allowed the privilege of naming the trump suit, or to lose a specific number, if there are no trumps. In either case, he proposes to play single-handed against the three other players.

The player who proposes the undertaking that is most difficult to accomplish is said to *overcall* the other players, and must be allowed to try. If he is successful, he wins the pool, and is paid a specific number of counters by each of his adversaries. If he fails, he must double the amount in the pool, and pay to each of the other players a specific number of counters.

ANNOUNCEMENTS The bids rank in the following order, beginning with the lowest. The bold-face type shows the words used by the players in calling their bids:

To win five tricks: **Boston**.

To win **Six Tricks**.

To win **Seven Tricks**.

To lose twelve tricks, after having discarded a card that is not to be shown: **Little Misère**.

To win **Eight Tricks**.

To win **Nine Tricks**.

To lose every trick: **Grand Misère**.

To win **Ten Tricks**.

To win **Eleven Tricks**.

To lose twelve tricks, after having discarded a card that is not to be shown, whereby the single player's remaining twelve cards are exposed face upwards on the table but are not liable to be called: **Little Spread**.

To win **Twelve Tricks**.

To lose every trick, whereby the single player's cards are exposed on the table but are not liable to be called: **Grand Spread**.

To win Thirteen Tricks: **Grand Slam**.

The object of the proposing player, if he is successful in his bid, is to win or lose the proposed number of tricks, whereas that of his three adversaries is to combine in order to prevent him from doing so. There are no honours, and the only factor in the count is the number of tricks taken. The highest card played of the suit led wins the trick, and trumps, if any, win against all other suits.

METHOD OF BIDDING The eldest hand has the first say, and after examining his cards and estimating the number of tricks he can probably take, making the trump to suit his hand, bids accordingly. It is not necessary for him to state which suit he wishes to make the trump, only the number of tricks he proposes to win. If he has no proposal to make, he says distinctly, *'I pass,'* and the other players in turn have an opportunity to bid. If any player makes a bid, such as six tricks, and any other player thinks he can make the same number of tricks with a trump the same colour as that of the turn-up, that is, Second Preference, he overcalls the first bidder by saying, *'I keep,'* or he may repeat the number bid, saying, *'Six here.'* This is simply bidding to win the number of tricks *in colour.* The original caller may hold his bid, or a third player may overbid both, by saying, *'I keep over you,'* or *'Six here.'* This means that he will undertake to win the number of tricks already bid, with the *turn-up* suit for trumps. In order to overcall a bid such as this, any other player would have to announce a greater number of tricks. For example, Z deals, and turns a heart. A calls six tricks, intending to name hearts trumps, but not saying so. B passes; Y says 'I Keep.' This announces to the table that Y will play with a red trump, and A knows he is bidding on diamonds. Z passes, and A says, 'I keep over you.' B then bids seven tricks, and if A will not risk seven tricks in hearts, B will be the successful bidder. If A bids seven tricks by keeping over B, the latter must know that it is useless for him to bid again unless he can make more tricks in diamonds than A can in hearts, because A's bid, being in first preference, will always outrank B's for the same number of tricks.

A player once having passed cannot come into the bidding again, except to call one of the misères. In the example just given, either Y or Z, after having twice passed, might have outbid the seven tricks by calling a little misère. This bid can, of course, be entertained only when it outranks any bid already made.

A player is not compelled to bid the full value of his hand; however, it is in his interests to go as near to it as he can with safety, because, as we will see presently, the more he bids, the more he is paid. For example, if he can make ten tricks, but bids only seven, he will be paid for the three over-tricks, if he makes them; however, the payment for seven bid and ten taken is only 22 counters whereas the payment for ten bid and ten taken is 42. Because he receives from each adversary, a player who underbid his hand in this way would lose 60 counters due to his timidity.

It sometimes happens that no one will make a proposal of any sort. It is very unusual to pass the deal. The trump is usually turned down, and a *Grand* is played, without any trump suit. This is sometimes called a *Misère Partout,* or 'all-round poverty', and the object of each player is to take as few tricks as possible.

METHOD OF PLAYING No matter who is the successful bidder, the eldest hand always leads for the first trick, and the other players must follow suit if they can, whereby the play proceeds exactly as in

Whist. The tricks should be carefully stacked, so that they can be readily counted by any player without calling attention to them. The laws provide a severe penalty for drawing attention to the score in this way. Suppose a player has called eight tricks. An adversary hesitates in his play, and another reaches over and counts the tricks in front of the caller, whereby he finds he has seven. This is tantamount to saying to the player who hesitates, 'If you don't win that trick, the call succeeds.' In this case, the single player may at once demand the play of the highest or lowest of the suit, or that the adversaries trump or refrain from trumping the trick.

In all calls except misères and slams, the hands should be played out, in order to allow the players to make what over-tricks they can; however, the moment a misère player takes a trick, or a slam player loses one, the hands are thrown up, and the stakes paid. It is usual to show the cards to the board, in order to satisfy each player that no revoke has occurred.

When Little Misère is called, each player discards one card, which must not be shown, and the hand is then played out with the remaining twelve cards.

When Spreads are called, the caller's cards must be placed face upwards on the table before a card is played. If it is a Little Spread, the discard of each player must remain unknown. The adversaries have no control over the way of playing the exposed cards, which cannot be called and can be played in any way that is suited to the judgement of the single player, provided he follows suit when he is able.

REVOKES If a player opposed to the caller revokes, but discovers his mistake in time to save himself, he may be called on by the single player for his highest or lowest of the suit led, or the card played in error can be claimed as an exposed card. If the highest or lowest of the suit is called, the card played in error is taken up.

If the caller revokes, and discovers his mistake in time, he is not liable to any penalty, unless an adversary has played to the next trick. In that case, the revoking card must be left on the table, and is liable to be called. When the single player revokes, he loses the call in any case, and at least one trick as well. He must also double the pool, and add to it a revoke forfeit of four red counters. For example, A bids eight tricks, and his adversaries detect and claim a revoke. Because he is supposed to have lost his bid, and one trick more, he can be said to have bid eight, and taken only seven; he loses 23 white counters to each of his adversaries, doubles the pool, and then pays a forfeit of four red counters. In some places, the forfeit is omitted, and in others it takes the place of doubling the pool. It is not usual to play the hand out after a revoke is claimed and proved.

If an adversary of the single player revokes, he and his partners must each pay the caller just as if he had been successful, and must also pay him for three over-tricks as forfeit, provided his bid was not more than nine tricks, because the bid and the over-tricks together must not exceed thirteen tricks. In addition to this, the individual player in fault must pay four red counters as forfeit to the pool. In some places he is made to double the pool; however, this is manifestly unfair, because he could not win the amount in the pool in any case, and therefore should not lose it.

In a Misère Partout, the revoking player pays five red counters to each adversary, and deposits a forfeit of four red counters in the pool. The hands are immediately thrown up if the revoke is claimed and proved.

CARDS PLAYED IN ERROR The single player is not liable to any penalty for cards played in error, or led out of turn, except the ones taken back to save a revoke; however, his adversaries are liable to the usual whist penalties for all irregularities of this type. The single player can forbid use of an exposed trump for ruffing, and can demand or prevent the play of an exposed card in plain suits, provided he does not ask the adversary to revoke. If a suit is led of which an adversary has an exposed card on the table, the single player may call on him to play his highest or lowest of that suit.

If a player has announced Little Misère, and one of the adversaries leads before the others have discarded, the caller may immediately claim the pool and stakes. If any adversary of a misère player leads out of turn, or exposes a card, or plays before his proper turn in any trick, the bidder may at once claim the pool and stakes. In all these cases, it is usual for the person in fault to pay a forfeit of four red counters towards the next pool.

In Misère Partout, there is no penalty for cards played in error or led out of turn.

PAYMENTS If the caller succeeds in winning the proposed number of tricks, he is paid by each of his adversaries according to the value of his bid, and the number of over-tricks he wins, if any. The various payments are shown in the following table:

Number of tricks bid by the player	Number actually taken by the player								
	5	6	7	8	9	10	11	12	13
Five	12	12	13	13	14	14	14	15	15
Six		15	16	16	17	18	19	20	20
Seven			18	20	21	22	23	24	26
Eight				23	24	26	28	29	31
Nine					32	34	36	39	41
Ten						42	45	48	52
Eleven							63	68	72
Twelve								106	114
Thirteen									166

The American system is not to pay the successful bidder for any over-tricks. This is in order to make him bid up his hand, and to save time, because hands do not have to be played out when the bidder has made or can show the number of tricks bid.

Tricks bid	5	6	7	8	9	10	11	12	13
Amount	10	15	20	25	35	45	65	105	170

If the caller fails in his undertaking, he must pay each adversary according to the number of tricks by which he failed to reach his bid. For example, a player who bids eight, and takes only seven, is said to be *'put in for'* one trick, and would have to pay each adversary 23 white counters. These payments are shown in the following table:

Tricks bid by the player	Number of tricks by which the player falls short of his declaration												
	1	2	3	4	5	6	7	8	9	10	11	12	13
Five	11	21	31	41	50								
Six	15	24	35	45	55	66							
Seven	19	29	40	50	60	72	82						
Eight	23	34	46	56	67	78	89	110					
Nine	33	44	57	68	82	92	103	115	127				
Ten	44	56	70	82	94	107	119	132	145	157			
Eleven	67	80	95	109	123	138	151	165	180	194	208		
Twelve	113	130	148	165	182	200	217	234	252	270	286	304	
Thirteen	177	198	222	241	262	284	305	326	348	369	390	412	433

Following is the same table reduced to the American decimal system, in which form it is commonly found in the clubs. It can be remarked in passing that the table is very illogical and inconsistent, because the payments bear no relation to the probabilities of the events. Some of the payments provide for impossibilities, unless the player has miscalled the trump suit, and is held to it; however, we have no authority to change the payments.

Tricks bid	Number of tricks the bidder is 'put in for'												
	1	2	3	4	5	6	7	8	9	10	11	12	13
Five	10	20	30	40	50								
Six	15	25	35	45	55	65							
Seven	20	30	40	50	60	70	80						
Eight	25	35	45	55	70	85	100	115					
Nine	35	45	55	65	80	95	110	125	140				
Ten	45	55	70	80	95	110	125	140	155	170			
Eleven	70	80	95	110	125	140	155	170	185	200	220		
Twelve	120	130	145	160	180	200	220	240	260	280	300	320	
Thirteen	180	200	220	240	260	280	300	320	340	360	390	420	450

If a misère is bid, the caller wins from or loses to each adversary according to the following table, if there are no over-tricks:

> Little Misère: .... 20 white counters.
> Grand Misère: .... 40 white counters.
> Little Spread: .... 80 white counters.
> Grand Spread: ....160 white counters.

It can be observed that each of these counters is twice the amount of the next lower.

When misère partout is played, the person who wins the largest number of tricks is the only loser, and must pay each of the other players the difference between the number of his tricks and theirs in red counters. The number of red counters lost will always be found to be three times the number of tricks taken, minus the number of tricks not taken. For example, A wins 4 tricks, three times which is 12; from this he deducts 9, the number he did not take, and finds his loss to be 3 red counters. Again: A wins 7 tricks, three times which is 21, minus 6 tricks not taken: a net loss of 15. No matter in what proportion the other tricks are divided between the other three players, this total payment will always be found to be correct. For example, A wins 6 tricks, Y 2, B 5 and Z none. A loses $6 \times 3 = 18 - 7 = 11$, of which he gives 4 to Y, 1 to B and 6 to Z.

If two players tie for the greatest number of tricks taken, they calculate their losses in the same way, but each pays only half the total. For example, A and Y each take 5 tricks, B takes 1 and Z 2. When the 7 red counters lost by A and Y are divided, a loss of 35 white counters is shown for each of them. If three players take four tricks apiece, they each pay the fourth player a red counter.

WINNING THE POOL   Besides the white counters won and lost by the players individually, the successful caller takes the pool, provided he has made a bid of seven tricks or better, which is called a *pool bid*. Any lower bid does not entitle him to the pool, unless the other players compel him to play the hand out. In order to save the pool, it is usual for the adversaries, before they play to the second trick, to say, *'I pay.'* If all agree to pay, the bidder must accept the amount of his bid without any over-tricks, and the pool is not touched. If a player has made a pool bid, and the adversaries, before they play to the second trick, agree to pay, they cannot prevent the caller from taking the pool; however, they save possible over-tricks. The agreement of the adversaries to pay must be unanimous.

Misère Partout does not touch the pool.

If the hand is played out, and the caller fails, he must double the pool, whether or not he has made a pool bid. If there is more than one pool, he must double the first one, which will of course contain the limit. This will simply have the effect of forming an additional pool to be played for.

When there are several pools on the table, a successful caller takes any of the pools that contain the limit. When there is only one pool on the table, he must be satisfied with its contents, however small.

At the end of the game, after the twelfth hand has been settled for, it is usual to divide the pool or pools equally among the players. However, sometimes a grand is played without trumps, whereby a thirteenth hand is made, and the pool is given to the player who wins the last trick.

METHODS OF CHEATING   Because there is no shuffling in Boston, and each player has the right to cut the pack, the cheat must be very skilful who can secure himself any advantage by having the last cut, unless he has the courage to use wedges. However, Boston is usually played for such high stakes that it naturally attracts people who have a high level of skill, and the system adopted is usually that of counting down. The cheat will watch for a hand in which there is little changing of suits, and will note the way of taking up the cards.

The next hand does not interest him, because he is busy studying the location of the cards in the still pack. When this comes into play on the next deal, he will follow every cut, and finally cut for himself so that the desired distribution of the suits will come about. Even if he fails to secure an invincible hand for bidding on himself, he knows almost so completely the contents of the other hands that he can bid them up, and afterwards play against them to great advantage.

It is unnecessary to say that if a cheat can mark the cards, the game becomes a walkover, even if he can recollect only the hand on his left.

SUGGESTIONS FOR GOOD PLAY Boston so closely resembles Solo Whist in matters such as bidding and playing single-handed against three other players that you can be referred to that game for the outlines of the principles that should guide you in estimating the probable value of your hand, playing for tricks or for misères, and combining forces with your partners for the purpose of defeating the single player.

For laws, see Whist Family Laws.

— —

BOSTON DE FONTAINEBLEAU

This game is sometimes incorrectly called French Boston. The latter will be described in its proper place.

CARDS Boston de Fontainebleau is played with a full pack of fifty-two cards. Two packs are usually used. The cards rank as in Whist, for both cutting and playing.

MARKERS These are not used: counters take their place. The counters are usually of the colours and values used in, and are distributed among the players as already described in, Boston.

STAKES As a guide to settling on the unit value, it can be noted that the largest amount possible to win or lose on a single hand is 2400 white counters; the smallest amount is 30, and the average is about 300.

THE POOL In addition to the counters won or lost on each hand, a pool is formed by the fact that each dealer in his turn places five counters in a small tray provided for the purpose. This pool can be increased by penalties, and so on, and the whole amount can be won under specific conditions, as in Boston. There is no limit to the amount of a single pool.

PLAYERS   The number of players, methods of *Cutting and Dealing* and so on , are the same as those already described in connection with Boston, except that no trump is turned for first preference: the suits always have a determined rank, whereby diamonds are first, hearts next, then clubs, and last spades. No-trump, or 'grand', out-ranks diamonds.

Twelve deals is a game, after which the players cut out if there are more than four belonging to the table, or if other candidates are waiting to play.

PENALTIES   Penalties for playing with more or fewer than the proper number of cards and so on are the same as for Boston.

OBJECTS OF THE GAME   These are identical to Boston, but instead of doubling the pool, the player who is unsuccessful in his undertaking pays into the pool the same amount that he loses to each of the other players.

ANNOUNCEMENTS   The bids rank in the following order, beginning with the lowest. The bold-face type shows the words used by the players in calling their bids. It will be noticed that the order is not the same as in Boston, and that an additional bid is introduced, called Piccolissimo.

To win 5 tricks: *Boston*.

To win *Six Tricks*.

To lose 12 tricks, after having discarded a card that is not to be shown: *Little Misère*.

To win *Seven Tricks*.

To win one trick, neither more nor fewer, after having discarded a card that is not to be shown, if there is no trump suit: *Piccolissimo*.

To win *Eight Tricks*.

To lose every trick, no trump suit: *Grand Misère*.

To win *Nine Tricks*.

To lose 12 tricks, after having discarded a card that is not to be shown, whereby the single player's remaining twelve cards are exposed face upwards on the table but not liable to be called: *Little Spread*.

To win *Ten Tricks*.

To lose every trick, no trump suit, whereby the single player's are exposed on the table but not liable to be called: *Grand Spread*.

To win *Eleven Tricks*.

To win *Twelve Tricks*.

To win 13 tricks: *Slam*.

To win 13 tricks, whereby the single player's cards are exposed face upwards on the table but not liable to be called: *Spread Slam*.

The object of the bidder, if he is successful in securing the privilege of playing, is to win or lose the proposed number of tricks, against the combined efforts of his adversaries. Having once made a bid, he must play it unless he is over-called.

METHOD OF BIDDING   The eldest hand has the first say, and after examining his hand, and deciding on the bid most appropriate to it, if any, he makes his announcement. If his proposal is to win a specific number of tricks with a specific suit for trumps, he must name the suit, saying, 'Eight Spades,' or 'Seven Diamonds,' as the case may be. If he proposes to play without any trump suit, he announces, 'Seven Grand,' or whatever the number may be. This bid overcalls one of the same number in diamonds. If the eldest hand has no proposal to make, he says, 'I pass,' and the other players in turn have an opportunity to bid. The bids outrank each other according to their order in the table on page 180–181, and the rank of the suits in which they are made. The players bid against each other, until all but one declare to pass; he then becomes the single player against the three other players.

A player having once passed cannot come into the bidding again, even to call a misère. In this way, the game differs from Boston. A player is not compelled to bid the full value of his hand, but it is in his interests to do so, and he should make the full announcement the first time he bids, because if he has had a good hand for ten tricks, and begins with a bid of seven, he cannot increase his proposal unless a player bids over him.

PARTNERS   Before playing, the successful bidder may call for a partner if he chooses to do so. The player who accepts him undertakes that the two together will win three tricks more than the number bid. For example, A has successfully bid seven in diamonds, and asks for a partner. If Y accepts him, these partners make no change in their positions at the table, but play into each other's hands, just as in Solo Whist, whereby B and Z are partners against them. A and Y together must win ten tricks, with diamonds for trumps.

If no one makes a proposal of any sort, *Misère Partout* is played, whereby there is no trump suit. The player or players who take the fewest number of tricks win or divide the pool. There are no other losses or gains in Misère Partout.

HONOURS   In any call in which there is a trump suit, the A K Q and J of trumps are honours, and can be counted by the successful bidder if he carries out his proposal. If the single player, or a caller and his partner, have all four honours dealt them, they score as for four over-tricks; if three, as for two over-tricks. Honours do not count for the adversaries under any circumstances.

In bidding on a hand, it must be remembered that although honours will count as over-tricks in payments, they cannot be bid on. If a player has nine tricks and two by honours in his hand, he cannot bid eleven. If he bids nine and fails to make so many, he cannot count the honours at all. In America, it has become less and less the custom to count honours.

A player who makes a bid can be compelled to play it; however, it is usual to allow him to pay instead of play, if he proposes to do so, either because he has overbid his hand or for any other reason.

METHOD OF PLAYING   No matter who is the successful bidder, the eldest hand always leads for the first trick, and the other players must follow suit if they can, whereby the play proceeds exactly as in Whist. Tricks should be carefully stacked, and there are the same penalties as in Boston for calling attention to the score. The methods of playing misères and spreads have already been described in connection with Boston. When piccolissimo is played, the moment the single player takes more than one trick, the hands are thrown up and the stakes paid.

REVOKES   The rules governing these and cards played in error are the same as for Boston. In piccolissimo, the penalties are the same as for misère.

PAYMENTS   If the caller succeeds in winning the proposed number of tricks, he is paid by each of his adversaries according to the value of his bid, as shown in the following table. Over-tricks, if any, and honours, if played, are always paid at the uniform rate of five white counters each. If the caller fails, he must pay each adversary the amount he would have won if he had been successful, with the addition of five white counters for every trick that he falls short of his proposal. For example, he bids nine hearts, and wins six tricks only. He must pay each adversary 115 white counters.

	No trump	The trump is			Extra tricks
		♣ ♠	♡	◇	
Boston: five tricks	....	10	20	30	5
Six tricks	....	30	40	50	5
Little misère	75				
Seven tricks	....	50	60	70	5
Piccolissimo	100				
Eight tricks	....	70	80	90	5
Grand misère	150				
Nine tricks	....	90	100	110	5
Little spread	200				
Ten tricks	....	110	120	130	5
Grand spread	250				
Eleven tricks	....	130	140	150	5
Twelve tricks	....	150	160	170	5
Slam: thirteen tricks	....	400	450	500	
Spread slam	....	600	700	800	

In America, the last two items are usually reduced, and are given as follows:

		♠ ♣	♡	◇	
Slam: thirteen tricks ...	....	250	300	350	
Spread slam	....	350	400	450	

Why a player should be paid more for spreads than for eleven or twelve tricks while the trick bid outranks the spreads is difficult to understand, but we have no authority to change the tables.

Misère Partout wins nothing but the pool.

If partners play, it is usual for the losers to pay the adversaries on their right, or, if partners sit together, to pay the adversary who sits next to them.

THE POOL Besides the white counters won and lost by the players individually, the successful player takes the pool. Successful partners divide it equally, regardless of the number of tricks bid or taken by each. If the partners fail, they must contribute to the pool an amount equal to that which they pay to one adversary. For example, A calls seven monds, and asks for a partner. Y accepts him, and the pair win only nine tricks. Each pays 135 counters to the adversary sitting next to him, and they then make up 135 more between them for the pool.

Asking for a partner is not a popular variation of the game, and is seldom resorted to unless the successful bid is very low, or has been made on a black suit.

If the adversaries of the caller declare to pay, before playing to the second trick, they can save nothing but possible over-tricks. The pool goes with every successful play.

If the single player is unsuccessful, he does not double the pool. as in Boston, but pays into it the same amount that he loses to each adversary, over-tricks and all, so that he really loses four times the amount shown in the table on page 181.

At the end of the game, or on the twelfth hand, if the caller does not succeed, he pays the pool as usual, and his adversaries then divide it among themselves.

The *Suggestions for Good Play* and so on are given in connection with Solo Whist and require no more detail for Boston de Fontainebleau.

The *Laws* vary so little from the ones used in the regular game of Boston that it is not necessary to give an additional code, for either Fontainebleau or French Boston, the latter which follows.

— —

FRENCH BOSTON

CARDS   French Boston is played with a full pack of fifty-two cards, which rank as in Whist, for both cutting and playing, except that the diamond Jack is always the best trump unless diamonds are turned up, in which case the heart Jack becomes the best trump, and the diamond Jack ranks next below the diamond Queen.

COUNTERS   These are used as in Boston, and their value is a matter of agreement before play begins.

THE POOL   This is made up by the dealer's contributing ten counters for the first eight rounds, and twenty for the last two. It is increased from time to time by penalties, and is won or lost by the players, just as in Boston. There is no limit to the pool. If any player objects to dividing it at the end of the game, it must be played for until a player wins it.

PLAYERS The number of players, their arrangement at the table and so on are precisely the same as for Boston.

CUTTING Instead of cutting for the first deal, any one of the players takes a pack of cards, and gives thirteen to each player in succession, face upwards. The player to whom he gives the diamond Jack deals the first hand, and has the choice of seats and cards. The other players sit as they please.

DEALING The cards are shuffled before every deal. The player on the left of the dealer cuts, and cards are given first to the player on the dealer's right, dealing from right to left. The cards can be dealt one at a time, or three at a time, or four at a time, whereby the last round is always dealt singly, and the last card is turned up. A misdeal loses the deal. Other irregularities are governed by the same laws as in Boston.

The deal passes to the right, and the next dealer is indicated by the position of the tray that contains the pool, which the dealer always passes to the player on his right, after putting in his ten or twenty counters.

Forty deals is a game, the first thirty-two of which are called 'simples', and the last eight 'doubles'. In the doubles, all stakes and contributions to the pool are doubled. If anything remains in the pool at the end, it is divided equally, unless a player demands that it be played for until won. These extra deals are simples.

RANK OF THE SUITS The suit turned on the first deal is called 'belle' for that game. The suit turned on each succeeding deal is called 'petite'. If belle turns up again, there is no petite for that deal. The suits are not first and second preference, as in Boston, but are used only to determine the value of the payments, and to settle which suits partners must name for trumps. The rank of the suits is permanent, as in Boston de Fontainebleau, but the order is hearts, diamonds, clubs and spades; hearts are highest. In France, the suits rank in this order in Boston de Fontainebleau, but in America diamonds outrank hearts.

OBJECTS OF THE GAME Each player in turn has an opportunity to announce that he is willing to undertake to win a specific number of tricks, if allowed the privilege of naming the trump suit, or to lose a specific number, if there is no trump suit. If he proposes to play alone, he may select any suit for trumps, but if he takes a partner, the trump suit must be belle or petite. The announcements outrank each other in a specific order, and the player who makes the highest must be allowed to play. If he succeeds in his undertaking, he wins the pool, and is also paid a specific number of counters by each of his adversaries. If he fails, he must double the pool, and pay each of his adversaries. The table of payments will be given later.

ANNOUNCEMENTS   The proposals rank in the following order, beginning with the lowest. The French terms are given in *bold-face type*:

Five tricks; or eight with a partner, in petite. *Simple in petite*.
Five tricks; or eight with a partner, in belle. *Simple in belle*.
Six tricks solo, in any suit. *Petite independence*.
Little misère. *Petite misère*.
Eight tricks solo in any suit. *Grand independence*.
Grand misère. *Grand misère,* or *misère sans ecart.*
Misère with four aces. *Misère des quatre as*.
Nine tricks in any suit. *Neuf.*
Nine tricks in petite. *Neuf en petite*.
Nine tricks in belle. *Neuf en belle*.
Little spread. *Petite misère sur table*.
Grand spread. *Grand misère sur table*.

METHOD OF BIDDING   The player to the right of the dealer has the first say. If he proposes to take a partner as in Solo Whist, he says, 'Je demande,' at the same time as he places one of his cards face downwards on the table. This card must not be shown or named, but must be of the suit that he proposes to make the trump. He is not allowed to announce the suit, so that any player who accepts him as a partner does so in ignorance as to whether he will play in belle or in petite. If the demand is accepted, the proposer and his partner make no change in their positions at the table, but must make eight tricks, just as in Solo Whist.

If a player cannot propose, he says, 'Je passe,' and each of the other players in turn from right to left have the opportunity to make a proposal. When any player proposes, any player in turn after him may accept, although this player might have already passed. If the fourth player proposes, the three other players have passed, and no one will accept him, he is bound to play solo against three such weak adversaries, and must make five tricks, either in belle or in petite. He is not allowed to play in a plain suit if he has made a simple 'demand'.

The only solo bids allowed are those for six, eight or nine tricks, which outrank each other. A player cannot bid seven to overcall six: he must go to eight; a player cannot *bid* five tricks without a partner, although, as we have just seen, he can be forced to *play* in that way.

When six, eight or nine tricks are bid, the suits outrank each other for equal numbers of tricks; however, because the suit called does not have to be the bidder's true intention, nor the same as the card laid on the table, the proposer must be careful that his play will be as good as his bid. For example, he intends nine tricks in spades, but proposes eight in diamonds. He cannot bid nine in diamonds, because that would be a better bid than he intends to play; however, the ruse might succeed in inducing a player not to bid against him, hoping diamonds is the true suit. It is a common artifice to bid the true suit, because few players will believe it to be such.

If clubs are belle, and diamonds petite, and a player who 'demands' is over-called by a demand in belle, or a call of six tricks, the first caller cannot advance his bid to six tricks except in the suit he has already laid on the table; however, he may accept the player's over-calling him rather than bid against him. After a player has once accepted or passed, he cannot bid misère.

If no one makes a proposition of any kind, the hands are thrown up; the next dealer contributes to the pool, and a fresh hand is dealt.

METHOD OF PLAYING As in Boston, the eldest hand has the first lead, and the other players must follow suit if they can, except in the misère des quatre as. When this is played, the bidder may renounce at pleasure for the first ten tricks.

GATHERING TRICKS When a partnership is formed, each partner gathers the tricks he takes. If the partnership loses, the partner who does not have his complement of tricks must pay the adversaries and double the pool. If the demander does not have five, and the acceptor has three, the demander pays. If the proposer has five, and the acceptor does not have three, the acceptor pays; however, they both win if they have eight tricks between them, no matter in what proportion. If neither has taken his proper share, they both must pay. When they are successful, they divide the pool.

SLAMS If a player has demanded, and not been accepted, and has been forced to play alone for five tricks, but wins eight, it is called a slam. But because he did not wish to play alone, his only payment, besides the pool, is 24 counters from each player if he played in petite, 48 if in belle, and double these amounts if the deal was one of the last eight in the game.

If two partners make a slam: thirteen tricks, they take the pool, and receive from each adversary 24 counters if they played in petite, 48 if in belle, and double if in one of the last eight hands in the game.

EXPOSED CARDS   The laws governing these are almost identical to those for Boston, with the additional rule that a player who allows a card to fall on the table face upwards before play begins can be forced to play independence in that suit.

REVOKES   The individual player who is detected in a revoke must double the pool, and pay both adversaries.

PAYMENTS   Payments are made according to the following table. The player who holds diamond Jack receives two counters from each of the other players in a simple, and four in a double, except in misères, in which the card has no value.

Misères are paid for according to the trump turned in the deal in which they are played. If a heart is turned, and little misère is played, the payment is 64 counters to or from each player. If a spade is turned, the payment is 16 only.

Three honours between partners count as three; four count as four. Being all in one hand does not increase their value.

The Bid	♠	♣	♢	♡
Five tricks alone, or partners' 8	4	8	12	16
Three honours	3	6	9	12
Four honours	4	8	12	16
Each extra trick	1	2	3	4
Six tricks, or petite independence	6	12	18	24
Three honours	4	8	12	16
Four honours	6	12	18	24
Each extra trick	2	4	6	8
Eight tricks, or grand independence	8	16	24	32
Three honours	6	12	18	24
Four honours	8	16	24	32
Each extra trick	4	8	12	16
Petite misère	16	32	48	64
Grand misère	32	64	96	128
Misère de quatre as	32	64	96	128
Misère sur table	64	128	192	256
Slam à deux (partners)	50	100	150	200
Slam seul (alone)	100	200	300	400
Slam sur table	200	400	600	800

— —

RUSSIAN BOSTON

This is a variation of Boston de Fontainebleau. A player who holds carte blanche declares it before playing, and receives ten counters from each of the other players. Carte blanche is the same thing as chicane in Bridge: no trump in the hand. However, in Bridge, the player is penalised for announcing it until after the hand is played.

The order of the suits is the same as in American Boston de Fontainebleau: diamonds, hearts, clubs and spades.

When a player bids six, seven or eight tricks, he is supposed to be still willing to take a partner, unless he specifies solo. When a partner accepts him, the combination must make four tricks more than the original proposal.

Four honours are paid for as four over-tricks, three honours as two over-tricks.

Piccolissimo is played, and comes between the bids of seven and eight tricks.

— —

GERMAN WHIST

CARDS   German Whist is played with a full pack of fifty-two cards, which rank as in Whist, for both cutting and playing.

PLAYERS   Two people play. They cut for the first deal, and the choice of seats.

DEALING   The dealer presents the pack to his adversary for cutting, and then gives thirteen cards to each player, one at a time, turning up the twenty-seventh card for the trump, and laying it on the talon, or remainder of the pack.

PLAYING   The non-dealer begins by leading any card he pleases, and his adversary must follow suit if he can. The winner of the first trick takes the trump card into his hand, and his adversary takes the card immediately under it, but without showing or naming it. Each player therefore restores the number of cards in his hand to thirteen. The card that is now on the top of the talon is turned up, and the winner of the next trick must take it, whereby his adversary takes the one under it, as before, and turns up the next. In this way, it will be seen that the winner of each trick must always get a card that is known to his adversary, whereas the loser of the trick gets one that remains unknown.

When the talon is exhausted, the thirteen cards in each hand should be known to both players if they have been observant, and the end game becomes a problem in double dummy.

STAKES   The game is usually played for so much a point, whereby the player who has won most of the tricks receives the difference between the number of his tricks and those of his adversary. Each game is complete in one hand.

In many ways the game resembles single-handed Hearts, except that in Hearts, none of the cards drawn are shown.

— —

CHINESE WHIST

CARDS   Chinese Whist is played with a full pack of fifty-two cards, which rank as in Whist, for both cutting and playing.

MARKERS   Ordinary whist markers are used for scoring the points.

PLAYERS   Two, three or four people can play Chinese Whist. When three play, the spade deuce is thrown out of the pack. Partners and deal are cut for from an outspread pack, as in Whist.

POSITION OF THE PLAYERS   When four people play, the partners sit opposite each other. When three play, the one who cuts the lowest card chooses his seat, and dictates the positions of the other two players.

DEALING   When four play, the pack is shuffled and cut as in Whist. The dealer then gives six cards to each player, one at a time, beginning on his left. These six cards are then spread face downwards on the table in front of the players to whom they have been dealt, but are not looked at. Six more are then dealt to each, one at a time, and these are turned face upwards, and sorted into suits. They are then laid face upwards on the top of the six cards that are lying on the table face downwards, so as to cover them. The last four cards are then dealt, one to each player. These last are retained in the hand, and must not be shown or named; they are usually called the *'down cards'*.

MAKING THE TRUMP　After examining the cards exposed on the table, and the down card in his own hand, the dealer has the privilege of naming any suit he pleases for trumps. No consultation with the partner is allowed.

METHOD OF PLAYING　The player to the left of the dealer begins by leading any one of his exposed cards, and the other players must follow suit if they can, either with one of their exposed cards or with their down cards. A player who has none of the suit led may either discard or trump. The highest card played of the suit led wins the trick, and trumps win all other suits. The side that wins the trick takes it in and arranges it just as in Whist. Before the next trick is led for, all cards that have been uncovered are turned face upwards. If any person has played his down card, he will have no card to turn up, because none has been uncovered. The cards cannot under any circumstances be shifted from their original positions. If a player has five cards face upwards, covering five cards face downwards, he cannot shift one of the exposed cards to the empty sixth place, and uncover another card. All covering cards must be gotten rid of in the course of play.

PENALTIES　Penalties for revokes, cards led out of turn and so on are the same as in Whist.

OBJECTS OF THE GAME　As in Whist, the object is to win tricks, and all tricks above six count one point towards game. Five, seven or ten points can be made the game, at the option of the players, but ten is the usual number. Honours are not counted except by agreement.

STAKES　It is usual to play for so much a point or a game. If points are played, the loser's score must be deducted from the winner's, and the difference is the value of the game won.

WHEN THREE PLAY　Eight cards are dealt to each person, and arranged face downwards, then eight more, arranged face upwards, and then one to each for down cards. There are no partnerships: each player plays for himself against the other players.

WHEN TWO PLAY　Twelve cards are dealt to each player and arranged face downwards, then twelve more, arranged face upwards, and then two down cards to each. It is usual to deal all the cards two at a time.

SUGGESTIONS FOR GOOD PLAY　Chinese Whist very closely resembles Dummy, and the main element of success is skilful use of tenace. Memory also plays an important part: it is especially necessary to remember what cards are still unplayed in each suit. While the down cards are held, a player cannot be sure of taking a trick by leading a card higher than any his adversary has exposed, because one of the down cards might be better. If a player is short of trumps, but has as many and better than those of his adversary, it is often good play to lead and draw the weaker trumps before the adversary turns up higher ones in order to protect them. For example, one player can have 10 8, and his adversary the 9 alone. If the 10 is led, the 9 will probably be caught, unless one of the adverse down cards is better. If the 10 is not led, the adversary can turn up an honour, and will then have major tenace over the 10 and 8.

The end game always offers some interesting problems for solution by the expert in tenace position, and in placing the lead.

— · —

AMERICAN-WHIST LAWS

Although the code of laws drawn up by the American Whist League, and finally approved and adopted at the Third Congress [in Chicago, 20 to 24 June 1893] refers exclusively to the parent game of Whist, its general provisions equally apply to all members of the whist family of games. We believe it will save much repetition and confusion to interlineate the exceptions that are necessary in order to cover the special features of important variations such as Boston, Cayenne and Solo Whist. When no exceptions are made, the law applies equally to these games and Whist. The unnumbered paragraphs show the inserted laws.

It is a common practice for the framers of laws to insert rules that are simply descriptive of the way of playing. We believe in adhering to the proper definition of a law, which is a rule that carries with it some penalty for its infraction, or that defines the rights of individual players. A statement such as that the Dummy player may not overlook his adversary's hand is not a law, because there is no penalty if he does so.

We are not responsible for the peculiar grammar used in both the American and the English Laws.

THE GAME

1. A game consists of seven points, and each trick above six counts one. The value of the game is determined by deducting the losers' score from seven.

In ***Boston,*** the game is finished in twelve deals.

In ***Cayenne,*** a game consists of ten points, and each trick above six counts towards game according to the table of values. Honours and Slams also count towards game. Every hand must be played out, and all points made in excess of the ten required to win the game are counted on the next game, so that it is possible to win two or three games in one hand. In Nullo, every trick over the book is counted by the adversaries. Players cannot count out by honours alone; they must win the odd trick or stop at the score of nine. If one side goes out by cards, the other cannot score honours. The rubber is won by the side that first wins four games of ten points each. The value of the rubber is determined by adding 8 points to the winners' score for tricks, honours and slams, and then deducting the score of the losers.

In ***Solo Whist,*** the game is complete in one deal, the value of it is determined by the player's success or failure in his undertaking, and it has to be settled for at the end of the hand, according to the table of payments.

FORMING THE TABLE

2. The players who are first in the room have the preference. If, because two or more arrive at the same time, more than four assemble, the preference among the last comers is determined by cutting, whereby a lower cut gives the preference over all who cut higher. A complete table consists of six, and the four have the preference play. Partners are determined by way of cutting, the highest two play against the lowest two, the lowest deals and has the choice of seats and cards.

Boston and ***Solo Whist,*** a table is complete with four players. In cutting for positions at the table, the lowest player has the choice of seats and cards, and the two highest players sit opposite each other.

If two players cut intermediate cards of equal value, they cut again, and the lower of the new cut plays with the original lowest.

4. If three players cut cards of equal value, they cut again. If the fourth has cut the highest card, the two lowest of the new cut are partners, and the lowest deals. If the fourth has cut the lowest card, he deals, and the two highest of the new cut are partners.

5. At the end of a game, if there are more than four belonging to the table, a sufficient number of the players retire to admit the people who are awaiting their turn to play. In determining which players remain in, the players who have played a lesser number of consecutive games have the preference over all who have played a

greater number. Between two or more who have played an equal number, the preference is determined by way of cutting, whereby a lower cut gives the preference over all who cut higher.

In *Boston, Cayenne* and *Solo Whist,* at the end of a game a new table has to be formed, whereby the players who are already in have no preference over fresh candidates.

6. To entitle a person to enter a table, that person has to declare his intention to do so before any one of the players has cut for the purpose of commencing a new game or of cutting out.

In *Boston, Cayenne* and *Solo Whist,* this rule does not apply.

CUTTING

7. In cutting, the ace is the lowest card. All the players have to cut from the same pack. If a player exposes more than one card, he must cut again. Drawing cards from the outspread pack can be resorted to in place of cutting.

SHUFFLING

8. Before every deal, the cards have to be shuffled. When two packs are used, the dealer's partner has to collect and shuffle the cards for the ensuing deal, and place them at his right hand. In all cases the dealer can shuffle last.

In *Boston* and *Cayenne,* two packs have to be used, and in Boston, there has to be no shuffling of either pack after the first deal.

9. A pack must be neither shuffled during the play of a hand nor shuffled so as to expose the face of any card.

CUTTING TO THE DEALER

10. The dealer has to present the pack to his right-hand adversary to be cut, the adversary has to take a portion from the top of the pack and place it towards the dealer, at least four cards have to be left in each packet and the dealer has to reunite the packets by placing the one not removed in cutting on the other.

11. If, in cutting or reuniting the separate packets, a card is exposed, the pack has to be reshuffled by the dealer, and cut again; if there is any confusion of the cards, or doubt as to the place where the pack was separated, there has to be a new cut.

In *Boston,* the pack has to be cut again, but not shuffled.

12. If the dealer reshuffles the pack after it has been properly cut, he loses his deal.

In *Boston, Cayenne* and *Solo Whist,* the misdealer has to deal again.

DEALING

13. When the pack has been properly cut and reunited, the dealer has to distribute the cards, one at a time, to each player in regular

rotation, beginning at his left. The last, which is the trump card, has to be turned up before the dealer. At the end of the hand, or when the deal is lost, the deal passes to the player next to the dealer on his left, and so on to each player in turn.

In *Solo Whist*, the cards are distributed three at a time until only four remain in the pack. These are dealt one at a time, and the last is turned up for trump.

In *Boston* and *Cayenne*, the cards are dealt four at a time for two rounds, and then five at a time. No trump is turned. After the cards have been dealt, the player opposite the dealer presents the still pack to be cut by the player on the dealer's left, and the top card of the portion left on the table is turned up.

In *Boston*, *Cayenne* or *Solo Whist*, the deal is never lost. The same dealer deals again with the same pack.

14. There has to be a new deal by the same dealer:
I. If any card except the last is faced in the pack.
II. If, during the deal or during the play of the hand, the pack is proved incorrect or imperfect; however, any prior score made with that pack will stand.

15. If, during the deal, a card is exposed, the side not in fault can demand a new deal, provided neither player of that side has touched a card. If a new deal does not take place, the exposed card is not liable to be called.

16. Anyone who deals out of turn, or with his adversaries' pack, can be stopped before the trump card is turned, after which the deal is valid, and the packs, if changed, remain so.

In *Boston* and *Cayenne*, the dealer has to be stopped before the last card is dealt.

MISDEALING

17. It is a misdeal:
I. If the dealer omits to have the pack cut, and his adversaries discover the error before the trump card is turned, and before they look at any of their cards.
II. If the dealer deals a card incorrectly, and fails to correct the error before he deals another.
III. If the dealer counts the cards on the table or in the remainder of the pack.
IV. If, having a perfect pack, the dealer does not deal to each player the proper number of cards, and the error is discovered before all have played to the first trick.
V. If the dealer looks at the trump card before the deal is completed.

VI. If the dealer places the trump card face downwards on his own or any other player's cards.

A misdeal loses the deal, unless, during the deal, either of the adversaries touches a card or in any other way interrupts the dealer.

In *Boston, Cayenne* and *Solo Whist*, the misdealer deals again with the same cards. In Boston, he forfeits a red counter to the pool for his error.

THE TRUMP CARD

18. The dealer has to leave the trump card face upwards on the table until it is his turn to play to the first trick; if it is left on the table until after the second trick has been turned and quitted, it is liable to be called. After it has been lawfully taken up, it must not be named, and any player who names it is liable to have his highest or his lowest trump called by either adversary. A player can, however, ask what the trump suit is.

This law does not apply to Boston or Cayenne.

In *Boston* and *Cayenne*, no trump is turned, but a card is cut from the still pack to determine the rank of the suits. See Law 13.

In *Cayenne,* the trump has to be named by the dealer or his partner after these two have examined their cards. The dealer has the first say, and can select any of the four suits; alternatively he can announce 'grand', whereby he plays for the tricks without any trump suit. In Cayenne, he can announce 'nullo', whereby he plays to take as few tricks as possible, there being no trump suit. If the dealer makes his choice, his partner has to abide by it, but if the dealer does not have a hand to justify him in deciding, he can leave the choice to his partner, who has to decide. A declaration once made cannot be changed.

IRREGULARITIES IN THE HANDS

19. If, at any time after all the players have played to the first trick, and the pack is perfect, a player is found to have either more or less than his correct number of cards and his adversaries have their right number, the latter, when this surplus or deficiency is discovered, can consult and will have the choice:

I. To have a new deal, or

II. To have the hand played out, in which case the surplus or missing card or cards are not taken into account.

If either of the adversaries also has more or less than his correct number, there has to be a new deal.

If any player has a surplus card by reason of an omission to play to a trick, his adversaries can exercise the foregoing privilege only after he has played to the trick following the one in which this omission occurred.

In *Boston,* if at any time it is discovered that a player opposed to the bidder has *fewer* than his proper number of cards, whether through the fault of the dealer, or through having played more than one card to a trick, he and his partners each have to pay the bidder for his bid and all over-tricks. If the bidder has *fewer* than his proper number of cards, he is put in for one trick at least, and his adversaries can demand the hand to be played out to put him in for over-tricks. In Misère Partout, any player who has *fewer* than his proper number of cards forfeits five red counters to each of the other players, and the hands are abandoned. If any player has *more* than the proper number of cards, it is a misdeal, and the misdealer deals again, after he has forfeited one red counter to the pool.

In *Solo Whist,* the deal stands good. If the player who has the incorrect number of cards is the caller or his partner, the hand has to be played out. If the caller makes good his proposition, he neither receives nor pays on that hand. If he fails, he has to pay. If the player who has the defective hand is the adversary of the caller, he and his partners have to pay the stakes on that hand, which can then be abandoned. If two players have an incorrect number of cards, and one of them is the caller, there has to be a new deal.

CARDS LIABLE TO BE CALLED

20. The following cards are liable to be called by either adversary:
I.   Every card faced on the table other than in the regular course of play, but not including a card led out of turn.
II. Every card thrown with the one led or played to the current trick. The player has to indicate the one led or played.
III. Every card held by a player in a way so that his partner sees any portion of its face.
IV. All the cards in a hand lowered or shown by a player so that his partner sees more than one card of the hand.
V.   Every card named by the player who is holding it.

In *Boston* and *Solo Whist,* there are no penalties for cards exposed by the single player, because he has no partner to take advantage of the information.

21. All cards liable to be called have to be placed and left face upwards on the table. A player has to lead or play them when called, provided he can do so without revoking. The call can be repeated at each trick until the card is played. A player cannot be prevented from leading or playing a card liable to be called; if he can get rid of it in the course of play, no penalty remains.

In *Boston* and *Solo Whist,* if the exposed card is a trump, the owner can be called on by his adversary not to use it for ruffing. If the suit of the exposed card is led, whether trump or not, the adversary can demand that the card be played or not played, or that the highest or lowest of the suit be played. If the owner of the exposed card has no other card of the suit, the penalty is paid.

Penalties have to be exacted by players in their proper turn, or the right to exact them is lost. For example, in Solo Whist, A is the proposer, B is the acceptor, and B has an exposed card in front of him. When Y plays, he should say whether or not he wishes to call the exposed card. If he says nothing, B has to await Z's decision.

22. If a player leads a card better than any his adversaries hold of the suit, and then leads one or more other cards without waiting for his partner to play, the latter can be called on by either adversary to take the first trick, and the other cards thereby improperly played are liable to be called; it makes no difference whether the player plays them one after the other, or throws them all on the table together: after the first card is played, the others are liable to be called.

23. A player who has a card liable to be called must not play another card until the adversaries have stated whether or not they wish to call the card liable to the penalty. If he plays another card without awaiting the decision of the adversaries, this other card is also liable to be called.

LEADING OUT OF TURN

24. If any player leads out of turn, a suit can be called from him or his partner the first time it is the turn of either of them to lead. The penalty can be enforced only by the adversary on the right of the player from whom a suit can be lawfully called.

If a player, so called on to lead a suit, has none of it, or if all have played to the false lead, no penalty can be enforced. If all have not played to the trick, the cards erroneously played to this false lead are not liable to be called, and have to be taken back.

In *Boston,* if the adversary of the bidder leads out of turn, and the bidder has not played to the trick, the latter can call a suit from the player whose proper turn it is to lead; or, if it is the bidder's own lead, he can call a suit when the adversaries next obtain the lead; or he can claim the card played in error as an exposed card. If the bidder has played to the trick, the error cannot be rectified. If the bidder leads out of turn, and the player on his left follows the erroneous lead, the error cannot be corrected.

In Misères, a lead out of turn by the bidder's adversary immediately loses the game, but there is no penalty for leading out of turn in Misère Partout.

PLAYING OUT OF TURN

25. If the third hand plays before the second, the fourth hand can also play before the second.

26. If the third hand has not played, and the fourth hand plays before the second, the latter can be called on by the third hand to play his highest or lowest card of the suit led or, if he has none, to trump or not to trump the trick.

In **Boston** and **Solo Whist**, if an adversary of the single player plays out of turn, the bidder can call on the adversary who has not played to play his highest or lowest of the suit led, or to win or not to win the trick. If the adversary of a Misère player leads or plays out of turn, the bidder can immediately claim the stakes. In Solo Whist, the individual player in fault has to pay for himself and his partners.

ABANDONED HANDS

27. If all four players throw their cards on the table, face upwards, no more play of that hand is permitted. The result of the hand, as then claimed or admitted, is established, provided that if a revoke is discovered the revoke penalty attaches.

In **Solo Whist**, if the bidder abandons his hand, he and his partner, if any, have to pay the stakes and settle for all over-tricks as if they had lost all the remaining tricks. If a player, not the bidder, abandons his hand, his partner or partners can demand the hand be played out with the abandoned hand exposed and liable to be called by the adversary. If they defeat the call, they win nothing, but the player who abandoned his hand has to pay the caller just as if he had been successful. If the partner or partners of the exposed hand lose, they have to pay their share of the losses.

REVOKING

28. A revoke is a renounce in error that is not corrected in time. A player renounces in error when he is holding one or more cards of the suit led and plays a card of a different suit.

A renounce in error can be corrected by the player who makes it, before the trick in which it occurs has been turned and quitted, unless either he or his partner, whether in his right turn or otherwise, has led or played to the following trick.

29. If a player corrects his mistake in time to save a revoke, the card improperly played by him is liable to be called; any player or

players who have played after him can withdraw their cards and substitute others, whereby the withdrawn cards are not liable to be called.

In *Boston,* if the bidder revokes and corrects himself in time, there is no penalty unless an adversary has played after him, in which case the bidder's card can be claimed as exposed. The player who followed him can then amend his play. If a player opposed to the bidder discovers and corrects a revoke made by himself or any of his partners, the bidder can either claim the card played in error as exposed or call on the revoking player for his highest or lowest of the suit led.

30. The penalty for revoking is transfer of two tricks from the revoking side to their adversaries; it can be enforced for as many revokes as occur during the hand. The revoking side cannot win the game in that hand; if both sides revoke, neither side can win the game in that hand.

In *Cayenne* and *Solo Whist,* as a penalty for a revoke, the adversaries of the revoking player can take from him three tricks, or deduct the value of three tricks from his score, or add the value of three tricks to their own score. The revoking players cannot score slams or game that hand. All slams have to be made independently of the revoke penalty.

In *Boston,* the penalty for a revoke on the part of the bidder is that he is put in for one trick, and has to pay four red counters into the next pool. If an adversary of the bidder revokes, he has to pay four red counters into the next pool, and he and his partners have to pay the bidder as if he had been successful. When a revoke is discovered in Boston, the hands are usually abandoned; however, the cards should be shown to the table, so that each player can be satisfied that no other revoke has been made. A player who revokes in Misère Partout pays five red counters to each of his adversaries, and the hands are then abandoned.

31. The revoking player and his partner can require the hand in which the revoke has been made be played out, and score all points made by them up to the score of six.

In *Boston,* the hands are abandoned after the revoke is claimed and proved.

In *Cayenne,* the revoking players have to stop at nine.

In *Solo Whilst,* the revoking players have to pay all the red counters involved in the call, whether they win or lose, but can play the hand out in order to save over-tricks. If the caller or his partner revokes, the two players must jointly pay the losses involved; however, if an adversary of the caller revokes, he individually has to pay the entire loss unless he can show that the callers would have won in spite of the revoke. If he is able to do this, his partners have to stand their share of the losses, but the revoking player individually has to pay for the three tricks taken as the revoke penalty. If the single player revokes, either on solo or abundance, he loses the red counters involved in any case, but can play the hand out in order to save over-tricks. If the single player in a misère or a slam revokes, the hand is abandoned and he has to pay the stakes. If an adversary of a misère or a slam revokes, he individually has to pay the whole stakes.

32. At the end of a hand, the claimants of a revoke can search all the tricks. If the cards have been mixed, the claim can be urged and proved, if possible; however, no proof is necessary, and the revoke is established, if, after it has been claimed, the accused player or his partner mixes the cards before the cards have been examined to the satisfaction of the adversaries.

33. The revoke can be claimed at any time before the cards have been presented and cut for the following deal, but not thereafter.

MISCELLANEOUS

34. Anyone, during the play of a trick and before the cards have been touched for the purpose of gathering them together, can demand that the players draw their cards.

35. If anyone, before his partner plays, calls attention in any way to the trick or the score, the adversary who is last to play to the trick can require the offender's partner to play his highest or lowest of the suit led, or, if he has none, to trump or not to trump the trick.

36. If any player says, 'I can win the rest,' 'The rest are ours,' 'We have the game,' or words to that effect, his partner's cards have to be laid on the table and are liable to be called.

37. When a trick has been turned and quitted, it must not again be seen until after the hand has been played. A violation of this law subjects the offender's side to the same penalty as in the case of a lead out of turn.

In *Boston, Cayenne* and *Solo Whist*, it remains the custom to permit looking at the last trick, except in Misères. The penalty in a misère game is the same as for a lead out of turn.

38. If a player is lawfully called on to play the highest or lowest of a suit, or to trump or not to trump a trick, or to lead a suit, and unnecessarily fails to comply, he is liable to the same penalty as if he had revoked.

39. In all cases in which a penalty has been incurred, the offender has to await the decision of the adversaries. If either of them, with or without his partner's consent, demands a penalty to which they

are entitled, this decision is final. If the wrong adversary demands a penalty, or a wrong penalty is demanded, no penalty can be enforced.

The following rules belong to the established code of Whist Etiquette. They are formulated with a view to discouraging and repressing specific improprieties of conduct, therein pointed out, which are not addressed in the laws.

1. No conversation should be indulged in during the play, except conversarion that is allowed in the laws of the game.

2. No player should in any way whatsoever give any intimation as to the state of either his hand or the game, or of either approval or disapproval of a play.

3. No player should lead until the preceding trick is turned and quitted.

4. No player should, after having led a winning card, draw a card from his hand for another lead until his partner has played to the current trick.

5. No player should play a card in any way so as to specifically call attention to it; nor should he demand that the cards be placed in order to attract the attention of his partner.

6. No player should deliberately incur a penalty because he is willing to pay it; nor should he make a second revoke in order to conceal one previously made.

7. No player should take advantage of information imparted by his partner through a breach of etiquette.

8. No player should object to referring a disputed question of fact to a bystander who professes himself to be uninterested in the result of the game and able to decide the question.

9. Bystanders should not in any way call attention to or give any intimation about the play or the state of the game during the play of a hand. They should not look over the hand of a player without his permission; nor should they walk around the table in order to look at the various hands.

ERRONEOUS SCORES

Any error in the trick score can be corrected before the last card has been dealt in the following deal; or, if the error occurs in the last hand of a game or rubber, it can be corrected before the score is agreed to. Errors in other scores can be corrected at any time before the final score of the game or rubber is agreed to.

BIDDING

In *Boston* or *Solo Whist,* any player who makes a bid has to stand by it, and either play or pay. If he makes a bid in error and corrects himself, he has to stand by the first bid unless he is overcalled, whereby he can either amend his bid or pass.

— —

ENGLISH-WHIST LAWS

THE RUBBER
1. The rubber is the best of three games. If the first two games are won by the same players, the third game is not played.

SCORING
2. A game consists of five points. Each trick, above six, counts one point.

3. Honours, that is, Ace, King, Queen, and Knave of trumps, are reckoned as follows.

If a player and his partner, either separately or conjointly, hold:

I.   The four honours, they score four points.

II. Any three honours, they score two points.

III. Only two honours, they do not score.

4. The players who, at the commencement of a deal, are at the score of four, cannot score honours.

5. The penalty for a revoke (*see* Law 72) takes precedence over all other scores. Tricks score next, and honours last.

6. Honours, unless claimed before the trump card of the following deal is turned up, cannot be scored.

7. To score honours is not sufficient: they have to be called at the end of the hand, and if so called, they can be scored at any time during the game.

8. The winners gain:

I.   A treble, or game of three points, when their adversaries have not scored.

II. A double, or game of two points, when their adversaries have scored less than three.

III. A single, or game of one point, when their adversaries have scored three or four.

9. The winners of the rubber gain two points (commonly called the rubber points), in addition to the value of their games.

10. If the rubber has consisted of three games, the value of the losers' game is deducted from the gross number of points gained by their opponents.

11. If an erroneous score is proved, the mistake can be corrected

before the conclusion of the game in which it occurred, and that game is not concluded until the trump card of the following deal has been turned up.

12. If an erroneous score, which affects the amount of the rubber, is proved, the mistake can be rectified at any time during the rubber.

CUTTING

13. The Ace is the lowest card.

14. In all cases, everyone has to cut from the same pack.

15. If a player exposes more than one card, he has to cut again.

FORMATION OF TABLE

16. If there are more than four candidates, the players are selected by way of cutting; the candidates who are first in the room have the preference. The four who cut the lowest cards play first, and cut again to decide on partners. The two lowest play against the two highest, and the lowest is the dealer, who has choice of cards and seats, and, having once made his selection, has to abide by it.

17. When there are more than six candidates, the ones who cut the two next-lowest cards belong to the table, which is complete with six players. When one of these six players retires, the candidate who cut the next-lowest card has a prior right to any aftercomer to enter the table.

CUTTING CARDS OF EQUAL VALUE

18. Two players who cut cards of equal value, unless the cards are the two highest, cut again; if they are the two lowest, a fresh cut is necessary in order to decide which of these two deals.

19. Three players who cut cards of equal value cut again; if the fourth (or remaining) card is the highest, the two lowest of the new cut are partners, and the lower of these two is the dealer. If the fourth card is the lowest, the two highest are partners, and the original lowest is the dealer.

CUTTING OUT

20. At the end of a rubber, if admission is claimed by any one candidate, or by two candidates, he who has, or they who have, played a greater number of consecutive rubbers than the others is, or are, out; however, when all have played the same number, they have to cut to decide on the outgoers; the highest are out.

ENTRY AND RE-ENTRY

21. A candidate who wishes to enter a table has to declare his intention before any of the players have cut a card, for the purpose of either commencing a fresh rubber or cutting out.

22. In the formation of fresh tables, the candidates who have neither belonged to nor played at any other table have the prior right of entry; the others decide their right of admission by cutting.

23. Anyone who quits a table before the conclusion of a rubber can, with the consent of the other three players, appoint a substitute in his absence during that rubber.

24. A player who cuts into one table while belonging to another loses his right of re-entry to the latter, and takes his chance of cutting in, as if he were a fresh candidate.

25. If anyone breaks up a table, the remaining players have the prior right to him of entry to any other table, and if there are not sufficient vacancies at the other table to admit all these candidates, they settle their precedence by cutting.

SHUFFLING

26. The pack must be neither shuffled below the table nor shuffled so that the face of any card can be seen.

27. The pack must not be shuffled during the play of the hand.

28. A pack, having been played with, must be neither shuffled by dealing it into packets nor shuffled across the table.

29. Each player has a right to shuffle, once only, except as provided in Rule 32, before a deal, after a false cut [*see* Law 34], or when a new deal [*see* Law 37] has occurred.

30. The dealer's partner has to collect the cards for the ensuing deal, and has the first right to shuffle that pack.

31. Each player after shuffling has to place the cards properly collected, and face downwards, to the left of the player who is about to deal.

32. The dealer always has the right to shuffle last; however, if a card or cards are seen during his shuffling, or while he is giving the pack to be cut, he can be compelled to re-shuffle.

THE DEAL

33. Each player deals in his turn, and the right of dealing goes to the left.

34. The player on the dealer's right cuts the pack, and, in dividing it, must not leave fewer than four cards in either packet. If, in cutting, or in replacing one of the two packets on the other, a card is exposed, or if there is any confusion of the cards, or a doubt as to the exact place in which the pack was divided, there has to be a fresh cut.

35. When a player whose duty it is to cut has once separated the pack, he cannot alter his intention; he can neither re-shuffle nor re-cut the cards.

36. When the pack is cut, if the dealer shuffles the cards, he loses his deal.

A NEW DEAL

37. There has to be a new deal:
I. If, during a deal, or during the play of a hand, the pack is proved to be incorrect or imperfect.
II. If any card, except the last, is faced in the pack.

38. If, during dealing, a card is exposed by the dealer or his partner, and neither of the adversaries has touched the cards, the latter can claim a new deal. A card exposed by either adversary gives that claim to the dealer, provided his partner has not touched a card. If a new deal does not take place, the exposed card cannot be called.

39. If, during dealing, a player touches any of his cards, the adversaries can do the same, without losing their privilege of claiming a new deal, should chance give them this option.

40. If, during dealing, one of the last cards is exposed, and the dealer turns up the trump before there is reasonable time for his adversaries to decide about a fresh deal, they do not thereby lose their privilege.

41. If a player, while dealing, looks at the trump card, his adversaries have a right to see it, and can exact a new deal.

42. If a player takes into the hand dealt to him a card that belongs to the other pack, the adversaries, when the error is discovered, can decide whether or not they will have a fresh deal.

A MISDEAL

43. A misdeal loses the deal.

44. It is a misdeal:
I. Unless the cards are dealt into four packets, one at a time in regular rotation, beginning with the player to the dealer's left.
II. If the dealer places the last (that is, the trump) card, face downwards, on his own or any other pack.
III. If the trump card does not come in its regular order to the dealer, but he does not lose his deal if the pack is proved to be imperfect.
IV. If a player has fourteen cards, and any of the other three players have fewer than thirteen.
V. If the dealer is under the impression he has made a mistake, and counts either the cards on the table or the remainder of the pack.

    VI. If the dealer deals two cards at once, or two cards to the same hand, and then deals a third card; however, if, before dealing that third card, the dealer can, by altering the position of one card only, rectify this error, he can do so, except as provided in the second paragraph of this Law.

    VII.If the dealer omits to have the pack cut to him, and the adversaries discover the error, before the trump card is turned up, and before looking at their cards, but not after they have done so.

45. A misdeal does not lose the deal if, during the dealing, either of the adversaries touches the cards before the dealer's partner has done so, but if the latter has first interfered with the cards, notwithstanding that either or both of the adversaries have subsequently done the same, the deal is lost.

46. If three players have their right number of cards, if the fourth player has fewer than thirteen cards and does not discover this deficiency until he has played any of his cards, the deal stands good. If he has played, he is as answerable for any revoke he might have made as if the missing card, or cards, had been in his hand; he can search the other pack for it, or them.

47. If a pack, during or after a rubber, is proved to be incorrect or imperfect, this proof does not alter any past score, game or rubber; the hand in which the imperfection was detected is null and void, and the dealer deals again.

48. Anyone who deals out of turn, or with the adversary's cards, can be stopped before the trump card is turned up, after which the game has to proceed as if no mistake had been made.

49. A player cannot shuffle, cut or deal for his partner, without the permission of his opponents.

50. If the adversaries interrupt a dealer while he is dealing, by either questioning the score or asserting that it is not his deal, and fail to establish this claim, should a misdeal occur, the dealer can deal again.

51. If a player takes his partner's deal and misdeal, the latter is liable to the usual penalty, and the adversary then deals who is next in rotation to the player who ought to have dealt.

THE TRUMP CARD

52. The dealer, when it is his turn to play to the first trick, should take the trump card into his hand; if it is left on the table after the first trick is turned and quitted, it is liable to be called. His partner can at any time remind him of the liability.

53. After the dealer has taken the trump card into his hand, it

cannot be asked for; a player who names it at any time during the play of that hand is liable to have his highest or lowest trump called.

54. If the dealer takes the trump card into his hand before it is his turn to play, he can be requested to lay it on the table; if he shows a wrong card, this card may be called, as also a second, a third, and so on, until the trump card is produced.

55. If the dealer declares himself to be unable to recollect the trump card, his highest or lowest trump can be called at any time during that hand, and unless it causes him to revoke, it has to be played; the call can be repeated, but not changed, that is, from highest to lowest, or vice versa, until this card is played.

CARDS LIABLE TO BE CALLED

56. All exposed cards are liable to be called, and have to be left on the table, but a card is not an exposed card when it is dropped on the floor, or elsewhere below the table. The following are exposed cards:

I.   Two or more cards played at once.
II. Any card dropped with its face upwards, or in any way exposed on or above the table, even though it is snatched up so quickly that no one can name it.

57. If anyone plays to an imperfect trick the best card on the table, or leads one that is a winning card as against his adversaries, and then leads again, or plays several of these winning cards, one after the other, without waiting for his partner to play, the latter can be called on to win, if he can, the first or any other of these tricks, and the other cards thereby improperly played are exposed cards.

58. If a player, or players, who is/are under the impression that the game is lost—or won—or for other reasons—throws his/their cards on the table face upwards, these cards are exposed, and are liable to be called, each player's cards by the adversary; however, if one player alone retains his hand, he cannot be forced to abandon it.

59. If all four players throw their cards on the table face upwards, the hands are abandoned, and no one can again take up his cards. If this general exhibition shows that the game might have been saved, or won, neither claim can be entertained, unless a revoke is established. The revoking players are then liable to the following penalties: they cannot under any circumstances win the game by the result of that hand, and the adversaries can add three to their score, or deduct three from the score of the revoking players.

60. A card detached from the rest of the hand so as to be named is liable to be called; however, if the adversary names a wrong card,

he is liable to have a suit called when he or his partner has the lead.

61. If a player who has rendered himself liable to have the highest or lowest of a suit called fails to play as requested, or if when he is called on to lead one suit he leads another, and has in his hand one or more cards of that suit demanded, he incurs the penalty of a revoke.

62. If any player leads out of turn, his adversaries can either call the card erroneously led or call a suit from him or his partner when it is next the turn of either of them to lead.

63. If any player leads out of turn, and the three other players have followed him, the trick is complete, and the error cannot be rectified; however, if only the second, or the second and third, have played to the false lead, their cards, when the mistake is discovered, are taken back; there is no penalty against anyone, excepting the original offender, whose card can be called; or he, or his partner, when either of them next has the lead, can be compelled to play any suit that is demanded by the adversaries.

64. In no case can a player be compelled to play a card that would oblige him to revoke.

65. The call of a card can be repeated until the card has been played.

66. If a player who is called on to lead a suit has none of it, the penalty is paid.

CARDS PLAYED IN ERROR, OR NOT PLAYED TO A TRICK

67. If the third hand plays before the second, the fourth hand can play before his partner.

68. If the third hand has not played, and the fourth hand plays before his partner does, the latter can be called on to win, or not to win the trick.

69. If anyone omits playing to a former trick, and this error is not discovered until he has played to the next, the adversaries can claim a new deal. Should they decide that the deal stands good, the surplus card at the end of the hand is considered to have been played to the imperfect trick, but does not constitute a revoke therein.

70. If anyone plays two cards to the same trick, or mixes his trump, or other card, with a trick to which it does not properly belong, and the mistake is not discovered until the hand is played out, he is answerable for all consequent revokes he might have made. If, during the play of the hand, the error is detected, the tricks can be counted face downwards, in order to ascertain whether there is among them a card too many. If this is the case, they can be

searched, and the card can be restored; the player is, however, liable for all revokes he might meanwhile have made.

THE REVOKE

71. The revoke is when a player who holds one or more cards of the suit led plays a card of a different suit.

72. The penalty for a revoke:

I.   Is at the option of the adversaries, who at the end of the hand can either take three tricks from the revoking player or deduct three points from his score; alternatively, they can add three to their own score.

II. Can be claimed for as many revokes as occur during the hand.

III. Is applicable to the score of only the game in which it occurs.

IV. Cannot be divided; that is, a player cannot add one or two to his own score and deduct one or two from the revoking player.

V.   Takes precedence over every other score; for example, the claimants two, and their opponents nothing; the former add three to their score, and thereby win a treble game, even if the latter have made thirteen tricks and held four honours.

73. A revoke is established if the trick in which it occurs is turned and quitted, that is, the hand removed from that trick after it has been turned face downwards on the table, or if either the revoking player or his partner, whether in his right turn or otherwise, leads or plays to the following trick.

74. A player can ask his partner whether he does not have a card of the suit that he has renounced. If the question is asked before the trick is turned and quitted, subsequent turning and quitting does not establish the revoke, and the error can be corrected, unless the question is answered in the negative, or unless the revoking player or his partner has led or played to the following trick.

75. At the end of the hand, the claimants of a revoke can search all the tricks.

76. If a player discovers his mistake in time to save a revoke, the adversaries, whenever they think fit, can call the card thereby played in error, or can require him to play his highest or lowest card to the trick in which he has renounced. Any player or players who have played after him can withdraw their cards and substitute others, whereby the withdrawn cards are not liable to be called.

77. If a revoke is claimed, and the accused player or his partner mixes the cards before they have been sufficiently examined by the adversaries, the revoke is established. The mixing of the cards only renders the proof of a revoke difficult, but does not prevent the claim and possible establishment of the penalty.

78. A revoke cannot be claimed after the cards have been cut for the following deal.

79. The revoking player and his partner can, under all circumstances, require the hand in which the revoke has been detected to be played out.

80. If a revoke occurs, is claimed and is proved, bets on the odd trick or on the amount of the score have to be decided by way of the actual state of the latter, after the penalty is paid.

81. If the players on both sides subject themselves to the penalty of one or more revokes, neither can win the game; each is punished at the discretion of his adversary.

82. In whatever way the penalty is enforced, under no circumstances can a player win the game by the result of the hand during which he has revoked; he cannot score more than four. (*See* Law 61.)

CALLING FOR NEW CARDS

83. Any player (when he pays for new cards) before, but not after, the pack is cut for the deal, can call for fresh cards. He must call for two new packs, of which the dealer takes his choice.

GENERAL RULES

84. When a player and his partner have an option of exacting from their adversaries one of two penalties, they should agree who is to make the election, but must not consult with each other as to which of the two penalties it is advisable to exact. If they do consult, they lose their right, and if either of them, with or without the consent of his partner, demands a penalty to which he is entitled, this decision is final.

[This rule does not apply to exacting the penalties for a revoke: partners have in that case, the right to consult.]

85. Anyone during the play of a trick, or after the four cards are played, and before, but not after, they are touched for the purpose of gathering them together, can demand that the cards be placed before their respective players.

86. If anyone, before his partner plays, calls attention to the trick— by saying that it is his, or by naming his card, or, without being required so to do, by drawing it towards him—the adversaries can require that opponent's partner to play the highest or lowest of the suit then led, or to win or lose the trick.

87. In all cases in which a penalty has been incurred, the offender is bound to give reasonable time for the decision of his adversaries.

88. If a bystander makes any remark whereby the attention of a player or players is called to an oversight that affects the score, he is

liable to be called on, by the players only, to pay the stakes and all bets on that game or rubber.

89. A bystander, by agreement among the players, can decide any question.

90. If a card or cards is or are torn or marked, either they have to be replaced by agreement or new cards have to be called at the expense of the table.

91. Any player can demand to see the last trick turned, and no more. Under no circumstances can more than eight cards be seen during the play of the hand, that is, the four cards on the table that have not been turned and quitted, and the last trick turned.

ETIQUETTE OF WHIST

The following rules belong to the established Etiquette of Whist. They are not called laws, because it is difficult—in some cases impossible—to apply any penalty to their infraction, and the only remedy is to cease to play with players who habitually disregard them.

Two packs of cards are invariably used at Clubs; if possible, this should be adhered to.

Anyone who has the lead and several winning cards to play should not draw a second card out of his hand until his partner has played to the first trick, because this act is a distinct intimation that the former has played a winning card.

No intimation whatever, by word or gesture, should be given by a player as to the state of either his hand or the game.

A player who requests the cards to be placed, or who demands to see the last trick, should make his request or demand for his own information only, and not in order to invite the attention of his partner.

No player should object to refer to a bystander who professes himself to be uninterested in the game and able to decide any disputed question of facts as to who played any specific card—whether honours were claimed although not scored, or vice versa.

It is unfair to revoke deliberately, and having made a revoke, a player is not justified in making a second in order to conceal the first.

Until the players have made bets as they wish, bets should not be made with bystanders.

Bystanders should make no remark; nor should they by word or gesture give any intimation of the state of the game until it is concluded and scored, and nor should they walk around the table in order to look at the various hands.

No one should look over the hand of a player against whom he is betting.

— —

DUMMY

Dummy is played by three players.

One hand, called Dummy's, lies exposed on the table.

The laws are the same as those of Whist, with the following exceptions.

I.   Dummy deals at the commencement of each rubber.

II. Dummy is not liable to the penalty for a revoke, because his adversaries see his cards; if he revokes, and the error is not discovered until the trick is turned and quitted, it stands good.

III. Because Dummy is blind and deaf, his partner is not liable to any penalty for an error whereby he can gain no advantage. Therefore, he can expose some or all of his cards—or can declare that he has the game, or trick, and so on, without incurring any penalty. If, however, he leads from Dummy's hand when he should lead from his own, or vice versa, a suit can be called from the hand that ought to have led.

— —

DOUBLE DUMMY

Double Dummy is played by two players, each of whom has a Dummy or exposed hand for his partner. The laws of the game do not differ from Dummy Whist, except in the special Law that there is no misdeal, because the deal is a disadvantage.

THE POKER FAMILY

— —

Poker is not the founding game but simply the most famous representative of a very ancient and always very popular family of games, all of which can be traced to one source: the old French game of Gilet, which was undoubtedly of Italian origin, and perhaps a variety of Primero. Gilet was changed to Brelan in the time of Charles IX, and although Brelan is no longer played, the word continues to be used in all French games to signify triplets, and 'brelan-carré' is the common French term for four of a kind in *le poker Amercain*. From Brelan can be traced the French games of Bouillotte and Ambigu, and the English game of Brag; however, the game of poker, as first played in the United States: five cards to each player from a twenty-card pack, is undoubtedly the Persian game of *as nas*.

The peculiar and distinguishing characteristic of Poker is well described by Seymour in his chapter about 'Brag', in the 'Court Gamester' of 1719: 'The endeavour to impose on the judgment of the rest who play, and particularly on the person who chiefly offers to oppose you, by boasting or bragging of the cards in your hand. Those who by fashioning their looks and gestures, can give a proper air to their actions, as will so deceive an unskilful antagonist, that sometimes a pair of fives, trays or deuces, in such a hand, with the advantage of his composed countenance, and subtle manner of overawing the other, shall out-brag a much greater hand, and win the stakes, with great applause and laughter on his side from the whole company.'

In quite a number of card games, the feature of pairs, triplets, sequences and flushes is retained, but the element of brag or bluff is omitted, so these games can hardly be considered to be fullblooded members of the poker family. Whiskey Poker, for example, truly has little or nothing in common with the true spirit of poker, and is simply the very ancient game of Commerce, which is played with five cards instead of three. The descriptions of this game in the earliest Hoyles manual betray its French origin, particularly in the use of the piquet pack, in the French custom of cutting to the left and dealing to the right, and in the use of the words 'brelan' and 'tricon'. In later descriptions of the 'new form' of Commerce, written in about 1835, we find 52 cards are used and dealt from left to right, and that the names of the combinations are changed to 'pairs-royal', 'sequences' and 'flushes'.

There seems to be little or nothing modern in the game of Poker except for the increased number of cards dealt to each player, whereby it is made possible for one to hold double combinations, such as two pairs, triplets with a pair, and so on. The old games were all played with three cards only, and the 'brelan-carré', or four of a kind, could be made only by combining the three cards held by the player who had the card that was sometimes turned up on the talon, or the remainder of the pack. The blind, the straddle, the raise, the bluff, table stakes and freeze-out are all to be found in Bouillotte, which flourished in the time of the French Revolution, and the 'draw' from the remainder of the pack existed in the old French game of Ambigu.

Poker was first mentioned in print in *Green's Reformed Gambler*, which contains a description of a game of poker played on a river steamer in June 1834. The author undertook a series of investigations with a view to discovering the origin of poker, the results of which were published in the *New York Sun* on 22 May 1904. It would seem that poker came from Persia to the United States by way of New Orleans. The French settlers in Louisiana, recognising the similarity between the combinations held in the newcomer from the East, *as nas*, and the combinations which they were already familiar in their own game of poque, called the Persian game poque, instead of *as nas*; the word 'poker' seems to be nothing but a mispronunciation of the French term, whereby it is divided into two syllables, as if it were 'po-que'.

There is no authoritative code of laws for the game of Poker, simply because the best clubs did not admit the game to their card rooms, and consequently decried the necessity for adopting any laws for its government. In the absence of any official code, the daily press was called on for hundreds of decisions every week. The author of this manual gathered and compared a great number of these newspaper rulings, and drew from them and other sources to form a brief code of poker laws, which will be found amply sufficient to cover all irregularities for which any penalty can be enforced, or that interfere with the rights of any individual player.

DRAW POKER

CARDS   Poker is played with a full pack of fifty-two cards that rank
A K Q J 10 9 8 7 6 5 4 3 2; the ace is the highest or lowest in play
  according to the wish of the holder, but ranks
below the deuce in cutting. In some localities a
special pack of sixty cards is used, whereby the
eight extra cards are elevens and twelves in each
suit, which rank above the ten and below the Jack.
It is very unusual to play Poker with two packs.

COUNTERS, OR CHIPS   Although counters not absolutely necessary, they are much more convenient than money. The most
common are red, white and blue circular chips, which should 'stack
up' accurately, so that equal numbers can be measured without
counting them. The red are usually worth five whites, and the blue
are worth five reds, or twenty-five whites. At the beginning of the
game, one player should act as banker, and be responsible for all
counters at the table. It is usual for each player to purchase, at the
beginning of the game, the equivalent of 100 white counters in
white, red and blue.

PLAYERS   Poker can be played by any number of people from two
to seven. When there are more than seven candidates for play, two
tables should be formed, unless the majority vote against it. In some
localities it is the custom for the dealer to take no cards when there
are eight players, because this is thought to make a better game than
two tables of only four players each. When the sixty-card pack is used,
eight players can take cards.

CUTTING   The players who will form the table, and their positions
at the beginning of the game, have to be decided by throwing
around a card to each candidate, face upwards, or by drawing cards
from an outspread pack. If there are more than eight candidates,
the four who cut the highest cards should play together at one table,
and the others at another table. If there is an even number of candidates, the tables divide evenly, but if the number is odd, the smaller
table is formed by the candidates who cut the highest cards.
   When the table is formed, the pack has to be shuffled and spread,
and positions drawn for. The player who cuts the lowest card has the

choice of seats, and has to deal the first hand. The player who cuts the next lowest has the next choice, and so on, until the players all are seated.

TIES   If the first cut does not decide, the players who tie have to cut again. If two or more players cut cards of equal value, the new cut will decide nothing but the tie, because even if one of the players who cuts to decide a tie draws a card lower than one previously cut by another player, the original low cannot be deprived of his right. For example, there are six players.

The first cut is:

5 ♠ FIVE	8 ♣ EIGHT	J ♦ JACK	7 ♥ SEVEN	K ♣ KING	8 ♦ EIGHT

The second cut is:

4 ♥ FOUR					2 ♣ TWO

The 5 and 7 have the first and second choice of seats, the 2 and 4 the third and fourth choice.

PLAYERS' POSITIONS   There are only three distinctive positions at the poker table: the *dealer*, the *pone* and the *age*. The pone is the player on the dealer's right, and the age is the one on his left.

STAKES   Before play begins, or a card is dealt, the value of the counters has to be decided, and a *limit* has to be agreed on. There are four limitations in Draw Poker, and they govern or fix the maximum of the four main stakes: the blind, the straddle, the ante, and the bet or raise.

The *blind* is the amount put up by the age before he sees anything, and should be limited to one white counter, because the blind is the smallest stake in the game. In some places it is permissible for the age to make the blind any amount he pleases within half the betting limit; however, this practice is a direct violation of the principles of the game, whereby it is required that the amount of the blind will bear a fixed proportion to the limit of the betting.

The *straddle* is a double blind, sometimes put up by the player to the left of the age, and similar to the blind, without seeing anything. This enables the player on the left of the straddler to double again, or put up four times the amount of the original blind. This straddling process is usually limited to one-fourth of the betting limit; that is, if the betting limit is fifty counters, the doubling of the blind has to cease when a player puts up sixteen, because another double would carry it to thirty-two, which would be more than half the limit for a bet or raise.

The *ante* is the amount put up by each player after he has seen his cards, but before he draws to improve his hand. The terms 'ante' and 'blind' are often confused. The blind is a compulsory stake, and has to be put up before the player has seen anything. He does not even know whether or not he will be dealt a foul hand, or whether it will be a misdeal. He has not even seen the cards cut. The ante, on the other hand, is a voluntary bet, and is a sort of entrance fee, which is paid before the hand is complete but after the first part of it has been seen. The ante is always twice the amount of the blind, whatever that might be. If the blind has been increased by the process of straddling, the ante has to be twice the amount of the last straddle, but must not exceed the betting limit. This is why the straddles are limited.

The largest *bet*, or *raise*, that a player is allowed to make is usually known as *the limit*. This limit is not the greatest amount that can be bet on one hand, but is the maximum amount by which one player can increase his bet over that of another player. For example, if no one has bet, A can bet the limit on his hand; B can then put up a similar amount, which is called *seeing* him, and can then *raise* him any other sum within the limit fixed for betting. If B raises the limit, it is obvious that he has placed in the pool twice the amount of the betting limit, but his *raise* over A's bet is within the betting limit. If another player raises B again, he is putting up three times the limit: A's bet, B's raise, and his own raise.

In the absence of any definite arrangement, it is usual to make the betting limit fifty times the amount of the blind; that is, if the value of the blind, or one white counter, is five cents, the limit of a bet or raise will be two dollars and a half, or two blue counters. This fixes the ante at two white counters, or ten cents, in the absence of straddles, and limits the straddling to the fourth player from the age, or sixteen white counters. This proportion makes for a very fair game, and gives a player some opportunity to vary his betting according to his estimate of the value of his hand. When the blind is five cents, the ante ten, and the limit twenty-five, the game ceases to be Poker, and becomes a species of *showdown*. It is universally admitted by good judges that a player can lose more money at 25 cent show-down than he can at two-and-a-half Poker.

There are several other variations in the way of arranging the stakes and the betting limits, but they will be better understood after the game itself has been described.

DEALING When the age has put up the amount of the blind, and the cards have been shuffled by any player who chooses to avail himself of the privilege, the dealer last, they are presented to the pone to be cut. The pone can either cut them or signify that he does not wish to do so by tapping the pack with his knuckles. If the pone declines to cut, no other player can insist on his doing so, nor do it for him. Beginning on his left, the dealer distributes the cards face downwards, one at a time in rotation, until each player has received five cards. The deal passes to the left, and each player deals in turn.

IRREGULARITIES IN THE DEAL The following rules about the deal should be strictly observed.

If any card is found faced in the pack, the dealer has to deal again. If the dealer, or the wind, turns over any card, the player to whom it is dealt has to take it; however, the same player cannot be compelled to take two exposed cards. If this combination occurs, there has to be a fresh deal by the same dealer. If the player exposes his cards himself, he has no remedy.

If any player receives more or fewer than his correct number of cards, and discovers the error before he looks at any card in his hand, or lifts it from the table, he can demand a fresh deal if no bet has been made; alternatively, he can ask the dealer to give him another from the pack if he has too few, or to draw a card if he has too many. Cards so drawn must not be exposed, but should be placed on the bottom of the pack.

If the number of the hands dealt does not agree with the number of players, there has to be a new deal.

If two or more cards are dealt at a time, the dealer can take back the card or cards improperly dealt if he discovers the error before he deals to the next player; otherwise, there has to be a new deal.

A misdeal does not lose the deal. The misdealer has to deal again.

If a player takes up his hand, or looks at any card in it, he is not entitled to any remedy. If he has more or fewer than the proper number of cards, his hand is foul and has to be abandoned, whereby the player forfeits any interest he might have in that deal, and any stake he might have put up on that hand. In all gambling venues, the invariable rule is to call a short hand foul, although there should be no objection to playing against a player who has only four cards, which cannot be increased to five, even by the draw.

STRADDLING During the deal, or at any time before he looks at any card in his hand, the player to the left of the age can *straddle the blind* by putting up double the amount put up by the age. The only privilege this secures to the straddler is that of having the last *say* as to whether or not he will make good his ante and draw cards. If he refuses to straddle, no other player can do so, but if he strad-dles, the player on his left can straddle him again by doubling the amount he puts up, which will be four times the amount of the blind. This will open the privilege to the next player on the left again, and so on until the limit of straddling is reached, but if one player refuses to straddle, no other following him can do so. Good players seldom or never straddle, because its only effect is to increase the amount of the ante.

METHOD OF PLAYING   When the cards are dealt, the players take up and examine their hands. The careful poker player always 'spreads' his cards before he takes them up, to be sure that he has neither more nor fewer than five, and he lifts them in such a way that the palm and fingers of his right hand conceal the face

SPREADING   SQUEEZING

of the first card, while the thumb of the left hand separates the others just enough to enable him to read the index or 'squeezer' marks on the edges.

The object of this examination is to ascertain the value of the hand dealt to him, and to see whether or not it is worthwhile trying to improve it by discarding specific cards and drawing others in their place. The player should not only be thoroughly familiar with the relative value of the various combinations that can be held at Poker; he should have some idea of the chances for and against better combinations being held by other players, and should also know the odds against improving any given combination by drawing to it.

The value of this technical knowledge will be obvious when it is remembered that a player might have a hand dealt to him that he knows is comparatively worthless as it is, and the chances for improv-ing it are only one in twelve, but he must bet on at odds of one in three, or abandon it. This proceeding would evidently be a losing game, because if the experiment were tried twelve times, the player would win once only, and would lose eleven times. This would be paying eleven dollars to win three; however, poker players are continually doing this.

RANK OF THE HANDS The various combinations at Poker outrank each other in the following order, beginning with the lowest. Cards that have a star over them add nothing to the value of the hand, and can be discarded. The figures on the right are the odds against this hand's being dealt to any individual player.

Five cards of various suits, not in sequence, and without a pair.

Even

One Pair. Two cards of one kind, and three useless cards.

34 to 25

Two Pairs. Two of one kind, two of another kind, and one useless card.

20 to 1

Threes. Three of one kind, and two useless cards.

46 to 1

Straight. All five cards in sequence, but of various suits.

254 to 1

Flush. All five cards of one suit, but not in sequence.

508 to 1

Full Hand. Three of one kind, two of another kind, and no useless cards.

693 to 1

Fours. Four cards of one kind, and one useless card.

4164 to 1

Straight Flush. Five cards of the same suit, in sequence with each other.

72192 to 1

Royal Flush. A straight flush that is ace high.

649739 to 1

When hands are of the same rank, their relative value is determined by the denomination of the cards they contain. For example, a hand without a pair, sequence or flush is called by its highest card: 'ace high' or 'Jack high', as the case may be. As between two of these hands, the one that contains the highest card would be the better, but either would be outclassed by a hand that has a pair in it, however small. A hand that has a pair of nines in it would outrank one that had a pair of sevens, even though the cards that accompanied the nines were only a deuce, three and four, and the ones that had the sevens were an ace, King and Queen. But if the pairs are alike in both hands, such as tens, the highest card outside the pair decides the rank of the hands, and if these are also alike, the next card, or perhaps the fifth, has to be considered. If the three odd cards in each hand are identical, the hands are a tie, and divide any pool to which each had a claim. Two flushes decide their rank in the same way. If both are ace and Jack high, and the third card in one is a nine, and in the other is an eight, the nine wins. In full hands, the rank of the triplets decides the value of the hand. Three Queens and a pair of deuces beats three Jacks and a pair of aces. In straights, the highest card of the sequence wins, not necessarily the highest card in the hand, because a player might have a sequence of A 2 3 4 5, which is only five high, and would be beaten by a sequence of 2 3 4 5 6. The ace has to either begin or end a sequence, because a player is not allowed to call this combination as Q K A 2 3 a straight.

It was evidently the intention of the people who invented Poker that the hands that are most difficult to obtain should be the best, and should outrank hands that occur more frequently. A glance at the table of odds on page 221 and above will show that this principle has been implemented with reference to the various denominations of hands; however, when we come to the members of the groups, the principle is violated. In hands that do not contain a pair, for example, ace high will beat Jack high, but it is much more common to hold ace high than Jack high; the exact proportion is 503 to 127. A hand of five cards that is only seven high but does not contain a pair is rarer than a flush; the proportion is 408 to 510. When we come to two pairs, we find the same inversion of probability and value. A player will hold 'aces up' that is a pair of aces and another pair that is inferior to aces twelve times as often as he will hold 'threes up'. In the opinion of the author, in all hands that do not contain a pair, 'seven high' should be the best instead of the lowest, and ace high should be the lowest. In hands that contain two pairs, 'threes up' should be the highest, and 'aces up' should be the lowest.

ECCENTRIC HANDS In addition to the regular poker hands, which are the ones already given, there are a few combinations that are played in some parts of the United States, especially in the south, either as a matter of local custom or by agreement. When any of these are played, it would be well for the person who is not accustomed to them to have a distinct understanding of exactly what combinations will be allowed and what hands they will beat. There are four of these eccentric hands as follows, and the figures on the right are the odds against their being dealt to any individual player.

Blaze. Five picture cards. Beats two pairs, but loses to three of a kind.

3008 to 1

Tiger. Must be seven high and deuce low, without a pair, sequence or flush. Beats a straight, but loses to a flush.

636 to 1

Skip, or Dutch Straight. Any sequence of alternate cards, of various suits. Beats two pairs and a blaze.

423 to 1

Round-the-Corner. Any straight in which the ace connects the top and bottom. Beats threes, but any regular straight beats it.

848 to 1

The rank of these extra hands has evidently been assigned by way of guesswork. The absurdity of their appraised value will be evident if we look at the first of them: the blaze, which is usually played to beat two pairs. Because it is impossible to have a blaze that does not contain two pairs of court cards, all that they beat is aces up or kings up. If it were ranked, as for other poker hands, by way of the difficulty of getting it, a blaze would beat a full hand.

All these hands are improperly placed in the scale of poker values, as will be seen by way of comparing the odds against them. In any games to which these eccentric hands are admitted, the rank of all the combinations would be as follows, if poker principles were followed throughout.

DENOMINATION	ODDS AGAINST
One pair	1/4 to 1
Two pairs	20 to 1
Three of a kind	46 to 1
Sequence or straight	254 to 1
Skip or Dutch straight	423 to 1
Flush	508 to 1
Tiger [Big or Little Dog]	636 to 1
Full hand	693 to 1
Round-the-corner straight	848 to 1
Blaze	3008 to 1
Four of a kind	4164 to 1
Straight flush	72,192 to 1
Royal flush [Ace high]	649,739 to 1

When the true rank of these eccentric hands is not allowed, what they will beat has to be decided according to local custom.

JOKER POKER, OR MISTIGRIS   It is not uncommon to leave the joker, or blank card, in the pack. The player to whom this card is dealt can call it anything he pleases. If he has a pair of aces, and the joker, he can call them three aces. If he has four clubs, and the joker, he can call them a flush, or he can make the joker fill out a straight. If he has four of a kind, and the joker, he can beat a royal flush by calling his hand five of a kind. In the case of ties, the hand that has the mistigris wins; that is, an ace and the joker will beat two aces.

A player who holds the joker can even call it a duplicate of a card that is already in his hand. For example, he might hold the A J 8 5 of hearts and the joker against the A K Q 7 3 of clubs. If he calls the joker the king of hearts, the club flush still beats him because it is queen next. He has to call it the ace, whereby his flush is made ace high.

PROBABILITIES When estimating the value of your hand as compared to that of any other player, before the draw, the theory of probabilities is of little or no use, and the calculations will vary with the number of players engaged. For example, if five are playing, someone should have two pairs every fourth deal, because in four deals, twenty hands will be given out. If seven are playing, it is probable that five of them will hold a pair of some kind before the draw. Unfortunately, these calculations are not of the slightest practical use to a poker player, because although three of a kind cannot be dealt to a player more than once in forty-five times on the average, it is quite a common occurrence for two players to have threes dealt to each of them at the same time. The considerations that must guide the player in judging the comparative value of his hand, both before and after the draw, have to be left until we come to the suggestions for good play.

THE ANTE The player to the left of the age is the one who has to make the first announcement of his opinion of his hand, unless he has straddled, in which case the player on the left of the last straddler has the first *'say'*. If he considers his hand good enough to draw to, let's say a pair of Kings, he has to place in the pool, or towards the centre of the table, double the amount of the blind, or of the last straddle, if any. This is called the ante, because it is made before playing the hand, whereas the blind is made before seeing it. The player is not restricted to double the amount of the blind or straddle: he can bet as much more as he pleases within the limit fixed at the beginning of the game. For example, if there has been only one straddle, he has to put up four white counters or pass out of the game for that deal. However, if he puts up the four, he can put up as many more as he pleases within the limit, which is two blues, or fifty whites. This is called *raising the ante*. If he does not care to pay twice the amount of the blind or straddle for the privilege of drawing cards in order to improve his hand, he has to throw his cards face downwards on the table in front of the player whose turn it will next be to deal. Reasonable time has to be allowed for a player to make his decision, but having made it, he has to abide by it; a hand once thrown down cannot be taken up again, and counters once placed in the pool, and the hand removed from them, cannot be taken out again, even though they were placed in the pool by mistake.

When the player who has the first say has made his decision, the player next to him on the left then has to decide. He has to put into the pool an amount equal to that deposited by the first player, or abandon his hand. Suppose there has been no straddle, and that all conclude to *stay*, as it is called. They each in turn put up two white counters until it comes to the age. The one white counter he has already put up as a blind belongs to the pool, but by adding one to it he can make his ante good, and draw cards, always provided no player has raised the ante. If any player has put more counters into the pool than the amount of the ante, all the other players have to put up a similar amount, or throw down their hands. Suppose five play, and A has the age. B antes two counters, and C puts up seven, the ante and a raise of five. If D and E come in, they have to put up seven counters also, and the age, A, has to put up six to make his ante good. It now comes to B, who has to either lose the two he has already put up or add five more to them. Let's suppose that D puts up the seven, and that E, the dealer, puts up twelve. This will force the age to put up eleven, B to put up ten, and C to put up five more. This will make each player's ante an equal amount: twelve counters, and they will then be ready to draw cards. No one can now raise the ante any further, because it is no one's turn to 'say'.

It will therefore be seen that every player in his turn can do one of three things, which are sometimes called the *a b c* of Poker: He can *Abdicate*, by throwing down his hand, and abandoning whatever money he has already placed in the pool; he can *Better*, by putting up more money than does any player before him, which is sometimes called 'going better'; or he can *Call*, by making his amount in the pool equal to the highest bet already made.

If any player increases the ante to such an extent that none of the other players care to call him, they naturally have to throw down their hands, and because there is no one to play against him, the one who made the last increase in the ante takes down all the counters in the pool. This is called *taking the pot*, and the cards are gathered, shuffled and dealt again, whereby the deal passes to the player who was the age.

DRAWING CARDS All the players who have made the ante good have the privilege of discarding, face downwards, as many cards as they please, in place of which they can draw others. The age has the first draw, and can take any number of cards from one to five, or can *stand pat*, refusing to draw any. A player cannot receive from the dealer more or fewer cards than he discards, so that if a person is allowed to play with a short hand, of four cards only, he will still have only four cards after the draw. If his hand was foul, it will remain so after the draw. In drawing, a player can keep or discard what cards he pleases. There is no rule to prevent his throwing away a pair of aces and keeping three clubs if he is so inclined; however, the general practice is for the player to retain whatever pairs or triplets he might have, and to draw to them. Four cards of a straight or a flush can be drawn to in the same way, and some players make a practice of drawing to one or two high cards, such as an ace and a king, when they have no other chance. Some hands offer opportunities to vary the draw.

For example, a player has dealt to him a small pair, but finds he also has four cards of a straight. He can discard three cards and  draw to the pair, or one card and draw to the straight, or two cards and keep his ace in the hope of making two good pairs aces up. The details of the best methods of drawing to various combinations will be discussed when we come to suggestions for good play.

In drawing cards, each player in turn who has made good his ante, beginning with the age, has to ask the dealer for the number of cards he wants. The demand has to be made so that every player can hear, because after the cards have been delivered by the dealer, no one has the right to be informed of how many cards any player drew. When the dealer comes to his own hand, he has to distinctly announce the number of cards he takes. He also has to inform any player who asks him how many cards he took, provided the question is put before the player who is asking it has made a bet, and it is put by a player who has made good his ante to draw cards.

In dealing the cards for the draw, the pack is not cut again, and the cards are dealt from the top, beginning where the deal before the draw left off. As each player asks for his cards, he has to discard the ones he wants replaced, and has to receive the entire number he asks for before the next player is helped. In some places, it is the custom for all players who have made good the ante to discard before any cards are given out. This is not good poker, because it prevents the dealer from seeing that the number discarded is equal to the number asked for. If any card is found faced in the pack, it has to be placed on the table among the discards. If any card is exposed by the dealer in giving out the cards, or is blown over by the wind before the player has touched it, the card must not be taken by the player under any circumstances, but has to be placed with the discards on the table. A player whose card is exposed in this way does not receive a card to take its place until all the other players have been helped. [The object of this rule is to prevent a dealer from altering the run of the cards in the draw.]

If a player asks for an incorrect number of cards and they are given to him, he has to take them if the next player has been helped. If there are too many, he has to discard before seeing them. If there are too few, he has to play them. If he has taken them up and has too many, his hand is foul, and shuts him out of that pool. If the dealer gives himself more cards than he needs, he is compelled to take them. For example, he draws three cards to a pair, but on taking up his hand finds he had triplets, and really wanted only two cards. He cannot change his draw, and has to take the three cards he has dealt off. There is a penalty for not following the strict rule of the game: each player, including the dealer, has to discard before he draws.

If the dealer gives any player more cards than he asked for, and the player discovers the error before he takes them up or looks at any of them, the dealer has to withdraw the surplus card, and place it on the top of the pack. If the dealer gives a player fewer cards than he asks for, he has to supply the deficiency when his attention is called to it, without waiting to supply the other players. If a player has more or fewer than five cards after the draw, his hand is foul, and he has to abandon it, together with all he might have already staked in the pool.

The dealer can be asked how many cards he drew, but is not allowed to say how many cards he gave to any other player. Each player has to watch the draw for himself.

The last card of the pack must not be dealt. When only two cards remain, the discards and abandoned hands have to be gathered, shuffled and presented to the pone to be cut, and the deal then has to be completed.

BETTING UP THE HANDS When all the players who made good the ante have been supplied with cards, the next player who holds cards on the left of the age has to make the first bet. If the age has declined to make good his ante, or has passed out before the draw, that does not transfer the privilege of having the last say to any other player, because the peculiar privilege of the age: having the last say, is given in consideration of the blind, which he is *compelled* to pay, and no other player can have that privilege, because no other player is obliged to play. Even if a player has straddled the blind, he has to still make the first bet after the draw, because he straddled of his own free will, and knew at the time that the only advantage the straddle would give him was having the last say as to whether or not he would make good his ante and draw cards.

If the player next to the age has passed out before the draw, the next player to the left who still holds cards has to make the first bet. The player whose turn it is to bet either has to do so or throw his hand face downwards in front of the player whose turn it will next be to deal. If he bets, he can put up any amount from one white counter to the limit: two blues. It then becomes the turn of the player next on his left who still holds cards to abdicate, better or call. If he calls, he does so by placing in the pool an amount equal to that staked by the last player, and it then becomes the turn of the next player on the left to say what he will do. However, if he goes better, he adds to the amount staked by the player on his right any other sum he sees fit, within the limit of two blues. Each player in turn has the same privilege, and the age has the last say.

Suppose five play, and that A has the age. B has straddled, and all but the dealer have made good the ante and drawn cards. There are sixteen white counters in the pool, and B's straddle has made the ante four instead of two. Suppose B bets a red counter, and C then throws down his hand. D *sees* B, by putting up a red counter, and then *raises* him, by putting up two blues, increasing his bet as much as the limit will enable him to. The age now has to abandon his hand or put up one red and two blues to call D, without knowing what B proposes to do. Let's suppose he sees D, and raises another two blues. B now has to retire, or put up four blues to call A, without knowing what D will do. He can raise the bet another two blues, or one blue, or a red, or even a white, if he is inclined to. If he declines to raise, he cannot prevent D from doing so, because D still has the privilege of replying to A's raise, and as long as a player has any *say* about anything, whether it is to abdicate, better or call, he can do any one of the three. It is only when there is no bet made, or when his own bet is either not called or not raised, that a player has nothing to say. Let's suppose B puts up the four blues to call A. It is now D's turn. If he puts up two blues, each will have an equal amount in the pool, and because no one will have anything more to say, the betting has to stop, and the hands have to be shown. However, if D raises A again, by putting up four blues instead of two, he gives A another say, and perhaps A will raise D in turn. Although B might have had quite enough of this, he either has to put up four more blues, the two raised by D and the other raise by A, or abandon his hand. If B throws down his cards, he loses all claim to what he has already staked in the pool: four blues and a red, besides his straddle and ante. Let's suppose he drops out, and that D just calls A, by putting up two blues only, making the amount he has in the pool exactly equal to A's: eight blues and a red, besides the antes. This prevents A from going any further, because it is not his turn to say anything. He is not asked to meet anyone's raise, nor to make any bet himself, but simply to show his hand, in order to see whether or not it is better than D's.

SHOWING HANDS   It is the general usage that the hand *called* has to be shown first. In this case, A's hand is called, because D was the one who called a halt on A in the betting, and stopped him from going any further. The strict laws of the game require that both hands be shown, and if there are more than two in the final call, all have to be shown to the table. The excuse usually made for not showing the losing hand is that the player who has the worse hand paid to see the better hand; however, it must not be forgotten that the player who has the better hand has paid exactly the same amount, and is equally entitled to see the worse hand. There is an excellent rule in some clubs that a player who refuses to show his hand in a call will refund the amount of the antes to all the other players, or pay all the antes in the next jackpot. The rule of showing both hands is a safeguard against collusion between two players, one of whom might have a reasonably good hand and the other nothing, but by mutually raising each other back and forth, they could force any other player out of the pool. The good hand could then be called and shown, whereby the cheater simply stated, 'That is good,' and threw down his hand. Professionals call this system of cheating 'raising out'.

When the hands are called and shown, the best poker hand wins, and their rank is determined by way of the table of values on pages 221–2. In the example just given, suppose that A, on being called by D, had shown three fours, and that D had three deuces. A would take the entire pool, including all the antes, as well as the four blues and one red staked by B after the draw. It might be that B would now discover that he had **laid down** the best hand, having held three sixes. This discovery would be of no benefit to him, because he abandoned his hand when he declined to meet the raises of A and D.

If the hands are exactly a tie, the pool has to be divided among the players who are in at the call. For example, two players show aces up, and each finds his opponent's second pair to be eights. The odd card has to decide the pool, and if that card is also a tie, the pool has to be divided.

If no bet is made after the draw, and each player in turn throws down his cards, the antes are won by the last player who holds his hand. This is usually the age, because he has the last say. If the age has not made good his ante, it will be the dealer, and so on to the right. There is no necessity for the fortunate player to show his hand:

the mere fact that he is the only one who holds any cards is prima facie evidence that his hand is the best. On the same principle, the player who has made a bet or raise that no other player will see wins the pool without showing his hand, because he must be the only one who has cards in his hand. This is because when a player refuses to see a bet, he has to abandon his hand, and with it all pretensions to the pool. If he wishes to call, but does not have enough money, he has to borrow it. He cannot demand a show of hands for what counters he has, except in table stakes.

During the betting, players are at liberty to make any remarks they see fit, and to tell as many cheerful lies about their hands as they please. A player can even miscall his hand when he shows it: the cards speak for themselves, just as the counters do, and what a player says does not affect either in the slightest. If a player says, 'I raise you two blues,' the statement amounts to nothing until the blues have been placed in the pool and the owner's hand has been removed from them. There is no penalty if a player, during the betting, tells his adversaries exactly what he holds; nor is he likely to lose anything by it, because no one will believe him.

JACKPOTS The addition of jackpots has probably done more to injure Poker than the trump signal has injured Whist. In the early days, when poker parties were small and four players were a common number, it was frequently the case that no one had a pair strong enough to draw to, and this deal was simply viewed as being a waste of time. To remedy this, it was proposed that whenever no player came in, each player should be obliged to ante an equal amount for the next deal, and just to demonstrate that there were some good hands left in the pack, no one was allowed to draw cards until someone had *Jacks or better* to draw to.

The result of this practice was to make jackpots larger than the other pools, because everyone was compelled to ante, and this seems to have prompted people who were always wanting to increase the stakes to devise excuses for increasing the number of jackpots. This has been carried so far that the whole system has become a nuisance, and has destroyed one of the finest points in the game of Poker: having the liberty of personal judgement as to every counter put into the pool, except the blind. The following excuses for making jackpots are now in common use.

After a Misdeal, some parties make it a jack, but the practice should be condemned, because it puts it in the power of any individual player to make it a jack when he deals.

The Buck is some article, such as a pen-knife, which is placed in the pool at the beginning of the game, and is taken down with the rest of the pool by whichever player wins it. When it comes to his deal, it is a jackpot, and the buck is placed in the pool with the dealer's ante, to be won, to be taken down and to make another jack in the same way.

The usual custom is to fix the amount of the ante in jackpots, whereby a red, or five whites, is the common stake. In some places, it is at the option of the holder of the buck to make the ante any amount he pleases within the betting limit. Whichever system is adopted, every player at the table has to deposit a similar amount in the pool. Players are sometimes permitted to *pass a jack*, that is, not to ante or take any part in the game until the jack is decided. If this is to be allowed, the fact should be understood at the beginning of the game.

The High Hand jackpot is played whenever a hand of an agreed value, such as a flush or a full, is shown to the board, that is, called. In some places, four of a kind calls for *a round of jacks*, whereby every player in turn makes it a jack on his deal.

ONLY TWO IN   It is a common custom in large parties of, say, six or seven players, to make it a jack when no one but the dealer will ante. Instead of allowing the blind to make his ante good, and draw cards against the dealer, each player contributes two white counters, the age adds one counter to his blind, and the cards are re-dealt for a jackpot. Another variety of this custom is when the blind is opposed by only one ante, to allow the age to make this player take down his two counters, and to pay two counters for him, to make it a jack. For example, five play, and A has the age. B and C pass, and D antes two counters. The dealer, E, says: 'I pass for a jack.' A then puts up three counters, one of which is added to his blind, and the other two players pay D's ante in the ensuing jack. D takes down his two counters, and the cards are re-dealt. This cannot be done if more than one player has anted, nor if the ante has been raised or the blind straddled. In the example just given, had D raised the ante to five counters and E passed, the age would have had to put up four more white counters and to draw cards, or would have had to allow D to win his blind.

PROGRESSIVE JACKS   In some localities, it is the custom to make the pair necessary to open a jackpot progress in value: Jacks or better to open the first round; Queens the next; then Kings; then Aces; and then back to Kings, Queens and Jacks again. This method is very confusing, and is not popular.

FATTENING JACKS When the original ante is two counters only, and no one holds Jacks or better on the first deal, each player has to contribute another white counter to 'fatten', and the cards are dealt again. This activity continues until the pot is opened, that is, until some player holds a hand as good or better than a pair of Jacks. The fattening process is followed when the dealer can make the original ante what he pleases; however, if the ante for jacks is a fixed sum, such as a red counter, it is not usual to fatten the pot at all. This saves all disputes as to *who is shy*, which are one of the greatest nuisances in Poker.

OPENING JACKS Because there is no age or straddle in any form of jackpot, the player to the left of the dealer has the first say, and has to examine his hand to see whether he has Jacks or better, that is, either an actual pair of Jacks or some hand that would beat a pair of Jacks if called on to do so, such as two pairs, a straight or triplets. In some localities, it is allowed to open jacks with a *bobtail*, that is, four cards of a flush or straight. If the player on the dealer's left does not have openers, or does not care to open the pot if he has, he says, 'I pass,' but does not abandon his hand. The next player on his left then has to declare. In some places, players are allowed to throw down their cards when they pass; however, in first-class games, a penalty of five white counters has to be paid into the pool by any player who abandons his hand before the second round of declarations, because it gives an undue advantage to players who have medium hands to know that they have only a limited number of possible opponents. For example, if six play, and the first three not only pass but throw down and abandon their cards, a player who has a pair of Jacks will know that he has only two possible adversaries to draw against him, whereby his chances will be so increased that his betting might be materially altered.

If no one acknowledges holding Jacks or better, the pot is fattened, and the cards are re-shuffled and dealt. The best practice is for the same dealer to deal again until someone gets Jacks or better. This is called *dealing off the jack*. If any player has forfeited his right in one deal, such as by having a foul hand, that does not prevent him from coming into the pot again on the next deal and from having rights equal to those of the other players.

If any player holds Jacks or better, he can open the pot, or 'the jack', for any amount he pleases within the betting limit. The expression 'open' is used because after one player has declared that he holds Jacks or better, all restrictions are removed, and the pool is then open to any player to come in and play for it, regardless of what he might hold. Each player in turn, beginning on the left of the opener, has to declare whether or not he will *stay*. If he stays, he has to put up an amount equal to that bet by the opener, and has the privilege of raising him if he sees fit. If he passes, he throws his cards face downwards on the table in front of the player whose turn it will next be to deal. If the opener is raised, and does not care to see that raise, he has to show his hand to the table before he abandons it, in order to demonstrate that he had openers. Some players show only the cards that are necessary to open, but the strict rules require the whole hand to be shown before the draw. When the jack is once opened, the betting before the draw proceeds exactly as in the ordinary pool. Any player on the right of the opener, who passed on the first round, can come in after the pot is opened. For example, E deals. A and B pass, but hold their hands. C opens, and D throws down his hand. E sees the opener's bet, and it then becomes the turn of A and B, who have passed once, to say whether or not they will play, now that the pot is opened.

When all the players who have declared to stay have deposited an equal amount in the pool, they draw cards to improve their hands, just as in the ordinary pool, whereby the player on the dealer's left is helped first. All the players who draw cards, except the opener, throw their discards into the centre of the table as usual, but the opener is always obliged to place his discard under the chips in the pool. This is so that he is able to show what he held originally, in case he should conclude to *split his openers* in order to try for a better hand. For example, he has opened with a pair of Jacks, but has four of one suit in his hand. Four other players have stayed, perhaps the bet has been raised, and he knows that his Jacks will probably be worthless, even if he gets a third. He therefore breaks the pair, and draws for a flush. Because the opener always places his discard under the chips in the pool, it is not necessary for him to betray his game by telling the whole table that he is drawing to a bobtail.

FALSE OPENERS If a player opens a jack without the hand to justify it, and discovers his error before he draws, according to the best usage his hand is foul, and he has to forfeit to the pool whatever amount he might have opened for, and any raises he might have stood. There are then three ways to play, as follows. *First*, players who have come in under the impression that the pot had been legitimately opened but who do not have openers themselves can withdraw their money and allow anyone to open it who has openers. This is very unfair to the players on the left of the false opener who have abandoned their hands. *Second*, players who have come into the pot after the false opening are allowed to stay in and play for it, no matter what their hands are. *Third*, when the false opening is discovered, each player is allowed to take down whatever amount he might have paid into the pool, including his original ante and all fatteners, and the false opener then has to make the entire amount good. The cards are then dealt afresh. This is a very harsh punishment for a very trifling and common error.

The second method is the most popular, and probably the fairest, and is now the universal rule.

If the false opener does not discover his mistake until he has drawn cards, his action is at least suspicious, and he should be compelled to put up the total amount in the pool, as in case three. In some localities, this type of player is barred from playing the next two jacks, but is compelled to ante his share in each.

BETTING JACKS When a jackpot has been properly opened, and all the players have declared whether or not they will stay, and have drawn cards, they proceed to bet on their hands. Because there is no age in jackpots, the rule is for the opener to make the first bet, or, if he has been raised out before the draw, the player next on his left who still holds cards bets first. The opener can decline to bet if he pleases, but if he does so, he has to show his openers, and then abandon his hand. If no bet is made, the last player who holds cards takes the pool without showing his hand. If a bet is made, each player in turn on the left has to abdicate, better or call, just as in the ordinary pool. At the conclusion of the betting, if there is a call, the best poker hand wins, naturally. If there is no call, the player who makes the last bet or raise takes the pool without showing his hand, unless he is the opener, when the whole hand does not have to be shown, because it is no one's business what the opener got in the draw, and no one has paid to see it. All he has to show is openers. However, if the opener is one of the players in the final call, he has to show his whole hand. If it is then discovered that he does not have openers, the false opener is compelled to ante for all the players at the table for another Jack. This is usually called giving them a 'free ride'.

The Kitty has become an almost universal adjunct to the pool. In clubs, it pays for the cards, and for an occasional round of refreshments; in small poker parties, it defrays the expense of the weekly supper. When the amount is excessive, or accumulates too rapidly, it is often used to give the players a 'free ride' by paying all their antes in a 'kitty jackpot'.

The kitty is usually kept by the banker, who takes a white counter out of every pool in which triplets or better are shown to the board, and a red counter out of every jackpot. These counters have to be kept apart from the other chips, and be accounted for at the end of the game by paying the kitty so much in cash, just as if it were one of the players.

Gambling and poker venues were supposed to derive their entire revenue from this source, and at the lowest-class ones, endless excuses were invented for taking out for the kitty. In many venues, there was a sliding scale for various hands, whereby one counter was taken for two pairs; two counters for triplets; three for straights or flushes; and a red for fours, jackpots and misdeals. It was not uncommon for the proprietors of these games to find thirty or forty dollars in the kitty after a night's play with 5 cent chips.

TABLE STAKES   This is one of several variations for arranging the stakes and the betting limit. In some localities, it is the custom to allow each player to purchase as many counters as he pleases; in others, it is the rule to compel each player to buy an equal number at the start: usually 200 times the amount of the blind. In table stakes, the betting limit is always the amount the player has in front of him, but no player is allowed to either increase or diminish that amount while he has any cards in front of him. Before the cards are dealt for any pool, he can announce that he wishes to buy counters, or that he has some to sell to any other player who wishes to purchase; however, for either transaction, the consent of all the other players has to be obtained. No player is allowed under any circumstances to borrow from another, nor to be 'shy' in any pot, that is, to say, 'I owe so many.' If he has any counters in front of him, his betting is limited to what he has; if he has none, he is out of the game, for that hand at least. Because a player cannot increase the amount he has in front of him during the play of a hand, it is best to keep on the table at all times as much as you are likely to wish to bet on any one hand.

It is the usual custom, and an excellent one, to fix on a definite hour for closing a game of table stakes, and to allow no player to retire from the game before that hour unless he is *decavé* (has lost all his capital). If he insists on retiring, whatever counters he has have to be divided among the other players, and if there are any odd ones after the division, they have to be put into the current pool.

In table stakes, any player can *call a sight* for what money or counters he has in front of him, even if another player has bet a much larger amount. For example, A has bet three dollars, and B has only two dollars in front of him, but wishes to call A. B calls for a sight by putting his two dollars in the pool, and A then has to withdraw his third dollar from the pool but leave it on the table to be called or raised by any other player. If C wishes to call A, or even to raise him, A and C can continue the betting independently of B's part of the pool. If C has even less money than B has, say, one dollar, he can still reduce the original pool more, leaving the two dollars aside for settlement between A and B, and A's third dollar still aside from that again for the decision of any other player.

Let's suppose that A and C continue the betting until one calls. When the hands are shown, if either A's or C's is better than B's, B loses his interest, but if B's is better than either A's or C's, he takes the part of the pool for which he called a sight, while A and C decide the remainder between them. For example, A calls C, and C shows three tens. Neither A nor B can beat it, and C takes everything. However, if B has three Jacks, and A only three fives, B takes the part of the pool for which he called a sight, and C takes the remainder.

If C has raised and bluffed A out, or has bet so much that A finally refuses to call, A has no interest in either pool, and C takes all the money outside the pool for which B calls a sight. If it then transpires, on the show of hands between B and C, that A has laid down a better hand than either of them, A is not entitled to claim the sight pool from B, because in laying down his hand he has practically acknowledged that C's hand is better, and has retired from the game. If B's hand is better than C's, B takes the sight pool.

FREEZE OUT   This might be called a variety of table stakes. At the start, each player is supplied with an equal number of counters, but no one is allowed to replenish his stock, or to withdraw or loan any part of it. As soon as any player has lost his capital, he is decavé, or *frozen out*, and has to permanently retire from the game. The other players continue until only one remains, who naturally has to win everything on the table. This is not a popular form of Poker, because it is sometimes a long time before a player who is frozen out can get into a game again.

SHOW-DOWN POKER   This is a variety of draw poker, in which each player takes the five cards dealt to him and turns them face upwards so all the other players can see them. Each player discards and draws in turn, and the eldest hand goes first. As soon as a hand is beaten, it is thrown into the deadwood, and all the drawn cards are dealt face upwards.

FLAT POKER   In this variety of the game, before the cards are dealt, the age puts up, for a blind, any amount he pleases within the limit. The players who are willing to bet a similar amount on the possibilities of their hands put up a similar amount. The players who decline are not given any cards. There are no straddles, raises or antes. Immediately after the deal, each player who is in the pool draws cards, and the age goes first. There are then two ways to play: the hands are shown and the best wins, or, beginning with the age, each player can say whether he will back his hand against the field, that is, all the other players in the pool. If he will, he has to put up as much as their combined stakes. He cannot be raised; however, if any one player or combination of players calls him, and one of them can beat his hand, the field divides the pool. For example, age makes it a blue, and three other players stay with him. After the draw, C puts up three blues against the field. D and A call it, and all show hands. If any of the three: A, B or D, can beat C, they divide the pool, whereby B gets his third, although he did not contribute to the call. This game is a pure gamble, except that a bold player can occasionally bluff the field off.

METHODS OF CHEATING Poker and its congeners have received more attention from 'card sharps' than has any other family of card games. It is generally believed that the derogatory term 'greek', as applied to a card sharp, had its origin in the 'Adam' of the poker family, which was a gambling game that Greeks introduced in Italy.

So many and varied are the methods of cheating at Poker that it is an axiom among gamblers that if a pigeon will not stand one thing, he will another. The best-informed players make it a rule never to play Poker with strangers, because they realise it is impossible for any but a professional gambler to know half the tricks used by the poker sharp. It is a notorious fact that even the shrewdest gamblers are continually being taken in by other players who are more expert than they. What chance, then, has the honest card player?

There are black sheep in all flocks, and it might be useful to give a few hints to players who are in the habit of playing in mixed company.

Never play with a player who looks attentively at the cards' face as he gathers the cards for his deal, or with a player who stands the pack on edge, with the cards' face towards him, and evens up the bunch by picking out specific cards, apparently because they are sticking up. Any pack can be straightened by pushing the cards down using your hand. The player who lifts them up is more than probably a cheat.

Never play with a player who looks intently at the pack and shuffles the cards slowly. If he is not locating the cards for the ensuing deal, he is wasting time, and should be hurried up.

Never play with a player who leaves the cut portion of the pack on the table, and deals off the other part. In small parties, this is a very common way of working what is known as **the top stock**. If this dealer is carefully watched, it will usually be found that he seizes the first opportunity to place the cut-off part on top of the part dealt from. The top stock is then ready for the draw, and the judicious player should at once cash his chips and retire from the game.

Never play with a player who continually holds his cards very close to his body, or who completely conceals his hand before the draw, or who takes great care to put his discard among previous discards, so that the exact number of cards put out cannot be counted. He is probably working a sleeve or vest hold-out. Some clumsy or audacious sharp will go so far as to hold out cards in their lap, or to stick them in a 'bug' under the table. One of the most successful poker sharps ever known, 'Eat-um-up Jake' Blackburn, who had a hand 'like a ham', could hold out five cards in his palm while he carried on all the operations of shuffling, dealing and playing his hand. These players require great dexterity and nerve to get rid of their 'deadwood', or surplus cards, without detection. **Holding out** is considered to be by the professional a most dangerous experiment, but is very common.

Never play with a player who keeps his eyes rivetted on the cards as he deals, and who deals comparatively slowly. He is probably using marked cards, or has marked the important ones himself during the play. Poker sharps who mark cards by scratching them with a sharp point concealed in a ring are obliged to hold the cards at a specific angle to the light in order to see the scratches. Cheats who dig points in the cards using their thumb nail depend on touch instead of sight. If you find these points on the cards, either dig other points on other cards or retire from the game.

Against the hold-out or marked cards there is no protection, because the dealer does not care how much the cards in the pack are shuffled or cut; however, every method of running up hands, or stocking cards, can be made ineffective if the pone will not only cut the cards but carefully reunite the packets. If the two parts are straightened after the cut, it will be impossible for the dealer to shift the cut and bring the cards back to their original position. The dealer will sometimes bend the top or bottom card so as to form a **bridge**, whereby he will be enabled to find the place at which the cards were cut. This can only be overcome by shuffling the cards instead of cutting them, which every player has the right to do. If you insist on shuffling, the cheat will do the same in his turn, and will run up hands to be dealt to himself. It is perfectly useless to endeavour to protect yourself against a poker sharp; the only remedy is to leave the game.

Many people have a strong prejudice against playing with a player who shuffles his chips. The mere fact of his being an expert at chip shuffling has nothing to do with the game of poker: the accomplishment is usually the result of having much experience at the faro table. The reason for the prejudice is that a chip shuffler is usually cold blooded and courageous, and seldom a loser at any game that requires nerve.

SUGGESTIONS FOR GOOD PLAY   Volumes might be written for the guidance of the poker player without improving his game one bit, unless he has at least one of four qualifications: control over his features and actions, judgement of human nature, courage, and patience. The player whose face or manner betrays the nature of his hand, or the effect of an opponent's bet or raise, will find everyone to beat his weak hands and no one to call his strong ones. Unless he is a reasonable judge of human nature, he will never be able to estimate the strength or peculiarities of the players to whom he is opposed, and will fail to distinguish a bluff from an ambuscade. Without courage, he cannot reap the full benefit of his good hands, and without patience, he cannot save his money in times of adversity.

Of one thing every player can rest assured: that Poker cannot be played by way of following mathematical formulas. Beyond the most elementary calculations of the chances in favour of specific events, the theory of probabilities is of no help. It is not necessary to call in a mathematician to prove that a player who habitually discards a pair of aces to draw to three cards of a suit will lose by way of the operation in the long run. Nor will any amount of calculation convince some players that they are wasting their money to stay in a jackpot in order to draw to a pair of tens, although this is the fact.

The various positions occupied by the player at the poker table can be briefly examined and some general suggestions offered for his guidance in each of them. In the first place, he should look out for his counters. It is always best for each player to place the amount of his ante or his bet immediately in front of him, so that there does not have to be a dispute about who is up or who is shy. Above all, it should be insisted that any player who has put counters in the pool once, and who has taken his hand from them, must not take them down again.

The Age is the most valuable position at the table, but is seldom fully taken advantage of. The age should never look at his hand until it is his turn to make good his blind. He can pick up his cards, but should use his eyes in following the manner and facial expression of the other players as they sort their cards. One of the greatest errors made by the age is in thinking he has to save his blind. The player who draws to nothing because he can do so cheaply will usually have nothing to draw at the end of the game. The age can usually afford to draw to four-card flushes, and to straights open at both ends, but should not do so when there are fewer than three players who have paid to draw cards, or when the ante has been raised.

If the age holds Kings or better before the draw, he should invariably raise the ante unless there are five players in the pool besides him, or unless some other player has already raised. If he holds two pairs, he should do all his betting before the draw. If any other player has raised, or his own raise is re-raised, the age has to use his judgement of the player and the circumstances. It is useless for the age to disguise his hand by way of manoeuvres such as holding up an odd card to a pair, unless he raises the blind at the same time. If he draws one or two cards only, and has not raised the blind, everyone will credit him for a small pair and an ace, or for a bobtail, and will inevitably call any bluff he might make. The age is the poorest position at the table for a bluff, but it is decidedly the best position in which to win large pots with moderate hands.

The Dealer has the next-best position to the age, and in large parties there is very little difference in the way in which the two positions should be played.

The *first bettor* has the worst position at the table, and should seldom come in on less than Queens. He should seldom raise the ante, even with two pairs, because he will only drive other players out. In this position, very little can be made out of good hands, because everyone expects to find them there, but the position offers many excellent opportunities for successful bluffing. A player in this position should never straddle. Many players endeavour to force their luck in this way, but it is a losing game, and the best players seldom or never straddle. Because he has to make the first bet after the draw, it is usual for the player in this position, if he has an average hand, to *chip along*, by simply betting a single counter and waiting for developments. With a strong hand, it is best to bet its full value at once, on the chance that the bet will be taken for a bluff and called.

OTHER POSITIONS As the positions go around the table from the first bettor to the age, they become more desirable, and not much has to be said about them beyond the consideration of the average strength necessary for a player to **go in** on.

GOING IN There is a great difference of opinion as to the minimum value of a hand that should justify a player in drawing cards if he can do so for the usual ante. In close games, many players make it a rule not to go in on less than tens, whereas in more liberal circles, the players will draw to any pair. In determining which course to follow, the individual has to be guided by his observation and judgement. Suppose five play, and A observes that B and C constantly draw to small pairs, whereas D and E never come in on less than tens. If A has the age, and B, D and E have anted, A can be sure there are at least two good hands against him, and will guide himself accordingly. However, if B and C are the only players in, A can safely draw to a small pair. It can be mathematically demonstrated that what is called an **average go-in hand** should be at least a pair of tens; however, a player who waits for tens in a liberal game, in which other players are drawing to ace high, will ante himself away if there are many jackpots, and will get no calls when he gets a hand.

BETTING Good players are guided by the general character of the game in which they take part. Some parties play a very liberal game, and the players bet high on medium hands, and give everyone a good fight. It is best to have liberal or lucky players on your right, because if they sit behind you, they will continually raise you, and you will be forced to either overbid your hand on the same liberal scale that they adopt or lose what you have already put up. If a liberal player sits on your right, you will often be able to make large winnings on moderate hands. In a close game, when the players bet in a niggardly way, the liberal player is at a great disadvantage, because he can win little or nothing on his good hands, but will lose large amounts when he runs up the betting on a good hand that is opposed to one that is better. When a liberal player finds a close player following him freely, he can be sure there is a very strong hand against him.

VARIETY Above all things, a player should avoid regularity in his play, because observant adversaries will soon learn his methods. The best players usually play two pairs pat, without drawing, about half the time. This gives them the reputation of betting on pat hands that are not genuine, and when they get a hand that is real, they will often succeed in getting a good bet, or even a raise, from the players who hold triplets or two large pairs, who have noticed them play two pairs pat. In the same way, it is advisable to hold up an odd card occasionally, without raising the ante, so that when you do hold triplets, and draw two cards, you will not frighten everyone at the table. The chances of improving a pair by drawing three cards are one in three, and by drawing two cards only are one in four. The difference is worth the moral effect of the variation in the play.

PROBABILITIES The endless poker statistics that have been published are of little or no value to the practical player, and there are only a few figures that are worth remembering. It is a general law in all games of chance that you should never do a thing you would not be willing to repeat under the same circumstances a hundred times. The best example of application of this law is in drawing to bobtails. If you have a four-card flush to draw to, the odds against getting it are about four to one, and unless you can obtain the privilege of drawing to it by paying not more than one-fifth of the amount in the pool, you will lose by it in the long run. The best players never draw to four-card flushes except when they have the age, and the ante has not been raised.

There are some players who pretend to be so guided by prob-abilities that they never go into a pool unless the chances in favour of their having a good hand after the draw are at least equal to the odds they have to bet by going into the pool. This is all non-sense, because no player knows when he goes into a pool how much it will cost him to get out, and the value of his individual hand is an unknown quantity at best, because it cannot be compared to the other hands. One thing only is certain: in the long run, the player who goes in with the strongest hand will have the strongest hand after the draw. This is an important thing to remember in jackpots, in which the value of at least one hand is known. If you draw to a pair that is smaller than Jacks, you do so with the full knowledge that the pair itself is not strong enough to win. Now, what are the odds against your winning the pool? Suppose you hold tens, and draw three cards. Your chance of improving your hand is slightly better than one in five. The opener of the jackpot has exactly the same chance, and if both of you draw cards a hundred times under these circumstances, he will beat you in the long run, to say nothing of the other players who might come in and beat both of you. It is therefore evident that in backing tens against openers, it is four to one against your beating the openers to begin with, and if you do beat them, the odds are still against your winning the pot. If there were five players, and the jackpots were all equal in amount, you would have to win one pot out of five in order to make your investment pay. Can you make this average when your original pair will not beat openers?

There are three principles with reference to the draw that should never be lost sight of, as follows.

(1) An average go-in hand is a hand that will win its proportion of the pools, according to the number playing, when all improvements and opposition are taken into account. This can be demonstrated to be a pair of tens.

(2) The draw is much more valuable to a weak hand than to a strong one, and weak hands will improve in much greater proportion than will strong ones. For example, the chances for a player to improve by drawing to a pair of Queens are one in three and a half. He can make two pairs, or triplets, or a full hand, or four of a kind. The chances of improvement for a player who draws to two pairs, say, Eights up, are only one in thirteen. This consideration leads players to adopt two lines of play: to bet all they intend to on two pairs before the draw, in order to prevent weaker hands from drawing cards and improving, or to discard the smaller pair in order to increase their chances of improvement.

(3) The smaller the number of players, the greater the value of the hands, and the larger the number of players, the greater the chance that any given hand will be beaten. When only two play, you can safely bet the limit on a pair of Eights, but in a party of eight players, they are hardly worth drawing to. For this reason, average hands should force the weaker out, and reduce the number of players *before the draw.*

For the benefit of people who are interested in these matters, **the probable improvement by the draw** can briefly be given.

It is 2½ to 1 against improving *a pair* by drawing three cards; the chances against making triplets or two pairs are 8 to 1, against a full hand 61 to 1, and against four of a kind 364 to 1. It is 4 to 1 against improving a pair by drawing two cards; the chances against triplets are 12 to 1, and 8 to 1 against two pairs.

It is 12 to 1 against making a full hand by drawing to *two pairs.*

It is 8 to 1 against improving *triplets* by drawing two cards, 14½ to 1 against a full hand, and 23 to 1 against four of a kind. It is 12 to 1 against improving if one card is drawn, 16 to 1 against the full, and 46 to 1 against four of a kind.

It is 11 to 1 against making a straight out of a sequence of four cards that is open in the middle, or at one end only. It is 5 to 1 against making a straight out of a sequence of four that is open at both ends.

IN-BETWEEN STRAIGHT OPEN-END STRAIGHT

It is 4½ to 1 against filling a four-card flush. It is 23 to 1 against filling a three-card flush. It is 95 to 1 against filling a two-card flush.

It is 3 to 1 against improving a four-card straight flush that is open at both ends. The chances against getting the straight or the flush have been given, and the odds against getting the straight flush are 24 to 1. The chance for getting a pair exists, but the pair would probably be worthless.

It is 4 to 1 against improving a four-card straight flush that is open in the middle or at one end only, and the odds against getting the straight flush are 46 to 1.

There are several minor or speculative draws that might be of interest. Drawing to an ace and a King, it is 3 to 1 against making a pair of either. It is 4 to 1 against making a pair of aces by drawing four cards to an ace, and 12 to 1 against making aces up, or better. It is 24 to 1 against making a straight by drawing to three cards of it, open at both ends. It is 12 to 1 against making either a straight or a flush by drawing to three cards of a straight flush, open at both ends.

HOW TO WIN AT POKER   There have been many alleged infallible receipts for winning at Poker. Proctor thought that refusing to go in on less than triplets would prove a certainty; however, in the same paragraph, he acknowledges that the adversaries would soon learn the peculiarity and avoid betting against the player. Triplets before the draw occur about once in every 45 hands. If five were playing, a player who was following Proctor's advice would have to blind 9 times, and ante in at least 12 jackpots in every 45 hands, to say nothing of fattening. This means an outlay of at least 75 counters. When the triplets came, would he get back 75 counters on them? He would probably win the blind, and one or two antes, but the moment he made his own ante good, every player who could not beat triplets, knowing his system, would lay down his hand.

An extensive observation of the methods of the best players has led the author to the conclusion that the great secret of success in Poker, apart from having a natural aptitude for the game and being a good actor, is *avoiding calling*. If you think you have the best hand, raise. If you think you do not have the best, lay it down. Although you might sometimes lay down a better hand than the one that takes the pool, the system will prove of immense advantage to you in two ways: in the first place, you will find it a great educator of your judgement, and in the second place, it will take almost any opponent's nerve. Once an adversary has learnt your method, it is a question not of his betting a red chip on his hand but of his willingness to stand a raise of two blues, which he will view as being inevitable if you come in against him at all. The fear of this raise will prompt many a player to lay down a moderately good hand without a bet, so that you have all the advantage of having made a strong bluff without having put up a chip. The system will also drive all but the most courageous players to call your hand on every occasion, because they are afraid of another inevitable raise, and it is an old saying that a good caller is a sure loser.

The theory of calling is to get an opportunity to compare your hand with your adversary's. Now, if you think that after the comparison yours will prove to be the better hand, why not increase the value of the pool? If, on the contrary, you fear that your adversary's hand will beat yours, why throw good money after bad ? If you don't think about it at all, and have no means of forming an opinion as to the respective merits of your hands, you are not a poker player, and have no business in the game.

BLUFFING There is nothing connected with Poker about which people have more-confused ideas as the subject of bluffing. The popular impression seems to be that a stiff upper lip and a cheerful expression of countenance, accompanied with a bet of five dollars, will make most people lay down three aces, and that this result will be brought about by way of the five-dollar bet, without any regard to the player's position at the table, the number of cards he drew, his manner of seeing or raising the ante, or the play of his adversaries before the draw. The truth of the matter is that for a bluff to be either sound in principle or successful in practice, the player has to select his opportunity carefully. The bluff has to be planned from the start and consistently played from the ante to the end. To use a common expression, 'The play has to be right for it, or the bluff will be wrong.'

There are many cases in which a bluff of 50 cents would be much stronger than one of five dollars; the difference depends on the player's position at the table, his treatment of the ante, and the number of cards he had drawn. As an example of when the play is right for a bluff, we will examine the following case. Five play in a jackpot. A and B have passed when C opens it for the limit. D and E pass out, but both A and B stay, and each draws one card. C takes two cards, and because it is his first bet, he puts up the limit on his three aces. A drops out, but B raises C the limit in return. Now, if C is a good player, he will lay down his three aces, even if he faintly suspects that B is bluffing, because B's play is sound in any case. He either could not or pretended he could not open the jack; however, he could afford to pay the limit to draw one card against openers, and could afford to raise the limit against an opener's evidently honest two-card draw; as a matter of fact, the whole play was a bluff, because B not only had nothing; he had nothing to draw to originally.

Another variety of the bluff, which is the author's own invention, will often prove to be successful with strangers, but can seldom be repeated in the same company. Suppose six play in a jackpot. A passes, and B opens it by quietly putting up his counters. C and D pass, and E, pretending not to know that B has opened it, announces that he will open it for the limit, although he does not have a pair in his hand. Naturally, he is immediately informed that it has been opened, whereby he unhesitatingly raises it for the limit. Whatever the other players do, E stands pat and looks cheerful. The author has never known this bluff to be called.

If he holds a strong hand, a player can often coax another player to raise him, by offering to divide the pool.

The successful bluffer should never show his hand. Even if he starts the game by bluffing for advertising purposes, hoping to get called on good hands later, he should neither show anything nor tell anything that the other players do not pay to see or know. Bluffing is usually more successful when a player is in a lucky vein than when he has been unfortunate.

— —

POKER LAWS

1. FORMATION OF TABLE   A poker table is complete with seven players. If eight play, the dealer has to take no cards, or a sixty-card pack has to be used. If there are more than seven candidates for play, two tables have to be formed unless the majority decide against it.

2. CUTTING   The players who will form the table and their positions at the beginning of the game can be decided by way of either drawing from an outspread pack or throwing around a card to each candidate, face upwards. If there are eight or more candidates, the tables will divide evenly if the number is even, and the players who cut the highest cards play together. If the number is odd, the smaller table will be formed by the players who cut the highest cards. In cutting, the ace is low. Any player who exposes more than one card has to cut again.

3. When the table is formed, the players draw from the outspread pack for positions. The lowest cut has the first choice and deals the first hand. The player who cuts the next lowest has the next choice, and so on until all the players are seated.

4. TIES If players cut cards of equal value, they have to cut again, but the new cut decides nothing but the tie.

5. STAKES Any player can be the banker and keep the kitty, if any. In Draw, Straight or Stud Poker, each player can purchase as many counters as he pleases. In Freeze-out, Table Stakes, Whiskey Poker and Progressive Poker, each player has to begin with an equal amount.

6. BETTING LIMITS Before play begins, limits have to be agreed on for the amount of the blind, the straddle and the ante in jackpots, as well as for betting or raising.

7. SHUFFLING Before the first deal, the pack has to be counted to see that it contains the proper number of cards. If the first dealer neglects this, he forfeits five counters to the pool. Before each deal, the cards have to be shuffled. Any player can shuffle, and the dealer goes last.

8. CUTTING TO THE DEALER The dealer has to present the pack to the pone [the player on his right] to be cut. The pone can either cut or signify he does not wish to do so by tapping the pack with his knuckles. If the pone declines to cut, no other player can insist on his doing so, nor do it for him. If he cuts, he has to leave at least four cards in each packet, and the dealer or the pone has to reunite the packets by placing on the other packet the packet that was not removed in cutting.

9. If in cutting or reuniting the packets a card is exposed, the pack has to be re-shuffled and cut.

10. If the dealer re-shuffles the pack after it has been properly cut, he forfeits five counters to the current pool.

11. DEALING BEFORE THE DRAW After the age [the player on the dealer's left] has put up the amount of the blind, the dealer distributes the cards face downwards, one at a time, in rotation, until each player has received five cards.

12. The deal passes to the left, except in jackpots, whereby it can be agreed that the same dealer will deal until the pot is opened.

13. MISDEALING A misdeal does not lose the deal; the same dealer has to deal again. It is a misdeal if the dealer fails to present the pack to the pone, or if any card is found faced in the pack, or if the pack is found imperfect, or if the dealer gives six or more cards to more than one player, or if the dealer deals more or fewer hands than there are players, or if the dealer omits a player while dealing, or if the dealer deals a card incorrectly and fails to correct the error before dealing another.

14. IRREGULARITIES IN THE HANDS If the dealer, or the wind, turns over any card, the player to whom it is dealt has to take it, but the same player cannot be compelled to take two exposed cards. If this combination occurs, there has to be a new deal. If the player exposes cards himself, he has no remedy.

15. If any player receives more or fewer than his proper number of cards, and discovers the error before he looks at any card in his hand, or lifts it from the table, he can demand a new deal if no bet has been made, or can ask the dealer to give him another card from the pack if he has too few, or can ask the dealer to draw a card if he has too many. Cards so drawn must not be exposed, but should be placed on the top of the pack. If a bet has been made, there has to be a new deal. If the player takes up his hand, or looks at any card in it, he has no remedy.

16. If a player takes up a hand that contains more or fewer than five cards, or looks at any card in it, the hand is foul, and he has to abandon it, whereby he forfeits any interest he might have in that pool. If one player has six cards and his neighbour four, and neither has lifted or looked at any card, the dealer can be called on to draw a card from the six hand and give it to the four hand.

17. STRADDLING During the deal, or at any time before he looks at any card in his hand, the player to the left of the age can straddle the blind by putting up double the amount put up by the age. If he straddles, the player on his left can double the amount again, provided he has not seen any of his cards, and so on until the limit of the straddling is reached. This limit must not exceed one-fourth of the betting limit. If any player in his turn refuses to straddle, no other player on his left can straddle.

18. THE ANTE After the cards are dealt, each player in turn, beginning with the one to the left of the age, or to the left of the last straddler, if any, has to either abandon his hand or put into the pool twice the amount of the blind or of the last straddle. When it comes to the turn of the age, and the straddlers, if any, they have to either abandon their hand, or make the amount they have in the pool equal to twice the amount of the blind or of the last straddle, if any.

19. RAISING THE ANTE Each player, when it is his turn to come in, can add to the amount of the ante any sum within the betting limit. This will compel any player who comes in after him to equal the total of the ante and the raise, or to abandon his hand, and will also give this following player the privilege of raising again by any other amount within the betting limit. If any player declines to equal the amount put up by any previous player, he has to abandon his hand, together with all his interest in that pool. Any player who has been raised in this way can raise again in his turn, and the game will not proceed until each player who holds cards has anted an equal amount.

20. WINNING THE ANTES If any player has put up an amount that no other player will equal, he takes whatever counters are then in the pool, without showing his hand, and the deal passes to the next player on the dealer's left. If only one player comes in, and the age declines to make good his ante, the player who has come in wins the blind, unless jackpots are played. If any player has straddled the blind or raised the ante, there can be no jackpot.

21. MAKING JACKS If no player will come in, it is a Natural Jack, and all the hands have to be abandoned, whereby each player puts up for the ensuing deal the amount agreed on. If no one has straddled the blind or raised the ante, and only one player has come in, the age can do one of four things: he can forfeit his blind; make the ante good; raise the ante; or demand that the single player who has come in will take down his ante, whereby the age puts up twice the amount agreed on for jackpots: once for himself and once for the player who came in. All the other players then have to put up for the ensuing deal. This is an Only-Two-In Jack.

22. DRAWING CARDS When two or more players have come in for an equal amount, and the others have abandoned their hands, each of them in turn, beginning with the one on the dealer's left, can discard any or all of the cards originally dealt to him and draw other cards in their place. The number discarded and drawn, if any, have to be distinctly announced by each player, including the dealer, and the fresh cards have to be given face downwards from the top of the pack, without any further shuffling or cutting. Each player has to receive the entire number he asks for before the next player is helped. No player will receive from the dealer more or fewer cards than he discards, so that if he is playing with a short hand, such as four cards only, he will still have four cards after the draw, and if his hand was originally foul, it will remain so.

23. EXPOSED CARDS   In dealing for the draw, if any card is found faced in the pack, or if any card is exposed by the dealer in giving out the cards, or is blown over by the wind before the player has touched it, these cards have to be placed on the table with the discards. The player whose card has been exposed does not receive another card in its place until all the other players, including the dealer, have been helped.

24. INCORRECT DRAWS   If any player asks for an incorrect number of cards, he has to take them, unless he discovers the error before the next player has been helped. If too many cards have been asked for, he has to discard before seeing them; if too few, and he lifts any of them, he holds a foul hand. No player is allowed to take back into his hand any card that has been discarded once. If he has taken up the cards, or has seen any of them, and has too many, his hand is foul, and has to be abandoned. If the dealer gives himself more cards than he needs, he has to take them, but if fewer, he can supply the deficiency, provided he has not looked at any of the drawn cards.

25. INCORRECT DEALING   If the dealer gives any player more or fewer cards than he asks for, and the player discovers the error before taking them up or seeing any of them, the dealer has to withdraw the surplus card and place it on the top of the pack. If the dealer gives a player fewer cards than he asks for, he has to supply the deficiency when his attention is called to it, without waiting to supply the other players. If the dealer gives cards to any player out of his proper turn, he can correct the error if none of the cards have been seen; otherwise, he cannot.

26. THE LAST CARD   The last card of the pack must not be dealt. When only two cards remain, and more than one card is asked for, the cards have to be mixed with the discards and abandoned hands, and all the cards shuffled together and presented to the pone to be cut. Discards of players who have yet to draw must not be gathered.

27. After the cards have been delivered by the dealer, no player has the right to be informed of how many cards any player drew, and any person, bystander or player who volunteers the information, except the player himself, can be called on to pay to the player against whom he informs an amount equal to that in the pool at the time. Any player who has made good the ante and drawn cards can, before making a bet, ask how many cards the dealer drew, and the dealer has to inform him.

28. BETTING AFTER THE DRAW The first player who holds cards on the left of the age has to make the first bet, whether or not he has straddled. If he declines to bet, he has to abandon his hand. The fact that the age is not playing makes no difference, because his privilege cannot be transferred to any other player. Bets can vary in amount from one counter to the betting limit. If no player will bet, the age takes the pool without showing his hand, or, if he has passed out before the draw, the last player on his right who holds cards wins the pool.

29. RAISING THE BETS If any player makes a bet, each player in turn on his left has to either bet an equal amount or abandon his hand. If any player bets an equal amount, he has the privilege of increasing the bet to any other sum within the betting limit. The players on his left then have to either meet the total amount of the original bet and the raise or abandon their hand. Any player who meets the amount already bet has the privilege of increasing it to any other amount within the limit, and so on, until no further raises take place. Any player whose bet has been raised has to abandon his hand or meet the raise, and has the privilege of raising again in return. If one player makes a bet or raise that no other player will see, he takes the pool without showing his hand, and the cards are shuffled and cut for the next deal.

30. CALLING THE BETS As long as one player raises another's bets, he gives that player the privilege of raising him again; however, if a player who has made a bet is not raised, and the other players simply bet an equal amount, the first bettor is called and all betting has to cease. The players then have to show their hand to the table, in order to decide which hand wins the pool.

31. Bets have to be actually made by placing the counters in the pool, and no bet is made until the player's hand has been withdrawn from the counters. Any counters once placed in the pool, and when the owner's hand is withdrawn, cannot be taken down again, except by the winner of the pool.

32. BETTING OUT OF TURN   If any player bets out of his turn, he cannot take down his counters again if he has removed his hand from them. If the player whose proper turn it was raises the bet, the player who bet out of turn has to either meet the raise or abandon his hand and all interest in that pool.

33. MOUTH BETS   Any player who states that he bets a specific amount but who fails to put up the actual counters in the pool cannot be called on to make the amount good after the hands are shown or the pool is won. If the players opposed to him choose to accept a mouth bet against the counters they have already put up, they have no remedy, because no value is attached to what a player says: his cards and counters speak for themselves. Any player who wishes to raise a mouth bet has the privilege of raising by mouth, instead of by counters, but cannot be called on to make the amount good after the hands are shown or the pool has been won.

34. SHOWING HANDS   When a call is made, all the hands have to be shown to the table, and the best poker hand wins the pool. Any player who declines to show his hand, even though he admits it is not good, has to pay an amount equal to the ante to each of the players at the table, or, if jackpots are played, has to put up for all of them in the next jackpot. When the hands are called, there is no penalty for mis-calling a hand: the cards, similar to the counters, speak for themselves.

35. RANK OF THE HANDS   The best poker hand is a *Royal Flush*: A K Q J 10 of the same suit, which beats:
   A Straight Flush: any sequence of five cards of the same suit.
   Four of a Kind: such as four 10s and an odd card.
   A Full Hand: three of a kind and a pair, such as three 8's and a pair of Q's, which beats:
   A Flush: five cards of the same suit, but not in sequence.
   A Straight: five cards in sequence, but of various suits. In straights, the Ace cannot be used to form combinations such as Q K A 2 3, but can be used as the bottom of 5 4 3 2, or the top of 10 J Q K. Straights beat:
   Three of a Kind: such as three K's and two odd cards.
   Two Pairs: such as two 9's and two 7's, with an odd card.
   A Pair: such as two Aces and three odd cards.
   If no pair is shown, the *Highest Card* wins.
   A short hand, such as four cards, cannot be claimed as either a straight or a flush.

36. TIES   In the case of ties, the highest of the odd cards decides it. Ultimate ties have to divide the pool. When combinations of equal rank are shown, the one that contains the highest cards wins, and the rank of the cards is A K Q J 10 9 8 7 6 5 4 3 2, so that two pairs: K's and 4's, will beat two pairs: Q's and J's. Three 5's and a pair of 2's will beat three 4's and a pair of aces.

JACKPOT LAWS

37. THE ANTES   There is neither age nor straddle in jackpots. Everyone at the table has to ante an equal amount. Any player can decline to ante, by saying, 'I pass this jack,' whereby the dealer will give him no cards.

38. OPENING   After the cards are dealt, each player in turn, beginning on the dealer's left, can open the pot for any amount he pleases within the betting limit, provided he holds a pair of Jacks or some hand better than a pair of Jacks. If he does not hold openers, or does not wish to open the pot with them, he has to say: 'I pass,' but must not abandon his hand, under penalty of paying five counters to the pool.

39. FALSE OPENERS   If a player opens a jack without the hand to justify it, and discovers his error before he draws, his hand is foul, and he forfeits whatever amount he might have already placed in the pool. The players who have come into the pool after the false opening stay in and play for the pot, regardless of the value of the hands dealt to them.

40. FATTENING   If no player will open, the cards are re-shuffled, cut and dealt, usually by the same dealer, and each player adds one counter to the pool.

41. COMING IN   If any player opens the pot for a specific amount, each player in turn, on his left, can come in by putting up a similar amount, regardless of the value of his hand. Any player on the right of the opener who passed on the first round can now come in. Any player who declines to put up the amount for which the pot is opened has to abandon his hand, and all his interest in the pool.

42. RAISING THE OPENER   Any player who comes into the pool has the privilege of raising the original opener any amount within the betting limit, and he can in turn be raised again, just as in the ordinary pools. If the opener declines to meet this raise, he has to show his entire hand before abandoning it. If he declines to do so, he has to pay the antes for all the other players for another jack. It is not enough to show openers before the draw: the whole hand has to be shown.

43. DRAWING CARDS Each player in turn who has come in, beginning on the left of the dealer, can discard and draw, in order to improve his hand. The opener is allowed to split his openers, provided it is the rule of the game that the opener will *always* put his discard under the chips in the pool, whether or not he intends to split. The opener's discard must never be gathered in with other discards when the pack runs short for the draw.

44. FALSE HANDS If a false opener does not discover his mistake until after he has drawn cards, his hand is foul and has to be abandoned. For a penalty, he has to put up an ante for each of the other players at the table for another Jack.

45. BETTING THE HANDS The opener makes the first bet, or, if he has withdrawn, the player next on his left makes it. If the opener declines to bet after the draw, he has to show his openers before abandoning his hand. He does not have to show the cards he has drawn. If no bet is made, the last player who holds cards takes the pool without showing his hand. If a bet is made, the game proceeds as in the ordinary pools. If the opener retires during the betting, he has to show his openers; if he is in the final call, he has to show his entire hand, whether or not it is the best. If he or any other player declines to show his hand when a call is made, he has to ante for all the other players for another jack.

46. SHY BETS If any player is shy in a jackpot, whether from failure to put up his ante, to fatten, or to substantiate his mouth bets with counters, nothing can be collected from him after a call has been made or the pot has been won.

— —

STRAIGHT POKER

Straight Poker or *Bluff* is played with a full pack of fifty-two cards and any number of players from one to eight. The arrangements for counters, seats and deal are exactly the same as in Draw Poker, but the method of anteing and betting up the hands is slightly different. There is no draw to improve the hand, and no such combination as a straight flush is recognised: four of a kind is the highest hand possible.

The ante and betting limit have to be decided before play begins. The first dealer is provided with a *buck*, which should be a pen-knife or a similar article. Before dealing, he puts up the amount of the ante for all the players, and then *passes the buck* to the player on his left, who must ante for all the players in the next pool. There is no variation of the amount of the ante under any circumstances, and the buck is passed around the table in this way irrespective of the deal, which is taken by the player who wins the pool. The laws for the deal and its irregularities are the same as in Draw Poker, except that it does not pass to the left.

When the cards are dealt, each player in turn, beginning with the one to the left of the dealer, can either bet or pass. If all pass, the holder of the buck antes, whereby a double pool is made, and passes the buck. The deal then passes to the left. If any player makes a bet, each player in turn, beginning with the one on his left, has to call it, raise it or abandon his hand. Players who have passed the first time now have to decide. The rules for seeing, raising, calling and showing hands are precisely the same as for Draw Poker.

Because of the absence of the draw, there is no clue as to the strength of an opponent's hand, except his manner and the amount of his bet. The hands shown are much weaker than the average of the ones in Draw Poker: they are about equal to hands that a player in that game would come in on. Triplets are very strong in Straight Poker, and two pairs will win three out of four pools in a five-handed game. The great element of success is bluff.

— —

STUD POKER

The arrangements for the cards, seats, antes, buck and so on are precisely as in Straight Poker; however, in dealing, only the first card is dealt face downwards, and the remaining four cards are turned up by the dealer as he gives them out. Each player in turn then looks at his *down card*, and the betting proceeds as in Straight Poker, whereby each player has the privilege of passing once before a bet is made.

A much more popular method is to stop the deal at two cards, whereby each player has received one face downwards and another face upwards. The best card showing then makes the first bet, and each player in turn has to meet it, raise it or pass out of that pool. If no one will call, the player who makes the bet takes the pool and the next deal. If a bet is made and called, the players in the call do not show their down cards, but are each given another card, face upwards, and the same betting process is gone through, whereby the best hand showing face upwards makes the first bet in each round. As long as two or more players remain in the pool, they are given more cards until they have five. The final betting is then done, and if a call is made, the down cards are shown, and the best poker hand wins the pool. Straight flushes do not count.

— · —

WHISKEY POKER

The arrangements for the cards, seats and so on, are the same as in Draw Poker. Each player is provided with an equal number of white counters, which can either have a value attached to them or simply represent markers. If the counters represent money, each player should have at least twenty; if they are only markers, five is the usual number.

If the game is played for money, each player puts one counter in the pool before the cards are dealt. There is no raising or betting of any kind.

An extra hand, called *the widow*, is dealt face downwards in Whiskey Poker. The dealer gives each player and the widow five cards, one at a time, beginning on his left, and deals to the widow just before he deals to himself. Each player in turn, beginning with the age, then examines his hand, and has the option of exchanging it for the widow, keeping it for the purpose of drawing to it, or risking his chances of winning the pool with it as it is.

If he wishes to exchange, he has to place his five cards face upwards on the table, and take up the widow, but not show it to any other player. The hand he abandons then becomes the widow. If he prefers to draw to his hand, he says, '*I pass,*' whereby the option of taking the widow is transferred to the next player. If he wishes to stand on the merits of the hand dealt to him, and not draw to it, he *knocks* on the table, whereby the option of taking the widow also passes to the next player on his left.

If any player takes the widow, the next player on his left can do any one of three things: he can discard from his own hand any card he pleases, taking one from the widow in its stead, whereby the card that he discards is placed on the table face upwards, and becomes part of the widow; or exchange his entire hand for the widow; or stand on the hand dealt him, and knock. Whether he draws one card, exchanges his entire hand or knocks, the next player on his left has the option of drawing, exchanging or knocking, and so on, until a player knocks.

If no player takes the widow until it comes to the dealer's turn, he has to either take it or turn it face upwards on the table. Even if the dealer knocks, he has to turn up the widow, and give each player an opportunity to draw from it or to exchange his entire hand for it.

When a player knocks, he signifies that no matter what the players following him might do, when it comes to his turn again the hands have to be shown. A player cannot draw and knock at the same time, but he can refuse to draw or exchange after another player has knocked, not before. In some localities, it is the rule to turn the widow face upwards at once if any player knocks before it is taken, whereby all the players after the knock are given an opportunity to draw or exchange; however, this is not the usual custom.

Suppose five play. E deals, and A passes; B takes the widow; C and D draw from B's abandoned hand, and E knocks—without drawing, naturally. A, who passed the first time, now has an opportunity to draw or exchange, and so have each of the other players in turn, up to D, but after D draws or exchanges, the hands have to be shown, because the next player, E, has knocked.

When the hands are shown, there are two ways to settle: if the counters have a money value, the best poker hand wins the pool, and the deal passes to the left; if the counters have no money value, there is no pool; however, the player who has shown the worst hand puts one of his counters in the middle of the table. This continues until a player has lost all five of his counters, and he is then called on to pay for the whiskey, or whatever refreshments might be at stake in the game—hence the name Whiskey Poker.

— —

PEEK POKER

This is a variety of Stud Poker, of which there are two forms, whereby seven cards are dealt to each player, or eight. In the first and original form of the game, two cards are dealt to each player, face downwards, then five face upwards. With eight cards, the last is also face downwards. The players draw, one card at a time, as in stud, and at the end, each player has to reduce his hand to five cards if he wishes to show for the pool.

—˙—

DEUCES WILD

This is an improvement on Joker Poker, or Mistigris. It can be played with the full pack of fifty-two cards, or the deleted pack of forty-four only, but if only forty-four, the cards taken out have to be the threes and fours whereby the deuces are left in.

The holder of one or more deuces can call these cards anything he likes, even if he has the duplicate of that card in his own hand. Two kings and a deuce can be called three kings. The king, jack, ten of clubs and two deuces can be called a straight flush, king high; or a royal flush, ace high.

Every pot is a jack, but there are no openers required. When the usual betting, drawing and calling are over, the hands are shown, and the best combination that can be made out of the cards and deuces, if any, wins. Five of a kind is a legitimate hand.

Sometimes the joker is added, in which case the four deuces and the joker would be the best possible hand. Any legitimate hand will win a tie with a hand made up of deuces or the joker, so that a pair of kings will beat king and deuce.

—˙—

THE WILD WIDOW

This is a variation of deuces wild. The game is practically draw poker, except that after each player has received four cards, one card is dealt to the table face upwards. Each player then gets his fifth card. The three cards of the same denomination as the widow, which is face upwards, are then 'running wild,' and any player who holds one or more of these cards can call it what he pleases, just as in deuces wild. The joker is sometimes added, so that there are four cards running wild.

— —

THE STRIPPED PACK

It is sometimes agreed to take out the deuces and treys and to play with only forty-four cards. This is to alter to some extent the established probabilities of the game.

— —

THIRTY-ONE

This game is sometimes called *Schnautz*. A pool is made up by any number of players. The dealer takes a pack of fifty-two cards and gives three to each player, face downwards, and three extra cards to the table, dealt face upwards. Each player in turn to the left can exchange one of his own cards for one of the cards on the table, whereby the object is to get a flush of three cards of some suit that has a pip value of thirty-one, or to get three of a kind.

The aces are worth 11, and the other court cards and the ten are worth 10 each. If no one can get a flush worth thirty-one, three of a kind wins the pool. If no one has three of a kind, the highest pip value shown in one suit wins. Drawing is kept up until a player knocks, after which only one more draw is allowed, and the knocker is not allowed to draw again. A player can knock without drawing at all if he wishes to prevent the other players from beating his original hand.

— —

BRAG

There are two varieties of this old English game: single- and three-stake Brag. Both are played with a full pack of fifty-two cards, and the positions of the players, arrangements for counters, decision of the betting limit and so on are the same as in Draw Poker. Three to twelve players can form a table.

There is a special value attached to three cards that are known as *braggers*. These again have a rank of their own: the best is the *ace of diamonds*, then the *Jack of clubs*, then the *nine of diamonds*. All other cards rank as in Poker. A player to whom any one of these braggers is dealt can call it anything he pleases. If he has a pair of nines and a bragger, or a nine and two braggers, he can call them three nines and bet on them as such. In this way, braggers resemble mistigris, which has already been described in connection with Draw Poker; however, in Brag, a natural pair or triplet outranks one made with the aid of a bragger. Three eights will beat an eight and two braggers.

The dealer has to put up an ante before the cards are cut. This ante can be any amount he pleases within the betting limit; no player can straddle or raise this ante until the cards are dealt. Beginning on his left, the dealer distributes the cards face downwards, and one at a time, until each player has received three. Beginning with the age, [eldest hand] each player in turn has to put up an amount equal to the dealer's ante or abandon his hand. He can, if he chooses, raise the ante any other amount within the betting limit. All players following him have to meet the total sum put up by any individual player, increase it or pass out. In this way, Brag is precisely similar to the betting after the draw in Poker.

If no one will see the dealer's ante, he has to be paid one white counter by each of the other players, and the deal passes to the left. If any player bets an amount that no other player will meet, he takes the pool without showing his hand. If a call is made, all the hands have to be shown, and the best brag hand wins.

Pairs and triplets are the only combinations of any value, and three aces are naturally the best hand; two aces and the club Jack are the next best. If none of the hands shown contains either a natural pair or a bragger, the highest card wins, and the ace ranks above the King. In the case of equal natural pairs, the highest card outside the pair wins. If the pairs tied are both made with a bragger, the highest bragger wins. Two odd cards, seven high, with the club Jack, would beat two cards seven high with the diamond nine.

THREE-STAKE BRAG   In this variation, each player puts up three equal amounts to form three equal pools. These amounts have to be invariable, and should be agreed on before play begins. The dealer then gives two cards to each player, one at a time, face downwards, and then a third card to each, face upwards. The highest card turned up in this way wins one of the pools, whereby the ace is the highest and the deuce the lowest. The diamond ace, being a bragger, outranks any other ace, the club Jack any other Jack, and the diamond nine any other nine. Ties are decided in favour of the eldest hand or the player nearest him on the left.

The players then take up the other two cards, without showing them, and proceed to brag on their hands as in single-stake Brag. The winner takes the second pool, but the players who pass out do not abandon their hands until the third pool is decided. If no bet is made for the second pool, it is won by the dealer.

All hands are shown in order to decide the last pool. Each player counts up the pip value of his three cards, reckoning the aces for eleven and court-cards as ten each. The player who comes nearest to thirty-one takes the third pool. Ties are decided in favour of the eldest hand, as before.

In some places, another variation is introduced by allowing the players to draw cards for the third pool, in order to increase the pip value of their hands. Beginning with the eldest hand, each player in turn pays into the pool a counter for each card he draws. These cards are given by the dealer face upwards, and one player has to be given all he requires before the next is passed to. If a player passes thirty-one, he is out of the pool. Some judgement is necessary in drawing in this way, because all the hands are exposed and each player knows exactly what he has to beat.

In *American Brag*, there are eight braggers: the Jacks and nines of each suit, and they are all of equal rank when used as braggers. Pairs or triplets formed with the aid of braggers outrank naturals, so that three Jacks are an invincible hand, and beat three aces. Two braggers and an ace outrank two aces and a bragger, but the absurd part of the arrangement is that three Jacks and three nines are a tie.

The method of playing differs from English Brag. If the players simply equal the dealer's ante, nothing unusual occurs, and all the hands are shown at once. However, if any player raises, and another sees this raise, these two immediately exchange hands, without showing them to the other players, and the one who held the worse hand retires from that pool, whereby the better hand is returned to its original holder, who then awaits a call or raise from the next player in order, and the entire amount staked remains in the pool. This lose-and-drop-out system is continued until only one player remains to dispute the pool with the dealer. If they come to a call, both hands are shown to the table. If the bragger is not called, he takes the pool without showing his hand.

COMMERCE

This old English game is evidently the forerunner of Whiskey Poker. It is played with a full pack of fifty-two cards, and the arrangements for the seats, counters and so on are the same as in Draw Poker. Three to twelve players can form a table. There are two methods of playing Commerce: with and without a widow. We will take the older form first.

WITHOUT A WIDOW   The counters have a money value, and each player deposits a counter in the pool. The dealer then distributes the cards one at a time, face downwards, until each player has three. The players then examine their cards, and each in turn, beginning with the eldest hand, can exchange one card. If he trades *for ready money*, he gives his card and one white counter to the dealer, and receives another card, face downwards, from the top of the pack. The discard is left on the table, and the counter is the dealer's perquisite. If he trades *for barter*, he passes his discard to the player on his left, who has to give one of his own counters in exchange before looking at the counter he is to receive. If the player will not exchange, he has to *knock* on the table, to signify that he will stand by the cards he has. If he exchanges, he takes up the offered card, and then has the privilege of trading for ready money or for barter himself. The trading goes on in this way around and around, until a player knocks, whereby all trading is immediately stopped and the hands are shown. The best hand wins the pool, whereby the rank of the various combinations is as follows, beginning with the highest.

TRIPLETS   Three aces are the highest, and three deuces the lowest. Pairs have no value.
Sequence Flushes   The ace is allowed to rank as the top or the bottom: Q K A, or A 2 3.
The Point   This is the greatest number of pips on two or three cards of the same suit in one hand, whereby the ace counts for eleven and the other court-cards for ten each. A single card of a suit does not count for the point. In the case of ties, a point made with three cards will beat one made with two cards. If the number of cards is also a tie, the dealer or the player nearest him on his left wins.

If no triplet is shown, the best straight flush wins. If there is no straight flush, the best point wins. The deal passes to the left, and a misdeal loses the deal, because the deal is an advantage, owing to the trade for ready money.

If the dealer does not win the pool, he has to pay one white counter to the player who does. If the dealer holds a combination of the same rank as the one that wins the pool, he has to pay one white counter to every other player at the table. For example, no triplet is shown, and a straight flush, Jack high, wins the pool. The dealer has a straight flush, 9 high, and has to pay one counter to every player at the table. If the dealer had no sequence flush, he would pay the winner of the pool only.

WITH A WIDOW　This is almost three-card Whiskey Poker. Each player is provided with three counters only, which are of no value, and three cards are dealt to each player and to the widow, face downwards, one at a time. The widow is turned face upwards immediately, and the dealer has the first say. Before he looks at the cards he has dealt to himself, he can exchange his whole hand for the widow; otherwise, the eldest hand has the first draw. No other player can exchange his whole hand, but each in turn can draw one card until a player knocks. The moment any player knocks, all drawing has to cease, and the hands are shown at once. Triplets, straight flushes and points determine the value of the hands, as already described, and the best hand takes the pool. The dealer makes no extra payments, because he has no perquisites. The first player to lose his three counters pays for the whiskey, and if two or more are frozen out at the same time, the one with the worst hand pays. The game is sometimes varied by playing freeze-out, whereby a value is attached to the three counters, and players who are decavé retire from the game until all the counters have been won by a single player.

Two other combinations are sometimes introduced in either form of Commerce: a flush, three cards of one suit, which rank next below the straight flush and a single pair that outrank the point.

Another variety of Commerce is variously known as *My Ship Sails* and *My Bird Sings*. The counters have a money value, and three are given to each player. Three cards are dealt, face downwards, and one at a time. There is no widow. The eldest hand can then exchange one card with the player on his left, who must give his card before seeing the one he is to receive. The exchange goes around to the left. The moment any player finds himself with a flush: three cards of the same suit, regardless of their value, whether dealt to him or made by exchange, he says, 'My Ship Sails,' whereby all exchange is stopped and the hands are shown. If there is more than one flush, the pips win, whereby ace counts for 11 and other court-cards for 10 each. If no player has secured a flush after two rounds of exchanges, the hands are shown, and the highest number of pips in the two-card flushes wins the pool. The elder hand wins ties.

— —

BOUILLOTTE
OR BRELAN

This is an old and famous French gambling game that is often referred to in stories of fast life in European society. It was the rage during and long after the French Revolution, but later had to share public attention with Baccara, and even with Le Poker Américain. It has many points in common with three-stake Brag, and is evidently descended from the same stock. Many people consider Bouillotte to be superior to Poker, because it offers the player many opportunities to speculate on winning aided by cards that are not in his own hand.

CARDS   Bouillotte is played with a piques pack, reduced to twenty cards, and only the A K Q 9 8 of each suit are retained. The ace is the highest card in play and in cutting. If five people play, the Jack of each suit is added; if only three play, the Queens are discarded, whereby the pack is reduced to sixteen cards. Two packs are usually used alternately.

   Counters   Counters or chips are used, as in Poker, instead of money. Any player can be the banker.

PLAYERS   Three, four or five people can play, but four is the proper number, and in all descriptions of the game it is supposed to be four-handed.

CUTTING   To decide the positions of the players, a sequence of cards is sorted out that is equal in number with the number of players. These cards are then shuffled, face downwards, and each player draws one. The highest of the sequence has the choice of positions, and so on down until all are seated. The player who draws the King deals the first hand.

STAKES   Each player purchases an equal number of counters from the banker, usually 100. This original *cave* cannot be added to or deducted from. As long as a single counter of it remains, the player has to call for a sight, just as in freeze-out or table stakes, and not until he is *decavé* [has lost everything] can he purchase another stake, the amount of which is usually at his own option.

BLIND AND STRADDLE Before the distribution of the cards, the dealer puts up a blind, usually five counters, which the player on his right has the privilege of straddling. If he straddles, he can be straddled again, and so on. In Bouillotte, the straddle practically buys from the dealer the privileges of the age. If it goes around until the dealer buys it back himself, the straddling then has to be stopped.

DEALING As in all French games, the cards are cut by the player on the dealer's left, and are dealt from right to left. Three cards are given to each player, one at a time, face downwards, and the thirteenth is then turned face upwards on the pack. This card is called the *retourne.*

MISDEALS If any card is exposed during the deal, either in the pack or in giving it to a player, it is a misdeal; however, the distribution of the cards is continued until each player has received three cards, whereby the exposed card is given out in its regular order. If any player can show triplets, he receives one white counter from each of the other players, and the hands are then abandoned. If more than one triplet is shown, the inferior does not pay the higher. If no triplet is shown, the cards are re-dealt. A misdeal does not lose the deal.

The deal passes to the right; however, if the player whose turn it is to deal has lost everything on the previous deal, and has just purchased another stake, the deal passes to the player beyond him. If a player withdraws from the table when it is his turn to deal, the deal passes to any newcomer who might take his place.

BETTING When the cards are dealt, each player in turn, beginning with the one to the right of the dealer, or to the right of the last straddler, if any, can do one of three things: equal the amount of the ante; increase the ante as much as he pleases within the limits of his cave; or pass, whereby he retains his cards but bets nothing. If any player *opens* the game by making a bet, the player on his right can equal or raise it; however, he cannot pass after the game is opened, unless he withdraws from the pool. Any player can call for a sight for the amount in front of him, but that does not prevent the other players from continuing the betting. If no one will open, the deal is void, and each player puts five counters in the pool for the next deal. If a player opens, and no one will equal or raise him, he wins the antes and straddles, if any. If any player makes a raise that no one will meet, he takes whatever is in the pool, unless a player has called for a sight for a small part of it.

CALLING AND SHOWING If only two players bet against each other, either can call the other and demand a show of hands at any time; however, if three or four are betting, the privilege of calling falls on each in turn from right to left. For example, A, B, C and D play. D blinds five counters, and deals. A passes, and B opens for five reds. C passes out, and D and A both meet the bet of five reds, but neither will raise it. This does not call B, who has the privilege of raising the bet if he pleases. Suppose he raises, and D and A both meet it. On this second round, when C has passed out, it is D's turn to say whether or not he will raise. On the next round it will be A's turn, and after that it will be B's second turn, and so on. If any player meets the bet but refuses to raise, although it is his turn, he still cannot call. If he does not avail himself of his privilege of raising, he has to *pass the word* to the player on his right, that is, transfer the privilege to him. If he declines, it is a call; if he raises, it goes on until every player has refused to avail himself of the privilege. If a player chooses to raise without waiting for his turn, he can naturally do so. One of the fine points of the game is knowing when to raise the bet yourself and when to pass the word.

RANK OF THE HANDS If a call is made, the hands are shown, and the best Bouillotte hand wins. There are only two classes of hand recognised in Bouillotte: the brelan and the point, but there are three kinds of brelans, which rank in the following order.

A Brelan Carré This is four of a kind: three in the player's hand, and the fourth turned up on the pack. If any player holds a brelan [three of a kind] of a denomination higher than the brelan carré, the player can turn up the card under the retourne, and if this makes his hand a brelan carré also, he wins the pool. In addition to winning the pool, the holder of a brelan carré receives from each player four white counters.

A Simple Brelan This is three of a kind in the player's hand, whereby three aces are the highest and three eights the lowest. In addition to winning the pool, the holder of a simple brelan receives one counter from each of the other players at the table. If two are shown, neither pays the other. If the brelan is formed by uniting the retourne with two cards in the player's hand, it is a *brelan favori*, and the holder of it receives an extra counter from every player at the table, whether or not he wins the pool. For example, the retourne is an eight, and a brelan of Queens is shown and wins the pool. Another player holds a pair of eights, and claims brelan favori. He does not pay the winning brelan, but receives one counter from its holder, and also from each of the other players. If the brelan favori wins the pool, it is paid two counters by each player. If two simple brelans are shown, the higher wins the pool, but both must be paid by each of the other two players, who did not hold brelans.

THE POINT   If no brelan is shown, the hands of all the players are shown, including the ones who passed out during the betting. This will expose thirteen cards, including the retourne. The pips in each suit are then counted, whereby the ace reckons for 11, court cards for 10 each, and the 9 and 8 at their face value. Whichever suit has the greatest number of pips is called the *suit that wins*, and the player who holds the highest card of it takes the pool, provided, naturally, that he was one of the players who backed his hand until the last call. If the player who holds the best card of the winning suit has dropped out during the betting, his cards count for the player who has the highest card of the suit among the players who backed their hands. For example, D deals and turns the heart 8. A and B have passed out, but C has made a bet that D has called. Neither has a brelan, so all four players show their cards, and it is found that they lie as follows.

Spades are the winning suit, but neither C nor D has a spade, and because neither A nor B is in the call, the spade suit cannot win anything. As between clubs and hearts, D's point is 40, and C's 38; D therefore wins the pool. C, naturally, had a great advantage in betting, because he knew four hearts were out: his own and the retourne, and all he feared was a brelan. A would have won the pool had he backed his hand, because he would have had the highest card of the winning suit.

CALLING FOR A SIGHT   Suppose four players have the following caves in front of them: A, 35; B, 60; C, 120; and D, 185. D blinds five, deals, and turns the heart 9. A puts up all his 35 counters. B passes out. C raises 50, and puts up 85, and D bets everything: 180 more than his blind. A demands a sight for his 35, and C puts up the remainder of his 120 and calls a sight for them. D then withdraws his superfluous 65, and it is a call. No one has a brelan, so all the hands are shown, and the cards lie as follows.

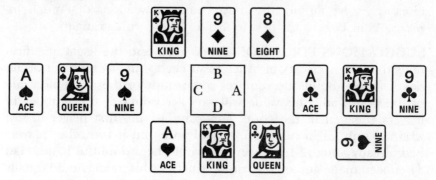

The point is exactly even for clubs and spades: 40 in each. In the case of ties, the dealer, or the player nearest him on the right, wins. In this case, A wins on account of his position, so clubs are the winning suit, and A has the best card of it. However, he can win from C and D only the amount for which he called a sight, that is, 35 counters. He therefore takes down 105 as his share of the pool, and leaves 170 to be decided between C and D. Now, although C has a better point than D, it is one of the principles of the game that the suit that wins cannot lose at the same time, and because D has a card of the winning suit, whereas C does not have one, D wins the remainder of the pool. If neither C nor D had a card of the winning suit, C would win from D on account of his better point.

If we transposed the club ace and spade ace, spades would be the winning suit, because the elder hand, A, had the best card of it; however, C would take the remainder of the pool, because he held a spade, whereas D did not hold one.

As it is, C is decavé, and has to purchase another stake or retire from the game. If C had lost this pool with a brelan in his hand, he would not be decavé, because after losing the pool, and all he had staked therein, B, who had passed out, would have to pay him for the brelan, and with this one white counter he would have to call for a sight in the next pool he entered.

METHODS OF CHEATING As in all games in which winning depends entirely on the cards held, and not on the way of playing them, Bouillotte offers many opportunities to the cheat. The small number of cards in the pack, and the consequent ease with which they can be handled, enable even the clumsiest card sharps to run up brelan carrés, make false shuffles, and shift cuts. There is one trick, called the poussette, which consists of surreptitiously placing more counters on the table when the player finds he has a hand worth backing. Marked cards, and packs trimmed to taper one way, biseautés, were among the most common weapons of French *tricheurs*. As in Poker, it is best to avoid playing with strangers.

SUGGESTIONS FOR GOOD PLAY   Beyond the usual qualifications that are necessary in order to succeed with any member of the poker family, Bouillotte requires some study of the probable value of the point, and this value will vary according to the number of players engaged in the coup. For example, the first player to say, who has only 21 in his hand, should ante, but if two other players had already anted, 31, or even 40, would be a doubtful hand. Had a bet been made and met by another player, this point should usually be laid down.

With good cards, it is always better for the eldest hand to pass, especially with a brelan, because he will then have an opportunity to judge the value of the hands against him, and can raise the bet to his advantage. Good players will not bet on an ace alone, unless the suit is turned up, nor on a point of 21 with a weak card of the turn-up suit. If three play in a pool, the point should be very strong to follow beyond the first raise, and if four players are engaged, it is almost a certainty that brelans will be shown.

When a player who has a brelan has frightened off his opponents with a big bet, it is usual to *stifle* the brelan, because it is considered to be more to the player's advantage to leave his adversaries under the impression that he might have been bluffing than to show the hand for the sake of the one white counter to which it entitles him. With three cards of one suit to the King, it is usual to bet high, in order to drive out anything but a brelan. Any player who holds ace and another of the suit will naturally abandon his hand, because his point is worth only 21 at the most, and the player who has three to the King will get the benefit of his cards when the point is counted.

— —

AMBIGU

CARDS   Ambigu is played with a pack of forty cards, whereby the K Q J of each suit are deleted. The cards rank in the order of their numerical value: the 10 is the highest and the ace the lowest. Two packs can be used alternately.

PLAYERS Any number from two to six can form the table, and the arrangements for seats, first deal and so on should be decided as in Bouillotte.

STAKES Each player begins with an equal number of counters, the value of which has to be determined beforehand. A betting limit should be agreed on, and one player should be the banker for the game.

BLIND Before the cards are dealt, each player deposits one counter in the pool; there is no straddle.

DEALING The cards are cut to the left and dealt to the right, and two cards are given to each player, one at a time, face downwards.

METHOD OF PLAYING Each player in turn, beginning on the dealer's right, examines his hand, and if satisfied with it says, 'Enough.' If not satisfied, he can discard one or both of his cards and receive others from the top of the pack. In either case, he places two white counters in the pool for his ante. When all have decided to stand or to draw, the remainder of the pack, exclusive of the discards, is re-shuffled and cut; each player is then given two more cards, one at a time, and face downwards. Each in turn examines his four cards, and if satisfied says, 'I play.' If not, he says, 'I pass.' If all pass, the dealer has the choice of two things: he can gather the cards and deal again, whereby each player puts another counter into the pool, or he can put up two white counters himself and compel the players to retain the cards dealt to them, whereby the dealer keeps his as well.

Any person who announces to play can put up as many counters as he pleases within the betting limit. If no person will stay with him, he takes back his raise, leaving the antes, and is paid two counters by the last player who refuses. If two or more declare to play, they can either meet the amount offered by the first player or raise him. If any player declines to meet a raise, he has to abandon his hand. If no one will call the last raise, the player who makes it takes the pool, and then shows his hand and demands payment from each of the other players for whatever combination he holds. If two or more players call, by making their bets equal, they again draw cards, whereby they have the privilege of either discarding any number from one to four or standing pat. After the draw, each in turn can pass or play. If all pass, the hands are abandoned, and the pool remains, whereby each player adds one counter for the next deal. This is to force players to bet on their hands. If a bet is made, the calling and raising proceeds as in Draw Poker.

When there are not enough cards to supply the players, the discards have to be gathered, shuffled and cut. Any player who has too many or too few cards has to abandon his hand as foul. Any player who shows his cards has to abandon his hand and forfeit four counters to the pool.

The general laws of Poker that govern all irregularities can be applied to Ambigu; however, it has to be remembered that French players are traditionally very much averse to penalties of all kinds, and if an error can be rectified without doing an injustice to any player, it is usual to set things right in the simplest way possible.

VALUE OF THE HANDS There are seven combinations of value in Ambigu, which rank in the following order, beginning with the lowest.

THE POINT This is the total number of pips on two or more cards of the same suit. A single card does not count for the point. Three cards of one suit are a better point than two cards, even if there are more pips on the two cards. If no higher combination than a point is shown, the player who has the winning point receives **one counter** from each of the other players at the table, besides winning the pool and everything in it. In the case of ties, the player who has two cards in sequence wins. For example, an 8 and a 7 will beat a 10 and a 5. If this does not decide it, the elder hand wins.

THE PRIME Four cards of different suits, sometimes called a Dutch flush, is a better hand than the point. If a prime is the best combination shown, the holder wins the pool and receives **two counters** from each of the other players. If the pips in the prime aggregate more than thirty, it is called **Grand Prime**, and the holder receives **three counters** instead of two from each of the other players. If two or more primes are shown, the one who has the highest number of pips wins. If this is still a tie, the elder hand wins.

A **Sequence** is a bobtail straight flush; that is, three of the four cards are in sequence, such as the 2, 3 and 4 of spades, with an odd card, such as a 9. This is a better combination than a prime, and the holder receives **three counters** from each player. In the case of ties, the highest sequence wins. If the sequence flush is one of four cards, it is a doublet.

A **Tricon**, or three of a kind, is better than a straight, and entitles the holder to *four counters* from each of the other players. Pairs have no value.

A *Flush* is four cards of the same suit, not necessarily in sequence, and is better than a tricon. The holder is paid *five counters* by each of the other players, and wins the pool.

DOUBLETS Any hand that contains a double combination will beat any single combination. For example, a player holds three of a kind, and the fourth card in his hand is of a suit different from any of his triplet. His hand is a double combination: prime and tricon, and will beat a flush. A sequence of four cards of the same suit is a double combination, and will beat anything but a fredon. When doublets are shown, the holder is paid for both combinations: *six* for tricon and prime, or *eight* for sequence and flush, as the case may be.

A *Fredon*, or four of a kind, is the best possible hand, and the holder is paid *ten or eleven counters* by each of the other players, according to the pip value of his cards. He is paid eight counters for fredon, and two for the prime, if it is smaller than 8's; however, he claims grand prime if he has four 9's, or four 10's, and gets eleven counters.

In the case of *ties* that cannot be decided by way of the pip values, the elder hand wins.

Even if a player has lost his entire stake in the pool, he has to pay the various combinations shown, and it is usual to reserve about ten counters for this purpose.

BETTING THE HANDS After the last cards have been drawn, the players proceed to bet on their hands precisely as in Poker. If a player makes a bet or raise that no one will call, he takes the pool, and then shows his hand and demands payment for the combination he holds. It is very unusual for a player to stifle a hand in Ambigu as he would at Bouillotte. If a call is made, the players in the call show and compare their cards, and the best hand wins the pool. Only the player who wins the pool can demand payment for combinations held.

THE EUCHRE FAMILY

——

This family embraces four of the best known and most popular games in the world, each of which has been considered to be the national game in its own country: Écarté in France, Napoleon in England, Spoil Five in Ireland, and Euchre in America.

It has always been the custom to trace the origin of Euchre to a variety of Triomphe, or French Ruff, which was probably introduced in America by the French residents of Louisiana, and to claim Écarté as its cousin and the French survivor of the parent game. In the opinion of the author, both the game and its name go to show that Euchre is of mixed stock and that it probably originated in an attempt to play the ancient Irish game of Spoil Five using a piquet pack. 'Euchre' is not a French word, but the meaning of it is identical to that of 'Spoil Five': both names signify that the object of the game is to prevent the maker of the trump from getting three tricks. In one game, he is 'spoiled'; in the other, he is 'euchred'. In the old game of Triomphe, in Écarté, and in the black suits in Spoil Five, the order of the court-cards in plain suits is the same: the ace ranks below the Jack. In Euchre, however, the Jack ranks above the ace when the suit is trumps, exactly as it does in Spoil Five. In the latter game, the five is the best trump; however, because there is no five in a piquet pack, that trump was probably disregarded, whereby the Jack was left the best. Taking up, or 'robbing' the turn-up trump, is another trait that is common to both Spoil Five and Euchre.

Spoil Five and Triomphe are mentioned in the earliest works about card games. Triomphe can be traced to the year 1520, when it was popular in Spain, and the origin of Maw, the parent of Spoil Five, is lost in the mists of Irish antiquity. It was the fashionable game during the reign of England's James I.

The old Spanish game of Triomphe, which is now obsolete, seems to have undergone several changes after its introduction in France.

At first, it was played by either two people or two pairs of partners. If one side had bad cards, it could offer to abandon the hand and allow the adversaries to count a point without playing. If the adversaries refused, they were obliged to win all five tricks or lose two points. It was compulsory to win the trick if possible, and to trump, overtrump or undertrump if the player had none of the suit led. This peculiarity survives in the games of Rams and Loo, which also belong to the euchre family.

After a time, we find a variation introduced in which any number from two to six could play, each for himself, and the player who first won two tricks out of the five marked the point. Later still, we find the ace ranking above the King and thereby becoming the best trump. If the ace was turned up, the dealer had the privilege of robbing it, or the holder of the ace of trumps could rob the turn-up and discard any card he pleased, just as in Spoil Five. However, in Triomphe, the dealer turned up another card, and if that was of the trump suit, the holder of the ace could rob that also, and so on until he turned a card of a different suit. This did not alter the trump but merely stopped the robbing process. Whether or not Triomphe borrowed this feature from Spoil Five or Maw it is now impossible to say.

Whatever its origin, Euchre has always been the most respectable member of the family, and the game that has best served the card-playing interest in social life. Spoil Five probably comes next with reference to respectability, but Écarté has often fallen into evil hands, and in some places the very name is viewed as being synonymous with gambling. The same is true of Napoleon, but to a lesser extent. Euchre, unlike the other members of the family, is not essentially a gambling game but belongs to the intellectual group of card games, a position we hope it can long maintain.

— · —

EUCHRE

CARDS   Euchre is played with what is commonly known as the piquet pack: thirty-two cards, whereby all cards below the 7 are deleted. In plain suits, the cards rank as in Whist, but in the trump suit, the Jack is the best and is called the *Right Bower*. The Jack of the same colour as the trump suit, red or black, is the second-best trump, and is called the *Left Bower*, so that if clubs were trumps, the rank of the nine cards in the trump suit would be as follows.

The rank of the cards in the other suits would be:

When the *Joker*, or blank card, is used, it is always the best trump, and ranks above the right bower. In cutting, the ace is low, and the other cards rank as in plain suits. A player who cuts the Joker has to cut again.

COUNTERS Counters or whist markers can be used for keeping the score, but it is much more common to use the small cards from the deleted portion of the pack. The game is five points, and the best method of scoring is to use the 4 and 3 of any suit. When the 3 is face upwards but covered by the 4 face downwards, it counts *one*. When the 4 is face upwards, covered by the 3 face downwards, it counts *two*. When the 4 is face downwards, covered by the 3 face upwards, it counts *three*. When the 3 is face downwards, covered by the 4 face upwards, it counts *four*.

ONE   TWO   THREE   FOUR

The number of pips exposed on the card that is face upwards is immaterial; the relative position of the two cards will always determine the score.

Rubber or game scores have to be kept on either a whist marker or a sheet of paper.

PLAYERS Euchre can be played by any number of people from two to seven, but in the seven-handed game, the full pack of fifty-three cards is used. Whatever the number of players, the players cut for positions at the table, for partners and for the deal.

CUTTING The cards are usually spread, face downwards, and each candidate for play draws a card.

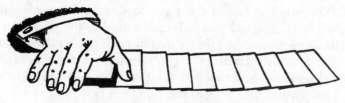

SPREADING THE PACK

When *two* or *three* play, the lowest cut has the choice of seats and takes the first deal. When *four* play, they cut for partners, and the two highest pair against the two lowest. The lowest has the choice of seats, and deals the first hand. When *five* or *seven* play, they have the choice of seats in their order, whereby the lowest goes first, and the lowest cut deals. When *six* play, the three lowest are partners against the three highest, whereby the lowest cut has the choice of seats, and the first deal.

TIES Players who cut cards of equal value cut again, but the new cut decides nothing but the tie.

PLAYERS' POSITIONS The *eldest hand*, or age, sits on the left of the dealer, and the pone sits on the dealer's right. There are no distinctive names for the other positions.

When *two* play, they sit opposite each other. When *three* play, each for himself, the game is known as *Cut Throat*, and the position of the players is immaterial. When *four* play, the partners sit opposite each other. When *five* or *seven* play, the maker of the trump in each deal selects his partners, and these players play against the other players without any change in their positions at the table. When *six* play, three are partners against the other three, and the opposing players sit alternately round the table.

STAKES If there is any stake on the game, its amount has to be settled before play begins. When *rubbers* are played, it is usual to make the stake so much a rubber point. If the winners of the game are five points to their adversaries' nothing, they win a *treble*, and count three rubber points. If the losers have scored one or two points only, the winners mark two points for a *double*. If the losers have reached three or four, the winners mark one for a *single*. The side that wins the rubber adds two points to its score for doing so, so that the largest rubber possible is one of eight points: two triples to nothing, and two added for the rubber. The smallest possible is one point: two singles and the rubber, against a triple. If the first two games are won by the same partners, the third game is not played.

DEALING Any player has the right to shuffle the cards, and the dealer goes last. The pack has to be presented to the pone to be cut, and he has to leave at least four cards in each packet. Beginning on his left, the dealer distributes the cards either two at a time and then three, or three and then two, to each player in rotation until all the players have five cards. Whichever number: two or three, that the dealer begins with, he has to continue giving the same number to every player, including himself, for the first round. After the cards are dealt, the next card is turned face upwards on the remainder of the pack, except in five- and seven-handed Euchre, in which no trump is turned. Each player deals in turn to the left, until the conclusion of the game or rubber.

IRREGULARITIES IN THE DEAL If any card is found faced in the pack, the dealer has to deal again. If the dealer exposes any card but the trump while he is dealing, the adversaries can demand a new deal by the same dealer. If any adversary of the dealer exposes a card, the dealer can elect to deal again. A player who deals out of turn can be stopped before the trump card is turned; however, after that, the deal has to stand, and afterward passes to the left in regular order. On completion of the deal, if any player has more or fewer than five cards, it is a misdeal, and the deal passes to the player on the misdealer's left.

The dealer loses his deal if he neglects to have the pack cut; if he deals a card incorrectly and fails to remedy the error before dealing another card; if he counts the cards on the table or the ones remaining in the pack; or if he deals two cards to one player and three to another in the same round.

If the pack is found to be imperfect, the deal in which the error is discovered is void, but all previous scores stand good.

MAKING THE TRUMP Although a card is turned up at the end of the deal, the suit to which it belongs is not necessarily the trump for that hand. Each player in turn, beginning on the dealer's left, whether he is an adversary or a partner of the dealer, can insist that the turn-up suit remain the trump, or can declare that he is indifferent as to which suit is the trump: the one turned up or some other. But if one player in his proper turn decides in favour of the turn-up, no player after him can alter the decision. When it comes to the dealer's turn, if no other player has decided to retain the suit turned up, he has to either let the trump remain as it is or insist on its being changed.

Because the individual or side that settles which suit will be the trump is said to **make the trump**, it will be necessary to describe the method of scoring in order to understand the principles that guide the players in deciding on the trump suit.

SCORING Euchre is played for tricks. If the side that makes the trump takes three or four tricks out of the five possible, it scores one point. If the side wins all five tricks, it scores two points for a **march**. If the player who makes the trump fails to win three tricks, he is **euchred**, and his adversaries score two points for the euchre. **When four play**, if the player who makes the trump declares to play **alone**, that is, without any assistance from his partner, who has to lay down his cards, the maker of the trump scores four points if he succeeds in winning all five tricks, and one point if he wins three or four tricks. However, if he fails to win three tricks, he is euchred, and the adversaries score two points. **When three play**, a lone hand counts three if the player wins all five tricks. **When two play**, five tricks is simply a march, and counts two points. **When five or seven play**, there are special scores for lone hands. When all five tricks are taken by one side, but not by an individual who is playing a lone hand, it is simply a march, and counts two points, no matter how many people are playing. When two or three people are playing, a march naturally has to be a lone hand, because there are no partnerships. As we will see later, there are some varieties of Euchre in which a lone hand can play against a lone hand, but this is not permitted in the ordinary game.

No one but the individual player who makes the trump can play alone.

Except in five- and seven-handed Euchre, the player who or the side that first reaches five points wins the game. If three people are playing, and two of them reach five points simultaneously by euchring the third, they both win a game. If they are playing for stakes, they divide the pool.

TAKING UP THE TRUMP After the trump is turned up, each player in turn examines his cards, and if he does not care whether or not the trump suit remains unchanged, he says, *'I pass.'* If all the players pass, the dealer has to decide. The dealer has the advantage of being allowed to take the trump card into his own hand and discarding one of his worthless cards in its place. If he thinks he can make three tricks with the turn-up suit for trumps, and his partner's probable assistance, or can win five tricks by playing alone, he discards any card he pleases, and places it under the remainder of the pack, face downwards, without showing or naming it. If the dealer decides to play alone, it is usual for him to pass his discard across the table to his partner, face downwards, so there can be no misunderstanding about his intention.

The dealer can take up the trump card at any time during the play of the hand, but it is usual to leave it on the pack until it is played to a trick. No one but the dealer can take the trump into his hand.

TURNING DOWN THE TRUMP   If the dealer fears that he and his partner cannot make three tricks with the turn-up suit for trumps, or would prefer to have the suit changed, he can pass. If he passes, he takes the trump card from the top of the pack, and places it face upwards, and partly under the pack, in a way whereby it can be distinctly seen.

TAKEN UP   TURNED DOWN

CHANGING THE TRUMP   It then becomes the turn of the other players, each in succession to the left of the dealer, to either name some other suit for the trump or pass a second time. If the suit of the same colour as that of the turn-up is named for the new trump, it is usual to say, *'I make it next.'* If a suit of a different colour is named, it is called *crossing the suit*, and some players, if a red suit is turned, will say, 'I *cross* to clubs.'

Any player who names a new suit can announce to play alone at the same time. The side that makes the new trump has to make at least three tricks, or will be euchred, and the adversaries will count two points. If a player names the suit that has just been turned down, he loses his right to make the trump, and if he corrects himself and names another suit, he debars not only himself but his partner from making the trump. When one player has named a new trump suit in his proper turn, his decision is binding on all the other players; however, if a player names a suit out of his proper turn, both he and his partner are debarred from making that suit the trump. If no one will name a new trump, the deal is void, and passes to the next player on the dealer's left.

ORDERING UP THE TRUMP Rather than pass the turn-up trump on the first round, any player who thinks it would be to his advantage to have the turn-up remain the trump can order the dealer to take it up. In doing so, he says, *'I order it,'* if he is an adversary, or, *'I assist,'* if he is the dealer's partner. In either case, the player who makes the trump can announce a lone hand at the same time. His side has to make at least three tricks, whether or not he plays alone, or it is a euchre, and the adversaries will count two points. In case an adversary of the dealer plays alone, he has to distinctly announce it when he orders up the trump. The usual expression is *'I order it alone.'* His partner then lays his cards face downwards on the table and takes no further part in the play of that hand. If he exposes any card of the abandoned hand, the adversaries can call on him to take up the hand and play it, whereby the exposed card is left on the table as liable to be called. This naturally stops the lone hand.

If the dealer's partner wishes to play alone instead of to assist, he says, *'I play this alone,'* and the dealer lays down his cards, whereby the trump is left on the pack.

PLAYING ALONE No player but the one who takes up, orders up or makes the trump can play a lone hand. If the dealer takes up the trump card of his own accord, he can play alone. If any player orders up or assists, he can play alone. Any player who makes a new trump after the first has been turned down can play alone. If one player orders up the trump, neither his partner nor his adversary can play alone, and if the dealer's partner assists, the dealer is prevented from playing a lone hand. In many clubs, the mistake is made of allowing the dealer to play alone on his partner's assist, or of letting the pone play alone after the dealer has been assisted, or of letting the partner of the player who makes the new trump play alone. This is not good Euchre, because an unfair advantage is thereby given to one side, as we will see when we come to the suggestions for good play, especially in connection with ordering up at what is called the 'bridge', that is, when the score is either 4 to 1 or 4 to 0.

METHOD OF PLAYING When the trump is settled, the eldest hand, or the player next to him on the left, if the partner of the eldest hand is playing alone, begins by leading any card he pleases, and the other players have to follow suit if they can. Failure to follow suit when a player is able is a *revoke*, if the error is not discovered and corrected before the trick in which it occurs is turned and quitted. If the player discovers his mistake in time, the card played in error has to be left on the table, and is liable to be called. When a revoke is discovered and claimed by the adversaries, it is usual to abandon the hand, and the adversaries of the revoking player can either deduct two points from his score or add two points to their own score, for every revoke made during the hand. The penalty cannot be divided. If both sides revoke, the deal is void, and the same dealer has to deal again.

Any player who has none of the suit led can either trump or throw away a card of another suit. The highest card played, if it is of the suit led, wins the trick; trumps win against all other suits; and a higher trump wins a lower. The winner of the trick can lead any card he pleases for the next trick, and so on, until all five tricks have been played. If the dealer takes the trump into his hand, any player who names it is liable to have his highest or lowest trump called, but a player can ask and has to be informed of what the trump suit is.

CARDS PLAYED IN ERROR   All cards led out of turn or played in error, or two or more cards played to a trick or dropped face upwards on the table are called *exposed cards*, and have to be left face upwards on the table. These cards have to be played when they are called by the adversaries, unless compliance with the demand would make the player revoke; however, the fact of their being exposed does not prevent their being gotten rid of in the course of play if the opportunity arises. Some people imagine that the adversaries can prevent an exposed card from being played, but this is not the case in Euchre. A person who is playing a lone hand is not liable to any penalty for exposing his cards, nor for leading out of turn, because he has no partner to derive any benefit from the information conveyed.

LEADING OUT OF TURN   If any person, who is not playing alone, leads out of turn, the adversaries can call a suit from the player in error, or from his partner, when it is next the turn of either of them to lead. The demand has to be made by the person who will be the last player on the trick in which the suit is called. If all have played to the lead before discovering the error, it cannot be rectified; however, if all have not played, the ones who have followed the false lead have to take back their cards, which are not liable to be called.

Any player can ask the other players to *draw cards* in any trick, provided he does so before the cards are touched for the purpose of gathering them. In answer to this demand, each player should indicate which card of the cards on the table he played. No one is allowed to see any trick that has been turned and quitted.

TAKING TRICKS As the tricks are taken, they should be neatly laid one on the other in a way so that any player at the table can count them. All tricks that belong to one side should be kept together. At the end of each hand, the score should be claimed and marked. Revokes have to be detected and claimed before the cards are cut for the following deal.

CUTTING OUT When the play is confined to four players, rubbers are usually played, and the table is complete with six people, whereby two look on and await their turn. At the end of a rubber, if there are more than four players belonging to the table, the ones who have just played cut to decide who will give place to the waiting players, and the players who cut the highest cards go out. If six belong to the table, there will be no more cutting out, because the players who are out for one rubber re-enter for the next, whereby they take the place of the players who have played two consecutive rubbers. If five belong to the table, the three who remained in for the second rubber have to cut to allow the fifth player to re-enter. At the end of the third rubber, the two players cut who have not yet been out, and at the end of the fourth rubber, the one who has played every rubber goes out without cutting. Partners and deal are cut for at the beginning of each new rubber.

METHODS OF CHEATING All the Euchre family of games, especially Écarté and Napoleon, present many opportunities to the cheat. This fact was so well known in Europe that it was considered extremely foolish for any person to play Écarté in mixed company. The small number of cards in the pack, and the custom of dealing two and three at a time, gives the dealer an opportunity to bunch four valuable cards, of which he can give himself three and turn up the fourth. False shuffles, shifted cuts and marked cards are formidable weapons. Body language between partners and variation in tone or words in passing are frequently used by card-sharps. One of the commonest devices in the United States is use of what are known as 'jack strippers'. These are two Jacks, usually both of the same colour, that can be withdrawn from any portion of the pack by the fingers of an expert, and placed on the top. When the card sharp deals, he places enough cards on these Jacks to supply the other players on the first round, so that the strippers will come to him. When only two people are playing, he strips these Jacks out and leaves them on the top when he cuts the cards, so that they will be dealt to him. Never play Euchre or Écarté with a player who cuts the pack using both hands.

Any person who is tempted to bet on any game in the Euchre family should remember the advice of a worldly-wise Parisian to his son: 'Until you have four eyes in your head, risk not your gold at Écarté.'

SUGGESTIONS FOR GOOD PLAY The main points for the beginner to understand are when to order up, when to assist, when to take up, when to play alone, and what to make the trump if it is turned down. His decision in each case will be largely governed by both his position at the table and the score. The following suggestions are for four players, whereby two are partners against the other two, and the players are playing without the Joker, because this is the most common form of the game. The general principles underlying these suggestions for the four-handed game will be found equally valuable in any form of Euchre.

ORDERING UP Although probabilities are of little practical value in Euchre, it might be well to remember that there are nine cards in the trump suit; however, because only two-thirds of the pack is dealt out, the average number of trumps among four players will be six. Of these, the dealer always has the advantage of being sure of one more than his share, and it is safe to reckon that the dealer holds at least two trumps. He can also be counted for a missing suit, because he will discard any losing card of an odd suit when he takes up the trump.

The Eldest Hand should not order up the trump unless he has cards such that he is reasonably certain of three tricks without any assistance from his partner, and cannot be sure of two tricks if the trump is turned down. When he holds one or two bowers, especially if he has cards of the next suit, that is, the suit of the same colour as that of the turn-up, he should always pass, because if the dealer takes it up, he will probably be euchred, and if he turns it down, the eldest hand will have the first say, and can make it next. It is seldom right to order up a bower, because the dealer will rarely turn down this card.

There are exceptional cases in which the eldest hand can order up with little or nothing. One of the most common cases is when the adversaries of the dealer are at the *bridge*, that is, when their score is 4, and the dealer's side has only 1 or 2 marked. It is obvious that if the dealer or his partner plays alone, he will win the game; however, if the trump is ordered up, the most he can score is 2 points for a euchre, and the player who orders up will then have a chance to go out on his own deal. For this reason it has come to be viewed as being imperative for the eldest hand to order up at the bridge, unless he holds the right bower, or the left bower guarded, or the ace twice guarded, any one of which combinations is certain to win a trick against a lone hand if the eldest hand does not lead trumps himself. Another case is when the score is 4 to 4, and the eldest hand has average trump strength and good side cards but nothing in the next suit. It is better to order it up and risk the game on this hand than to take the chance of the dealer's turning it down.

The Pone, who is the partner of the eldest hand, orders up at the bridge on exactly opposite principles. The fact that the eldest hand did not order up shows that the dealer cannot make a lone hand. This should indicate to the pone that his partner has a certain trick in trumps, and if the pone holds any good trumps himself, he can often guess what his partner's trumps are. For example, the ace is turned, and the pone holds the left bower guarded. The eldest hand has to have the right bower, or four trumps to the King. If the eldest hand has passed at the bridge and the pone has strong trumps himself, especially the ace or left bower and two small trumps, he should order up the trump, not to save the game but to be sure of winning it by preventing the dealer from turning it down. If the pone does not order up at the bridge, the eldest hand can infer that he is weak in trumps.

When it is not a bridge, the pone should be guided by the same principles as the ones given for the eldest hand, because he can be sure that his partner will make it next if it is turned down, unless he has a certainty of three tricks by crossing.

If a player calls his partner's attention to the fact that they are at the bridge, both partners lose their right to order up.

ASSISTING The dealer's partner usually assists on plain-suit cards, such as two aces, rather than on trumps. The score and the turn-up trump will often be a guide as to whether or not to assist. For example, if the score is 1 all or 2 to 1, and a bower is turned, it is rarely right to assist, because the dealer is thereby prevented from playing alone. If the partner has good suit cards, they might be useful to make a march; if he has strong trumps, especially if he is sure of three tricks, he should play alone rather than assist. If the score is 3 in the dealer's favour, he does not require a lone hand in order to win the game, and with two reasonably certain tricks in his own hand, the dealer's partner should assist, because they might win the game by a march.

If the dealer's side is at the bridge, the score is 4 to 1 or 4 to 0 in their favour, and the eldest hand passes, the dealer's partner has to be on the alert to prevent the pone from playing a lone hand. He should assist unless a bower is turned, or he has it himself, or holds cards whereby, combined with the turn-up, he is sure of a trick. For example, the dealer's partner has the King and two other trumps, and the ace is turned. It is impossible for the pone to make a lone hand, even if he has both bowers, and the ace is bare, because he cannot catch the King, even if his partner leads the trump through it. However, if a small trump was turned, the pone might easily make a lone hand with both bowers and the ace.

TAKING UP The average expectation of the dealer is something more than two trumps, including the turn-up. With more than two trumps, or with two strong trumps, and a reasonably certain trick in a plain suit, the dealer should take up the trump. Three trumps of any size and an ace in plain suits is a strong take-up hand. It is better to take up the trump with only one plain suit in the hand, and small trumps, than with two strong trumps and two weak plain suits. The score will often decide the dealer in taking up the trump. For example, at 4 all, it is useless to turn anything down unless you have a certain euchre in the next suit, and nothing in the turn-up. Even then, the adversaries are almost certain to cross the suit and go out. With the score 3 all, the dealer should be very careful about taking up on a weak hand, because a euchre loses the game. If he is weak, but has a chance in the next suit, or a bower in the cross-suits, he should turn it down. It is a common stratagem to turn it down for a euchre when the dealer is better in the next suit, and has only 2 to go.

PLAYING ALONE The dealer has the best chance to get a lone hand, but the eldest hand is more likely to succeed with one, on account of the advantage of the lead. It is an invariable rule for any player to go alone when he has three certain tricks, unless he is 3 up and can win the game with a march. A lone hand should be played with both bowers and the ace, no matter how worthless the other cards; or with five trumps to the ace without either bower; or with two high trumps and three aces in plain suits; or with three good trumps and two aces. The theory of this is that although the march might be made with the partner's assistance, if the partner has the cards necessary to make a march, the adversaries have little or nothing, and there is a very good chance to make a lone hand if three tricks of it are certain. Both bowers and the ace, with only the seven and eight of a plain suit, have made many a lone hand. If the lone player is not caught on the plain suit at the first trick, the adversaries can either discard it in order to keep higher cards in the other suit or have none of it from the first. There is always a chance, and it should be taken.

The dealer's partner, and the pone, should be very careful in playing lone hands, and should never risk them except with three certain tricks, no matter what suit is led first.

With three sure tricks, some players make it a rule to play alone, provided both of the two other cards are of the same suit.

MAKING THE TRUMP When the trump is turned down, the general rule is for the eldest hand to make it next. The exceptions are when he has nothing in the next suit but has at least two certain tricks in the cross-suit and a probable trick in a plain suit. It is safer to make it next with a weak hand than to cross it on moderate strength, because the presumption is that neither the dealer nor his partner had a bower in the turn-down suit and therefore have none in the next suit. If this is the case, it is very likely that one or both are strong in the cross-suits, and it is not considered to be good policy to cross the suit unless you are so strong in it that you are reasonably certain of three tricks. Some players invariably make it next, regardless of their hands, unless they can play alone in the cross-suit. In taking on this habit, they are exposed to the common artifice of the dealer's turning it down for a euchre. A dealer who holds a bower and three cards of the next suit will often turn it down and trust to the eldest hand to make it next, whereby the dealer will be given four trumps instead of two. The eldest hand should be on his guard against this when the dealer's side has 3 scored.

The dealer's partner, on the other hand, should cross the suit almost as invariably as the eldest hand should make it next, because if his partner cannot take up the trump, and the eldest hand cannot make it next, their hands have to be weak, and if it is passed to the pone, he will probably turn out to have a lone hand. The best chance is to cross the suit, unless the player has three certain tricks in his own hand by making it next, such as five trumps to the ace, or four trumps and a plain-suit ace. With these cards, he should play alone.

The pone should never make the trump unless he has three certain tricks and is willing to play a lone hand. Be wary if the dealer turns it down, and both the eldest hand and the dealer's partner pass a second time.

LEADING The general principle of leading is to make tricks while you can. It is useless to save up tenaces in plain suits, because there are only five tricks to play, two of which are certain to fall to the trumps, and it is very improbable that any player will lead up to you a small card of a plain suit that will go around twice. It is seldom right to lead small cards of a plain suit. There is a better chance to make a trick with the King by leading it than by keeping it guarded. In the trump suit, tenaces are very strong and should be preserved, especially if the tenace is over the turn-up trump. There is a familiar example of the importance of tenace when only two play, whereby one person holds the major tenace in trumps and hearts, and has to win three tricks, no matter which player leads. The cards in one hand are as follows.

The cards in the other hand are as follows.

If the player who has the major tenace has to lead first, all he has to do is force his adversary with the plain suit: spades. Whatever the adversary leads, the player who has the major tenace simply wins it, and forces again. If the player who has the four trumps has the first lead, it does not matter what card he plays: the player who has the major tenace wins it, and forces with the plain suit. As long as the major tenace in trumps is not led away from, it has to win three tricks in trumps.

LEADING TRUMPS With strong cards in plain suits, the eldest hand can often lead trumps to advantage if the dealer's partner has assisted, especially if the turn-up trump is small. It is seldom right to lead trumps if the dealer has taken up the trump of his own accord, but an exception is usually made when the eldest hand holds three trumps, and two aces in plain suits. The best chance for a euchre is to exhaust the trumps, so as to make the aces good for tricks. If the pone has ordered up the trump, the eldest hand should lead trumps to him immediately, but the pone should not lead trumps to his partner if the eldest hand has ordered up at the bridge. If a bower is turned, the dealer's partner should lead a small trump at the first opportunity.

In playing against a lone hand, the best cards in plain suits should always be led, and trumps should never be led. In playing alone, it is best to lead winning trumps as long as they last, so as to force discards, whereby intermediate cards will often be left in plain suits that are good for tricks.

SECOND HAND You should play the best card you have second hand, and cover everything led if you can. With King and another card or Queen and another card, it is usually best to put up the honour second hand, on a small card led.

TRUMPING It is seldom right to trump partners who win cards, unless the partner has ordered up the trump and you think you can lead through the dealer to advantage. In playing against a lone hand, it is sometimes good play to trump your partner's ace with an unguarded left bower or ace of trumps, because the dealer might thereby be prevented from getting into the lead with a small trump, and a King or Queen of trumps might thereby be saved in your partner's hand. If you do not trump, the dealer will probably get in and swing the right bower, and your trump will be lost.

If your partner has ordered, made or taken up the trump, and you have only one trump, even a bower, you should trump with it at the first opportunity. Trump everything second hand, unless it takes the right bower for a doubtful trick, or breaks into the major tenace in trumps.

DISCARDING It is best to throw away singletons, unless they are aces. If you have two cards of equal value, but of different colours, one of which has to be discarded, it is usual to keep the one of the same colour as the turn-up when you are playing against the dealer. You should discard suits that the adversaries are trumping. If your partner discards a suit in which you have a high card, keep that suit, and discard another. If you have both ace and King of a plain suit, discard the ace, in order to show your partner that you can win a trick in the suit. It is very often important to discard correctly when you are playing against a lone hand, especially if the lone player leads trumps for the fourth trick. It is a common practice for modern players to signal in the discard if they have a certain trick in a suit. This is done by discarding two cards in another suit, the higher before the lower. For example, you have two aces, spades and diamonds. The dealer plays alone on hearts, and trumps your spade ace the first time. If you have two clubs, such as King and ten, discard the King first, and then the ten, and your partner will know you can stop the diamond suit. He should thereby be advised to keep his clubs.

— —

CUT-THROAT EUCHRE

The main element in the three-handed game is playing to the score. The player who has the strong hand always has to be kind to the underdog, and partnerships are always formed against the player who has the high score. Suppose *A*, *B* and *C* are playing, and that *A* has 3 points to his adversaries' nothing on *B's* deal. It is in the interests of *A* to euchre *B*; however, it is in the interests of *C* to let *B* make his point, because if *B* is euchred, *A* wins the game. When *B* has made his point, *C* deals, and it is then in the interests of *B* to let *C* make his point. Suppose *C* makes a march: 3 points, whereby he is put on a level with *A*. On *A's* deal, it is *C's* game to euchre him, but *B* has to let *A* make his point, so that instead of being opposed by both *B* and *C*, as he was a moment ago, *A* finds a friend in *B*, and the two who were helping each other to beat *A* are now cutting each other's throats. On *B's* deal, *A* does not wish to euchre him, because although that would win the game for both *A* and *C*, *A*, who now has 4 points up, does not wish to divide the pool with *C* while he has such a good chance to win it all himself. Suppose *B* makes his point. *A* will do all he can to euchre *C*, but *B* will oppose the scheme, because his only chance for the game is that *A* will not be able to take up the trump on his own deal, and that *B* will make a march.

— —

SET-BACK EUCHRE

This is simply a reversal of the ordinary method of scoring, whereby the players start with a specific number of points, usually ten, and deduct what they make on each deal. The peculiarity whereby the game is given its name is that if a player is euchred, he is *set back* two points, and his adversaries count nothing. The revoke penalty is settled in the same way. The game is usually counted using chips, whereby each player starts with ten and places in the centre of the table the chips he is entitled to score.

— —

BLIND EUCHRE

Each player is for himself, and a widow of two cards is dealt. The player who takes the widow practically orders up the trump and has to play against all the other players after discarding two cards. If no one will take the widow, the deal is void.

— —

PENALTY EUCHRE

Five players are each provided with twelve counters. An extra hand of five cards is dealt face downwards, for a widow. Each player in turn can exchange the hand dealt to him for the widow, or for the hand abandoned by anyone who has taken the widow, whereby the cards are always face downwards. The turned trump is not taken up by the dealer but is left on the pack. The eldest hand leads for the first trick, and every player is for himself, whereby each holds his own tricks.

At the end of the hand, each player who has not taken a trick receives a counter from each of the other players, whether or not they have taken tricks. Then all the players who have won tricks put back into the pool a counter for each trick they have taken. The first player who gets rid of his twelve counters wins the game.

— —

AUCTION EUCHRE

This form of the game is sometimes erroneously called *French Euchre*, because French people know nothing about Euchre in any form. Auction Euchre is exactly the same as the ordinary four- or six-handed game, except that the trump is not turned up: the players bid in turn for the privilege of naming the trump suit. The bidder names the number of tricks he proposes to take. There is no second bid, and the player who has made the highest bid names the trump suit. No matter who is the successful bidder, the eldest hand leads for the first trick. The number of points won or lost on the deal is the number of points bid, even if the bidder accomplishes more. If a player has bid 3, and he and his partner take 4 or 5 tricks, they count 3 only. If they are euchred, whereby they have failed to make the number of tricks bid, the adversaries count the number of points bid. Fifteen points is usually the game.

This is probably the root of the much better games of five- and seven-handed Euchre, which will be described further on.

— ◦ —

PROGRESSIVE EUCHRE

This form of Euchre is especially well suited to social gatherings. Its peculiarity is in the arrangement and progression of a large number of players originally divided into sets of four, and playing, at separate tables, the ordinary four-handed game.

APPARATUS   A sufficient number of tables to accommodate the assembled players is arranged in order and numbered consecutively, whereby number one is called *the head table* and the lowest of the series is called *the booby table*. Each player is provided with a blank card, to which the various coloured stars can be attached as they accrue in the course of play. These stars are usually of three colours: red, green and gold. The head table is provided with a bell, and each table is supplied with one pack of cards only. It is usual to sort out the thirty-two cards used in play, and the four small cards for markers, before the guests arrive.

DRAWING FOR POSITIONS   Two packs of differently coloured cards are used, and from the two black suits in each a sequence of cards is sorted out that is equal in length to the number of tables in play. For example, if there are sixteen ladies and sixteen gentlemen, or thirty-two players in all, they will fill eight tables, and all the clubs and spades from the ace to the eight inclusive should be sorted out. These cards are then thoroughly shuffled and presented, face down-wards, to the players to draw from. The ladies take only the red-back cards, the gentlemen only the blue. The number of pips on the card drawn indicates the number of the table at which the player is to sit, and the players who draw cards of the same suit are partners for the first game.

PLAYING   When all the players are seated, the deal is cut for at each table, and play begins. There is no cutting for partners, because that has been settled in the original drawing. Five points is a game, and after that number is reached by either side at the head table, the bell is struck. Lone hands are usually barred at the head table, so as to give the other tables time to make a specific number of points, and so as to avoid ties. On the tap of the bell, all play immediately ceases, even if the players are in the middle of a deal. If the players at any but the head table have reached five points before the bell rings, they play on, and count all points they have made until the bell taps.

PROGRESSING The partners who win the game at the head table each receive a gold star, and retain their seats for the next game. The losing players at the head table go down to the booby table. All the winning players at the other tables receive red stars, and go to the table next in order above, whereby the players at table number two go to number one. The players who lose and remain at the booby table each receive a green star.

CHANGING PARTNERS At all but the head table, the partners who progress to the next table divide, whereby the lady who has just lost at each table retains her seat and takes for her partner the gentleman who has just arrived from the table below. At the head table, the newly arrived pair remain as partners, but at the booby table, the players who have just arrived from the head table divide. When all the players are seated, they cut for the deal, and play is resumed until the next bell tap.

TIES In the case of ties in points at any table when the bell taps, the players who have won the most tricks on the next hand are declared the winners. If that is also a tie, the ladies cut to decide it, whereby the lowest cut goes up. In cutting, the ace is low, and the Jack ranks below the Queen.

PRIZES Six prizes are usually provided for large companies. The lady and gentleman who have the most gold stars take the first prizes, the most red stars win the second prizes, and the most green stars win the booby prizes. One player cannot win two prizes. In the case of ties for the gold stars, the accompanying red stars decide it; if that is also a tie, the player who has the fewest number of green stars wins, and if that is still a tie, the players have to cut for it.

The host decides the hour at which play will cease and is the referee in all disputes.

— —

MILITARY EUCHRE

The host arranges each table as a fort that is marked by a distinguishing flag and a number of small duplicate flags. The partners who sit east and west progress around the room from table to table, and play one game of five points at each; no lone hands are allowed. The winners of each are given a little flag from the losers as a trophy. By the time the E and W pairs have made the circuit of all the tables and gotten home again, the game is ended, whereby the victors are the fort that has captured the greatest number of flags.

— —

RAILROAD EUCHRE

Railroad Euchre is the name given to any form of the four-handed game in which every expedient is used in order to make points rapidly.

CARDS   A pack of twenty-five cards is used, whereby all cards below the 9 are deleted and the Joker is added. The Joker is always the best trump.

PLAYERS   There are four players, whereby two are partners against the other two. Partners, deal and seats are cut for as in the ordinary game.

DEALING   The cards are distributed as in the ordinary game, but it is usual to agree beforehand on a suit that will be the trump if the Joker is turned up.

PLAYING ALONE   The main peculiarity in Railroad Euchre is in playing alone. Any player who announces to play alone, whether or not the dealer has the privilege of passing a card, face downwards, to his partner. In exchange for this, but without seeing it, the partner gives the best card in his hand to the lone player, whereby he passes it to him face downwards. If he does not have a trump to give him, he can pass him an ace, or even a King. Even if this card is no better than the one discarded, the lone player cannot refuse it. If the dealer plays alone, he has two discards: the first in exchange for his partner's best card, and then another, in exchange for the trump card, after he has seen what his partner can give him. In this second discard, he can get rid of the card passed to him by his partner. If the dealer's partner plays alone, the dealer can pass him the turn-up trump, or any better card he might have in his hand.

When any person has announced to play alone, either of his adversaries can play alone against him, whereby his partner's best card is discarded and taken in the same way. If the lone player who makes the trump is euchred by the lone player opposing him, the euchre counts four points. It is considered imperative for a player who holds the Joker or the right bower guarded to play alone against the lone hand, and take his partner's best: because it is evident that the lone hard cannot succeed, there is a better chance to euchre it with all the strength in one hand than divided.

If any player, in his proper turn, announces to play alone and asks for his partner's best, the partner cannot refuse; nor can he propose to play alone instead.

SCORING   With the exception of the four points for euchring a lone hand, the scoring is exactly the same as in the ordinary four-handed game; however, there are one or two variations that are sometimes agreed on beforehand in order to make points even more rapidly.

LAPS   If a player makes more points than are necessary to win the game, the additional points are counted on the next game, so that there is always an inducement to play lone hands, even with 4 points up.

SLAMS   If one side reaches five points before the other has scored, it is a slam, and counts *two games*.

When laps and slams are played, it is sometimes agreed that if a person plays alone without taking his partner's best card, or the dealer plays alone without taking up the trump or asking for his partner's best, and this player succeeds in winning all five tricks with a pat hand, it counts *five* points. If he fails to win all five tricks, the adversaries count *one*. If he is euchred, they count *three*, but they are not permitted to play alone against him.

JAMBONE   Any person who plays a lone hand can announce, 'Jambone,' and expose his cards face upwards on the table. The adversaries then have the right to call any card they please, either for the lead or in following suit; however, they cannot make the player revoke; nor can they consult, or in any way expose their hands. If a lead is required, it has to be called by the person on the jambone player's left. If a card is called on a trick, it has to be called by the person on the jambone player's right. If in spite of these difficulties the jambone player succeeds in winning five tricks, he scores *eight* points. If he wins three or four only, he counts *one* point. If he is euchred, he loses *two*. It is not allowable to play alone against a jambone.

JAMBOREE This is the combination of the five highest trumps in one hand, and has to be only announced and shown in order to entitle the holder to score *sixteen* points. If the combination is held by the dealer, it can be made with the assistance of the turn-up trump, and any player can make it with the assistance of his partner's best; however, it does not count unless the holder of it has made the trump. If a player who has a pat Jamboree is ordered up, all he can score is a euchre.

As in other forms of Euchre, no one but the maker of the trump can play alone or announce, 'Jambone,' or 'Jamboree.' Lone hands are very common in Railroad Euchre, and ordering up to prevent lone hands is even more common.

— - —

SEVEN-HANDED EUCHRE

CARDS Seven-handed Euchre is played with a full pack of fifty-three cards, including the Joker. The cards in plain suits rank as at Whist, but the Joker is always the best trump, and the right and left bowers are the second and third best, respectively.

COUNTERS One white and four red counters are necessary. The white counter is passed to the left from player to player in turn, in order to indicate the position of the next deal. The red counters are placed in front of the maker of the trump and his partners, in order to distinguish them from their opponents. Markers are not used: the score is kept on a sheet of paper. The score is usually kept by a person who is not playing, so that none of the players in the game can know how the various scores stand. If an outsider is not available for scoring, there are two methods. The first is for one player to keep the score for the whole table, and to inform any player of the state of the score if he is asked to do so. The other is to have a dish of counters on the table, whereby each player is given the number he wins from time to time. These counters should be placed in a covered receptacle so they cannot be counted by their owner and so that no other player will know how many he has. Because it is very seldom that a successful bid is fewer than five, and never fewer than four, counters marked as being worth 4, 5, 6 and 7 each will answer every purpose, and will pay every bid made.

CUTTING　　The players draw cards from an outspread pack for the choice of seats, and the players who cut the lowest cards have the first choice. The lowest cut of all deals the first hand, and passes the white counter to the player on his left, whose turn it will be to deal next. Ties are decided in the usual way.

DEALING　　The cards are dealt from left to right, whereby two are given to each player for the first round, then three, and then two again, until each player has received seven cards. The four cards remaining in the pack are then placed in the centre of the table, face downwards, and form the *widow*. No trump is turned.

The rules that govern all irregularities in the deal are the same as in ordinary Euchre.

MAKING THE TRUMP　　When the cards are dealt, each player in turn, beginning with the eldest hand, bids a specific number of points, and at the same time names the suit he wishes to make the trump. There is no second bid, and the suit named by the highest bidder has to be the trump for that deal. The successful bidder takes the widow, selects from it what cards he pleases, and discard other cards in their stead, so as to restore the number of his cards to seven. He then places a red counter in front of him, and chooses his partners, whereby he passes a red counter to each of them. These counters have to be placed in front of the players in order to distinguish them as belonging to the bidder's side, but the players make no changes in their respective positions at the table. Each player should bid on the possibilities of his hand, however small, so as to guide the other players in their selection of partners.

PARTNERS　　If the bidder has proposed to take not more than five tricks out of the seven possible, he chooses two partners, and these three play against the remaining four. If he has bid to make *six* or *seven* tricks, he chooses three partners, and these four play against the remaining three. Partners cannot refuse to play.

PLAYING ALONE　　If a player thinks he can take all seven tricks without having any partners, he can bid *ten*, which would outrank a bid of seven, but this bid has to be made before he sees the widow. If a player thinks he can win all seven tricks without having either a widow or partners, he can bid *twenty*, which is the highest bid possible. When twenty is bid, the cards in the widow have to remain untouched.

PLAYING   The successful bidder has the lead for the first trick. The general rules for following suit and so on are the same as in ordinary Euchre. The bidder takes in all the tricks won by himself and his partners, and one of the adversaries should gather for that side. If a player on either side *revokes*, the adversaries score the number bid, and the hand is abandoned.

SCORING   If the bidder is successful in his undertaking, he and his partners, if any, are credited by the scorer with the number of points bid, but no more. If a player bids five, and his side takes seven, it counts them only five points. If the player who makes the trump fails to reach his bid, he is euchred, and the adversaries are credited with the number of points bid.

PRIZES   It is usual to give two prizes for each table in play: one for the highest number of points won during the evening, and one for the smallest number, whereby the latter is usually called the 'booby' prize.

SUGGESTIONS FOR GOOD PLAY   It is very risky to bid seven without having the Joker, whereby the odds are 11 to 1 against finding it in the widow. A bid of ten should not be made without having both the Joker and the Right Bower, and all the other cards winners and trumps. To bid twenty, a player should have a practically invincible hand that contains at least five winning leads of trumps.

The first bidders are always at a disadvantage, because they know nothing of the contents of the other hands; however, after one or two players have made a bid, the players who follow them can judge reasonably well how the cards lie. For example, the seven players are *A B C D E F G*. *A* deals, and *B* bids 2 in hearts. *C* and *D* pass. *E* bids 3 in clubs, and *F* bids 4 in hearts. It is evident that *F* is bidding on *B*'s offer in hearts and intends to choose him for a partner. *G* finds in his hand four good spades and the Joker, but neither Bower. He can safely bid 5 or 6, and take *E* for a partner if he is successful, because *E* very probably has one or both of the black Bowers. If he bids 5 only, the dealer, *A*, has an excellent chance to bid 6 in hearts, and to take *B* and *F* for two of his partners, and *G* for the third partner, whereby he trusts to find *G* with the Joker, or at least protection in one or both black suits.

If the successful bidder has had no previous bids to guide him in his choice of partners, he should take the players who have the lowest scores, if the scores are known, because it is to his advantage to avoid advancing the players who are perhaps already ahead. When the scores are not known, there is nothing but luck to guide a player, unless he has a very good memory and knows which players are probably behind.

LEADING If the successful bidder wants 6 or 7 tricks, and holds the Joker, he should lead it at once. If he does not have the Joker, he should begin with a low trump and give his partners a chance to play the Joker on the first round. If the leader cannot exhaust the trumps with one or two rounds, it will sometimes be to his advantage to lead any losing card he might have in the plain suits, in order to let his partners win the trick if they can. When you are playing alone, it is absolutely necessary to exhaust the trumps before you open a plain suit.

Partners should avail themselves of the methods that are common to four-handed Euchre in order to support each other in trumps and plain suits. The discard should invariably be from weakness if the player is the bidder's partner and from strength if the player is opposed to him.

EUCHRE FOR FIVE PLAYERS This is practically the same as the seven-handed game, but the pack is reduced to 28 cards, all of which are below the Eight in each suit being deleted. The Joker is not used. Five cards are dealt to each player, by two and three at a time, and the three remaining cards form the widow. The player who bids *three* tricks takes only one partner. The player who bids *four* or *five* tricks takes two partners. A player who intends to take the widow but no partners can bid *eight*, and a player who intends to take neither widow nor partners can bid *fifteen*. In this form of Euchre, the scores are usually known, and 100 points is game.

In some clubs, it is the practice for the successful bidder to select one of his partners by asking for the holder of a specific card. For example, B has the lead and has bid five in hearts, whereby he holds the three best trumps, the club ace and a losing spade. Rather than select his partners at random, he asks for the spade ace, and the player who holds that card has to say, 'Here,' on which the bidder will pass him a counter and thereby mark him as one of his partners.

— • —

CALL-ACE EUCHRE

In this variety of euchre, each player is for himself with reference to the final score. The one who takes up the trump or orders it up, or who makes it after it is turned down, can call on the best card of any suit but the trump. The player who holds the best card of that suit has to be his partner, but does not declare himself. When the highest card of the suit asked for falls in play, the partner is disclosed.

Because the whole pack is not dealt out, it often happens that the ace, or even both the ace and the king, of the suit called for are in the talon. If it turns out that the caller himself has the highest card of the suit, he has no partner.

When six play, thirty-two cards are used, and only one card remains unknown. When five play, the sevens are thrown out. When four play, the eights are also discarded.

If the maker of the trump does not wish to have a partner, he can either say, 'Alone,' or ask for a suit of which he himself holds the ace.

If the maker of the trump and his partner get three tricks, they score 1 point each. If they win all the tricks, they score 3 points each if there are five or six in the game, and 2 points if there are not more than four players. If the partnership is euchred, each of the other players at the table scores 2 points.

For a lone hand who wins all five tricks, the player scores a point for as many players as there are at the table, including himself. Euchres score 2 for every player other than the lone hand. A lone hand who makes only three or four tricks, scores 1.

— —

500, OR BID EUCHRE

In this variety of euchre, the joker is always used. When there is a trump suit, it is the best trump, but when there are no trumps, it is a suit by itself, but still a trump. The player who holds it cannot trump with it as long as he can follow suit, but when he has none of the suit led, he can trump with the joker if he likes. When the joker is led in a no-trump hand, the leader has to name the suit he wishes played to it.

Five hundred is supposed to be a game for three players, but sometimes two play against two as partners.

The dealer gives ten cards to each player: three and then two at a time, as in the ordinary game of euchre; however, after dealing the first three cards to each, he lays off three cards face downwards for a widow. This widow is taken in hand by the successful bidder, who discards three cards in its place.

The players bid for the privilege of either naming the trump suit or playing without any trump but the joker. The number of tricks bid must not be fewer than six, and the suit has to be named at the same time. The player who has the most valuable game, regardless of the number of tricks or the suit, is the successful bidder, because a bid of seven in hearts, for example, is worth more in points than a bid of eight in clubs, as will be seen in the following table. The greater number of tricks counts.

If trumps are:	6 tricks	7 tricks	8 tricks	9 tricks	10 tricks
Spades	40	80	120	160	200
Clubs	60	120	180	240	300
Diamonds	80	160	240	320	400
Hearts	100	200	300	400	500
No-trumps..............	120	240	360	480	600

The successful bidder always leads for the first trick, after he has taken the widow and discarded. After the hand is played, he has the first count. If he has made as many as he bid, he scores it, but he cannot score more than he bid unless he succeeds in winning every trick. In that case, he scores 250 if his bid was fewer than 250, but if his bid was more than 250, he gets nothing extra for winning every trick.

Any player but the bidder who wins a trick scores ten points for it, so it is necessary for each player to keep separate the tricks he individually wins.

If the bidder fails, he loses, or is set back, as many points as he bid, and scores nothing for the tricks he takes; however, he can play the hand out in order to prevent the other players from scoring, because his adversaries still get ten points for each trick they win.

Five hundred points is game, and because the bidder has the first count, he can go out first, even if an adversary has also won enough tricks to reach 500.

— —

EUCHRE LAWS

1. SCORING A game consists of five points. If the players who make the trump win all five tricks, they count *two* points towards game; if they win three or four tricks, they count *one* point; if they fail to win three tricks, their adversaries count *two* points.

2. If the player who makes the trump plays *alone*, and makes five tricks, he counts as many points as there are players in the game: two if two play, three if three play, four if four play, and so on. If he wins three or four tricks only, he counts one; if he fails to win three tricks, his adversaries count two.

3. THE RUBBER This is the best of three games. If the first two games are won by the same players, the third game is not played. The winners gain a *triple*, or three points, if their adversaries have not scored; a *double*, or two points, if their adversaries are fewer than three scored; and a *single*, or one point, if their adversaries have scored three or four. The winners of the rubber add two points to the value of their games, and deduct the points made by the losers, if any; the remaining points are the value of the rubber.

4. FORMING THE TABLE A Euchre table is complete with six players. If more than four assemble, they cut for the preference, whereby the four lowest play the first rubber. Partners and deal are then cut for, whereby the two lowest pair against the two highest. The lowest deals, and has the choice of seats and cards.

5. TIES Players who cut cards of equal value cut again, but the new cut decides nothing but the tie.

6. CUTTING OUT At the end of a rubber, the players cut to decide who will give way to the players who are awaiting their turn to play. After the second rubber, the players who have played the greatest number of consecutive games give way; ties are decided by way of cutting.

7. CUTTING In cutting, the ace is low, and the other cards rank K Q J 10 9 8 7, whereby the King is the highest. A player who exposes more than one card, or who cuts the Joker, has to cut again.

8. SHUFFLING Every player has a right to shuffle the cards, and the dealer goes last.

9. DEALING The dealer has to present the pack to the pone to be cut. At least four cards have to be left in each packet. If a card is exposed in cutting, the pack has to be re-shuffled and cut again. If the dealer re-shuffles the pack after it has been properly cut, he loses his deal.

10. Beginning on his left, the dealer has to give to each player in rotation *two* cards on the first round, and *three* on the second; or three to each on the first round, and two on the second. When five cards have been given to each player in this way, the next card is turned up for the trump. The deal passes to the left.

11. There has to be a new deal by the same dealer if any card but the trump is found faced in the pack, or if the pack is proved to be incorrect or imperfect; however, any previous scores made with the imperfect pack stand good.

12. The adversaries can demand a new deal if any card but the trump is exposed during the deal, provided they have not touched a card. If an adversary exposes a card, the dealer can elect to deal again. If a new deal is not demanded, cards exposed in dealing cannot be called.

13. The adversaries can stop a player from dealing out of turn or with the wrong pack, provided they do so before the trump card is turned, after which the deal stands good.

14. MISDEALING A misdeal loses the deal. It is a misdeal if the cards have not been properly cut, if the dealer gives two cards to one player and three to another in the same round, if the dealer gives too many or too few cards to any player, if the dealer counts the cards on the table or the ones remaining in the pack, or if the dealer deals a card incorrectly and fails to correct the error before dealing another. If the dealer is interrupted in any way by an adversary, he does not lose his deal.

15. THE TRUMP CARD After the trump card is turned, each player in turn, beginning with the eldest hand, has the privilege of passing, assisting or ordering up the trump. If a player passes, and afterwards corrects himself by ordering up or assisting, both he and his partner can be prevented by the adversaries from exercising their privilege. If a player calls his partner's attention to the fact that they are at the bridge, both partners lose their right to order up the trump.

16. The dealer can leave the trump card on the pack until it is gotten rid of in the course of play. If the trump card has been taken up or played, any player can ask, and has to be informed of by the dealer, what the trump suit is; however, any player who names the trump card can be called on by an adversary to play his highest or lowest trump.

17. If the dealer takes up, or is ordered up, he has to *discard* a card from his own hand, and place it under the remainder of the pack. When this discard has been quitted, it cannot be taken back.

If the dealer has not discarded until he has played to the first trick, he and his partner cannot score any points for that hand.

18. If the eldest hand leads before the dealer has quitted his discard, the dealer can amend his discard, but the eldest hand cannot take back the card led.

19. If the dealer takes up the trump to play alone, he has to pass his discard across the table to his partner. If he fails to do so, the adversaries can insist his partner play with him and thereby stop the lone hand.

20. MAKING THE TRUMP   If the dealer does not take up the trump, he has to place it under the remainder of the pack, face upwards, so it can be distinctly seen. Each player in turn, beginning on the dealer's left, then has the privilege of naming a new trump suit.

21. If any player names the suit already turned down, he loses his right to name a suit, and if he corrects himself and names another suit, neither he nor his partner is allowed to make that suit the trump. If a player names a new trump suit out of his proper turn, both he and his partner are forbidden to make that suit the trump.

22. If no one will name a new trump, the deal is void and passes to the next player on the dealer's left.

23. IRREGULARITIES IN THE HANDS   If any player is found not to have his correct number of cards, it is a misdeal; however, if he has played to the first trick, the deal stands good, and he cannot score anything in that hand.

24. EXPOSED CARDS   The following cards are exposed cards, have to be left face upwards on the table, and are liable to be called by the adversaries.
   I. Every card faced on the table in other than the regular course of play.
   II. Two or more cards played to a trick. The adversaries can elect which cards will be played.
   III. Any card named by the player who holds it.

25. If an adversary of a person who is playing alone exposes a card, the lone player can abandon the hand and score the points. If the partner of the lone player exposes a card, the adversaries can stop the lone hand by compelling the player in error to play with his partner, whereby the exposed card is left on the table.

26. CALLING EXPOSED CARDS   The adversary on the right of an exposed card has to call it before he himself plays. If it will be the turn of the player who holds the exposed card to lead for the next trick, the card, if wanted, has to be called before the current trick is turned and quitted. If a player has an exposed card and the lead play from his hand before the previous trick is turned and quitted, the card so led can also be claimed as exposed.

27. LEADING AND PLAYING OUT OF TURN   If a player leads when it was his partner's turn, a suit can be called from his partner. The demand has to be made by the last player to the trick in which the suit is called. If it was the turn of neither to lead, the card played in error is exposed. If all have played to the false lead, the error cannot be rectified. If all have not followed, the cards erroneously played have to be taken back, but are not liable to be called.

28.   If an adversary of a lone player leads out of turn, the lone player can abandon the hand and score the points.

29.   If the third hand plays before the second, the fourth hand can play before his partner, either of his own volition or at the direction of the second hand, who can say, 'Play, partner.' If the fourth hand plays before the second, the third hand can call on the second to play his highest or lowest of the suit led, or to trump or not to trump the trick.

30. REVOKING   A revoke is either a renounce in error that is not corrected in time or non-compliance with a performable penalty. If a revoke is claimed and proved, the hand in which it occurs is immediately abandoned. The adversaries of the revoking player then have the option of either adding two points to their own score or deducting two points from his score. If both sides revoke, the deal is void. If one person is playing alone, the penalty for a revoke is as many points as would have been scored had the lone hand succeeded.

31.   A revoke can be corrected by the player who makes it before the trick in which it occurs has been turned and quitted, unless the revoking player or his partner, whether in his right turn or otherwise, has led or played to the following trick.

32.   If a player corrects his mistake in time to save a revoke, the card played in error is exposed, but any cards subsequently played by other players can be taken back without penalty.

33. PLAYING ALONE   No one but the individual maker of the trump can play alone.

34. The dealer has to announce his intention to play alone by passing his discard over to his partner. Any other player who intends to play alone has to use the word 'alone' in connection with his ordering up or making the trump, as in 'I order it, alone,' or 'I make it hearts, alone.'

35. The partner of a player who has announced to play alone has to lay his cards on the table, face downwards. If he exposes any of his cards, the adversaries can stop the lone hand, and compel him to play with his partner, whereby the exposed card is left on the table and is liable to be called.

36. The lone player is not liable to any penalty for exposed cards, nor for a lead out of turn.

37. If either adversary leads or plays out of turn, the lone player can abandon the hand and score the points.

38. MISCELLANEOUS No player is allowed to see any trick that has been turned and quitted once, under penalty of having a suit called from him or his partner.

39. Any player can ask the other players to indicate the cards played by them to the current trick.

40. A player who calls attention in any way to either the trick or the score can be called on to play his highest or lowest of the suit led, or to trump or not to trump the trick during the play in which the remark was made.

— ◼ —

ÉCARTÉ

Écarté is usually described as a very simple game, but unfortunately the rules governing it are very complicated, and because no authoritative code of law exists, disputes about trifling irregularities are very common. In the following directions, the author has selected what seems to be the best French usage. The code of laws adopted by some of the English clubs is unfortunately very defective and in many ways out of touch with the true spirit of the French game. English players are very fond of penalties, whereas French players try to establish the status quo.

CARDS Écarté is played with a pack of thirty-two cards, which rank

K Q J A 10 9 8 7. When two packs are used, the adversary shuffles one while the other is being dealt.

MARKERS   In France, the game is always marked with the ordinary round chips or counters, never with a marker. Because five points are the game, four of these counters are necessary for each player.

PLAYERS   Écarté is played by two people, who sit opposite each other. One is known as the dealer, and the other is known as the pone, the adversary, the elder hand, the non-dealer, the leader or the player.

THE GALLERY   In clubs in which Écarté is made a feature, and in which there is a great deal of betting on the outside by the spectators, it is not usual to allow more than one game between the same players, whereby the loser gives place to one of the people who have been backing him, who is called a *rentrant*. This is known as playing the *cul-levé*. Any person in the gallery is allowed to draw attention to errors in the score, and can advise the player he is backing, or can even play out the game for him if he resigns. The player does not have to take the advice given to him, which has to be offered without discussion and by way of pointing only, not by way of naming the suit or cards. If a player will not allow the gallery to back him, and takes all bets himself, no one can overlook his hand nor advise him without his permission, and he does not have to retire if he loses the game.

CUTTING   The player who cuts the highest écarté card deals the first hand, and has the choice of seats and cards. If a person exposes more than one card in cutting, the lowest is taken to be his cut. If he does not cut, or will not show his cut, he loses the first deal.

STAKES   Écarté is played for so much a game. If the gallery is betting, all money offered has to be placed on the table, and if the bets are not taken by the players, the bets can be covered by the opposing gallery.

DEALING   It is usual for the dealer to invite his adversary to shuffle the cards, but if two packs are used, this is not necessary. The dealer has to shuffle the pack and present it to his adversary to be cut. At least two cards have to be left in each packet, and the upper part of the pack has to be placed nearer the dealer. Five cards are given to each player, and the eleventh card is turned up for the trump. The cards are distributed two and three at a time, or three and then two, and in whichever way the dealer begins, he has to continue during the game. If he intends to change his way of dealing in the following game, he has to advise his adversary of this when he is presenting the cards to be cut.

MISDEALING A player who deals out of turn, or with the wrong cards, can be stopped before the trump is turned. However, if the trump has been turned, and neither player has discarded or played to the first trick, the pack has to be set aside, with the cards as dealt, and the trump has to be turned, to be used for the ensuing deal. The other pack is then taken up and dealt by the player whose proper turn it was to deal. If a discard has been made, or a trick played to, the deal stands good, and the packs, if changed, have to remain so.

There has to be a new deal if any card but the eleventh is found faced in the pack. If the dealer exposes any of his own cards, the deal stands good. If he exposes any of his adversary's cards, the non-dealer can claim a fresh deal, provided he has not seen any of his cards.

It is a misdeal if the dealer gives too many or too few cards to either his adversary or himself. If the hands have not been seen, and the pone discovers he has received more than five cards, he has the choice to either discard the superfluous cards at hazard or claim a misdeal, which loses the deal. If the pone has received fewer than the proper number, he can either supply the deficiency from the remainder of the pack, without changing the trump card, or claim a misdeal. If the dealer has given himself too many or too few cards, the pone can claim a misdeal; or can draw the superfluous cards from the dealer's hand, face downwards; or can allow the dealer to supply the deficiency from the remainder of the pack, without changing the trump.

If the cards have been seen, the pone, because he has an incorrect number, can supply or discard in order to correct the error, or can claim a misdeal. If he discards, he has to show the cards to the dealer. If the dealer has an incorrect number, the pone can draw from his hand, face downwards, looking at the cards he has drawn (as the dealer has seen them); or can allow the dealer to supply the deficiency; or can claim a misdeal.

When any irregularity is remedied in this way, the trump card remains unchanged.

If the dealer turns up more than one card for the trump, his adversary has a right to select which card will be the trump, or the adversary can claim a new deal by the same dealer, provided he has not seen his hand. If he has seen his hand, either he has to claim a misdeal or the eleventh card has to be the trump, whereby the other exposed card is set aside.

If the pack is found to be imperfect, all scores previously made with it stand good.

TURNING THE KING   If the King is turned up, the dealer marks one point for it immediately. If a wrong number of cards has been dealt, and a King is turned, it cannot be scored, because it was not the eleventh card.

PROPOSING AND REFUSING   When the cards are dealt, the pone examines his hand, and if he thinks it is strong enough to win three or more tricks, he stands, that is, plays without proposing, and says to the dealer, *'I play.'* If he thinks he can improve his chances by drawing cards, and gives the dealer the same privilege, naturally, he says, *'I propose,'* or simply *'Cards.'* In reply, the dealer can either accept the proposal by asking, *'How many?'* or refuse by saying, *'Play.'* If he gives cards, he can also take cards himself, after having helped his adversary. If he refuses, he has to win at least three tricks or lose two points, and if the pone plays without proposing, he has to make three tricks or lose two points. The hands on which a player should stand, and the ones on which the dealer should refuse, are known as *jeux de règle*, and will be found in the suggestions for good play.

A proposal, acceptance or refusal once made cannot be changed or taken back, and the number of cards asked for cannot be corrected.

DISCARDING   If the pone proposes, and the dealer asks, 'How many?', the elder hand discards any number of cards from one to five, and places them on his right. These discards, once quitted, must not again be looked at. A player who looks at his own or his adversary's discards can be called on to play with his cards exposed face upwards on the table but not liable to be called. The number of cards discarded have to be distinctly announced. The trump is then laid aside, and the cards are given from the top of the pack, without more shuffling. It is considered to be imperative that the player who has proposed take at least one card, even if he proposed with five trumps in his hand. When the pone is helped, the dealer then announces how many cards he takes, and places his discards on his left. The dealer, if asked, has to inform his adversary of how many cards he took, provided the question is put before he plays a card.

After he has received his cards, the pone can either stand or propose again, and the dealer can either give or refuse; however, these subsequent stands or refusals do not carry with them any penalty for failure to make three tricks. If these repeated discards exhaust the pack, so that there are not enough cards left to supply the number asked for, the players have to take back a sufficient number from their discards. If the dealer has accepted a proposal, and finds there are no cards left for himself, that is his own fault: he should have counted the pack before he accepted. The trump card cannot be taken into the hand under any circumstances.

MISDEALING AFTER DISCARDING   If the dealer gives the pone more or fewer cards than he asks for, he loses the point and the right to mark the King, unless it was turned up.

If the dealer gives himself more cards than he wants, he loses the point and the right to mark the King, unless he turned it up. If he gives himself fewer cards than he wants, he can make the deficiency good without penalty; however, if he does not discover the error until he has played a card, all tricks for which he has no card to play have to be considered to have been won by his adversary.

If the pone asks for more cards than he wants, the dealer can play the hand or not, as he pleases. If he plays, he can draw the superfluous card or cards given to the pone, and look at them if the pone has seen them. If the dealer decides not to play, he marks the point. In either case, the pone cannot mark the King, even if he holds it.

If the pone asks for fewer cards than he wants, he has to play the hand as it is, and can mark the King if he holds it; however, all tricks for which he has no card to play have to be considered to have been won by his adversary.

If a player plays without discarding, or discards for the purpose of exchanging, without advising his adversary of the fact that he has too many or too few cards, he loses two points and the right of marking the King, even if turned up.

If either player, after discarding and drawing, plays with more than five cards, he loses the point and the privilege of marking the King.

If the dealer forgets himself in dealing for the discard, and turns up another trump, he cannot refuse his adversary another discard, if he demands it, and the exposed card has to be put aside with the discards.

If any cards are found faced in the pack when the discard is being dealt for, the deal stands good if the cards will fall to the dealer. However, if the exposed card will go to the pone, he has the option of either taking it or claiming a fresh deal by the same dealer.

During all the discards, the trump card remains the same.

MARKING THE KING   When the discards are settled, the first and most important thing before play begins is to mark the King. If the King is turned up, the dealer marks one point for it immediately. If the pone holds it, he has to *announce* and mark it before he plays a card. If he leads the King for the first trick, he still has to announce it by saying distinctly, 'I mark the King,' and unless this announcement is made before the King touches the table, the King cannot be marked. So important is this rule that in some European casinos it is found printed on the card tables. When the King has been properly announced, it can be actually marked with the counters at any time before the trump is turned for the following game.

If the dealer holds the King, he has to announce it before his adversary leads for the first trick. It is in order that so there can be no surprises in this way, the elder hand is required to say distinctly, 'I play,' before he leads a card. The dealer then has to reply, 'I mark the King,' if he has it; if he does not, he should say, 'Play.' A player is not compelled to announce or mark the King if he does not choose to do so.

If a player announces and marks the King when he does not hold it, his adversary can take down the point erroneously marked, and mark one himself, for penalty. This does not prevent him from marking an additional point for the King if he holds it himself. For example, the pone announces King, and marks it, at the same time as he leads a card. Because the pone has not notified the dealer that he was about to play, the dealer cannot be deprived of his right to mark the King himself, if he holds it. The dealer marks the King, marks another point for penalty, and takes down the pone's point that was erroneously marked. If the player who announces the King without holding it discovers his error before a card is played, he simply amends the score and apologises, and there is no penalty. If any cards have been played after an erroneous announcement of the King, these cards can be taken back by the adversary of the player in error, and the hand is played over again.

METHOD OF PLAYING   The elder hand begins by leading any card he pleases, at the same time as he announces the suit: 'Hearts', 'spades' or whatever it might be. This announcement has to be continued at every trick. If a player announces one suit and leads another, his adversary can demand he take back the card played and lead the suit announced. If he has none of the announced suit, the adversary can call a suit. If the adversary is satisfied with the card led but improperly announced, he can demand it remain as played.

RENOUNCING   When a card is led, the adversary not only has to follow suit; he has to win the trick if he can. If he can neither follow suit nor trump, he can discard any card he pleases. If a player does not follow suit, or declines to win the trick when he is able to do so, it is a renounce, and if he makes the odd trick, he counts nothing; if he makes all five tricks, he counts one point only, instead of two. If he trumps the trick when he can follow suit, he is subject to the same penalty. There is no such thing as a *revoke* in Écarté. When it is discovered that a player has not followed suit when he was able to or that he has lost a trick he could have won, the cards are taken back and the hand is played over again, with the foregoing penalty for the renounce.

The highest card played, if it is of the suit led, wins the trick, and trumps win all other suits.

LEADING OUT OF TURN   If a player leads out of turn, he can take back the card without penalty. If the adversary has played to the erroneous lead, the trick stands good.

GATHERING TRICKS   The tricks have to be turned down as taken in, and any player who looks at a trick once it is turned and quitted can be called on to play with the remainder of his hand exposed but not liable to be called.

ABANDONED HANDS   If, after taking one or more tricks, a player throws his cards on the table, he loses the point; if he has not taken a trick, he loses two points. However, if the cards are thrown down to claim the point or the game, and the claim is good, there is no penalty. If the cards are abandoned with the admission that the adversary wins the point or the game, and the adversary cannot win more than is admitted, there is no penalty.

SCORING   A game consists of five points, which are made by tricks, by penalties and by marking the King. A player who wins three tricks out of the five possible counts one point towards game, and a player who wins all five tricks, which is called *the vole*, counts two points. The player who holds or turns up the King of trumps can mark one point for it, but is not compelled to do so.

If the pone plays without proposing, and makes three or four tricks, he counts one point; if he makes the vole, he counts two points. However, if he fails to make three tricks, the dealer counts two.

If the dealer refuses the first proposal, he has to make three tricks to count one point; if he makes the vole, he counts two points. However, if he fails to win three tricks, the player who was refused counts two points.

If the dealer accepts the first proposal and gives cards, subsequent proposals and refusals do not affect the score; the winner of the odd trick scores one point, and the winner of the vole scores two points.

In no case can a player make more than two points in one hand by tricks. If the dealer refuses the first proposal, and the pone makes the vole, it counts two points only. If the pone plays without proposing, and the dealer marks the King and wins the vole, it counts him only three points altogether.

The player who first reaches five points wins the game. If a player has four scored, and turns the King, that wins the game, provided the King was the eleventh card. Rubbers are seldom played.

CHEATING The methods of cheating at Écarté would fill a volume. There are many tricks that although not exactly fraudulent are definitely questionable. For example, a player asks the gallery whether or not he should stand, and finally concludes to propose, all the while fully intending to draw five cards. Another player will handle his counters as if he is about to mark the King; will then effect to hesitate; and will finally re-adjust the counters and ask for cards, whereby he probably takes four or five cards, because he has absolutely nothing in his hand. The pone will ask the dealer how many points he has marked, knowing perfectly well that the number is three. On being informed of this, he concludes to ask for cards, as if he were not quite strong enough to risk the game by standing, when as a matter of fact he wants five cards and is afraid that the vole will be made against him.

There are many simple little tricks practised by the would-be card sharp, such as watching how many cards a player habitually cuts and then getting the four Kings close together in a position in the pack so that one of them is almost certain to be turned. Body-language signals between people on opposite sides of the gallery who are nevertheless in partnership are often translated into advice to the player, to his great benefit. Besides these, all the machinery of marked cards, reflectors, shifted cuts, wedges, strippers and false shuffles are at the command of the cheat, who can always handle a small pack of cards with greater freedom, and to whom the fashion of dealing in twos and threes is always welcome. The honest card player does not have a chance in a thousand against the professional at Écarté.

SUGGESTIONS FOR GOOD PLAY French players claim that any person can become an expert at a game such as Piquet simply by dint of long practice, but that the master of Écarté has to be a born card player, because no game requires to such an extent the exercise of individual intelligence and finesse. Although this might be true, there are many points about the game that may be learnt by the novice and that will greatly improve his play.

There are two things the beginner should master before he sits down to the table for actual play: the hands on which it is right to stand or to play without proposing, and the hands on which it is right to refuse or to play without giving cards. These are called stand hands, or *jeux de règle*, and the player should be able to recognise them on sight.

In the following paragraphs, the words **dealer** and **player** will be used to distinguish the adversaries at Écarté.

The principles underlying the jeux de règle are the probable distribution of the cards in the trump suit and the fact that the odds are always against the dealer's holding two or more. There are thirty-two cards in the Écarté pack, of which eight are trumps, and one of these is always turned up. The turn-up and the player's hand give us six cards that are known, and leave twenty-six unknown. Of these unknown cards, the dealer holds five, and he can get these five in 65,780 ways. The theory of the jeux de règle is that there is only a specific number of these ways whereby he will be given two or more trumps. If the player holds one trump, the odds against the dealer's holding two or more are 44,574 to 21,206, or slightly more than 2 to 1. If the player holds two trumps, the odds against the dealer's holding two or more are 50,274 to 15,506, or more than 3 to 1. It is therefore evident that any hand that is certain to win three tricks if the dealer does not have two trumps has odds of two to one in its favour, and all these hands are called jeux de règle. The natural inference from this is that these hands should always be played without proposing, unless they contain the King of trumps.

The exception in the case of holding of the King is made because there is no danger of the dealer's getting the King, no matter how many cards he draws, and if the player's cards are not strong enough to make it probable that he can win the vole, it is better for him to ask for cards, in the hope of improving his chances. If he is refused, he stands an excellent chance to make two points by winning the odd trick.

Although it is the rule for the player to stand when the odds are two to one in his favour for making the odd trick, and to ask for cards when the odds are less, there are exceptions. The chances of improving by taking in cards must not be forgotten, and it has to be remembered that the player who proposes runs no risk of penalty. He also has the advantage of scoring two for the vole if he can get enough cards to win every trick, whereas the dealer gets no more for the vole than for the odd trick if the player does not propose. Some beginners have a bad habit of asking for cards if they are reasonably certain of the point. Unless they hold the King, this is not wise, because the player cannot discard more than one or two cards, but the dealer can take five and then stands a fair chance of getting the King, which would not only count a point for him but would effectually stop the vole for which the player was drawing cards.

The most obvious example of a jeux de règle is one trump, a winning sequence of three cards in one suit, and a small card in another. For example, hearts trumps:

1   44,724 to 21,056

If the dealer does not hold two trumps, it is impossible to prevent the player from winning the point with these cards, because he only has to lead his winning sequence until it is trumped and then trump himself in again. With this hand, the player will win 44,724 times out of 65,780.

There are about twenty hands that are usually known as jeux de règle, and every écarté player should be familiar with them. In the following examples the weakest hands are given, and the trumps are always the smallest possible. If the player has more strength in plain suits than is shown in these examples, or higher trumps, there is so much more reason for him to stand. However, if he does not have the strength indicated in plain suits, he should propose, even if his trumps are higher, because it has to be remembered that strong trumps do not compensate for weakness in plain suits. The reason for this is that from stand hands, trumps should never be led unless there are three of them; they are to be kept for ruffing, and when you have to ruff it, does not matter whether you use a seven or a Queen. The King of trumps is naturally led, but a player does not stand on a hand that contains the King.

In the following examples, the first suit given is always the trump, and the next suit is always the one that should be led, beginning with the best card of it if there is more than one. The figures on the right are the number of hands in which the player or the dealer will win out of the 65,780 possible distributions of the twenty-six unknown cards. These calculations are taken, by permission of Mr Charles Mossop, from the eighth volume of the *Westminster Papers,* in which all the variations and their results are given in full.

						PLAYER WINS	DEALER WINS
2	7 ♣ SEVEN	8 ♣ EIGHT	7 ♥ SEVEN	8 ♥ EIGHT	9 ♥ NINE	47,768	18,012
3	7 ♥ SEVEN	8 ♥ EIGHT	K ♠ KING	7 ♠ SEVEN	7 ♦ SEVEN	46,039	19,741
4	7 ♠ SEVEN	8 ♠ EIGHT	7 ♦ SEVEN	7 ♣ SEVEN	Q ♥ QUEEN	43,764	22,016
5	7 ♦ SEVEN	8 ♦ EIGHT	8 ♣ EIGHT	7 ♣ SEVEN	K ♥ KING	45,374	20,406
6	7 ♣ SEVEN	8 ♣ EIGHT	8 ♦ EIGHT	9 ♦ NINE	Q ♠ QUEEN	44,169	21,611
7	7 ♥ SEVEN	8 ♥ EIGHT	9 ♣ NINE	10 ♣ TEN	J ♦ JACK	43,478	22,302
8	7 ♠ SEVEN	8 ♠ EIGHT	10 ♥ TEN	A ♥ ACE	A ♣ ACE	44,243	21,537
9	7 ♦ SEVEN	8 ♦ EIGHT	A ♠ ACE	J ♠ JACK	8 ♥ EIGHT	44,766	21,014
10	7 ♣ SEVEN	8 ♣ EIGHT	K ♠ KING	J ♠ JACK	7 ♦ SEVEN	44,459	21,321
11	7 ♥ SEVEN	8 ♥ EIGHT	K ♠ KING	A ♦ ACE	9 ♣ NINE	44,034	21,746
12	7 ♠ SEVEN	8 ♠ EIGHT	J ♠ JACK	10 ♣ TEN	10 ♥ TEN	43,434	22,346

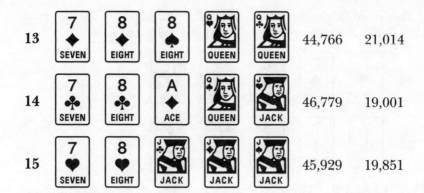

The player should always stand on a hand that contains three trumps, not including the King, and should lead the trump:

An example of a hand that contains only one trump has already been given, and some hands are jeux de règle that contain no trumps. The strongest of these is the King of each plain suit, and any queen. Lead the K Q suit:

The odds in favour of this hand are greater than in any other jeux de règle. Another hand that is recommended by Bohn is this, the odds in favour of which have not been calculated. The player is to begin with the guarded King:

Another hand is any four court cards, not all of which are Jacks, unless one is the trump Jack guarded. In the example, the Queen should be led:

There are two hands that are usually played with only one trump, from both of which the best card of the long suit is led:

THE LEADER There are a great many more opportunities to make the vole than most players are aware of, especially with reference to jeux de règle. When the vole is improbable or impossible, tenace is very important, and all tenace positions should be made the most of. In example hand number 5, for example, if the clubs were the Queen and ace, it would be better to begin with the heart King than to lead away from the minor tenace in clubs. Observe the lead in example hand number 4. Many tenace positions cannot be taken advantage of because the player has to win the trick if he can. For example, several discards have been made, and each player suspects that the other holds three trumps, with three tricks to play. The Queen is led, and the adversary holds K A 7. If he could pass this trick, he has to lie tenace; however, because he has to win it with the King, he gives tenace to his adversary, who evidently has J and another card.

When the dealer is four, the player can stand on much weaker hands.

It is usually best to lead from guarded suits in preference to single cards. Lead the best of a suit if you have it. If the third trick is the first you win, and you have a trump and another card, lead the trump, but if you have won two tricks, lead the plain suit.

THE DEALER When the player asks for cards, the dealer knows that his adversary probably does not hold a jeux de règle. The dealer must not be too sure of this, however, because proposals are sometimes made on very strong hands in order to either try for the vole or make two points on the refusal. The dealer should assume he is opposed by the best play until he finds the contrary to be the case, and it is safest to play on the assumption that a player who proposes does not have a jeux de règle.

For all practical purposes, it can be said that the dealer can refuse to give cards with hands that are slightly less strong than ones on which the player would stand. The general rule is for the dealer to give cards unless he is guarded in three suits; or has a trump, and is safe in two suits; or has two trumps, and is safe in one suit. If the dealer has only one suit guarded, and one trump, he has to take into account the risk of being forced and of having to lead away from his guarded suit.

There are eight recognised hands on which the dealer should refuse. The full details of the calculations can be found in the ninth volume of the *Westminster Papers*. As in the case of the player, the weakest trumps have been taken for the examples, and the weakest holdings in plain suits have been taken. If the dealer has better plain suits, or stronger trumps, he naturally has so much more in his favour if he refuses. The first column of figures are the number of times in 65,780 that there will be no proposal, so that the dealer has no choice but to play. The other columns are the number of times the dealer or the player will win if the player proposes and the dealer refuses.

The first suit given in each example is the trump.

No.	Cards	No Proposal	Dealer Wins	Player Wins
22	7♣ 8♣ 9♣ 7♦ 7♠	6,034	36,974	22,772
23	7♥ 8♥ A♠ 8♠ 7♠	9,826	38,469	17,485
24	7♠ 8♠ K♥ 7♥ 7♣	8,736	41,699	15,345
25	7♦ 8♦ Q♣ 7♣ 7♥	9,256	40,524	16,000
26	7♣ 8♣ 7♦ 8♦ Q♠	10,336	37,484	17,960
27	7♥ 8♥ 8♣ 9♣ J♦	9,776	37,439	18,565
28	7♠ 8♠ 9♥ 10♥ 10♣	9,776	36,909	19,095

29  9,776   36,733 19,271

In giving cards, some judgement of human nature is necessary. Some players habitually propose on strong hands, and it is best to give to them reasonably freely.

DISCARDING The general principles of discarding are to keep trumps and Kings and to let everything else go. If you hold the trump King, you can discard freely in order to strengthen your hand for a possible vole. If you have proposed once, and hold the King, and feel reasonably sure of the point, you can propose again on the chance of getting strength enough to make the vole.

When only two cards can be discarded, it is a safe rule to stand on the hand: either to play without proposing or to refuse cards, unless you hold the King.

There are no authoritative laws for Écarté, and the various French and English codes are not in agreement. The code adopted by the English clubs is not in accord with the best usage, and many contingencies are not provided for in it. All that is essential in the laws will be found embodied in the aforementioned description of the game.

— —

POOL ÉCARTÉ

Pool Écarté is played by three people, each of whom contributes an agreed sum, which is called a *stake*, to form a pool. The players then cut to decide who will play the first game, whereby the lowest écarté card goes out. The players then cut for the first deal, the choice of seats and cards, and so on, exactly as in the ordinary game.

The winner of the first game retains his seat; the loser pays into the pool another stake, which is equal to the first, and retires in favour of the third player, who is called the *rentrant*. The rentrant takes the loser's seat and cards, and cuts with the successful player for the first deal. The loser of the second game adds another stake to the pool, and retires in favour of the waiting player.

The pool is won by any player who wins two games in succession. If the winner of the first game also won the second, he would take the pool, which would then contain five stakes: the three originally deposited and the two added by the losers of the two games. A new pool would then be formed by each of the three who deposit another stake, and all the players cut to decide who will sit out for the first game.

In some places, only the two players who are actually engaged contribute to the pool, whereby the loser retires without paying anything more, and the rentrant contributes his stake when he takes the loser's place.

The outsider is not allowed to advise either player during the first game, nor to call attention to the score; however, in the second game, he is allowed to advise the player who has taken his seat and cards. This is on the principle that he has no right to choose sides in the first game, but that after that, he has an interest in preventing his former adversary from winning the second game, so as to preserve the pool until he can play for it again himself.

— ◄—

NAPOLEON

OR NAP

This is one of the simplest and most popular game of the euchre family. Few games became as widely known in such a short time, or were in as much vogue among all classes of society. So far as the mere winning and losing goes, the result depends largely on luck, and skill is of small importance. Except in a long series of games, the average player has little to fear from the most expert.

CARDS Napoleon is played with a full pack of fifty-two cards, which rank A K Q J 10 9 8 7 6 5 4 3 2, whereby the ace is highest in play but ranks below the deuce in cutting.

COUNTERS Because each deal is a complete game in itself, it has to be settled for in counters, to which some value is usually attached. One player is selected for the banker, and before play begins, each of the other players purchases from him a specific number of counters, usually fifty. When any player's supply is exhausted, he can purchase more, from either the banker or another player.

In many places, counters are not used, and the value of their game is designated by way of the coins that take their place. In 'penny nap', English coppers are used in settling; sixpences are used in 'sixpenny nap'; and so on. In America, nickel and quarter nap are the usual forms.

PLAYERS Any number from two to six can play, but four is the best game. If five or six play, it is usual for the dealer to give himself no cards.

CUTTING The players draw from an outspread pack to form the table, and for choice of seats. A lower cut gives preference over all higher; the lowest cut has the first choice of seats, and deals the first hand. Ties cut again, but the new cut decides nothing but the tie.

In some places, the players take their seats at random, and a card is then dealt to each face upwards; the lowest card or the first Jack takes the deal.

DEALING Any player has a right to shuffle the cards, and the dealer goes last. The cards are then presented to the pone to cut, and at least four have to be left in each packet. Beginning at his left, the dealer gives each player in rotation two cards on the first round and three on the next, or three on the first and two on the next. No trump is turned. In some places, the cards are distributed one at a time until each player has five; however, this plan is not popular, because the hands run better and the bidding is livelier when the cards are dealt in twos and threes. The deal passes to the left, and each player deals in turn.

MISDEALING A misdeal does not lose the deal in Napoleon, because the deal is a disadvantage. For this reason, if any player begins to deal out of turn, he has to finish, and the deal stands good. If any card is found faced in the pack, or is exposed by the dealer; or if too many or too few cards are given to any player; or if the dealer does not give the same number of cards to each player in the same round; or if the dealer fails to have the pack cut, it is a misdeal, and the misdealer has to deal again using the same pack.

BIDDING Beginning on the dealer's left, each player in turn bids for the privilege of naming the trump suit, whereby he states the number of tricks he proposes to win, playing single-handed against the three other players and leading a trump for the first trick. In bidding, the trump suit is not named; only the number of tricks is. If a player proposes to win all five tricks, he bids *nap*, which is the highest bid possible, and precludes any more bidding, except in some of the variations that will be described later on. If a player will not make a bid, he says, *'I pass.'* When a bid has been made, any following player has to either increase it or pass. If all pass until it comes to the dealer, he is bound to bid at least one trick, and to either play or pay. The hands are never abandoned except in the case of a misdeal.

In some places a *misère* bid is allowed, which outranks a bid of three tricks, and is beaten by one of four. There is no trump suit in misère, but the bidder, if successful, has to lead for the first trick.

Any bid once made can neither be amended nor recalled, and there is no second bid.

METHOD OF PLAYING The player who bids the highest number of tricks has the first lead, and the first card he plays has to be one of the trump suit. The players have to follow suit if they are able, but do not have to win the trick unless they choose to do so. The highest card played of the suit led wins the trick, and trumps win all other suits. The winner of the trick leads again for the next trick, and so on, until all five tricks have been played. After the first trick, any suit can be led.

The bidder gathers all tricks he wins, and stacks them so they can be readily counted by any player at the table. One of the other side should gather all tricks won by the adversaries of the bidder. A trick once turned and quitted cannot again be seen. In some places, players have a very bad habit of gathering tricks with the cards face upwards, whereby they turn down one card only. This always results in many misdeals, on account of cards' being continually found faced in the pack.

The hands are usually abandoned when the bidder succeeds in his undertaking, or shows cards that are good for his bid against any play. If it is impossible for him to succeed, because when he bids four and the adversaries have won two tricks, the hands are thrown up, because nothing is paid for under- or over-tricks. Players should show the remainder of their hands to the board, as evidence that no revoke has been made.

IRREGULARITIES IN HANDS If a player, before he makes a bid or passes, discovers that he holds too many or too few cards, he has to immediately claim a misdeal. If he has either made a bid or passed, the deal stands good, and the hand has to be played out. If the bidder has his right number of cards and succeeds, he has to be paid. If he fails, he neither wins nor loses, because he is playing against a foul hand. If the bidder has more than his right number of cards, he has to pay if he loses, but he wins nothing if he succeeds. If he has fewer than his right number of cards, he is simply supposed to have lost the trick for which he has no card to play.

PLAYING OUT OF TURN If any adversary of the bidder leads or plays out of turn, he forfeits three counters to the bidder, independently of the result of the hand, and receives nothing if the bid is defeated. If the bidder leads out of turn, the card has to be taken back, unless all the players have followed the erroneous lead, in which case the trick is good. There is no penalty if the bidder plays out of turn.

REVOKES When a revoke is detected and claimed, the hands are immediately abandoned, and the individual player in fault has to pay all the counters, depending on the result. If he is the bidder, he pays each adversary; if he is opposed to the bidder, he pays for himself and for each of his partners. In England, it is the rule to take back the cards and play the hand over again, as at Écarté, whereby the revoking player pays all the stakes according to the result. This is often very unfair to the bidder, and leads to endless disputes as to who held specific cards that have been gathered into tricks. Sometimes, the difference between a seven and an eight in a specific player's hand will change the entire result.

PAYMENTS If the bidder succeeds in winning the specified number of tricks, each adversary pays him a counter for every trick bid. If he bid three tricks, they pay him three counters each; four counters each for four tricks bid; and the value of three tricks for a misère. If he fails to win the specified number of tricks, he pays each adversary; three counters if he bid three tricks, or a misère; four if he bid four. Any player who bids nap, and who succeeds in winning all five tricks, receives ten counters from each adversary, but if he fails, he pays only five to each adversary.

When penny nap is played, whereby the settlement is in coins, it is usual to make naps win a shilling or lose sixpence, in order to avoid handling a lot of coins.

SUGGESTIONS FOR GOOD PLAY In calculating his chances for success in winning a specific number of tricks, the player will often have to take into consideration the probability of specific cards' being out against him. This will vary according to the number of players engaged. For example, if four are playing, and the bidder holds K Q of a plain suit, the odds against the ace of that suit's being out against him are about 2 to 1. Because it would be impossible for any person to remember all the jeux de règle for three tricks in Napoleon, each player has to learn from experience the trick-taking value of specific hands. Trump strength is, naturally, the great factor, and the bidder should count on finding at least two trumps in one hand against him. Nap should never be bid on a hand that is not reasonably sure of winning two rounds of trumps, with all other cards but one winners. One trick can always be risked in a nap hand, such as A Q of trumps, or a King, or even a Queen or Jack in a plain suit; the odds against the adversaries having a better card are slightly increased by the odds against their knowing enough to keep it for the last trick.

If the bid is for three tricks only, tenaces, or guarded minor honours in plain suits, should be preserved. After the first trick, it will sometimes be advantageous for the player to get rid of any losing card he might have in plain suits. It is seldom right to continue the trumps if the bidder held only two originally, unless he has winning cards in two plain suits, in which case it might be better to lead even a losing trump to avert the possibility that adverse trumps will be made separately.

In playing against the bidder, leave no trick to your partners that you can win yourself, unless a small card is led, and you have the ace. In opening fresh suits, do not lead guarded honours; prefer aces or singletons. If the caller requires only one more trick, it is usually best to lead a trump. If you have three trumps, including the major tenace, pass the first trick if a small trump is led; or, if you remain with the tenace after the first trick, be careful to avoid the lead.

Discards should indicate weakness, unless you can show command of a suit such as A K, or K Q, by discarding the best of it. Your partners will thereby be directed to let that suit go and to keep the other suits. It is usually better to keep a guarded King than a single ace. The player on the right of the bidder should get into the lead if possible, especially if he holds one or two winning cards. These will either give his partners discards or enable them to overtrump the bidder.

In playing misères, it is better to begin with a singleton, or the lowest of a safe suit. An Ace or King two or three times guarded is very safe for a misère, because it is very improbable that any player will be able to lead the suit more than twice, and if the bidder's missing suit is led, the high card can be gotten rid of at once.

In playing against a misère, discards are important, and the first should be from the shortest suit, and always the highest card of it. A suit in which the bidder is long should be continued, in order to give partners discards. More money is lost in Napoleon by playing imperfect misères than in any other way.

VARIATIONS The foregoing description applies to the regular four-handed game, but there are several variations in common use.

Better bids than 'nap' are sometimes allowed, on the understanding that the bidder will pay double or treble stakes if he fails but will receive only the usual amount if he is successful. For example, one player bids *Nap*, and another holds what he considers to be a certainty for five tricks. In order not to lose this opportunity, the latter bids *Wellington*, whereby he is bound to pay ten counters to each player if he fails. Another might outbid this again by bidding *Blucher*, whereby he is bound to pay twenty to each if he loses but to receive only ten if he wins. In England, the bidder, if successful, receives double or treble stakes for a Wellington or a Blucher, which is simply another way of enabling any person who has a nap hand to increase the stakes at pleasure, because a player who had a certain five tricks would naturally bid a Blucher at once, thereby trebling his gains and shutting off all competition at the same time. This variation is not to be recommended, and benefits no one but the gambler.

POOLS Napoleon is sometimes played with a pool, whereby each player contributes a specific amount, usually two counters, on the first deal. Each dealer in turn adds two more; revokes pay five, and leads out of turn three. The player who first succeeds in winning five tricks on a nap bid takes the pool, and a fresh pool is formed. If a player bids nap and fails, he is usually called on to double the amount then in the pool, as well as to pay his adversaries.

Purchase Nap, which is sometimes called *Écarté Nap*, is a variation of the pool game. After the cards are dealt, and before any bids are made, each player in turn, beginning on the dealer's left, can discard as many cards as he pleases, whereby the dealer gives him others in their place. For each card so exchanged, the player pays one counter to the pool. Only one round of exchanges is allowed, and bids are then in order. When a player has once refused to buy, or has named the number of cards he wishes to exchange, he cannot amend his decision. Any player who wins five tricks on a nap bid takes the entire pool. This is a very good game, and increases both the bids and the play against them.

WIDOWS Another variation is to deal five cards in the centre of the table, face downwards, whereby the dealer gives the cards to the widow just before he helps himself in each round. Any player in his proper turn to bid can take the widow, and from the total of ten cards so obtained select five on which he has to bid nap, whereby he discards the other cards face downwards.

PEEP NAP In this variety of the pool game, one card only is dealt to the widow, usually on the first round. Each player in turn, before bidding or passing, has the privilege of taking a private peep at this down card, on paying one counter to the pool. The card is left on the table until the highest bidder is known, and this bidder then takes the card into his hand, whether or not he has paid to peep at it. He then has to discard in order to reduce his hand to five cards. If a player bids nap, it usually pays the players following him to have a peep at the down card in case the bidder retains it in his hand.

— —

SPOIL FIVE

Spoil Five is one of the oldest of card games, and is usually conceded to be the national game of Ireland. It is derived from the yet older game of Maw, which was the favourite recreation of England's James I. The connecting link seems to have been a game called Five Fingers, which is described in the *Compleat Gamester*, first published in 1674. The Five Fingers was the five of trumps, and was also the best, whereby the ace of hearts came next. In Spoil Five, the Jack of trumps comes between these two.

CARDS   Spoil Five is played with a full pack of fifty-two cards. The rank of the cards varies according to the colour of the suit, and the trump suit undergoes still further changes, whereby the heart ace is always the third-best trump. In the plain suits, the K Q J retain their usual order, and the King is the best. The rank of the spot cards, including the aces of diamonds, clubs and spades, is usually expressed by way of the phrase *Higher in red; lowest in black*; that is, if several cards of a suit, not including a King, Queen or Jack, are played to a trick, the highest card will win if the suit is red, and the lowest if the suit is black.

This will give us the following order for the plain suits, beginning with the highest card in each.

No change			Highest in red								
♡ K	Q	J	10	9	8	7	6	5	4	3	2
◇ K	Q	J	10	9	8	7	6	5	4	3	2	A
			Lowest in black								
♣ K	Q	J	A	2	3	4	5	6	7	8	9	10
♠ K	Q	J	A	2	3	4	5	6	7	8	9	10

In the trump suit, the same order of cards is retained, except that four cards are always the best trumps. These are the Five, Jack and ace of the suit itself, and the ace of hearts, whereby the latter is always the third best. This gives us the rank of the cards as follows, when the suit is trump.

	No change						Highest in red							
♡5 J		♡	A K Q	10	9	8	7	6	5	4	3	2		
◇5 J	♡A	◇	A K Q	10	9	8	7	6	5	4	3	2		
							Lowest in black							
♣5 J	♡A	♣	A K Q	2	3	4	5	6	7	8	9	10		
♠5 J	♡A	♠	A K Q	2	3	4	5	6	7	8	9	10		

COUNTERS Spoil Five is played with a pool, for which counters are necessary. One player should act as the banker, and the other players should purchase from him, whereby each player begins with 20 counters. Coins can take the place of counters, and shillings are the usual points.

PLAYERS Any number from 2 to 10 can play, but 5 or 6 is the usual game.

CUTTING This is unknown in Spoil Five. The players take their seats at random, and one of them deals a card face upwards to each player in succession. The first Jack takes the first deal. Some note should be made of the player who gets the first deal, because the rules require that when the game is brought to an end, the last deal be made by the player on the right of the first dealer.

THE POOL Before play begins, each player deposits one counter in the pool, and to this amount each successive dealer adds a counter until the pool is won, when all contribute equally to form a new one. In some places, it is the practice for each successive dealer to put up for all the players, whether or not the pool is won. This simply makes for larger pools.

DEALING Any player has the right to shuffle the pack, and the dealer goes last. The cards are then presented to the pone to cut, and as many cards as there are players have to be left in each packet. Beginning on his left, the dealer gives five cards to each player; two on the first round and three on the next, or three and then two. After all are helped, the next card is turned up on the remainder of the pack, and the suit to which it belongs is the trump for that deal.

MISDEALING If there is any irregularity in the deal that is not the dealer's fault, such as that any card except the trump is found faced in the pack, or the pack is found to be imperfect, the same person deals again. However, if the dealer neglects to have the pack cut, or deals too many or too few cards to any player, or exposes a card in dealing, or does not give the same number of cards to each player on the same round, or counts the cards on the table or the ones remaining in the pack, it is a misdeal, and the deal passes to the next player on the misdealer's left. In some places, the misdealer is allowed to deal again if he forfeits two counters to the pool.

ROBBING THE TRUMP CARD   If the trump card is an ace, the dealer can discard any card he pleases in exchange for it. He can take up the ace when he plays to the first trick, or can leave it on the pack until it is gotten rid of in the course of play. When an ace is turned, the eldest hand, before leading, should call on the dealer to discard if he has not already done so. If the dealer does not want the trump, he answers, 'I play these.'

If the trump card is not an ace, any player at the table who holds the ace of trumps is bound to announce the fact when it comes to his turn to play to the first trick. The usual plan is for him to pass a card to the dealer face downwards, and in return the dealer will give him the turn-up trump. If the holder of the ace does not want the turn-up, he has to tell the dealer to turn the trump down, whereby it is shown that he could rob but does not wish to. If the holder of the ace of trumps plays without announcing it, he not only loses his right to rob; his ace of trumps becomes of less value than any other trump for that deal, and even if it is the ace of hearts, he loses the privileges attached to that card.

METHOD OF PLAYING   The eldest hand begins by leading any card he pleases. It is not necessary to follow suit except in trumps; however, if a player does not follow suit when he is able to do so, he has to trump the trick, or it is a revoke. If he cannot follow suit, he can trump or discard at his pleasure. The highest card played of the suit led wins the trick, and trumps win all other suits. The winner of the first trick leads any card he pleases for the next, and so on, until all five tricks have been played. Each player gathers his own tricks, because there are no partnerships.

RENEGING   The three highest trumps have special privileges in the matter of not following suit. Any player who holds the Five or Jack of the trump suit, or the ace of hearts, but who has no smaller trump with them, can refuse to follow suit if any inferior trump is led; however, if he also has a smaller trump, he has to play one or the other. If a superior trump is led, the player has to follow suit in any case. For example, if the Five of trumps is led, no one can refuse to follow suit, no matter what trumps he holds, but if the Jack is led, and any player holds the Five alone, he does not have to play it to the inferior trump lead. If the heart ace is led, and one player holds the Jack alone and another the Five alone, neither of these cards has to be played, because the trump led is inferior to both of them. If a superior trump is played in following suit, such as the Five played on an Eight led, the holder of the lone Jack of trumps or ace of hearts does not have to play it, because the lead was inferior. This privilege of reneging is confined to the three highest trumps.

OBJECTS OF THE GAME   In Spoil Five, there are three things to play for. If any one person can win three tricks, he takes the pool. If he can win all five tricks, he not only gets the pool; he receives an extra counter from each of the other players. If he has no chance to win three tricks, he has to bend all his energies to scattering the tricks among the other players, so that no one will be able to get the three tricks necessary to win the pool. When this is done, the game is said to be *spoiled*, and because that is the object of the majority in every deal, it gives the game its name. In the older forms of the game, the winner of three tricks counted five points, and if he could be prevented from getting three tricks, his five points were spoiled.

JINK GAME   When a player has won three tricks, he should immediately abandon his hand and claim the pool, because if he continues playing, he has to *jink it*, and get all five tricks or lose what he has already won, whereby the game is spoiled just as if no one had won three tricks. It is sometimes a matter for nice judgement whether or not to go on, and, for the sake of an extra counter from each player, to risk a pool already won. The best trump is often held up for three rounds in order to coax a player to go on in this way.

IRREGULARITIES IN THE HANDS   If, during the play of a hand, it is discovered that anyone holds too many or too few cards, that hand is foul and has to be abandoned, whereby the holder forfeits all right to the pool for that deal. The players who have their right number of cards finish the play without the foul hand, but any tricks already won by the holder of the foul hand remain his property.

IRREGULARITIES IN PLAY   If any player robs when he does not hold the ace, leads or plays out of turn, reneges to the lead of a higher trump; renounces in the trump suit, revokes in a plain suit, or exposes a card after any player has won two tricks, he loses all his right and interest in the current pool, which he cannot win, either on that or any subsequent deal, but to which he has to continue to contribute when it comes to his turn to deal. After the pool has been won, and a fresh one formed, the penalty is removed.

SUGGESTIONS FOR GOOD PLAY   Observation, quickness and good judgement of character are the essentials for success in Spoil Five, and the last mentioned is probably the most important. The peculiar order of the cards, the privilege of renouncing when you are holding a card of the suit led, and the right of passing inferior trump leads are very confusing to the beginner, but if you practise, the routine and strategy of the game will soon become familiar.

The player should first make up his mind whether he will try to win the pool or spoil it. Attention should especially be paid to the player who robs, because he has to have at least the ace and the turn-up in trumps, and is more likely to require spoiling than is any other player. When a player wins a trick, some judgement will be necessary to decide whether he is trying for the pool himself or simply spoiling it for someone else. When he wins two tricks, every other player at the table has to combine against him.

With only one small or medium trump, it is better to use it at the first opportunity. Unless the player has some hopes of winning the pool himself, he should trump all doubtful cards, that is, cards that can win the trick if not trumped. With two good trumps, it is better to wait for developments: even if you cannot win the last three tricks yourself, you can effectually spoil any other player. Do anything you can to prevent the possibility of a third trick's being won by a player who has already won two.

— —

FORTY-FIVE, OR FIVE AND TEN

These names are given to Spoil Five when it is played by two people only or by four or six people divided into two equal partnerships. There is no pool, because one side or the other has to win three tricks every deal. The side that wins the odd trick counts five points towards game, or ten points if it wins all five tricks. Forty-five points is game. In another variation, each trick counts five points, and the winners' score is deducted from the losers', so that if one side wins four tricks, it counts fifteen towards game. When this way of counting is adopted, the players count out; that is, if each side is 35 up, the first to win two tricks counts out.

Minor variations are sometimes introduced, such as robbing with the King if the ace is not in play, and counting five for the dealer's side if the ace or King is turned up.

— —

RAMS

OR RAMMES

This game seems to be the connecting link between the more strongly marked members of the Euchre family and Division Loo.

CARDS Rams is played with the euchre pack: thirty-two cards, which rank as at Écarté: K Q J A 10 9 8 7. It became the fashion, however, to adopt the rank of the cards in the piquet pack: A K Q J 10 9 8 7.

PLAYERS Any number from three to six can play, but when six play, the dealer takes no cards. The general arrangements for the players, first deal, counters, and so on are exactly the same as in Spoil Five.

THE POOL Each successive dealer puts up five counters, to either form or augment the pool.

DEALING When the cards have been properly shuffled and cut, five are given to each player: two the first round and three the next, or three the first round and two the next. An extra hand, known as the *widow*, is dealt face downwards in the centre of the table. The dealer gives cards to the widow just before dealing to himself in each round. When all are helped, the next card is turned up for the trump. Irregularities in the deal are governed by the same rules as in Spoil Five.

DECLARING TO PLAY Each player in turn, beginning with the eldest hand, can either play or pass. If he passes, he lays his cards face downwards in front of him, and takes no more part in that deal unless a general rams is announced. If he plays, he engages himself to take at least one trick or forfeit five counters to the pool. He can play with the hand originally dealt to him, or can risk getting a better hand by taking the widow in exchange. If he exchanges, his original hand is dead, and must not be seen by any player. If any player takes the widow, the players following him have to play the hand dealt to them or pass out. In some clubs, the eldest hand is obliged to play, with either his own hand or the widow.

If all pass except the pone, he has to play against the dealer, with either the cards dealt to him or the widow. If he declines to play, he has to pay the dealer five counters, and the pool remains. The dealer has to play if he is opposed by only one player, but if two other players have announced to play, the dealer can play or pass as he pleases. If he plays, he can discard and take up the trump card. No other player can rob the trump.

METHOD OF PLAYING The eldest hand of the people who have declared to play begins by leading any card he pleases. Each player in turn has to head the trick, that is, play a higher card if he can. If he has two higher, he can play either. If he has none of the suit led, he has to trump if he can, even if the trick is already trumped by another player. For example, hearts are trumps, and A leads a club. B follows suit, but neither C nor D has a club. Suppose C trumps with the King, and that the only trump D has is the Queen: he has to play it on the trick, and thereby lose it to C's King. When a player can neither follow suit nor trump, he can discard any card he pleases. The winner of the trick leads for the next trick, and so on until all five tricks have been played.

PENALTIES There is only one penalty in Rams: to win nothing on the deal, and to forfeit five counters to the next pool. This is inflicted for playing with more or fewer than five cards, for exposing any card, for leading or playing out of turn, for renouncing, and for refusing to head or trump a trick when you are able to do so.

DIVIDING THE POOL Pools can be simple or double. The usual custom is to compel everyone to play when the pool is a simple, whereby it contains nothing but the five counters put up by the dealer. When there are more than five counters in the pool, they have to be a multiple of five, and the pool is called a double. In double pools, the players can play or pass as they please. No matter how many counters are already in the pool, the dealer has to add five.

Each player gathers in the tricks he wins, and at the end of the hand, he is entitled to take one-fifth of the contents of the pool for every trick he has won. If he has played his hand, and failed to get a trick, he is ramsed, and forfeits five counters to form the next pool, in addition to the counters that will be put up by the next dealer. If two or more players fail to win a trick, they each have to pay five counters, and if the player whose turn it will be to deal next is ramsed, he will have to put up ten: five for his deal and five for the rams.

GENERAL RAMS If any player thinks he can win all five tricks, with the advantage of the first lead, he can announce a general rams when it comes to his turn to pass or play. This announcement can be made either before or after the widow is taken. When a general rams is announced, all at the table have to play, and the players who have passed and laid down their hands have to take them up again. If the widow has not been taken, any player who has not already refused it can take it. The player who announced general rams has the first lead. If he succeeds in getting all five tricks, he not only gets the pool; he receives five counters in addition from each player. If he fails, he has to double the amount then in the pool, and pay five counters to each of his adversaries. Any player who takes a trick that spoils a general rams gets nothing from the pool, and it is usual to abandon the hands the moment the announcing player loses a trick.

— · —

ROUNCE

This is an American corruption of Rams. It is played with the full pack of fifty-two cards, which rank as in Whist, and any number of players from three to nine. Six cards are dealt to the widow, one of which has to be discarded by the player who takes it. All pools are alike, there is no difference between simples and doubles, and there is no such announcement as general rounce. There is no obligation to head the trick, nor to trump or under-trump, but the winner of the first trick has to lead a trump if he has one.

— · —

BIERSPIEL

This was a popular form of Rams among German students. Three crosses are chalked on the table in front of each player, which represent five points each. When a trick is won, a beer-soaked finger wipes out the centre of a cross, and reduces its value to four. Successive cancellings of the remaining arms of the cross as tricks are taken gradually reduce it to nothing, and the player who is last to wipe out his third cross pays for the beer. No player is allowed to look at his cards until the trump is turned, and the dealer gives the word of command: 'Auf.' The seven of diamonds is always the second-best card of the trump suit, and ranks next below the ace. If it is turned up, the dealer turns up the next card for a trump, and when it comes to his turn, he can take both cards into his hand and discard others in their place. If the dealer passes, the eldest hand can take up the trump. If only two declare to play, a trump has to be led for the first trick; if three play, trumps have to be led twice; and if four play, trumps have to be led three times. If the leader has no trump, he has to lead his smallest card, face downwards, whereby a trump is called for from any of the other players who have one. All penalties are made by way of adding fresh crosses to the delinquent's score.

— —

LOO
OR DIVISION LOO

This was at one time the most popular of all-round games at cards; however, its cousin Napoleon seems to have usurped its place in England, whereas Poker has eclipsed it in America. There are several varieties of the game, but the most common form is Three-card Limited Loo, which will be first described.

CARDS Loo is played with a full pack of fifty-two cards that rank A K Q J 10 9 8 7 6 5 4 3 2, whereby the ace is the highest.

COUNTERS Because Loo is a pool game, counters are necessary. They should be of two colours: white and red, and one red is worth three whites. The object of this is to provide for an equal division of the pool at all times. One person should act as the banker, to sell and redeem all counters. Each player should begin with 18 red and 6 white, which is equal to 20 reds.

PLAYERS Any number of people from three to seventeen can play, but eight is the usual limit, and five or six make the best game. The players take their seats at random.

CUTTING A card is dealt around to each player, face upwards, and the first Jack takes the first deal.

THE POOL Each successive dealer places three red counters in the pool. The pool is added to from time to time by way of penalties for infractions of the rules, and by way of forfeitures from players who have failed in their undertakings. These payments are always made in red counters, and the number is always three or six. When the pool is divided, it sometimes happens that a player is not allowed to withdraw his share. In these cases, the red counters that represent it should be changed for their value in white ones, so that the forfeited share can be divided in three parts.

The difference between *Limited Loo* and *Unlimited Loo* is in the amounts paid into the pool. In Limited Loo, the penalty is always three or six red counters. In Unlimited Loo, it is the same for irregularities, and for infraction of the rules; however, any player who fails in his undertaking has to put up for the next pool an amount equal to that in the current pool. When two or more fail on successive deals, the pool increases with surprising rapidity. A player at 25 cent Loo has been known to lose $320 in three consecutive deals.

DEALING   When the pack has been properly shuffled and cut, the dealer gives three cards to each player, one at a time in rotation, beginning on his left. The first deal, and every deal in which the pool contains only the three red counters put up by the dealer, is known as a *simple*, and no trump card is turned up until one or two tricks have been played to. If there are more than three red counters in the pool, it is known as a *double*, and an extra hand has to be dealt for the *widow*. After all have been helped, the next card in the pack is turned up for a trump. The dealer gives cards to the widow just before he helps himself in each round.

IRREGULARITIES IN THE DEAL   If the pack is found to be imperfect, or any card except the trump is found faced in the pack, the same dealer has to deal again without penalty. If the dealer neglects to have the pack cut, re-shuffles the pack after it has been properly cut, deals a card incorrectly and fails to correct the error before dealing another, exposes a card in dealing, gives any player too many or too few cards, or deals a wrong number of hands, it is a misdeal, and he loses his deal and forfeits three red counters to the current pool. The new dealer adds his three counters as usual, and the pool becomes a double.

METHOD OF PLAYING   A description of the method of playing will be better understood if it is divided into two parts, because it varies in both simple and double pools.

In Simple Pools, no trump is turned and no widow is dealt. If the dealer inadvertently turns a trump, he forfeits three red counters to the current pool, but it remains a simple. If he deals a card for a widow, and fails to correct himself before dealing another card, it is a misdeal.

The eldest hand leads any card he pleases, and the other players have to not only follow suit; they have to head the trick if they can. This does not necessarily mean that they will play the best card they hold of the suit led; it means that they will play a better one than any already played. The cards are left in front of the players. If all follow suit the winner of the trick leads any card he pleases for the next trick. If all follow suit to that again, the winner leads for the next, and if all follow suit again, that ends it, and the winners of the several tricks divide the pool. All the players who have not won a trick are *looed*, and have to contribute three red counters each for the next pool, which, added to the three to be deposited by the next dealer, will make the ensuing pool a double. However, if in any trick any player is unable to follow suit, as soon as the trick is complete, the dealer turns up the top card on the remainder of the pack, and the suit to which it belongs is the trump. If any trump has been played, the highest trump wins the trick. In any case, the winner of the trick has to lead a trump for the next trick if he has one. When all three tricks have been played, the winner of each trick is entitled to one-third of the contents of the pool. The players who have not won a trick are looed, and have to contribute three red counters each for the next pool. This is called a ***Bold Stand***.

In Double Pools, an extra hand is dealt for the widow, and a trump is turned. No player is allowed to look at his cards until it comes to his turn to declare. The dealer, beginning on his left, asks each player in turn to announce his intentions. The player can ***stand*** with the cards dealt to him, can ***take the widow*** in exchange, or can ***pass***. If he passes or takes the widow, he gives his original hand to the dealer, who places it on the bottom of the pack. If he takes the widow or stands, he has to win at least one trick, or he is looed, and will forfeit three red counters to the next pool.

If all pass but the player who has taken the widow, he wins the pool without playing, and the next deal has to be a simple. If only one player stands, and has not taken the widow, the dealer, if he will not play for himself, has to take the widow and play to defend the pool. If he fails to take a trick, he is not looed; however, the payment for any tricks he wins has to be left in the pool, and the red counters for them should be changed for white ones, so that the amount can be easily divided at the end of the next pool.

FLUSHES If any player in a double pool holds three trumps, whether they are dealt to him or found in the widow, he has to announce it as soon as all have declared whether or not they will play. The usual custom is to wait until the dealer declares, and then to ask him, 'How many play?' The dealer replies, 'Two in', 'Three in', or, 'Widow and one', as the case may be. The player who has the flush then shows it, and claims the pool without playing, whereby each of the players who is 'in' is looed three red counters. If two players hold a flush in trumps, the elder hand wins, whether or not his trumps are better, but the younger hand, who holds another flush, is not looed.

LEADING In all double pools, the eldest hand of the people playing has to lead a trump if he has one. If he has the ace of trumps, he has to lead that, or if he has the King and the ace is turned up. The old rule was that a player had to lead the higher of two trumps, but it is obsolete. The winner of a trick has to lead a trump if he has one. Each player in turn has to head the trick if he can. If he has none of the suit led, he has to trump or over-trump if he can, but he does not have to under-trump a trick already trumped.

IRREGULARITIES AND PENALTIES There is only one penalty in Loo: to win nothing from the current pool, and to pay either three or six reds to the next pool. If the offender has won any tricks, the payment for them has to be left in the pool in white counters, to be divided among the winners of the next pool.

The offences are divided: some are paid for to the current pool, such as the ones for errors in the deal, whereas others are not paid until the current pool has been divided. If any player looks at his hand before it is his turn to declare, or the dealer does so before asking the other players whether or not they will play, or if any player announces his intention out of his proper turn, the offender in each case forfeits three red counters to the current pool, and cannot win anything that deal; however, he can play his hand in order to keep counters in the pool. If he plays and is looed, he has to pay.

REVOKES If a player, when he is able to do so, fails to follow suit, or to head the trick, or to lead trumps, or to lead the ace of trumps (or King when ace is turned), or to trump a suit of which he is void, the hands are abandoned on discovery of the error, and the pool is divided as equally as possible among the people who declared to play, with the exception of the offender. Any odd white counters have to be left for the next pool. The player who is in fault is then held guilty of a revoke, and has to pay a forfeit of six red counters to the next pool. The reason for the division of the pool is that there is no satisfactory way to determine how the play would have resulted had the revoke not occurred. It is impossible to take back the cards and replay them, because no one would have a right to judge how much a person's play was altered by way of his knowledge of the cards in the other hands.

If a player, having already won a trick, renders himself liable to any penalty, as for exposing a card, leading or following suit out of turn, or abandoning his hand, he is looed for three red counters, which are payable to the next pool, and the payment for the tricks he has won has to be left in the pool in white counters.

IRISH LOO

In this variation, no widow is dealt, and there is no distinction between simple and double pools. A trump is always turned up, and the dealer asks each player in turn, beginning on his left, whether or not he will play, whereby he takes up the cards of the players who decline to stand. He then announces his own decision, and proceeds to ask the people who have declared to play whether or not they wish to exchange any of the cards originally dealt to them. The usual question is simply 'How many?' and the player names the number of cards he wishes to exchange, if any, at the same time as he discards others in their place. The number first asked for cannot be amended or recalled. The trump is laid aside, and the cards called for are dealt from the remainder of the pack, without more shuffling. In all other ways, the game is Three-card Loo.

FIVE-CARD LOO

This is Irish Loo with some additional variations. Each red counter should be worth five white ones, and the players will require about fifty red counters each at starting. The dealer puts up five red counters. Any player who holds a flush of five cards in any suit can immediately claim the pool, and every person at the table, whether playing or not, is supposed to be looed, and pays five red counters to the next pool. If two players hold flushes, the elder hand wins, even if the younger hand holds a flush in trumps.

Another variation is to make the club Jack, which is known as *Pam*, always the best trump. Combined with four cards of any suit, this card will make a flush. If any player leads the trump ace, the holder of Pam has to pass the trick if he can do so without revoking. The old usage was for the holder of the trump ace to notify any player who held Pam to pass, if he wished him to do so; however, that is quite superfluous, because no player wants to lose his ace of trumps, and it goes without saying that he wants Pam to pass it.

THE ALL-FOURS FAMILY

— – —

All Fours is to be found among the oldest games of cards, and is the parent of a large family of variations, all of which are of American origin. The youngest member of the family, Cinch, has become one of the most popular games in the United States. The main defect in Cinch has been the method of scoring, in which too much was left to luck. In the following pages, the author has attempted to remedy this.

The name 'All Fours' seems to have been varied at times to 'All Four' and was derived from four of the five points that counted towards game; the fifth point, for 'gift', has apparently been overlooked. The game was originally ten points up, and the cards were dealt one at a time. According to the descriptions in some of the older Hoyles manuals, the honours and Tens of the plain suits did not count towards game; however, this is evidently an error, because we find in the same editions the advice to trump or win the adversary's best cards in plain suits. This would obviously be a mere waste of trumps if these plain-suit cards did not count for anything.

All Fours seems to have been popular with all classes of society at one time or another. In Cotton's *Compleat Gamester*, it is given as being among the main games in Cotton's day: 1674. Daines Barrington, writing a hundred years later, writes about All Fours in connection with Whist. 'Whist,' he states, 'seems never to have been played on principles until about fifty years ago; before that time [1735] it was confined chiefly to the servants' hall, with All Fours and Put.' Another writer tells us that Ombre was the favourite game of the ladies, and Piquet of the gentlemen *par excellence;* clergymen and country squires preferred Whist, 'while the lower orders shuffled away at All Fours, Put, Cribbage, and Lanterloo.' In 1754, a pamphlet was published that contained 'Serious Reflections on the dangerous tendency of the common practice of Card-playing, especially the game of All Four.'

— —

ALL FOURS

SEVEN-UP, OR OLD SLEDGE

CARDS　Seven-up is played with the full pack of fifty-two cards, which rank A K Q J 10 9 8 7 6 5 4 3 2; the ace is the highest, in both cutting and play.

COUNTERS　Each player or side should be provided with seven counters. As the points accrue, these counters are gotten rid of by placing them in a pool in the centre of the table. By this method, a glance will show how many each side or player has 'to go', that is, how many will put him out.

PLAYERS　Two, three or four people can play. When three play, the game resembles Cut-throat Euchre: each for himself. When four play, two are partners against the other two, and the partners sit opposite each other. The player on the dealer's left, or his adversary if only two play, is always spoken of as the eldest or elder hand. The player on the dealer's right is the pone.

CUTTING　If there are four players, they cut for partners, deal and choice of seats. The two lowest are partners against the two highest; the highest cut has the choice of seats, and deals the first hand. When two or three play, they cut for seats and deal. In cutting, the ace is high. Ties cut again, but the new cut decides nothing but the tie.

STAKES　If there is any stake, it is for so much a game. Rubbers are never played.

DEALING　Each player has the right to shuffle the pack, whereby the dealer goes last, and the cards are then presented to the pone to cut. At least four cards have to be left in each packet. Beginning on his left, the dealer gives six cards to each player: three on the first round and three more on the second, whereby the next card is turned up for the trump and left on the remainder of the pack. If this card is a Jack, the dealer counts one point for it immediately; however, if any player is found to have an incorrect number of cards, and announces it before he plays to the first trick, the Jack cannot be counted, because it could not have been the proper trump.

In *Pitch, or Blind All Fours,* no trump is turned. The first card led or 'pitched' by the eldest hand is the trump suit for that deal.

MISDEALING If any card is found faced in the pack, or the pack is proved to be imperfect, the same dealer deals again. If he deals without having the cards cut, or gives too many or too few cards to any player, it is a misdeal, and the deal passes to the next player on the misdealer's left. If the dealer exposes a card, the adversaries can elect to either have the deal stand or have a new deal by the same dealer. In *Pitch*, a misdeal does not lose the deal, because the deal is no advantage.

BEGGING When the deal is completed, and the trump is turned, the eldest hand looks at his cards, and the other players leave theirs untouched. If the eldest hand is not satisfied, he says, *I beg,* and the dealer, after examining his own hand, has the option of giving him a point or *running the cards*. If he decides to give the point, he says, *Take it,* and the eldest hand immediately scores one for the *gift*. If the dealer will not give, he lays the trump card aside, and deals three more cards to each player, including himself, whereby he turns up another trump. If this is a Jack of another suit, the dealer scores a point for it at once. If it is of the same suit as that first turned up, the Jack cannot be scored, because the dealer has declined to have that suit for the trump. When the same suit is turned up a second time, the card is laid aside. Three more cards are given to each player, and another trump is turned, and so on until a different suit comes up for the trump. If the pack is exhausted before another suit turns up, the cards have to be *bunched*, and the same dealer deals again.

The dealer's partner and the pone are not permitted to look at their cards until the eldest hand and the dealer have decided whether to stand or run the cards. Among strict players, if a person looks at his hand before the proper time, the adversaries score a point. The object of this rule is to prevent the possibility of any expression of satisfaction or disapproval of the turn-up trump.

No second beg is allowed, but when only two play, if either player is dissatisfied with the new trump, he can propose to *bunch the cards*. If the proposition is agreed to, the cards are re-shuffled and dealt again by the same dealer. If three play, the dealer has to give a point to both adversaries if he refuses to run the cards, although only one begs. The dealer cannot give a player enough to put him out.

DISCARDING When the cards have been run, the usual practice is to discard all superfluous cards, whereby each player reduces his hand to six, with which he plays. In some clubs, it is the rule to keep all the cards if only nine are in each hand, but to discard down to six if two or more rounds were dealt after the first trump was turned.

OBJECTS OF THE GAME   The object in Seven-up is to secure specific points that count towards game. As its name implies, the game is won when a player has put up seven of his counters, each of which represents a point. There are six ways of making these points, and it is possible for one player to make five of them in one deal; however, he cannot by any possibility make seven. The following count one point each.

1st. Turning up the *Jack* of trumps.

2nd. Being *given* a point by the dealer.

3rd. Holding the *Highest* trump.

4th. Holding the *Lowest* trump.

5th. Winning a trick with the *Jack* of trumps in it.

6th. Making the majority of the pips that count for what is called *Game*.

Turning the Jack is entirely a matter of chance, and should not occur more than once in thirteen deals. If a Jack is turned every few deals, you can be sure that unfair methods are being used. Nothing is more common among advantage players than turning up Jacks every few deals.

Begging is resorted to by a player who holds no trumps, or such indifferent ones that it is very unlikely they will be either High or Low. If he has anything better, such as very high or low cards in other suits, this hand is called 'a good hand to run to', and the player begs, hoping the new trump will better fit his hand. If he has nothing better in other suits than in the turn-up, it will still be slightly in his favour to beg, unless he has trumps enough to give him some hope of making the point for Game. It is a fatal error to beg on good cards, and gamblers have a saying that he who begs a point today will beg a stake tomorrow.

High and *Low* count to the player to whom these cards are dealt, and there is no chance to alter the fortunes of the deal except by begging and running the cards. These two points can both be made by way of the same card, if it is the only trump in play, because High is counted for the best trump out during the deal, and Low is counted for the lowest, no matter what the cards are.

Catching the Jack, or saving it, is one of the main objects of the game, and as a rule, a player who holds the Jack should lose no opportunity to save such a valuable counting card. On the other hand, a player who holds higher trumps will often have to use good judgement as to whether to lead them to catch the Jack, if it happens to be out, or to keep quiet until the last few tricks, when, if the Jack is not out, these trumps can be useful to win cards that count for Game.

The Game is usually known as *the gambler's point*, because it is the only point that has to be played for in every hand, and its management requires more skill than all the other points put together. The cards that count for Game are the four honours and the Ten of each suit. Every ace counts 4, every King 3, every Queen 2, every Jack 1, and every Ten 10. After the last card has been played, each player turns over the tricks he has won, and counts up the pip value of the court cards and Tens he has won. Whoever has the highest number counts the point for Game. For example, two are playing. The elder hand has taken in an ace, two Kings and a Jack, which are collectively worth 11. The dealer has taken in a Queen and a Ten, which are worth 12, so the dealer marks the point for Game. If both players have the same number, or if there is no Game out, which rarely happens, the non-dealer scores Game. If three play, and Game is a tie between the two non-dealers, neither scores. The non-dealer is given the benefit of counting a tie for Game as an offset to the dealer's advantage in turning Jacks. When no trump is turned, as in Pitch, no one can count Game if it is a tie.

METHOD OF PLAYING   The eldest hand begins by leading any card he pleases. If a trump is led, each player has to follow suit if he is able. When a plain suit is led, he does not have to follow suit if he prefers to trump, but if he does not trump, he has to follow suit if he can. If he has none of the suit led, he can either trump or discard. This rule is commonly expressed by saying that a player can *follow suit or trump*. The highest card played of the suit led wins the trick, and trumps win all other suits. The winner of the trick takes it in, and leads for the next one, and so on until all the cards have been played. The tricks themselves have no value except for the court cards and Tens they contain.

Because High, Jack and Game are always counted by the player who holds these points at the end of the play, there can be no question about them; however, serious disputes sometimes arise as to who played Low. The best method of avoiding this is for each player, as the game proceeds, to announce and claim the lowest trump that has so far appeared, and rather than give it to the current trick, to leave it turned face upwards in front of him if it is of no counting value. For example, four are playing, and a round of trumps comes out, whereby the six is the lowest. The player who holds it announces,

'Six for Low', and keeps the card face upwards in front of him until a smaller trump appears. It often happens that a player holds a 7 or an 8, and having no idea that it will be Low, takes no notice of it. At the end of the hand, it is found that both the 7 and the 8 are out, whereby the 7 is Low, and the holders of these two cards get into an argument as to which card each of them held.

SCORING When the last card is played, the various points for High, Low, Jack (if in play) and the Game are claimed, and the player who or the side that holds them puts a counter in the pool for each. The side that first gets rid of its seven counters wins the game. If both sides make points enough to win the game on the same deal, High goes out first, then Low, then Jack, and then Game. As already noticed, one card can be both High and Low; the Jack can be High, Low, Jack; and it is even possible, if there is no other trump or counting card in play, for the Jack to be High, Low, Jack, and the Game.

In the variety known as *All Fives*, the score is kept on a cribbage board, and part of it is pegged as the hand progresses. A player who wins a trick that contains any of the following cards in the trump suit pegs them immediately. For the trump ace, 4 points; for the King, 3; for the Queen, 2; for the Jack, 1; for the Ten, 10, and for the Five, 5. After the hand is over, all these cards are counted over again in reckoning the point for Game, whereby the Five of trumps counts 5. Sixty-one points is game.

IRREGULARITIES IN PLAY The most serious error in Seven-up is the *revoke*. If a player does not follow suit when he is able, it is a revoke unless he trumps the trick. A player who holds two small trumps and the Ten of a plain suit can trump both the ace and the King of that suit rather than give up his Ten. However, if on the third round the Queen is led, and he cannot trump it, he has to play his Ten if he has no other card of the suit.

The only points affected by the revoke are Jack and Game. *If the Jack is not in play*, there is only one point that can be affected by the revoke: the score for Game, and the revoke penalty is one point, which the adversary can add to his own score or deduct from the score of the revoking player. The adversary can also score the point for Game if he makes it; however, it cannot be scored by the revoking player, who can mark only High or Low if he holds either or both of these points.

If the Jack is in play, two points can be affected by a revoke. The player in fault cannot score either Jack or Game, and the penalty for the revoke is two points, in addition to which the adversary of the revoking player can score either or both Jack and Game if he makes them.

The revoking player cannot win the game that hand, no matter what he scores, but must stop at six. A revoke is established as soon as the trick in which it occurs has been turned and quitted, or a card has been led or played to the next trick.

EXPOSED CARDS When four play, all exposed cards have to be left on the table, and these cards are liable to be called by the adversaries if they cannot be previously gotten rid of in the course of play. All cards led or played out of turn are exposed, and are liable to be called. If two or more cards are played to a trick, the adversaries can select which will remain; the other card is exposed.

METHODS OF CHEATING Few games lend themselves more readily to the operations of the cheat than Seven-up. Turning Jacks from the bottom of the pack; setting up the half-stock for the beg; dealing yourself more than six cards, and dropping on the tricks already won the ones that count for Game; getting the A J 10 and 2 of a suit together during the play of a hand, then shifting the cut to get them on the next deal, whereby the Jack is turned up; marked cards; strippers; wedges; and reflectors are only a few of the tricks that are in common use. Players who are not expert enough to deal seconds or shift cuts will sometimes resort to trifling advantages such as abstracting one of the Tens from the pack, so that they can know a suit from which a small card can always be led without incurring any danger of the adversary's making the Ten. One very common swindle in Seven-up is known as **the high hand**, which consists of giving the intended victim the A K J 10 9 2 of trumps and then inducing him to bet that he will make four points. No matter how skilful the player is, he will find it impossible to save both Jack and Game.

—— · ——

CALIFORNIA JACK

This is a variety of Seven-up for two players, in which the number of cards in the hand is constantly restored to six by way of drawing from the remainder of the pack.

The trump suit is cut for before the cards are shuffled and dealt. The usual method is to cut for seats and deal, and the highest cut determines the trump suit at the same time. After each player has been given six cards, three at a time, the remainder of the pack is turned face upwards on the table, and the winner of each trick takes the top card, whereby his adversary takes the next one. When the stock is exhausted, the last six cards are played as in the ordinary game of Seven-up.

Seven points is game, and the points are the same as in Seven-up; however, everything, including Low, counts to the player who wins it.

Shasta Sam is California Jack with the remainder of the pack turned face downwards, and is a much better game on that account.

AUCTION PITCH
SELL-OUT, OR COMMERCIAL PITCH

This very popular round game derives its name from the fact that the first card led or 'pitched' is the trump suit, and that the privilege of pitching it belongs to the eldest hand, who can sell it out to the highest bidder.

The number of *cards* and their rank is the same as in Seven-up: A K Q J 10 9 8 7 6 5 4 3 2, whereby the ace is the highest in both cutting and play.

PLAYERS Any number from four to seven can play, each for himself, and five is considered to be the best game. The players cut for choice of seats, whereby the highest cut takes the first choice and the deal.

COUNTERS Each player should be provided with seven white counters to mark the game. If stakes are played for, red counters are used in order to make up the pool, whereby one player acts as the banker to sell and redeem all red counters.

DEALING Six cards are dealt to each player, three at a time, but no trump is turned. All the rules for irregularities in the deal are the same as in Seven-up, but a misdeal does not lose the deal under any circumstances.

OBJECTS OF THE GAME As in Seven-up, the object of each player is to get rid of his seven counters, one of which he is entitled to put into the pool for each of the following points. For holding the *highest* trump in play, for holding (having dealt to him) the *lowest* trump in play, for winning a trick with the *Jack* of trumps in it, and for making the greatest number of the pips that count for the *game* point. The details of these points have already been explained in connection with Seven-up. If the count for Game is a tie, no one scores it.

BIDDING   The eldest hand sells. If he pitches without waiting for a bid, he has to make four points or he will be set back that number. Each player in turn, beginning on the left of the eldest hand, bids for the privilege of pitching the trump, whereby he names the number of points he thinks he can make. If he will not bid, he has to say distinctly, *I pass.* After a bid has been made, any following player has to bid higher or pass. There are no second bids. The highest number any player can bid is four, whereby he will be required to make High, Low, Jack and the Game against the combined efforts of all the other players. The eldest hand has to either accept the number bid or pitch the trump himself, and make as many points as the highest bidder offered him. If the eldest hand accepts, he pushes into the pool as many counters as he is bid, and the successful bidder pitches the trump. If no bid is made, the eldest hand has to pitch and trump himself.

A bidder is not allowed to give the seller enough points to put him out, and if he does so by mistake, he forfeits his right to bid at all for that deal. If the seller has only two points to go, and a player is able to bid three or four, he loses nothing by bidding one point only, because no one can overbid him, and he is entitled to count all he makes. The only risk he runs is that the seller can afford to refuse one point, and will go out on his own pitch. To remedy this, it is the custom in some clubs to allow a player to bid the full value of his hand. If the seller accepts, he scores to within one point of game, but if he refuses, he has to make as many points as bid, even if he does not actually want them. It is one of the fine points of the game for the seller to refuse when the number of points offered would put the bidder out if he were successful.

There is no penalty for bidding out of turn. If a player chooses to expose to a preceding player what he is prepared to bid, that is usually to his own disadvantage.

BIDDING TO THE BOARD   Modern players usually adopt the practice of bidding to the board, and the eldest hand has the first bid. In this form of the game, the points bid count to no one, and anyone can bid up to four, no matter what the scores are. No one can claim the privilege of pitching the trump for as many points as bid, because each player in turn has to bid higher or pass.

PLAYING   The successful bidder has the first lead, and whatever card he plays, whether or not by mistake, is the trump suit for that deal. After that, the winner of the trick can lead any suit he pleases. A player has to follow suit in trumps if he is able to do so; however, in a plain suit, he can trump if he chooses, although he holds a card of the suit led. If he does not trump, he has to follow suit if he can. If he has none of the suit led, he can trump or discard as he pleases. The highest card played of the suit led wins the trick, and trumps win all other suits.

SCORING   At the end of the hand, the various players claim the points made, and score them by placing white counters in the pool. If the bidder makes any points in excess of the number bid, he scores them. The first player to get rid of his seven white counters wins the pool, and takes down all the red counters it contains. The white counters are then re-distributed, and the players cut for the first deal of the new game.

If two players can count out on the same deal, and one of them is the bidder, he wins the pool if he has made good his bid. If neither of the ties is the bidder, the points count out in their regular order: High first, then Low, then Jack, and finally Game. For example, seven are playing. A sells to B, who bids two. B and C each have two to go. B pitches a trump of which C has both High and Low; however, if B makes Jack and Game, he wins the pool, because he bid only two points, and made them. This is usually expressed by way of the rule *Bidder goes out first.*

SETTING BACK   If the player who pitches the trump fails to make the number of points bid, he is set back, and scores nothing for any points he might have made. A player who is set back, for either overbidding his hand or refusing to sell and failing to make the number of points offered to him, has to withdraw from the pool as many white counters as were bid, and add them to his own. For example, it is A's sell. A and B each have two to go. B bids three, which A refuses, and pitches the trump himself. A makes only two points; B scores one point; and a third player D, scores another point. B and D score one point each, but A scores nothing for the two points he made, and has to take three white counters from the pool, which will make him five to go. Had the bid that A refused been two only, he would have won the game, because he made two points. In many clubs, it is the custom for a player who is set back to add a red counter to the pool.

IRREGULARITIES IN PLAY   If any adversary of the player who pitches the trump leads or plays out of turn, he can be called on by the bidder to play his highest or lowest of the suit led, or to trump or not to trump the trick. If any player but the pitcher has followed the erroneous lead, the cards have to be taken back, but if the pitcher has followed, the error cannot be rectified.

In the case of a *revoke*, the hand is played out as if the revoke had not occurred, and each player except the person in error counts whatever points he makes. If the pitcher of the trump fails to make the number of points bid, he cannot be set back, but has to be allowed to score any points he makes. The revoking player is then set back the number of points bid, and forfeits a red counter to the pool. If no bid was made, he is set back two points.

— —

SMUDGE

In this variation of auction pitch, any player who is not in the hole wins the game at once if he can bid four points and make it.

— —

PEDRO

Pedro, Pedro Sancho, Dom Pedro and Snoozer are all varieties of Auction Pitch, in which specific counting cards are added, and secondary bids are allowed.

Everything counts to the player who wins it, instead of to the one to whom it is dealt. The game point is scored by the player who wins the trick that contains the Ten of trumps. If that card is not in play, there is no Game.

In *Pedro Sancho*, the Five and Nine of trumps count their pip value in scoring, so that 18 points can be bid and made on one deal: one each for High, Low, Jack and Game, and fourteen more for the Nine and Five of trumps. These two trumps have no special rank. The Ten will win the Nine, and the Six will take the Five. In some places, all the cards in the pack are dealt out, which makes for a much better game in any form of Pedro.

The eldest hand sells, as in Auction Pitch. If a player's first bid is raised, he can raise again in his proper turn.

Fifty points is game, and the players are usually provided with two varieties of counters for scoring: one worth five points, and the other worth one. The rank of the points in scoring is High, Low, Jack, Ten (Game), Five and Nine. The revoke penalty is to be set back the number of points bid, or ten points if there is no bid, and the player in fault cannot score anything that hand. In all other ways, the rules are the same as in Auction Pitch.

In *Dom Pedro, or Snoozer*, the Joker is added to the pack, and the Three, Five and Nine of trumps count their pip value in scoring. The Joker, or Snoozer, counts fifteen, so that thirty-six points can be bid and made on one deal. The Joker is the lowest trump, so that the deuce of trumps will win it, but it will win any trick in plain suits. Fifty or a hundred points is the game. In counting out, the order of precedence is High, Low, Jack, Ten (Game), Three, Five, Nine and Snoozer.

— — —

CINCH
DOUBLE PEDRO, OR HIGH FIVE

This is viewed as being the most important variety of All Fours, and could have supplanted the parent game altogether. Cinch is one of the pedro variations of Auction Pitch, the differences being that no one sells and that there is added the always popular American feature of a draw in order to improve the hand.

The derivation and meaning of the name Cinch seems to be very much misunderstood. Many people assume it is simply a name for the Left Pedro, but this is not the case. Cinch is a Mexican word for a strong saddle-girth, and when used as a verb it refers to the way of adjusting the girth on a bucking broncho so that no amount of kicking will get the horse free. The word is used in this sense to describe one of the main tactics of the card game, which is to 'cinch' specific tricks, so that the adversary cannot possibly get either of the Pedroes free.

CARDS Cinch is played with a full pack of fifty-two cards that rank A K Q J 10 9 8 7 6 5 4 3 2. When the suit is trumps, the 5 retains its natural position, and is known as the *Right Pedro*; however, the 5 of the same colour as that of the trump suit, which is known as the *Left Pedro*, ranks between the 5 and the 4 of the trump suit. The ace is highest in both cutting and play. Whist players, who took up Cinch as a side issue, were in the habit of making the ace lowest in cutting, but this practice was out of harmony with all other members of the Seven-up family of games.

COUNTERS The score is usually kept on a sheet of paper; however, it is more convenient to provide each side with 8 red and 11 white counters, which represent 51 points, whereby the whites are worth 1, and the reds 5 each. A good pull-up cribbage board is better still.

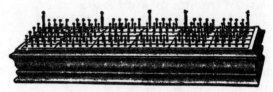

PULL-UP GAME COUNTER

PLAYERS Any number from two to six can play, but the regular game is for four persons, two of whom are partners against the other two. The player on the dealer's left is the *eldest hand*, and the *pone* is on the dealer's right.

CUTTING The players draw from an outspread pack for partners, seats and deal. The two lowest play against the two highest; the highest cut has the choice of seats and cards, and deals the first hand. Partners sit opposite each other.

DEALING Each player has the right to shuffle the pack, and the dealer goes last. The cards are then presented to the pone to cut, and at least four cards have to be left in each packet. Beginning on his left, the dealer gives nine cards to each player, three at a time in three separate rounds. No trump is turned, and the remainder of the pack is left on the table face downwards.

MISDEALING If any card is found faced in the pack, the cards have to be re-shuffled and dealt again. If the dealer exposes a card in dealing, or turns up a trump by mistake, the adversaries can elect to have a new deal by the same dealer, or to let the deal stand. If the dealer gives too many or too few cards to any player, or fails to give the same number of cards in each round, it is a misdeal, and the deal passes to the next player on the left. Any player who deals out of turn, or with the wrong cards, can be stopped before the last three cards are dealt, but after that, the deal stands good. If a misdeal is not discovered until after a bid has been made, the deal stands good if three players have their right number of cards. The deal passes in regular rotation to the left.

OBJECTS OF THE GAME   The game is fifty-one points, and the side that first pegs that number, or that gets rid of its fifty-one counters, is the winner. Fourteen points are made on every deal, as follows.

1 for *High*, the ace of trumps.
1 for *Low*, the deuce of trumps.
1 for the *Jack* of trumps.
1 for the Ten of trumps, or *Game*.
5 for the Five of trumps, or *Right Pedro*.
 5 for the Five of the same colour, or *Left Pedro*.
14 points altogether, all in the trump suit.

All these points, including Low, count to the player who wins them, and not to the players to whom they are dealt. This saves endless disputes.

BIDDING   Beginning with the eldest hand, each player in turn, after examining his nine cards, can make *one bid* for the privilege of naming the trump suit. The peculiarity of this bidding is that nobody sells: the bids are made *to the board*, as it is called. The bidder announces the number of points he thinks he can make (with his partner's assistance) but does not name the trump suit. If a player will not bid, he says, *'I pass.'* After a bid has been made in its proper turn, any following player has to bid higher or pass. No one is allowed to bid more than fourteen points. There are no second bids, and a bid once made cannot be amended or withdrawn. The player who has made the highest bid is called on to name the trump suit.

IRREGULAR BIDS   If any player bids before the eldest hand has bid or passed, both the player in error and his partner lose their right to make any bid that deal, but the partners not in error have to bid against each other for the privilege of naming the trump suit. If the eldest hand has decided, and the pone bids without waiting for the dealer's partner, the pone loses his bid, and the dealer can bid before his partner, without penalty. If the dealer bids before his partner has decided, both he and his partner lose their right to bid that deal; however, the pone is still at liberty to overbid the eldest hand for the privilege of naming the trump. If the dealer's partner has bid, and the dealer bids without waiting for the pone, the dealer loses his right to bid for that deal.

If a player whose partner has not yet bid names the trump suit, his partner loses the right to bid. If no bid is made, the dealer can name any suit he pleases, without bidding. If any player exposes a card before the trump suit is named, the adversaries can elect to have a new deal by the same dealer.

DISCARDING AND DRAWING When the trump suit is named, each player discards and leaves *face upwards* on the table as many cards as he pleases. He has to discard three, in order to reduce his hand to six cards. If he discards more than three, he has to draw from the remainder of the pack in order to restore the number of his cards to six, so that after the discard and draw, each player at the table will have exactly six cards, although nine were originally dealt to him.

The dealer, beginning on his left, gives to each player in turn as many cards from the top of the pack as might be necessary to restore the number in his hand to six. When it comes to the dealer's turn, rather than take cards from the top of the pack, he can search the remainder of the pack, and take from it any cards he pleases. This is called *robbing the deck*. If he finds in his own hand and the remainder of the pack more than six trumps, he has to discard the ones he does not want, and show them face upwards on the table with the other discards.

If any player discards a trump, his partner has the right to call his attention to it, and if the player has not been helped to cards, or has not lifted the cards drawn, the trump erroneously discarded can be taken back; otherwise, it has to remain among the discards until the hand has been played, when, if it is of any counting value, it has to be added to the score of the side that makes the trump.

Although there is no law to that effect, it is considered to be imperative that each player except the dealer discard everything but trumps. This is partly because no other cards are of the slightest use, and partly because one of the points of the game is that the number of trumps held by each player before the draw should be indicated by way of his discard.

METHOD OF PLAYING The player who has named the trump suit begins by leading any card he pleases. If a trump is led, everyone has to follow suit if he is able to do so, and it has to be remembered that the Left Pedro is one of the trump suit. When a plain suit is led, any player can trump if he chooses, although he holds one of the suit led, but if he does not trump, he has to follow suit if he can. If he has none of the suit led, he can trump or discard at pleasure. The highest card played of the suit led wins the trick, and trumps win all other suits. The Five of trumps, or any higher card, will win the Left Pedro, but the Left Pedro will win the Four of trumps, or any lower card. The winner of the trick gathers it in, turns it face downwards, and leads for the next trick, and so on, until all six tricks have been played. The tricks themselves have no value, and do not have to be kept separate. The last trick turned and quitted can be seen, but no other.

IRREGULARITIES IN PLAYING   If, during the play of a hand, any player is found to have too many cards, his hand is foul, and neither he nor his partner can score any points for that deal; however, they can play the hand out in order to prevent the adversaries from scoring everything. If he has too few cards, there is no penalty.

If a player leads out of turn, and the three other players follow him, the trick stands good. If all the players have not followed the false lead, their cards have to be taken back, but only the leader's card is liable to be called. If it was the turn of the partner of the player in error to lead, the adversary on his right can call on him to lead or not to lead a trump, but cannot specify the plain suit. If it was the turn of either adversary of the player in error to lead, the card led in error is simply exposed.

If the third hand plays before the second, the fourth can also play before the second. If the fourth hand plays before his partner, and third hand has not played, the trick can be claimed by the adversaries, regardless of who wins it, but the player who actually wins it leads for the next trick.

If a player has a card of the suit led, and neither follows suit nor plays a trump, it is a *revoke*, and, if it is detected and claimed by the adversaries, neither the player in error nor his partner can score any points that hand; however, the hand can be played out in order to prevent the adversaries from scoring everything. If an adversary of the bidder revokes, the bidder's side scores all points it makes, regardless of the number bid. For example, A has bid nine, and Y revokes. A–B make eight only, which they score, and Y–Z score nothing. When a player renounces, his partner should ask him whether he is void of the suit.

If any player abandons his hand, the cards in it can be exposed and called by the adversaries. The practice of throwing down the hand as soon as you renounce to trumps cannot be too strongly condemned.

All *exposed cards*, such as cards dropped on the table, two or more cards played at once, cards led out of turn, or cards named by the player who holds them, have to be left face upwards on the table, and are liable to be called by the adversaries, unless they can be previously gotten rid of in the course of play. If the exposed card is a trump, the adversaries can prevent its being played, but the holder of it is not liable for a revoke in these cases.

SCORING When the last card has been played, each side turns over all the tricks won, and counts the points they contain: High, Low, Jack, Game, Right Pedro and Left Pedro. Everything, including Low, counts to the side that wins it. The number of points won or lost is determined by way of deducting the lower score from the higher, whereby the difference is the number of points won on that deal. If it is a tie, neither side scores. If either side has incurred a penalty that prevents it from scoring any points it might have won, the adversaries have nothing to deduct, and score all they make.

If the side that named the trump fails to make as many points as it bid, it scores nothing, and the number of points bid is scored by the adversaries, in addition to any points the adversaries might have made in play. For example, A–B are partners against Y–Z. B has bid to make 8, and named hearts for trumps. A–B make 10, which is 2 more than they bid, and Y–Z get the other 4, which leaves A–B 6. These are scored by placing one red and one white counter in the pool. However, suppose A–B got only 5 points, and Y–Z 9. A–B would score nothing, because they did not make good their bid, whereas Y–Z would score the 9 points actually won, and the 8 points bid in addition, or 17 altogether.

The old way of scoring was to *set back* the side that failed to make the number bid; however, that system of counting entirely destroyed the interest in the game when one side got much behind, because that side could not recover in time to prevent the other side from *sweating out*, as it is called. Suppose A–B have been set back 18 points on two failures, and that Y–Z have made 16 points on these two deals, and 23 on their own bids. The score will stand as follows: A–B 64 to go, and Y–Z 12 to go. Even if we suppose that A–B make 11 on each of the next four deals, they will have 20 to go, whereas Y–Z will be out. Again, A–B want 15, and Y–Z want 2. Even if A–B can bid 12 and make it, Y–Z will sweat out.

In the case of the system of scoring recommended here, this sweating out is impossible, and it is not uncommon for a side that wants one to go to be beaten by an adversary that wants forty-nine.

The side that first pegs out on a cribbage-board, or that gets rid of its fifty-one counters, wins the game. When the game is counted on a pull-up cribbage marker, it is usual to start with ten up, and to peg out to the game-hole, or sixty-one.

VARIATIONS There are quite a number of minor differences in the way of playing Cinch. Sometimes, instead of there being discarding and drawing, after the successful bidder has been ascertained but before he names the trump, four more cards are given to each player, including the dealer. Having seen thirteen cards, the bidder names the trump suit, and the hands are then reduced to six cards each player. This method gives no clue to the number of trumps originally held, and deprives the dealer of one of the greatest advantages of his position: robbing the deck.

Another method is to discard and draw after the trump is named, but to make the dealer take his cards from the top of the pack in order to complete his hand, without seeing what he is to get. This often leaves counting cards in the remainder of the pack, which have to remain face downwards, and be kept separate from the discards. These points count for neither side, but any points found among the discards can be counted by the side that makes the trump, as in the ordinary game. Owing to the uncertainty as to the number of points actually in play, the result is controlled more largely by luck than skill.

In some places, the *first lead* from the successful bidder has to be a *trump*. This makes the game too much like Auction Pitch, and spoils some of the finer points in leading.

Low is sometimes counted for the person to whom it is dealt. This rule causes endless confusion and disputes.

The old method of *scoring* has already been mentioned. Another variation is that if the bidder's side does not make at least 8 points, it cannot score anything, no matter what it bid. If both sides score 7, and neither has bid more than 7, neither scores. If one side bids 6, and makes 8, it scores 8, but the adversaries score the 6 they make. If the side that bid 6 had made 6 only, it would score nothing, whereas its adversaries would mark the 8 they made. The only good result of the 6 bid in this case is to prevent the adversaries from scoring for a failure, because had 7 been bid, and only 6 made, the adversaries would have scored the 7 bid in addition to the 8 they made, or 15 in all. This system, although better than the old way, because it never sets players back, enables one side to sweat out, because if the bidder does not make 14, the adversaries have to count something every deal.

Five or six players, each for himself, can play what is called *Auction Cinch*, or *Razzle-dazzle*. Only six cards are dealt to each player: three on the first round and three on the second. The privilege of naming the trump suit is then bid for as usual. After the trump is named, superfluous cards are thrown out, and other cards are drawn in their place, whereby the hands are restored to six cards each. The successful bidder then calls on the holder of any given card to be his partner. The person who holds the card named cannot refuse, and says, 'I play with you.' The partnership thereby formed plays against the combined forces of the other players, but without changing seats. The maker of the trump leads first, any card he pleases. For example, A B C D E are playing. C bids 8 and names clubs. After the draw, he finds he holds A J 10 5 2 of trumps. He calls for the club King as his partner, and leads his Pedro at once for the King to take it in. He is then certain to catch the other Pedro, or to save three of the four points for High, Low, Jack and the Game. People who have played Seven-handed Euchre will at once recognise the similarity between the two games. Both are excellent round games for the family circle.

PROGRESSIVE CINCH   This is played by way of dealing one round at each table, that is, four deals, whereby each player has the deal once only. The ordinary game of Cinch is played, and the pair who have the fewest points to go at the end of the four deals progress to the next-higher table. Ties cut to decide, and high goes up. On arriving at the next table, the partners divide, and another game of four deals is played, whereby the winning pair again progress. The general arrangements for the original positions of the players, and the prizes to be given, are the same as in Progressive Euchre, and have been fully described in connection with that game.

BLIND CINCH   Instead of each player's being given thirteen cards at once, the hands are dealt in two parts. First of all, nine cards are dealt to each player, three at a time. Four cards are then dealt in front of each player, but are not to be touched until the bidding is finished. The highest bidder takes up his four extra cards and then names the trump, after which he discards down to six cards for play. The other players then take up their four cards and discard down to six, and the game proceeds as in regular cinch.

SIXTY-THREE   In this variation, nine cards are dealt to each player, three at a time. After the bidding, the players discard and fill up again to six cards. Players are allowed several bids, and each player raises in turn if he is raised. The highest bid possible is sixty-three points, and these can be made as follows: high, low, Jack and ten of trumps count 1 each; pedros count 5 each; King of trumps counts 25; trey of trumps counts 15; and nine of trumps counts 9. Game is 150 points.

WIDOW CINCH   Six players cut for partners, two on a side. Each player has two adversaries between himself and his partner. The dealer gives each player eight cards, four at a time, and four cards are dealt to the table after the first round to the players. These four cards are the widow. The successful bidder can take the widow before he names the trump, and all the players then discard down to six cards.

SUGGESTIONS FOR GOOD PLAY   There is a great diversity of opinion about bidding. Some people always bid six on an ace, if they hold neither of the Pedroes. This is based on the sound principle that the odds are five to four in favour of your partner's having one of the Pedroes, which he will immediately give up if you lead the ace. The odds are five to two that your partner will hold one or more of any three named counting cards that you do not hold. If you have no Pedro, you should count on your partner for one, and if you have King and Queen, you can risk his having a guard to it, and bid as if you were sure of getting his Pedro home. If you have none of the points for High, Low, Jack or Game, or only one of them, count on your partner for one at least, and bid accordingly.

It is very difficult to give exact rules for bidding, and the state of the score has much to do with it; however, as a general rule, it is much better to bid on *catching cards* than on the points themselves. For example, A K Q of trumps should be good for eight points; some players habitually bid twelve on them, because they reckon to catch both Pedroes and one of the minor points. This is risky unless there are one or two small trumps with the A K Q. On the other hand, two Pedroes, with Jack and Low, are not worth bidding more than five on, because it is very unlikely that you will save more than one of the Pedroes, if that. The very fact that you bid five diminishes your chances, because you betray the fact that your only hope is to save a well-guarded Pedro. Having a lot of experience with players who bid their hands correctly will give a player a very good idea of what the bidder has in his hand. To the partner, this is a great point, because it enables him to judge when to give up points himself, and when to play for his partner to throw them to him.

The number of cards asked for by each player should be very carefully noted, because it will frequently happen that the entire trump suit can be located by this means. It is useless to keep anything but trumps, because tricks, as such, have no value, and every card you draw increases your chances of getting another trump.

The most important point in the game is to *cinch* every trick in which an adversary plays after you, that is, to play some trump higher than a Pedro, if the Pedroes have not been played, and you do not hold them yourself. Examples of cinching will be found in the illustrations of hands. If your partner leads a certain winning trump, such as the ace, or the King if the ace is gone, give him the best counting card you have, but if you have two, and one of them is Low, give up the lower card first: you may catch something with the Jack or Ten. If your partner leads any trump higher than the Five, play your smallest trump unless the second hand covers, in which case you have to cinch the trick, in order to prevent the fourth hand from giving up a Pedro on his partner's trick.

If you are forced to win your partner's first lead of trumps, return the best trump you have, unless it is the Jack or Ten, in which case you have to be guided by the number of points you are playing for and your chances of making them if you lose the card you lead.

If your partner begins by leading a plain suit, you have to cinch the trick if you can, and if the second hand follows suit, any trump better than the Five will do. If the second hand puts on a trump, you have to cinch higher.

If the player on your right renounces to trumps, get into the lead if possible, and play your best cards in plain suits. This might give your partner a tenace position over the player on your left.

If your partner begins with a high card in trumps, not the ace, credit him with the sequence below it, and put in your Pedro at the first opportunity. For example, your partner leads King, won by the ace second hand. Whatever this player leads, put in your Pedro, if you have one: your partner has to have Queen of trumps.

Playing to the score is very important. Do not attempt to get more than the number bid until that is assured. On the other hand, if it is certain that the adversary cannot make good his bid, do not let him get as close to it as possible: play boldly to win all you can, because every point he makes is simply lost.

Following are a few example hands, which will give you a very good idea of some of the fine points in the game.

Number 1. A bids 8 on hearts.
The draw: A 2; Y 2; B 4; Z 5.

Number 2. A bids 8 on hearts.
The draw: A 2; Y 3; B 4; Z 4.

A	Y	B	Z	TRICK	A	Y	B	Z
♣ Q	♣ 3	♡ 8	♣ 5	1	♡ 3	♡ 7	♡ 10	♡ 8
♡ 2	♡ 6	♡ Q	♡ 4	2	♡ Q	♡ 2	♡ 4	♡ 9
♡ 10	♡ J	♣ J	♡ 9	3	♡ 6	♡ J	A ◊	♣ 4
♡ K	5 ◊	2 ♠	4 ♠	4	♣ 2	7 ♠	K ◊	6 ♠
♡ A	♡ 7	6 ♠	♣ 9	5	♡ K	♡ A	♣ 3	♣ 6
♡ 3	♡ 5	10 ♠	K ◊	6	♡ 5	5 ◊	2 ◊	♣ 10

Number 1   Y's draw shows that he holds at least four trumps, so A has to trust his partner to cinch the first trick and return the trump. [See our suggestions for good play.] At trick 3, Z cinches, to make A play a high trump. It is evident to A that neither B nor Z holds either Jack or Seven of trumps, so both these cards have to be with Y. Because B has no more trumps, the adversaries have to have both Pedroes, and Y has to have one, because he holds four trumps. If they are divided, A can catch both by cinching this trick with the King and leading the Ace; however, if Y has both Pedroes, this course would lose Jack, Game and one Pedro. If A cinches this trick with the Ten, thereby enabling Y to win with the Jack, A has to catch both Pedroes, no matter how they lie, provided Y leads the trump Seven, because A will refuse to win it.

Y sees his danger, and by leading a Pedro to A, forces him to either pass it or get into the lead and free the other Pedro.

A–B score nothing: Y–Z score 7 for Jack, Game, Pedro, and 8 in addition, for points bid but not made by A–B: 15 altogether.

Number 2   At trick 2, Y sees that he cannot save Low, and the lead would be a great disadvantage, because either A has all the remaining trumps or Y's partner has an unguarded Pedro. At trick 3, A knows that if Y has Ace, and Z Pedro, A can still make his bid by catching Jack and saving his own Pedro. If the Pedro is not with Z, the small trump is still the best lead, because it puts the lead on A's left. B gets rid of cards that might get him into the lead to his partner's disadvantage. Unfortunately, Z is unable to take the lead away from Y at trick 4. Because Y is still in the lead, there is no necessity for A to save his Pedro, because Y cannot possibly catch it, and A has to catch Y's, no matter how Y plays.

A–B score 10 points: Low, Game and both Pedroes – 12, from which they deduct the 2 points made by Y–Z.

Number 3. A bids 12 on hearts. The draw: A 3; Y 5; B 3; Z 2.				TRICK	*Number 4.* A bids 8 on hearts. The draw: A 2; Y 4; B 4; Z 4.			
A	Y	B	Z		A	Y	B	Z
♥ A	♥ 3	5 ♦	♥ 6	1	♥ A	♥ 6	♥ J	♥ 3
♥ K	♥ 4	♥ 8	♥ 10	2	♥ 8	♥ 7	♥ 4	♥ 9
♥ 2	♥ 7	♥ 9	♥ J	3	♥ Q	♥ 2	4 ♦	♥ K
♣ Q	♣ K	♣ 3	♣ J	4	Q ♠	♣ 2	♣ A	♣ 9
8 ♠	♣ A	♣ 10	2 ♦	5	5 ♦	♥ 5	♣ J	♣ 7
♥ Q	Q ♠	K ♦	♥ 5	6	♥ 10	4 ♠	J ♦	2 ♦

Number 3 At the second trick, A knows that his partner still holds another trump, because he drew only three cards. This trump has to be the 9. Z holds two more trumps, and they have to be the Jack and the Right Pedro, because Z would not throw away Game if he had anything smaller. The 7 has to be with Y, and if A now leads trump Queen, he will leave the Pedro good over his Deuce, thereby leaving him only 8 points, whereas he has bid 12. If A leads the Deuce, his partner's nine will cinch the trick, and Z can make only the Jack.

A–B score 10. The 12 actually taken make good the bid; however, the 2 points won by the adversaries have to be deducted, thereby leaving 10 to be scored by A–B.

Number 4 At the third trick, a hasty or careless player would have been only too glad of the opportunity to get in his Pedro. However, Y reasons that there are only two trumps unaccounted for: the Ten and the Left Pedro. If B has one, it has to fall to this trick. He cannot have both, because A drew only two cards. If A has both, Y has to catch his Pedro, no matter how A plays, and as long as Y does not get into the lead himself, he cannot lose his own Pedro. At trick 5, A naturally places the Pedro with Z, because Y did not save it on the King, and it is perfectly natural for A to trump with his Pedro, intending to lead the Ten to catch Z's.

A–B score nothing, not having made good their bid. Y–Z score Right and Left Pedro, and Low, 11 points, whereby the 8 points bid but not made by A–B are added, making 19 altogether.

— —

CINCH LAWS

FORMATION OF TABLE A cinch table is complete with six players. If more than four assemble, they cut for preference, and the four highest play the first game. Partners and deal are then cut for, and the two lowest pair against the two highest. Partners sit opposite each other. The highest deals, and has the choice of seats and cards. The Ace is high, in both cutting and play. A player who exposes more than one card has to cut again.

TIES If the first cut does not decide, the players who cut equal cards cut again, but the new cut decides nothing except the tie.

CUTTING OUT At the end of the game, the players cut in order to decide who will give way to the people awaiting their turn to play, and the lowest cuts go out. After the second game, the players who have played the greatest number of consecutive games give way, and ties are decided by way of cutting.

DEALING Every player has the right to shuffle the cards, and the dealer goes last. The dealer has to present the pack to the pone to cut. At least four cards have to be left in each packet. If a card is exposed in cutting, the pack has to be re-shuffled, and cut again. If the dealer re-shuffles the pack after it has been properly cut, he loses his deal.

Beginning on his left, the dealer has to give to each player in rotation three cards at a time for three rounds. No trump is turned. The deal passes to the left.

There has to be a new deal by the same dealer if any card is found faced in the pack, or if the pack is proved to be incorrect or imperfect; however, any previous cutting or scores made with the imperfect pack stand good.

The adversaries can demand a new deal if any card is exposed during the deal, provided they have not touched a card. If an adversary exposes a card, the dealer can elect to deal again. If a new deal is not demanded, cards exposed in dealing cannot be called.

The adversaries can stop a player from dealing out of turn, or with the wrong pack, provided they do so before the last three cards are dealt, after which the deal stands good.

MISDEALING A misdeal loses the deal. It is a misdeal if the cards have not been properly cut, if the dealer does not give the same number of cards to each player on the same round, if the dealer gives too many or too few cards to any player, if the dealer counts the cards on the table or the ones remaining in the pack, or if the dealer deals a card incorrectly and fails to correct the error before dealing another. If the dealer is interrupted in any way by an adversary, he does not lose his deal.

BIDDING After receiving his nine cards, each player in turn, beginning on the dealer's left, announces the number of points he will undertake to win if he is allowed to name the trump suit. No player is allowed to bid more than fourteen points. If he will not bid, he has to say, 'I pass.' A bid having been regularly made, any following player has to bid higher or pass. There are no second bids. A bid once made can neither be amended nor withdrawn.

IRREGULAR BIDS If any player bids before the eldest hand has bid or passed, both the player in error and his partner lose their right to bid, but the side not in error has to bid in order to decide which of the partners will name the trump. If the eldest hand has decided, and the pone bids without waiting for the dealer's partner, the pone loses his bid, and the dealer can bid before his partner bids. If the dealer bids without waiting for his partner, both lose their bids, but the pone can overbid the eldest hand.

If the dealer's partner has bid, and the dealer bids without waiting for the pone, the dealer loses his bid.

If a player whose partner has not yet bid names the trump suit, his partner loses his bid.

If a player bids with more than nine cards in his hand, his bid is lost, and the adversaries have to draw the superfluous cards from his hand, face downwards, whereby the cards are placed in about the middle of the undealt portion of the pack.

If no bid is made, the dealer can name any trump he pleases, without bidding.

If any player exposes any of his cards before the trump suit is named, the adversaries can elect to have a new deal by the same dealer.

DISCARDING   When the trump is named, each player has to put out at least three of his cards, and can discard as many more as he pleases. All these discards have to be placed on the table face upwards. If a player discards a trump, his partner can call his attention to it, and it can be taken back, provided the player has not been helped to cards, or has not lifted the cards drawn.

DRAWING   The players having discarded, the dealer, beginning on his left, has to give to each player in turn from the top of the pack, face downwards, as many cards as might be necessary to restore the number in each hand to six.

ROBBING THE DECK   When it comes to the dealer's turn to draw cards, rather than take them from the top of the pack, face downwards, he can search the remainder of the pack, and take from it any cards he pleases in order to restore the number in his hand to six. If he finds in his own hand and in the remainder of the pack more than six trumps, he has to discard the ones he does not want, face upwards on the table.

IRREGULAR DRAWING   If a player asks for too many or too few cards, and does not discover his error until the next player has been helped, if he has too few he can make his hand good from the discards, but must not take a trump therefrom. If he has too many, the adversaries have to be allowed to draw the superfluous ones at random, face downwards, and place them on the top of the pack.

PLAYING   The maker of the trump has to lead for the first trick, any card he pleases. If a trump is led, all the players have to follow suit if they are able. If a plain suit is led, a player can trump, even when he is holding a card of the suit led; however, if he does not trump, he has to follow suit if he can; otherwise, or he is liable to the penalty for a revoke.

The last trick turned and quitted can be seen, but no other.

IRREGULARITIES IN THE HANDS   If any player is found to have an incorrect number of cards, it is a misdeal if no bid has been made. If a bid has been made, the deal stands good if three players have their right number of cards. If the first trick has been played to by a person who holds too many cards, neither he nor his partner can score anything that hand, but they can play the hand out in order to save what points they can. If a player has too few cards, there is no penalty, but he should draw from the discard in order to make up the deficiency, whereby only plain-suit cards are available.

EXPOSED CARDS   The following are exposed cards, which have to be left face upwards on the table, and are liable to be called by either adversary: every card faced on the table in other than the regular course of play; two or more cards played to a trick, whereby the adversaries can elect which will be played; and any card named by the player who holds it.

The adversary on the right of an exposed card has to call it before he himself plays. If it will be the turn of the player who holds the exposed card to lead for the next trick, the card, if wanted, has to be called before the current trick is turned and quitted. If a player who has the lead, and who has an exposed card in front of him, plays before the previous trick is turned and quitted, the card so led can also be claimed as exposed.

If a trump is exposed after the trump suit has been named, the adversaries can prevent the playing of this card, but the holder of it is not liable to any penalty for a revoke under these circumstances.

LEADING OUT OF TURN   If a player leads when it was his partner's turn, the partner can be called on by his right-hand adversary to lead or not to lead a trump, but a specified plain suit cannot be called. If it was the turn of neither of the partners in error to lead, the card played in error is simply exposed. If all the players have played to the false lead, the error cannot be rectified. If all have not followed, the cards played to the false lead can be taken back, and are not liable to be called.

PLAYING OUT OF TURN   If the third hand plays before the second, the fourth can also play before the second, either of his own volition or on the direction of the second hand, who can say, 'Play, partner.' If the fourth hand plays before the second, and the third hand has not played, the trick can be claimed by the adversaries, no matter who actually wins it; however, the actual winner of it has to lead for the next trick.

If any player abandons his hand, the cards in it can be claimed as exposed, and can be called by the adversaries.

THE REVOKE   A revoke is a renounce in error that is not corrected in time, or non-compliance with a performable penalty. It is a revoke if a player has one of the suit led, and neither follows suit nor trumps.

A person who is prohibited from playing an exposed trump is not liable to any penalty if it causes him to revoke.

A revoke is established when the trick in which it occurs has been turned and quitted, or when either the revoking player or his partner, whether in his right turn or otherwise, has led or played to the following trick.

If a revoke is claimed and proved, the revoking side cannot score any points that deal, but it can play the hand out in order to prevent the adversaries from making points.

If an adversary of the bidder revokes, the bidder's side scores whatever points it makes that deal, regardless of the number bid.

A player can ask his partner whether or not he has a card of the suit in which he renounces and does not trump, and the player can correct his error if the question is asked before the trick is turned and quitted. However, if he answers in the negative, there is no remedy.

DRAWING CARDS   Any player can ask the other players to indicate the cards played by them to the current trick, but he has to confine himself to the expression 'Draw cards.'

IRREGULAR REMARKS   A player who calls attention in any way to the trick or the score can be called on to play his highest or lowest of the suit led, or to trump or not to trump the trick during the play of which the remark is made.

SCORING   A game consists of fifty-one points, fourteen of which have to be made on every deal, as follows.

1 for *High*, or the Ace of trumps.
1 for *Low*, or the Deuce of trumps.
1 for the *Jack* of trumps.
1 for *Game*, or the Ten of trumps.

5 for *Right Pedro*, or the Five of trumps.

5 for *Left Pedro*, or Five of the same colour as that of the trump suit. All points count to the side that wins them.

Any trumps found among the discards at the end of the hand count for the side that made the trump.

At the end of the hand, the number of points won by each side is added up, and the lower is deducted from the higher, whereby the difference is scored by the winners of the majority. If the result is a tie, neither scores. For example, if A–B make 11, Y–Z have to make the remaining 3, which deducted from 11 leaves 8 points for A–B to score.

If the side that names the trump suit fails to make as many points as it bids, it scores nothing for that deal, and the number bid is scored by the adversaries, in addition to any other points the adversaries might have made in play. The number bid and the number actually won have to be compared before the points made by the adversaries are deducted.

The side that first makes fifty-one points wins the game.

HEARTS

— — —

Hearts is supposed by some people to be an entirely new game; however, its leading principle, losing instead of winning tricks, is to be found in many other card games, some of which are quite old. Slobberhannes, Enflé, Schwellen, Polignac and The Four Jacks all belong to the same family, but most of them have given way to the more popular game of Hearts.

There are several varieties of Hearts, but the main arrangements are the same in all, and the main differences are in the way of settling at the end of the hand.

CARDS Hearts is played with a full pack of fifty-two cards, which rank A K Q J 10 9 8 7 6 5 4 3 2; the ace is the highest in play, but in cutting, ranks below the deuce. There is no trump suit.

When three people play, the deuce of spades is thrown out of the pack; when five play, both the black deuces are laid aside; and when six play, all four deuces are discarded. It is usual to play with two packs, whereby one pack is shuffled while the other is being dealt.

COUNTERS Every deal is a game in itself, and has to be settled for in counters immediately. It is usual for each player to begin with fifty counters, which are purchased from a person who it is agreed on will act as the banker. When only two play, the game can be scored on a pull-up cribbage board, and settled for at the end.

PLAYERS Any number from two to six people can play, but four is the usual number, whereby each plays for himself against all the other players. The players on the dealer's right and left are known as the pone and the *eldest hand*, respectively.

STAKES The value of the counters has to be agreed on before play begins, and the method of settling should also be understood, because Sweepstake Hearts and Howell's Settling are entirely different games, and require totally different methods of play.

CUTTING If seven players assemble, it is usual to make up a table in which the dealer takes no cards. If there are more than seven candidates for play, two tables have to be formed.

Players draw from an outspread pack for the choice of seats and cards, whereby the lowest cut has the first choice, and the other players follow in their order. The player who cuts the lowest card takes the first deal, and the deal afterwards passes in regular rotation to the left.

In cutting, the ace is low. Any player who exposes more than one card has to cut again.

TIES If the first cut does not decide, the players who are tying have to cut again, but the new cut decides nothing except the tie.

DEALING Any player has the right to shuffle the pack, and the dealer goes last. The cards are then presented to the pone to cut, and he has to leave at least four in each packet. The cards are dealt from left to right, one at a time to each player in rotation until the pack is exhausted. No trump is turned. In Two-handed Hearts, the dealer stops when each player has received thirteen cards. The deal passes to the left.

MISDEALING It is a misdeal if the dealer omits to have the pack cut and the error is discovered before the last card is dealt, if the dealer deals a card incorrectly and does not remedy the error before dealing another, or if the dealer counts the cards on the table or the ones remaining in the pack, or if it is discovered before all have played to the first trick that any player has too many or too few cards. A misdeal loses the deal unless one of the other players has touched the cards, or has in any way interrupted the dealer.

If any card is exposed by the dealer, the player to whom it is dealt can demand a new deal, provided he has not touched any of his cards. Anyone who deals out of turn, or with the wrong cards, can be stopped before the last card is dealt. After that, the deal stands good, and the packs, if changed, have to remain so.

IRREGULAR HANDS If, after the first trick has been played to, any two players are found to have more or fewer than their correct number of cards, and the pack is perfect, the one who has fewer has to draw, face downwards, from the hand of the one who has more, and each has to pay five counters into the pool.

OBJECTS OF THE GAME As a general proposition, the object of each player is to avoid getting any hearts in the tricks he takes in. In some varieties of the game, his object has to be to take no hearts; in others, it will be to take fewer than do his adversaries, and in others it will be to take fewer than four. After a person has taken in one or more hearts, his object will be to *load* the other players, that is, to see that they also get some hearts, or it might be to see that a given player takes at least one heart, or that no one but himself takes any. The way in which a person has to vary his play in accordance with these objects will be discussed when we come to the suggestions for good play. In the meantime, it is necessary to bear in mind only the general principle that the object of the game is to avoid winning any tricks that contain hearts.

METHOD OF PLAYING   When the cards are dealt, the player to the left of the dealer begins by leading any card he pleases, and the other players have to follow suit if they can. The highest card played, if it is of the suit led, wins the trick. There is no trump suit. If a player has none of the suit led, he can discard anything he pleases. The winner of the trick takes it in and leads for the next trick, and so on until all the cards have been played. The tricks themselves have no value as such, and do not have to be kept separate.

IRREGULARITIES IN PLAY   If any player omits to play to a trick, and plays to a following one, he is not allowed to correct his error, but is compelled to take the thirteenth or last trick, with whatever hearts it might contain. If a player is found during or at the end of a hand to be a card short, and all the other players at the table have their right number and have played to the first trick, the player who has the short hand is compelled to take the last trick, with whatever hearts it might contain.

EXPOSED CARDS   If a person leads or plays two cards to one trick, he is allowed to indicate the card he intended, but he has to leave the other one face upwards on the table. All exposed cards are liable to be called by any player at the table, and if one player calls this card, his decision is binding on the other players. A player who has an exposed card in front of him has to play it when called on, provided he can do so without revoking, but he cannot be prevented from getting rid of the exposed card in the course of play, if the opportunity arises.

LEADING OUT OF TURN   If a player leads out of turn, he can be called on to lead or not to lead a heart when it is next his turn to lead. This penalty can be enforced by only the player on his right. If all have played to the false lead, the error cannot be rectified, but if all have not played, their cards have to be taken back, and are not liable to be called.

If any person plays out of turn in any trick, the player on his left, not having played, can demand that the card be taken back, and after the proper player has played, the player in error can be called on to play his highest or lowest of the suit led, or not to discard a heart. If the person on the left of the player in error was the leader in the trick, either he or the player whose proper turn it was to play can demand the penalty.

REVOKING   Any player who fails to follow suit, when he is able to do so, can amend his error if he discovers his mistake before the trick in which it occurs has been turned and quitted. The card played in error then becomes an exposed card. The players who have played after him have the privilege of withdrawing their cards and substituting others, without penalty. If the revoking player does not discover his error in time, the hand has to be played out, and if the revoke is detected and claimed, the player in error has to pay all the losses on that hand. If the revoking player wins the pool himself, he has to pay the thirteen counters to the pool, and leave them for a *Jack*. If he divides the pool with another player, he has to pay his co-winner six counters, and put up the other seven for a Jack.

If two or more players revoke in the same hand, each has to pay the entire losses in that hand as if he were alone in error, so that if two revoke and a third wins the pool, the latter receives twenty-six counters instead of thirteen. In Auction Hearts, the revoking player also has to refund the amount put up by the bidder. A revoke has to be claimed and proved before the pool is divided. Non-compliance with a performable penalty is the same as a revoke.

SETTLING   After the last card has been played, each player turns over his tricks, counts the number of hearts he has taken in and announces it. Players should be careful not to gather or mix the cards until all thirteen hearts have been accounted for. Each player then pays into the pool for the number of hearts he has taken in, according to the system of settlement agreed on before play began. The pool is then taken down by the player or players who win it, and the deal passes to the left. The game is at an end any time the players wish to stop, after a hand has been settled for, but it is usual to agree on a definite time.

There are two ways of settling at the end of the hand, each of which has its good points.

SWEEPSTAKE HEARTS   After the hand has been played, each player announces the number of hearts he has taken in, and pays into the pool one counter for each. All thirteen hearts having been paid for, any player who has taken no hearts wins the entire pool; two players who have taken none divide the pool. If all the players have taken hearts, or if one player has taken all thirteen, the pool remains, and forms a *Jack*. This can be won by only a single player in some subsequent deal who takes no hearts, and all the other players have taken at least one heart. These jack pools are naturally increased thirteen counters every deal until a player wins the whole amount. Some clubs make it a Jack after two players have divided a pool, and use the odd counter as a starter. It will be found that natural Jacks occur quite frequently enough without having to resort to this expedient.

HOWELL'S SETTLING   The great objection to the method of settling at Sweepstake Hearts is that it makes the game almost entirely one of chance. No matter how good a player you might be, good luck alone will bring success. In a four-handed game, it is possible for one player to take in only 58 hearts in 60 deals and to still be 46 counters behind, whereas another player might take in 500 hearts in 60 deals and be 46 counters ahead. It might be claimed that the player who has 46 counters ahead at the end was the better player, because he won; however, most people will agree that a player who takes in only 58 hearts in 60 deals is a much better player than one who has taken in 500 hearts in the same time.

It was to remedy this defect, and to give skill its proper percentage of value, that Mr E. C. Howell of Boston proposed the method of contributing to and dividing the pools that is now known as Howell's Settling.

Each player begins with an equal number of counters, usually 100. At the end of the hand, after the hearts have been counted and announced, each player pays into the pool, for every heart he holds, as many counters as there are players besides himself. For example, A, B, C and D play. A takes three hearts, B and C take five each, and D takes none. There being three players besides himself, A puts up three times three, or 9 counters. B and C put up 15 each, and D none, so that there are 39 in the pool. Each player then takes out of the pool 1 counter for every heart he did ***not*** hold when the hearts were announced. D, having taken no hearts, gets 13 counters. A, having taken three hearts only, is entitled to 10 counters for the 10 hearts he did not hold, and B and C get 8 each. This exhausts the pool. There are no Jacks in this way of settling.

Matters can be facilitated by having counters of different colours, whereby the white is the unit, and the red represents the number it will be necessary to pay for one heart. Practice will make the players so familiar with the amount of the various profits or losses that they simply pay or take what is due to them.

The first time this is played, it looks like a reasonably severe game for a player who takes in a large number of hearts on one deal, but it will be found that he rapidly recovers. During a sitting of any length, the player who takes in the smallest number of hearts has to be the winner. In the case mentioned in connection with Sweepstake Hearts, in which one player lost 46 counters and another won 46, in 60 deals, the result at Howell's Settling would have been that the player who took in only 58 hearts would be 548 counters ahead, and would not instead have 46, whereas the one who took in 500 hearts would lose 1220 counters, not win 46.

METHODS OF CHEATING   Under the rule for dealing the cards one at a time, the cheat has to be very skilful in order to secure any advantage in Hearts. However, when it is the practice to deal the cards three at a time, and four on the last round, it is an easy matter to get four small hearts together on the bottom of the pack. Any person who is observed to hold three or four small hearts every time he deals should be carefully watched, and it will usually be found that he gathers the small hearts from the hands of the other players while the pool is being divided. Marked cards are of little use to the cheat in Hearts, because so much depends on what a player holds, and so little on his play.

— —

VARIETIES OF HEARTS

Before proceeding to suggestions for good play, it will be better to describe some of the variations of the game in common use, because what would be good play in one variation would not be in another.

TWO-HANDED HEARTS   The two players having cut for the deal, thirteen cards are given to each, one at a time, and the remainder of the pack is left on the table, face downwards. The dealer's adversary, usually called the pone, begins by leading any card he pleases, and the dealer has to follow suit if he can, as in the ordinary game. The winner of the trick takes it in, but before leading for the next trick, he draws one card from the top of the pack lying on the table, thereby restoring the number of his cards to thirteen. His adversary then draws the next card, and the cards are played and drawn in this way until the pack is exhausted. The thirteen cards remaining in the hands of the two adversaries are then played, and after the last trick has been won, each turns over his cards and counts the number of hearts he has taken in. The object of the game is to take fewer hearts than does your opponent, and the method of settling is either for the greater number to pay the lesser the difference or for the first six hearts taken by the loser to count nothing, but for all above six to be paid for. The most popular way is to peg up the difference on a cribbage board, and to settle at the end of the sitting.

THREE-HANDED HEARTS The deuce of spades is discarded, and seventeen cards are dealt to each player, one at a time, after which the game proceeds in the usual way. There are several methods of settling. Howell's method is undoubtedly the best, but Sweepstakes is very common. An excellent way is for the player who takes the largest number of hearts to pay the two other players as many counters as he has hearts in excess of theirs. If two players have an equal number, both pay the low player. There are no Jacks.

AUCTION HEARTS This is usually played by four people, although five or six can form a table. After the cards have been dealt in the usual way, the player to the left of the dealer examines his cards, and determines which suit he would prefer to play to get clear of. It might be that if the game were to get rid of clubs instead of hearts, his hand would be a very good one, whereas if the suit were to remain hearts, it would be a very bad hand. Because the pool will contain thirteen counters to a certainty, he can afford to pay something for the better chance he will have to win it if he is allowed to make clubs the suit to be avoided, instead of hearts. He bids whatever amount he is willing to pay for the privilege of changing the suit, without naming the suit he prefers. The next player then has a bid, and so on in turn, whereby the dealer bids last. There are no second bids.

The player who makes the highest bid pays into the pool the amount he has bid. He then names the suit to be avoided, and leads for the first trick, regardless of his position with reference to the deal. The dealer's position is a great advantage, on account of its having the last bid.

After the hand is played, the players who have taken in any cards of the suit announced to be avoided pay one counter to the pool for each of them. If any one player gets clear, and each of the other players has at least one of the tabooed suit, he takes the entire pool. If two get clear, they divide the pool, and leave any odd counter to form the basis of a Jack, as in Sweepstakes. If one player takes all thirteen, it is a Jack; however, rather than sell the next choice to the highest bidder, the player who named the suit on the hand that made the pool a Jack has the choice of suits again for the next deal, and has to select a suit without paying anything more for it, until a player wins what he paid for the choice in the first place; that is, the pool has to be won before the choice can be sold again.

The general principles of the game are for the players to combine against the successful bidder and to spare no effort to prevent him from winning the pool.

SPOT HEARTS   In this variation, when the hearts are announced at the end of the hand, the spots on them are the units of value, whereby the Jack is worth 11, the Queen 12, the King 13 and the Ace 14. This adds nothing to the interest or skill of the game; rather, it tends to create confusion and delay, owing to the many disputes as to the correctness of the count.

The total to be accounted for in each deal is 104. In settling, the player who has the smallest number collects from each of the other players the amount they have in excess of his. If two or more players have an equal number, or none at all, they divide the amount collected from each of the others. For example, four play, A has 8 points, B 24, C 18, and D 54. Because 8 points is the lowest, B pays A 16, C pays him 10, and D pays him 46. If A and B had 8 each, C 32, and D 56, C would pay 24, and D 48, and A–B would divide the amount between them.

The main variation in play arises from the fact that a player who has to win a heart trick cannot always afford to play his highest heart as in the ordinary game.

JOKER HEARTS   In this variation, the heart deuce is discarded, and the Joker takes its place. The Joker occupies a position between the Jack and the Ten in value, with the added peculiarity that it cannot be discarded on a plain suit, because if it is, it wins the trick unless there is a higher heart in the same trick. If a player has the Joker dealt to him, his only chance to get rid of it is to play it on a trick in which hearts are led, or to discard it on a plain suit on which some other player has already discarded a heart higher than the Ten. Under these circumstances, the holder of the Joker is allowed to discard it, even if he has one of the suit led, and because the Joker is in the trick, the player who discarded the higher heart is compelled to take it in.

In settling, the Joker is worth five counters. If the player to whom it was dealt takes it in, he pays these five counters to the pool. If another player gets the Joker, he has to pay the five counters to the player who got rid of it. The remainder of the pool is then divided in the usual way. This is a most exasperating game.

DISCARD HEARTS   This is sometimes called *Black Jack*, or *Black Lady*. If it is the Jack, it is worth ten hearts; if it is the Queen, it is worth thirteen hearts.

After the cards are dealt, each player in turn lays out three cards that he does not want, and the player on his left is obliged to take them, after having discarded himself. No player can look at what he will get until he has discarded himself.

The Black Jack or Lady holds its rank as a spade when spades are led; however, the moment any other suit is led, of which the player is void, the player can discard the Black Jack or Lady, just as he would get rid of a heart. If hearts are led and the player has no hearts, he can play the Black Jack or Lady to the trick, because it ranks below the deuce of hearts.

PROGRESSIVE HEARTS   The general arrangements for the players and their positions are exactly the same as the ones already described in connection with Progressive Euchre. The players at each table cut for the deal, and play begins with the tap of the bell at the head table. Only one deal is played at each table.

There are no counters. At the end of the hand, the ladies compare their cards, and the lady who has the fewer hearts goes to the next-higher table. The gentlemen then compare their cards in the same way, so that one lady and one gentleman go up from each table at the end of every hand. They take the seats vacated by the players who leave the table they go to. All ties are determined by way of cutting, whereby the players who cut the lower cards go up. In cutting, the ace is low.

Each player is provided with a score card, to which the gold, red and green stars are attached as in Euchre. The gold stars are given to the players at the head table who have the fewest hearts. The players who move from other tables receive red stars, and the ones who take in the most hearts at the booby table receive green stars. Prizes are given to the ladies and gentlemen who have the greatest number of each variety of star, but the same player cannot win two prizes. If there is a tie in one class, the number of other stars has to decide, whereby equal numbers of gold are decided by the majority of red on the same card, red ties by the greater number of gold, and green ties by the fewest number of gold stars.

HEARTSETTE   Heartsette differs from hearts only in the addition of a widow. When four play, the spade deuce is deleted; twelve cards are given to each player, and the remaining three form the widow, which is left face downwards in the centre of the table. When any other number play, the full pack is used. If there are three players, three cards are left for the widow; two cards are left when five play, and four when six play. The player who wins the first trick takes in the widow, with any hearts it might contain. He is entitled to look at these cards, but must not show or name them to any other player. The game then proceeds in the usual way. Payments are made to the pool for all hearts taken in, and the pool is then won or divided, or remains to form a Jack, just as in Sweepstake Hearts. The main difference in the game is that the other players do not know whether or not the winner of the first trick is loaded, and he is the only player who knows how many or what hearts are still to be played.

DOMINO HEARTS   In this variation, six cards only are dealt to each player, and the remainder of the pack is left face downwards on the table. When a player is unable to follow suit, he has to draw cards from the stock, one at a time, until he can. The last player who has any cards left in his hand has to take what is left of the stock, if any. The hearts taken in are then counted as usual. Thirty-one points is game, and the winner is the player who has the fewest hearts scored when another player reaches thirty-one.

SUGGESTIONS FOR GOOD PLAY   A good player, after sorting his hand, carefully estimates its possibilities. The hand might be such that it is evidently impossible to avoid taking some hearts. The player then has to decide whether he will play to give each of the other players hearts or take all the hearts himself. If he succeeds in either object, he has a chance to win back his money in the ensuing Jack. In deciding on his chances to get clear without taking a single heart, the player first has to consider the advisability of beginning with a heart, or with a plain suit. If hearts, he should know the probability that the heart he leads will not win the trick; if a plain suit, he should know the probability that the suit will go around one or more times without hearts' being discarded on it, especially if he intends to lead high cards. These chances then have to be balanced one against the other and the more favourable cards selected.

LEADING HEARTS ORIGINALLY   When your hearts are so small as to be absolutely safe, such as the 7 5 3 2, it might be supposed that the best play would be to lead them at once, in order to get a large number of hearts out of your way. But with these cards, it is usually much better play, unless you have a very dangerous hand in plain suits, to reserve these small hearts until you have a more definite idea, from the fall of the cards, to whom you are giving them. These cards are especially useful for getting rid of the lead at dangerous stages in the end-game.

When the plain-suit cards are high or dangerous, but the hearts are reasonably safe, it is usually better to lead the hearts, and to continue leading them every time you get in. By following these tactics, it is quite possible for you to take almost every trick in the plain suits, and yet to win the pool by rapidly exhausting the hearts.

If you lead the ♡ 4, the only chance for it to win is that one player has no hearts, and that the 2 and 3 are divided. The odds against this combination of circumstances will vary according to the number of hearts you hold with the 4, but can be generally stated on the average as about 50 to 1. It is usually considered to be a safer lead than a high card of a plain suit, even if you have only three of the suit.

If your only heart is the 5, and you propose to lead it, the chances that the 2, 3 and 4 are not each in separate hands are about 19 in 25, or 19 to 6 against it, which is about 3 to 1. If you lead the 5, the odds against your winning the trick decrease as the number of hearts you hold with the 5 increases. If you have four hearts, and the 5 is the lowest, the odds against its winning the trick, if you lead it, are about 29 to 11. If you have eight hearts, and the 5 is the lowest, it is about an even chance. If your only heart is the 6, it is about an even chance that it will win the trick; however, the odds against you increase rapidly with the number of additional hearts you hold. If you propose to lead the 7, the chances it will win the trick are 2 to 1 under the most favourable circumstances, which are when it is your only heart. These odds against you increase rapidly with the number of additional hearts that you hold.

LEADING PLAIN SUITS ORIGINALLY   It will often happen that you will have to decide between the lead of a comparatively dangerous heart and a risky plain suit. If you know about probabilities, you should be able to select the safer course. The odds against getting a heart on the first round of a plain suit depend on how many cards of the suit you hold. If you lead an Ace, or any card that is sure to win the trick, the odds against your getting a heart on it are as follows.

If you have 4 cards of the suit, 22 to 1.
        "   5   "   15 to 1.
        "   6   "   7 to 1.
        "   7   "   4 to 1.
        "   8   "   2 to 1.

These odds can be slightly increased by taking into account the fact that players who cannot follow suit do not always discard hearts, because they perhaps have more dangerous cards to get rid of.

The odds against a suit's going around a second time can be influenced by the cards played to the first round; however, it sometimes happens that you have to calculate in advance for two rounds of a suit, regardless of the cards that might be played by other players. This is especially the case when you fear that the suit will be led to you, and you have cards that have to win two rounds. If you have 4 cards of the suit the odds *against* your getting a heart in two rounds are 2 to 1. The odds in *favour* of your getting a heart in two rounds are:

> If you have 5 cards of the suit, 4 to 3.
>   "   6   "   2 to 1.
>   "   7   "   6 to 1.

As an example of the value of having a thorough knowledge of these odds, suppose a careful player had to win two rounds of a plain suit, of which he held six cards, or to lead the ♡ 7, whereby he had three higher. The suit would be the better play, because it takes in only one heart, whereas the lead of the heart might take in four.

The following table shows the exact number of times in 1000 deals that a heart would probably be discarded on a plain suit led, according to the number of cards in the suit held by the leader, and the number of times the suit was led:

Cards held by the leader	1, 2, 3, 4	5	6	7	8
Times hearts will be discarded:					
On first round	44	63	122	200	315
On second round	358	430	659	857	1000
On third round	842	1000	1000	1000	1000

This shows that 158 times in 1000, when the leader has 1, 2, 3 or 4 cards of the suit, it will go around three times, because 158 is the balance necessary to bring our last figure, 842, up to 1000. If we reduce this to a small fraction, the odds are about 5⅛ to 1 that a suit will not go around three times without affording to some player the chance of discarding hearts on it. This calculation shows the hopeless nature of all hands that contain at least three cards of each suit, unless the smallest card in every suit is below a 6, because if any one of the suits is led three times, it is even betting that you will have to win the third round, and 5⅛ to 1 that you get a heart on it if you do.

PLAIN-SUIT LEADS   The favourite lead with most heart players is a singleton, or, failing that, a two-card suit. This is a mistake, unless the singleton is a high card, because if the adversaries are sharp players, they will at once suspect the nature of the lead, and carefully avoid the suit. However, if you wait until another player opens the suit, the suit will very probably be led twice in succession. The best original plain-suit lead is one in which you are moderately long but have small cards enough to be safe, and from which you can lead intermediate cards that probably will not win the first trick.

Having very little experience in playing Hearts will convince anyone that it is best, in plain suits, to play out the high cards first. This agrees with the theory of probabilities, because although the odds are 22 to 1 against your getting a heart on the first round of a plain suit of which you have 4 cards, the odds are only 2 to 1 against it on the second round, and on the third round they are 5⅛ to 1 in favour of it. Accordingly, on the first round, most players put up their highest card of the suit led, no matter what their position with reference to the leader, but in doing so, they often run needless risks. The object in Sweepstake Hearts is to take none, and the most successful players will be found to be the ones who play consistently with the greatest odds in their favour for taking none.

Suppose you hold a suit such as A 10 9 7 4 2. This is a safe suit, because it is very improbable that you can be compelled to take a trick in it. The best lead from this suit is the 10 or 9. If the suit is led by any other player, the same card should be played, unless you are the fourth hand, and have no objection to the lead. This avoids the risk, however slight, of getting a heart on the first round, which would be entailed by playing the ace. In Sweepstake Hearts, it is a great mistake to play the high cards of a suit in which you are safe, because no matter how small the risk, it is an unnecessary one. In the case we are considering, when you have six cards of the suit, the odds are 7 to 1 against your getting a heart if you play the ace first round; that is, you will probably lose one pool out of every eight if you play it. Take the greatest odds in your favour, when you have only four cards of a suit: they are 22 to 1 against your getting a heart the first round, so that you would lose by it only once in 23 times. However, this is a heavy percentage against you if you are playing with players who do not run these risks, because you give up every chance you might otherwise have in 5 pools out of every 110.

When you have a dangerous hand in hearts, but one absolutely safe long suit, it is often good play to begin with your safe suit, whereby you retain any high cards you might have in other suits in order to get the lead as often as possible for the purpose of continuing your safe suit, which will usually result in one or more of the other players' getting loaded.

When you have at least three of each plain suit, it is obvious that you cannot hope for any discards, and that you have to take into account the probability of having to win the third round of one or more suits, with the accompanying possibility of getting hearts at the same time. If you have the lead, this probability has to be taken into account before any of the other players show their hands, and because it can be set down as about 5⅛ to 1 that you will get a heart, any better chance that the hand affords should be taken advantage of.

It will often occur that a player's attention has to be so concentrated on getting clear himself that he has no opportunity to scheme for 'loading' the other players. However, if it unfortunately happens that he is compelled to take in one or more hearts, he should at once turn his attention to taking them all, or to loading the other players, with a view to making a Jack of the pool. If he succeeds in either object, he has another chance for his money.

It is usually bad policy to return the suit opened by the original leader. He has picked that out as his safest suit, and although he might be the only one safe in it, by continuing it you are reducing your chances to two players, when you might share them with all three.

FOLLOWING SUIT   When a player is not the original leader, his policy becomes defensive. This is due to the fact that because the first player is plotting to give hearts to everyone but himself, each of the other players has to be a prospective victim, and should do his best to avoid the traps prepared by the player who plans the opening of the hand.

When you are second or third player, the first time a suit is led, it is usually best to play your highest card, unless you are safe in the suit, or have so many cards that there is danger of getting a heart, even on the first round. As fourth player, you should always play your highest card, unless there is already a heart in the trick, or some decided disadvantage in the lead. The risks you run in playing high cards while you are following suit have to be judged by way of the same probabilities we examined in considering the original lead. The fact that one or more players have already followed suit, and perhaps the cards they have played, might enable you to arrive at a yet closer estimate of your chances. It is usually conceded that the odds against a player who holds up on the first round are about 1 to 11; that is, in 12 pools, he will sacrifice his chances of one simply by holding up.

After one or two tricks have been played, the conditions might be such that it becomes necessary to hold up, in order to win the second round. This is especially the case after you have been loaded, and are anxious to keep a specific player out of the lead. For an example, see illustrative hand number 4 on page 389, in which Y holds up the ◇ King to keep A from getting in and leading another round of hearts. In the same hand, Z tries hard to make the pool a Jack by holding up the ♣ Q. If A had not been entirely safe in diamonds, the stratagem would have succeeded.

In following suit, it is important to keep count of the cards played, in order to avoid the unwitting lead of a suit of which the other players have none. The suits that require close watching are the ones in which you have nothing smaller than a six or eight. You should be careful to note which player seems to have the smaller cards, after the suit has been led once or twice, and be on the watch to take the lead away from him in other suits if you can; otherwise, he might load you by leading the small cards of your dangerous suit, in which he is safe. When this danger is apparent, it is best to retain, until the second round, high cards such as Kings and Queens of the suits led. Even if you have four of the suit, you run only a 2 to 1 risk in winning the second round instead of the first, as against a certainty that you will be out of the pool at once if the dangerous player gets the lead. For an example of this, see B's play in illustrative hand number 2 on page 388.

When you have a certain safe card, and other cards of another suit that are not absolutely safe, it is better to keep the safe card, in order to be sure of getting rid of the lead if you are put in on your dangerous suit.

In following suit, the most annoying hand you can hold is one that contains at least three cards of each suit, none of which are below a 6. There is no hope of a discard, unless two players make a fight in another suit, which they lead four or five times in order to load each other, regardless of the escape of the other players. This very seldom occurs, and never occurs among good players. With this hand, escape is almost impossible, and it is usually best to make the losses as small as possible. Many good players, with this hand, will deliberately take in hearts on the plain suits, hoping to escape with only one or two in each trick, rather than have to carry the whole load by getting into the lead at the end. It should never be forgotten that when you have to inevitably take some hearts, it is cheaper to take them in on plain suits than to win heart tricks.

CONTROL OF THE LEAD One of the strongest points in good heart play is the proper control of the lead at specific times. A player whose hand contains no commanding cards, and who is unable to do anything but follow suit on the first two or three rounds, will often find himself compelled to win one of the later rounds with a small card, whereby he takes in one or two hearts with it, and this misfortune usually overtakes him, because a specific player gets into the lead at a critical period of the hand. If he sees the impending danger, and has K, Q or J of a suit led, he will not give up his high card, even if the ace is played to the trick, but will retain it in order to prevent the possibility that the dangerous player will get into the lead on the second round of the suit. In doing this, he naturally decreases the odds against his getting hearts, by deliberately winning the second round. However, 2 to 1 in his favour is a much better chance than the certainty, almost, that he will be loaded if a specific player is given the opportunity to lead a certain suit again. See B's play in illustrative hand number 2 on page 388, and Y's in number 4 on page 389.

A player might have no desire to prevent any specific adversary from getting the lead, but might be simply anxious to carry out a specific line of play. In order to do this, it might be essential that he have some direction of the course of the hand. This is impossible if his play is confined to following suit helplessly, whatever is led. He has to be able to assume the lead himself in order to change the course of the play so as to better suit his game.

Let's suppose he has a dangerous hand in plain suits, but is safe in hearts, and decides that his best chance is to lead hearts at every opportunity; or that he has a specific safe suit that it is manifestly to his advantage to have led as often as possible. The other players, being the ones who are to suffer from this line of play, will naturally prevent it if possible, and in order to carry out the plan in spite of their opposition, it will be necessary for the individual player to gain the lead a specific number of times, and to thereby force his game on them.

Again, a player might know that he can load a specific adversary if he can get in and lead a specific suit or card, or know that by giving one player the lead, that player can load another. In these cases, commanding cards have to be held or retained, in order to give the player control of the lead.

When a player is attempting to take all thirteen hearts, the control of the lead, especially in the end game, is very important, because the design of each of the other players will be to get the lead into some other hand, in the hope that they will load the player who has it, and thereby at least divide the pool.

THE DISCARD   One of the most important elements in heart play is the discard. The beginner is too apt to discard hearts at every opportunity, but having a bit of experience will teach him that even a 3 in a plain suit might be a better card to part with.

The most important thing in discarding is to reduce the odds against your winning the pool. Let's suppose you have the A K Q of a plain suit. It is 5⅛ to 1 that you get a heart if this suit is led a third time. If you can get a discard, the odds are at once reduced to 2 to 1 in your favour, that being the probability that you will escape, even if you have to win two rounds. This is a very large percentage, and should never be lost sight of. If you have a choice between two dis-cards, one being from the K Q J 2 of hearts, and the other from the K Q J of a plain suit, select the plain suit. You can improve your chances little or none in the hearts, whereas you not only bring the odds to your side in the plain suit; you secure a chance of discarding on the third round of it.

Following the same principle, it is evidently good play to discard from a suit that has been led once or twice, if you have a dangerous card or cards in it. Even if you have a safe tenace in a suit, such as 4 and 2, and the 5 and 3 are still out somewhere, it is better to discard from it if there is the slightest danger of your getting the lead. Tenaces are only safe when they are led up to.

In *Howell's Settling*, the object is not so much to load the other players as to escape yourself. It is never advisable to attempt to take all thirteen hearts, because there are no Jacks; however, there are many cases in which it is better to deliberately take three or four, in order to avoid the chance of taking six or eight. For an example of these tactics adopted by two players, see illustrative hand number 3 on page 389. On the same principle, there are often cases in which it is advisable to take a trick with one heart in it, in order to get rid of a dangerous card, whereby you might be brought in several hearts later on. The general principles of leading and discarding are the same as in Sweepstake Hearts, but it is not necessary to take these desperate chances in order to escape entirely.

THREE-HANDED HEARTS   This game is more difficult to play than any other form of the game, partly because there are so many rounds of each suit, and partly because the moment one player refuses, the exact cards of that suit in the two other players' hands are known to each of them.

There is usually a great deal of cross-fighting in the three-handed game, during which one player escapes by getting many discards. When all three have refused, whereby each has a different suit, the end game becomes a question of generalship, and preservation of one or more commanding cards with which to control and place the lead is usually the key to the situation. A player who has no high cards for the end game, unless he is quite safe, is almost certain to be loaded in the last few tricks.

TWO-HANDED HEARTS Before opening the hand, the player should carefully consider what suits are safe and what are dangerous. It is usually best to preserve the safe suits and to lead the dangerous ones, which you should clear your hand of, if possible. It is of great advantage to have a missing suit, and equally disadvantageous to have a number of a suit of which your adversary is probably clear. If a card of a missing suit is drawn, it is usually best to lead it at once, so as to keep the suit clear; however, in doing so, be careful to first place the card among the other cards in the hand; otherwise, your adversary will detect it is a missing suit.

The lead is a disadvantage if you have safe hearts; however, towards the end of the stock, from which cards are drawn, it is an advantage to have commanding cards, with which you can assume the lead if necessary.

There is some finesse in determining whether or not to change the suit often in the leads. If you have a better memory than your adversary's, it might be well to change often, but if not, it might assist you to keep at one suit until you are afraid to lead it again.

In Two-Handed Hearts, keeping count of the cards is the most important matter, because the real play comes after the stock is exhausted, and the moment that occurs, you should know every card in your adversary's hand. The exact number of each suit should be a certainty, if not the exact rank of the cards. Until you can depend on yourself for this, you are not a good player. The last thirteen tricks are usually a problem in double-dummy, but the advantage will always be found to be with the player who has carefully prepared himself for the final struggle by preserving specific safe suits and getting rid of the suits in which it became evident that his adversary had the small and safe cards.

Some very pretty positions arise in the end game, whereby it is often possible to foresee that four or five tricks have to be played in a specific way in order to ensure that the lead is properly placed at the end, so that the odd hearts can be avoided.

AUCTION HEARTS The cards having been cut and dealt, the player to the left of the dealer, whom we will call A, examines his hand, and determines which suit he would prefer to play to get clear of. Let's suppose his hand consists of the ♡ A K 8, ♣ J 6 5 4 3 2,

◇ K 4 and ♠ 7 3. If the suit remains hearts, he is almost certain to take in a number, but if it is changed to clubs, he is almost as certain of getting clear. The hand is not absolutely safe, because hearts might be led two or three times before the clubs in the other hands were exhausted by the original leader, whose game would be to lead small clubs. Because the pool will contain thirteen counters to a certainty, he can afford to bid in proportion to his chances of winning it for the privilege of making clubs the suit to be avoided, instead of hearts.

It might be assumed, if the odds were 10 to 1 that the player would get clear if the suit were clubs, that he could therefore afford to bid ten times the amount of the pool, or 130, for his chance. Theoretically this is correct, but should he lose a pool such as this, he would have to win ten other pools to get back his bid alone, to say nothing of the amounts he would lose by paying his share in pools won by other players. Let's suppose him to win his share: one-fourth of all the pools. While he is winning the ten pools necessary to repair his single loss, he has to stand his share of the losses in the thirty others, which would average about 128 counters. This has to show us that even if a player has a 10 to 1 chance in his favour, he has to not only calculate on losing that chance once in eleven times; he has to make provision for the amounts he will lose in other pools. Experience shows that a bid of 25 would be about the amount a good player would make on this hand we are considering, if the pool were not a Jack, and he had first say.

The next player, Y, now examines his hand. Let's suppose he finds ♡ 6 4 3, ♣ A K 10, ◇ 8 7 5 3 and ♠ 6 5 4. If the first bidder is offering on clubs, it is evident he will lead them, because the successful bidder has the original lead in Auction Hearts, and it is equally evident that if he does so, a player who has A K 10 will have to pay for most of the pool. If any of the other suits is the one bid on, B has as good a chance for the pool as does anyone, at least to divide it. With two men yet to bid, a good player would probably make himself safe by shutting out A's bid, and probably offer 26.

Let's suppose B then to examine his hand and to find ♡ J 10, ♣ Q 9 8 7, ◇ A 10 9 and ♠ 10 9 8 2. Being unsafe in everything, he passes, and practically submits to his fate, his only hope being that the pool will result in a Jack. Z then examines his hand, and finds ♡ Q 9 7 5 2, ♣ none, ◇ Q J 6 2 and ♠ A K Q J. He sees at once that on spades he would lose everything, and that on diamonds he would have a very poor chance. On clubs, the result would depend on how often spades were led. In hearts, he has a very good hand, especially because he has a missing suit to discard in. Because he is the last bidder, he can make sure of the choice for 27, which he bids, and pays into the pool. The result of the play is given in illustrative hand number 4 on page 389. (As the cards happen to lie, had A been the successful bidder and made it clubs, Z would have won the pool.)

ILLUSTRATIVE HANDS

Number 1. Sweepstake Hearts
A leads for the first trick,

Number 2. Sweepstake Hearts
A leads for the first trick,

A	Y	B	Z	TRICK	A	Y	B	Z
10 ♠	Q ♠	8 ♠	K ♠	1	♣ A	♣ K	♣ 10	♣ Q
♣ J	♣ A	♣ 4	♣ K	2	♣ 5	♣ 2	♣ 9	♣ J
6 ◊	A ◊	J ◊	Q ◊	3	10 ◊	J ◊	9 ◊	A ◊
5 ◊	K ◊	10 ◊	9 ◊	4	Q ◊	8 ◊	K ◊	4 ◊
4 ◊	3 ◊	2 ◊	8 ◊	5	2 ♠	J ♠	A ♠	9 ♠
♣ 9	♣ 7	♣ 3	♣ Q	6	Q ♠	10 ♠	K ♠	8 ♠
♣ 6	♣ 5	♣ 2	♣ 10	7	♡ A	7 ◊	3 ◊	♡ Q
3 ♠	6 ♠	4 ♠	J ♠	8	♡ 10	♡ 4	♡ 3	♡ 5
2 ♠	5 ♠	♡ K	9 ♠	9	♣ 4	♡ K	♣ 6	♣ 7
♡ A	♡ Q	♡ 10	♡ 5	10	♡ 9	7 ♠	♡ J	5 ♠
♡ 7	♡ 7	♡ 9	7 ♠	11	♡ 7	♡ 2	♣ 8	♡ 8
♡ 6	♡ 8	♡ 4	♣ 8	12	♡ 6	6 ♠	6 ◊	4 ♠
A ♠	♡ 2	♡ 3	7 ◊	13	♣ 3	5 ◊	2 ◊	3 ♠

A 4   Y 6   B 2   Z 1
making it a Jack.

A 4   Y 5   B 0   Z 4
whereby B wins the Pool.

Number 1. 2nd Trick: Z sees that with this hand, escape is impossible. Because his main danger is in being loaded with hearts at the end, he clears his hand as rapidly as possible. *9th Trick:* The ♠ A is held up, and it looks as if A were safe in that suit with A 5 2. If Z now leads the ♡ 5, and A gets into the lead, returning the spade, Z has to take every other trick. *10th Trick:* If Z now leads ♠ 7, he loads A, but if his ♡ 5 wins the next trick, he takes all the rest of the hearts, and Y and B divide the pool. If he leads the ♡ 5 first, he cannot get more than four hearts, and the other players inevitably make a Jack of it. *11th Trick:* Y sees that if he underplays the 7 led, B will win the pool, because he has nothing but hearts, and A has only one more. He keeps A out of the lead by winning two rounds, so as to be sure of loading B, thereby making it a Jack. The ending is very well played.

Number 2. A has an even chance to escape, and it is better for him to be third or fourth player in hearts than to lead them. ***3rd Trick:*** B sees from the fall of the clubs that Y has no more, and that A is safe in them and will lead them again, so he holds up ◊ K in order to keep A out of the lead. ***7th Trick:*** Because A's hand can now be counted to contain either the 7 4 3 of clubs and four dangerous hearts or the 4 3 of clubs and five hearts, B's game is clearly to lead diamonds, in order to load Y and Z. His only dangerous card, the ♡ J, will go on the next round of spades, which have to be led again in the next two or three tricks.

	Number 3. Howell's Settling Z dealt, and A leads for the first trick.			TRICK	Number 4. Auction Hearts A, the successful bidder, names Hearts.			
A	Y	B	Z		A	Y	B	Z
10 ◊	J ◊	9 ◊	K ◊	1	♡ 5	♡ 8	♡ 6	♡ J
7 ◊	6 ◊	8 ◊	Q ◊	2	Q ◊	4 ◊	8 ◊	A ◊
♣ 4	♣ 9	♣ J	♣ A	3	J ◊	K ◊	7 ◊	10 ◊
♣ 2	♣ 8	♣ 5	♣ K	4	A ♠	7 ♠	6 ♠	10 ♠
J ♠	8 ♠	K ♠	A ♠	5	♡ 7	♡ A	♡ 4	♡ 10
5 ♠	7 ♠	Q ♠	10 ♠	6	K ♠	3 ♠	5 ♠	9 ♠
4 ♠	6 ♠	3 ♠	2 ♠	7	♡ Q	♡ K	♡ 3	♣ 9
♡ 5	♡ 3	♡ 8	♡ 4	8	♡ 9	♣ J	♣ 10	♣ Q
♡ A	♡ J	♡ 7	5 ◊	9	Q ♠	♣ 6	4 ♠	8 ♠
♡ 9	♡ 2	♡ K	♣ Q	10	J ♣	♣ 5	♣ A	2 ♠
A ◊	♡ 10	♡ 6	9 ♠	11	6 ◊	♣ 4	5 ◊	9 ◊
4 ◊	♣ 3	♡ Q	♣ 10	12	2 ◊	♣ 3	♣ K	♣ 8
2 ◊	♣ 7	3 ◊	♣ 6	13	♡ 2	♣ 2	3 ◊	♣ 7

A 3	Y 2	B 7	Z 1	A 0	Y 7	B 1	Z 5

Z wins 9, Y 5 and A 1, and B loses 15.   A wins the pool.

Number 3. A begins with the intermediate cards of his safe suit. ***8th Trick:*** Y is afraid to lead away from his club tenace, because it might be at once led back to him. ***9th Trick:*** Z seizes this opportunity to get rid of the very dangerous ◊ 5. If A does not play the ♡ A now, it is quite possible he will take every trick, except one in diamonds. ***10th Trick:*** If A leads the ◊ 2, and hearts are led again, he has to take all the remaining hearts. By taking three at once, he can escape the rest. B sees that if he passes this trick, A will at once lead the ◊ 2, and he will take all the remaining hearts, so he takes these three and throws the lead to Y, who has no chance to injure him. *11th Trick*: Z keeps two clubs, hoping that if Y gets in and leads clubs, B will discard a diamond instead of a heart, in which case Z would get clear.

Number 4. A, with his dangerous suit of spades, clears up the hearts at once. *6th Trick*: The second round of spades betrays A's dangerous suit to the other players. *7th Trick*: A has to risk division of the King and 3, because if they are in one hand, nothing will save him. Z keeps ◇ 9 and ♣ Q in order to be sure of getting a lead, because he is the only player who can load A by putting him in on spades at the end, thereby making him take in his own hearts. *8th Trick*: B cannot risk playing the high clubs while there is any chance for him to win the pool. He can count A to be safe in diamonds, with two hearts and two spades. *10th Trick*: A clears his hand of the very dangerous spade before leading his tenace in diamonds. *12th Trick*: A will not give up the heart until he is sure that B does not have the ♣ 7.

— —

SLOBBERHANNES

CARDS   Slobberhannes is played with a Euchre pack: thirty-two cards, and all cards below the Seven are deleted. The cards rank A K Q J 10 9 8 7, and the ace is the highest in both cutting and play. There is no trump suit.

COUNTERS   Each player is provided with ten counters, and points are marked by way of placing these counters in the pool. The player who first loses his ten counters also loses the game. If stakes are played for, counters of a different colour have to be provided, and the player who loses the game has to pay as many counters to each of the other players as they have points still in front of them. One player is usually the banker, and sells and redeems all money counters. The other money counters are redistributed at the end of each game.

PLAYERS   Any number from four to seven can play; however, the two black Sevens have to be deleted if there are more than four players. When seven play, the dealer takes no cards. All the preliminaries of seats, cards and deal are settled as in Hearts.

DEALING   The entire pack is distributed, whereby the dealer gives each player in rotation two or three cards in each round. No trump is turned. All irregularities in the deal are governed by the same laws as in Hearts, but a misdeal does not lose the deal under any circumstances. The same dealer has to deal again.

OBJECTS OF THE GAME The object in Slobberhannes is to avoid taking either the first or the last trick, or any trick that contains the Queen of clubs. The player who wins any of these loses one point, and if he wins all three of them, he loses an extra point, or four points altogether. The penalty for a revoke is also the loss of a point.

METHOD OF PLAYING The eldest hand begins by leading any card he pleases, and the other players have to follow suit if they can. The highest card played, if it is of the suit led, wins the trick, and the winner takes it in and leads for the next trick. The player who wins the first trick has to pay for it immediately, in order to avoid disputes. The tricks that are neither the first nor the last trick have no value, unless they contain the club Queen, which has to be paid for as soon as it is taken in.

There is a good deal of play in manoeuvring to get rid of cards that might win the last trick or that would take in the club Queen. Naturally, the Ace and King of clubs are dangerous cards, and unless the player who holds them has enough small cards to make him safe in that suit, he should be on the alert for opportunities to discard.

— —

POLIGNAC
QUATRE-VALETS, OR FOUR JACKS

CARDS AND PLAYERS When Polignac is played by four people, a Piquet pack is used, and eight cards are dealt to each player, 3–2–3 at a time. When five play, the two black Sevens are deleted, and six cards are given to each player. When six play, each person receives five cards. When seven play, the dealer takes no cards. In France, the cards usually rank as in Écarté: K Q J A 10 9 8 7; however, in England and America, it is more usual to preserve the order in Piquet: A K Q J 10 9 8 7. There is no trump suit. All the preliminaries are settled as in Hearts or Slobberhannes.

COUNTERS Each player is provided with ten or twenty counters, as can be agreed on, and the player who first loses his counters loses the game, and pays to each of the other players any stake that might have been previously agreed on: usually a counter for each point they have yet to go when he is decavé.

OBJECTS OF THE GAME The object of the game is to avoid winning any trick that contains a Jack, especially the Jack of spades, which is called **Polignac**. The moment any player wins a trick that contains a Jack, he pays one counter into the pool. If he takes in Polignac, he pays two counters. The eldest hand begins by leading any card he pleases, and the other players have to follow suit if they can. The highest card played, if it is of the suit led, wins the trick, and the winner leads for the next trick. If a player has none of the suit led, he can discard anything he pleases.

The game is sometimes varied by adding a *general*, or *capot*. Any player who thinks he can win all the tricks announces capot before the first card is led. If he is successful, he loses nothing; however, each of the other players have to pay five counters into the pool: one for each Jack, and one extra for Polignac. If the capot player fails to win every trick, each player pays for whatever jacks he has taken in.

— – —

ENFLÉ

OR SCHWELLEN

When Enflé is played by four people, the Piquet pack of thirty-two cards is used. If there are more than four players, sufficient cards are added in order to give eight to each person. The rank of the cards and all other preliminaries are the same as in Hearts. There is no trump suit.

The cards are dealt 3–2–3 at a time. The eldest hand leads any card he pleases, and the other players have to follow suit if they can. If all follow suit, the highest card played wins the trick, which is turned face downwards, and the cards in it are dead. The winner leads for the next trick, and so on. However, if any player is unable to follow suit, he is not allowed to discard, but has to immediately gather up the cards already played, and take them into his own hand with the cards originally dealt to him. The players following the player who renounces to the suit led do not play to the trick at all, but wait for him to lead for the next trick. If any player fails to follow suit on the next trick, or on any subsequent trick, he gathers the cards already played, takes them into his hand, and leads for the next trick. The play is continued in this way until a player gets rid of all his cards and therefore wins the game.

Enflé is usually played for a pool, to which each player contributes an equal amount before play begins. The game requires considerable skill and memory to play it well, because it is very important to remember the cards taken in hand by specific players and the ones that are in the tricks turned down.

— —

THE LAWS OF HEARTS

1. **Formation of table.** The people who are first in the room have the preference. If more than the necessary number assemble, the choice will be determined by way of cutting, whereby the people who cut the lowest cards have the right to play. Six people is the largest number that can play at one table. The player who cuts the lowest card has the deal.

2. In cutting, the Ace is low. Players who cut cards of equal value have to cut again. All have to cut from the same pack, and any person who exposes more than one card has to cut again. Drawing cards from an outspread pack is equivalent to cutting.

3. A complete Heart pack consists of fifty-two cards, which rank in the order A K Q J 10 9 8 7 6 5 4 3 2, and the Ace is highest in play. In Three-Handed Hearts, the spade deuce is thrown out. In Five-Handed, both the black deuces are laid aside. In Six-Handed, all four deuces are discarded. In Joker Hearts, the heart deuce is replaced by the Joker.

4. When two packs are used, the player next but one on the dealer's left has to collect and shuffle the cards for the next deal, and place them on his right. The dealer has the privilege of shuffling last.

5. The dealer has to present the pack to his right-hand adversary to cut. Not fewer than four cards will constitute a cut.

6. In the case of any confusion or exposure of the cards in cutting, or in reuniting them after cutting, the pack has to be shuffled and cut again.

7. If the dealer re-shuffles the cards after they have been properly cut, or looks at the bottom card, he loses his deal.

8. After the cards have been cut, the dealer has to distribute them one at a time to each player in rotation, beginning at his left and

continuing until the pack is exhausted, or in Two-Handed Hearts, until each player has thirteen cards.

9. The deal passes to the left.

10. There has to be a new deal by the same dealer if the pack is proved to be incorrect, either during the deal or during the play of a hand; or if any card is faced in the pack, or is found to be so marked or mutilated that it can be named. In the last case, a new pack has to be used.

11. If a card is exposed during the deal, the player to whom it is dealt can demand a new deal, provided he has not touched any of his cards. If the deal stands, the exposed card cannot be called.

12. Anyone who deals out of turn can be stopped before the last card is dealt. After that, the deal has to stand, and the packs, if changed, have to remain so.

13. It is a misdeal if the dealer omits to have the pack cut, and the error is discovered before the last card is dealt, or if the dealer deals a card incorrectly and fails to remedy it before dealing another, or if the dealer counts the cards on the table or the ones remaining in the pack, or if it is discovered before all have played to the first trick that any player does not have his proper number of cards and the pack is perfect.

14. A misdeal loses the deal unless one of the other players has touched his cards, or has in any way interrupted the dealer.

15. If, after the first trick is played to, any two players are found to have more or fewer than their correct number of cards, and the pack is perfect, the player who has fewer will draw from the hand of the one who has more, and each will pay a forfeit of five counters into the pool.

16. If a player omits to play to any trick, and plays to the following one, he will not be allowed to correct the error, but will be compelled to take in the last trick, with whatever hearts it might contain.

17. If a player is found during or at the end of a hand to be a card short, all the other players have the right number, and all have played to the first trick, he will be compelled to take in the last trick.

18. If a player leads or plays two cards to a trick, he has to indicate the card intended, and leave the other face upwards on the table. Any card exposed, except in the proper course of play, or any card named by the player who holds it, has to be left face upwards on the table.

19. A player has to lead or play any exposed card when called on to do so by any other player, provided he can do so without revoking. He cannot be prevented from playing an exposed card, and if he can get rid of it in this way, no penalty remains.

20. If a player leads out of turn, a suit can be called from him when it is next his proper turn to lead. This penalty can be enforced only by the player on his right. If he has none of the suit called, or if all the players have played to the false lead, no penalty can be enforced. If all have not played to the false lead, the cards can be taken back, and are not exposed cards.

21. If the third hand plays before the second, the fourth hand can demand that the card be taken back, and can call on the third hand to play the highest card he has of the suit, or he can call on him not to discard hearts. If the fourth plays before the third, the second player can demand the penalty.

22. When the first player to any trick has led, the other players have to follow suit if they can. If a player revokes, and discovers the error before the trick in which it occurs has been turned and quitted, he can amend his play, and the card played in error becomes an exposed card. Any players who have played after him can withdraw their cards and substitute others, whereby the cards first played are not exposed.

23. If the revoke is discovered during the play of the hand, the hand has to be played out, and at the end, the revoking player has to pay all losses in that hand. If the revoking player wins the pool himself, he has to pay to the pool thirteen counters, and leave them for a Jack. If he divides it, he has to pay the other winner six counters, and leave up seven for a Jack.

24. If two or more players revoke in the same hand, each has to pay the entire losses in the hand, as if he were alone in error, so that if two revoke, and a third wins the pool, he receives twenty-six counters instead of thirteen. In Auction Hearts, the revoking player has to pay the amount of the bid in addition.

25. The claimant of a revoke can search all the tricks at the end of a hand. The revoke is established if the accused player mixes the cards before the claimants have time to examine them.

26. A revoke has to be claimed before the tricks have been mixed, in preparation for shuffling for the next deal.

27. If a player is lawfully called on to lead a specific suit, or to play the highest of it, and unnecessarily fails to comply, he is liable to the penalties for a revoke.

28. Any trick once turned and quitted must not again be seen until the hand is played. Any player who violates this rule is subject to the same penalties as for a lead out of turn.

29. In settling at the end of the hand, the player who has taken no hearts [each of the other players having taken at least one heart] wins the pool. When two players have taken none, and the other two

each have at least one, they divide it, and the odd counter remains until the next pool. When three players have taken none, the thirteen counters remain in the pool, thereby forming a Jack, that can be won only by one player who takes no hearts, whereby each of the other players has taken at least one heart. During the time the Jack is played for, and until it is won, each player has to add to the pool by paying for the hearts he takes in each hand.

30. In Auction Hearts, the player to the left of the dealer has the first bid, the dealer bids last, and there is no second bid.

THE BÉZIQUE FAMILY

—⁃—

This family includes three of the most popular games: Bézique itself, Binocle, and Sixty-Six. These are all comparatively modern games, but are descended from very old stock, whereby the best known of the ancestors are Marriage, Matrimony, and Cinq-Cents. The etymology of the word *Bézique* is very much disputed. Some people claim it is from the Spanish *basa*, and afterwards *basico*: 'a little kiss', which refers to the union of the spade Queen and the diamond Jack, and the various marriages in the game. This was afterwards *Basique*, transformed by the French to *Besique*, and by the English to *Bézique*. One English writer thought the word was from *bésaigne*: 'the double-headed axe'.

Judging from the rank of the cards, which is peculiar to German games, Bézique might have originated in an attempt to play Binocle with a piquet pack, because Binocle seems to have originally been played with a full pack of fifty-two cards. One German writer stated that the game was of Swiss origin, and that the Swiss probably got it from Spain. In one writer's opinion, the name Binocle was derived from *bis*: until, and *knochle*: the knuckle, which would imply that the original meaning was 'until some one knuckled', that is stopped the game by knocking on the table with his knuckles. This interpretation seems far-fetched, but if is correct, it would sustain the opinion that Binocle was derived from the old game of Cinq-Cents, in which the player knocked with his knuckles in order to announce he had made enough points to win the game. In the opinion of the author, the word *binocle* is a German mispronunciation of the French word *binage*, which was the term used in Cinq-Cents for the combination of spade Queen and diamond Jack, as will be noted if the description of Cinq-Cents is referred to. Stopping the play is a prominent feature of Sixty-Six, which is another variation of Bézique and the connecting link between Binocle and Skat. In Sixty-Six, the combination known as Bézique, or binocle, is omitted; so is the sequence in trumps. Binocle, played with sixty-four cards, is simply Bézique, including a slight difference in the counting value of the various combinations. Sometimes twelve cards are given to each player.

Great confusion seems to have existed when the game of Bézique was introduced in England, in the winter of 1868–69, owing to the fact that many people rushed into print with their own private opinions of the rules, which were first given by a Dr Pole, in 1861. No one knew whether 'the last trick' was the absolute last trick or the last one before the stock was exhausted. Whether the highest or lowest cut dealt was also a matter of dispute. Cavendish got both these wrong in the first edition of his *Pocket Guide*, but corrected himself without explanation or apology in the second edition. It was then the custom of many players to attach no value to the trump suit until the stock was exhausted, so that until the last eight tricks, there was no such thing as trumping a trick in order to win it. Disputes also arose as to counting double combinations, whereby many people contended that a double marriage should be as valuable as a double bézique. Time and experience have finally settled all these points, and the rules of the game are now practically uniform in all countries.

— —

BÉZIQUE
OR 64-CARD BINOCLE

There are two forms of Bézique in common use: the ordinary game, which will be first described, and the variation known as Rubicon Bézique, which is to Bézique proper what Railroad Euchre is to Euchre.

CARDS Bézique is played with two packs of thirty-two cards each, whereby all below the Seven are deleted and the two packs are then shuffled together and used as one pack. It is better to have both packs of the same colour and pattern, but it is not absolutely necessary. The cards rank A 10 K Q J 9 8 7 and the Ace is the highest in both cutting and play.

COUNTERS Special markers are made for scoring in Bézique, but the score can easily be kept by means of counters. Each player should be provided with four white, four blue and one red, together with a special marker such as a 5 cent piece or a button. The button stands for 500 points, each blue counter for 100, the red counter for 50, and the white counters for 10 each. At the beginning of the game, the counters are placed on the left of the player, and are passed from left to right as the points accrue, whereby smaller denominations are exhanged for higher when necessary. Many people find it more convenient to peg the game on a pull-up cribbage board, they start at 21, count each peg as 10 points, and go twice around to the game hole.

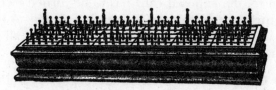

A PULL-UP BÉZIQUE MARKER

STAKES   Bézique is played for so much a game: 1000 points up, or for so much a point, whereby the score of the loser is deducted from that of the winner. When a party of five games is agreed on, it is usual to have an extra stake on the odd game, and when three games have been won by the same player, the party is at an end. It is usual to count it a double game if the loser has not reached 500 points.

PLAYERS   Bézique is played by two people, one of whom is known as the *dealer* and the other as the *pone*. They cut for choice of seats and deal, whereby the player who cuts the highest card has the first choice and elects whether or not to deal himself. In cutting, the cards rank as in play, and the ace is the highest. If a player exposes more than one card, he has to cut again.

DEALING   The cards are thoroughly shuffled and presented to the pone to cut. At least five cards have to be left in each packet. The cards are then dealt three at a time for the first round, two for the next, and three for the last, whereby each player receives eight cards. The seventeenth card is then turned up for the trump. If this card is a Seven, the dealer scores 10 points for it at once. The trump card is laid on the table by itself, and the remainder of the pack, which is called the *stock* or *talon*, is slightly spread, in order to facilitate the process of drawing cards from it, and to be sure that none of the cards remaining in the undealt portion are exposed. In 64-card Binocle, twelve cards are sometimes dealt to each player.

MISDEALING   A misdeal does not lose the deal, but in some cases a new deal is at the option of the adversary. If the dealer exposes a card that belongs to either the adversary or the stock, the pone can demand a new deal, but if either player exposes any of his own cards, the deal stands good. If too many cards are given to either player, there has to be a new deal. If too few, the pone can claim a fresh deal, or allow the dealer to supply the missing cards from the top of the stock, without changing the trump card. If any card but the trump is found to be faced in the pack, there has to be a new deal. If a card faced in the stock is not discovered until the first trick has been played to, the exposed card has to be turned face downwards, without disturbing its position. If a pack is found to be imperfect, the deal in which the error is discovered is void, but all previous cuts or scores made with that pack stand good.

METHOD OF PLAYING   The pone begins by leading any card he chooses, to which his adversary can play any card he pleases. A player is not obliged to follow suit, nor to trump, but can renounce or trump at pleasure until the stock is exhausted, after which the method of play undergoes a change. If a player follows suit, the higher card wins the trick, and if identical cards are played to the same trick, such as two Jacks of clubs, the leader wins. Trumps win plain suits. The winner of the trick takes in the cards, and turns them face downwards; however, before he leads for the next trick, he has the privilege of announcing and scoring any one of specific combinations he might hold in his hand. After this, or in the absence of any announcement, and before leading for the next trick, he draws a card from the top of the stock and places it in his hand, without showing or naming it. His adversary draws the next card, so that each player restores the number of cards in his hand to eight. This method of drawing from the stock is open to many objections, and in France the pone always draws first, no matter who wins the trick.

All combinations announced and scored have to be laid face upwards on the table; however, the cards still form part of the player's hand, and can be led or played at any time, although they must not again be taken in hand until the stock is exhausted.

OBJECTS OF THE GAME   The reasons for winning or not winning specific tricks will be better understood in connection with the description of the various combinations that count towards game, and the way of scoring them.

BRISQUES   The aces and Tens of each suit are called brisques and count ten points each towards game. Except for the purpose of getting or keeping the lead, there is no object in winning any trick that does not contain a brisque. Every brisque taken in should be scored at once by the player who wins the trick: 10 points for an ace or Ten, and 20 points if there are two of these cards in the same trick.

A player who holds or draws the *Seven of trumps* has the privilege of exchanging it for the turn-up trump and scoring 10 points at the same time but he has to make the exchange immediately after winning a trick and before drawing his card from the stock. If the turn-up card is a Seven, or one exchange has already been made, the exchange can still be made and scored. He cannot score the Seven and make a declaration at the same time.

DECLARATIONS The combinations that can be announced and scored during the play of the hand are divided into three classes: Marriages and Sequences, Béziques, and Fours of a kind. Only one combination can be scored at a time, and it has to be announced immediately after the player who holds it has won a trick, and before he draws his card from the talon. If he draws without announcing, it is equivalent to saying he has no declaration to make. Having drawn his card, even if he has not looked at it, he cannot score any declaration until he wins another trick.

The combinations and their values are as follows.

CLASS A

King and Queen of any plain suit: *Marriage* 20
King and Queen of trumps: *Royal Marriage* 40
Sequence of five highest trumps: *Sequence* 250

CLASS B

Spade Queen and diamond Jack: *Bézique* 40
Two spade Queens and diamond Jacks: *Double Bézique* 500

CLASS C

Any *four Aces* 100
Any *four Kings* 80
Any *four Queens* 60
Any *four Jacks* 40

The four court-cards in class C can all be of different suits, or any two of them can be of the same suit.

Many misunderstandings arise with reference to the way and order of making declarations, most of which can be avoided by way of remembering the following rules.

The player who makes the declaration has to have won the previous trick, and has to make his announcement before drawing his card from the stock. When the stock is exhausted, so that there is no card to be drawn, no announcement can be made.

Only one declaration can be scored at a time, so that a trick has to be won for every announcement made, or the combination cannot be scored. This does not prevent a player from making two or more announcements at the same time, but he can score only one of them.

A player cannot make a lower declaration with cards that form part of a higher one already made in the same class. For example, marriages and sequences belong to the same class. If the sequence has been declared, a player cannot take from it the King and Queen and score a marriage; nor can he add a new Queen to the King already in the sequence, and announce a marriage, because the higher combination was scored first. However, if the marriage is first announced, the A 10 J can be added and the sequence scored, after winning another trick.

Cards once used in combination cannot be used again in combinations of equal value of the same class. For example, four Kings have been declared, and one of them has afterwards been used in the course of play. The player cannot add a new King to the three remaining and announce four Kings again. A marriage in spades has been declared, and the King has been gotten rid of in play. A new King of spades will not make another marriage with the old Queen. A bézique has been scored, and the Jack has been gotten rid of in play, whereby a new Jack of diamonds will not make another bézique with the old Queen.

Some judgement is necessary in making announcements, and the question of time is often important. Suppose hearts are trumps, and the winner of the trick holds double bézique, sixty Queens, and a royal marriage:

He cannot lay all these cards down at once and claim 600 points. Nor can he lay down four Queens and two Jacks, and score 560, nor four Queens and a King, and score 100. He can announce them if he chooses to expose his hand in that way, but he can score only one combination, and has to win a separate trick in order to score each of the other combinations. It would be better for him to select one of the combinations and declare it, and to wait until he won another trick to declare the next one. A beginner would be apt to declare the highest count first: 500 for the double bézique; however, under the rule whereby a player is prevented from making a declaration that forms part of a higher one of the same class already made, he would lose the 40 points for the single bézique. It would be better to declare the single bézique first, and score 40 points for it, and after winning another trick, to show the other bézique, and score 500 points more for the double combination. A player is not allowed to score 40 for the second bézique and then 500 for the two béziques combined, because if new announcements are made in the same class, at least one new card has to be added from the player's hand when the announcement is made, even if it is not scored until later.

DOUBLE DECLARATIONS   It frequently happens that a player is forced to make two declarations at the same time, although he can score only one of them. For example, a player has announced and shown four Kings, one of which is the King of spades. On winning another trick, he shows and scores bézique. One of the bézique cards forms a marriage with the spade King, and because the combinations belong to different classes, both can be scored, although the same card is used in each; however, the player cannot score the second combination until he wins another trick. Under these circumstances, it is usual to declare both combinations, whereby you score the more valuable and repeat the one left over until an opportunity arises to score it. In this case, the player would say, 'Forty for bézique, and twenty to score.' If he lost the next trick, he would continue to repeat at every trick, 'Twenty to score,' until he won a trick.

A player who has a score in abeyance in this way is not obliged to score it if he has anything else to announce. A player who has twenty to score might pick up the sequence in trumps before he wins another trick, and would be very foolish to lose the chance to score 250 for the sake of the 20 already announced. If he had time, he would probably declare, 'Royal Marriage, forty, and twenty to score.' On winning another trick, he would add the A 10 J of trumps and announce, 'Two-fifty in trumps, and twenty to score,' still carrying on the small score for a future opportunity.

A player can lay down and score eighty Kings, and afterwards sixty Queens, whereby the remaining Kings form marriages. In this case, he would score the sixty points first and declare the two or three marriages remaining. In the same way, he can have announced four Kings, and after playing away two of them, leaving two Kings of spades, he can declare double bézique and claim the two marriages 'to score'. In all these cases it has to be remembered that the cards declared must still be on the table when the time comes to score them. If, in the case just given, one of the cards forming either of the marriages was gotten rid of in the course of play, that marriage could not afterwards be scored, although it had been properly announced. If the stock is exhausted before the player who has a score in abeyance can win another trick, the score is lost.

It is often very important for a player to know how much time he has to score. When the talon is spread, it is comparatively easy to judge how many more tricks remain to be played. The English laws allow a player to count the stock; the French do not. A trick once turned and quitted cannot again be seen, and the players are not allowed to count the number of tricks they have won.

The last card of the stock is taken by the player who wins the trick, and the turn-up trump goes to his adversary.

THE LAST EIGHT TRICKS When the stock is exhausted, the players take back into their hands all the cards remaining of the combinations that have been laid on the table. The winner of the previous trick then leads any card he pleases, but his adversary now has to not only follow suit; he has to win the trick if he can, with either a superior card of the same suit or a trump. The same rule applies to all the remaining tricks. Brisques still count for the winner of the trick that contains them, and should be scored as soon as made. The winner of the last trick of all scores ten points for it immediately, in addition to any brisques it might contain.

IRREGULARITIES IN PLAY If a player leads out of turn, and his adversary plays to the lead, whether intentionally or otherwise, the trick stands good. If the adversary calls attention to the error, the card led out of turn can be taken back without penalty.

If a player has too many cards after playing to the first trick, his adversary can either claim a fresh deal or compel him to play without drawing from the talon, until the number of cards in his hand is reduced to eight; the player who has too many cards is not allowed to make any announcements until he has his right number of cards. If a player has too few cards, his adversary can either claim a fresh deal or allow him to make good the deficiency by drawing from the stock.

After the stock is exhausted, any player who fails to follow suit or to win a trick, when his is able to do so, can be compelled to take back his cards to the point where the error occurred, and to re-play the hand. In France, he is penalised by counting nothing from that point onwards, for either brisques or the last trick.

IRREGULARITIES IN DRAWING   If a player has forgotten to take a card from the talon, and has played to the next trick, his adversary can elect to call the deal void, or to allow him to draw two cards next time.

If a player has drawn two cards from the stock, instead of one, he has to show the second one to his adversary if he has seen it himself. If he has not seen it, he can put it back without penalty. If he draws out of turn, he has to restore the card improperly drawn, and if it belongs to his adversary, the player in error has to show his own card. If both players draw the wrong cards, there is no remedy.

If the loser of any trick draws and looks at two cards from the stock, his adversary can look at both cards of the following draw, and can select either for himself. If he chooses the second card, he does not have to show it.

If, on account of some undetected irregularity, an even number of cards remains in the stock, the last card must not be drawn. The winner of the trick takes the last but one, and the loser takes the trump card.

IRREGULAR ANNOUNCEMENTS   If a player announces four of a kind and has only three, as, for example, laying down three Kings and a Jack and declaring four Kings, his adversary can compel him not only to take down the score erroneously marked but to lead or play one of the three Kings. A player can be called on to lead or play cards from any other erroneous declarations in the same way; however, if the player has the right card or cards in his hand, he is permitted to amend his error, provided he has not drawn a card from the stock in the meantime.

SCORING   It is better to score all points as soon as they are made. The game is usually 1000 points. Some players do not count the brisques until the last trick has been played, but the practice is not to be recommended. Scores erroneously marked have to be taken down, and the adversary can add the points to his own score.

Suggestions for Good Play will be found under Binocle.

— —

FOUR-HANDED BÉZIQUE

In this variation, four people can play: each for himself, or two against two, whereby partners sit opposite each other. Four packs of thirty-two cards each are shuffled together and used as one pack. Triple bézique counts 1500. When a player wins a trick, either he or his partner can declare everything in the hand, but only one combination can be scored at a time. The advantage of showing all the combinations in the hand is that they can be built up by either partner. For example, one partner has declared bézique and royal marriage, and scores the marriage only. His partner wins the next trick and adds A 10 J to the marriage, thereby scoring the sequence, or perhaps shows three Kings or Queens, thereby making fours.

The players usually divide after the stock is exhausted, and for the last eight tricks, each takes one of his former adversaries for a partner, but without changing seats. The game is usually 2000 points up.

— —

THREE-HANDED BÉZIQUE

Three people play, each for himself. Two packs of thirty-two cards each and one of thirty-one cards are shuffled together. Triple bézique counts 1500, and the game is usually 2000 points.

The deleted card from the third pack should be an Eight.

— —

POLISH BÉZIQUE

This differs from the ordinary game in only the value of the tricks taken. The winner of each trick, rather than turn it down after counting the brisques, takes from it any court-cards it might contain, and the Ten of trumps. He lays these cards face upwards on the table, apart from the cards declared from his own hand, and uses them to form combinations, which may be scored in the usual way. The main difference is that cards so taken in tricks cannot be led or played to subsequent tricks; nor can they be taken in hand at the end of the stock. Combinations can be completed either by cards in the player's hand or by cards won in subsequent tricks.

— —

CINQ-CENTS

This might be described as Bézique using one pack of cards. All the regulations are the same as in the modern form of Bézique, but there is an additional count: 120, for a sequence of the five highest cards in any plain suit. Bézique is called *Binage*, and naturally there are no double combinations. Cards that have been used in one combination cannot be used in any other, even of a different class.

Brisques are not scored as they are won, but after the hand is over and ten points have been counted for the last trick, each player turns over his cards and counts up the value of the points they contain. In this final count, the Ace reckons for 11, the Ten for 10, the King for 4, the Queen for 3, and the Jack for 2, no matter what the suit, so that there are 120 points to be divided between the players. It is usual for only one to count, whereby the other takes the difference between his total and 120.

From this it might be imagined that no notice was taken of the counting value of the cards taken in during the progress of the play. Early in the game this is true, but towards the end, each player has to keep very careful mental count of the value of his tricks, although he is not allowed to score them. When either player knows, by adding the mental count of his tricks to his scored declarations, that he has made enough points to win the game, he stops the play by knocking on the table, with either his knuckles or his cards. He then turns over his tricks and counts the points they contain in order to show his adversary he has won the game. Even if his adversary also has enough points to go out, the player who knocked wins the game, provided his count is correct. If the player who knocks is mistaken, and cannot count out, he loses, no matter what his adversary has.

If neither player knocks, and at the end of the hand both players are found to have enough points to put them out, neither player wins the game, which has to be continued for 100 points more; that is, because 500 points are the usual game, they have to be made 600 in this case. If both players reach 600 without knocking, the game has to be continued to 700. If neither player knocks, and only one player has enough points to go out, he wins the game on its merits.

As the name implies, 500 points are game.

—•—

PENCHANT

Penchant is a complicated form of Cinq-cents and Bézique. It is played with a single pack of thirty-two cards, which rank as at Piquet: A K Q J 10 9 8 7, whereby the ace is highest in both cutting and play.

CUTTING The higher cut has the choice of seats, and the lower cut deals the first hand.

DEALING After the cards have been cut by the pone, the dealer gives one card to his adversary, then one to the stock, and then one to himself, all face downwards. Two more cards are then given to the stock, one card to the pone, two cards to the stock again, and one card to the dealer. This is continued, whereby two cards are given to the stock between the ones given to each player, until the last round, when only one card is dealt to the stock. This will result in each player's receiving six cards, and twenty cards being left in the centre of the table for the talon. No trump is turned. Very few players trouble themselves with this method of dealing: they prefer to deal three cards to each player alternately, and leave the remaining twenty for the stock.

PLAYING All the regulations for leading, following suit, drawing from the talon and so on are the same as in Bézique, but the declarations and their values are quite different.

BRISQUES There are twelve brisque cards, and the Seven of each suit is added to the usual Aces and Tens. The brisques are not scored as taken in, except in the last six tricks. At the end of the hand, all the brisques are counted, whether or not already scored in the last six tricks, and the player who has more than six brisques counts ten points for each above six. If each has six brisques, neither scores. By this method, a player can make and score several brisques in the last six tricks, all of which he will reckon over again in the total count at the end.

DECLARATIONS The winner of any trick, previous to the exhaustion of the stock, can announce and lay on the table any one of ten combinations, which are divided into three classes. These are as follows, including the number of points he is entitled to score for each.

CLASS A: DIFFERENT SUITS

Any four of a kind, such as four Tens 100
Any three of a kind, such as three Queens 30
Any pair, such as two Nines 20

CLASS B: THE SAME SUIT

Any sequence of five, that contains K Q J 250
Any sequence of four, that contains K Q J 40
Any sequence of K Q J 30
King and Queen of any suit 20
Queen and Jack of any suit 20
Any flush of five cards that contains K Q J 50

CLASS C: PENCHANTS

Any Queen and Jack of different suits 10

The sequences and flushes in class B all have to be of the same suit, and penchant cards have to be of different suits.

If the winner of any trick has no declaration to make, he signifies it by drawing the top card from the stock. His adversary, before drawing his card from the stock, can then declare a penchant, if he has one; however, no other combination can be declared by the player who does not win the trick. If the winner of the trick makes any declaration, the loser cannot declare.

The Jack of the first penchant declared makes the *trump suit* for that deal, no matter which player announces it. Trumps do not increase the value of any combination, and are useful only to win plain-suit tricks.

All declarations are scored immediately, either on a marker or with counters. It will be observed that with the exception of sequences of five cards, fours and penchants, the count is ten points for each card in the combination. Only one declaration can be made at a time.

Any card laid on the table for one declaration can be used again in future declarations, provided the player who makes the new announcement adds at least one fresh card from his hand. A player who has a marriage and a penchant on the table cannot afterwards score for the pair of Queens, but if he adds a Queen from his hand, he can score the triplet.

Pairs, triplets and fours are divided into two classes, whereby the major is formed of court-cards and the minor is formed of cards below the Jack. Minor combinations cannot be scored if the adversary has on the table cards that form a major combination of the same or greater value in the same class, that is, in class A. For example, if your adversary has two Queens on the table, you cannot announce any pair below Jacks. His Queens do not have to have been announced as a pair: they can be parts of a marriage and a penchant. However, if you have on the table a pair as good as his, you can score minor pairs. For example, he has two Kings on the table, and you have two Aces. Your Aces cancel his Kings, and you can score any minor pair, but he cannot. If you have a minor triplet to declare, such as three Eights, no major pair of his will bar it, because your triplet counts more than his pair. No minor combination on his side will bar you; it has to be one of court-cards, and it has to be better than any cards you have laid on the table yourself.

THE LAST SIX TRICKS　　After the stock is exhausted, the second player has to follow suit if he is able, and has to win the trick if he can. As already explained, brisques won in the last six tricks are scored as they are taken in, and after the last card is played, all the brisques are re-counted, whereby the player who holds more than six scores ten points for each above that number. There is no score for winning the last trick.

Four deals are a game At the end of the fourth deal, the lower score is deducted from the higher, and the difference is the value of the game in points. If the lesser score is not at least 400 points, the winner doubles the difference in his favour.

In the only textbook about this game, many technical terms are introduced that have no meaning to the ordinary card player, and that have therefore been omitted from this description.

Suggestions for Good Play are found under Binocle.

— —

RUBICON BÉZIQUE

Rubicon Bézique bears the same relation to the ordinary game that Railroad Euchre does to Euchre proper; in fact, the game might well be called Railroad Bézique, because its main peculiarity is the rapid accumulation of large scores. The game seems to have originated in France, but is now very popular wherever Bézique is played.

CARDS　　Rubicon Bézique is played with four piquet packs of thirty-two cards each, and all cards below the Sevens are deleted from an ordinary pack. The four packs, which should be of the same pattern and colour, are shuffled together and used as one pack. The cards rank A 10 K Q J 9 8 7, and the ace is the highest, in both cutting and play.

MARKERS   The game can be kept on a bézique marker, a pull-up cribbage board or with counters. Markers have to be made to score at least 5000 points. When a cribbage board is used, it is usual to count the outside row of pegs as 10 each, the inner row as 100 each, and the game pegs in the centre as 1000 each. If counters are used, there have to be for each player four white to mark 10's, one red to mark 50, nine blue to mark 100s, and four copper to mark 1000 each. These counters are moved from left to right of the player as the points accrue. In whatever way the count is kept, it should be distinctly visible to both people, because playing to the score is very important.

STAKES   Rubicon Bézique is played for so much a hundred points, and in settling up, all fractions of a hundred are disregarded, unless they are necessary to decide the game. Ten cents a hundred was the usual stake, and sixpence in England. Games are seldom worth fewer than one or two thousand points.

PLAYERS   Rubicon Bézique is played by two people, one of whom is known as the *dealer* and the other as the *pone*. They cut for seats and deal, and the player who cuts the higher card has first choice and elects whether or not to deal himself. In cutting, the cards rank as in play, and the ace is the highest. If a player exposes more than one card, he has to cut again.

DEALING   The cards are thoroughly shuffled and presented to the pone to cut. At least five cards have to be left in each packet. The dealer then distributes the cards three at a time, first to his adversary and then to himself, for three rounds, so each player receives nine cards. No trump is turned, but the first marriage declared and scored is the trump suit for that deal. The undealt portion of the pack, called the *stock* or *talon*, is slightly spread between the two players and slightly to the left of the dealer. If in spreading the stock any card is found to be exposed, there has to be a new deal by the same dealer.

MISDEALING   A misdeal does not lose the deal, but in some cases a new deal is at the option of the pone. If the dealer exposes a card that belongs to his adversary or the stock, the pone can demand a new deal, but if either player exposes any of his own cards, the deal stands good. If too many cards are given to either player, and the error is discovered before the dealer plays to the first trick, there has to be a new deal. If either player has too few cards, the pone can demand a new deal, or can allow the dealer to supply the deficiency from the top of the stock. If any card is found to be exposed in the pack, there has to be a new deal. If any card faced in the stock is not discovered until the first trick has been played to by the dealer, the exposed card has to be turned face downwards, without disturbing its position. If the pack is found to be imperfect, the deal in which it is discovered is void, but all previous scores or cuts made with that pack stand good.

METHOD OF PLAYING The pone takes up and examines his nine cards. If he finds himself to be without King, Queen or Jack of any suit, he immediately shows his hand to the dealer, and marks fifty points for *carte blanche*. Whether or not he has carte blanche, he begins the play by leading any card he pleases. If the dealer has carte blanche, he has to show and score it before playing to the first trick. Players are not obliged to follow suit, nor to trump, but can renounce or trump at pleasure until the stock is exhausted, after which the method of play undergoes a change. Until the first marriage is declared and scored, there is no trump suit. If the second player in any trick follows suit, the higher card wins. Trumps win plain suits. If identical cards are played to the same trick, such as two club aces, the leader wins.

The tricks are left face upwards on the table until an ace or a Ten is played, because tricks that do not contain either of these cards are of no value. When an ace or a Ten is played, the winner of the trick gathers in all the cards that have accumulated, and turns them face downwards in front of him. These counting cards are called *brisques*, and if a player neglects to gather the brisques he wins, his adversary can do so when he next wins a trick, whether or not the trick he wins contains a brisque: the fact that there is a brisque on the table is sufficient.

DECLARING The winner of any trick, before leading for the next trick, has the privilege of announcing and scoring any one of specific combinations he might hold in his hand. After this, or in the absence of any announcement, and before leading for the next trick, he draws one card from the top of the stock, and places it in his hand, without showing or naming it. His adversary then draws the next card, so that each restores the number of cards in his hand to nine. This method of playing, announcing and drawing is continued until the stock is exhausted.

If a player who has already announced carte blanche finds that the first card he draws from the stock is not a King, Queen or Jack, he shows it to his adversary, and scores another fifty points for another carte blanche. This can be continued until he draws one of these cards. Carte blanche cannot be scored at all unless it is held before a card is played; that is, it has to be dealt to the player originally.

All combinations announced and scored have to be left face upwards on the table, but the cards still form part of the player's hand, and can be led or played at any time, although they must not again be taken in hand until the stock is exhausted.

The first marriage announced and scored, no matter by which player, makes the *trump suit* for that deal; however, a player who has a marriage on the table is not obliged to announce it if he does not wish to make that suit the trump.

IRREGULARITIES IN PLAY   If a player leads out of turn, and his adversary plays to the lead, whether intentionally or otherwise, the trick stands good. If the adversary calls attention to the error, the card led out of turn can be taken back without penalty.

If, after playing to the first trick, one player is found to have more than his right number of cards, the English rules state that the game is to be immediately abandoned, and the adversary of the player in error is to add 1300 points to his score at the time the error is discovered, together with all the points already scored by the player in error; however, the latter amount must not exceed 900.

The same penalties are enforced if one player has too many cards and the other too few, but in the latter case, the hand is played out, and the player not in fault scores all he can.

If both players have more than their right number of cards, the deal is void. If either has less than his proper number, and his adversary has the right number, the deal stands good, and there is no penalty except that the player who has the right number of cards wins and scores for the last trick. If both players have fewer than the right number, the deal stands good, and the actual winner of the last trick scores it.

It will be observed that these rules are quite different from the French rules, which have been given in connection with the ordinary game of Bézique. In France, it is always the custom to establish the *status quo*, if possible, and to assume that the error was quite unintentional. In England, all laws are based on the assumption that your adversary is a rogue, and the penalties are absurdly severe, but we have no authority to change them.

IRREGULARITIES IN DRAWING   If a player has forgotten to take his card from the talon, and has played to the next trick, the English laws compel him to play the remainder of the hand with eight cards; the French laws give his adversary the option of calling the deal void or of allowing the player in error to draw two cards from the stock next time.

If a player draws two cards from the stock, instead of one, he has to show the second card to his adversary if he has seen it himself. If it was his adversary's card, he has to also show his own card. If he has not seen it, he can put it back without penalty. If he draws out of turn, he can restore the card improperly drawn, and if it belongs to his adversary, the player in error has to show his own card. If both players draw the wrong cards, there is no remedy.

If the loser of any trick draws and looks at two cards from the stock, his adversary can look at both cards of the following draw, and can select either card for himself. If he chooses the second card, he does not have to show it.

If, on account of some undetected irregularity, an odd number of cards remain in the stock, the last card must not be drawn.

OBJECTS OF THE GAME   Each game is complete in one deal, and the score of the loser is deducted from that of the winner. The combinations that can may be declared and scored are the same as in Bézique, but owing to the use of four packs of cards, double combinations are much more frequent, and triple combinations are not uncommon.

The main concern of the player has to be, first of all, to save himself from a rubicon, that is, either to reach 1000 points or to score as few points as possible. If he does not reach 1000, his adversary will take whatever points he has scored and add them to his own, besides 1300 in addition for rubicon and brisques. For example, at the end of the hand, A has scored 1200, and B has only 700. B is rubiconed, and his 700 points are added to A's 1200, together with 1300 more for a rubicon game and brisques, whereby A is given a grand total of 3200 points to nothing. Had B reached 1000, he would have saved his rubicon, and A would have scored the difference only, or 200 points, plus 500 for the game: 700 altogether.

BRISQUES   The aces and Tens of each suit are of no value unless it is necessary to count them in order to either decide a tie or save a rubicon. They are never scored during the play of the hand.

DECLARATIONS   The combinations that can be announced and scored during the play of the hand are divided into three classes: A, Marriages and Sequences; B, Béziques; and C, Fours. Only one combination can be scored at a time, and it has to be announced and laid on the table immediately after the player who holds it has won a trick and before he draws his card from the talon. If he draws without announcing, it is equivalent to saying he has no declaration to make. Having drawn his card, even if he has not looked at it, he cannot score any declaration until he wins another trick. The various combinations and their values are as follows.

CLASS A

King and Queen in any plain suit: *Marriage* 20
King and Queen of trumps: *Royal Marriage* 40
Five highest cards in a plain suit: *Sequence* 150
Five highest cards in trumps: *Royal Sequence* 250

CLASS B

Spade Queen and Diamond Jack: *Single Bézique* 40
Two spade Queens and diamond Jacks: *Double Bézique* 500
Three spade Queens and diamond Jacks: *Triple Bézique*   1500
Four spade Queens and diamond Jacks:
    Quadruple Bézique 4500

CLASS C

Any four Aces 100
Any four Kings 80
Any four Queens 60
Any four Jacks 40

Besides the aforementioned combinations, there is the score of fifty points for carte blanche, which can be announced only before the first trick is played to, and the score of fifty points for the winner of the last trick of all.

In class A, the first marriage declared naturally has to count 40, because it is the trump suit for that deal. In class C, the four court-cards can be of different suits, or any two or more of them can be of the same suit.

The rules governing declarations are as follows.

The player who makes the declaration has to have won the previous trick, and has to make his announcement before drawing his card from the stock. When the stock is exhausted, so that no cards remain to be drawn, no announcements can be made.

Only one declaration can be scored at a time, so that a trick has to be won for every announcement made, or the combination cannot be scored. This rule does not prevent a player from making two or more announcements at the same time, but he can score only one of them.

A player cannot make a lower declaration with cards that form part of a higher combination already shown in the same class. For example, marriages and sequences belong to the same class. If a sequence has been declared, the player cannot take from it the King and Queen, and score for the marriage; nor can he add a new Queen to the King already used in the sequence, because the higher combination was scored first. The same rule applies to lower and higher béziques. However, if the lower combination is first shown and scored – the marriage – the A 10 J can be added afterwards, on winning another trick, and the sequence can be scored. This rule does not apply to cards that belong to combinations in different classes. A Queen used in class A can be used over again in both the B class and the C class.

RE-FORMING COMBINATIONS The main peculiarity of Rubicon Bézique is that combinations that have been laid on the table and scored can be broken up, re-formed and scored again indefinitely. For example, a player has declared royal sequence, and scored 250 points for it. He can play away the Ace, thereby breaking up the sequence, and on winning the trick can lay down another Ace, thereby re-forming the sequence and scoring 250 points again. He might repeat the process with the Ten, King, Queen and Jack, and in six successive tricks would score this royal sequence six times, thereby making 1500 points out of it. In actual play, it is not necessary to go through the formality of playing away a card from the combination on the table and then replacing it, because it amounts to the same thing if the new card in the hand is led or played and the fresh combination is claimed.

Marriages, béziques and fours can be broken up and re-formed in the same way. After declaring 100 Aces, the player can lead or play another Ace, and claim another 100 Aces, thereby scoring them when he wins a trick. In this way, eight Aces actually held might score 500 points. In the bézique combinations, a new card simply re-forms the single bézique. In order to score double, triple or quadruple bézique, all the cards that form the combination have to be on the table at one time, but can be played and scored one after the other, cumulatively. For example, a player who holds quadruple bézique and who shows all eight cards at once would score 4500 only; the minor béziques would be lost. If he had time, and could win enough tricks, he might show the single first, thereby scoring 40; then the double, thereby scoring 500; then the triple, thereby scoring 1500; and finally the quadruple, thereby scoring 4500; whereby he would be yielded a grand total of 6540 points. He might declare marriage in hearts, and afterwards play three more heart Queens, thereby scoring each marriage, and then three heart Kings, thereby scoring three more marriages. These would all be new combinations.

DOUBLE DECLARATIONS   These are carried forward in the way already described for the ordinary game. Suppose a player has two spade Kings on the table, and shows double bézique. He naturally marks the more valuable score: 500, and simply claims the marriages by saying, 'With twenty and twenty to score.' On winning another trick, he is not compelled to score the previous announcement if he has any other or better to make. He might have two more Queens, and would announce, 'Sixty Queens, with twenty and twenty to score.' If he scores one of the announcements held over, he still carries on the other announcement.

When announcements are carried forward in this way, it has to be remembered that the cards have to still be on the table when the time comes to score them. If one of them has been led or played, or the stock is exhausted before the player wins another trick, the score held over is lost.

TIME   On account of the great number of combinations possible in Rubicon Bézique, it is very seldom that a player succeeds in scoring everything he holds. He is allowed to count the cards remaining in the talon, provided he does not disturb their order. This count is often important towards the end of the hand. For example, you know from the cards you hold, and from the ones played, that your adversary has to have in his hand the cards that will make a double bézique on the table into a triple bézique, which would give him 1500 points. If, on counting the stock, you find only six cards remain, and you have three specific winning trumps to lead, you can shut out his 1500 by exhausting the stock before he can win a trick.

IRREGULAR ANNOUNCEMENTS   If a player announces a combination that he does not show, such as fours when he has only three, which he might easily do by mistaking a Jack for a King, his adversary can compel him to not only take down the score erroneously marked but lead or play one of the three Kings. A player can be called on to lead or play cards from other erroneous declarations in the same way; however, if he has the right card or cards in his hand, he is permitted to amend his error, provided he has not drawn a card from the stock in the meantime.

THE LAST NINE TRICKS When the stock is exhausted, all announcements are at an end, and the players take back into their hands all the cards on the table that might remain from the combinations declared in the course of play. The winner of the previous trick then leads any card he pleases, but for the last nine tricks, the second player in each not only has to follow suit; he has to win the trick if he can, with either a superior card or a trump. Any player who fails to follow suit or to win a trick, when he is able to do so, can be compelled to take back his cards to the point at which the error occurred, and to replay the hand from that point onwards. In France, he is penalised by way of counting nothing from that point onwards, for either brisques or the last trick.

The winner of the *last trick* scores fifty points for it immediately.

SCORING Each deal is a complete game in itself, and the winner is the player who has scored the most points for carte blanche, combinations and the last trick. The brisques are not counted, unless they are necessary in order to either decide a tie or save a rubicon.

The value of the game is determined by way of deducting the lower score from the higher, and then adding 500 points to the remainder. In this deduction, all fractions of a hundred are disregarded. For example, A's score is 1830, and B's is 1260. A wins 1800, minus the 1200 scored by B, which leaves 600; to this have to be added the 500 points for game, whereby the total value of A's game is made 1100 points.

If the scores are very nearly equal, being within one or two hundred points of each other, the tricks taken in by each player are turned over, and the brisques are counted, whereby each player adds to his score ten points for every brisque he has won. Suppose that after the last trick had been played and scored, A's total was 1260 and B's 1140. This is close enough to justify B in demanding a count of the brisques. It is found that A has seven only, whereas B has twenty-five. This shows B to be the winner of the game: he has a total score of 1390 to A's 1330.

If the difference between the final scores is fewer than 100 points, after adding the brisques and throwing off the fractions, the player who has the higher score adds 100 points for bonus. In the case just given, B's final score is equal to A's, after dropping the fractions from both, so he would add 100 for bonus to the 500 for game and win 600 points altogether.

RUBICONS If the lower score is fewer than 1000 points, no matter what the higher score is, the loser is rubiconed, and all the points he has scored are *added* to the score of the winner rather than deducted.

In addition to this, the winner adds a double game, or 1000 points, for the rubicon, and 300 points for all the brisques, no matter who actually won them. For example, A's score is 920 and B's 440. It is not necessary to count the brisques in order to see that A wins and B is rubiconed. A adds B's 400 to his own 900, thereby making his score 1300, and to this total he adds 1300 for rubicon and brisques, thereby making the value of his game 2600 points altogether.

The loser is not rubiconed if he can bring his total score to 1000 by adding his brisques. Suppose A has 1740 and B 850. The brisques are counted, and it is found that B has eighteen, thereby making his score 1030 and saving his rubicon. A adds his fourteen brisques, therby making his total 1880, thereby making the value of his game 1800, minus B's 1000, plus 500 for the game, or 1300 altogether.

If B's brisques did not prove sufficient to save the rubicon, A would count them all. Suppose that in the foregoing case B had taken in only eleven brisques, thereby leaving his total 990. Because this does not save the rubicon, the game is reckoned as if the brisques had not been counted at all, and A wins 1800, plus B's 800, plus 1300 for rubicon and brisques: 3900 altogether.

If the player who is rubiconed has scored fewer than 100 points, the winner takes 100 for bonus, in addition to the 1300 for rubicon and brisques.

When a series of games is played between the same individuals, it is usual to keep the net results on a sheet of paper, whereby the hundreds only are set down, and to settle at the end of the sitting.

Suggestions for Good Play are found under Binocle.

CHINESE BÉZIQUE   This is Rubicon Bézique whereby six packs of cards are shuffled together and used as one pack. The counts run into enormous figures, and 6000 is not an uncommon score for the winner.

In *CHOUETTE BÉZIQUE,* one of several players agrees to take all bets, and has the choice of deal and seats without cutting. His adversaries can consult in playing against him. If the chouette player wins, one of his opponents takes the loser's place, but if he loses, the same player opposes him for the next game. The adversaries usually cut in order to decide which of them will play the first game against the chouette player, whereby the highest card has the privilege. If there are four players, two can play against two, and each player consults with his partner and shares his bets.

BINOCLE

—•—

The word *Binocle* is spelt in many ways, all of which are, however, phonetic equivalents of the correct way. The word is probably derived from the French word *binage*, which was the name given to the combination known as *binocle*, and which seemed to be a better term than *cinq cents*, because the game was no longer 500 points up. In all German works about card games, the name is spelt as we spell it in this book, but the pronunciation of the initial *b* in the German is so near that of *p* that *Pinocle* is nearer the correct spelling than any other form. There is no authority for the introduction of the *h*, whereby some people have been led to think that the word is a compound of *bis* and *knochle* and has given rise to the forms *binochle*, *pinochle*, *pinuchle*, *pinucle*, *penucle*, *penuchle*, *penuckle* and *pinuckel*, all of which can be found in various works about card games.

CARDS   Binocle is played with two packs of twenty-four cards each, whereby all cards below the Nine are deleted and the two packs are then shuffled together and used as one pack. The cards rank A 10 K Q J 9, and the Ace is the highest, in both cutting and play.

COUNTERS   The game is 1000 points, and is usually scored using counters, whereby each player is provided with four white counters worth 10 each, four blue counters worth 100 each, one red counter worth 50, and a coin or button that represents 500. These counters are placed on the left of the player at the beginning of the game, and are moved over to his right as the points accrue. The game is sometimes kept on a cribbage board, whereby each player starts at 21 and goes twice around to the game-hole, and each peg is reckoned as 10 points.

STAKES   Binocle is played for so much a game of 1000 points, and the moment either player either actually reaches or claims to have reached that number, the game is at an end. If his claim is correct, he wins; if it is not, his adversary takes the stakes, no matter what the score is.

PLAYERS   Binocle is played by two people, one of whom is known as the dealer and the other as the pone. They cut for the choice of seats and deal, and the player who cuts the higher card can deal or not, as he pleases. It is usual for the player who has the choice to make his adversary deal. A player who exposes more than one card has to cut again.

DEALING   After the cards are thoroughly shuffled, they are presented to the pone to cut. At least five cards have to be left in each packet. The dealer then distributes the cards four at a time for three rounds, whereby he gives to his adversary first and then to himself. The twenty-fifth card is turned up for the trump. If this card is a Nine, the dealer claims *dix*, and counts ten for it immediately. The trump card is laid aside, and the remainder of the pack, which is called the *stock*, or *talon*, is slightly spread, in order to facilitate the process of drawing cards from it, and to be sure that none of the cards remaining in the stock is exposed. The trump is usually placed face upwards under the last card of the stock.

In *64-card Binocle*, the Sevens and Eights are added to the pack. There are then two ways to play. If eight cards are dealt to each player, the game is simply Bézique, except for some minor details related to the combinations and their value; these are usually disregarded, and the regular game of Bézique is played. If twelve cards are dealt to each player, the game is the same as the one about to be described, but eight cards are added to the pack, and the Seven takes the place of the Nine for dix.

MISDEALING   If the dealer exposes a card that belongs to either his adversary or the stock, the pone can demand a new deal, but if either player exposes any of his own cards, the deal stands good. If too many cards are given to either player, and the error is discovered before the dealer plays to the first trick, there has to be a new deal. If either player has too few cards, the pone can demand a new deal, or can allow the dealer to supply the deficiency from the top of the stock. If any card is found to be exposed in the pack, there has to be a new deal. If a card faced in the stock is not discovered until the first trick has been played to by the dealer, the exposed card has to be turned face downwards, without disturbing its position. If the pack is found to be imperfect, the deal in which it is discovered is void, but all previous scores and cuts made with that pack stand good. In all misdeals, the same dealer deals again.

METHOD OF PLAYING After the trump is turned, the pone begins by leading any card he pleases. The second player is not obliged to follow suit, nor to trump, but can renounce or trump at pleasure until the stock is exhausted, after which the method of play undergoes a change. If the second player follows suit in any trick, the higher card wins. Trumps win plain suits. If identical cards are played to the same trick, such as two club Jacks, the leader wins.

The winner of the trick takes in the cards, and turns them face downwards, but before he leads for the next trick, he has the privilege of announcing and scoring any one of specific combinations he might hold in his hand. After this, or in the absence of any announcement, and before leading for the next trick, he draws a card from the top of the stock, and places it in his hand, without showing or naming it. His adversary then draws the next card, so that each player restores the number of cards in his hand to twelve. This method of playing, announcing and drawing from the talon is continued until the stock is exhausted. The A 10 K Q J of each suit have specific counting values, which will be described further on.

All combinations announced and scored have to be laid face upwards on the table; however, the cards still form part of the player's hand, and can be led or played at any time, although they must not again be taken in hand until the stock is exhausted.

IRREGULARITIES IN PLAY If either player leads out of turn, and his adversary plays to the lead, whether intentionally or otherwise, the trick stands good. If the adversary calls attention to the error, the card can be taken back without penalty.

If at any time it is discovered that a player has too many cards, his adversary can either claim a fresh deal or compel him to play without drawing from the talon until the number of his cards is reduced to twelve. The player who has too many cards is not allowed to make or score any announcements until he has his right number of cards. If a player has too few cards, his adversary can either claim a fresh deal or allow him to make good the deficiency by drawing from the stock.

Any player who looks at any but the last trick turned down forfeits his entire score for 'cards'.

IRREGULARITIES IN DRAWING If a player has forgotten to take a card from the talon, and has played to the next trick, his adversary can elect to either call the deal void or allow him to draw two cards next time.

If a player has drawn two cards from the stock instead of one, he has to show the second card to his adversary if he has seen it himself. If it was his adversary's card, he has to show his own card also. If he has not seen it, he can put it back without penalty. If he draws out of turn, he has to restore the card improperly drawn, and if it belongs to his adversary, the player in error has to show his own card. If both draw the wrong cards, there is no remedy, and each has to keep what he gets. If the loser of any trick draws and looks at two cards from the stock, his adversary can look at both cards of the following draw, and can select either for himself. If he chooses the second card, which his adversary has not seen, he does not have to show it.

If, on account of some undetected irregularity, an even number of cards remains in the stock, the last card must not be drawn. The winner of the trick takes the last card but one, and the loser takes the trump card.

OBJECTS OF THE GAME   The aim of each player is to reach 1000 points before his adversary does, and the one who first reaches that number and announces it wins the game. Points are scored for *dix*, *melds*, the *last trick* and *cards*, which are the counting cards in tricks won.

MELDS   The various combinations that are declared during the play of the hand are called *melds*, from the German word *melden*: 'to announce'. These melds are divided into three classes: *A*, Marriages and Sequences; *B*, Binocles; and *C*, Fours. Only one combination can be announced at a time, and it has to be melded immediately after the player who holds it has won a trick, and before he draws his card from the stock. If he draws without announcing, even if he has not seen the card drawn, he cannot meld anything until he wins another trick. The melds and their values are as follows.

CLASS A

King and Queen of any plain suit: *Marriage*	20
King and Queen of Trumps: *Royal Marriage*	40
The five highest trumps: *Sequence*	150

CLASS B

Spade Queen and diamond Jack: *Binocle*	40
Two spade Queens and diamond Jacks: *Double Binocle*	80
King and Queen of spades, and diamond Jack: *Grand Binocle*	80

CLASS C

Four Aces of different suits	100
Four Kings of different suits	80
Four Queens of different suits	60
Four Jacks of different suits	40
Eight Aces	200
Eight Kings	160
Eight Queens	120
Eight Jacks	80

The third meld in class B is not often played in the United States. The count for it is the same: 80 points, whether or not the marriage in spades is the trump suit. It will be observed that the court-cards in class C have to be of different suits in Binocle, whereas in Bézique, any four court-cards can be declared. The following rules govern all classes of declaration.

The player who makes the declaration has to have won the previous trick, and has to meld before drawing his card from the stock. When the stock is exhausted, so that no cards remain to be drawn, no more announcements can be made.

Only one meld can be scored at a time, so that a trick has to be made for every announcement made, or the combination cannot be scored, and a fresh card has to be played from the hand for every fresh meld. This is a very important rule, and not very well understood. Suppose a player holds four Kings and four Queens. The total count for the various combinations these cards will make is 220: two plain-suit marriages, 20 each; royal marriage, 40; four Kings, 80; and four Queens, 60. Because only one combination can be scored for each trick won, and because the player has to lay down at least one fresh card for each successive meld, it is evident that if he begins with the 80 Kings and then marries each of them in turn, when he comes to the fourth Queen, he will have to sacrifice the 20 for a marriage in order to score the 60 for the four Queens. He cannot score both, or he will not be complying with the rule about the fresh card from the hand for every meld. That is why four Kings and four Queens are never worth 240 but only 220.

A player cannot meld cards that have already been used in order to form higher combinations in the same class; however, he can use cards melded in lower combinations in order to form more valuable ones in the same class, provided he adds at least one fresh card from his hand. The principle is that cards can be **added** to melds already shown but cannot be **taken away** in order to form other combinations in the same class. For example, royal marriage has been melded and scored. The player can *add* to this the Ace, Ten and Jack of trumps in order to make the sequence, which is a more valuable combination in the same class. But if the first meld is the sequence, he cannot *take away* from the sequence the card or cards in order to form a marriage. A new Queen added to the King already in the sequence will not make a marriage, because it is not the Queen that is added to the sequence but the King that is taken away.

The same rule applies to the binocles. If a player has scored double binocle, he cannot afterwards take away two cards in order to meld a single binocle; however, if the single binocle has been melded and scored first, he can add two more cards and score the double binocle. He cannot score the second single and then claim the double, because a new card has to be added in order to form a new meld in the same class.

If four Kings are melded and scored, the other four can be added later, but if the eight Kings are first melded, the score for the four Kings is lost.

Cards can be taken away from one combination in order to form less valuable combinations in another class. For example, four Jacks have been melded; the diamond Jack can be taken away in order to form a binocle with the spade Queen. If spades are trumps, and the sequence has been melded, the Queen can be taken away in order to form a binocle, because the binocle is in a different class of melds; however, the Queen cannot be used to form a marriage, because the sequence and the marriage are in the same class. Because there are three classes, one card can be used three separate times. The spade Queen, for example, can be used in a marriage in binocle and in four Queens, and these melds can be made in any order.

Cards once used in combinations cannot again be used in melds of equal value that belong to the same class, and combinations once broken up cannot be re-formed by way of addition of fresh cards. For example, four Kings have been melded, and one of them has been used in the course of play. The player cannot add a new King to the three remaining and meld four Kings again. A marriage in hearts has been melded, and the King has been played away. A new King will not make another marriage with the old Queen. A binocle has been melded, and the Jack has been played; another Jack will not make a new binocle with the old Queen.

DOUBLE DECLARATIONS When a player makes a meld that contains specific cards that will form a counting combination with other cards already on the table, it is called a *double declaration*, that is, a meld in two classes at the same time. For example, a player has melded and scored four Kings, and on winning another trick, melds binocle. Two of the cards on the table form a marriage in spades, and because the marriage is in a different class from either of the other melds, he can claim it and score it; however, if he does, he will lose the score for the binocle, because he is prevented by way of the rule about a fresh card from the hand for each individual meld. The only way to secure both scores would be to meld the marriage first, and to afterwards lay down the Jack and meld the binocle.

TIME   On account of the number of combinations possible, and the fact that there are only twelve tricks to be played before the scores for announcements are barred, it frequently happens that a player does not have time to score everything he holds. He is allowed to count the cards remaining in the talon, provided he does not disturb their order, and it is often important to do so towards the end of a hand.

SCORING DIX   If a player holds or draws the Nine of trumps, he has the privilege of exchanging it for the turn-up card and of scoring ten points for dix. The exchange has to be made immediately after winning a trick and before drawing his card from the stock. If the turn-up is a Nine, the exchange can still be made and scored, and if one player has already exchanged a Nine for the turn-up, the second Nine can still be exchanged for the first, and scored. A player cannot score dix and any other combination at the same time. For this reason, a player whose time is short will often forego the dix score altogether unless the trump card is valuable.

IRREGULAR MELDS   If a player announces a combination he does not show, such as fours when he has three only, which he can easily do by mistaking a Jack for a King, his adversary can compel him to not only take down the score erroneously marked but lead or play one of the three Kings. A player can be called on to lead or play cards from other erroneous declarations in the same way, but if he has the right card or cards in his hand, he can amend his error, provided he has not drawn a card from the stock in the meantime.

THE LAST TWELVE TRICKS   When the stock is exhausted, all announcements are at an end, and the players take back into their hands all the cards on the table that might remain from the combinations declared in the course of play. If a player takes up his cards before playing to the last trick, he can be called on to lay his entire hand on the table.

The winner of the previous trick then leads any card he pleases; however, for the last twelve tricks, the second player in each not only has to follow suit; he has to win the trick if he can, with either a superior card or a trump. Any player who fails to follow suit or to win a trick, when he is able to do so, can be compelled to take back his cards to the point at which the error occurred, and to replay the hand from that point onwards. The penalty for the *revoke* varies in different places, but the general rule is for the revoking player to lose his entire count for 'cards'.

The winner of *the last trick* scores ten points for it, and the players then turn over the tricks they have taken and count their score for 'cards'.

CARDS The five highest cards in each suit count towards game for the player who wins them. The Ace is worth 11 points, the Ten 10, the King 4, the Queen 3 and the Jack 2, no matter what the suit is, so that there are 240 points for cards to be divided between the players in each deal. It is usual for only one player to count, whereby the other players check him and take the difference between the total and 240. Cards are not scored as the tricks are taken in but after the hand is over and the 10 points have been scored for the last trick.

From this, it might be imagined that no notice was taken of the counting value of the cards taken in during the play. Early in the game, this is true, but towards the end, each player has to keep very careful *mental count* of the value of his tricks, although he is not allowed to make any note of it nor to score it. When either player knows, by adding his mental count to his score for melds and dix, that he has made enough points to win the game, he stops the play by knocking on the table. He then turns over his tricks and counts his cards, in order to show his adversary he has won the game. Even if both adversaries have enough points to go out, the player wins who knocks first, provided his count is correct. If the player who knocks is mistaken, and cannot count out, he loses the game, no matter what his adversary's score is.

If neither adversary knocks, and at the end of the hand both players are found to have points enough to put them out, neither wins the game. If the game is 1000 points, it has to be continued to 1250. If both reach that point without knocking, the game has to be continued to 1500. If neither knocks, and only one has enough points to put him out, he wins the game on its merits.

SCORING The game is usually 1000 points. All scores for dix, melds and the last trick are counted as soon as made; however, the players are not allowed to keep any record of the score for cards nor to go back over their tricks in order to refresh their memory. Any player who goes back further than the last trick turned and quitted forfeits his entire score for cards. The player who first correctly announces he has reached 1000 points wins the game, no matter what his adversary's score may be, but if the announcement is incorrect, he loses the game.

If a player scores more than he is entitled to, as, for example, scoring 80 for four Queens, his adversary can take down the superfluous score, 20 points in this example, and can add it to his own score for a penalty.

CHEATING Apart from the usual weapons of false shuffles, strippers cut in order to locate or pull out the binocle cards, and the opportunities always offered to the cheat when the cards are dealt three or four at a time, the Bézique family of games is especially adapted to use of marked cards. These will show the philosopher the exact value of both the cards in the next draw, and will enable him to vary his play accordingly. It is for this reason that in France the top card of the stock is always drawn by the same player, no matter which card wins the trick. In Rubicon Bézique, a person should be very familiar with the movements peculiar to dealing seconds before he ventures to play in a public venue; otherwise, he might find his adversary with the most astonishing run of repeated combinations, and will be rubiconed almost every game.

Never play with a player who cuts the pack with both hands, watches the cards closely as he deals, or looks intently at the top of the stock before he plays to the current trick. Players who have a nervous affection that makes them pass over too many counters at once also bear watching. Colour blindness can lead them to take over a blue counter instead of a white one in a close game.

SUGGESTIONS FOR GOOD PLAY The general principles of play are much the same in all the Bézique family of games.

It is usually best to give your adversary the deal, because the first lead is often an advantage, especially if the turn-up is valuable, and you have a dix, or if you want to make the trump in Rubicon Bézique.

It is seldom right to make the trump unless you have one or two of the sequence cards with the marriage.

THE LEAD This is a disadvantage unless you have something to declare, or there is a brisque in the trick, or you can get home the Ten of a plain suit. The Tens are of no value in plain suits except as brisques, because they enter into no combination with other cards except in Penchant, Cinq-cents and Rubicon. If the trick is of no value, or you have nothing important to declare, you should get rid of your small cards, and lead them when you do not want to retain the lead. The lead is sometimes necessary in order to prevent your adversary from declaring, especially towards the end of the hand. If you have led a brisque and won the trick, it is better to lead another brisque in the same suit than to change.

Aces are better leads than Kings or Queens, because the court-cards can be married, and you might never get 100 Aces. Kings are better leads than Queens, especially if the Queens are spades. Jacks are better than either, but the Jack of diamonds should be kept as long as possible. If you have to decide between two combinations, one of which you have to sacrifice, lead the one that is of the smaller value, or the one least likely to be restored. For example, if your adversary has shown one or two Kings, but no Ace, and you have three of each, you are more likely to get 100 Aces than 80 Kings.

If you hold duplicate cards, especially in trumps, you should play the card on the table, not the one in your hand.

BRISQUES   Beginners often overlook the importance of brisques. Every time you allow your adversary to take in a brisque you might have won, you make a difference of twenty points in the score. While you are hugging three Aces, waiting for a fourth, your adversary might get home all his Tens, and then turn up with your fourth Ace in his hand.

DISCARDING   It is usually best to settle on one of two suits or combinations, and to discard the others, because you cannot play for everything. Once you have settled on what to play for, it is usually bad policy to change unless something better turns up.

Your adversary's discards will often be a guide as to the combinations he hopes to make, and will show you that you do not have to keep specific cards. For example, if a binocle player discards or plays two heart Kings, it is unlikely he has either of the Queens, and you can reasonably hope for 60 Queens; however, it will be impossible for you to make anything out of your Kings but marriages. In Bézique, in which Kings can be of the same suit in fours, you will have a slightly better chance for 80 Kings on account of your adversary's discards, because he definitely has no more, because he would not break up three Kings.

DECLARING   It is often a nice point to decide whether or not you can afford to make minor declarations while you are holding higher ones in your hand. In Rubicon, many players will give up the trump marriage if they have the sequence, especially with a good chance of re-forming it several times using duplicate cards. The number of cards in hand will often be the best guide. In Rubicon, if you held trump sequence and double bézique, it would be better to declare the sequence first, and to lead the card you drew. One of the trump sequence on the table would then be free to regain the lead and declare the double bézique, but if the bézique were declared first, the sequence might have to be broken into in order to regain the lead. With a plain-suit sequence and four Aces, you should declare the Aces first: they will then be free to win tricks for the purpose of making other declarations.

It is seldom right to show the bézique cards in other combinations, and four Jacks is a very bad meld, because it shows your adversary that he cannot hope for double bézique. By holding up bézique cards, even if you know they are of no use to you, you can lead your adversary to break up his hand, hoping to draw the card or cards you hold.

TRUMPS Small trumps can be used to advantage in winning brisques, but you should keep at least one small trump to get the lead at critical periods of the hand, or to make an important declaration. It is bad policy to trump in to make minor declarations, unless your time is short. It is seldom right to lead the trump Ace, except at the end of the hand, or when you have duplicates; however, leading high trumps to prevent an adversary from declaring more is a common stratagem, if you know from the cards in your hand, and the ones played, that your adversary might get the cards in order to meld something of importance.

THE LAST TRICKS Before you play to the last trick, you should give yourself time to note the cards your adversary has on the table, and should compare them with your own, so you can play the last tricks to advantage. If you wait until after playing to the last trick, he might gather up his cards so quickly that you will be unable to remember them. In Rubicon, it is not always advisable to win the last trick. If your adversary is rubiconed in any case, you can add 100 points to your own score by giving him the 50 for the last trick, whereby he might be put across the line into another hundred.

THREE-HANDED BINOCLE

When three people play, the entire pack is dealt out, whereby sixteen cards are given to each player, four at a time, and the last card is turned up for the trump. There is no stock. Each person plays for himself, and has to keep his own score. A triangular cribbage-board is very useful for this purpose.

DIX   Each player in turn, beginning on the dealer's left, can show the Nine of trumps if he holds it, and exchange it for the trump card. If two Nines are shown by different players, the player on the dealer's left takes the turn-up trump. Even if the dealer has a Nine himself, he is not allowed to keep the turn-up trump. If the same player holds both Nines, he can score twenty on winning a trick. A player who has 990 up is not out if he turns up the Nine. He has to win a trick.

MELDS   All the combinations have the same value as in the ordinary game, but all melds are laid on the table before a card is played. When he lays down his cards, a player can make as many combinations with them as he can, just as he would in the ordinary game if he had plenty of time. If he has the trump sequence, he can lay down the marriage first, then the A 10 J. If he has double binocle, he can lay down the single first, and then the other, and claim the count for both singles. Four Kings and four Queens count 220. The trump sequence counts 190.

No player is allowed to meld after he has played to the first trick. If he discovers he had more to meld, but has played a card, the unannounced score is lost. An interesting variation is sometimes introduced by way of allowing the other players to claim any score overlooked by the one who melds.

The total number of points claimed by each player is announced but not scored. The player has to win a trick before he can score anything, but the first trick he wins entitles him to score everything he has announced, including dix. It is usual to put the melds on a slate, and to rub them out if the player does not win a trick.

PLAYING   The melds are all taken in hand again before play begins. The eldest hand leads for the first trick any card he pleases, and the other players have to follow suit if they are able, and have to win the trick if they can, with either a higher card or a trump. If the third hand cannot win the trick, he is still obliged to follow suit if he can; however, if he has none of the suit led, and the second hand has already put on a better trump than any held by third hand, the latter has to under-trump if he can. The winner of one trick leads for the next, as in the ordinary game. The winner of the sixteenth or last trick counts ten points for it at once.

SCORING   The points for dix, melds and the last trick are all scored using the counters in the ordinary way, but the score for cards has to be kept mentally. The moment any player correctly announces he has reached 1000 points, he wins the game, no matter what the other players have scored. If his claim is not correct, he retires, and the two remaining players finish alone. If neither player wins the game that deal, the two players play the next deal as in ordinary two-handed Binocle, using a stock, whereby the ultimate winner takes the stakes. If it has been agreed that the lowest score pays when the first player goes out, the game is ended as soon as one player retires. If two players reach 1000 points without either having claimed the game, they both have to go on to 1250, but if the third player reaches and announces 1000 before either of the others reaches 1250, he wins the game.

THE REVOKE   The individual player in error loses his entire score for 'cards'. The bidder cannot be set back if either adversary revokes. He can demand that the hand be played out if he thinks he can get a good score.

FOUR-HANDED BINOCLE

Four people can play, each for himself, or two against two as partners, sitting opposite each other. All the cards are dealt, twelve to each player, four at a time, and the last card is turned up for the trump.

MELDS   Melds are not made until the player who holds them has played to the first trick. The eldest hand leads and then melds, the second player plays and then melds, and so on. The card played to the first trick can still be reckoned in the melds.

PLAYING   The general rules of play are the same as in the three-handed game, and players are obliged to follow suit and to win the trick if they are able to do so. The fourth player has to win his partner's trick if he can, and any player who cannot follow suit to a trick that is already trumped has to under-trump if he is unable to over-trump.

SCORING   There are three ways to score. In the first way, each player has to individually win a trick in order to score his melds. In the second way, when either partner wins a trick, the melds in both hands can be scored. In both these ways, the melds are kept separate. In the third way, when a player wins a trick, he can combine his melds with the ones of his partner in order to form fresh combinations, and the scores are made as if the melds of the two partners were in one hand; however, cards previously played to the tricks cannot be used in these fresh combinations. The cards have to still be on the table, unplayed. For this reason, in this style of game, the melds are not taken up until one of the partners wins a trick.

— —

AUCTION BINOCLE

In this variation, each of three or four players is for himself. The forty-eight cards are dealt out, four at a time, but no trump is turned. Beginning on the dealer's left, each player in turn bids a specific number of points for the privileges of naming the trump suit and having the lead for the first trick. There are no second bids. If all the players pass, the dealer has to bid twenty.

As soon as the trump is named, every player at the table makes his own melds, which will be good if he wins a trick. The rules for play are the same as in the ordinary three and four hand.

If four play as partners, two against two, the eldest hand always leads for the first trick, no matter who the successful bidder is.

The bidder always has the first count at the end of the hand, and it is usual to play this game so many deals instead of so many points. At the end of six deals, for example, the highest score is the winner.

USING A WIDOW Sometimes this game is played using a widow: three cards when three play, and four cards when four play. Each player is allowed three bids, whereby the eldest hand has the first right to hold the play for the same amount, and the successful bidder turns the widow face upwards, so that all can see what it contained. He then takes the widow into his hand and discards what he pleases, face downwards, in order to reduce his hand to the same number of cards as that of the other players. The trump is not named until after this discard. The bidder has the first lead and also the first count. Six deals is a game.

The bidder always has the first count, and if he makes good his bid, with the aid of any points laid away in the widow, he scores all he makes. No melds can be scored unless the player who makes them wins a trick. Non-bidders then score their melds and points taken in tricks. Each player in turn has to follow suit and has to head the trick if he can. If he cannot follow suit, he has to trump, and if he cannot beat a trump already played, he has to under-trump, if he can.

If either of the bidder's opponents leads out of turn, the bidder cannot be set back. He can let the error stand or call on the proper player to lead. If a player fails to follow suit, or to trump or win a trick when required to do so, it is a revoke, and the entire score is forfeited for 'cards'. The melds are not lost by a revoke, but if the bidder has not enough to cover his bid by melds, and revokes, he is set back the entire amount of the bid.

If the bidder leads before discarding, his opponents have to rectify the error before they play a card, or there is no penalty. If a wrong number of cards is in the widow, and the opponents have their right number, the bidder is set back the amount of his bid.

-- -- --

SIXTY-SIX

Sixty-six is one of the simplest forms of Bézique, and is an extremely good game for two people using one pack of cards.

CARDS   Sixty-six is played with a pack of twenty-four cards, and all cards below the Nine are deleted. The cards rank A 10 K Q J 9, and the Ace is the highest, in both cutting and play.

MARKERS   The game can be kept using the small cards in the unused portion of the pack or using a whist marker or counters. Anything that will score up to seven points will do.

PLAYERS   The regular game is played by two people, one of whom is known as the dealer and the other as the pone. They cut for seats and deal, and the highest cut has the choice.

STAKES   Sixty-six is played for so much a game, or for so much a point, whereby the loser's score is deducted from the winner's. If the loser has not scored at all, it is usually counted a double game.

DEALING   When the cards have been shuffled and presented to the pone to cut, the dealer gives six cards to each player, three at a time, and deals first to his adversary. There are several ways of making the trump, one of which should be agreed on before play begins. One way is for the pone to draw a card from the top, the middle or the bottom of the talon, after the dealer has given each player his six cards. Another way is for the dealer to turn up the seventh card, after dealing the first round of three to each player. Another, and the one usually adopted in the United States, is for the dealer to turn up the thirteenth card for the trump, after giving six cards to each player. The trump card is left face upwards on the table, and is usually placed under the remainder of the pack, which is slightly spread, face downwards, for the players to draw from.

The general rules for irregularities in the deal are the same as in Binocle. A misdeal does not lose the deal.

OBJECTS OF THE GAME The object of the game, as its name implies, is to count sixty-six. If a player can get sixty-six before his adversary, he counts one point towards game. If he gets sixty-six before his opponent gets thirty-three, which is called *schneider*, he counts two. If he gets sixty-six before his adversary wins a trick, which is called *schwartz*, he counts three. The player who first makes seven points in this way wins the game.

A player can reach sixty-six by winning tricks that contain specific counting cards; by holding and announcing marriages, which are the King and Queen of any suit; and by winning the last trick.

The various counts for these tricks are as follows.

For King and Queen of trumps: *Royal Marriage* 40
For King and Queen of any plain suit: *Marriage* 20
For the Ace of any suit 11
For the Ten of any suit 10
For the King of any suit 4
For the Queen of any suit 3
For the Jack of any suit 2
For the last or twelfth trick 10

The marriages count for the player who holds and announces them; all other points count for the player who actually wins them. The last trick does not count unless it is the twelfth, that is, not unless every card is played.

METHOD OF PLAYING The pone begins by leading any card he pleases. The second player in any trick is not obliged to follow suit, even in trumps, but can renounce or trump at pleasure until the players cease to draw from the stock. If the second player follows suit, the higher card wins the trick. Trumps win all other suits.

DRAWING The winner of the trick takes in the cards, and turns them face downwards; however, before he leads for the next trick, he draws a card from the top of the stock, and places it in his hand without showing or naming it. His adversary then draws the next card, so that each restores the number of cards in his hand to six.

THE TRUMP If either player holds or draws the Nine of trumps, he can exchange it for the turn-up at any time, provided he has already won a trick. This does not have to be the trick immediately before exchanging, and he does not have to wait to get the lead before making the exchange. For example, a player who holds the Nine, and who has to play to his adversary's lead, can win the trick with the turn-up card, thereby leaving the Nine in its place, provided he has won a previous trick. There is no count for dix, as in Bézique and Binocle, and the player is not obliged to exchange unless he wishes to do so. If the Nine is the last card in the stock, it is, naturally, too late to exchange it, and the player who draws it has to keep it.

MARRIAGES If a player holds both King and Queen of any suit, he can count 20 points towards 66 for the marriage, or 40 for royal marriage, by leading either of the marriage cards. It is not necessary for the King or Queen so led to win the trick, but the player who declares a marriage has to have the lead, and has to have won a trick; otherwise, he cannot count it. The pone can declare a marriage on his first lead; however, it will not count unless he wins a subsequent trick, and if his adversary gets to 66 before the pone gets a trick, the marriage is lost, and the pone is schwartz.

If the 20 or 40 claimed for the marriage is enough to carry the player's count to 66 or beyond, the marriage has to be only shown and claimed, without leading it, and the remaining cards are then abandoned, provided the count is correct. Only one marriage can be shown but not led in this way.

In the ordinary course of play, it is not necessary to show both cards of the marriage unless the adversary asks to see them. The player simply leads the King or Queen, and says, 'Twenty,' or 'Forty,' as the case may be. If he leads a King or Queen without claiming any count, it is evident he does not have a marriage. If he has simply forgotten to claim it, he cannot amend the error after his adversary has played to the trick, and the score is lost. To avoid disputes, careful players leave one of the marriage cards face upwards among their cards, as a reminder that a marriage was claimed in that suit, by either the player who has the card turned or his adversary.

COUNTING A player is not allowed to make any record of his progress towards sixty-six, but has to keep his count mentally. It is highly important to keep both your own and your adversary's count, so you can always know how many each of you wants to reach 66. A player is not allowed to go back over his tricks in order to refresh his memory, and if he looks at any trick but the last one turned and quitted, he loses the privilege of 'closing'.

All *irregularities* in playing and drawing are governed by the same rules as in Binocle.

THE LAST SIX TRICKS After the stock is exhausted, marriages can still be led or shown, and scored; however, the second player in each trick has to follow suit if he can, although he is not obliged to win the trick unless he chooses to do so. If all the cards are played, the winner of the last or twelfth trick counts 10 for it towards his 66.

ANNOUNCING SIXTY-SIX If neither of the players has claimed to have reached 66 until after the last trick is played, both turn over their cards and count their points. If only one has reached 66, he counts one or two points, according to his adversary's count. If neither has reached 66, which is possible if no marriages have been declared, or if both have 66 or more and neither has claimed it, neither side scores, but the winner on the next deal adds one to whatever he might make. For example, A and B are adversaries, and the last trick is played without either player's announcing he is sixty-six. On counting, it is found that A has 48 points and a marriage: 68 altogether, whereas B has 72 points and the last trick: 82 altogether. Neither player counts anything. On the next deal, let's suppose that A makes 66 before B gets out of schneider, whereby A will be given two points. To these he adds one for the tie on the last deal, and scores three altogether.

CLOSING Closing is turning the trump card face downwards on the remainder of the pack, which signifies there will be no more drawing from the stock, and that the second player in each trick has to follow suit if he can, although he is not obliged to win the trick.

A player can close only when he has the lead, but if he has the lead, he can close at any time. The pone can close before leading for the first trick, or after winning the first trick, and before drawing from the stock. The leader can close after one or more tricks have been played, and can close without drawing from the stock, or he can draw and then close. If the leader closes without drawing, his adversary has to play without drawing.

When the stock is closed, the player who holds the Nine of trumps can still exchange it for the trump card, whether or not he is the closer, provided he has previously won a trick. It is usual for the closer, if he does not hold the Nine himself, to take up the trump card and offer it to his adversary. This is an intimation that he is about to turn it down if his adversary does not want it. It is sometimes better not to exchange when the game is closed, because the adversary might thereby be given a good counting card if he can catch all your trumps.

There is no score for the last trick when the game is closed, because the number of tricks played will then be fewer than twelve.

Because closing gives peculiar advantages to the closer, there are specific forfeits if a person closes and fails to reach 66. There are three varieties of closing, which are as follows.

If, during the play of the hand, either player thinks he has reached 66, he closes, and turns over the tricks he has already won. If he is correct, he scores one point, two points or three points, according to the condition of his adversary's count. However, if he is not correct, and has not quite reached 66, his adversary scores two points in any case, and if the non-closer had not won a trick up to the time the stock was closed, he scores three, because that is the number the closer would have won had he been correct in his count.

If a player thinks he would have a better chance to reach 66 first if his adversary was compelled to follow suit, he can close the stock. For example, A's mental count is 35, and he holds in his hand a marriage and the Ace of another plain suit but no trumps. If he closes at once, and leads the Ace, his adversary will have to follow suit, and the 11 points will put the closing player to 46. He can then show his marriage, without leading it, and claim 66. However, if the adversary turns out to have none of the suit led, and trumps the Ace, A might never reach 66, and B counts two points.

A player can close, hoping to make schneider or schwartz. For example, A knows his score is 13, and B has 32. A has royal marriage and Ace of trumps in his hand, and the Nine is turned up. If A closes, and thereby compels B to follow suit, he has to catch the Jack or Ten of trumps by leading the Ace. If he catches the Jack, that will put him to 26, and showing the royal marriage will put him 66 and make B schneider. If B has no trump, one of the marriage cards can be led without any fear of losing it, and that will put A to 66, even if B plays a Nine to both leads. However, if A leads the ace of trumps without closing, B is not compelled to follow suit, and might play the Nine of a plain suit to the Ace of trumps. If A then closes or plays on without closing, B might win one of the marriage cards with the Ten, and not only get out of schneider but reach 66 in plain suits before A can win another trick.

On the same principle, a player might think he can reach 66 before his adversary can win a trick, provided he can compel him to follow suit. With two plain-suit Aces and the royal marriage, the pone would close before playing to the first trick, trusting to catch at least 4 points with his two aces and to then show the marriage, thereby making his adversary schwartz.

Some judgement is necessary in deciding whether or not to draw before closing. If a player is allowed to draw, he can get a trump, or a guard to one you suspect he has. Suppose he has exchanged the Nine for the Ten, and you have Ace and royal marriage: it is very likely that the Ten is unguarded, and if you close without drawing, you might catch it, which will make your three trumps alone good for 68. This also shows that the player should not have taken up the Ten until he wanted to use it.

Nothing is gained by closing, except that the adversary is compelled to follow suit, because if you close in order to make him schwartz, and he gets a trick, you count two only; if you close in order to make him schneider, and he gets out, you count one only. If you fail in the first case, he counts three, and any failure will give him two points.

THREE-HANDED SIXTY-SIX

This is exactly the same as the ordinary game, except the dealer takes no card, but scores whatever points are won on the hand he deals. If neither of the other players scores, either because each has made 65 or one has failed to claim 66, the dealer scores one point, and the other players get nothing. The dealer cannot go out on his own deal. He has to stop at six, and win out by his own play.

There are two ways to settle. Each player can pay a specific amount to the pool, and the first player out take it all, or, after one player is out, the two remaining players finish the game, and the loser pay both or settle for the refreshments, as the case may be. If the first player goes out when it will be his turn to deal, he has to deal the next hand.

FOUR-HANDED SIXTY-SIX

This game is sometimes called *Kreutz-marriage*, owing to the German fashion of dealing the cards in the form of a cross; however, because the cards are not dealt that way, and marriages are not scored in the United States, the name is not appropriate in that country.

The pack is increased to thirty-two cards by way of addition of the Sevens and Eights. After the cards are cut by the pone, the dealer gives three to each player on the first round, then two, and then three again, whereby the last card is turned up for the trump. In Germany, the dealer first gives two cards to his partner, then two to his left-hand adversary, then two to his right-hand adversary, and finally two to himself. This is continued for four rounds, so that each player receives eight cards, and the last card is turned up for the trump. The turned-up trump belongs to the dealer, and cannot be exchanged.

In this form of the game, the players not only have to follow suit; they have to win the trick if they can, and have to trump and over-trump if possible. A player is even obliged to win his partner's trick. Owing to this rule, a player who has good plain-suit cards will usually attempt to exhaust the trumps as rapidly as possible.

The *counting cards* are the same as in Sixty-six, and the winner of the last trick counts 10. Because there is no stock, there is no closing, and because marriages are not counted in the United States, the 66 points have to be made on cards alone.

The scores for *schneider* and *schwartz* are the same as in Sixty-six, and seven points are game. There are 130 points made in every deal, so if one side gets more than 66 and fewer than 100, its adversaries have to be out of schneider, and the winners count one. More than 100 but fewer than 130 are schneider, and count two. If the winners take every trick, thereby making 130 points, they score three. Some-times an extra point is scored for winning the Ten of trumps, but this count is quite foreign to the game.

NATIONAL GAMES

—·—

There are some games of cards that do not seem to belong to any specific family; they stand apart from other games, and since they were invented they have been played with only trifling variations, thereby giving rise to no offshoots that bear other names. They were usually the most popular games with the middle and lower classes in the countries in which they were found, and can still be considered to be distinctly national in character. Games that become popular with 'the masses' always last longer than others, and the rules governing them are much better understood and more firmly established. In the course of the nineteenth century, the English aristocracy ran the gamut of Quadrille, Ombre, Whist, Écarté, Bézique, Piquet, Rubicon and Bridge, whereas the middle classes stuck steadily to Cribbage for almost the entire period from about 1700 to 1900.

Six of these popular games are strikingly typical of the national character, in both their construction and the way of playing them. They are Skat in Germany, Cribbage in England, Piquet in France, Conquian in Mexico, Calabrasella in Italy, and Cassino in the United States. They are all excellent games, and have deservedly survived much more pretentious rivals.

With the exception of Skat, little is known about the exact origin of any of these games, although most of them can be traced by way of their resemblance to more ancient forms. Skat is the most modern and remains the most popular, and many people think it is superior to Whist. The game seems to have originated among the farmers of Thuringia, a province of Saxony, and was probably a variation of the Wendish game of Schapskopf. The first mention of Skat that could be found was in an article in the *Osterländer Blättern*, in 1818. Thirty years later, Professor Hempel of Altenburg published the rules and principles of the game under the title *Das Skatspiel, von J. F. L. H.* He reportedly learnt the game from a friend, who had been taught it by a Wendish coach driver he employed. The game spread rapidly, and soon became popular all over Germany, although many minor variations were included in the details of play. In order to settle these issues, a Skat congress was finally held in Altenburg in 1886. This was succeeded by other congresses in Leipzig and Dresden, and the result of these meetings was to weed out all the minor differences in play and settle on a universal code of laws for the game, which is called Reichs-Skat.

In the United States, Reichs-Skat is no longer played; the value of some of the games is changed, and all the bidding is by Zahlen-reizen. In all the textbooks about Skat that have been examined, this fact has been entirely overlooked.

—·—

SKAT

The etymology of the word *Skat*, sometimes spelt *Scat*, is a matter of doubt, but the most plausible explanation is that it is a corruption of one of the terms in the parent game of Taroc; *scart*, from *scarto*: 'what is left'; or *scartare*: 'to discard or reject'. *Matadore* is another word from the game of Taroc, which is still retained in Skat. Other people attribute the word to *Skatt*, the Old-German or Anglo-Saxon word for money, or the modern-German word *schatz*: 'a treasure', referring to the forms of the game in which good counting cards are laid aside in the skat for the count at the end of the hand. This derivation would account for both spellings of the word: with a *k* and with a *c*.

You are advised to make yourself familiar with the German terms in the following description, because they are in common use wherever skat is played. Many American players who use the English language in bidding by figures adhere to the German names for the suits and positions at the table.

CARDS Skat is played with a pack of thirty-two cards, and all cards below the Seven are deleted. The rank of the cards differs according to whether the players are attempting to win or lose tricks. If the object is to win tricks, it is known as a 'game'; if the object is to lose, it is called a 'nullo'. In nullo, the cards rank in their natural order: A K Q J 10 9 8 7, and the Ace is the highest. In the various 'games', the four Jacks are always the best trumps, and are known as *Wenzels*.

The other cards follow the usual German rank: A 10 K Q 9 8 7, and the Ace is the highest in plain suits.

The German names for the cards are as follows. *Jack:* Wenzel, Bauern, Bube, Jungen, or Unter. *Ace:* As, or Daus. *Ten:* Zehn. *King:* König. *Queen:* Dame, Ober, or Königen. *Nine:* Neun. *Eight:* Acht. *Seven:* Sieben. The most common terms are Bube, As, Zehn, König, Dame and so on. The words Unter and Ober for the Jack and Queen refer to the way of marking the suits on the German cards. In the Queens, the mark of the suit is always above the figure, which has a single head; in the Jacks, the suit mark is always under the figure. This distinction is necessary, because in the German cards the Queen is a male figure. The King has two suit marks, one on each side of the head. When the French or American double-head cards are used, with suit-marks in both corners, the words *ober* and *unter* have no meaning: *Dame* and *Bube* are used instead.

RANK OF THE SUITS   In addition to the rank of the cards themselves, the suits outrank each other, except in Nullo, whereby clubs are always the best, then spades, hearts and diamonds. Germans have various names for the suits, whereby the one first given in each instance is in common use among modern Germans. *Clubs:* Kreuz, Trefle, Eicheln, Eckern, or Braün. *Spades:* Pique, Schüppen, Laub, or Grün. *Hearts:* Hertzen, Cœur, or Roth. *Diamonds:* Carreau, Schellen, Eckstein, Ruthen, or Gelb. In the German notation of card games and problems, the suits are indicated by way of the French terms: clubs, *tr* for trefle; spades, *p* for pique; hearts, *co* for cœur; and diamonds, *car* for carreau. The cards are indicated by way of the initials A K D B Z 9 8 7, which stand for As, König, Dame, Bube, Zehn and so on. The winning card in each trick is always printed in full-face type.

The cards of each suit are divided into two parts, known as counting cards: *Zahlkarten*, and cards that have no counting value: *Fehlkarten*, or Ladons. The counting cards and their values are as follows. Ace 11, Ten 10, King 4, Queen 3, and Jack 2. These are used in reckoning up the value of the tricks won by each side in counting towards 61 in all the 'games', but not in Nullo. The Seven, Eight and Nine have no counting value.

The rank of the suits has no influence on their trick-taking powers, nor on the value of the Zahlkarten, but increases or diminishes the value of the 'game' played for. When any suit is made the trump, it takes precedence over the three other suits only insofar as trumps will win other suits, and the suits that are not trumps are equal in value with reference to trick taking. Because the four Wenzels are always the highest trumps, there will always be eleven cards in the trump suit, and seven in each of the plain suits, so that if clubs were trumps, the rank of the cards would be as follows.

In any of the other suits, the rank would be:

MATADORES The club Jack is always the best trump, and every trump card in unbroken sequence with the club Jack is called a Matadore, provided the sequence is in the hand of the same player. This rule holds whether the sequence was in the hand originally dealt to the player or whether part of it is found in the Skat, if he becomes possessed of the Skat cards. For example, Clubs are trumps, and a player holds these cards:

He has only one Matadore; however, because the Skat cards will belong to him if he has made the trump, he might find in them the spade Jack, which would complete his sequence, thereby giving him six Matadores instead of one. Because one side or the other has to have the club Jack in every deal, there always has to be a specific number of Matadores, from one to eleven. If the player who makes the trump has them, he is said to play *with* so many; if his adversaries hold them, he is said to play *without* just as many as they hold. The difficult thing for the beginner in Skat to understand is that whether or not a player holds the Matadores, the number of them has exactly the same influence on the value of his game. If one player held these cards:

and wished to make hearts trumps, he would be playing 'with two'. If another player wished to make the same suit trumps with these cards:

he would be playing 'without two', and the value of each game would be exactly the same, no matter which player actually made the trump. Matadores have to be held; they do not count if they are won from the adversaries in the course of play.

MARKERS   Counters of any kind are not used in Skat, because the score is kept on a writing pad, which should be ruled into vertical columns for the number of players engaged.

PLAYERS   Skat is played by three people. If there are four at the table, the dealer takes no cards, but shares the fortunes of the players who are opposed to the single player, whereby he wins and loses on each hand whatever they win and lose. If there are five or six at the table, the dealer gives cards to the two players on his left and the player next to him on the right. The players who hold no cards share the fortunes of the two who are opposed to the single player.

After the table is formed, no one can join the game without the consent of all the players who are already in, and then only after a *round*, that is, after each player at the table has had an equal number of deals. If any player cuts into a table during the progress of a game, he has to take his seat at the right of the player who dealt the first hand. When six people present for play, it is much better to form two tables, but some people object to playing continuously, and prefer the dealer to have a rest when more than three play.

There are always three active players in Skat. The player who makes the trump is called *the player*, or Spieler; the two opposed to him are called the *adversaries*, or Gegners; and the ones who hold no cards are called *im Skat*, or Theilnehmer. Of the three active players, the player who leads for the first trick is called *Vorhand*, the second player is called *Mittelhand*, and the third is called *Hinterhand*. The person sitting on the dealer's right, to whom the cards are presented to cut, is called the *pone*.

No person is allowed to withdraw from the game without giving notice in advance, and he can retire only at the end of a round of deals. It is usual to give notice at the beginning of a round, by saying, 'This is my last.'

CUTTING   Positions at the table are drawn for, and the cards rank as in play: Jacks are the best, and the suits outrank each other in order, so that there can be no ties in cutting. The lowest cut has the first choice of seats, and also deals the first hand. It is usual for the player sitting on the right of the first dealer to keep the score, so that players can always know when a round ends.

STAKES   Skat is played for so much a point, and the single player wins from or loses to each of the other players at the table. A cent a point was considered to be a reasonably stiff game, and half a cent was more common in good clubs. Many people played for one-fifth, or even one-tenth of a cent a point. At half a cent a point, ten dollars usually covered a run of reasonably bad luck in an evening's play.

DEALING   At the beginning of the game, the cards should be counted and thoroughly shuffled, and shuffled at least three times before each deal thereafter. The dealer presents the pack to the pone to cut, and at least five cards have to be left in each packet. The cards are dealt from left to right in rotation, and the deal passes to the left in regular order.

Only three people at the table receive cards, no matter how many players are in the game. If there are four players, the dealer gives himself no cards. If there are five or six players, the first two on the dealer's left and the pone receive cards. The other people at the table are said to be 'im Skat', because they are laid aside for that deal.

The cards can be distributed in several ways, but whichever way the first dealer selects has to be continued during the game, by both the original dealer and the other players at the table. Ten cards are given to each player, and two are dealt face downwards in the centre of the table for the Skat. No trump is turned. The cards have to be dealt, three cards to each player, then two to the Skat, then four to each player again, and finally three.

IRREGULARITIES IN THE DEAL   If the pack is found to be imperfect, the deal in which the error is discovered is void, but any previous scores or cuts made with that pack stand good. If the cards have not been cut, or if a card is found faced in the pack, or if the dealer exposes a card in dealing, any active player who has not looked at his cards can demand a fresh deal by the same dealer. If the dealer gives too many or too few cards to any player, he has to shuffle and deal again. If the error is not discovered until the hand is partly played out, the deal is void, and the misdealer deals again.

A misdeal does not lose the deal under any circumstances, but it is usual to exact a penalty of ten points for a misdeal.

OBJECTS OF THE GAME   The object of each player is to obtain the privilege of attempting to complete a specific task, which is known as his 'game', and which he has to be able to carry through successfully against the combined efforts of the other two players. The more difficult the task undertaken, the greater the number of points scored for it, and the player who will undertake the game that is of the greatest value of the ones offered has to be given the privilege of trying it. In order to determine which player this is, the players can all bid for the privilege by naming a specific number of points, which is usually well within the actual value of the game they intend to play. If a bidder meets with opposition, he gradually approaches the true value of his game, and the player whose game is worth the most will naturally be able to bid the greatest number of points, and has to be selected as the player, whereby the other two players are his adversaries.

GAMES   These games are divided into two main classes: the ones in which the player undertakes to win, and the ones in which he tries to lose. When he plays to lose, it is to lose every trick because there is no trump suit, and the cards in each suit rank A K Q J 10 9 8 7. These games are called *Null*, or Nullo, and *Null Ouvert*, whereby the latter is played with the successful bidder's cards exposed face upwards on the table but not liable to be called. The moment the bidder wins a trick in a Nullo, he loses his game. Nullos are quite foreign to Skat, and seem to have been introduced as a consolation for players who always hold bad cards.

When *Ramsch* is played, the object is to take fewer cards than do either of the other players, but the cards rank as in the ordinary game, except that the four Jacks are the only trumps.

In all other games, the successful bidder undertakes to win; however, his success depends not on the number of tricks he takes in but on the total value of the counting cards contained in these tricks. The total value of all the counting cards is 120 points, and in order to be successful, the single player has to win at least 61. If he succeeds in winning 61 or more points, he wins his game, whatever it is. If he can get 91 points, he wins a double game that is called *schneider*. If he can take every trick, he wins a treble game, which is called *schwartz*. It is not enough to win 120 points, because if the adversaries win a single trick, even if it contains no counting cards, they save the schwartz.

If the single player fails to reach 61, he loses. If he fails to reach

31, he is schneider, and if he fails to take a trick, he is schwartz. These various results increase the value of the game, as will presently be noted.

There are four varieties of game in which the successful bidder plays to win, whereby the difference is in the way of using the skat cards and making the trump. These games are called *Fragé, Tourné, Solo,* and *Grand,* and outrank each other in the order given, whereby Fragé is the lowest. The first three: Fragé, Tourné and Solo, are each again divided into four parts, according to the suit that is trumps, whereby a Tourné in clubs is better than one in spades, a Solo in hearts is better than one in diamonds, and so on. This is in accordance with the rank of the suits already mentioned in the paragraph devoted to that subject.

In a *Fragé,* or Simple Game, the successful bidder takes both the skat cards into his hand, then declares which suit will be the trump, whereby he discards two cards face downwards for his schatz, or treasure, before play begins. The two cards thereby laid aside count for the single player at the end of the hand, provided he takes a trick, and they cannot be won by the adversaries unless they make the single player schwarz. Fragé is no longer played.

In a *Tourné,* the successful bidder turns one of the skat cards face upwards on the table before looking at the second card. He can turn over whichever card he pleases, but the one he turns fixes the trump suit for that hand. If the card turned over is a Jack, he can change to a Grand, but he has to do so before he sees the second card in the Skat.

If the player does not like the first card he turns, he does not have to show it, but can put it in his hand and turn the other card. This second card has to be the trump, or a Grand can be played if the card is a Jack. In case the game is lost after taking the second card, it costs double. This is called *Passt mir Nicht.*

In a *Solo,* the skat cards are not touched: the successful bidder names the trump to suit the hand of ten cards originally dealt to him. The Skat belongs to him, as in Fragé and Tourné, but he must not see its contents until the hand is played out, when any points and Matadores it might contain will count for him.

In a *Grand,* there is no trump suit: the four Jacks are the only trumps in play. These four cards preserve their relative suit value, whereby the club Jack is the best, and they are still Matadores. There are four varieties of Grand: a tourné player can make it a Grand if he turns up a Jack. This is called a *Grand Tourné.* A player can make it a grand without seeing either of the skat cards. This is called a *Grand Solo.* A player can announce a Grand and lay his cards face upwards on the table, exposed but not liable to be called. This is called a **Grand Ouvert**. A Fragé cannot be played as a Grand under any circumstances. A player can announce **Gucki Grand**, which means he will take both the skat cards into his hand at once, in order to get the privilege of laying out any two cards he pleases, but that Jacks will be the only trumps. If a Gucki Grand is lost, it costs double.

A player can announce a **Gucki Nullo**, in which he takes both the skat cards into his hand and lays out any two cards he pleases. This loses double if it is not successful.

Revolution is seldom played. It is a Nullo in which the adversaries put their twenty cards together as one hand to see whether they can make the player take a trick.

Uno and **Duo** are Grands, in which the single player engages to take one trick in Uno, or two in Duo, neither more nor less.

GAME VALUES   Each of the aforementioned games has what is called a unit of value, which is afterwards multiplied several times according to the number of Matadores and whether the game was schneider or schwarz.

These unit values are as follows, beginning with the lowest.

Suits Trumps:			Jacks Trumps:	No Trumps:
	Turn	Solo	Turned Grand 12	Gucki Nullo 15
◇	5	9	Gucki Grand 16	" if played open 30
♡	6	10	Solo Grand 20	Solo Nullo 20
♠	7	11	Open Grand 24	" if played open 40
♣	8	12	Ramsch 20	Revolution 60

When one player takes no trick in a Ramsch, the player who has the greater number of points loses 30. If two players take no trick, the loss is 50 points.

All Guckis lose double if they fail, so that if a player announces a Gucki Nullo and loses it, he will lose 30, but if he won it, he would get 15 only. If a player has a Gucki Null Ouvert, he has to announce it is to be played open before he touches the skat cards. It is then worth 30 if won and 60 if lost.

Passt-mir-nicht tournees all lose double if they fail, but win the usual number of points if they succeed.

MULTIPLIERS   The aforementioned values are simply the standard counting values of these various games. In calculating the actual value of a player's game, in order to see how much he can safely offer in the bidding, and how much he would win if successful in his undertaking, these standard values are multiplied as follows.

Five classes of game are recognised, beginning with the lowest, in which the player gets the necessary 61 points but does not make his adversaries schneider. This is simply called 'game', and because it always has to be either won or lost, it is a constant factor. The value of the game is 1, and each better game is numbered in regular order, whereby the five varieties are as follows.

The Game, 1. Schneider, 2. Schwarz announced or Schwarz, 3. Schwarz after announcing Schneider, 4. Schwarz announced, 5.

These numbers are added to the number of Matadores, and the total thereby found is multiplied by the unit value of the game. For example, a player has obtained the privilege of playing on a bid of thirty. His game is a Solo in hearts, in which he holds the three highest Matadores and announces schneider in advance. His game multiplier is therefore 3 (for the announced schneider), to which he adds 3 more for the Matadores: 6 altogether. Because the unit value of a heart Solo is 10, he could have gone on bidding to 60 had it been necessary, and he will win 60 from each of his adversaries if he succeeds in reaching 91 points in the counting cards he takes in in his tricks, together with what he finds in the Skat.

If his adversaries got to 30 with their counting cards, he would have lost 60 to each of them, although he bid only 30, because he announced his game as schneider, and did not make it. Had he not announced the schneider, and reached 91 or more in his counting cards, he would have won a game worth 50, thereby losing the extra multiplier by not announcing the schneider in advance, because a schneider made without announcing it is worth only 2.

In reckoning the value of a game, it is always safer to bid on playing 'with' than 'without' Matadores in a Solo or Tourné, because, although you might have a hand 'without four', you might find a Wenzel in the Skat, and if it is the club Jack, you lose three multipliers at once.

BIDDING   The players have to be familiar with the way of computing the various games in order to bid with judgement and without hesitation. Suppose you hold the three highest Matadores with an average hand that is not strong enough in any one suit to play a Solo but is good enough for a Tourné. Your smallest possible game will be diamonds with three, which will be worth 5 multiplied by 4: 1 for the game, and 3 for the Matadores: 20 points. If you can get the game on any bid less than 20 you are absolutely safe, provided you can reach 61 in your tricks. However, the opposition of another player might irritate you [*reizen*] and provoke you to bid 24, or even 28, in the hope of turning a heart or a spade. If you go beyond 20, and turn a diamond, you have to either find the fourth Matadore in the Skat or make your adversaries schneider, in order to secure another multiplier. If you fail, you lose 24, or 28, according to your bid.

The great difficulty in Skat is to judge the value of a hand, so as to neither under-bid it nor over-bid it, and also to get all out of it that it is worth. A person who plays a Fragé in hearts when he could easily have made it a Solo reduces the value of his game only 80 per cent. A player who has the four Wenzels, A K Q 9 8 of diamonds, and a losing card, would be foolish to play a diamond Solo with five, schneider announced, worth 72, while he had in his hand a sure Grand, with four, schneider announced, worth 140. Naturally, the schneider is not a certainty. The risk is that the Ten of diamonds will be guarded, and that an Ace and a Ten will make, both of them on your losing card, or one of them on the diamond Ten. A careful player would be satisfied with 100 on this hand, because if he fails to make the announced schneider, he loses everything.

A player is not obliged to play the game he originally intended to, if he thinks he has anything better; however, he has to play a game worth as much as he bid, or the next higher, and having once announced his game, has to play it.

Suppose the Vorhand has a spade Solo with two, and on being offered 33 says, 'Yes,' thinking the bidder will go on to 36, instead of which he passes. It is very probable that the bidder has a spade Solo without two, and will defeat a spade Solo announced by the Vorhand. If the Vorhand has almost as good a game in hearts, he should change, hoping to make schneider or find another Matadore in the Skat. If he loses the game, a heart Solo with two costs 30 points; however, because the Vorhand refused 33, and the next-best game he could have made with a heart Solo is 40, that is the amount he loses, although he refused only 33.

METHOD OF BIDDING   The Vorhand always holds the play, and the Mittelhand always makes the first bid, or passes, whereby the Hinterhand says nothing until the propositions made by the Mittelhand have been finally refused or passed by the Vorhand. The usual formula is for the Vorhand to say, 'How many?' or 'I am Vorhand,' whereupon the Mittelhand bids or passes. If the Vorhand has as good a game as offered him, he says, 'Yes,' and the Mittelhand has to bid higher or pass. If the Vorhand does not have as good a game, he can either pass or bluff the bidder into going higher by saying, 'Yes.' As soon as one passes, the other turns to the Hinterhand, who has to either make a higher bid than the last or pass. The survivor of the first two has to either say, 'Yes,' to the offers made by Hinterhand or pass. The final survivor then announces his game. It is usual for the last one to pass to signify he is done by pushing the skat cards towards the survivor, thereby indicating that they are his and that he is the player. If a player is offered a game equal to his own, he can still say, 'Yes,' but if he is offered a better game and still says, 'Yes,' he runs the risk of being compelled to play.

The old German way of bidding, which was adopted at the Skat Congresses in Altenburg, Leipzig and Dresden, was to bid in suits, whereby a bid of club Solo outranked one of spade Solo, no matter what it was worth. This has long been obsolete, and the objection to it was that a player might get the play on a game of much inferior value. A player who had a spade Solo, six Matadores and schneider announced could offer only a spade Solo, without mentioning its value, and although his game was worth 99, he could be outbid by an offer of Nullo, which was then worth only 20. This is contrary to the spirit of the game, whereby it is required that the person who offers the game of the greatest value will be the player. The rank of the bids in the old German game was as follows, beginning with the lowest.

> Fragé, in the order of the suits.
> Tourné, in the order of the suits.
> Grand Tourné.
> Solo in diamonds, hearts and spades.
> Nullo, worth 20.
> Solo in clubs.
> Grand Solo, worth 16.
> Null ouvert, worth 40.
> Grand ouvert.

The multipliers were the same as the ones used in the modern game, but the player had no means of using them in his bids. It will be observed that in the modern value of the various games, the old rank is sought to be preserved by way of assuming the lowest possible bid on any given game.

In some parts of Germany, it is still the custom to reckon Solos at the tourné values, whereby one multiplier for 'out of hand' is simply added. A spade Solo with two would thereby be reckoned 'with two, one for game, one for out of hand; four times seven, or twenty-eight.' Note that seven is tourné value for spades.

THE SKAT CARDS   When the successful bidder is determined, the skat cards are pushed towards him, and the way in which he uses them limits the game he is allowed to play. Although the player has to win or lose a game worth as many as bid, he can attempt to win as many more as he pleases. If he has gotten the play on a bid of ten, that does not prevent him from playing a club Solo, with schneider announced. However, if he has bid or refused eleven, and plays a tourné in diamonds, he has to make schneider or play with or without two Matadores in order to bring his multipliers up to three. If both these fail him, he loses 15: the next-higher game than his bid that is possible in a diamond tourné.

Because Fragé is no longer played on account of its small value, if the player takes both the skat cards into his hand at the same time, without showing them, his game has to be a Gucki Grand, unless he has previously announced it is a Gucki Nullo. When his game is announced, he lays out any two cards he pleases for his skat, so as to play with ten only.

If the player turns over either of the skat cards, his game is limited to a tourné. If he turns a Jack, he can change to Grand but not to Grand Ouvert. Neither schneider nor schwarz can be announced in any game in which the skat cards are used. A tourné player has to lay out two skat cards in order to reduce his hand to ten cards.

If the player neither turns over nor takes into his hand either of the skat cards, he can play any of the suit Solos, Grand Solo, Grand Ouvert, Nullo, or Null Ouvert. He can announce schneider or schwarz in any Solo.

Any player who looks at the skat cards before the beginning of the play is debarred from bidding that deal, and is penalised ten points in the score. In addition to this penalty, either of the other players can demand a fresh deal. If a player looks at the skat cards during the play of a hand, the play is immediately stopped, and if he is the single player, he can count only the points taken in up to that time, exclusive of the skat. These points are deducted from 120, and his adversaries claim the difference. The game is then settled, according to this count, exactly as if the hand had been played out. If an adversary of the single player looks at either of the skat cards during the play of a hand, the single player can at once stop the game, and his adversaries can count only the points they have taken in in tricks up to that time. If they have no tricks, they are schwarz; if they do not have 30 points, they are schneider.

When four or more play, any person who holds no cards can be penalised ten points for looking at the skat cards.

METHOD OF PLAYING   When the successful bidder has disposed of the skat cards and announced his game, the Vorhand leads any card he pleases for the first trick. The Vorhand should be careful not to lead until the player has laid out or discarded for the Skat in a Gucki or a Tourné. Players have to follow suit if they can, but are not obliged to win the trick. If they have none of the suit led, they can trump or discard at pleasure. The highest card played, if it is of the suit led, wins the trick, and trumps win all other suits. The winner of the first trick leads for the next, and so on, until all the cards have been played, or the game is acknowledged as won or lost, and abandoned. In a Grand, if a Jack is led, players have to follow suit with the other Jacks, because Jacks are trumps.

ABANDONED HANDS   If the single player finds he has over-bid himself, or that he cannot make as good a game as bid, he can abandon his hand in order to save himself from being made schneider or schwarz, provided he does so before he plays to the second trick. A Solo cannot be abandoned in this way, because the rule is made only to allow a player to get off cheaply who has been unlucky in finding nothing in the Skat to suit his hand. For example, a player has risked a Tourné with a missing suit, and turns up that suit. He can abandon his hand at once, thereby losing his bid or the next-higher game but escaping schneider.

IRREGULARITIES IN THE HANDS   If, during the play of a hand, any person is found to have too many or too few cards, and the other players having their right number, it is evident there has been no misdeal if the pack is perfect and there are two cards in the Skat. If the player in error has too few cards, probably from having dropped a card on the floor or having played two cards to the same trick, he loses in any case, but the adversary can demand to have the hand played out in order to try for schneider or schwarz, and the last trick, with the missing card, has to be considered as having been won by the side not in fault. If the player in fault is opposed to the single player, his partner suffers with him. If the player discovers his loss, he is not allowed to pick the card from the floor and replace it in his hand if he has in the meantime played to a trick with a wrong number of cards.

PLAYING OUT OF TURN   The usual penalty in the United States for leading or playing out of turn is loss of the game if the error is made by the adversaries of the single player. If it is made by the player himself, the card played in error has to be taken back, and if only one adversary has played to the false lead, he can also take back his card. If both adversaries have played, the trick stands good. The single player suffers no penalty, as it is only to his own disadvantage to expose his hand.

THE REVOKE   If a player revokes, and is one of the adversaries of the single player, the game is lost for the player in error; however, he can count the points in his tricks up to the time the revoke occurred, in order to save schneider or schwarz. In Nullos, the game is lost the moment the revoke is discovered.

SEEING TRICKS   The tricks have to be kept separate as they are taken in, and any player is allowed to look at the last trick turned and quitted. Any player who looks at any trick other than the last can be penalised ten points.

PLAYING OUVERTS   The rules of the game require Ouverts to be exposed face upwards on the table before a card is played.

SCORING   The score should always be kept by the player sitting on the right of the first dealer. This will mark the rounds. The score sheet should be ruled into vertical columns, one column for each player at the table.

Each player is charged individually with his losses and gains, whereby the amounts are added to or deducted from his score, and a plus or a minus mark is placed in front of the last figure, so that the exact state of each player's score will be evident at a glance.

The score of the single player is the only one put down, and it is charged to him as a loss or a gain at the end of each deal.

If there are four players, a line is drawn under every fourth amount entered in each person's account. If three play, the line is drawn under every third amount. This system of scoring will show at once whose turn it is to deal, if the total number of amounts under which no line is drawn are counted up. For example, three people play, and A dealt the first hand. In the first three columns are shown the amounts won and lost in the three rounds, whereas the last three columns show the way in which these losses and gains were entered on the score sheet.

Points won and lost			Score card		
1st Round	2nd Round	3rd Round	A	B	C
A won 33	A lost 16	C lost 36	+ 33	+ 40	+ 55
C won 55	B won 40	B won 48	+ 17	+ 88	+ 67
C won 12	A lost 24	C lost 12	− 7		+ 31
					+ 19

At the end of the second round, a line was drawn under A's account, which then contained three items, and after the first game in the third round, a line was drawn under C's account.

If we suppose the game to be stopped at this point, the scores would be balanced as follows.

A	B	C
− 7	+ 88	+ 19
− 95	+ 95	+ 26
− 26	+ 69	− 69
− 121	+ 164	− 43

We take the three scores and bring them down on one line. We draw a line under them, and proceed as follows. First, we take A, who has lost 7 to B, and from whom B has also won 88. This gives us 95-minus for A and 95-plus for B. We then compare A and C, and find that A owes C 26: put down as minus for A, and plus for C. We now compare B and C, and find that B wins the difference, which is 69 points: put down plus for B, and minus for C. We then add up in order to see that the scores balance.

The same method can be used when four play, but some people prefer to call the lowest score zero, and thereby make all the other scores plus. Suppose the final scores were as follows.

A	B	C	D
+ 186	+ 42	+ 344	+ 116
+ 144	0	+ 302	+ 74 = 520
+ 4	4	4	4
+ 576	0	+ 1208	+ 296
− 520	− 520	− 520	− 520
+ 56	− 520	+ 688	− 224

If B is zero, his points are to be taken from the ones of each of the other players, because B is plus. If the low score is a minus, the points have to be added to each of the other points. The three totals are added, and found, in this case, to be 520, which is the total of B's loss. We now multiply the scores by the number of players engaged, in this case four, and from the product, we deduct the 520 already found. The scores then balance.

When Skat is played for the League stake, which was one-fourth of a cent a point, the results can be found in a still shorter way by way of adding up all the scores and taking an average, whereby this average is the sum divided by the number of players. Take the results just given, for example.

A	B	C	D
186	42	344	116 = 688 ÷ 4 = 172
172	172	172	172
+ 14	− 130	+ 172	− 56

The average is simply deducted from each score, and the remainder is the amount won or lost, in cents.

CHEATING   As in all games in which the cards are dealt in groups, the cheat will find many opportunities in Skat. The clumsiest shuffler can usually locate some of the Wenzels at the top or bottom of the pack, before presenting it to be cut, and if the players do not insist on the cards always being dealt in the same way, the card sharp can secure to himself two or more Wenzels, either in his hand or in the Skat. Any person who deals the cards sometimes three at a time, and again five at a time, should be stopped immediately, and no excuses such as changing his luck should be listened to for a moment. Any person who habitually picks up the cards with their faces towards him, and straightens them by lifting them from their positions in the pack, should be stopped at once, and requested to straighten the cards face downwards.

Dealing seconds is very difficult when the cards have to be 'pinched' in threes and fours. A second dealer who holds back a Wenzel on the top can give his adversary two cards underneath without knowing it. Marked cards are of advantage only when the dealer plays, and are of little use beyond telling him what he can turn up for a trump, or what he will find in the Skat. The rule for having four in the game, if possible, is one of the greatest safeguards, unless the dealer is in secret partnership with one of the players.

SUGGESTIONS FOR GOOD PLAY   The main things to master in Skat are the values of the hands, the principles of bidding on them, the best methods of playing them, and the proper methods of combining forces with your partner for the time being, in order to defeat the single player.

BIDDING   Some people attach a great deal of importance to the odds for and against specific cards' being in the Skat. If a player who does not have three is forced to risk finding a Matadore in the Skat, it is usually enough for him to know that the odds are about 3 to 1 against it. It is much more important for him to consider what cards might make against him, and what they would count. It is often necessary to estimate very closely the number of points that have to fall on a specific number of leads. For example, you are the Vorhand, and hold these cards:

Even if you find the Ace and Ten with the best Wenzel in one hand against you, you have an almost certain club Solo, because if you lead a Wenzel, your adversary has to either take it or give you the Ace or Ten. If he wins it, and his partner gives him a Ten of another suit, and they then proceed to make both the Aces and Tens of your weak suits, that will give them only 56 points, and you will make every other trick. The only thing that could defeat you is for one player on the fourth trick to lead a suit of which his partner had none. This would require one player to have all the spades and the other all the hearts, which is almost impossible.

Another familiar example is the following. You are the Vorhand who has these cards:

Although you cannot possibly win more than six tricks, and have to lose every trick in the red suits, you have an invincible Grand, because the adversaries do not have a sufficient number of Fehl-karten to give you in order to avoid adding 16 points to the 46 you already have in your hand, which must make you 62 before they get a trick.

It is better to bid on a doubtful Solo than on a risky Tourné, and if you have a choice of two numerically equal suits, it is better to bid on a suit that contains small cards than on one that contains A 10. In bidding Tournés, you have to remember that the more cards you hold of a suit, the less your chance to turn up one.

It is not good play to bid a Solo on four or five trumps unless you have some aces in the other suits. A Grand can be bid even without a trump, if you have the lead, and hold four aces, or three aces and four Tens. A Grand with any two Wenzels is safe if you have two good suits. A Nullo should never be bid unless the player has the Seven of his long suit.

Some risk has to be taken in all bids, and a player who never offers a game that is not perfectly safe is called a *Maurer:* one who builds on a solid foundation. The player who offers the most games will usually win the most unless he is a very poor player.

LEADING   The single player should almost always begin with the trumps, in order to get them out of his way. With a sequence of Wenzels, it is a common artifice to begin with the lowest, hoping the second player will fatten the trick by discarding a Ten or an Ace, under the impression that the Hinterhand can win it. This style of underplay is called *Wimmelfinte*, and the Mittelhand should beware it. With only one Wenzel and the Ace and Ten, it is better to begin with a small trump. If you find all the trumps in one hand against you, or tenace over you, you should stop leading trumps, and play forcing cards.

If you have no Wenzels, it is usually best to lead your smallest trumps. If you have only Ace Ten and small trumps, and know the adversaries have one Wenzel and one trump better than your small one, lead your Ten, so they cannot make both trumps. In playing for a schneider, it is often advisable to continue the trumps, even after the adversaries are exhausted, so they will not know which suit to keep for the last trick.

LAYING OUT THE SKAT   In a Fragé or a Tourné, some judgement is required in discarding for the Skat. It is often necessary to lay aside the Ace and Ten of trumps if there is any danger the adversaries will catch them. Unguarded Tens should always be laid out, and it is a good general principle to get rid of one suit entirely, so you can trump it. It is a common practice to put in the Skat the Ace and Ten of a suit of which you also hold the King. When you lead the King, if Mittelhand has none of the suit, he is sure to fatten the trick for his partner, thinking he must have Ace or Ten. With the Ten, King and small cards of a plain suit, lay the Ten and King in the Skat.

THE ADVERSARIES   These players should combine against the single player by getting him between them if possible. If you sit on the left of the player, lead your short suits up to him, but if you sit on his right, lead your longest suit through him. Try to force out his trumps on your plain-suit cards if you can, and avoid giving him discards of his weak suits. With a long trump suit, it is often advantageous to lead it through the player but seldom right to lead it up to him.

In Solos, the adversaries should lead Aces and winning cards, and change suits frequently. If you are playing against a Grand, and have two trumps, one of which is the best, lead it, then play your long suit; however, if you have the two smallest trumps, lead the long suit first, and force with it every time you get in.

The partners should always scheme to protect each other's Tens by keeping the Aces of plain suits. For this reason it is very bad play to fatten with the Ace of a suit of which you do not have the Ten, or to play an Ace third hand when there are only small cards in the trick, and the Ten of the suit has not been played and you do not hold it.

If the player is void of a suit, continue leading it, no matter what you hold in it. This will either weaken his trumps or, if he is between you, give your partner discards.

If the player leads a Wenzel, it is usually best to cover it if you can, but do not play the club Jack on the diamond Jack unless you want the lead very badly.

When the single player does not lead trumps, but plays his Aces and Tens, Germans call it *auf die Dörfer gehen*: 'getting to the villages', or 'getting home', which is equivalent to the expression 'getting out of the woods' or 'getting in out of the rain'. When the single player runs for home in this way, it is usually best to lead trumps through him at the first opportunity.

In playing against a Nullo, the great point is to give your partner discards. If you find that the player's long suit is yours also, continue it until your partner has discarded an entire suit, if possible. If you then have the small card of the discarded suit, you can defeat the Nullo at once.

FATTENING   Germans call fattening *Wimmeln,* or 'swarming' the points together in one trick. It is always advisable to get rid of Tens in this way, or Aces of suits in which you hold both Ace and Ten; however, it is bad play to fatten with the Ace of a suit of which you do not have the Ten, unless the trick wins the game from the player or saves a very probable schneider.

The following ***illustrative hands*** will give you a very good idea of the way in which the various forms of the game are played: they show the difference in the play of a Tourné, Solo and Grand.

A TOURNÉ   A, the Vorhand, has refused ten with the following cards, and the Hinterhand has passed without a bid.

A concludes to play a Tourné, and turns the heart ♡ Q, whereby he finds the ◊ King in the Skat. He lays out the ♠ 10 and ♠ 9 in the Skat, and expects to make 12 points: a heart Tourné, with one Matadore. The play is given in the margin as follows. A is the player, and is also the Vorhand, and has the lead for the first trick. Hearts are trumps.

A TOURNÉ

	A	B	C	A wins
1	♣J	♡7	J ♢	4
2	♡Q	♡A	♡8	–
3	K ♢	9 ♢	Q ♢	7
4	♡J	J ♠	A ♠	–
5	♡10	♡9	7 ♠	10
6	A ♢	♣7	8 ♢	11
7	7 ♢	K ♠	10 ♢	–
8	♣K	♣10	♣9	–
9	♡K	Q ♠	8 ♠	7
10	♣A	♣Q	♣8	14
♠ 10 and ♠ 9 in the Scat.				10
A wins 63.				

The way in which A exhausts the trumps, and makes both his Ace and his King of diamonds should be carefully studied. At trick 8, if he put on the ace of clubs, B might have the 8, and he would lose both his King and the Queen on the Ten, thereby giving him only 60 points. It has to be remembered that A knows every card out against him, because he has seen the skat cards. A wins his 12 points: a heart Tourné with one.

A SOLO. The Vorhand has refused a bid of 18, and announces spade Solo with the following cards.

A SOLO

	A	B	C	A wins
1	8 ♠	K ♠	♡J	–
2	♣A	♣K	♣7	15
3	9 ♠	Q ♠	10 ♢	–
4	7 ♢	A ♢	Q ♢	–
5	8 ♢	K ♢	♣Q	–
6	♡A	♡K	♡8	15
7	♡10	♡7	♡9	10
8	10 ♠	7 ♠	♣8	10
9	J ♠	♣J	♡Q	–
10	A ♠	J ♢	♣9	–
♢ 9 and ♣ 10 in the Scat.				10
A wins 60.				

He has the lead for the first trick, and naturally begins with the trumps. The play is given in the margin.

C wins the first trick, and leads his long suit through the player. In the last three tricks, A coaxes B to win the Ten of trumps, but if B does so, he gives up the advantage of his tenace over the player, which is now the only chance to defeat him. B knows that if he wins the Ten of trumps, B and C can make only 59 points, because A will save his trump Ace.

A, having failed to reach 61, loses a spade Solo without one: twice 11, or 22 points, which was the game he has to have won to be as good as the offer of 18 that he refused.

A GRAND B bids, both the Vorhand and the Hinterhand pass, and B announces a Grand, with the following cards.

A GRAND

	A	B	C	B wins
1	♣ 10	♣ A	J ◇	–
2	8 ♠	A ◇	7 ◇	11
3	♡ A	9 ♠	10 ♠	–
4	♣ 7	10 ◇	9 ◇	10
5	♣ 8	♡ J	Q ◇	5
6	♣ 9	J ♠	♡ 9	2
7	♡ 7	K ◇	♡ Q	7
8	♣ Q	♣ J	♡ K	9
9	♣ K	A ♠	7 ♠	15
10	♡ 10	Q ♠	K ♠	–
◇ 8 and ♡ 8 in the Scat.			–
B wins 59.			

The play is given in the margin. In a Grand, the four Jacks are the only trumps.

A has the first play, and as he leads through the player, he begins with his long suit, of which he knows that the Ace alone is out, and it might be in the skat. If the player has the Ace, C will probably trump it. If the player does not have the Ace, it is just possible he will not trump the Ten.

C, leading up to the player, opens his short weak suit. At trick 3, C knows that A has to have the Ten of hearts; otherwise, he would not fatten with the Ace. Because this shows that A can stop the heart suit, C guards the spades and lets all his hearts go.

B loses a very strong Grand, which has to have been successful if C had had one club, or if A had led anything but the club Ten. A Grand with three Matadores is worth 4 times 20, or 80 points, which is what B loses, although he can have bid only 10 or 12 in order to get the play.

— —

AMERICAN SKAT

In this now frequently played variation, the highest bidder always sees the skat before announcing his game. Although it is a gucki, it does not have to be a grand, but it can be solo or nullo if he likes. If he wins the game, he announces the scores as usual, but if he loses, he always loses double. He can announce schneider or schwarz after discarding for the skat. If he makes an announced schneider, rather than simply add a multiplier, it doubles the value of his game. An announced schwarz trebles it.

For example, spade solo with 1, schneider announced. His game is 1 for game, 1 for schneider, without 1, $3 \times 11 = 33$, doubled for announcing schneider: 66. If it is lost, it costs 132. If he makes schwarz after announcing schneider, it adds one multiplier: 77. The smallest possible game is a diamond with or without 1, worth 18: 36 if lost. The largest game possible to lose is a grand with four, schwarz announced, which costs 1008.

THE LAWS OF SKAT

THE GAMES

1. Following are the Unit values of the various games.

Frage will not be allowed. Tournee in diamonds 5, in hearts 6, in spades 7 and in clubs 8. Solo in diamonds 9, in hearts 10, in spades 11 and in clubs 12. Turned grand 12, gucki grand 16, solo grand 20 and open grand 24. Gucki nullo 15, open gucki nullo 30, solo nullo 20, open solo nullo 40, and revolution, if played, 60. Uno and duo, if played, will be worth 20, or if played open 40.

2. When there are trumps, the unit value of the game will be multiplied as follows. 1 for game; 2 for schneider; 3 for announcing schneider, or for making schwarz without having made any announcement; 4 for schwarz after having announced schneider; and 5 for announcing schwarz. To each of these multipliers will be added one for each matadore, 'with' or 'without'.

3. In tournees, if the player says, 'Passt-mir-nicht' to the first card and takes the second, he loses double if he loses his game. In guckis, whether grand or nullo, the player loses double if he loses his game.

4. The value of Ramsch will be 20 points, to be charged to the player who loses the game. If one player takes no trick, the loser will be charged 30 points. If two players take no trick, the loser will be charged 50 points. The winner of the last trick takes the skat cards. If there is a tie between two for high score, the winner of the last trick will be the loser. If the last trick is taken by the low score, and the other tricks are tied, the two high scores lose 20 points each. If all three are tied at 40 points each, there is no score.

5. In all games that are played 'open', the hand of the single player has to be laid face upwards on the table before either adversary plays a card; however, the adversaries will not be allowed to consult, nor dictate to the player what cards he will play.

FORMATION OF TABLE

6. Any number from three to six can form a table, but there will be only three active players in each deal, and they will be known, respectively, as the Vorhand, the Mittelhand and the Hinterhand. The players who hold no cards will share the fortunes of the players opposed to the single player whose score is put down.

7. There will be as many deals in each round as there are players

at the table, and no person will be allowed to withdraw from the game during a round unless the players consent to having a substitute and this substitute be found.

8. Newcomers can enter the table only after the conclusion of a round and with the consent of the other players. The new candidate for play has to take his seat so he will have the deal.

9. If seats are drawn for, the lowest skat card will have the first choice. The next lowest will sit on his left, and so on. In cutting, the cards and suits rank as in play. The player who draws the lowest card will deal the first hand, and the score will be kept by the player on his right.

10. The game will come to an end only at the conclusion of a round, and any player who wishes to stop has to give notice before the beginning of a round.

CARDS

11. There are thirty-two cards in the pack, the rank and value of which are as follows. Jack 2; ace 11; ten 10; king 4; queen 3; and the nine, eight and seven have no counting value.

12. The suits will always outrank each other in the same order: clubs, spades, hearts and diamonds. The four jacks, or Wenzels, which are always the four best trumps, will outrank each other in the same order.

13. In Nullo, the cards rank A K Q J 10 9 8 7, and the suits and jacks are all of equal rank.

DEALING

14. When four or more play at the same table, the dealer takes no cards, but gives cards to the two players sitting immediately on his left and the player next to him on his right.

15. When only three play, the Hinterhand will deal the cards.

16. The deal passes in regular order to the left.

17. After being thoroughly shuffled, the pack has to be presented to the pone (the player sitting on the dealer's right) to cut, and at least three cards have to be left in each packet. Any player can demand a right to shuffle the cards before they are dealt, but the dealer will have the last shuffle before presenting the cards to be cut. If any card is exposed in cutting, there has to be a new cut.

18. The dealer will give each active player cards, three at a time for the first round, face downwards, beginning on his left. He will then lay aside, face downwards, two cards for the skat. Each player will then receive four cards at a time for the second round, and finally three cards at a time for the last round.

19. If any card is found faced in the pack, or if the pack is proved

to be incorrect or imperfect, there has to be a new deal. An imperfect pack is one in which there are duplicate or missing cards, or cards so torn or marked that they can be identified by their back.

20. If a player deals out of turn, the deal has to stand if it is complete; otherwise, there has to be a new deal by the right dealer. When the deal stands, the next deal has to be by the player who should have dealt, and subsequent deals have to be arranged so that there will be the right number to each round. A player who deals out of turn can be penalised 10 points.

ERRORS IN DEALING

21. There are no misdeals. No matter what happens, the same dealer has to deal again if it was his proper turn to deal.

22. If a card is exposed by the dealer during the deal, there has to be a new deal or if the cards of the players become confused so that the dealer cannot separate them.

23. If the dealer gives too many or too few cards to any player, or neglects to lay out the skat cards in their proper turn, or does not give the right number of cards in each round, or gives three to one player and four to another, or fails to present the pack to be cut, there has to be a new deal, and the dealer is charged 10 points for the error.

THE SKAT CARDS

24. Any active player who takes up or sees either or both the skat cards when he is not entitled to do so will be debarred from bidding that deal. If any but an active player looks at either of the skat cards, 10 points will be deducted from his score.

25. If any Kiebitz (an onlooker who does not belong to the table) looks at either of the skat cards, he can be called on to pay the value of the game.

26. If an active player looks at the skat cards during the play, not having laid out the cards from his own hand, his game is lost if he is the single player. If he is opposed to the player, the player's game is won, but can be played out in order to see whether he can make schneider or schwarz.

27. If an active player takes one or both of the skat cards into his hand by mistake, before the bidding begins, the dealer will draw from his hand, face downwards, enough cards to reduce his hand to ten, and the player in fault will be charged 25 points' penalty and be debarred from bidding for that deal. If, in three-hand, the player in fault is the dealer, the Vorhand will draw.

28. If the successful bidder takes both of the skat cards into his hand together, or picks them up together, he will be obliged to play

a Gucki Grand, unless he has announced to play Nullo. If he puts the first card into his hand without showing it, he will be obliged to turn up the second card and play Passt-mir-nicht.

29. The player can turn up either of the skat cards, but if he exposes both, he has to play the suit of higher value.

30. If he turns a jack, he can either play in suit or announce a turned Grand.

31. A player who turns up a seven cannot announce a Nullo unless it has been previously agreed to play turned Nullos, which are worth 10 points.

32. The player who takes the skat cards has to lay out two cards in their place before a card is led. If he neglects to lay out for the skat before he plays to the first trick, or if he lays out more or fewer than two cards, and not discover the error until the first trick has been turned and quitted, he will lose his game.

BIDDING

33. All bidding will be by way of numbers that represent the value of some possible game, and the lowest bid allowed will be 10.

34. The Mittelhand has to bid to the Vorhand, and the Vorhand has to either undertake as good a game as that offered him or pass. If the Vorhand passes, the Hinterhand bids to the Mittelhand, and the Mittelhand has to either undertake as good a game as that offered or pass. If the Mittelhand passes, when bidding to the Vorhand, the Hinterhand has to bid to the Vorhand: but the Hinterhand is not allowed to say anything until either the Mittelhand or the Vorhand has passed.

35. Any figure once named cannot be recalled. A player having once passed cannot come into the bidding again.

36. The survivor of the bidding will be known as the Player, and will have the privilege of naming the game to be played; the two other active players are his adversaries.

37. If no bid is made, and the Vorhand will not undertake to play any game against the two other players, they have to play Ramsch.

ANNOUNCEMENTS

38. The player, if he does not use the skat cards, can announce any suit for the trump, or can play a Grand or Nullo.

39. If he wishes to announce schneider or schwarz, he has to do so when he names the game to be played, and before a card is led. All Open Grands are compulsory 'schwarz announced'.

40. The way of taking up the skat cards, when the player uses them, is sufficient announcement for a Tournee, Passt-mir-nicht or Guckser, but a Gucki Nullo has to be announced before the skat

cards are touched, and open Gucki Nullo has to be announced before the skat cards are seen.

41. The player is not allowed to announce either schneider or schwarz in any game in which he uses the skat cards.

42. The adversaries cannot announce schneider or schwarz under any circumstances.

43. No player but the Vorhand can announce Ramsch, and then only when no bid has been made.

PLAYING

44. In Tournee, but not in Solo, Grand or Nullo, the player can, in order to avoid the possibility of being made schneider, abandon his game as lost before playing to the second trick. The adversaries are then bound to score it as a 'game' lost, even if they could have made the player schneider.

45. No matter who the single player is, the Vorhand will always lead for the first trick. The winner of one trick leads for the next, and so on, and each player in turn has to follow suit if he can.

46. If, during the play of the hand, any player is found to have a wrong number of cards, and the other players have their right number, only the players who have their right number can win the game. If it is the player who has a wrong number, his game is lost. If it is one of his adversaries, the player's game is won.

47. If the single player leads out of turn, the cards have to be taken back if the trick is not complete and the adversary who has not played demands it. If both adversaries have played to the false lead, the trick stands. If an adversary has played to his false lead, the player cannot take it back unless the other adversary permits it.

48. If an adversary of the player leads out of turn, and the player calls attention to it, the player can immediately claim his game as won and abandon the hand, or can insist that the play proceed with a view to making the adversaries schneider or schwarz. Whether or not he proceeds, his game is won, and he can either let the false lead stand or insist on a lead from the proper hand.

49. If, during the progress of the hand, the player lays his cards on the table, face upwards, and announces he has won his game by reaching 61 or 91, whichever might be necessary in order to make good his bid, and it is proved he is mistaken, he loses his game, even if he could have taken up his cards again and won it.

50. If an adversary lays his cards on the table, face upwards, and claims to have already defeated the player's game, all that adversary's cards will be taken by the player and counted with the tricks already taken in by the player. If the adversary is found to be in error, the

player will score his game as won, even if he would have lost it had it been continued.

51. If the single player gives up his game as lost, and lays his cards on the table, the adversaries will take all these cards and add them to their own, and count their cards to see whether they have also made the player schneider.

THE REVOKE

52. If the single player revokes, and does not discover the error before the trick is turned and quitted, he loses his game. If he discovers the error and corrects it in time, there is no penalty, but any adversary who plays after him can amend his play.

53. If either adversary of the player revokes, the player can claim his game as won, but can insist on playing the hand out in order to see whether he can make schneider or schwarz. Even if the single player has over-bid his hand, he wins his game if either adversary revokes.

LOOKING BACK

54. Any active player can see the last trick turned and quitted, provided no card has been led for the next trick. If a player looks back at any other trick, or counts his cards, he loses the game, but either of the other players can insist on playing on in order to see whether they can make schneider.

55. If an adversary of the player tells his partner how many points they have taken in, or asks him to fatten a trick that is his, or calls attention in any way to the fact that the partner's play should be this way or that, the single player can at once claim his game as won and abandon his hand.

SCORING

56. The single player wins his game if he reaches 61 points. He wins schneider if he makes 91. He wins schwarz if he gets every trick.

57. If the adversaries reach 30, they are out of schneider. If they reach 60, they defeat the player. If they get to 90, they make him schneider, and if they win every trick, they make him schwarz.

58. The value of the game having been calculated according to Law Number 2, the amount won or lost will be entered on the score pad under the name of the individual player, and each following item will be added to or deducted from the previous total, so that the last entry will at all times show the exact state of the player's score.

59. At the end of the sitting, each player wins from or loses to each of the other players at the table the full amount of his score.

60. In every case in which a player loses his game, he loses what he would have won had he been successful, regardless of the amount he might have bid. However,

61. If the player fails to win a game equal to the amount he has bid, he loses the value of the next-higher game that would have made good his bid, because in no case can a player lose less than he bid, and in every case he has to lose some multiple of the game, which he declared to play.

— · —

FROG

This is a very popular game in Mexico, and seems to be an elementary form of Skat, which it resembles in many ways. Even the name might be a corruption of the simple game in Skat, which is called *frage*. The main differences are that there are four cards added to the pack for frog, and that the players win or lose according to the number of points they get above or below 61, rather than compute the value of the game by way of matadores.

PLAYERS   Three, four or five can play, but only three are active in each deal. If four play, the dealer takes no cards. If five play, he gives cards to the two on his left and the one on his right.

CARDS   There are thirty-six cards in the pack, which rank A 10 K Q J 9 8 7 6. Each Ace is worth 11, Tens 10, Kings 4, Queens 3, and Jacks 2. This gives us 120 points in the pack, and the object is to get 61 or more.

DEALING   Anyone can deal the first hand, after which the deal passes to the left. Three cards are given to each player the first round, then three for the widow, then two rounds of four cards each to the players, so that there are three hands of eleven cards each, and three cards in the widow.

THE GAMES   Each player in turn, beginning on the dealer's left, can offer to play one of three games, and the highest offer has to be accepted. A player cannot increase his own bid unless he is over-bid. The highest bidder becomes the single player, who is opposed to the two other players.

Frog In this, hearts have to be trumps. The single player turns the widow face upwards in order to show what it contained, then takes the three cards into his hand. He then has to discard in order to reduce his playing hand to eleven cards again. Any points in the cards he lays away will count for him at the end of the play.

The player on the dealer's left always leads for the first trick, any card he pleases. The other players have to follow suit if they can, but are not obliged to head the trick. If a player cannot follow suit, he has to trump, and if the third player also cannot follow suit, he has to play a trump, but is not obliged to over-trump unless he wants to.

When the eleven tricks are played, each side turns over the cards taken in and counts the points. For every point the single player gets over 60, he has to be paid a counter by each of the other players who held cards. However, if he does not get 60, he has to pay each of the other players at the table, including the ones who held no cards, if any, a counter for every point his adversaries get over 60.

Chico This outbids Frog. The player who offers this game can name any suit for the trump except hearts, but must not touch the widow, although the points in it will count for him at the end. Each point under or over 60 is worth two counters in Chico.

Grand This outbids Chico and is the highest bid possible. Hearts have to be trumps, and the player who offers this game must not touch the widow until the play is finished. Every point under or over 60 in a Grand is worth four counters.

The bidder has to play the game he names. He cannot bid Frog and play Chico, or bid Chico and play Grand. The settling up of the scores at the end, if the payments are not made at once in counters, is the same as in Skat.

— ◆ —

CRIBBAGE

Cribbage is not only one of the oldest card games; it enjoys the distinction of being quite unlike any other game, both in the way of playing it and in the system of reckoning the points. It is also peculiar because it is one of the very few really good games that require no effort of the memory: judgement and finesse are the main qualities required for success.

There are two main varieties of the game: *Five-* and *Six-card* Cribbage, and these are divided according to the number of players. The earlier writers agree in speaking of the five-card game as being the more scientific, but the more modern writers are in favour of the six-card game, which is definitely the more common and popular. The skill in Five-card Cribbage is limited to laying out for the crib and securing the 'go'; however, in Six-card Cribbage, although the scientific principles applicable to the crib remain the same as in the five-card game, there is abundant room for display of skill all through, whereby the hand is as important as the crib, and the play is sometimes more important than either. The six-card game will be described first.

CARDS   Cribbage is played with a full pack of fifty-two cards, which have no rank except the order of their sequence: K Q J 10 9 8 7 6 5 4 3 2 A, whereby the Ace is always the lowest, in either cutting or play. The cards also have a counting or pip value, whereby the three court-cards: K Q J, and the 10, are worth ten points each. All other cards, including the Ace, retain their face value. There are no trumps, and the four suits are therefore equal in value at all times.

MARKERS   The game is 61 points, and is scored or 'pegged' on a cribbage-board, which has a double row of 30 holes on each side and a game-hole at each end. The players are each provided with two pegs, and score the points as they accrue by advancing their pegs from left to right according to the number of points they make. For example, one player makes 6 for his first count. He places one of his pegs in the sixth hole from the left-hand end of the board. He then makes 4, and places the second peg four holes in advance of the first, whereby it will be shown that his total score is ten points. The third time, he makes 2, which he scores by lifting out the back peg and putting it two holes in advance of the first one. This system of pegging not only shows the total number of points made by either player; it enables the adversary to check the count, because glancing at the distance between the two pegs will show the number of points pegged last time.

When a player reaches the extreme right of the board: 30 points, he crosses over to the inner row of holes, and goes down from right to left. On reaching the end of the second row, he still has one more row to go in order to get into the game-hole, which is in the middle of the board.

When one player reaches his game-hole before the other turns the corner, it is called a *lurch*, and counts two games.

The pegs are so often lost or mislaid it is much more convenient to use a *pull-up* cribbage-board, in which every hole is provided with its own peg, which can be raised in order to indicate the count. The back pegs can be either left standing or pushed down again.

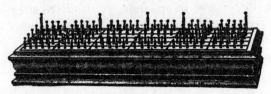

The board is always placed midway between the players.

If three people play, a triangular board is necessary. This is provided with three sets of holes and three game-holes.

When a cribbage-board is not at hand, the game can be kept by way of ruling a sheet of paper into ten divisions and marking them with the figures 1 to 0 on each side:

0	6	8	ㄥ	9	ϛ	ㄣ	Ɛ	ㄥ	I
1	2	3	4	5	6	7	8	9	0

Each player used to be provided with two coins: one silver and one copper (or different-size coins), whereby the copper coin could be advanced from point to point in order to count units and the silver coin marked the tens.

PLAYERS   Cribbage is distinctly a game for two players, although three can play, each for himself, or four, whereby two are partners against the other two. When two play, one is known as the *dealer* and the other is known as the non-dealer, or *pone*.

CUTTING   The players cut for the choice of seats, and for the first deal. The lowest cut has the choice, and deals the first hand. The Ace is low. If a player exposes more than one card, he has to cut again. Ties are also decided by way of cutting again.

STAKES   Cribbage is played for so much a game, and lurches count double. Players can either settle at the end of each game or score on a sheet of paper. In the pull-up cribbage-boards, there are nine extra pegs for counting games won. These are placed in a line with the player's game-hole at each end.

DEALING   The cards are shuffled and presented to the pone to cut, and he has to leave at least six cards in each packet. Six cards are dealt to each player, one at a time in rotation, beginning with the player on the dealer's left if there are more than two players. No trump is turned, and the remainder of the pack is placed face downwards at the end of the cribbage-board on the dealer's left.

IRREGULARITIES   It is a misdeal if any card is found faced in the pack, or if the pack is found to be imperfect, and there has to be a fresh deal by the same dealer. Any previous cuts or scores made with the imperfect pack stand good. A player who deals out of turn can be stopped before the non-dealer lifts his cards from the table. The penalty for dealing out of turn is two points, if the error is detected in time; otherwise, the deal stands good.

If the dealer neglects to have the pack cut, exposes a card in dealing, gives too many or too few cards to any player, deals a card incorrectly and fails to remedy the error before dealing another, or exposes one of his adversary's cards, the non-dealer scores two points by way of penalty. The non-dealer also has the option of demanding a fresh deal by the same dealer or of letting the deal stand. If the error is simply an irregularity in the way of dealing, or an exposed card, the pone has to decide without looking at his cards. If either player has too many or too few cards, the pone can look at the hand dealt to him before deciding whether or not to have a fresh deal; however, if it is the pone himself who has too many or too few cards, he has to discover and announce the error before lifting his cards from the table; otherwise, he will not be entitled to the option of letting the deal stand. If the pone has too many cards, he can return the surplus to the top of the pack, without showing or naming them. If the dealer has too many cards, the pone can draw from his hand face downwards, and return the surplus to the top of the pack; however, the pone cannot look at the cards so drawn unless the dealer has seen them. If there are too few cards, and the pone elects to have the deal stand, the deficiency has to be supplied from the top of the pack.

THE CRIB When the cards are dealt, each player takes up his six cards and examines them with a view to laying out two cards, face downwards, for the crib, thereby leaving himself four cards with which to play. The four cards that form the crib, two from each hand, always belong to the dealer, and it is usual for each player, in discarding for the crib, to slip his two cards under the end of the cribbage-board opposite the one occupied by the remainder of the pack.

Cards once laid out for the crib, and the hand removed from them, cannot be taken up again. A penalty of two points can be scored by the adversary for each card so taken up again, whether or not it is returned to the player's hand. If either player confuses his cards in any way with the ones of the crib, his adversary scores two points, and can also claim a fresh deal.

If it is not discovered that a player has too many cards until he comes to lay out for the crib, the same rules apply that are given for misdealing, but if he has too few cards, there is no remedy, because he has lifted his hand. He has to lay out two cards for the crib and play with what remain, and his adversary scores two points' penalty at the same time.

THE STARTER When both players have discarded for the crib, the non-dealer cuts the remainder of the pack, and the dealer lifts the top card from the portion left on the table, turning it face upwards. When the two portions are again united, the turned card is placed face upwards on the pack, and is known as the starter, because it forms the starting-point in the count for every hand and crib. At least four cards have to be left in each packet in cutting for the starter. If the starter is found face upwards, there has to be a new deal.

If the starter is a Jack, the dealer immediately pegs two points *for his heels.* If he does not peg these two holes before he plays a card, the score is lost. If the Jack of the same suit as that of the starter is found in the hand or crib of any player, it is called ***his nobs***, and when the hand is reckoned up after the play is over, one point can be scored for it.

If the dealer exposes more than one card after the pack has been properly cut, his adversary can choose which of the exposed cards will be the starter.

In order to understand the motives that govern the players in discarding, and the influences the starter has on the value of the hands and crib, it will be necessary to describe the objects of the game, before giving the method of play.

OBJECTS OF THE GAME   The main object in Cribbage is to form and preserve various counting combinations. As these combinations occur in the course of play, or are shown in the hand or crib after the play is over, their value in points is pegged on the cribbage-board, and the player who first pegs a sufficient number of these combinations to reach a total of 61 points wins the game.

There are five main varieties of these counting combinations: Pairs, Triplets, Fours, Sequences, and Fifteens, besides some minor counts that will be discussed in their proper place.

The various counting combinations in Cribbage can arise in two ways. They can be formed by combining the cards played by one person with the ones played by his adversary, or they can be found in the individual hand or crib after the play is over. In the latter case, the starter is considered as part of each hand and crib, whereby each of them is increased to five available counting cards.

PAIRS   A pair is any two cards of the same denomination, such as two Fives or two Queens, and its counting value is always the same: 2 points. *Triplets*, usually called Pairs Royal, Proils or Prials, are any three cards of the same denomination, such as three Nines. Their value is the number of separate pairs that can be formed with the three cards, which is three, so the combination is always worth 6 points. The pairs that can be formed with three Nines, for example, would be as follows.

Fours, sometimes called Double Pairs Royal, or Deproils, are any four cards of the same denomination, such as four Fours, and their counting value is the number of separate pairs that can be formed with the four cards, which is six. The combination is therefore always worth 12 points. The combinations of four cards, arranged in pairs, are as follows.

Whether the aforementioned combinations are formed during the play of the hand or are found in the hand or crib after the play is over, their counting value is exactly the same.

SEQUENCES Any three or more cards that follow each other in numerical order will form a sequence. A sequence can also run into the court-cards, such as 9 10 J, 10 J Q, or J Q K, but Q K A is not a sequence in Cribbage. The counting value of a sequence is one point for each card in it. Sequences formed in the course of play always have to be single, although the cards that form them do not have to fall in regular order. The cards found in the hand or crib can be double, and the ones formed with the aid of the starter can be treble or quadruple.

The method of computing the value of double and treble sequences should be thoroughly understood, so that these combinations can be counted at sight. A few examples will show that each combination belongs to a specific class, to which the same counting value is always attached. These classes are distinguished by the number of duplicates of the sequence cards.

  If you hold three cards that form a sequence, and also have a duplicate of any one of them, no matter which, it is evident that by substituting the card of equal value you can form another sequence. These combinations are therefore always worth 8 points: 6 for the *double*

run, as it is called, and 2 for the pair, no matter what the cards are that form the combination.

     If the five cards in the hand and starter together contain a run of three with two duplicates, it is evident that three separate sequences can be formed by using each of the duplicates alternately. These combinations are always worth 15 points: 9 for the triple run of three, and 6 for the pair royal.

     If the duplicates are of two different cards, no matter which, it will be found that four different sequences of three cards each can be formed by changing the Aces and Threes alternately. These combinations are therefore always worth 16 points: four runs of three, worth 12; and 4 points for the two separate pairs.

     If the five cards contain one sequence of four, and one duplicate, the combination will always be worth 10 points: 8 for the double run of four, and 2 for the pair.

The aforementioned combinations should be thoroughly familiar to every player, so he can know the exact value of the combination the moment he sees the length of the sequence and the number of duplicates.

TWO-CARD FIFTEENS Any combination of two or more cards, the total face value of which is exactly 15, is called *fifteen-two*, because each fifteen so formed is worth two points in the pegging. There are only three combinations of two cards that will form fifteen: a Five with any court-card or Ten, a Nine and a Six, and an Eight and a Seven. The way of counting duplicates is the same as that used for the pairs and sequences, and the player should be equally familiar with each variety of combination. The fifteens formed by *two cards* only are the simplest, and should be studied first.

   It is obvious that if there is in the hand or the starter a duplicate of either of the cards that form the fifteen, no matter which, another fifteen cards can be formed, and the combination will therefore always be worth 6 points: 4 for the two fifteens, and 2 for the pair. It must not be forgotten that in the case of *tenth cards*, as they are called, the duplicates cannot form pairs, as for example with K J 5. The fifteen is duplicated, but there is no pair.

If there are two duplicates of either card, the combination will always be worth 12 points: 6 for the three fifteens, and 6 more for the pair royal.

If the duplicates are of two different cards, the combination is still worth 12, because four different fifteens can be formed by combining each Nine with each Six separately, and there are two single pairs.

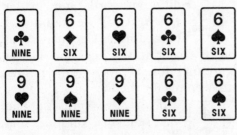

The same is true of any combinations of two-card fifteens in which all five cards are of value; they are both of the same pegging value: 20 points. If there are three duplicates of one card in the original fifteen, the four separate fifteens will be worth 8, and the double pair royal 12. If there are two duplicates of one card, and one of the other, six separate fifteens can be formed by combining each Nine with each Six, pegging 12, and the pair royal of one card with the single pair of the other will add 8 more.

THREE-CARD FIFTEENS can be formed in fifteen ways, ranging from 10 4 A to 5 5 5. If you hold any of these combinations, and have a fourth card that is a duplicate of any of the three cards that form the fifteen, the value of the combination will depend on how many cards you can replace with the duplicate card.

If you have an extra tenth card, you can replace the other tenth card once only, and the total value of the combination is therefore 6 points, which is expressed by the formula 'Fifteen-two, fifteen-four, and a pair'.

If your combination was 9 3 3, and you had another 9, the same thing would be true; however, if your duplicate is a Three, there are two cards that can be replaced, and the combination is therefore worth 12: 6 for the three fifteens, and 6 more for the pair royal.

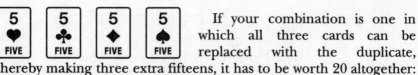 If your combination is one in which all three cards can be replaced with the duplicate, thereby making three extra fifteens, it has to be worth 20 altogether: 8 for the four fifteens, and 12 for the double pair royal.

 If you have two duplicates of any one card in the original combination, there are only two extra fifteens, and the combination will be worth 12: 6 for the three fifteens, and 6 more for the pair royal.

 If you have duplicates of two different cards, you can form four fifteens, because you can replace the Seven first, then the Six, and then put the first Seven back again with the new Six. This will make the combination of the same value as if you had three duplicates of one card, 12 points: 8 for the four fifteens, and 4 for the two single pairs.

COMBINATIONS The beginner's greatest difficulty is in counting hands that contain all three varieties of counts: pairs, sequences, and fifteens. However, if he is familiar with the values of the various combinations taken separately, he will have no difficulty in computing them when they are found together. A regular order should be observed in going over the hands, so that nothing will be forgotten. Most players begin with the fifteens, because these are more liable to be overlooked, and then reckon the value of the runs and pairs together.

Take the following four examples.

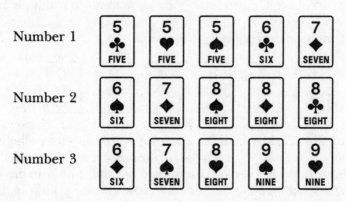

Number 4

Number 1 contains a fifteen in addition to the three runs of three and the pair royal, and is therefore worth 17 altogether. Numbers 2 and 3 each contain three fifteens; however, Number 2 is worth 21 points on account of the three runs of three and the pair royal, whereas Number 3 is worth only 16: a double run of four and a single pair. Number 4 contains four fifteens in addition to the four runs of three and two single pairs, and is therefore worth 24 points.

The best combination that can be held in hand or crib is three Fives and a Jack, whereby the Five is of the same suit as that of the Jack for a starter. We have already noted that the four Fives by themselves are worth 20, to which we have to add the four extra fifteens made by combining the Jack with each Five separately, and one more point for his nobs: 29 altogether. If the Jack were the starter, the combination would be worth 30 to the dealer, but his heels would have to be counted before a card were played.

FLUSHES In addition to the aforementioned combinations, if all four cards in the hand are of the same suit, the player can peg four points for the flush; if the starter is also of the same suit, he can peg five points. A flush does not count in the crib unless the starter is of the same suit, whereby it counts five points. Flushes are never made in play.

LAYING OUT FOR THE CRIB Having this knowledge of the objects of the game, and the various counting combinations, we can note that each player should keep the cards that count the most for him, or that are most likely to form good combinations with different starters.

Suppose the non-dealer holds these cards:

If he puts the two Eights in his adversary's crib, he not only gives him two very good cards, which go to form a great many valuable combinations; he leaves himself absolutely nothing but 2 points for a single fifteen, formed by the 9 and 6. It would be a little better, but still very bad play, for him to discard the 8 and 6, thereby leaving himself a sequence of four cards and a fifteen: 6 points altogether. He might do slightly better by discarding the 10 and 8, thereby leaving himself a run of four, and two fifteens: 8 points altogether. If he discards either the 10 and the 9, or the 10 and the 6, he will leave himself a double run of three, a pair, and two fifteens: 12 altogether. Of these two discards, the discard of the 10 and 6 is better than that of the 10 and 9, because the 10 and 9 might help to form a sequence in the adversary's crib, whereas the 10 and 6 are so far apart they are very unlikely to be of any use.

Cards that are likely to form parts of sequences are called *close cards*, and cards that are too widely separated to do so are called *wide cards*.

METHOD OF PLAYING When the crib is laid out, and the starter is cut, the pone begins by playing any card he pleases. The card he selects he lays face upwards on the table on his own side of the cribbage-board, and at the same time announces its pip value: two, five or ten – whatever it might be. It is then the dealer's turn to play a card from his hand, which is also laid face upwards on the table, but on the dealer's side of the cribbage-board. Rather than announce the pip value of this second card, the dealer calls out the total value of the two cards taken together. The pone then lays another card on the table face upwards and on the top of the first, which is not turned face downwards, and at the same time announces the total pip value of the three cards so far played, whereby the dealer plays again, and so on.

If at any time the total pip value of the cards played is exactly 15 or 31, the player who plays the card that brings it to that number pegs two points for it at once. If any counting combination, such as a pair, pair royal or sequence is formed by the cards played, its value is pegged by the person who plays the card that completes the combination; however, neither player is allowed to play a card that will make the total pip value of the cards played pass 31. The method of forming and pegging these various combinations in play will be better understood if they are described separately. A card once played cannot be taken up again, unless it passes 31.

PAIRS If the first card played by the pone is a 6, and the dealer also has a 6, the latter will probably play it, and announce, 'Twelve, with a pair,' and peg two holes. If the pone holds a third six, he will immediately play it, and announce, 'Eighteen, with a pair royal,' and peg six holes for the three pairs that can be formed with the three Sixes, although he does not hold all of them. If the dealer is fortunate enough to hold the fourth Six, he might rejoin with,

'Twenty-four, with a double-pair-royal.' This will entitle him to peg twelve more holes, although he has already pegged the single pair.

SEQUENCES   Suppose the first card played by the pone is a 4. The dealer plays a 2, and announces, 'Six.' The pone plays a 3, and announces, 'Nine, with a run of three,' and pegs three holes for the sequence formed in play. The dealer plays an Ace, 'Ten, with a run of four,' and pegs four holes for the sequence of four cards made in play, all of which are face upwards on the table, although he holds only two of them.

FIFTEENS   The pone then plays a 5, which, added to the 10 just announced by the dealer, makes 15, with a run of five cards: seven holes to peg altogether. (This is quite independent of the sequence previously scored, just as the double pair royal was of the previous single pair.) The dealer now plays a deuce, and announces seventeen. This card does not form any sequence with the cards that have gone immediately before it, because if the order of play is retraced, it will be found that another deuce is encountered before we reach the Four. This illustrates the rule already given, that sequences formed in play always have to be single, and cannot be reckoned with substitute cards, such as pairs royal; if they could, the last player in this case might claim a double run of five and a pair.

The pone now plays another 4, which forms the sequence afresh if we go back to the third card played. He announces, 'Twenty-one, with a run of five,' and pegs five holes more. The dealer plays a 3, and also claims a run of five, which he pegs, and because that is the last card to be played in that hand, he also pegs one hole for ***last card***.

The total score of the dealer is now 10 points, and that of the pone is 15. The cards they held, and the order in which they were played, are as follows.

Pone:

Dealer:

SHOWING   In order to illustrate the way of counting the hands, which is called showing, let's suppose the starter to be a Queen, and that the pone discarded an Ace and a Ten for the crib, whereby the dealer laid out two Jacks.

The non-dealer always has the first show, as an offset to the advantage of the dealer's crib. The pone therefore shows his hand, which, combined with the starter, is as follows.

This is worth 10 holes, the run of three with one duplicate is always worth 8, and the fifteen formed by the starter and the Five counts 2 more. This puts the pone's total score to 25 points.

The dealer then counts, and shows his hand first. This, with the starter, is as follows.

This is worth 14 holes. In addition to the run of three with one duplicate, three fifteens can be formed by combining the starter and a Three with each of the deuces, then taking the starter and the Ace with both the deuces together. This puts the dealer's total score to 24, and the crib is still to count. This is as follows, with the starter.

This is worth 9 holes: 8 for the run of three, with one duplicate and 1 for his nobs. There are no fifteens, and the Ace is worthless. This puts the dealer three holes around the corner and on the homestretch for the game-hole.

The deal now passes to the player who was the pone, and the next crib will belong to him.

Beginners often experience difficulty in deciding when a run has been made in play and when it has not. If there is any dispute about it, the cards should be placed as shown in these illustrations, and if any duplicate is encountered before the run is complete, it cannot be pegged.

Take the following examples.

There is no sequence, because we encounter a duplicate deuce before we reach the Five. If the last player had a Five to play now, it would make a run of five cards, stopping at the deuce of hearts. Take the following.

There is no sequence; however, had the pone played his Five for his second card, the dealer would have pegged two runs: one of four, and one of six, besides the last card, the pone thereby making one run of five and a pair, as follows.

It will be seen that had the dealer not played his Ace and kept his Six at the last, the pone would have pegged eleven holes on him instead of seven.

GO, AND THIRTY-ONE When a person has no card that he can play without making the total pip value of all the cards played more than 31, he has to say to his adversary, 'Go.' This means, 'Go on and play, because I cannot.' If his adversary has no cards left, the player has to say, 'Go' to himself. When a person is told to go, he has to play as many cards as he can without passing 31. If he reaches 31 exactly, he scores two points; if he cannot quite reach it, he scores one point for the go. The principle is that if 31 cannot be made by either player, the one who plays the card that brought the count nearest to it will count one for it, even if he has told himself to go. There is no count for 'last card' if it makes 31. However, the 'last card' counts if it makes 15.

If a player tells another to go when he can still play himself, he forfeits two points, and his adversary can, if he chooses, take back the cards to the point at which the error occurred and have them played over again. The same penalty can be enforced against a player who pegs for a go when he can still play.

Suppose the first card played is a Jack. The dealer, who holds two Nines, an Eight and a Five, plays the Five and pegs 2 for the fifteen. The pone plays a Nine, and announces the total as twenty-four. The dealer cannot pair this Nine, because it would run the count past 31; nor can he play the Eight, so he says, 'Go.' The pone pegs the go without playing, which shows he is also unable to play, having nothing as small as a Seven.

Both players then turn down the cards already played, and the player whose turn it is to play begins all over again with his remaining cards or card, whereby he announces its face value and his adversary plays after him until either their cards are exhausted or they reach another 31.

To continue the aforementioned example, let's suppose the dealer to play one of his Nines. The pone plays a Jack, and announces 'Nineteen.' The dealer plays his remaining Nine, and calls 'Twenty-eight.' The pone tells him to go, and he pegs one. These three cards are turned down. The pone then plays a Ten, and the dealer marks one for the last card. The hands and crib are then shown.

If either player can reach exactly 31, he scores two points for it, whether or not he has been told to go. Suppose the pone begins with a Nine. The dealer plays a Six and pegs 2 for the fifteen. The pone pairs the Six, calls 'Twenty-one,' and pegs 2 for the pair. The dealer, who has two Fives and a Four in his hand, plays the Four, and calls 'Twenty-five,' hoping the pone has no small card, whereby the dealer will be enabled to make a run of three with one of his Fives if he is told to go. However, the pone plays a Five, and calls, 'Thirty, with a run of three.' The dealer tells him to go, and he plays an Ace, pegging two holes for the 31. The cards are all turned down, and because the pone has no cards, the dealer plays his two Fives, and pegs a pair and the last card. The pair counts in this case because the adversary has no cards to interfere with it. A run of three might be played and scored in the same way, because the scores for combinations made in play are determined by the order in which the cards are played, irrespective of who plays them.

IRREGULARITIES IN HANDS If a player is found to have too many or too few cards, after he has laid out for the crib, his adversary pegs two points, and can also claim a fresh deal. If the deal is allowed to stand, superfluous cards have to be drawn at random by the adversary, who can look at the card or cards so drawn before placing them in the pack. If either player is found to have too few cards after having laid out for the crib, he has no remedy. His adversary pegs two points, and the short hand has to be played and shown for what it is worth.

IRREGULAR CRIBS   If the superfluous card is found in the crib, and the non-dealer had the short hand, the dealer can reckon all the combinations he can make in the six-card crib; however, if it was the dealer who had the short hand, the superfluous crib is void. If the crib contains a superfluous card, and both of the players have their right number, the non-dealer pegs two holes for the evident misdeal, and the crib is void. If both players have their right number, and the crib is short, it has to be shown for what it is worth, but the non-dealer pegs two holes for the evident misdeal.

IRREGULAR ANNOUNCEMENTS   There is no penalty if a player announces a wrong number as the total of the cards played, provided he does not peg an erroneous fifteen or thirty-one. If the following player does not correct the announcement, but plays and adds to it, the error cannot be rectified. If any holes are pegged for an erroneous announcement, the adversary can demand they be taken down again, and can add the number to his own score.

MISCOUNTING   If a player over-counts his hand, crib or play, and pegs the points erroneously claimed, his adversary can call attention to the error and demand the superfluous points be taken down again, and can add them to his own score as penalty. If a player neglects to peg the full value of his hand, crib or play, his adversary can add the neglected points to his own score, after pointing out the omission. If a player is mistaken in exacting either of these penalties, he not only has to take down what he pegged; he has to allow his adversary to peg the same number as that of the penalty.

None of these corrections can be claimed until the player in error has pegged and quitted the score, that is, removed his fingers from the front peg. The claim should always be prefaced by the word *Muggins*. If the error is one of omission in play, the adversary has to play his own card before claiming muggins. If it is in the hand or crib, the adversary has to wait until the points claimed are pegged and quitted. If there are no points claimed, he has to wait until the cards are turned face downwards, thereby acknowledging that there is evidently nothing to score. A player is not allowed to tell his adversary whether or not he has counted his hand or crib correctly until it is pegged.

NINETEEN   Because it is impossible to hold 19 in hand or crib, it is a common practice for a player, when he has nothing at all to score, to announce, 'Nineteen.' The numbers twenty-seven, twenty-six and twenty-five are also impossible.

PEGGING   Neither player is allowed to touch the other's pegs. If the score is erroneous, the player in fault has to be called on to remedy it himself. A player whose pegs are touched by his adversary can score two holes for penalty. If a player removes his adversary's front peg, the latter can immediately claim the game. If a player displaces his own front peg, he has to place it behind the other. If both players displace their front pegs, as by accident, they can agree to replace them where they believe them to have stood, but if they cannot agree, they have to call the game void.

PEGGING OUT   In pegging during the play, the first player to reach his game-hole wins, no matter what either player has in hand or crib. If neither player can peg out in play, the non-dealer has the first show. If he cannot show out, the dealer proceeds to count his hand and then his crib. If he cannot show out, there has to be a new deal.

CHEATING   The greatest advantage at Cribbage is to secure good starters, and for this purpose the cheat adopts various methods of trimming and marking the cards so he can secure a starter that is exactly suited to his hand. After trimming specific cards slightly longer or shorter than others, the pack to be cut can be presented to the pone in such a way that he will unconsciously lift them by either the ends or the sides, according to the wish of the dealer, and thereby uncover a starter that is exactly suited to the dealer's hand or crib. When the card sharp has the cut, he can naturally uncover any card he pleases. With marked edges, the pone can cut down to a card of any desired denomination. Some audacious gamblers make it a rule to get a starter by simply removing the top card and turning up the next one. Needless to say, the second card has been carefully pre-arranged. Any person who fingers the pack longer than necessary in cutting starters, or who cuts sometimes by the edge and sometimes by the side, will bear watching. Marked cards and second dealing are great weapons in a game in which so much depends on having knowledge of the adversary's hand and on securing good counting cards for yourself.

SUGGESTIONS FOR GOOD PLAY   In the six-card game, the hand is more valuable than the crib, because you know what it contains, whereas the crib is largely speculative. In the five-card game, in which there are only three cards in the hand and four in the crib, it is usual to sacrifice the hand very largely for the possibilities of the crib, because of the much larger scores that can be made with five cards: the starter and four in the crib.

BAULKING   In both games, it is the duty of the pone to baulk the dealer's crib as much as possible, by laying out cards that are very unlikely to be worth anything, in either making fifteens or filling up sequences. Pairs it is impossible to provide against, and the chance of making a flush is remote, but should be avoided if there is any choice. The best baulk is a King and Nine, and tenth cards and Aces are also very good cards to lay out. Cards that are at least two pips apart, called *wide cards*, are better than *close cards*, because the latter can form sequences. Fives are very bad discards, as are any cards that form a five or a fifteen.

THE CRIB   In laying out for his own crib, the dealer should preserve his own hand as much as possible; however, other things being equal, the best cards to lay out are pairs, close cards and cards that form fives, such as Fours and Aces. It these elements can be combined, so much the better. An Eight and a Seven, for example, are not only close cards, being only one pip apart; they form a fifteen. The same is true of a trey and deuce.

KEEPING   In selecting the hand to keep, much depends on the score. Early in the game, you want a counting hand; near the end, especially if you have only four or five points to go, you want a pegging hand, that is, one in which every card is different, so you can pair several cards or make fifteens with almost anything the pone might lead. In keeping a counting hand, much depends on whether it is good in itself or it requires a starter. In reckoning on the possibilities of the starter, it must never be forgotten that there are sixteen tenth cards in the pack, and that they are therefore the most probable starters of all. It is better to keep sequences open at both ends than the sequences open in the middle. With two Sevens and two Eights, either a Six or a Nine will make your hand worth 24; however, with two Eights and two Sixes, nothing but a Seven will improve your hand more than 4 points. Sequences are the best to keep, especially the ones of three cards with a duplicate. After them, pairs royal are valuable, and next to them, cards that will make a number of fives in various combinations, such as two Threes and two deuces.

LEADING   There are two systems of playing, known as *playing off* and *playing on*, and they are selected according to the player's position in the score. Long experience has shown that in six-card

Cribbage, the average expectation of the non-dealer for his hand and play is 12 points, and that for the dealer, in hand, crib and play it is 17. This being so, each player having had a deal, the players' scores should be about 29. If a player is 29 or more, he is said to be *at home*; and if he is seven or more points ahead of his adversary on even deals, he is said to be *safe at home*. When a player is safe at home, he should play off, that is, take no chances of scoring himself that might give his adversary a chance to make a still better score. This is usually found in the method of playing sequences. A player who avoids playing cards that might lead up to a run is said to play off. If he invites the run, hoping to make it longer himself, he is said to play on. When a player is behind, it is better for him to play on and to seize every chance to score, especially with sequences. Because it is considered to be an advantage to be ahead on the first deal, most players prefer a forward game on the opening hand.

PLAYING OFF   In this, it is best to play cards on which it is unlikely your adversary can score. Lead Aces, Twos and Threes, which cannot be made into fifteens. Do not pair his cards unless you have a card that will make you a double pair royal (without passing 31), should he make a pair royal on you. Do not play close cards that he might turn into sequences.

Never play a card that will allow the adversary to make a double score, such as a pair and a fifteen, or a sequence and a fifteen at the same time. Plays such as the following are all bad plays. 9 on 3; 7 on A; 6 on 3, 4 or 5; 5 on 5; 4 on 7; 3 on 9; and A on 7. All these expose you to the immediate rejoinder of a double count. Naturally, if you have the card to make a pair royal in return, that is another matter, and is playing on, not playing off.

Do not play a card that brings the pip count to 5 or 21 if you can help it, because any tenth card will enable your adversary to peg two holes. Be slightly wary about pairing the first card played, unless you have a third of the same denomination. If you have a choice between a pair and a sequence, your decision will depend on whether you are playing off or on. If you are playing off, make the pair, and take no chances of long runs.

PLAYING ON   In this, you play to give your adversary a count, hoping to make a better yourself. It is always advantageous to play one of a pair, and to begin with one end of a sequence. If he pairs your first card, you can reply with a pair royal. If he plays to make a sequence, you can sometimes hold him off until you get the score, and he will be unable to continue the run without passing 31. Play one of two cards that form a five, such as 3 and 2, and 4 and A. If he plays a tenth card to it, you can peg fifteen. In playing on, you should make all the sequences possible, taking chances of your adversary's being able to continue the run. If you think he is leading you on, you have to be guided by the state of the score as to how much you can risk.

Towards the end, you have to reckon reasonably closely how many points you can afford to risk your adversary's making without putting him out. If you have enough in your hand to get out on the show, you should not attempt to make a single point in play. Pair nothing, because he might come out with a pair royal, and make no runs, because he might extend them. However, if you do not have enough to show out, you have to take every chance to peg the difference, because if you cannot get out in play and first show, the dealer not only has both hand and crib against you; he has the first show on the next deal. In six-card Cribbage, the usual pegging for the play is five holes for the dealer, and four or five for the non-dealer. By adding this expectation to your show, you can see how many you can hope to peg yourself, and how many the dealer will probably be on hand, crib and peg altogether. The hands should average 7 points, the cribs 5.

— —

FIVE-CARD CRIBBAGE

In this form of the game, only five cards are dealt to each player, one at a time. Two of these are laid out for the crib, and the three remaining are used in play, exactly as in the six-card game.

THREE FOR LAST   The non-dealer on the first hand of each game is allowed to peg three holes as a compensation for the advantage his adversary derives from having the first deal. Although the rules allow these three holes to be pegged at any time during the game, the holes should be put up immediately, in order to avoid disputes.

There is no more play after a go is declared or either player has reached 31. The score for 31 is two holes, and for the go one hole. Great importance is attached to the score for the go in five-card Cribbage, because so little is made in play that every point counts.

THE CRIB   This is the most important thing in the five-card game, and it is much more important to baulk your adversary's crib than to preserve your own hand. The best baulking cards are a King with a 10, 9, 8, 7, 6 or A. Never lay out a Jack, nor two cards that form a five, nor any pair, nor any two close cards. In laying out for your own crib, Fives, Sevens and Eights are the best. Any pair, any two cards that make five or fifteen, and any close cards are also good. Keep pairs royal and runs in your hand, and do not forget that a flush of three counts in the hand; however, the starter has to agree to make a flush in the crib.

PLAYING OFF AND ON   The pegging in play is usually small: 2 for the dealer, and an average of 1½ for the non-dealer, hence the importance of the go. The average hand is slightly fewer than 5, the crib about 5. The player is at home if he has pegged 17 in two deals: his own and his adversary's. He is safe at home if he is 7 ahead or his adversary is 7 behind.

In Five-card Cribbage, more than any other game, it is true that a game is never won until it is lost. Take the following example, in which the pone is 56 up, and the dealer has pegged only 5 holes altogether. The separated cards show the cards laid out for the crib, and the odd card is the starter.

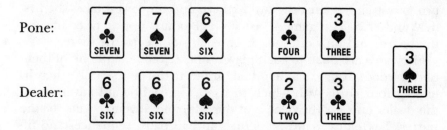

The pone leads a Seven, and afterwards pairs the dealer's Six, thereby pegging to 58. The dealer pegs 6 for the pair royal, and is told to go. This enables the dealer to make a double pair royal and 31, thereby pegging fourteen holes more. (The last card does not count when a go or 31 is pegged.) On the show, the pone has only a pair, which puts him to 60, within one of the game-hole. The dealer shows 12 in hand and 17 in crib, thereby making him 54 up. In the next deal, the player who wanted one could not peg, whereby his adversary secures a fifteen and a go, and shows out with a pair and a fifteen: 61 up and game.

— —

THREE-HANDED CRIBBAGE

Five cards are dealt to each player, then another, face downwards, for the foundation of the crib. Each player then lays out one card in order to make the dealer's crib up to four. The starter is cut by the player on the dealer's left, and the game proceeds as in six-card Cribbage, whereby the eldest hand has the first show and the dealer has the last.

— —

FOUR-HANDED CRIBBAGE

When four play, they cut for partners, choice of seats, and deal; the two lowest pair against the two highest, and the lowest takes the first deal and crib. The game is usually 121 points up, or twice around the board, and only one player on each side keeps the score.

Five cards are dealt to each player, one at a time, and one of them is discarded from each hand in order to form the crib, thereby leaving four cards with which to play. The right-hand adversary of the dealer cuts for the deal, and the left-hand adversary cuts for the starter. The eldest hand plays first, and all pairs, sequences and fifteens are scored by the side that makes them. If a player says, 'Go,' his left-hand neighbour has to play or pass the go to the next player on his left. In this way, it can pass entirely around the table to the last player, who will then peg for it.

In this game, there is a great deal more in the play than in either hand or crib. The average hand and crib is the same as in six-card Cribbage: 7 for the hand and 5 for the crib, but the play for the partners will run to 8 or 10 holes. Either side should be at home with 48 to 50 on two deals: four individual hands of 7 each, four plays of five each, and one crib of 5.

— —

SEVEN-CARD CRIBBAGE

This form of the game for two players differs from the other forms only in the number of cards dealt to each player, which is seven. Two cards are laid out for the crib, and five are kept for playing. There being six cards in each hand, with the starter, the counting combinations sometimes run into high figures, so it is usual to play the game 121 or even 181 points up.

There are no authoritative *Laws* for Cribbage, but the aforementioned descriptions contain all the regulations that are in force at the best venues.

PIQUET

— · —

Piquet is supposed to have been introduced during the reign of England's Charles VII, and was designed as a motif for a ballet of living cards that was performed in the palace of Chinon. Of the etymology of the word *piques* little or nothing is known, but the game itself is one of the perennials that have survived much more pretentious rivals, and, thanks to its intrinsic merits, it has never since its invention ceased to be more or less à la mode.

There are several varieties of Piquet, but the straightforward game for two players, sometimes called *Piquet au Cent*, or 100 points up, is the most common and popular, and will be described first.

CARDS Piquet is played with a pack of thirty-two cards, and all cards below the Seven are deleted. The cards rank A K Q J 10 9 8 7, and the Ace is the highest in both cutting and play. There is no trump in Piquet, and all suits are equal in value. Two packs are sometimes used, one by each player in his proper turn to deal.

The cards have a specific pip-counting value, whereby the Ace is reckoned for 11, other court-cards for 10 each, and the 7 8 9 10 for their face value.

MARKERS Because the scores are not put down until the end of the hand or play, the game is usually kept on a sheet of paper, or can be marked on a cribbage-board.

PLAYERS Piquet is played by two people, who sit opposite each other. They are known as the dealer, and the elder hand or pone.

CUTTING The players cut for seats and cards, whereby the lower cut has the choice, and deals the first hand. If a player exposes more than one card, the lowest of the exposed cards have to be taken as his cut. Ties are decided by way of cutting a second time.

494

STAKES   Piquet is played for so much a game of 100 points, but if the loser has not reached 50 points, he is lurched and loses a double game.

DEALING   When the cards are shuffled, they are presented to the pone to cut, and at least two cards have to be left in each packet. Twelve cards are dealt to each player, either two or three at a time, but whichever method is first selected has to be maintained throughout the game. In England, the cards are always dealt by twos. No trump is turned. The remaining eight cards are placed face downwards on the table, whereby the five top cards are laid cross-wise on the three at the bottom. These eight cards are called the talon or stock. Each player deals in turn.

IRREGULARITIES IN DEALING   If the pack is proved to be imperfect, the deal is void, but all previous scores or cuts made with that pack stand good. A misdeal does not lose the deal under any circumstances. If a card is found faced in the pack, there has to be a fresh deal with the same cards. If a player deals out of turn, and detects the error himself before he sees any of his cards, he can insist on his adversary's dealing, even if the adversary has seen his cards. Because the deal is a disadvantage, the adversary is not bound to correct the player in error.

If the dealer gives too many or too few cards to either player, a new deal is at the option of the adversary. The error will naturally be detected when it is found that there are only seven cards in the talon. If the non-dealer elects to have the deal stand, the error in the player's hand has to be remedied in the discard, as will presently be described, and the stock has to be divided 4–3 or 5–2, according to which player has too many cards.

CARTE BLANCHE   When the cards are dealt, each player takes up his twelve cards and sorts them into suits. If the pone finds himself without a K Q or a J, he should immediately claim 10 points for carte blanche. If the dealer holds carte blanche, he does not declare it until the pone has discarded.

DISCARDING   The five cards on the top of the talon belong to the pone, and he can discard from his hand any number of cards from one to five, and replace them by an equal number from the top of the stock. He has to take at least one card, and has to take from the talon in the natural order of the cards. If he has elected to let a deal stand in which he has been given thirteen cards, he is entitled to four cards only from the talon, and in all cases has to leave himself with twelve cards after his discard and draw are completed. If he does not take all five cards, he has to announce distinctly how many he leaves, because if he fails to do so, the dealer is not liable for having too many cards.

The dealer then discards, and first declares carte blanche if he holds it. In England, he does not have to draw at all, and in France he has to draw at least one card. Besides the three cards that belong to him, he is entitled to take as many as he pleases of the cards left by the pone, and in drawing from the talon, he has to take the cards in the order in which they come. If two cards are left by the pone, for example, and the dealer wants three only, he has to take the two left by the pone and one of his own three, and leave the two others face downwards on the table. The number of cards in hand after the discard and draw has to be exactly twelve. Only one discard is allowed, and having been made it cannot be changed after the stock has been touched.

If the pone does not take all the cards to which he is entitled, he is allowed to look at the cards that remain of the first five that were on the talon, but on no account can he look at any of the dealer's three. If the dealer leaves any cards in the stock, he has a right to look at them, but the pone cannot see them until he has led for the first trick, or announced the suit he will lead. If he announces a suit, and after seeing the cards in the stock does not lead that suit, the dealer can call a suit. If the dealer does not look at the remaining cards, the pone also cannot see them.

Each player keeps his discards separate from those of his adversary, and is allowed to refer to them at any time during the play of the hand, but on no account can he see his adversary's discards, unless that adversary has mixed with them one or more of the unseen cards that were left in the stock, and afterwards picks up and looks at his discard, including the card the other adversary is entitled to see. For example, the dealer leaves a card without looking at it. This he afterwards mixes with his discard. Now, if he looks at his discard, he naturally sees the card left in the stock, and the pone can demand to see not only the card left but the entire discard. The same rule applies to the pone if he takes into his discards an unseen card of the stock.

IRREGULAR DISCARDS   If a player discards fewer cards than he intended, it is too late to remedy the error if he has touched the stock. If he discards too many cards, as the dealer frequently will by laying out five instead of three, he can take them back if he has not touched the ones in the stock; however, if he touches any card in the stock, he has to play with the short hand if there are not enough cards left in the stock to make his hand up to twelve.

IRREGULAR DRAWING If the pone draws one of the three cards that properly belong to the dealer, he loses the game, and if the dealer draws any of the first five, before the pone has announced that he leaves them, the dealer loses the game. The dealer has no right to touch any part of the stock until the pone has discarded and drawn; however, if the pone draws without making any announcement about leaving cards, the dealer has a right to assume that five cards have been taken, and that only three remain in the stock. For example, the pone discards five cards, but draws four only, without saying anything. The dealer proceeds to discard and draw. He has naturally taken one of the pone's cards, but it is too late to remedy the error or claim a penalty, and the pone has to play with eleven cards. It is evident that the dealer will have too many cards, but because he has been led into the error by his adversary, he has to be allowed to discard in order to reduce his hand to twelve.

If a player takes a card too many from the stock, he can replace it if he has not put it with the other cards in his hand. If he has seen it, he has to show it to his adversary. If the superfluous card has been taken into the hand, the player has to have too many cards, and can score nothing that deal. This does not prevent the adversary from scoring anything he might have in hand or play, even if it is inferior.

If a player is found to have too few cards after the draw, he can still play and count all he can make, but cannot win a capot, because he has no card for the last trick, which has to be won by his adversary.

THE STOCK If a player looks at one of his adversary's cards in the stock before or during the draw, he can count nothing that hand. If he looks at a card left in the talon after the draw, which he is not entitled to see, his adversary can call a suit from him as many times as he has seen cards. If a card of the talon is accidentally exposed, the player to whom it would naturally belong can demand a fresh deal.

OBJECTS OF THE GAME In order to understand the principles that guide players in discarding, the objects of the game first have to be explained. There are three classes of counting combinations at Piquet, and the player who holds the better of each class scores it. These combinations are Point, Sequence, and Fours and Triplets.

THE POINT This is the suit that has the greatest pip value, whereby the Ace is reckoned as 11, court-cards as 10 each, and the 10 9 8 7 at their face value. If one player's best suit contains five cards, worth 48 points, and his adversary has a suit worth 51, the latter suit would be the only one to count, and would be called the point for that deal.

The value of the point is the number of cards that go to make it. In England, players count a point that contains the 7 8 and 9 as worth one less than the number of cards. This is a modern invention, is unknown to the older writers about the game, and is not always played.

SEQUENCE   Three or more cards of the same suit, if they are next in value to each other, form a sequence. The French terms are usually used to designate the number of cards in the sequence: Tierce, Quatrième, Quinte, Sixième, Septieme, and Huitième. In many English works about cards, quinte is erroneously spelt without the *e*, and 'quart' is given for a sequence of four. If you intend to use the French language at all, it might as well be used correctly.

Sequences outrank each other according to the best card, if they are of equal length, so that a quinte to a King would be better than a quinte to a Queen; however, a longer sequence always outranks a shorter one, regardless of the high cards. The player who holds the best sequence is entitled to score it, together with any inferior sequences he might hold in other suits. If his adversary holds intermediate sequences, they are of no value. For example, one player holds a quinte to the Jack in spades, a tierce to the Ten in hearts, and a tierce to the Nine in clubs, whereas the other holds a quatrième majeure (A K Q J) in hearts, diamonds and clubs. None of the latter are of any value, but all the cards in the other hand are good. If the best sequence is a tie, no sequences can be scored by either player.

The value of a sequence is ten more than the number of cards that go to form it, provided that number exceeds four. A tierce counts 3 only, and a quatrième 4 only, but a quinte is worth 15, a sixième 16, and so on.

FOURS AND TRIPLETS   Any four cards of the same denomination, higher than a Nine, are called a Quatorze, and three of any kind higher than the Nine are called a Trio, or sometimes a Brelan. Because a trio is seldom mentioned without naming the denomination, it is usual to say, 'Three Kings,' or 'Three Jacks,' as the case may be. The 7 8 and 9 have no value except in point and sequence. The player who holds the quatorze of the highest rank can score any inferior ones he might hold, and also any trios. If his adversary holds any intermediate ones, they are of no value. In the absence of any quatorze, the best trio decides which player will count all the trios he might have in his hand, whereby his adversary counts none. For example, one player holds four Tens and three Jacks, and his adversary holds triplets of Aces, Kings and Queens. None of the latter would be of any value, because the lowest quatorze is better than the highest trio, and the player who has the four Tens could also count his three Jacks. Pairs have no value.

The value of any quatorze is 14, as its name implies. Trios are worth 3 only.

In discarding, the object is to secure the best counting combinations, and also to retain cards that will win tricks in play. The combinations take precedence over each other in scoring, whereby the first is always Carte Blanche, then the Point, then Sequence, and finally the Quatorze or Trio.

DECLARING Carte blanche has to be announced and shown before a discard is made. Each player having discarded and drawn, the elder hand proceeds to announce any counting combinations he holds, which he has to declare in regular order, beginning with the point. In announcing the point, the suit is not mentioned; only its value is. The sequences are defined by way of the number of cards and the highest: 'sixième to the King', for example. The fours and trios are defined in the same way: 'four Kings' or 'three Jacks'.

To each of these declarations, as they are made in regular order, the dealer has to reply, *'Good,' 'Equal,'* or *'Not good.'* If the point is admitted to be good, the holder scores it, not by putting it down on the score sheet, but simply by beginning his count with the number of points it is worth. If the point is equal, neither player scores it, and secondary points have no value under any circumstances. If the point declared by the elder hand is not good, it is not necessary for the dealer to say how much better his point is: that will come later. To each of the other declarations, replies are made in the same way, except that fours and trios cannot be 'equal'. As each combination is admitted to be good, the elder hand adds it to his count. For example, his point is 51, good; his sequence is five to the Ace, good; and his triplet of Aces is good. These are worth 5, 15 and 3, respectively, and his total count is 23, if he has no minor sequences or trios. This is not put down but simply announced.

The strict rules of the game require the player whose combination is acknowledged to be good to show it; however, among good players, this is quite unnecessary, because each usually knows by his own cards what his adversary should and probably does hold.

The elder hand, having finished his declarations and announced their total value in points, leads any card he pleases. If this card is a

Ten or better, he claims one point for leading it, even if he does not win the trick, and adds this point to his score.

An illustration will probably make the aforementioned processes clearer. The elder hand, after the draw, holds these cards:

$$\heartsuit \text{ A K Q J}: \clubsuit \text{ A K Q}: \diamondsuit \text{ A K Q 7}: \spadesuit \text{ A}.$$

He announces, 'Forty-one.' 'Not good.' 'Quatrième to the Ace.' 'Not good.' Then 'Quatorze Aces,' which he knows is good and which admits of his counting his triplets of Kings and Queens. These are worth collectively 20 points, and on leading one of his Aces, he announces 'Twenty-one.'

The dealer, before playing a card, proceeds to claim the count for the combinations that are good in his own hand, which is as follows.

$$\clubsuit \text{ J 10 9 8}: \diamondsuit \text{ J 10 9}: \spadesuit \text{ K Q J 10 9}.$$

The point is worth 5, the quinte 15, the quatrième 4, and the tierce 3: 27 altogether. His trios of Jacks and Tens are shut out by the superior combinations in the elder hand.

Having claimed these 27 points, and their correctness having been admitted by the elder hand, the dealer proceeds to play a card. If either player has forgotten to declare anything before he plays, the count is lost.

SINKING A player is not obliged to declare any combination unless he wishes to do so, and he can sink a card if he thinks it would be to his advantage to conceal his hand. Sinking is calling only part of a combination, as, for example, calling 51 for his point when he really has 61, calling a quinte when he has a sixième, or calling a trio when he has a quatorze. Sinking is usually resorted to only when the player knows from his own hand and discards that what he declares is still better than anything his adversary can hold; however, it has to be remembered that the part of the declaration that is sunk in this way is lost.

IRREGULAR DECLARATIONS If either player claims a combination he does not hold, and does not remedy the error before he plays a card, he cannot count anything that deal, and thereby loses any other declarations he might have made that are correct. His adversary then counts everything in his hand, whether or not his combinations were inferior. He also counts for what he wins in the tricks.

If the elder hand's declaration is admitted by the dealer to be good, it is good, even if the dealer afterwards proves to have a better point, sequence, quatorze or trio. If any combination named by the elder hand is not actually his best, he cannot amend his declaration after the dealer has replied to it. This is in order to prevent a player from getting information to which he is not entitled. If he holds three Kings and three Tens, for example, and announces the Tens in order to find out whether or not his adversary has three Queens or Jacks, and the dealer says, 'Not good,' the three Kings are lost, and the dealer scores his own trios.

It sometimes happens that in order to keep a good point or sequence, a player will discard one card of a quatorze originally dealt to him, or one of a trio, of which he afterwards draws the fourth. He can score only the trio, naturally; however, his adversary, having none of that denomination in either his hand or discards, knows that four were possible, and after playing a card, has a right to ask the suit of the card that was discarded.

METHOD OF PLAYING The elder hand can lead any card he pleases, and announces the suit at the same time. The dealer is bound to follow suit, if he is able, but is not obliged to win the trick. Because there are no trumps, the higher card, if it is of the suit led, wins the trick. If the second player does not follow suit, the leader wins. The winner of one trick leads for the next, and so on until all twelve tricks are played.

Every time a card is played that is better than a Nine, the leader counts one for it, and adds the number to the total value of his score as already announced. If the second player wins the trick with any card better than a Nine, he also counts one, but if the trick is won by the player who led, there is no extra count for winning it. The winner of the *last trick* counts one for it, in addition to his count for winning it with a card better than a Nine. If the leader wins it, he gets the one extra.

If each player wins six tricks, there is no more scoring, but if either player wins the *odd trick*, he adds to his score ten points for *cards*, in addition to all other scores. If either player wins all twelve tricks, which would be the case in the illustrative hand just given, he adds to his score forty points for the *capot*; however, these forty points include the scores for both the last trick and the odd trick.

A card once laid on the table cannot be taken back, unless the player has renounced in error. There is no revoke in Piquet, and if a player has one of the suit led, he has to play it. If he fails to do so, when the error is discovered, the cards have to be taken back and replayed.

REPIC If either player is able to reach 30 by successive declarations, beginning with the point, all of which are admitted by his adversary to be good, he adds 60 to his score, thereby making it 90 instead of 30, and this is irrespective of what his adversary might have in minor or inferior combinations. The important thing to remember in repic is that declarations always count in regular order, whereby carte blanche takes precedence over everything, followed by the point, sequences, and quatorze or trio. Suppose elder hand to hold the following cards.

$$\heartsuit \text{ K Q J 10 9; } \clubsuit \text{ A K Q; } \diamondsuit \text{ A Q 9; } \spadesuit \text{ Q.}$$

If the quinte to the King is admitted good for the point, it has to be good for the sequence as well. That is 20. The four Queens have to be good, because the adversary cannot have any quatorze. This makes the total 34, plus 60 added for repic: 94 altogether, to which he will add one for leading the first card, if it is above a Nine.

Suppose the elder hand had the following cards.

$$\heartsuit \text{ A K Q J 8; } \clubsuit \text{ A K; } \diamondsuit \text{ A K; } \spadesuit \text{ A K 10.}$$

If his point is good, that and his four Aces and Kings will make him 33 altogether; however, his sequence is not good, because the dealer holds five diamonds to the Queen, which comes in order before the score for quatorze, and therefore saves the repic. Suppose that with the aforementioned cards the elder hand was told that even his point was not good. He would count 29 for the 14 Aces, 14 Kings, and the card led. If the dealer had a sixième in diamonds, and a quinte in clubs, for example, he would claim a repic: 96 points, in spite of the 29 announced by the elder hand, because point and sequence score before quatorze.

Equalities do not save the repic. Take the following hands.

Elder: $\heartsuit$ A J 10 9 8; $\clubsuit$ 10; $\diamondsuit$ 10; $\spadesuit$ A J 10 9 8.
Dealer: $\heartsuit$ K Q; $\clubsuit$ A K Q; $\diamondsuit$ A K Q J 7; $\spadesuit$ K Q.

The point is equal. The quatrième to the Jack is not good, and the four Tens are not good, so the elder hand leads a card, and counts, 'One.' The dealer then claims repic: 95 points, which is good, although the elder hand had an equal point.

PIC If either player can reach 30 in hand and play combined, before his adversary scores anything, 30 points are added for the pic. Pic can never be made by the dealer unless the elder hand leads a card smaller than a Nine: he has to make repic if anything. To make pic, the elder hand has to reach 30 in the regular order of scoring. Suppose he holds these cards.

$$\heartsuit \text{ A 9; } \clubsuit \text{ A K Q J; } \diamondsuit \text{ K Q J 10 9; } \spadesuit \text{ K.}$$

If the dealer acknowledges the point to be good, everything else in the hand has to be good as well. This will give the elder hand 27 before playing a card: 5 for the point, 15 and 4 for the sequences, and 3 for the Kings. By leading out the A K and Q, 3 more points are secured, whereby the dealer has nothing to score, so the elder hand reaches 30 and makes the pic, whereby he counts 60 and still has the lead. Equalities do not save pic.

According to the strict rules of the game, a player who is playing for pic is not allowed to count 30 at all, but has to jump from his last count, 29, to 60, or he loses the pic; however, this is seldom or never insisted on.

SCORING　When the last card is played, the total number of points made by each player is put down on the score sheet, or marked on a cribbage-board, and if neither player has reached 100 points, the deal passes to the one who was elder hand on the last deal.

The order of scoring should be carefully observed, in order to determine which goes out first, and whether or not a player is lurched: Carte blanche, The Point, Sequence, Quatorze or Trio, Repic, Points for Leading or Winning, Pic, the Odd Trick, and Capot.

If one player reaches 100 before his adversary has reached 50, it is a *lurch*, and counts a double game.

ABANDONED HANDS　If a player throws down his cards, he can still take them up again, unless he or his adversary has mixed his cards with the discards or with the remainder of the talon.

SUGGESTIONS FOR GOOD PLAY　The main points for the beginner are good discarding and taking advantage of tenace positions in the play, so as to secure the count for cards, which is often important.

ELDER HAND　In discarding, the pone should consider what there might be against him. If it is unlikely that he will lose a pic or repic, he should try for the *point*, which very often carries with it the sequence. It has to be remembered that there are only eight cards in each suit, and by comparing the ones you hold with the ones your adversary might hold, it is comparatively easy, in most hands, to estimate the possible scores against you. Next to the point, the most important thing is the score for *cards*. The point will save pic and repic, but the cards will make the greatest difference in the score in the long run. Sequences are always valuable, especially the ones that are Ace high in the elder hand, because they enable the elder hand to win a succession of tricks in play.

The elder hand should risk a good deal if he has a reasonable chance to make a pic or repic, which will often settle the game. If there is any choice as to what to keep of two nearly equal chances, always preserve the combination that will be most likely to secure the count for cards.

In *Leading*, it is best to begin with the point, unless you know you are leading up to either tenace or high cards that will bring in a long adverse suit. The piquet player soon learns the importance of tenace and fourchette, and can sometimes see how things have to be managed for five or six tricks ahead, so as to secure the odd trick. Tenace is the best and third best of any suit, such as A Q, whereas a fourchette is any two cards within one of each other, such as K J, or Q 10, and the lead from these combinations should always be avoided. If you have the odd trick in hand, make it at once, before you risk anything else, because the only difference between the odd trick and eleven tricks is the count for each card led in the tricks.

THE DEALER   The first thing to guard against is a long run of winning leads from the elder hand, which might make the odd trick, or even capot. Because there are no trumps, it is very important that the dealer keep guarded Kings and twice guarded Queens. The main thing for the dealer to remember is that if he cannot stop a long suit in the elder hand, he will have to provide in advance for a specific number of discards, and these have to be planned so that guards will be preserved in the other suits. He should also get his hand into condition such that when he does get into the lead, he will not have to lead away from tenaces or guarded Kings. Careful attention to his adversary's declarations, and a comparison of his own hand with his discards, will usually guide the dealer to a correct conclusion as to what to keep and what to throw away in playing to tricks.

— • —

PIQUET NORMAND
FOR THREE PLAYERS

In this form of the game, the players cut for seats and deal. The cards are dealt by twos and threes until each player has ten, whereby two cards remain for the talon. The dealer can lay out any two cards in exchange for these, but no other player is allowed to touch them, nor to see the discards.

The elder hand makes the first declarations. He makes repic and counts 90 if he can reach 20 without playing a card, and makes pic, 60, if he can reach 20 in hand and play, under the same conditions as in the game for two players. Most tricks count 10, and if it is a tie, each trick counts 5. Capot counts 40 if all the tricks are taken by one player, but if two players take them all between them, the tricks count 20 each.

The game can be played for a pool, first player out to take all, or it can be agreed that after one player has retired, the other players will decide it between them by playing it out in the ordinary two-handed game.

— —

PIQUET VOLEUR
FOR FOUR PLAYERS

The players cut for partners, whereby the two lowest pair against the two highest, and the lowest cut takes the first deal. Partners sit opposite each other. All the cards are dealt out, two and three at a time, and each player receives eight cards.

The elder hand declares first, but rather than announce one thing at a time and await the reply of his adversaries, he declares everything, then plays a card. Suppose the cards are distributed as follows, whereby Z is the dealer.

$\spadesuit$ K Q J 10
$\diamondsuit$ J 10 9 8

$\heartsuit$ A; $\spadesuit$ A; $\diamondsuit$ A Q   Y $\heartsuit$ K Q J; $\diamondsuit$ K 7
$\clubsuit$ A Q J 10   A   B $\clubsuit$ K 9 8
              Z

$\heartsuit$ 10 9 8 7
$\spadesuit$ 9 8 7; $\clubsuit$ 7

A announces 41 for his point, sequence of three to the Queen, four Aces, and says, 'I play a club,' which is his lead for the first trick. If the second player admits all these to be good, he says nothing, but plays a card. In this case, Y would announce four to the King, and four to the Jack, and would play a spade, having no club. B would then announce three Kings, which are good on account of his partner's having four Aces; however, both of the sequences are shut out by Y's better declarations. The dealer, Z, then declares four to the Ten and three to the Nine, both of which sequences are made good by his partner's holding the best sequence at the table.

When the first trick is played, each person at the table shows what he has claimed, so his adversaries can verify the count. A would then gather up the first trick, and announce the total score for his side, which would be 22: 4 for the point, 14 Aces, 3 Kings, and 1 for the card led. He would then play another club, and announce 22. This his partner would win but would not count, because he is on the same side that has already counted for the lead. If the play is followed up, it will be found that A–B make a capot. The adversaries will then score 15 for their three sequences of four and their one sequence of three.

No point of fewer than 30 can be announced.

PIC AND REPIC   If one player, or two partners together, reach 20 in counting, without playing, they count 9 for the repic. If they reach 20 in declarations and play together, they count 60 for the pic. Carte blanche in the hand of one or other partner can count towards pic or repic, and if two partners each held carte blanche, they would be entitled to 90 points for the repic, no matter what the adversaries held, because carte blanche takes precedence over all other scores.

— · —

PIQUET A ECRIRE

This game somewhat resembles Skat in the way of playing and settling. Any number from three to seven sit around the table, but only two play, and the losses of each individual are charged to him on a score sheet ruled off for the purpose. The players can take turns, whereby each person plays two deals, the first with the person on his left and the second with the person on his right. Alternatively, it can be agreed that the loser in each deal will give way to a new player, whereby the winner of most points in each deal will continue. The game is usually arranged for a specific number of tours or deals, at the end of which the scores are balanced and settled for.

— ● —

RUBICON PIQUET
FOR TWO PLAYERS

The main difference between this game and the usual form Piquet, au cent, is in the way of declaring. The usual method used in England and the United States is as follows.

The Point is scored by the player who holds the greatest number of cards in the suit, and the pip value is resorted to only in order to decide ties. This is done in order to conceal, if possible, the nature of the cards held. When the numerical value is asked for, only the last figure is given: 'seven,' for example, if the point is 47.

If the point is good, the elder hand immediately names the suit. If it is not good, the suit is not named, and the elder hand proceeds to call his *sequences*. If they are good, the suits have to be named, and it is the same for quatorze and trio.

UNDERCALLING   If a player holds an inferior sequence, quatorze or trio, which he knows is better than any his adversary can possibly hold, he can call it, and afterwards score the better combination, provided he is correct in estimating the inferior combination that he called as *good against the cards*. However, if the adversary can demonstrate that the inferior announcement was not actually good against the cards, and that it was possible for him to hold a better combination, the score for the higher combination is lost. For example, a player holds four Kings and three Aces, and on glancing over his hand and discards sees that his adversary cannot hold any quatorze, so he declares the three Kings instead of the four Aces. Suppose he mistook a Nine for a Ten, and overlooked the fact that his adversary might have had four Tens: the score for the four Kings would be lost, but the three Aces would be good if his adversary had discarded a Ten and did not actually hold four. In the ordinary game, the higher combination is lost if it is not called.

In play, every card led, whatever its value, counts one, and winning the trick also counts one. The last trick counts two, the capot forty. Pic and repic are reckoned as in the ordinary game.

SCORING   Rather than play 100 points up, six deals is a game, whereby each player deals three times. The lower score is then deducted from the higher, and 100 points are added to the difference in order to determine the value of the game, which is usually played for so much a point.

If the result of the six deals is a tie, two more deals have to be played. If they also result in a tie, the game is void.

RUBICONS If either player fails or both players fail to reach 100 points in the six deals, the player who has the most is the winner, and adds to his own score all the points made by the loser, plus 100 in addition for game. For example, A has 113 scored, and B has 80. A wins 113 + 80 + 100 = 293 altogether. Again: A has 88, and B has 84. A wins 88 + 84 + 100 = 272 altogether. Again: A has 180, and B has 142. A wins the difference in the scores: 38 + 100 = 138 altogether.

— —

IMPÉRIAL
OR PIQUET WITH A TRUMP

Impérial differs from Piquet in some minor details, although the leading principle is the same. There are no discards, sequences of court-cards are the only sequences that count, tierces are worthless, and a trump suit is added.

The *cards* rank K Q J A 10 9 8 7, whereby the K Q J A and 7 of trumps are called honours, and in all sequences the four highest cards in the suit are the only cards that count.

COUNTERS Each player is supplied with six white and four red counters, which are passed from left to right as the points accrue. Each red is worth six white, and when all six white counters have been passed over, they have to be returned, whereby a red one is passed over in their place. When all the counters, four red and six white, have been passed over, the game is won.

DEALING Twelve cards are given to each player, two or three at a time, and the twenty-fifth card is turned up for the trump. If this is an honour, the dealer marks one white counter for it. There are no discards.

IMPÉRIALS Specific combinations of cards are known as impérials, and the player marks one red counter for each of them. The best impérial is carte blanche, which is sometimes marked as a double impérial, and is worth two reds. A sequence of K Q J A in any suit is an impérial. An impérial de retourne can be formed in the dealer's hand if the turn-up trump completes his sequence or makes four of a kind. An impérial tombée, or de rencontre, is made when the player who holds the King and Queen of trumps catches the Jack and Ace from his adversary. Four Kings, Queens, Jacks, Aces or Sevens in one hand are an impérial, but the Eights, Nines and Tens have no value.

DECLARING   The elder hand announces his point, as in Piquet, and arrives at its value in the same way, whereby the Ace is reckoned for 11 and so on. The dealer replies, 'Good,' or 'Not good,' as the case may be, but there are no equalities. If the point is a tie, the elder hand counts it. The point is worth a *white* counter. The impérials are then called, and each impérial is worth one *red* counter. The sequences are called first, whereby in trumps the sequence is 'good', naturally, then the fours are called, the best of which are four Kings and the lowest four Aces. In plain-suit sequences, there are no 'equals', and the elder hand counts ties as an offset to the advantages of the deal.

PLAYING   The elder hand leads a card, and the dealer then declares and marks any impérials he might have that are good, after which he plays a card. No impérials can be claimed or scored after the holder has played a card. The second player in each trick has to win the trick if he can, with either a higher card or a trump. For each honour in trumps in the tricks won, the player marks a white counter at the end of the hand. The winner of the odd trick scores as many white counters as he has tricks in excess of his adversary's. If either player makes capot (all twelve tricks), he scores two red counters.

SCORING   When one player reaches six white counters and changes them for a red, his adversary has to take down any white counters he might have scored. For example, the pone has 2 reds and 4 whites up, and the dealer has 1 red and 5 whites. The pone scores two whites, thereby reaching six and advancing his score to 3 reds, which are sometimes called impérials. The dealer has to take down his white counters, thereby losing that count altogether and leaving himself 1 red. The only exception to this is that at the beginning of the hand, if both have impérials combinations in hand, neither side takes down its white counters.

In *Counting out*, the following order of precedence has to be observed. The turn-up trump (if it is an honour). The Point. Impérial in hand, sequences first. Impérial de retourne. Impérial tombée. Honours in tricks. Odd tricks.

— ◦ —

CASSINO

This is a very old and always popular game, which was much improved way of introduction of the variations known as Royal and Spade Cassino, the latter of which is an especially lively game. Similar to Euchre, Cassino is eminently respectable, and is one of the few card games that are unhesitatingly admitted to the domestic circle.

CARDS Cassino is played with a full pack of fifty-two cards, which have no rank in play, because their pip value or face value is the only element of importance. In cutting for positions at the table, or for partners in the four-handed game, the Ace is the lowest card, and the other cards ranks upwards to the King in the order of their sequence.

MARKERS When a specific number of points is agreed on as a game, the score can be kept with counters, on a sheet of paper or on a cribbage-board. If each hand is a game in itself, it is settled for immediately, in either counters or money.

PLAYERS Any number from two to four can play, each for himself, or four can play two against two, whereby partners sit opposite each other. The players on the dealer's right and left are known as the pone and the eldest hand, respectively.

CUTTING The players draw from an outspread pack for positions at the table, whereby the lowest card has the choice and deals the first hand. If the first cut does not decide, the players who are tying have to cut again. If a player exposes more than one card, he has to cut again. The ace is low.

STAKES Cassino can be played for so much a game or so much a point and it can be agreed that the game will be a specific number of points or be complete in one deal, or that the player who makes the most points on each deal will score one, and the player who first makes a specific number in this way, such as five, will be the winner. If points are played for, the lower score is usually deducted from the higher, and the difference is the value of the game. It is sometimes agreed that if the winner has twice as many points as does his adversary, he will be paid for a double game.

DEALING   After the cards have been properly shuffled, they have to be presented to the pone to cut, and he has to leave at least four in each packet. Beginning on his left, the dealer distributes four cards to each player in two rounds of two at a time, and gives two cards to the table just before helping himself in each round. No trump is turned, and the remainder of the pack is left face downwards on the dealer's left. The four cards dealt to the table are then turned face upwards, and the play begins. After all four cards given to each person have been played, the dealer takes up the remainder of the pack, then, without any more shuffling or cutting, deals four more cards to each player, two at a time, but gives none to the table. When these four cards have been played, four more are dealt in the same way, and so on, until the pack is exhausted, after which the deal passes to the left in regular rotation.

IRREGULARITIES IN THE DEAL   If the pack is proved to be imperfect, or if a card is found faced in the pack, there has to be a fresh deal by the same dealer. If a player deals out of turn, he has to be stopped before the cards on the table are turned face upwards.

A misdeal loses the deal. It is a misdeal if the pack has not been cut, or if the cards are shuffled after the pack has been properly cut, or if the dealer deals a card incorrectly and fails to remedy it before dealing to the next player, or if the dealer deals too many or too few cards to either any player or the table.

If a card is exposed during the deal, an adversary can claim a fresh deal. If, after the cards on the table have been faced, a card is exposed by the dealer, or is found faced in the pack, the player to whom it would be dealt can reject it, whereby it then has to be placed in the middle of the stock, and the player has to be given the top card. If a card is exposed in the last round, the dealer has to take it, and allow the player to whom it would have been dealt to draw a card from the dealer's hand, face downwards. If the player draws the exposed card, he has to keep it.

If the dealer gives any player an incorrect number of cards in any round after the first, and does not detect and correct the error before he deals to the next player, he cannot count anything that hand. The number of cards in each hand has to be restored to four, by either drawing from them, face downwards, or adding from the stock. If any player lifts his cards before the dealer has helped all the players, including himself, a misdeal cannot be claimed.

OBJECTS OF THE GAME   The object in Cassino is to secure specific cards and combinations of cards that count towards game. These are as follows.

	Points
Most *Cards* taken in.	3
Most *Spades* taken in.	1
The Ten of diamonds: *Big Cassino*.	2
The deuce of spades: *Little Cassino*.	1
The *Ace* of any suit.	1
A *Sweep* of all the cards on the table.	1

The way in which these points are secured will become evident from the description of the method of playing the hands.

METHOD OF PLAYING   Beginning on the dealer's left, each player in turn plays a card from his hand, and places it face upwards on the table. Only one card can be played at a time, and each person has to play in his proper turn until all four of his cards are exhausted. After receiving fresh cards, the eldest hand again plays first, and so on for every round. Under some conditions, each player in his proper turn can take up specific cards from the table, together with the card played from his hand, whereby he turns the cards face downwards in front of him. He is entitled to count all the points contained in the cards taken in or won in this way. These conditions are that he can match or *pair* a card or cards on the table, and that he can *combine* two or more cards on the table so as to make their total pip value equal to that of the card he plays, and that he can *build* a card in his hand on a card on the table so as to make the cards total pip value agree with that of a second card that is still in his hand.

PAIRING   If the person whose turn it is to play holds in his hand any card of a denomination similar to that of any of the cards on the table, he can play the card from his hand, face upwards, then gather it in again, together with all similar cards, whereby he turns them face downwards in front of him. For example, he holds an Eight, and there are one or two Eights on the table. He plays the Eight from his hand, and then gathers in all the Eights.

COMBINING   If a player holds any card that is not a K Q or J, and the pip value of it is equal to that of two or more cards on the table, he can play the card from his hand, then gather it in again, together with the two or three cards that collectively equal it in pip value. For example, he holds a 9, and a 4, a 3 and a 2 are on the table. He can combine these three cards, call attention to the fact that their collective value is 9, play the 9 from his own hand, then gather in and turn down all four cards. An 8 and an Ace, or a 6 and a 3 might be gathered in the same way, or two of these combinations might be gathered at the same time: 3, 2, 6, 7, for example, which would make two nines, and all of these cards might be gathered by a player who holds a 9 in his hand.

Pairs and combinations can be taken in together. For example, among the cards on the table are a 4, a 6, and a 10, and the player holds a 10. He can gather in not only the pair of Tens but the combinations that equal a 10.

BUILDING   A player might have in his hand two cards, the lower of which, if added to a card on the table, would build up its value to that of the higher card that is still in the player's hand. For example, a player holds a 9 and a 2, and there is a 7 on the table. He can place the 2 on the 7, and announce the total value: 'Nine,' whereby the other players will be notified that these two cards cannot be separated; however, he cannot take the cards in until it again comes round to his turn to play, because he is allowed to play only one card at a time, and has played his card in making the build.

If any other player following him holds a 9, he is entitled to take in this build, but cannot separate the two cards that form it. A player who holds either a 7 or a 2 cannot touch either of the cards in the build, because they are no longer a 7 and a 2: for all practical purposes, they are a 9.

INCREASING BUILDS   If any player held an Ace and a 10 in his hand, he could increase the 9 build to a 10 build, by putting his Ace on the 7 and 2 and announcing the total value: 'Ten.' Any following player would then be unable to win the build with anything but a 10, and the player who originally built it a 9 would lose it unless he also held a 10 in his hand. If the build remains a 9 until it comes around again to the player who originally built it, he can then take it in with his 9, or he might himself increase it to 10, if he had an Ace and a 10 in his hand; however, in order to do this, the player has to have in his hand the cards to win both the original and the increased build. A player who holds in his hand a 10, 3 and 2, but no 8, cannot build a 5 on the table to an 8 and afterwards advance it to 10. He has to have the 2 3 8 and 10 all in his own hand in order to do this.

Some players imagine that a player cannot increase his own build in this way, even if he has both the cards for the first and the last build, but there is no reason why a player should be denied a privilege that is freely granted to his adversary. If any player can legitimately make or increase a build, all the players can do so, provided they have the proper cards.

DOUBLE BUILDS When two cards of the same denomination, or two builds of the same value are put together as one, they cannot be increased. For example, a player holds 7 and 3, and there are on the table a 5 2 and 4. He places his 3 on the 4, gathers the 5 and 2 together, and announces the build as 'Two Sevens'. This cannot be increased to 8, 9 or 10 under any circumstances, and nothing but a 7 will win it.

Pairs can be doubled in the same way. If a player has two Nines in his hand, and there is one Nine on the table, he can build on the latter with one Nine of his own and announce, 'Two Nines,' whereby any player will be prevented from building either of the Nines to 10, and the builder will be entitled to take in both cards with his third Nine when it comes around to his turn. If any other player at the table holds the fourth Nine, he can naturally take in the build.

It is necessary to distinguish between building and combining. In combining cards, the cards already on the table are gathered together; in building, or increasing a build, a card has to be played from the hand. If one player has made a build of any description, it cannot be interfered with or increased except by other cards from a player's hand, whereby the cards from the table are not available. For example, one player has built a 5 by combining two Aces on the table with a 3 from his hand. On the table are also a 2 and a 4, and a following player holds a 9 and a 7. He cannot use the deuce on the table to increase the build from 5 to 7, nor the 4 to increase it to 9, because that would not be building from his hand; however, if he held the 4 and 9 in his hand, he could build on the 5.

The simple rule to be remembered is that no combination of cards once announced and left on the table can be changed, except by way of addition of a card from the hand of a player.

TAKING IN Any player who has made a build is obliged to win it when it is next his turn to play, to win something else, or to make another build. For example, the player has built a 5 into a 9 with a 4, and holds another 4: if another 5 appears on the table before it comes to his turn to play, he can build it into a 9 also, with his other 4, and announce, 'Two Nines.' Alternatively, if a player lays out a 4, he can pair it and take it in, and leave his 9 build until the next round. In the same way, a player can increase or win another player's build rather than take in his own. An opponent's build can be increased by cards from the hand only.

In the four-handed game, partners can take in each other's builds, or make builds that can be won by the card declared in the partner's hand. For example, one player builds an 8, and his partner holds Little Cassino. If there is a 6 on the table, the Cassino can be built on it, and 'Two Eights,' called, although the player has no 8 in his own hand: the 8 already built by his partner is sufficient. If a player has built a 9 that has been taken in by an adversary, and he still holds the 9 he built for, his partner can build for the declared 9 in the same way.

SWEEPING   If at any time a player is able to win everything on the table with one card, it is a sweep, and counts a point. For example, He holds an 8, and there are on the table four cards only: 5 3 6 and 2. By combining the 6 and 2, and the 5 and 3, two Eights will be formed, and the sweep is made. Sweeps are usually marked by leaving the cards with which they are made face upwards at the bottom of the tricks taken in by the player. Sweeps made by opposite sides are sometimes turned down in order to cancel each other.

TRAILING   When a player cannot pair, combine or build anything, he has to play a card. This is called trailing because he is simply following along and waiting for opportunities. In trailing, it is usually the best policy to play the smaller cards, except Aces and Little Cassino: because other players will probably also trail small cards, these can be combined and won with the larger cards kept in the player's hand.

LAST CARDS   In the last round, all the cards remaining on the table are won by the player who takes the last trick, but it does not count as a sweep unless it would have been a sweep under any circumstances. The last trick is usually made by the dealer, who always keeps back a court-card if he has one, in order to pair one already on the table.

IRREGULARITIES IN PLAY   If any person plays out of his proper turn, the card so played is laid aside as exposed, until it comes to his turn, whereby it is simply placed on the table with the other cards. The player in error is not allowed to build or combine the card, nor to win anything with it.

If a player gathers in a card that does not belong to the combination or build, he has to return not only the card improperly taken up but all other cards taken in with it, together with his own card, whereby the latter, however, is laid out separately from the other cards. If the combination was his own build, it has to be broken up, but if an adversary's, it has to be restored and left as it was.

If a player takes in a build with a wrong card, or takes in a wrong combination, or gathers cards to which he is not entitled, the error has to be challenged and proved before the next trick is taken in by another player, because only the last trick gathered can be seen.

If a player makes a build without the proper card in his hand to win it, when the error is discovered, the combination has to be broken up, and the adversaries can take back the cards they have played in following the erroneous build, and amend their play. If, however, another player has won the erroneous build, there is no penalty, nor any remedy.

SHOWING   After the last card has been played, each player counts his cards face downwards and announces the number. The player who has the most cards scores the three points for cards. If it is a tie, neither player scores. The cards are then turned face upwards, and the spades are counted and claimed, followed by all the points for Cassinos and Aces. It should be remembered that the total number of points to be made in each hand, exclusive of sweeps, is eleven, and that the total of the claims made has to agree with that number.

SCORING   There are several methods of scoring. The old way was to play 11 points up, whereby the lower score was deducted from the higher at the end of each deal. If one side reached 11 before the adversary reached 6, it was a lurch, and counted as a double game. The common method is to count every hand a game, and to settle for it in counters.

—·—

21-POINT CASSINO

This game is usually either marked with counters or pegged on a cribbage-board. Nothing is scored until the end of the hand, whereby each side reckons and claims its points. In order to avoid disputes, there should be a previous understanding as to what points go out first in a close game. In the absence of any agreement to the contrary, the points count out in the following order. Cards first, then Spades, Big Cassino, Little Cassino, Aces, and Sweeps. If the Aces have to decide it, the spade Ace goes out first, then clubs, hearts, and diamonds. If the sweeps have to decide it, only the difference in the number of sweeps counts, and if there is none, or not enough, the game is not ended, and another deal has to be played.

It is better to agree to *count out* in 21-point Cassino, whereby each player keeps mental count of the number of cards and spades he has taken in, together with any 'natural' points. The moment he reaches 21, he should claim the game, and if his claim is correct, he wins, even if his adversary has 21 or more. If he is mistaken, and cannot show out, he loses the game, no matter what his adversary's score is. If neither player claims out, and both players are found to be claimed out, neither player wins, and the game has to be continued to 32 points, and so on: eleven points more each time until one player claims to have won the game.

SUGGESTIONS FOR GOOD PLAY   The main thing in Cassino is to remember what has been played, especially in the counting and high cards, such as Aces, Eights, Nines and Tens. In making pairs and combinations, give preference to the ones that contain spades, and if you have to trail, do not play a spade if you can help it. If three Aces have been taken in, play the fourth Ace, if you hold it, at the first opportunity, because it cannot be paired; however, if there is another Ace to come, keep yours until you can make a good build with it. As between cards that were on the table and cards trailed by an adversary, take in the cards trailed if you have a choice. Take in the adversary's build in preference to your own, if you can, and build on his build at every opportunity. If Big Cassino is still to come, avoid trailing cards that will make a Ten with the cards on the table. Go for 'cards' in preference to everything else, and always make combinations that take in as many cards as possible. If you have a Nine, and the cards on the table are 2 2 5 7, take in the 2 2 5 in preference to the 2 7. It is considered to be bad policy to take in three court-cards, because all sweeps are thereby stopped when the fourth court-card appears.

— —

ROYAL CASSINO

The only difference in this form of the game is that the three court-cards: K Q J, have a pip value, and can be used in combining and building, whereas in the ordinary game, they can be used in pairs only. The Jack is worth 11, the Queen 12, and the King 13 so that a 9 and 2 can be taken in with a Jack, or a 6 4 and 3 with a King. In the same way, a Queen will win Jack and Ace, or a King will win a Jack and deuce. The aces are sometimes valued at 14 each.

— —

SPADE CASSINO

In this interesting variation, every spade counts one point towards game. The spade Jack counts one in addition to its being a spade, and the extra point so made takes the place of the count for 'spades' in the ordinary game, so that 24 points are made in every hand, exclusive of sweeps: Cards 3, Big Cassino 2, Little Cassino 1, the four Aces 4, the spade Jack 1, and 13 spades. It has to be remembered that the spade Jack and deuce count 2 points each: the extra point is for the spade.

The game is scored on a cribbage-board, and every point is pegged immediately, that is, every spade, every Ace, the Cassinos and the sweeps. There is nothing to count at the end of the hand but the cards. Sixty-one points is game, once around the board and into the game-hole.

— —

DRAW CASSINO

In this variation, no more cards are dealt after the first round: each player keeps his hand filled to four cards by drawing a card from the top of the stock as soon as he plays one from his hand. The stock is left on the table, face downwards, slightly spread, for convenience in slipping off the top card as it is drawn.

— —

CONQUIAN

The etymology of this word is Spanish: *con quién* which means 'with whom'. However, of the game it stands for, little or nothing is known except it is a great favourite in Mexico and in all the American States that border it, especially Texas. It is an excellent game for two players. It is quite different from any other game in its principles, and requires very close attention and a good memory in order to play it well. In its finer points, especially in judgement of what the adversary holds or is playing for, it ranks with the best games, and has become quite popular.

CARDS   Conquian is played with the Spanish pack: forty cards, and the 8 9 10 of each suit is deleted. In the United States, it is much more common to play with a pack of forty cards from which the three court-cards: K Q J, have been discarded, thereby leaving each suit an unbroken sequence from the Ace to the Ten. Some people play with the full pack, but this spoils the game, because it is then possible to win on a sequence of a single suit. There are no trumps, and the cards have no value as to rank: a sequence of 6 7 J is no better than one of 2 3 4. The Ace is not in sequence with the King.

COUNTERS   Each player should be supplied with at least ten counters, which can be used in settling at the end of each deal.

PLAYERS   Conquian is played by two people, one of whom is known as the dealer and the other as the pone. If there are three at the table, the dealer takes no cards and has no part in the game for that hand.

CUTTING   Seats and deal are cut for, and the lowest cut has the choice and deals the first hand. The Ace is low, the King high.

STAKES   Each deal is a game in itself, and the loser pays one counter for it. If the game is a tie, called a *tableau*, each player puts up a counter for a pool, and the winner of the next game takes the pool, in addition to the counter paid by his adversary. If the next game is also a tableau, each player adds another counter to the pool, and so on until the game is won.

DEALING   Ten cards are dealt to each player in five rounds of two at a time, and the twenty cards remaining in the stock are laid on the table face downwards, between the players but slightly to the left of the dealer. The stock can be slightly spread, in order to facilitate the process of drawing cards from it.

OBJECTS OF THE GAME   The object of each player is to form triplets, fours and sequences, by combining the cards dealt to him with others drawn from the stock. These combinations are laid on the table, face upwards, and the player wins the game who first suc-ceeds in laying down eleven cards in this way.

SEQUENCES   These all have to be of the same suit, and cannot be shorter than three cards. The Ace is not in sequence with the King, but the 7 is next below the Jack. A sequence once started can be added to from time to time as the cards are drawn from the stock.

TRIPLETS   These are any three cards of the same denomination, and can be increased to *Fours* at any time, by adding the other card.

BORROWING   A player who has four of a kind on the table can borrow any one of the four to use in a sequence; however, he cannot borrow one of three, because no combination can consist of fewer than three cards. In the same way a player can borrow the card at either end of a sequence of at least four cards, if he can use it in order to make a triplet. He cannot borrow an intermediate card, nor a card of a sequence of three cards only, because three cards have to be left in order to maintain the sequence; however, if he had a sequence of at least five cards on the table, he might borrow the top of it in order to make one triplet, then the next card in order to make another triplet.

METHOD OF PLAYING   When the cards are dealt, each player sorts his hand into sequences and triplets, and determines what cards he wants in order to complete his runs, so he can be on the lookout for them. The pone then draws the top card from the stock and turns it face upwards on the pack. If this card can be used in combination with any of the cards in his hand, he draws it over to his side of the table, and takes from his hand the cards that complete the combination of three cards, thereby leaving them all face upwards. Even if he has enough cards in his hand to increase the combination to four or more cards, he should not show them. The cards drawn from the stock must never be taken into the hand.

Let's suppose the pone holds these cards: ♡ J 7 6 4, ♣ 5 3 2, and ◇ K 7 5, and that the ♡ 5 is the first card he draws. He can use this card in three ways: by making a run of three with the ♡ 4 and ♡ 6, or a run with the ♡ 6 and ♡ 7, or a triplet with the two other 5's. In this case, he would probably lay out the 6 and 7, and make the run of three. If he draws the ♡ Q later on, he can use it by continuing the sequence with his Jack, or if the ♡ 3 appears he can use it with his ♡ 4.

PASSING   If the pone cannot use the card drawn, or does not wish to, he draws it from its position on the top of the stock and places it between himself and the dealer, still face upwards. The dealer then decides whether or not he wants it, and if he does not want it, he 'passes' it by turning it face downwards and pushing it to his right. Cards once passed in this way cannot be seen again by either player. The player who passes the card turns up the next card on the stock. If he does not want it, he places it on the table between himself and his adversary, and if his adversary also does not want it, he turns it down and passes it to the pile of deadwood, and turns up the top card of the stock again. In this way, it will be noted that each player has to decide on two cards in succession: the one drawn but not used by his adversary, and the one he draws himself. This process is continued until the stock is exhausted, whereby the game is ended.

DISCARDING   If a player uses any card drawn from the stock in this way, it is obvious he has too many cards, and in order to reduce his hand and show-downs to ten cards, he has to discard something, unless he can show down everything remaining in his hand, in which case he would have eleven cards down, and win the game. In discarding, the card thrown out is placed at the disposal of the adversary, as if it were the card drawn from the stock, and if the adversary does not want it, he passes it and draws another. It should be observed that the player who draws the card from the stock always has the first refusal of it. This is sometimes very important, because both players often need the same card.

In the aforementioned example, the player's best discard would be his ◊ K, which is too far removed from the other cards in the suit to make a run possible, and there is no mate to it with which to start a triplet. If the adversary could use this King, he would have to discard in his turn, and the card so thrown out would be at the disposal of the other player, just as if it had been drawn from the stock.

FORCING   A player does not have to use any card drawn, but if he has on the table any combination in which it can be used, his adversary can force him with it, even after it has been declined. For example, a player has eight cards down: two sequences of four small cards each, and a pair of Kings in his hand. Another King will make him game; however, if he has to depend on his sequences to put him out, he will have to get three more cards. Suppose he draws a card that will fit one of his sequences: however, it is to his advantage to pass it; on laying it on the table, his adversary can take it up and force him with it, by placing it at the end of his sequence and at the same time saying, 'Discard.' In the same way, a player who holds one of the cards of his adversary's show-down sequence or triplet can force after using a card, by placing his discard on his adversary's sequence instead of laying it on the table. If it is laid on the table, the adversary can pass it at once, by turning it down, and it is then too late to compel him to use it. Suppose you think your adversary holds two cards of an unplayed sequence and has a triplet on the table. If you can use one of these sequence cards in his hand to advantage, and can force him by giving him the fourth card of his triplet, which is of no use to you, you should do so; however, you have to remember that you cannot force except after you have used a card yourself, because you are not allowed to discard under any other circumstances.

If a player looks at any of the cards that have been passed and turned down, his adversary can take up and examine the remainder of the stock, but without disturbing the position of the cards therein, and without showing the cards. If a player looks at any of the cards in the stock except the one he draws, his adversary can look at all of the cards. If a player draws out of turn, his adversary simply claims the card.

SHOWING   After the last card is drawn from the stock and passed, each player shows the remainder of his hand, and because neither can combine his cards so as to get eleven down, it is a tableau, and each puts a counter in the pool for the next hand. The deal passes from one player to the other in rotation as long as they continue to play.

SUGGESTIONS FOR GOOD PLAY   Observation of the cards passed will usually show what the adversary is keeping and what he has no chance for. Towards the end of the stock, each player should know what the other holds in his hand by way of the cards that have not appeared in the drawing. If a player does not have a good chance to get eleven cards down himself, he should play for a tableau, by using nothing that will compel him to discard cards that might put his adversary out. It should be remembered that a player cannot get eleven cards down in one suit, and careful observation of the cards passed will often show that his runs are blocked, whereby the cards necessary to continue them have been turned down.

One peculiar feature of the game is that a player cannot block his adversary and at the same time win the game, because as long as he holds up the card his adversary wants, he cannot get eleven cards down himself. His only chance is that he might be able to use the card his adversary requires. For example, he holds two 8's, one of which will make his adversary eleven cards down by completing a sequence. If there is another 8 to come, the player who has the pair can use both his 8's, and win; however, if there is no other 8 to come, it is impossible for the player who has the two 8's to win without first putting his adversary out.

—·—

CALABRASELLA

This was a very popular game with the middle classes and the unoccupied clergy in Italy, and is one of the very few good card games for three players. Had the game been better known, it would have become a great favourite, especially with people who were fond of the whist family, because Calabrasella is an excellent training school for using cards of re-entry, long suits and tenace positions in the end game. In the combination of two players against the third player, its tactics very closely resemble Skat, and many interesting and difficult positions occur in every game.

CARDS   Calabrasella is played with the Spanish pack: forty cards, and the 10 9 and 8 of each suit is discarded. The cards rank 3 2 A K Q J 7 6 5 4; the 3 is the highest, and the 4 the lowest, in both cutting and play. There are no trumps.

MARKERS   The game can be scored by paying and taking in counters, whereby each player is provided with about fifty counters at the beginning of the game, which are purchased from a banker; however, the better way is to keep account of the gains and losses of the single player in each deal, in the way already described in connection with Skat, whereby the account is balanced at the end in the same way.

PLAYERS   Calabrasella is played by three people, two of whom are partners against the third player in each hand. If four play, the dealer takes no cards but shares the fortunes of the partners who are opposed to the single player, just as in Skat. The players on the right and left of the dealer are known as the pone and the eldest hand, respectively.

CUTTING   The players cut for seats and deal, and the lowest card has the first choice and deals the first hand. A player who exposes more than one card has to cut again.

STAKES   The game is played for so much a point. The largest win or loss for the single player is 140, but this amount is almost impossible, and the average payment is 10 or 20.

DEALING   The cards are presented to the pone to cut, and at least four cards have to be left in each packet. The dealer then distributes the cards to the players four at a time, until player each has twelve, and four remain in the stock or talon, which is left on the table face downwards. No trump is turned. The deal passes to the left.

There are no misdeals. If the cards are not properly distributed, or four cards are not left in the talon, the same dealer has to deal again, without penalty.

OBJECTS OF THE GAME   The main objects of the game are to win the last trick and to secure counting cards in the other tricks in the course of play. There are 35 points to be played for in every deal. The six highest cards in each suit: 3 2 A K Q J, have a counting value, whereby the Ace is worth 3, and the other cards 1 each. The last trick counts 3.

DECLARING   The eldest hand examines his cards and determines whether or not he will *stand*, that is, play single handed against the two other players. If he will not, he says, '*Pass*,' and the next player decides. If all three players pass, the deal is void and passes to the next player on the left. If any player stands, he asks for the 3 of any suit he pleases, and if either adversary holds it, he has to give it up. If it is in the stock, the player cannot ask for any other card. If he has all four 3's in his hand, he can ask for a 2, but for no lower card. The adversary who gives the card asked for has to receive a card in exchange from the hand of the single player, but this card must not be shown to the other adversary.

DISCARDING   Having given a card in exchange for the 3 asked for, the single player has to discard at least one more card, face downwards on the table, and can discard as many as four cards. The four cards remaining in the stock are then turned face upwards, and the single player can select from them as many cards as he has discarded; however, he is not allowed to amend his discard in any way. The cards he does not take, if any, are turned down again and placed with his discards, thereby forming a stock of four cards, which must not be seen or touched until the last card is played, whereby the stock becomes the property of the side that wins the last trick, and any counting cards it might contain are reckoned for that side.

PLAYING   When discards are settled, the eldest hand leads any card he pleases, and the other players have to follow suit if they can, but no one is obliged to win a trick if he has a smaller card of the suit led and does not want the lead. The two adversaries of the single player do their best to get him between them, and combine their forces to prevent him from winning tricks that contain counting cards, especially Aces. Whatever tricks they win are placed together, and the counting cards contained in them reckon for their joint account. The tricks have no value as such, except the last trick.

SHOWING The winner of the last trick takes the stock, and each side then turns over its cards and counts the total value of the points won. The lower score is deducted from the highest, and the difference is the value of the game. If all 35 points are won by either side, they count double: 70.

SCORING If the single player loses, he loses to both adversaries, and if he wins, he wins from both. His score is the only one put down, and the amount is preceded with a minus or plus sign according to the result. If he secures 23 points, he wins 11; if he takes in 16 only, he loses 3. If the amount is less than 18, it has to be a loss; if it is 18 or more, it has to be a gain. The method of balancing the scores at the end is found fully explained in connection with Skat.

IRREGULARITIES The penalty for a revoke is loss of 9 points, which are taken from the score of the side in error at the end of the hand, and are added to the side not in fault. If the final score is 24 to 11, for example, in favour of the single player, and one of the partners has revoked, the score is 33 to 2, and the player wins 31 points. If any player turns over the stock before he has announced to stand and has discarded at least one card, he loses 35 points to each adversary, and the deal is void. If an adversary of the single player turns over the stock before the player has discarded, there is no penalty, and the player can discard as he pleases. If an adversary of the single player leads or plays out of turn, the player can abandon the hand at that point, and claim the stock and last trick, whereby the adversaries are entitled to count only the points they have won up to the time the error occurred.

SUGGESTIONS FOR GOOD PLAY The general tactics of the game are extremely similar to the ones used in Whist and Skat. The player establishes his long suit as rapidly as possible, and preserves his tenaces and cards of re-entry. The adversaries of the player should lead short suits up to him and long suits through him, and every opportunity should be taken advantage of to discard counting cards on the partner's tricks, especially Aces, which are not the best of the suit but count the most. Both sides scheme to get their hands in shape for winning the last trick, which usually makes a difference of ten or twelve points in the score, owing to the high cards held back and the cards found in the stock. Each side should keep mental count of its score, so as to know whether or not it has to win the last trick to get to 18. The exposure of the stock, the number of cards discarded by the player, and the suits that are led and avoided will all prove to be useful guides in determining where the strength or weakness in each suit lies, and proper advantage should be taken of all these inferences.

Some judgement is required in selecting the suit in which the 3 is to be asked for, and the single player has to plan in advance for all his discards: one for the exchange, and the ones for the stock. The player's position at the table makes quite a difference. The leader has an advantage with a good long suit, but with tenaces it is better to be the third player, and very bad to be the second hand.

Some pretty positions arise in the end game through refusal of players to win tricks that would put them in the lead and thereby lose them the last trick and the stock. After the first few tricks, everything has to be arranged with a view to securing that last trick, but the importance of getting home with Aces must never be overlooked. The Aces count 12 points in every hand, and the side that can get in three out of the four has 6 points the best of it.

— • —

VINT

Although some people think this game is the forerunner of bridge and might class it as one of the whist family, it is at present so little known outside of Russia, where it is the national game, that the author has thought it best to group it with other games that are distinctly national in character.

Vint has been variously described as bridge without a Dummy and as auction whist. It resembles bridge in the making of the trump, and whist in the manner of the play.

CARDS Vint is played with the full pack of fifty-two cards, which rank from the A K Q down to the deuce. Two packs are usually used.

PLAYERS A table is complete with four players, and if there are more than four candidates for play, the selection has to be made by way of cutting. All the rules for formation of tables, cutting, ties and so on are the same as in bridge. The lowest cut takes the deal, and partners sit opposite each other.

DEALING The dealer presents the pack to be cut, then gives thirteen cards to each player, one at a time. No trump is turned. The deal passes to the left. All irregularities are governed by the same laws as in bridge.

MAKING THE TRUMP   Each player in turn, beginning with the dealer, bids to make a specific number of tricks, from seven to thirteen, with a suit of his own choosing, which he names when he makes his bid. The suits outrank each other in the order of hearts, diamonds, clubs and spades, whereby hearts are the best. No trumps are higher than hearts. A bid of seven tricks is usually called 'one' in hearts, or whatever the suit is. A bid of 'two' means to win eight tricks, or two over the book.

BIDDING   If a player wishes to go over the first offer made, he has to either bid the same number of tricks in a better suit or increase the number of tricks. No player can increase his own bid unless he is over-bid in the interval, but there is no limit to the number of times that players can outbid each other. Observe that the dealer can bid or pass, and that each player after him in turn can bid or pass. The highest bidder has to abide by his announcement as to both the number of tricks and the suit.

THE PLAY   No matter who dealt the cards, the player to the left of the highest bidder always leads for the first trick. Each player in turn has to follow suit if he can, and the highest card played, if it is of the suit led, wins the trick; trumps win all other suits. The winner of one trick leads for the next, and so on. There is no Dummy hand as in bridge.

SCORING   Although the bidding is for so many 'odd' tricks, or tricks over the book, every trick taken is counted when it comes to the scoring; however, it is the number of tricks bid, not the rank of the suit, that determines the value. Every trick won by the same partners:

in a bid of 'one' is worth 10
in a bid of 'two' is worth 20
in a bid of 'three' is worth 30
in a bid of 'four' is worth 40
in a bid of 'five' is worth 50
in a bid of 'six' is worth 60
in a bid of 'seven' is worth .... 70.

Both sides score. If the highest bid was 'two in diamonds', and the bidder's side won nine tricks, they would score 9 times 20, or 180, whereas their adversaries would score 4 times 20, or 80.

As soon as either side reaches 500, it wins the game, even if the players are in the middle of a hand, but the hand has to be played out in order to see how many points are won by each side. It should be observed that although the bidder's side can make nine or ten tricks, the adversaries can win the game if they get enough to count out before the bidder, by reaching 500 first.

TRICKS AND HONOURS The score for tricks and for honours has to be kept separate: usually above and below the line, as in bridge. All trick points, which are the only points that count towards game, are placed below the line, and the honour points are placed above it.

For winning a game, 1000 points are added in the honour column. The side that first wins two games of 500 points each adds 2000 rubber points in the honour column.

SLAMS If a little slam: 12 tricks, is made but has not been bid, it is worth 1000 points in honours. If a little slam: 6 tricks, has been bid and is made, it is worth 5000 more points for bidding it, or 6000 points altogether. If a grand slam, 13 tricks, is made but not bid, it is worth 2000 honour points. If a little slam is bid and a grand slam is made, it is worth 7000 altogether. If a grand slam is bid and made, it is worth 12,000 altogether.

LOST GAMES If the bidder fails to make good, his adversaries score 100 times the value of the tricks as penalty, in the honour column; the scores for the tricks actually won stand at their regular value below the line. Suppose the bid to be three in diamonds, thereby making the tricks worth 30 each, and that the bidder's side gets the odd trick only. Although the bidder has failed to make good, he scores below the line for the seven tricks he took, at 30 each, and the adversaries score for the six they took, also at 30 each. Then, as the bidder fell short by two tricks of making good, his adversaries score these two tricks at 3,000 points each, penalty, in the honour column.

HONOURS The honours are the A K Q J 10 of trumps and the four Aces, whereby the Aces are always honours; however, when there is a no-trump declaration, they are the only honours. This makes the Ace of trumps count double, when there is a trump suit: once as one of the five honours in trumps, and once as an Ace.

Each honour is worth ten times as much as a trick. If the bid was three in clubs, the tricks would be worth 30 each and the honours 300 each. The side that has the majority of Aces and of honours scores for all it holds, not for the majority or difference. Suppose the bidder's side has three honours in clubs and three Aces: the other side has to have only two honours and one Ace; therefore, the bidder scores for six honours, at 300 each.

If the Aces and honours in trumps are so divided that each side has a majority of one or the other, they offset. Suppose the bidder to hold four Aces and two honours. The adversaries have to have the majority of trump honours. The number of their trump honours, which is three, is then deducted from the number of the bidder's Aces: four, thereby leaving the bidder's side only one honour to the good. Three honours on one side and three Aces on the other would be a tie, and no honours to score.

If the Aces are a tie, the side that wins the most tricks scores them. Suppose the bidder has three honours and two Aces. He scores five honours if he wins the odd trick; otherwise, he scores one honour only, whereby the Aces are a tie and he has only one more honour than his adversaries have.

In no-trump hands, the honours are worth 25 times the value of the tricks. If Aces are easy, neither side scores. If one side has three Aces, they are all scored. Suppose the bid to have been 'Two at no-trumps': the Aces are then worth 25 times 20, and three of them are worth 1500 points.

CORONETS   A sequence of three or more cards in any suit: trumps or plain, held by an individual player, is a coronet. Three or four Aces in one hand is also a coronet. When there is a trump suit, three Aces or three of a plain suit in sequence are worth 500 in the honour column. Each additional card is worth 500 points more. A sequence of K Q J 10 9 would be worth 1500. In the trump suit, and in all the suits when there are no trumps, these coronets are worth double, and each additional card is therefore worth 1000 more points.

RUBBERS   As soon as one side wins two games, the first rubber is ended. The partners then change, without cutting, in such a way that at the end of three rubbers, each player will have had each of the other players for a partner. At the end of the third rubber, the losses and gains are ascertained for each individual, and are settled for.

LAWS   The laws that govern the game are almost identical to the ones for Bridge.

— —

PREFERENCE

This is a simplified form of Vint, for three players, using a 32-card pack. The cards rank A K Q J 10 9 8 7, and the suits rank Hearts, diamonds, clubs and spades. Hearts are always *preference*. There are no hands played without a trump suit.

If four people play, the dealer takes no cards. The three active players make up a pool, whereby each players puts in an equal amount at first, and the bidder puts into it as many as he bids for the privilege of naming the trump suit.

Anyone can deal the first hand, after which the deal passes to the left. Three cards are given to each player the first round, then two cards are laid off for a widow, then four cards to each player, then three cards to each player. Beginning on the dealer's left, each player in turn can name the trump if he thinks he can take at least six of the ten tricks to be played for. Bids outrank each other in the order of the suits, and hearts are always preference. The number of tricks is not mentioned. In the case of there being no bids, each player in turn has a second chance to bid for the widow. These bids are made in counters, to be put into the pool. The highest bidder takes the widow, lays out two cards, then names the trump suit.

The players agree on a value for the tricks won, and payments are made from the pool accordingly. These payments can vary according to the rank of the trump suit.

—-—

RED DOG

Any number can play, using a full pack of cards, and each player contributes one counter to the pool. When the entire pool is won, a fresh pool has to be made up. Five cards are dealt to each player, one at a time. The remainder of the pack is placed in the middle of the table, face downwards. The player to the left of the dealer looks at his cards. If he passes, he pays a counter forfeit to the pool.

Each player has one chance to bet or pass. All the cards are then gathered up, and the deal passes. If a player bets, he can bet from one chip up to as many chips as there are in the pool. He bets that he holds a card of the same suit as that of the card on the top of the stock, but of higher rank, whereby the cards rank from the ace and king down to the deuce. When the bet is made, the dealer turns the top card face upwards.

Suppose it is the club ten. If the better can show a higher club, he wins from the pool as many chips as he bet. If he fails, his bet goes into the pool. The turned card and the better's hand are then thrown into the discard, without showing any more cards, and it is the turn of the next player to bet or pass. It is clear that two reasonably high cards in two suits are a safe bet, whereas four aces would be a certainty. Remembering cards shown is a feature of the game.

ODD GAMES

—•—

There are quite a number of odd card games that come and go as favourites from time to time and pass around the world from one country to another under many names. The origin of most of these games is lost in the weedy undergrowth of variations, but the main family trait in some of them can be traced back to the alpha of cards.

Among the oldest of games was Ombre, immortalised by the writer Pope, and the only survivor of it is a variation played by the older Germans, under the name of Solo: a game that still faintly resists the exterminating influence of Skat. The ancient and honourable games of Comète, Hoc and Nain Jaune survive to the present day in a large and prosperous family, ranging from Commit to Fan Tan, the latter today which is quite a favourite among people who like simple and amusing games, free from mental effort. Fan Tan is unfortunately named, because many people confuse it with the Chinese banking game, and it would be much better under its older name: Play or Pay.

Among the many games that everyone has heard of, and that many thousands of people have been advised to play, is one that, strange to say, is not to be found described in any work about card games: Old Maid. There was a time when the result of this game was supposed to be final and conclusive, and parties of young men were known to substitute a Jack or King for the discarded Queen, in order to learn what the future had in store for them. Under these circumstances, the game naturally became Old Bachelor.

For people who believe in the verdict of the cards, there are other sources of information. Fortune telling, whether for the purpose of amusement or self-deception, has undoubtedly interested many people in all stations of life ever since Eittella first explained the art, way back in the sixteenth century. The meanings attached to the cards individually and the way the cards are arranged are all that can be given in a work of this kind. The qualifications for success in foretelling the future do not depend as much on the cards as on good judgement of human nature, unlimited assurance, a glib tongue and a measure of ingenuity in making a connected story out of the disjointed sentences formed by the chance arrangement of specific cards, to which an arbitrary or fanciful meaning is attached.

Speculation is considered by some people to be an excellent training school for the commercial instincts of the younger members of a family: it teaches them to form correct estimates as to the value of specific articles offered for sale in a fluctuating market. Authors is a very good game for the family circle, and does not require special cards, because the ordinary pack is easily adapted to the distinctions of the game.

Patience, or Solitaire, has probably claimed the attention of every card player at some time or another, and you cannot fail to be impressed by the number and ingenuity of the patience games that have been invented. One of the most expensive works about cards ever published is devoted exclusively to Solitaire.

Among all these odd games, you should be able to find something to amuse all types of card players. The only apparatus required in any of them is a pack of cards and a few counters, and for the latter, corn or coffee-beans are an excellent substitute.

— —

SIX-BID SOLO

This is the American development of the old German game of heart solo, and somewhat resembles Frog, which has already been described. Six-bid solo is a very popular game in America's western states.

CARDS The pack is thirty-six cards, which rank A 10 K Q J 9 8 7 6. These cards have a counting value: aces are worth 11 each, tens 10, kings 4, queens 3 and jacks 2. The value of the entire pack is therefore 120, and the object of the player is to get at least 60 of these points in play.

PLAYERS Three players take an active part, but if there is a fourth player at the table, when he deals, he takes no cards, but is paid if the bidder fails, without having to pay if the bidder wins.

COUNTERS It is necessary to have chips of some sort in order to pay the various games; otherwise, some careful bookkeeping will have to be done.

OBJECTS   The object of the game is to secure the privilege of playing a specific game, in which the bidder thinks he can secure the necessary 60 points out of the 120 in the pack. There are six games, or bids, that outrank each other according to their value in payments.

DEALING   The cards can be thrown around, or cut for the first deal, which is unimportant. After the pack has been properly shuffled and cut, the dealer gives four cards to each player, including himself, then three to each and three to the table for the 'widow', then four to each player again.

BIDDING   The player to the left of the dealer has the first bid and can name any one of the six following games, which he will undertake to make against two adversaries, or be set back a specific amount. The lowest bid is solo.

SOLO   If no one bids higher, the player names any suit but hearts for the trump, and the player to the left of the dealer leads any card he pleases. At the end of the play, the bidder adds the cards in the widow to the tricks he has taken in. For every point he has taken in beyond 60, he gets 2 chips from each opponent. If he fails to reach 60, he pays 2 to each opponent.

HEART SOLO   This is a better call than solo. If the bidder takes in more than 60 points, he is paid 3 chips for each point. He loses 3 chips for each point below 60.

MISERE   There are no trumps, and the player undertakes to avoid taking in a single counting card in play, whereby the cards in the widow are disregarded. This game wins or loses 30 chips as a lump payment.

GUARANTEE SOLO   The player can name any suit for trumps. If he calls hearts, he has to take in at least 74 points, and for any other suit, 80 points. This game wins or loses 40 chips.

SPREAD MISERE   There are no trumps, and the widow is disregarded. The player to the left of the bidder leads, the second player plays, then the bidder lays his cards on the table, face upwards but plays them to suit himself. This game wins or loses 60 chips.

CALL SOLO   The bidder can ask for any card he wishes, and if it is not in the widow, it has to be given to him in exchange for any card he pleases. The trump is then named, and the bidder has to take every trick. If he named hearts, the game is worth 150; if he named any other suit, the game is worth 100 only.

— —

AUTHORS

This game was originally played with cards that bore the names of various authors and other famous people, arranged in groups; however, the game is much simpler when played with an ordinary pack of fifty-two cards.

Any number of people can play. The cards are shuffled and spread, and the person who draws the lowest card deals the first hand. The ace is low. Each player then deposits a counter in the pool, and the cards are distributed one at a time until the pack is exhausted. If some players have a card more than others do, it makes no difference.

The *object* of the game is to secure tricks that consist of four cards of the same denomination, such as four 6's or four K's, and the player who has the most tricks of this kind wins the pool. Ties divide it.

The player on the left of the dealer begins by *asking* for a specific card, which has to be of the same denomination as that of one already in his hand. For example, he holds the spade Ten. He can ask anyone at the table for any of the other three Tens, but has to designate the suit and ask a specific player for the card wanted. If the player asked has the card, he has to immediately surrender it, and the player to whom it is given can then ask again: any player for any card, always provided the asker has a card of the same denomination as that in his own hand.

If the person asked does not have the card demanded, the privilege of asking is transferred to him, and he can ask any person at the table for any card of the same denomination as that of one already in his own hand. If he has just been asked for a Ten, for example, and has a Ten, but it is not of the suit asked for, he might turn on his questioner and get a Ten from him, if he could guess the right suit.

As soon as any player gets together four cards of the same denomination, he lays them face downwards the table in front of him, and they form a trick.

Having a good memory is necessary to play this game well, because it is very important to recall who has asked for specific cards and which players were unable to supply them. It is a legitimate artifice in the game to ask for a card you already have in your own hand, although you know it will lose your guess, because it might be the only way to prevent another player from drawing several valuable cards from you. For example, you hold the Fives of diamonds and spades, and have asked for and received the Five of clubs. If you ask for the heart Five, and miss it, the player who has that card can draw all your cards; however, if you ask for the spade Five, and he gets into the ask, he will at once betray the fact that he holds the fourth Five by asking you for the club Five, but he will never think of asking you for the spade Five, because you asked for it yourself. If you can get into the ask again, you can immediately make a trick in Fives.

— · —

SPECULATION

Any number of people fewer than ten can play, whereby each player contributes an agreed number of counters to the pool, and the dealer pays double. The full pack of fifty-two cards is used, and the cards rank from the A K Q down to the 2.

In *dealing*, the cards are distributed from left to right, one at a time, until each player has received three. The next card on the top of the pack is turned up, and the suit to which it belongs is the trump and forms the basis of speculation for that deal. If the turn-up card is an ace, the dealer takes the pool immediately, and the deal passes to the left. If the turn-up card is a K Q or J, the dealer offers it for sale, before a card is looked at, and can accept or refuse the amount offered. Whether or not the card is sold, all the cards that have been dealt out are turned face upwards, and the highest card of the turn-up suit wins the pool. If the card is not an honour, the dealer proceeds to sell it before any player is allowed to look at any of the cards dealt. If anyone buys the dealer's turn-up card, the purchaser places it on his own cards, and leaves it face upwards. Whether or not it is sold, the elder hand proceeds to turn up the top card of his three cards. If this is not a trump, the next player on his left turns up his top card, and so on until a trump is turned that is better than the one already exposed. The player who possesses the original turn-up does not expose any more of his cards until a better trump is shown. As soon as a better trump appears, it is offered for sale, and after it is sold or refused, the cards are turned up again until either a better trump appears or all the cards have been exposed. The holder of the best trump at the end takes the pool.

——

OLD MAID

Strange to say, this oft quoted and continually derided game is not mentioned in any work about cards, a singular omission that we hasten to redress.

Any number of young ladies can play, and a pack of fifty-one cards is used, whereby the Queen of hearts is deleted. Any player can deal the cards, which are distributed one at a time until the pack is exhausted, and if every player does not have the same number, it does not matter. Beginning with the eldest hand, each player sorts her cards into pairs of the same denomination, such as two Fives, two Jacks, and so on, and all pairs so formed are laid on the table face downwards, without showing them to the other players. All the cards laid out in this way are left in front of the player, in order to discover errors, if any. Three of a kind cannot be discarded, but four of a kind can be considered as two pairs.

When the discarding of pairs is complete, the dealer begins by spreading her remaining cards to resemble a fan, and presents them, face downwards, to her left-hand neighbour, who has to draw one card at random. The card so drawn is examined, and if it completes a pair, the two cards are discarded. Whether or not it forms a pair, the player's cards are spread and presented to the next player on the left, to be drawn from in the same way.

This process of drawing, forming pairs and discarding is continued until it is found that one player remains who has one card. This card is naturally the odd Queen, and the unfortunate holder of it is the Old Maid, but only for that deal.

——

LIFT SMOKE

The number of players has to be limited to six, and each player deposits a counter in the pool. A full pack of fifty-two cards is used. The cards rank from the ace down to the deuce, as in Whist. If there are four players, six cards are dealt to each player, one at a time; if five play, five cards are dealt to each player, and if six play, four cards are dealt to each. The last card that falls to the dealer is turned up for the trump, and the remainder of the pack is placed in the centre of the table as a stock to draw from.

The eldest hand leads for the first trick, and the other players have to follow suit if they can. The highest card played, if it is of the suit led, wins the trick, and trumps win all other suits. The winner of each trick draws the top card from the talon, and leads again. When any player's cards are exhausted, he withdraws from the game, and the other players continue. The player who remains to the end, who has a card when his adversary has none, wins the pool. If two players remain with a card each, the winner of the trick draws from the stock, and the card so drawn wins the game, whereby the player's adversary has no card.

— ● —

EARL OF COVENTRY

This game is sometimes called Snip Snap Snorem, by people who are not of a poetical turn of mind. Any number of people can play, and a full pack of cards is dealt, one at a time. If some players have a card more than the others do, it does not matter. The eldest hand lays on the table any card he pleases, and each player in turn pairs or matches it, if he can, with another card of the same denomination, thereby accompanying the action with a rhyme. Suppose the first card played is a King: the person who plays it would say, 'There's as good as King can be.' The first player to lay down another King would say, 'There is one as good as he.' The player who holds the third King would say, 'There's the best of all the three,' and the holder of the fourth King would then triumphantly exclaim, 'And there's the Earl of Coventry.'

The fortunate holder of the Earl of Coventry in each round has the privilege of leading a card for the next trick, and the first player to get rid of all his cards wins one counter from the other players for every card they hold. The words 'Snip, Snap, Snorem,' can be substituted for the aforementioned rhymes if time is short.

Jig is a variation of Earl of Coventry in which the next card higher in sequence and suit has to be played, if the player has it, until four cards are shown. The player who lays down the last card of the sequence of four cards starts a fresh sequence, and the winner is the player who can first get rid of all the cards originally dealt to him. All the other players then pay him a counter for each card they have left.

COMMIT

The etymology of this word has been quite overlooked by people who have described the game. The word is from the French, *cométe*: 'a comet'; however, instead of being an equivalent in English, it is simply a phonetic equivalent: *Commit*, instead of *Comet*. Tenac informs us that the game was invented during the appearance of Halley's comet, and the idea of the game is that of a string of cards forming a tail to the card first played, a feature that is common to quite a number of the older card games.

Commit is played by any number of people, with a pack of fifty-one cards, whereby the Eight of diamonds is deleted. The players draw for positions at the table and for the first deal, and make up a pool. The cards have no value except the order of their sequence in the various suits. The ace is not in sequence with the King; it is below the 2. The dealer distributes the cards, one at a time to each player in rotation, as far as they will go, and leaves any odd cards on the table face downwards, in order to form what are known as *stops*. Because it is desirable to have a number of these stops, it is usual to give only nine cards to each person when there are five players.

The eldest hand begins by leading any card he pleases, which he lays face upwards in the centre of the table. If he holds any other cards in sequence above it, he has to play them, and when he can no longer continue the series, he says aloud, 'Without the Jack,' or whatever the card might be that he fails on. The player on his left then has to continue the sequence in the same suit, if he can, or has to say, 'Without the Jack.' When the sequence reaches the King, it is stopped, and the player who held the King receives a counter from each player at the table. The same player then begins another sequence with any card he pleases. If a sequence is opened with an ace, a counter can be demanded from each player at the table.

If a sequence is stopped, which it will be if the card necessary to continue it is in the stock, or if the diamonds are run up to the Seven, the person who plays the last card before the stop is entitled to begin another sequence. If any player who is unable to continue a sequence in his proper turn holds the Nine of diamonds, he can play that card, and the player following him is then at liberty to either continue the original sequence or play the Ten of diamonds, thereby following up that sequence. When the Nine of diamonds is played, the holder receives two counters from each player at the table; however, if it is not gotten rid of in play, the holder of it has to pay two counters to each of the other players.

The first player to get rid of all his cards wins the pool, and the cards remaining in the other hands are then exposed. Any player who holds a King has to pay a counter for it to each of the other players.

— —

MATRIMONY

Any number of people can play, and a full pack of fifty-two cards is used. Each player should be provided with an equal number of counters, to which a trifling value can be attached. A strip of paper is placed in the centre of the table, marked as follows.

Matrimony	Intrigue	Confederacy	Pair	Best

Any King and Queen is *Matrimony*; any Queen and Jack is *Intrigue*; and any King and Jack is *Confederacy*. And any two cards of the same denomination form a *Pair*, and the diamond ace is always *Best*.

The players draw, and the lowest card deals, whereby ace is low. The dealer then takes any number of counters he chooses, and distributes them as he pleases on the various divisions of the layout. Each player then takes a number of counters one less than the dealer's, and distributes them according to his fancy.

The cards are then cut, and the dealer gives one card to each player, face downwards, then another, face upwards. If any of the latter are the diamond ace, the player to whom it is dealt takes everything on the layout, and the cards are gathered and shuffled again, whereby the deal passes to the left and the new dealer begins a fresh pool. If the diamond ace is not turned up, each player in turn, beginning with the eldest hand, exposes his down card. The first player to discover Matrimony in his two cards takes all that has been staked on that division of the layout. The first player to discover Intrigue or Confederacy takes all on that, and the first player to expose a Pair takes that pool. The ace of diamonds is of no value except as one of a pair, if it is one of the cards that were dealt to the players face downwards. The pool for it remains until the card is dealt to a player face upwards. Any of the pools that are not won have to remain until the following deal, and can be added to.

—-—

POPE JOAN

This game is a combination of the layout in Matrimony and the way of playing in Commit. There are a great many ways of dividing the layout, but the following is the simplest. Five cards are taken from an old pack and laid out in the centre of the table, or their names are written on a sheet of paper.

The cards are thrown around for the deal, and the first Jack deals. The cards are distributed one at a time, whereby the full pack of fifty-two cards is used. The following table indicates the number of cards to be given to each player, and the number left in the stock in order to form stops.

3 Players,	15 cards each		7 in the stock			
4	"	12	"	4	"	"
5	"	9	"	7	"	"
6	"	8	"	4	"	"
7	"	7	"	3	"	"
8	"	6	"	4	"	"

Before the deal, the dealer has to dress the layout, by putting one counter on the Ten, two on the Jack, three on the Queen, four on the King, and five on the Pope, which is the Seven (or the Nine) of diamonds.

The eldest hand begins by leading any card he pleases, and if he has the cards in sequence and suit with it and above it, he continues to play until he fails. He then says, 'No six,' or whatever the card is that he stops on. The next player on his left then continues the sequence if he can, and if he cannot, he says, 'No six,' also, and the next player is passed to. If no one can continue, the card has to be in the stock, which remains on the table face downwards and unseen. When one sequence is stopped in this way, the last player has the right to begin another sequence with any card he pleases.

The object of the game is twofold: to get rid of all the cards before any other player does so, and to get rid of the cards that appear on the layout. If the duplicate of any of these cards can be played, the holder of the card at once takes all the money staked on it; however, if he fails to get rid of it before a player wins the game by getting rid of all his cards, the player who is found to have one of the layout cards in his hand at the end has to double the amount staked on that card, to which the next dealer will add the usual contribution.

The player who first gets rid of all his cards collects from the other players a counter for every card they hold. These cards have to be exposed face upwards on the table, so that all the players can see who has to double the various pools. If any of the layout cards are in the stock, the pool simply remains, without doubling.

There are a great many variations of Pope Joan. Sometimes a layout very similar to that in Matrimony is used, whereby Pope takes the place of Pair, and Game takes the place of Best. A trump is turned by the dealer, and Matrimony is King and Queen of trumps, Intrigue is Queen and Jack of trumps, and Confederacy is King and Jack of trumps. The player who holds these cards will naturally be able to play both of them if he can play one in a sequence, and will take the pool for the combination. If he holds one card and another player holds the other, they divide the pool. If one of the cards is in the stock, the pool remains. In some places, it is the custom to remove the Eight of diamonds, as in Commit, in order to form an extra and known stop. The player who first gets rid of his cards takes the pool on Game, and the holder of Pope takes that pool if he can get rid of the card in the course of play; if he cannot, he has to double the pool, exactly as with the honours in trumps.

— —

NEWMARKET
BOODLE, MICHIGAN, OR STOPS

This game, which is sometimes called Boodle, is Pope Joan without the pope. The four cards that form the layout are the tableau, but there is no 7. Each player puts a counter on each card in the tableau, and the dealer puts two cards. The whole pack is dealt out, one card at a time; an extra hand is dealt out, one card at a time; and an extra hand is dealt to the dealer's left for a 'widow', in order to form 'stops'. The dealer is usually allowed to sell this hand without looking at it, if he does not care to exchange his own for it. The other players bid for it. The player to the left of the dealer plays the first card.

The player has to begin with the lowest card in his hand of the suit he selects. He is not restricted as to the suit, but has to play all he has in sequence, then name the card he fails on. If any other player has that card, the sequence has to be continued until it gets up to the ace, or a stop is reached, whereby no one can play. The player who comes to a stop has to change the suit, if he can, and begin with the lowest card he holds in it.

If, in the course of play, any of the four cards on the layout can be gotten rid of, the player who holds them takes the pool in that card. If he is left with the card in his hand at the end, it remains until the next deal. The first player to get rid of all his cards receives one counter from the other players for each card they hold, and the usual chips are placed on the cards in the tableau again, whether or not the ones already placed there have been won.

SPIN This is Newmarket, with one variation. The player who holds the diamond ace is allowed to play it in order to get the privilege of stopping one suit and opening another. For example, the sequence in spades has run to the Nine, and one player holds both spade Ten and diamond ace. If this player sees that another player is very likely to win the game at any moment, and he has a pool card to play, he might stop the spade sequence by playing both the Ten and the diamond ace together, thereby announcing *Spin*. He can then play a pool card, or begin a new sequence with the lowest of the suit in his hand. He cannot play the diamond ace unless he can play to the sequence first.

SARATOGA This varies from Newmarket in only the method of making up the pool. Rather than leave players to distribute their stakes at pleasure, each player is compelled to place an agreed amount on each of the pool cards, as in Pope Joan.

— —

POCHEN

This is a round game for any number of players from three to six, using a 32-card pack. The layout has a centre division for pools and seven other divisions around it, marked, respectively, A, K, Q, J, 10, Marriage and Sequence. Each player dresses the layout by placing a counter in each of the eight divisions. The dealer then gives cards, three then two at a time, as far as they will go equally, and turns up the next card for the trump.

The holders of the five highest trumps show them and take the corresponding pools: Ace of trumps the A pool, and so on. If any player holds both K and Q of trumps, he takes the pool for marriage. The player who holds the highest and longest sequence in any suit takes the pool for sequence, but the sequence has to be at least three cards. Pools not won remain until the next deal.

After all the pools around the edge are decided, the players bet for the centre pool, or pochen. Any player who has a pair, or three of a kind, who wishes to bet on them, puts as many counters as he pleases into the centre pool, and any player who is willing to bet against him has to put in a similar amount. There is no raising these bets, and the players in order to the left of the dealer have the first say as to betting, or passing. The higher pair wins. Threes beat pairs, and four of a kind is the best hand possible.

When this pool is settled, the play of the cards follows. The eldest hand leads any card he pleases, and each player in turn to the left has to follow in sequence and suit, playing the 10 on the 9, the J on the 10, and so on, until the K is reached. The player who has the King, or the highest card if the King is in the stock, starts again with any card he pleases. Any player who cannot continue the sequence in his turn has to pass for that round.

As soon as one player gets rid of his last card, the game is at an end, and every player at the table has to pay him a counter for each card held. The deal then passes to the left, and the layout is dressed for the next hand.

— —

RANTER GO ROUND

This is a round game for any number of players, who make up a pool or stake to be played for. A full pack of fifty-two cards is used, and each player has three markers. The dealer gives one card to each player, face downwards. This card is examined, and if it is not satisfactory, it is passed to the player on the left, whereby the object is to avoid holding the lowest card at the table.

If the player on the left holds any card but a king, he is obliged to exchange. If the player who is forced to exchange gives an ace or a deuce, he announces it, but the player who demands the exchange is not allowed to say what he gives, because the card might be passed on. Each player in turn to the left can exchange, or pass, which means he is satisfied with his card.

When it comes around to the dealer, he cannot exchange, but can cut the pack and take the top card. All the cards are then turned face upwards, and the lowest card shown loses a counter. The deal passes to the left. When all the players but one have lost all their markers, the survivor takes the pool.

— —

FIVE OR NINE

This game, which is sometimes called Domino Whist, is simply Pope Joan or Matrimony without the layout. Any number of people can play, and the full pack of fifty-two cards is used, whereby the cards are dealt in proportion to the number of players, as in Pope Joan.

The eldest hand has to begin by laying out the Five or Nine of a suit in order to start the first sequence. If he has neither of these cards, he has to pass, and the first player on his left who has a Five or Nine has to begin. The next player on the left then has to continue the sequence in the same suit if he can, but can play either up or down, whereby he lays the card on the right or left of the starter. If a Five is led, he can play a Four or Six. Only one card is played at a time by each person in turn. Any person who is not able to continue the sequence can start another if he has another Five, but cannot start a sequence with a Nine unless the first starter in the game was a Nine. He is also at liberty to start a new sequence with a Five or Nine rather than continue the old sequence; but he has to play if he can: one or the other. If he is unable to play, he has to pay one counter into the pool, which is won by the first player who gets rid of all his cards. The winner is also paid a counter for every card held by the other players.

— — —

FAN TAN

This is the simplest form of Stops, and requires no layout. Any number of players can take part, and a full pack of fifty-two cards is used. The players cut for deal and seats, and low has the choice. Ace is low. The players are provided with an equal number of counters, and before the cards are dealt, each player places an agreed number of cards in the pool. All the cards are dealt. If some players have more than others do, it does not matter.

The eldest hand begins by playing any card he pleases, and the next player on his left has to either play the next card above it or put one counter in the pool. Only one card is played at a time, and after the sequence has arrived at the King, it has to be continued with the ace and to go on until the suit is exhausted. The person who plays the thirteenth card of any suit has to start another sequence, in any suit and with any card he pleases. The player who first gets rid of all his cards takes the pool.

The great trick in this game is to provide for the last suit to be played, and in order to have the selection of the second suit, it is usual for the eldest hand to begin with the higher of two cards next in value to each other, whereby he will be made the last player in that suit. Each suit is turned face downwards as it is exhausted.

— — —

SOLITAIRE

All games of Solitaire are played with the full pack of fifty-two cards. The games can be roughly divided into two classes: games in which the result is entirely dependent on chance and cannot be changed by the player after the cards have been shuffled and cut, and games that present opportunities for exercising judgement and skill, whereby the choice of several ways to the same end is offered to the player at various stages. The first class is naturally the simpler, but is the less satisfactory, because it is nothing more than a game of chance.

Of the many hundreds of patience games, it is possible to give only a few of the best known.

TAKE TEN   Shuffle and cut the cards, and deal out thirteen face upwards in two rows of five each and one row of three. Any two cards, the pip value of which equals 10, can be withdrawn from the tableau, and other cards can be dealt from the top of the pack in their place. Only two cards can be used in order to form a 10. The K Q J 10 of each suit have to be lifted together, and none of these cards are touched until all four cards of the same suit are on the table together. When no cards can be lifted, the game is lost.

The object in most patience games is to arrange the cards in sequences. An ascending sequence is one in which the cards run from A 2 3 up to the King, and a descending sequence is one in which the cards run down to the ace. Sequences can be formed of one suit or of mixed suits, according to the rules of the game.

THE CARPET   Shuffle and cut the pack. Deal twenty cards in four rows of five cards each, face upwards. This is the carpet. Any aces found in it are taken out and used to form a fifth row, at either the bottom or the side. The holes made in the carpet by removing the aces are then filled up from the pack. Cards are then taken from the carpet to build on the aces in ascending sequence, following suit, and the holes in the carpet are continually filled up with fresh cards from the top of the pack. As other aces appear, they are laid aside in order to start the sequence in the suit to which they belong. When you are stopped, deal the cards remaining in the pack in a pile on the table by themselves, face upwards. If any card appears that can be used in the ascending sequences, take it, and if this enables you to make more holes in the carpet, do so. However, after you have been driven to deal this extra pile, holes in the carpet can no longer be filled from the pack: they have to be patched up with the top cards on the extra pile until it is exhausted.

FOUR OF A KIND   Shuffle and cut the pack, then deal out thirteen cards face downwards in two rows of five each and one row of three. Deal on the top of these cards until the pack is exhausted, whereby you will be given four cards in each pile, face downwards. Imagine that these piles represent, respectively, the A 2 3 4 5 in the first row, the 6 7 8 9 10 in the second row, and the J Q K in the third row. Take the top card from the ace pile, turn it face upward, and place it, still face upwards, under the pile to which it belongs.

If it is a Jack, for example, it will go face upwards under the first pile in the third row. Then take the top card from the second pile, and so on, and keep the left hand as a marker on the pile last drawn from. When you come to a pile that is complete, and all the cards are face upwards, you can skip it and go on to the next pile. If at the end you find that the last card to be turned up lies on its proper pile, and requires only turning over, you win, but if you have to remove it to another pile, you lose.

TRY AGAIN Shuffle and cut the pack, and deal the cards face upwards into four heaps. You are not obliged to deal to each pile in succession, but can place the cards on any of the four piles, according to your judgement or pleasure. In dealing out in this way, it is not good policy to cover one card with a higher card, unless you are compelled to do so. Every time you come to an ace, separate it from the other cards, and place it in a new row, as a foundation for an ascending sequence, which can be continued regardless of the suit of the cards used. The top cards of the four piles are used in order to build up the sequence. After an ace has appeared, the player can examine the cards in any or all of the piles, but their order cannot be disturbed. The object in looking at the cards is to select either the pile that is least likely to stop you or the pile that has the fewest cards in it.

TAKE FOURTEEN Shuffle and cut the pack, and deal the cards one at a time, face upwards, into twelve piles. Continue dealing on the top of these twelve until the pack is exhausted. This will give you four piles that contain one card more than the other piles contain. Then take off any two of the top cards that will make 14, and reckon the Jack as 11, the Queen as 12, the King as 13, and all the other cards at their face value. Only two cards have to be used in order to make 14. If you succeed in taking off all the cards in this way, you win. You are at liberty to look at the underneath cards in the various piles, but you cannot disturb their positions.

THE IDIOT'S DELIGHT This is supposed to be the best of all solitaires. A full pack of fifty-two cards is thoroughly shuffled, cut and dealt face upwards. Nine cards are placed in a row from left to right. On these, eight cards are placed from left to right, then seven, six and so on down to one. There will now be a triangle of forty-five cards, with a row of nine at the top and a file of nine at the left. The remaining seven cards are placed apart, all face upwards, and can be used at any time the player wishes.

As soon as an ace is free at the bottom of any vertical file, it is placed above the triangle, to be built on in suit and sequence up to the king. It is not compulsory to build. Only one card can be moved at a time from one file to another, and only the bottom card of the file can be moved. All cards so moved have to be placed on a card of a different colour, and in descending sequence, such as a red seven on a black eight. If a card cannot be so placed, it cannot be moved except to go into a space. Spaces are made by getting all the cards away from one vertical file to other files or to the aces. Once cards are built on, the aces cannot be taken back again under any conditions.

Spaces can be filled by any card, but it is obvious that kings cannot be moved except into spaces. The object is to get the entire fifty-two cards built up on the aces. This should be done about once in every three or four attempts.

— · —

KLONDIKE

This game is sometimes mistakenly called 'Canfield', but that is a distinct game, described elsewhere, in which there are separate piles for stock and foundations.

Shuffle the full pack of fifty-two cards, and cut and turn up the top card. Lay six more cards in a row to the right of the first card, but all face downwards. On the second card of this row, place another card face upwards; then cards face downwards on the remaining five of the top row. On the third pile from the left, place another card face upwards, then four more cards face downwards to the right. Continue this until you have seven cards face upwards, whereby you will be given twenty-eight cards in your layout.

Take out any aces that are showing, and place them in a row by themselves for 'foundations'. Build up on these aces in sequence and suit to kings. On the layout, build in descending sequence: red on black, and black on red, and turn up the top card when any pile is left without a faced card on it. If there is more than one card face upwards on any pile, the cards have to be removed together or not at all. Spaces can be filled with only kings.

The stock is run off three cards at a time, and any card that shows can be used. The pack can be run through in this way until no cards showing can be used, but there has to be no shuffling or rearrangement of the cards. Sometimes it is the rule to run through the pack once only, and to turn up one card at a time.

The object of the game is to see how many cards can be built on the ace row. A better average can usually be obtained when the pack is run off three at a time with the privilege of running through again and again as long as any card can be used.

— —

FORTUNE TELLING

Whatever the arrangement used for laying out the tableau in fortune telling, the result of the reading will always be dependent on the person's ability to string together in a connected story the meanings that are attached to the various cards. According to Eittella, the founder of all fortune telling, only thirty-two cards should be used, and it is essential they be single heads, because a court-card standing firmly on its feet is a very different thing from one standing on its head. If single-head cards are not at hand, the lower part of the double-head cards has to be cancelled in some way.

Following are the interpretations of the various cards, whereby the letter *R* means that the card is either reversed or standing on its head.

HEARTS   Ace. The house, or home.

King. A benefactor. *R.* He will not be able to do you much good, although he means well.

Queen. Everything that is lovely in a woman. *R.* You will have to wait a while for realisation of your hopes.

Jack. A person who might be useful to you. *R.* He will not prove to be of much account.

Ten. A pleasant surprise.

Nine. Reconciliation.

Eight. Children.

Seven. A good marriage. *R.* Fair to middling.

CLUBS   Ace. Profits from business or gambling.

King. A just man, who has taken a fancy to you. *R.* Something will interfere with his good intentions.

Queen. Your best girl. *R.* She is jealous.

Jack. A probable marriage. *R.* It might have to be postponed.

Ten. Success in business. If followed by ◊ 9, the note will not be paid when it is due; if followed by the ♠ 9, you will lose the entire account.

Nine. Success in love.

Eight. Great anticipations.

Seven. Trifling love affairs. *R.* They will get you into trouble.

DIAMONDS   Ace. A letter, or a written notice.

King. A person to beware. *R.* The person will annoy you in any case.

Queen. A shrew or gossip. *R.* She will make you tired.

Jack. A bearer of bad news. *R.* Worse news than what you expected.

Ten. An unexpected journey.

Nine. That expected money will not come to hand.

Eight. Some surprising actions on the part of a young man.

Seven. Success in lotteries, gambling or speculation. *R.* The amount will be very small.

SPADES   Ace. Love affairs.

King. Police or sheriffs. *R.* Loss of a lawsuit.

Queen. A happy and deceptive widow. *R.* She is fooling you.

Jack. A disagreeable young man. *R.* He will do you an in injury or an injustice of some kind.

Ten. Prison.

Nine. Vexatious delays in business matters.

Eight. Bad news. If followed by the ◊ 7, quarrels.

Seven. Quarrels that will be lasting unless the card is followed by some hearts. *R.* Family rows.

COMBINATIONS   4 aces, death; 3 aces, dissipation; 2 aces, enmity.

4 Kings, honours; 3 Kings, success in business; 2 Kings, good advice.

4 Queens, scandal; 3 Queens, dissipation: 2 Queens, friendship.

4 Jacks, contagious diseases; 3 Jacks, idleness; 2 Jacks, quarrels.

4 Tens, disagreeable events; 3 Tens, change of residence; 2 Tens, loss.

4 Nines, good actions; 3 Nines, imprudence; 2 Nines, money.

4 Eights, reverses in business or love; 3 Eights, marriage; 2 Eights, trouble.

4 Sevens, intrigues; 3 Sevens, pleasure; 2 Sevens, small affairs and gossip.

THE CONSULTATION   There are several ways of telling fortunes, but one example will suffice. The most important thing is to know what your client wants to be told, and the next is to be sure that the client cuts the cards with her left hand.

The cards are shuffled, presented to be cut, then counted off into sevens, whereby every seventh card is laid face upwards on the table, and the six intermediates are placed on the bottom of the pack each time. When twelve cards have been obtained in this way, they are laid out in a row and examined to see whether the card that represents the questioner is among them. If it is not, the cards have to be gathered, shuffled, cut and dealt again. A married man who has light hair would be the ◇ K, and who has dark hair the ♣ K. If the man claims to be single, he would be the ♡ J. If your client is a woman, the ♡ Q will apply to blondes, the ♣ Q to brunettes. Do not ask whether she is married, and take no notice of any rings she might be wearing.

When you have obtained the necessary twelve cards, the more you know about the consultant's history, hopes and prospects, and the better you can judge her character, the less attention you have to pay to the cards, and the more satisfactory the result of the consultation will be. It is not necessary to stick too closely to the meanings of the cards, nor to their combinations: the great thing is to tell your client what she wants to hear.

In order to confirm the truth of the pleasing story you have built on the twelve cards, the cards have to be gathered together, shuffled, presented to be cut with the left hand, then divided into four packets of three cards each. The first packet is for the Person, the second is for the House, the third is for the Future, and the fourth is for the Surprise. Each packet is successively turned up, and its contents are interpreted in connection with the part of the questioner's life it represents. In case there is nothing very surprising in the last pack, it is well to have a few generalities on hand, which will be true of a person's future six times out of ten. The expert at fortune telling has a stock of vague suggestions that are supposed to be given by the cards, and that are framed so as to draw from the client the drift of her hopes and fears. Once the scent has been smelt, most of the fortune telling is in the nature of confirming the client's own views of the situation. Nevertheless, when it is well done, by a good talker, fortune telling is very amusing, especially in a small group.

BANKING GAMES

—

There are two distinct classes of banking game: ones that can be played without any apparatus but a pack of cards and some counters, and ones that require a permanent establishment and expensive paraphernalia. Among the first, probably the best-known banking games are Vingt-et-un, Baccara, Blind Hookey and Fan Tan, the latter which requires only one card the face of which is never seen. In the second class of games, which are often called table games, the best known are probably Faro, Keno, Roulette, Rouge et Noir and Chuck Luck.

Each of these games has a number of offshoots, and the distinctions between the original and the variation are sometimes so minute they are hardly worth mentioning. As a matter of reference, and for the convenience of people who hear these variations spoken about, the games' names and main characteristics are given herein.

Banking games, which are properly so called, are games in which one player is continually opposed to all the other players. In round games, each player is for himself, but no player is selected for the common enemy. In partnership games, the sides are equally divided, and any advantage in the deal or lead passes alternately from one side to the other. In other games, the single player that might be opposed to two or three other players usually takes the responsibility on himself, and for one deal only, so any advantage he might have is temporary. In banking games, on the contrary, one player is selected as opposed to all the other players, and the opposition is continual. If there is any advantage in being the banker, it is supposed to be a permanent one, and if the banker has not gone to any special expense in securing the advantages of his position, he is obliged to surrender the position from time to time and give the other players a chance. This is the rule in Vingt-et-un, Baccara and Blind Hookey. If the banker is not changed occasionally, he retains his position on account of the expense he has been put to in order to provide the apparatus for the play, as in Faro, Keno, Roulette and Rouge et Noir. To justify this expenditure, he has to have some permanent advantage, and if no advantage or 'percentage' is inherent in the principles of the game, any person who is playing against this banker is probably being cheated.

In the gaming venues of Monte Carlo, everything is perfectly fair and straightforward, but no games are played in them except the ones in which the percentage in favour of the bank is evident and openly acknowledged. In venues of Faro, there is no advantage of this type, and no honest faro bank can exist. It is for this reason that the game is not played in the Monte Carlo venues, in spite of the many thousands of Americans who begged the managers to introduce it. The so-called percentage of 'splits' in the venues of Faro is a mere sham, and any candid dealer will admit that they do not pay for the petrol to get to the venues. Roulette, Rouge et Noir, Keno and Chuck Luck are all percentage games, although the banker in Chuck Luck is seldom satisfied with his legitimate gains.

The peculiarity about all percentage banking games is that no system, as a system, will beat the games. The mathematical expectation of loss is so nicely adjusted to the probabilities of gain that the player always has to get just slightly the worst of it if he will only play long enough. Take any system of martingales, and suppose for the sake of illustration that in 1000 coups, you will win 180 counters. The mathematical expectation of the game is such that just about once in a thousand coups, your martingale will carry you to a point at which you will lose 200 counters, thereby leaving you only 20 behind on every 1000 if you keep on playing. Every system has been carefully investigated, and enormous labour has been expended on compilation of tables in which every number rolled at Roulette and every coup raked in at Rouge et Noir is recorded for a long period of time. However, the result of all systems is found to be the same: the bank succeeds in building up its percentage like a coral island, and the player's money disappears like water in the sand.

— • —

VINGT-ET-UN

Any number of people can play Vingt-et-un, and a full pack of fifty-two cards is used. The **cards** have no rank, but a counting value is attached to each card, whereby the ace is reckoned as 11 or 1, at the option of the holder; all court-cards are reckoned as 10 each; and the other cards are reckoned at their face value.

The cards are thrown around for the first deal, and the first ace takes it. The dealer is also the banker. Each player is provided with a specific number of *counters*: usually 25 or 50, and a betting limit is agreed on before play begins. The players on the dealer's right and left are known as the pone and the eldest hand, respectively.

The *object* of the game is to get as near 21 as possible in the total pip value of the cards held.

STAKES　Before the cards are dealt, each player except the dealer places before him the amount he bets on his chances for that deal. This amount can either be at the option of the player, within the betting limit, or a fixed sum, such as one counter. In one variation, each player is allowed to look at the first card dealt to him before making his bet and receiving a second card. When it comes to the dealer's turn, he does not stake anything on his card, but has the privilege of calling on all the other players to *double* the amount they have placed on theirs. Any player who refuses to double has to pass over to the dealer the stake already put up and to stand out of the game for that hand.

Another variation is to allow any player whose second card is of the same denomination as that of the first to separate the cards, and to place on the second card a bet equal in amount to the one on his first card, whereby afterwards he draws to each card separately, as if the cards were two different hands.

DEALING　When the bets are made, the cards are shuffled and presented to the pone to cut, and four have to be left in each packet. Two cards are given to each player, including the dealer, one at a time in two rounds. If the dealer gives too many cards to any player, in either the first deal or the draw, he has to correct the error at once. If the player has seen the superfluous card, he can keep any two cards he chooses of the ones dealt to him. If the dealer gives himself too many cards, he has to keep them all. The last card in the pack must not be dealt. If there are not enough cards to supply the players, the discards have to be gathered up, shuffled together and cut.

NATURALS　When all the cards are dealt, the dealer first examines his hand. If he has exactly 21 cards: an Ace and a tenth card, which is called a natural, he shows the natural at once, and the players have to pay him twice the amount they have staked in front of them, unless they also have a natural, whereby the game is a stand-off. If the dealer does not have a natural, each player in turn, beginning with the eldest hand, examines his two cards to see how closely their total value approaches 21. If the player has a natural, he exposes it immediately, and the dealer has to pay him double the amount staked. It is sometimes the rule for the holder of a natural, if the dealer does not have one, to take the stakes of all the other players, but this variation is not in favour.

DRAWING   If no natural is shown, each player in turn can either draw another card or stand on the two cards dealt to him, which are not shown under any circumstances. If he is content, he says, 'I stand.' If he wants a card, he says, 'One,' and the dealer gives him a card, face upwards. If the pips on the card drawn, added to the cards already in the player's hand, make his total greater than 21, he is créve, and passes over to the dealer his stake, thereby throwing his cards in the centre of the table, still face downwards. If the total is not 21, he can draw another card, and so on until he either is créve or stands. When the first player is disposed of in this way, the dealer goes on to the next player, and so on until he comes to himself. He turns his two cards face upwards, and either draws or stands, to suit himself. If he overdraws, all the other players expose their first two cards in order to show they have 21 or fewer, and he then pays each of them the amount they have staked. If he stands, either before or after drawing, the other players expose their cards in the same way, and the ones who have the same number are tied, and win or lose nothing. The players who have fewer than the dealer has lose their stake; the ones who have more than the dealer has, but still not more than 21, have to be paid by the dealer. When the result is a tie, it is called *paying in cards*.

THE BANKER   The banker for the next deal can be decided on in various ways. The old rule was for one player to continue to act as the banker and to deal the cards until one of his adversaries held a natural, if the dealer had no natural to offset it. When this occurred, the player who held the natural took the bank and the deal until someone else held a natural. Another way was to agree on a specific number of rounds for a banker, after which the privilege was drawn for again. Another was for one player to remain the banker until he had lost or won a specific amount, whereby the privilege was drawn for again. The modern practice is for each player to be the banker in turn, whereby the deal passes in regular rotation to the left. When this is done, there has to be a penalty for dealing twice in succession, and the penalty is usually fixed at having to pay ties, if the error is not discovered until one player has drawn cards; if it is discovered before that, it is a misdeal.

POOLS   Vingt-et-un is sometimes played with a pool. Each player contributes one counter at the start, and the pool is afterwards fed by way of penalties. Every player who is créve puts in a counter, whereby all ties with the dealer pay one counter, and the dealer pays one counter for any irregularity in dealing. The pool can be kept to pay for refreshments, similar to the kitty used in Poker, or can be won by the first natural shown, as can be agreed.

PROBABILITIES   The only point in the game is for a player to know what hands to stand on and what to draw to. The dealer is guided by the cards dealt to other players and by what the players ask for. The other players should stand on 17 but draw on 16. In practice, it has been found that the odds are about 2 to 1 in favour of drawing at 16, and 3 to 1 for drawing at 15. The rules for drawing and so on are more fully described in connection with the very similar game of Baccara.

— • —

MACAO

In this variety of Vingt-et-un, only one card is dealt to each player, court-cards and tens count nothing, and the Ace is always worth one. The number to be reached is 9, instead of 21, and if a player has a 9 natural, he receives from the banker three times his stake; if he has an 8 natural, he receives double; and if he has a 7 natural, he is paid. If the banker has an equal number of points natural, it is a tie, and if the banker has a 7, 8 or 9 natural, he receives from each of the other players once, twice or three times the amount of their stakes. If none of these naturals is shown, the players draw in turn, as in Vingt-et-un, and the dealer receives from the players who have fewer points than he has, or who are créve, and pays the players who have more points but have not passed 9.

— • —

FARMER

Any number of people can play. All the 8's and all the 6's except the ♡ 6 are discarded from a pack of fifty-two cards. All court-cards count for 10, the ace counts for 1, and all other cards count at their face value. A pool is then made up by way of each player's contributing one counter. This is the farm, and is sold to the highest bidder, who has to put into it the price he pays for it. This bidder then becomes the farmer and deals one card to each player, but takes no card himself.

The object of the players is to get as near 16 as possible, and each in turn, beginning on the dealer's left, has to take at least one card. After looking at it, he can ask for another card, and so on until he either is créve or stands. If a player overdraws himself, he says nothing about it until all the players are helped, whereby the hands are exposed. Any player who has exactly 16 points takes the farm and all its contents. If there is more than one 16, the one that is made with the assistance of the ♡ 6 wins; otherwise, the one that is made with the fewest cards wins. If this is a tie, the eldest hand wins. If no one has exactly 16 points, the farm stays with its original owner, deal after deal, until exactly 16 points are held by a player.

Whether or not anyone wins the farm, when the hands are exposed, all players who have overdrawn have to pay to the player who owned the farm at the beginning of that deal as many counters as they have points more than 16. These payments do not go into the farm but are clear profits. The players who have fewer than 16 points pay nothing to the farmer but the player who is nearest ♡ 6 receives a counter from each of the other players. Ties are decided by way of possession of the 16, or the fewest cards, or the eldest hand, as already described. If the farm remains in the same hands, the farmer deals again and collects his profits until he loses his farm. When the farm is won, it is emptied, and re-sold as at the beginning of the game.

— —

QUINZE

This is a form of Vingt-et-un for two players, but the number of points to be reached is 15 instead of 21. Court-cards are reckoned as 10 points, and the ace is reckoned as 1 point only. Each player stakes an agreed amount every time, then the dealer gives one card to his adversary and one to himself. The pone can either stand on the first card or draw, but does not say anything if he overdraws. The dealer then draws or stands, and both players show their cards. The player who is nearest 15 points wins; however, if the result is a tie, or if both players have overdrawn, the stakes are doubled and another hand is dealt, whereby the deal passes from player to player in rotation.

— • —

BACCARA

This very popular variation of Vingt-et-un originated in the south of France and came into vogue during the latter part of the reign of France's Louis Philippe. It is neither a recreation nor an intellectual exercise but simply a means for rapid exchange of money, and is well suited to impatient people. The word *Baccara* is supposed to mean 'nothing' or 'zero', and is applied to the hands in which the total pip value of the cards ends with a cypher.

There are two forms of the game in common use: Baccara a deux tableaux and Baccara chemin de fer. The first will be described first.

PLAYERS   Baccara can be played by any number of people from three to eleven. The people who are first in the room have the preference and should immediately inscribe their name. The first eleven people form the table, and the privilege of being the banker is sold to the highest bidder, that is, to the one who will put up the most money to be played for. The remaining ten people draw for choice of seats at the table, whereby the first choice is for the seat immediately on the right of the banker, and then for the first seat on his left. Five players are arranged on each side of the banker in this way, right and left alternately, according to the order of their choice. Sometimes an assistant or croupier is seated opposite the banker, in order to watch the bets, gather and shuffle the cards and so on. A waste basket is placed in the centre of the table for receiving cards that have been used in play.

If no one bids for the bank, the bank has to be offered to the first person on the list of players; if he declines, it is offered to the next person, and so on. The amount bid for the bank is placed on the table, none of it can be withdrawn, and all winnings are added to it. If no bid is made, the banker can place on the table any amount he thinks proper, and that amount, or what remains of it after each coup, is the betting limit. When the banker loses all he has, the bank is either sold to the next-highest bidder or offered to the next player on the list. If the banker wishes at any time to retire, the person who takes his place should begin with an amount equal to that in the bank at that time.

COUNTERS   Each of the players should be provided with a specific number of counters, all of which have to be sold and redeemed by the banker or his assistant.

CARDS   Three packs of fifty-two cards each are shuffled together and used as one pack. The players shuffle as much as they please, the banker goes last, then the banker presents the cards to any player he pleases in order to have them cut. The banker can burn one or two cards if he pleases, that is, turn them face upwards on the bottom of the pack.

OBJECT OF THE GAME   The court-cards and Tens count nothing, but all other cards, including the Ace, are reckoned at their face value. The object is to secure cards the total pip value of which will most closely approach the number 8 or 9. An 8 made with two cards is better than a 9 made with three.

STAKES   Each player in turn, beginning with the first on the right of the banker, and after him the first on the left, and so on, right and left alternately, can bet any amount he pleases until the total amount bet equals the capital in the bank at the time. When this amount is reached, it is useless to place more bets, because they might not be paid. For this reason, Baccara is a very slow game when there is not much money in the bank. After all the players have made what bets they wish, outsiders can place bets on the result if they choose to do so.

Either the players or the gallery can bet on either side of the table, which is divided down the middle by way of a line that sections it into two parts, right and left, hence the name Baccara a deux tableaux. A person who wishes to bet on both sides at once places his money *à cheval*, that is, across the line. If one side wins and the other loses, a bet placed in this way is a stand-off; if both sides lose, the bet is lost; and if both sides win, the bet is won.

When the banker loses, he pays the players in their order, right and left alternately, beginning with the players who hold cards, until his capital is exhausted. Any more bets are disregarded. If any player bets on the opposite side of the table to the one on which he is seated, his bet is not paid until all five of the players on that side have been settled with, because the bet is viewed as being that of an outsider and one that does not belong to that side of the table. If the player who actually holds cards is not the one nearest the banker, he is still the first one to be paid, followed by the players beyond him in order. For example, the third player holds cards: after him, the fourth and fifth are paid, and then the first and second, each alternately with a player on the other side of the table.

BANCO   Each player in turn, beginning with the one to whom cards will be dealt first, has the right to go banco, that is, to challenge the banker to play for his entire capital at a single coup. This proposition takes precedence over all other propositions. If the bank loses this coup, it has to be either put up to the highest bidder again or offered to the next player on the list. If it wins, the same player or any other player can make a similar offer for the next coup, which will now be for double the first amount, naturally; however, no player is allowed to offer banco more than twice in succession.

DEALING   When the cards are cut, the banker takes a convenient number of them in his hand, or better, spreads them face downwards on the table, and slips off the top card, whereby he gives it to the player next to him on the right, face downwards. The next card, he gives to the player on his left, and the next, to himself. He gives another card to the right, to the left, and to himself, after which the players take them up and examine them. Ten cards have to remain in the stock for the last deal.

IRREGULARITIES   After the first card is dealt, no bets can be made or changed. The cards have to be held so they will at all times be in full view of the players. Any card found faced in the pack is thrown in the waste basket. Any card once separated from the pack has to be taken. If neither of the players wants it, the dealer has to take it himself. If the cards are dealt irregularly, the error can be rectified if they have not been looked at, but any player can amend or withdraw his bet before the cards are seen. If the error is not detected in time, the player who holds cards can play the coup or not as he pleases, and all bets on his side of the table are bound by his decision. If a player holds one card too many, he can either refuse the coup or retain whichever two of the three cards he pleases, whereby he throws the third card into the waste basket and does not show it. If the banker has too many cards, the players can amend their bets, after which the banker's cards are exposed, and the card taken from him, whereby he will be left with the smallest point, because the drawn card is thrown in the waste basket. If the banker gives himself two cards whereas either player has been given one only, the player has to be given another card, and the banker also has to take another. If the players have not amended their stake before the error was corrected, the first two cards dealt to the banker are thrown in the waste basket, and the third card is his point for that deal. If the banker gives the second card to either player before dealing the first to himself, he has to give the second one to the other player as well, then take his own. This single card then has to be thrown in the waste basket, but the banker can play out the hand as if he had two cards that counted 10 or 20, that is, baccara.

SHOWING If any one of the three people who hold cards finds he has a point of 8 or 9, it has to be shown at once, and the other two hands are then exposed. If the banker has 8 or 9, and neither of the other players has as many, the bank wins everything on the table. If either player has more than the banker has, all the bets on that side of the table have to be paid. If either player has as many as the banker, all the bets on that side of the table are a stand-off. If either player has fewer than the banker, all the bets on that side of the table are lost. If a player wrongly announces 8 or 9, he cannot draw cards unless his point was 10 or 20.

DRAWING If none of the three players can show 8 or 9, the banker has to offer a card to the player on his right. The card has to be slipped off the pack and offered face downwards. If the player on the right refuses it, it is offered to the player on the left, and if he also refuses it, the banker has to take it himself. If the player on the right takes it, the player on the left can also ask for a card; however, whether or not he does so, the banker is not obliged to draw unless he chooses, after the first card offered has been taken by either player. When the card is taken, it is turned face upwards and left on the table in front of the person to whom it belongs. Only one card can be drawn by any player, and all the hands are then exposed. Ties are a stand-off. The banker pays all bets on the side that is nearer 9 than he is, and wins all on the side that is not as near 9 as he is. The players on the opposite sides of the table have nothing to do with each other: each wins or loses with the banker alone.

It should be observed that if a player had 4 originally and draws a 9, his point is not 13 but 3, because all 10's count for nothing. There is no such thing as being créve, as in Vingt-et-un.

IRREGULARITIES If the banker gives two cards, face upwards, to the player on his right, the player can retain which card he pleases and throw the other into the waste basket. If two cards are given to the player on the left, he can select which card he pleases, and the banker has to take the other.

ORDER OF PLAYING When the coup is finished and all bets are paid, all the cards that have been used are thrown into the waste basket, and the stakes are placed for the next coup. The banker deals again, from the top of the stock, without any further shuffling or cutting of the cards. If the player on the right won the first coup, the banker deals to him again, but if he lost, the banker deals to the next player beyond him, that is, the second from the banker, on his right. The same applies to the player on the left. If the player on the right or left wins the second coup, the cards are dealt to him again for the third coup. If he loses, they are dealt to the next player beyond him, and so on, until all five players have both held cards and lost a coup, after which the banker deals to the one nearest him again.

It will thereby be noted that there are in each coup only two active players, and that all stakes made on the game are made on the result of the players' hands.

SUGGESTIONS FOR PLAYING   By way of giving justice to the players who are backing him, the player is supposed to draw or not to draw, according to the laws of probabilities, which are exactly the same as in Vingt-et-un. If he has four points, which would be 5 below 9, he should draw, just as he would if he had 16 in Vingt-et-un, which would be 5 below 21. If he has 5 or more, he should stand; however, if he has 5 exactly, it is a matter of judgement, whereby drawing a card is sometimes good play, especially if it is likely to lead the banker to overdraw himself. In some clubs, there is a law that a player has to draw if his point is less than 5, and has to stand if it is more than 5; otherwise, he has to pay a fine.

Because no one is backing the banker, he is at liberty to play as badly as he pleases, and is really the only player who has an opportunity to exercise any judgement in the matter of drawing. If a player refuses a card, the banker might be able to judge whether or not he has 6 or 7 by way of his habit of drawing or not drawing at 5. If he is known to be a player who draws at 5, it is useless for the banker to stand at 5, unless he thinks he can beat the player on the other side of the table, and there is more money on that side. If the player who is demanding a card has been given a 10, the banker should stand, even at 3 or 4. If he has been given an ace, the banker should stand at 4; if a 2 or 3, the banker should stand at 5; and if the player is given a 4, the banker should draw, even if he has 5. If a player has drawn a 5, 6 or 7, the banker should draw, even if he has 5 or 6. If the player draws an 8 or 9, the banker should stand at 4 or 5, sometimes even with 3.

It has to be remembered that the banker should have a sharp eye as to the relative amounts staked on each side of the table, because they will often decide which player he should try to beat. For example, the banker has 5, the player on his right has drawn a 10, and the player on his left has drawn a 7. The banker has an excellent chance to win all the bets on the right, and should have a certainty of standing off with them. Unless the bets on the left very much exceeded them, the banker would be very foolish to risk losing everything by drawing to 5, simply in order to beat the player on his left.

BACCARA CHEMIN DE FER   In this variation, each player in turn on the left becomes the banker, whereby he takes the deal as soon as the first banker loses a coup. The banker gives cards to only the player on his right and himself. If this player will not go banco, each of the other players in order beyond him can do so. If no one goes banco, each player in turn to the right makes what bets he pleases, within the limit of the bank's capital. If the banker wins the coup, he deals again, and so on until he loses, whereby the deal passes to the player on his left. The banker, after winning a coup, can pass the deal to the player on his right, if he chooses to do so, provided that player will put up an amount equal to the amount that is in the bank at that time. When this player loses a coup, the bank has to go to the player to whom it would have gone in regular order, that is, the player on the left of the player who transferred his privilege.

Six packs of cards are usually used in Chemin de Fer, and the cards are placed in a wooden box, from which each dealer takes as many cards as he wants.

CHEATING   Baccara is 'honeycombed' with trickery. Dishonest players, in collusion with the banker, have specific means of informing him of their point, so he can win all the money staked on that side of the table by the other players. This can be done in many ways. The player can ask the player sitting next to him whether or not he should draw, whereby it is shown he has 5. Alternatively, he can make a movement as if to expose his first two cards, then correct himself. This shows the banker that the player has baccara and is pretending he thought he had 9. In addition to this system of communication, which Parisians call *tiquer*, marked cards, second dealing and prepared stocks that can be either palmed on the true cards or substituted therefor are all in common use. If Baccara is honestly played, it is one of the fairest of all banking games, but the opportunities for cheating are so many and so easily availed of, and the money to be won and lost so great, especially in Chemin de Fer, that few people who know anything about cheating at cards can resist the temptation to practice it at Baccara.

The Laws of Baccara are very long and complicated. Because no official code exists, and each gambling club makes its own house rules, it is not necessary to give them here: the directions contained in the aforementioned description are sufficient for playing any game honestly.

— —

BLIND HOOKEY

This game is sometimes called Dutch Bank. Any number of people can play, and a full pack of fifty-two cards is used. The cards rank from the A K Q down to the deuce. Any player can shuffle, and the dealer goes last. The pack is then cut, and the reunited parts are placed in the centre of the table. The players then cut the pack into several packets, none fewer than four cards, all of which remain on the table face downwards. A player then pushes one of the packets towards the dealer, and bets are made on the other packets. Any player, except the dealer, can bet what he pleases on any packet.

After all the bets are made, all the packets, including the dealer's, are turned face upwards, whereby the bottom card of each packet is exposed. Any packet in which a card lower than the dealer's is disclosed loses all bets placed on it. Any packet that shows a card better than the dealer's wins from him. The dealer takes all ties. The deal then passes to the next player on the left. Sometimes only three packets are cut, one of which is pushed to the dealer.

This game was a great favourite with card sharps, especially on ocean steamers. They used packs in which the cards were trimmed long and short, so a confederate could cut the cards by the ends, or by the sides for high or low cards, whereby he afterwards pushed one of the high cuts towards the dealer.

— —

CHINESE FAN TAN

This is apparently the fairest of all banking games, because there is absolutely no percentage in favour of the banker except that the players have to do the guessing.

The person who is willing to put up the largest amount of money to be played for is usually selected to be the banker. He is provided with a large bowlful of beans, counters, buttons, small coins or objects of which many of similar size and shape can be easily obtained. A rectangular card is placed in the centre of the table, and the players stake their money on either its corners or its edges. These corners are supposed to be numbered in rotation from 1 to 4, whereby the figure 1 is on the right of the banker.

A bet placed on any of the corners takes in the number it is placed on and the next higher as well, so that a bet on the corner 1 would be on the numbers 1 and 2, on 2 would be on 2 and 3, and on 4 it would be on 4 and 1.

```
              X
 ┌─────────────┐
 │ 3        2  │
 │             │
 │ 4        1  │
 └─────────────┘
```

In this illustration, the bet would be on 2 and 3.

If the bet is placed on the edge of the card, it takes in the next-higher number only.

```
 ┌─────────────┐
 │ 3        2  │
 │             X
 │ 4        1  │
 └─────────────┘
```

In this illustration, the bet is on the number 2 and no other number.

After all the bets have been placed, the banker takes a large handful of the beans or counters from the bowl, and places them on the table, whereby he counts them off rapidly into fours. The number of odd counters that remains decides which number wins, and if no odd counters remain, 4 wins. If there were 2 or 3 counters over, the banker would pay all bets on the corners 1 and 2, even money. If there were 2 over, he would pay all bets on the edge of the card between 1 and 2 at the rate of three for one, and so on. The counters are then returned to the bowl, and bets are placed for another coup.

Sometimes the banker will draw a handful of beans from the bowl and place them on the table, whereby he covers them with either a saucer or his cap. He then bets any player that there will be 1, 2, 3 or 4 beans left, whereby the player takes his choice and is paid three for one if he guesses correctly.

— —

FARO

This is one of the oldest banking games, and is supposed to be of Italian origin. It belongs to the same family as that of Lansquenet, Florentini and Monte Bank. Under the name of Pharaon, it was in great favour during the reign of France's Louis XIV, and came to the United States by way of New Orleans. When it was originally played, the dealer held the cards in his left hand, and any bets once put down could not again be taken up until they were decided. In addition to splits, the dealer took hockelty.

When it is played nowadays, Faro requires extensive and costly apparatus, and the engraved counters used are often worth more than their playing value.

A full pack of fifty-two cards is shuffled and cut by the dealer then placed face upwards in a dealing box, the top of which is open. The cards are drawn from this box in couples, by pushing them one at a time through a slit in the side. As the cards are withdrawn in this way a spring pushes the remainder of the pack upwards. The first card in sight at the beginning of each deal is called *soda*, and the last card left in the box is *in hoc*.

The first card withdrawn is placed about 10 centimetres (6 inches) from the box, and the second is laid close to the box itself.

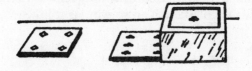

Each two cards withdrawn in this way are called a *turn*, and there are twenty-five turns in each deal, whereby Soda and Hoc are dead cards. When the first turn is being made, the Soda begins the pile that is further from the box, and the next card taken out is called a *loser*, which is placed close to the box. The card left face upwards in the box is the *winner* for that turn, so that there has to be a winner and a loser for every turn: the loser outside the box and the winner left in it. On the next and all following turns, the winning card on the previous turn will be placed on the same pile as that of the Soda, so that it will be possible at any time to decide which cards have won and which have lost.

The Object of the Game is for the players to guess whether the various cards on which they place their money will win or lose. The players are at liberty to select any card they please, from the ace to the King, and to bet any amount within the established limit of the bank.

THE LAYOUT   All bets are made using counters of various colours and values, which are sold to the players by the dealer and can be redeemed at any time. These counters are placed on the layout, which is a complete suit of spades, enamelled on green cloth, whereby space is left between the cards for the players to place their bets. The ace is on the dealer's left.

There are a great many ways of placing bets in Faro. For example, a player can make bets that cover twenty-one combinations of cards, all of which would play the Ten to win, as follows.

If the first bet is supposed to be flat on the Ten itself, 2, 3 and 4 would take in the card next to the Ten; 5 would take in the cards on each side with the Ten; 6 and 7 would take in the three cards behind which the bets are placed, whereby the Ten is one in each instance; 8 and 9 would take in the Ten, and the card one remove from it in either direction; 10 and 11 are the same thing, but placed on the other card; 12 to 17 inclusive take in the various triangles of which the bet is the middle card; 18 and 19 take in the four cards surrounding them; 20 and 21 are *heeled* bets, whereby the bottom counter is flat on the corner of the card, and the remaining counters are tilted over towards the card diagonally across from the card on which the bet is placed, whereby both cards are played to win. In addition to these twenty-one bets, other bets might be made by way of heeling bets that would take specific cards to lose and the Ten to win. Bets can also be *strung* behind odd or even cards on the side next to the dealer. These show that the player bets that the next case-card that comes will win if it is an even card and lose if it is an odd, that is, if he places his string behind an even card.

If the player thinks a card will win, he bets it *open*, that is, with nothing but his counters. If he wants to play a card to lose, he *coppers* it, by placing a checker or button on his chips. If a player wishes to reach two cards that are widely separated, such as the deuce and the Seven, and does not have enough money to bet on both, he can ask the dealer for a *marker*, which is a flat, rectangular piece of ivory. This is placed on the card to be played with the same money, and the dealer can either trust his memory for the bet or place another marker on the bet.

After the dealer has waved his hand in preparation for pushing the top card from the box, no bet can be made or changed. After the turn is made, the dealer first picks up all the bets he wins, then pays all he loses, after which he waits for the players to rearrange their bets for the next turn. Between each turn, a player can make any change he pleases. A lookout sits on the right of the dealer in order to see he pays and takes correctly and to watch that no bets are changed and no coppers slipped off during the turn.

SPLITS   If two cards of the same denomination win and lose on the same turn, it is a split, and the dealer takes half the bets on the split card, no matter whether it is bet to win or lose. Splits should come about three times in two deals if the cards are honestly dealt. In *'Stuss'* (dealt without a box), the bank takes splits.

KEEPING CASES   As the cards are withdrawn from the box, they are marked on a case-keeper, which is a suit of thirteen cards that have four buttons running on a steel rod opposite each of them. As the cards come out, these buttons are pushed along, so that the player can know how many of each card are still to come and what cards are left in for the last turn. In brace games, when the cards are pulled out two at a time in order to change the run of them, the case-keeper is always a confederate of the dealer, and is signalled what cards have been pulled out under the cards shown, so he can secretly mark them up. A bet placed or left on a card of which no card is left in the box is called a *sleeper*, and is public property, whereby the first player who can get his hands on it keeps it.

When only one card of any denomination is in the box, it is obvious that this card cannot be split, and that the bank has no advantage over the player. These cards are called **cases**, and the betting limit on cases is only half the amount allowed on other cards. It is not considered to be *comme il faut* for a player to wait for cases, and people who play regularly usually make a number of small bets during the early part of the deal, then bet high on the cases as they come along. A player who goes on the principle that the dealer can cheat players who bet high, and who follows and goes against the big bets with small ones, or who plays one-chip bets all over the board, hoping to strike a good spot to fish on, is called a *piker*, and when a game runs small this way, the dealers call it a *piking game*.

KEEPING TAB In addition to the case-keeper, score-sheets are provided on which the players can keep a record of what cards win and lose on each turn. These tabs are printed in vertical columns, about five deals to a sheet. A dot indicates the soda card, and a dash indicates hoc. All winners are marked with a down stroke and all losers with a cypher. The diagram in the margin on page 561 will give a very good idea of a faro tab for a complete deal. The Queen was soda, the Five split out, and the Eight was in hoc.

A	0	0	1	0
2	0	1	1	1
3	0	0	1	1
4	1	0	0	0
5	0	0	X	
6	1	1	1	1
7	0	1	1	0
8	1	1	0	–
9	0	1	0	1
10	0	0	0	0
J	1	1	1	0
Q	.	0	1	0
K	1	0	1	1

SYSTEMS On the way in which the cards will go, a great many systems of play are based. There are sixteen ways for a card to 'play', which are simply the permutations of the stroke and the cypher arranged in rows of four at a time. If a player is betting **three on a side**, he will take each card as it becomes a case, and bet that it either wins three times and loses once or loses once and wins three times. In the aforementioned deal, he would have bet on the A 3 4 6 9 J to lose on the fourth card out of the box, and would have bet on the case-cards of the 2 7 8 10 Q K to win. The Soda, it has to be remembered, is really a winning card. Of these bets, he would have won five out of twelve, and taken back his money on the 8, because that card was left in hoc. Were **break even** being played, these bets would have been exactly reversed, because all the cards would have played either to win and lose an equal number of times or to *win* or *lose out*, that is, to do the same thing all four times.

Another favourite system is colours. The player takes a definite card, such as the soda, or the first winner or loser, as his starter, and whatever the colour of the third card of each denomination is, that is, the card that makes it a case, he plays it to win or lose, according to the system of colours he is playing. Many players reverse on the last turn.

When a player bets one card to lose and another to win, and loses both bets on the same turn, he is *whipsawed*.

THE LAST TURN If three different cards are left in for the last turn, the players can *call the turn*, whereby they name the order in which they think the cards will be found. Suppose the three cards left in the box are the 9 8 2: these can come in six ways, as follows.

$$9\ 8\ 2 \qquad 9\ 2\ 8 \qquad 8\ 9\ 2 \qquad 8\ 2\ 9 \qquad 2\ 9\ 8 \qquad 2\ 8\ 9$$

The odds against any one of these ways are 5 to 1, but the dealer pays 4 for 1 only. In calling the turn, the bet is strung from the selected loser to the selected winner. If the third card intervenes, the bet is strung away from it, in order to show it goes around the layout to the other card.

If there are two cards of the same denomination in the last turn, it is called a *cat-hop*, and because it can come only three ways, the dealer pays 2 for 1. Suppose the cards are 8 8 5: they can come as follows.

$$8\ 8\ 5 \qquad 8\ 5\ 8 \qquad 5\ 8\ 8$$

If three cards of the same denomination are left, the call is by the colour and is paid 2 for 1. Suppose two black and one red card are left. These can come as follows.

$$B\ B\ R \qquad B\ R\ B \qquad R\ B\ B$$

The bets are placed on the dealer's right for red first, on his left for black and red, and in front of him for two blacks.

CHEATING If Faro were honestly played, it would be one of the prettiest banking games in the world. Unfortunately, though, the money to be made at this game is so great that the richest prizes in the gambling world are offered to the players who can handle the cards so as to 'protect the money of the house'. All systems are not only worthless; they are dangerous to use when they are opposed to the skill of the modern faro dealer. A first-class 'mechanic' used to be able to get from one to two hundred dollars a week, and a percentage of the profits; however, it is hardly necessary to state that he was not paid that amount for simply pulling cards out of a box. Before venturing to 'buck the tiger', you should get someone show you how fifty-three cards are shuffled up so as to make the last turn come the way that there is most money in it for the house. Watch the movements carefully, so you will know them the next time you see them in a fashionable house, which you imagine to be 'dead square'. If you see a dealer who has a shuffling board as thick as his dealing box, don't play against that game. If you see a dealer take up the cards already taken from the box and slip them one under the other, as if to straighten them up, the sooner you cash your chips the better, because you are up against a brace game, no matter where it is dealt.

The proprietors of some fashionable 'clubs', especially at 'watering places', pretend to be above all things such as cheating in faro, and become indignant at the suggestion that there is anything crooked in their establishment. The author has but one reply to them: if it is true that there is nothing unfair in your game, let me put a clerk in the dealer's place to shuffle and pull out the cards, and let your people simply see to paying and taking bets.

The boast of all these fashionable gambling houses is that they never won a person's money except in a square game. Strange to say, this is generally true, and the explanation is very simple. If you are losing, there is no necessity to cheat you, so you lose your money in a square game. If you are winning, it is the bank's money, not yours, that the person would win if he started to cheat you, and because the dealer is paid to 'protect the money of the house', as it is called, he is perfectly justified in 'throwing the harpoon into you' for a few deals, just to get his own money back; however, he is very careful not to cheat you out of any of your own money. You can lose if you like, but you cannot win: faro banks are not run that way.

— —

ROUGE ET NOIR
OR TRENTE-ET-QUARANTE

The banker and his assistant, called the croupier, sit opposite each other at the sides of a long table, on each end of which are two large diamonds: one red and the other black, separated by a square space and a triangle. Any number of people can play against the bank, whereby they place their bets on the colour they select: red or black.

Six packs of fifty-two cards each are shuffled together and used as one pack, whereby the dealer takes a convenient number of cards in his hand for each deal. When the players have made their bets, and cut the cards, the dealer turns one card face upwards on the table in front of him, at the same time as he announces the colour he deals for, which is always for **black first**. The dealer continues to turn up cards one by one, announcing their total pip value each time, until he reaches or passes 31. Court-cards and Tens count 10 each, and the ace and all other cards count for their face value. When 31 has been reached or passed for black, the **red** is dealt for in the same way, and whichever colour most closely approaches 31 wins. Suppose 35 was dealt for black, and 38 for red: black would win. The number dealt must never exceed 40.

The colour of the first card dealt in each coup is noted, and if the same colour wins the coup, the banker pays all bets placed on the space marked **Couleur**. If the opposite colour wins, he pays all bets in the triangle marked **Inverse**. All bets are paid in even money, because there are no odds in this game.

Although black is the first colour dealt for, both it and inverse are ignored in the announcement of the result: red and colour are the only colours mentioned, win or lose.

If the same number is reached for both colours, it is called a **refait**, and is announced by way of the word *Apres*, which means that all bets are a stand-off for that coup. If the refait happens to be exactly 31, however, the bank wins half the money on the table, no matter how it is placed. The players can either pay this half at once or move their entire stake into the first prison, which is a little square marked out on the table, and which belongs to the colour they bet on. If they win the next coup, their stake is free; if they do not, they lose it all. If a second refait of 31 occurs, they have to lose a fourth of this imprisoned stake, and the remainder is moved into a second prison, to await the result of the next coup, which would either free it or lose it all.

PROBABILITIES   It has been found that of the ten numbers that can be dealt: 31 to 40, the number 31 will come more frequently than any other number. The proportions are as follows.

31: 13 times	36: 8 times
32: 12 times	37: 7 times
33: 11 times	38: 6 times
34: 10 times	39: 5 times
35: 9 times	40: 4 times

The 31 refait also comes more frequently than any other refait. Although the odds against it are supposed to be 63 to 1, the bankers expect it about twice in three deals, and each deal will produce from 28 to 33 coups.